BRITAIN YESTERDAY
AND TODAY
1830 to the Present

A HISTORY OF ENGLAND

General Editor: Lacey Baldwin Smith

THE MAKING OF ENGLAND: TO 1399

C. Warren Hollister
Robert C. Stacey
University of Washington, Seattle
Robin Chapman Stacey
University of Washington, Seattle

THIS REALM OF ENGLAND: 1399–1688

Lacey Baldwin Smith
Northwestern University

THE AGE OF ARISTOCRACY: 1688–1830

William B. Willcox
Walter L. Arnstein
University of Illinois, Urbana-Champaign

BRITAIN YESTERDAY AND TODAY: 1830 TO THE PRESENT

Walter L. Arnstein
University of Illinois, Urbana-Champaign

BRITAIN YESTERDAY AND TODAY

1830 to the Present

Eighth Edition

Walter L. Arnstein
University of Illinois, Urbana-Champaign

HOUGHTON MIFFLIN COMPANY   BOSTON   NEW YORK

Editor-in-Chief: Jean Woy
Associate Editor: Leah Strauss
Associate Production/Design Coordinator: Lisa Jelly
Senior Cover Design Coordinator: Deborah Azerrad Savona
Manufacturing Manager: Florence Cadran
Senior Marketing Manager: Sandra McGuire

Cover design: Walter Kopec
Cover art: Ginner, Charles (1878–1952), *Picadilly Circus*. 1912. Tate Gallery,
  London/Art Resource, NY.

Printed in the U.S.A.

Library of Congress Catalog Card Number: 00-133909

ISBN: 0-618-00104-2

123456789-QUF-04 03 02 01 00

To Charlotte

Contents

Illustrations

Maps

Graphs and Charts

Foreword

Carl Becker once complained that everybody knows the job of the historian is "to discover and set forth the 'facts' of history." The facts, it is often said, speak for themselves. The businessperson talks about hard facts; the statistician refers to cold facts; the lawyer is eloquent about the facts of the case; and the historian, who deals with the incontrovertible facts of life and death, is called a very lucky fellow. Those who speak so confidently about the historian's craft are generally not historians themselves; they are readers of textbooks that more often than not are mere recordings of vital information and listings to dull generalizations. It is not surprising, then, that historians' reputations have suffered; they have become known as peddlers of facts and chroniclers who say, "This is what happened." The shorter the historical survey, the more textbook writers are likely to assume godlike detachment, spurning the minor tragedies and daily comedies of humanity and immortalizing the rise and fall of civilizations, the clash of economic and social forces, and the deeds of titans. Anglo-Saxon warriors were sick with fear when Viking "swift sea-kings" swept down on England to plunder, rape, and kill, but historians dispassionately note that the Norse invasions were a good thing; they allowed the kingdom of Wessex to unite and "liberate" the island in the name of Saxon and Christian defense against heathen marauders. The chronicler moves nimbly from the indisputable fact that Henry VIII annulled his marriage with Catherine of Aragon and wedded Anne Boleyn to the confident assertion that this helped produce the Reformation in England. The result is sublime but emasculated history. Her subjects wept when Good Queen Bess died, but historians merely comment that she had lived her allotted three score years and ten. British soldiers rotted by the thousands in the trenches of the First World War, but the terror and agony of that holocaust are lost in the dehumanized statistic that 765,399 British troops died in the four years of war.

In a brief history of even one "tight little island," the chronology of events must of necessity predominate, but if these four volumes are in any way fresh and up-to-date, it is because their authors have tried by artistry to step beyond the usual confines of a textbook and to conjure up something of the drama of politics, the humdrum of every day life, and the pettiness, as well as the greatness, of human motivation. The price paid will be obvious to anyone seeking total coverage. There is relatively little in these pages on literature, the fine arts, or philosophy, except as they throw light on the uniqueness of English history. On the other hand, the complexities, uncertainties, endless variations, and above all the accidents that bedevil the design of human events — these are the very stuff of which history is made and the "truths" that this series seeks to narrate and preserve. Moreover, the flavor of each volume varies according to the tastes of its author. Sometimes the emphasis is political, sometimes economic or social, but the presentation is always impressionistic — shading, underscoring, or highlighting to achieve an image that will be more than a bare outline and will recapture something of the smell and temper of the past.

Even though each book was conceived and executed as an entity capable of standing by itself, the four volumes were designed as a unit. They tell the story of how a small and insignificant outpost of the Roman Empire hesitantly, and not always heroically, evolved into the nation that has probably produced and disseminated more ideas and institutions, both good and bad, than any state since Athens. Our hope is that these volumes will appeal both individually, to those interested in a balanced portrait of particular segments of English history, and collectively, to those who seek the majestic sweep of the story of a people whose activities have been wonderfully rich, exciting, and varied. In this spirit this series was originally written and has now been revised for a seventh time, not only to keep pace with new scholarship but, equally important, to keep it fresh and thought-provoking to a world becoming both more nostalgic and more impatient of its past.

Time has not left this series untouched since its inception in 1966. As the four volumes have changed over seven revisions, so also have their authors. William B. Willcox of the University of Michigan and Yale University, a decade before his death in 1985, turned responsibility for revising volume III, *The Age of Aristocracy*, over to Walter L. Arnstein of the University of Illinois, and now, five revisions later, this volume belongs to him although Willcox's name still appears on the title page. In September of 1997 C. Warren Hollister, the author of volume I, *The Making of England*, died, and the series has been fortunate in persuading Robin and Robert Stacey of the University of Washington to take on the revision of the volume. A new generation is emerging to keep our four volumes abreast of the changing needs and interests of educators and students.

The writing of history is always a collective enterprise, and so the authors of this series would like to thank the following reviewers who made valuable suggestions for the eighth edition: Lorraine Atreed, Holy Cross College; Joel D. Benson, Northwest Missouri State University; Katherine French, SUNY–New Paltz; Amy M. Froide, University of Tennessee–Chattonooga; Helen Hundley, Wichita State University; Susan K. Kent, University of Colorado; Newton Key, Eastern Illinois University; Fred M. Leventhal, Boston University; Muriel C. McClendon, University of California–Los Angeles; and Joseph P. Ward, University of Mississippi.

Lacey Baldwin Smith

Preface

This book is the product of teaching courses over four decades—at Roosevelt University, Northwestern University, the University of Chicago, and the University of Illinois at Urbana-Champaign—that surveyed the history of modern Britain. More distantly, it reflects the influence of my own teachers, among them Professor Oscar I. Janowsky of the City College of New York and Professors Herman Ausubel and J. Bartlett Brebner of Columbia University. More immediately, it is the product of much—if never quite enough—reading of relevant books, articles, and reviews; of impressions gathered during several lengthy sojourns in the British Isles since 1956; and of the imaginative suggestions of Professor Lacey Baldwin Smith.

The decision to produce new editions of the volume at regular intervals—this eighth edition is being published precisely thirty-five years after the first edition appeared—has allowed me to correct factual errors, to rethink and rephrase numerous paragraphs and chapter subsections, and to retitle and rearrange numerous chapters. I have also sought to take into account the explosion of historical work on various facets of the social and cultural history of Victorian Britain and on numerous aspects of twentieth-century history in general, for which until a few years ago the relevant cabinet and personal papers were closed to researchers.

For the sixth, seventh, and eighth editions, I have rewritten sections dealing with numerous topics throughout the volume, ranging from the changing patterns of gender relations and popular culture to the history of medicine, from the implications of the Irish Famine to the conduct of the Crimean War, and from Britain's involvement in World War I to the British role in both the origins of the Cold War in the 1940s and its closing stages during the late 1980s and early 1990s. Chapter 22 seeks to place the entire Margaret Thatcher era into provisional historical perspective, and a new Chapter 23 introduces the "Tony Blair Era" and British society at the onset of the new millennium.

This book rests on the assumption that, even in the twenty-first century, students may still benefit from becoming acquainted with the history of a national community other than the one to which they belong and from being introduced to the lives and actions of multi-dimensional human beings as well as to abstract social and economic forces. The framework remains predominantly but not pedantically chronological, and political history retains a significant, but in no sense exclusive, place. Social and economic developments are clarified by charts, tables, and photographs as well as by words, and political and diplomatic events are enlivened by cartoons. Analogies drawn from American history are deliberately included. The volume may therefore serve as an appropriate companion to the student of English literature or as a guide to the tourist wishing to put places and events into context. The completely revised bibliography is intended to provide interested students with sources in which they may learn more about virtually every theme, event, or person mentioned in the book. The aim has been to provide balance without excluding controversy. The names and dates of modern British history are not in dispute, but interpretations often conflict, and I have made no attempt to disguise that fact.

I remain in debt for their helpful suggestions to the late Professor William B. Willcox of Yale University, the late Professor Charles Mullet of the University of Missouri, the late Professor Robert Zegger of Northeastern Illinois State University, Professor R. J. Q. Adams of Texas A & M University, Professor Marjorie Morgan of Southern Illinois University, Professor Fred Leventhal of Boston University, as well as to several reviewers chosen by Houghton Mifflin Company. Two University of Illinois colleagues also gave cogent advice: Professor Paul W. Schroeder on Chapters 4 and 6, and Professor Richard W. Burkhardt on Chapter 5. Dr. Alan E. O'Day of the University of North London provided useful suggestions on Chapter 9.

It is with great pleasure that I also acknowledge the work of a number of University of Illinois doctoral students who, in matters both menial and substantive, have assisted me with the preparation of successive editions of this volume. Dr. Prudence Moylan (now of Loyola University, Chicago) aided me with the second, and Dr. Randall E. McGowen (now of the University of Oregon) did so with the third. In comparable fashion Dr. James Filkins (now of Chicago's Dr. Robert Stein Institute of Forensic Medicine) assisted me with the fourth edition, Dr. Chet DeFonso (now of Northern Michigan University) with the fifth, Dr. John Beeler (now of the University of Alabama) with the sixth, Dr. Christopher Prom (now of the University of Illinois Archives) with the seventh, and Mr. David Kamper with the current revision.

During that long-ago era before computers and word processors, my wife did much of the typing—on a manual typewriter no less—for the original edition and spotted many a fuzzy thought and long-winded sentence. Prior to proofreading the most recent editions, she made numerous additional useful suggestions, including the reminder that during the nineteenth and twentieth centuries, the Scottish experience differed significantly on occasion from that of other parts of the United Kingdom. In appropriate if utterly conventional fashion, however, I take full responsibility for what ultimately appears on the printed page.

W. L. A.

About the Author

Walter L. Arnstein holds a Ph.D. from Northwestern University. He is Professor Emeritus at the University of Illinois at Urbana-Champaign, where from 1968 to 1998 he taught British History; in 1989 the university also named him Jubilee Professor of the Liberal Arts and Sciences. He has held fellowships at Clare Hall of Cambridge University and at the Institute for Advanced Studies in the Humanities of the University of Edinburgh. He has served as President of the Midwest Victorian Studies Association, the Midwest Conference on British Studies, and the North American Conference on British Studies. He has also served on the editorial boards of the *American Historical Review, The Historian,* and *Albion.* His other publications include *The Bradlaugh Case* (1965; new ed., 1984), *Protestant Versus Catholic in Mid-Victorian England* (1982); as co-author, *The Age of Aristocracy: 1688–1830* (8th ed., 2001); as editor and contributor, *Recent Historians of Great Britain* (1990); as editor and compiler, *The Past Speaks: Sources and Problems in British History Since 1688* (1981; second ed., 1993); and, as author, eight articles about Queen Victoria.

BRITAIN YESTERDAY AND TODAY

1830 to the Present

PART ONE

THE AGE
OF IMPROVEMENT
1830 to 1851

A MODEL TEXTILE MILL OF THE 1830s
This factory, with work rules displayed prominently on the walls, was located at
Tewkesbury in the west of England. *(The Granger Collection)*

CHAPTER 1

Reform or Revolution?

Change and continuity are the contrasting colors on a historian's palette, and any society at any time contains some elements of each. The Britain of 1830 was the product of a heritage receding into the mists of early Anglo-Saxon and Celtic times and of the ferment created by dramatic population growth as well as by the blast furnace, the steam engine, and the factory town. The age of Augustan placidity and unquestioned aristocratic predominance was only yesterday. The age of the iron horse was just beginning. The age of mass production, mass housing, mass transportation, and mass destruction was yet to come.[1]

Alexis de Tocqueville and the Britain of 1830

Most of the people of Britain were too close to the momentous forces of their age, which found nineteenth-century industrialists competing for pride of place with eighteenth-century squires, to perceive the full import of the change or to provide a balanced appraisal of their own society. That task was taken on by a shrewd and perceptive Frenchman, Alexis de Tocqueville, who was soon to immortalize his name with a classic description and interpretation of the United States of Andrew Jackson's day: *Democracy in America*. Tocqueville never wrote a similar study of the British Isles, but the notes he took on two trips across the Channel during the early 1830s provide a revealing, if partial, account of British society in transition.[2]

Tocqueville surveyed an England still largely rural and unaccustomed to the roar and clatter of the steam locomotive, but he sensed that the future was being molded by the extraordinary changes taking place in commerce and industry — not by the apparently sluggish growth in farm production. Consequently he concentrated his attention on London and a

---

[1]Asa Briggs, *The Age of Improvement, 1783–1867* (1958), remains a reliable general account of Britain during the first half of the nineteenth century. Eric J. Evans, *The Forging of the Modern State, 1783–1870* (1983), is largely topical in approach. Norman Gash, *Aristocracy and People: Britain 1815–1865* (1979), stresses politics at the national level.

[2]Alexis de Tocqueville, *Journeys to England and Ireland*, trans. by George Lawrence and K. P. Mayer, ed. by K. P. Mayer (1958).

3

number of provincial cities. He was fascinated by the forces that continued to attract the rural populace to the cities and the factories and by the boundless energy displayed by industrialists and workers alike in expanding cities like Birmingham. "These folk never have a minute to themselves," he reported. "They work as if they must get rich by the evening and die the next day." Although appalled by the housing conditions in some of the growing industrial towns and depressed by the number of English people dependent on poor relief, Tocqueville appraised the average standard of living in England as superior to that of his native France.

England was for Tocqueville a bustling commercial country; at the same time, it remained intensely aristocratic and conscious of differences in social status. It was clear to the Frenchman, however, that the English aristocracy differed markedly from that of pre-Revolutionary France. It was smaller yet more accessible and, as a consequence, more highly respected. Because a wealthy merchant could hope that one day his son or grandson might become a peer himself, he did not distrust the aristocracy en masse. Analogously, the custom of primogeniture — in which the younger children received allowances but only the eldest son inherited his father's titles and estates — resulted in a continual seeping down of aristocratic sons and daughters into the middle classes, bringing to English upper-class society a cohesion that did not exist in France. Certain professions had become the traditional preserve of the younger sons of the aristocracy. In the case of Tocqueville's friend, Lord Radnor, the eldest son inherited title and fortune, the second son became canon of Salisbury Cathedral, the third a captain in the navy, and the fourth a banker in London. Had there been additional sons, they might well have found comparable openings in the law, in the army, or as administrators in India. Tocqueville ultimately was struck less by distinctions between classes based on heredity or law than by differences based on wealth. Material gain seemed to him a primary motive among all classes.

Although he considered the English a "naturally religious" people, Tocqueville described the established Church of England as "immensely rich, very badly organised and full of great abuses." Its bishops seemed to be the staunch defenders of government of and by the well-off and well-connected. Such people felt at home amid the carpets and upholstered pews of many Anglican churches. They also were accustomed to observing family prayers at home, with both male and female servants assembled in hierarchical order of precedence.

Although many of the English were used to receiving spiritual truths from their social superiors, others paid little heed to an established church that, in the words of Archbishop William Howley, left the slum-dwellers of cities like Manchester and Leeds "in a state of heathen darkness." The dissenting denominations — Presbyterian, Congregationalist, and Baptist — had recovered from their eighteenth-century doldrums and were growing in number more quickly than the established church. So were the Methodist sects, those late-eighteenth-century evangelical offshoots from the Church of England. Yet the nonreligious were growing at a similar rate and, in a city like Manchester, with a population of 300,000, only one inhabitant in four attended church on Sunday. Many a worker who had labored for twelve hours each weekday preferred to spend Sunday in bed or in a neighborhood pub.

Tocqueville realized that, for all of Britain's monarchical trappings, the center of British politics and the very soul of the kingdom resided in Parliament, that most exclusive and aristocratic club in all of Europe. Membership in the House of Commons was restricted to a minority of the propertied classes; the process of getting into the house could be incredibly expensive, and once there an M.P. received no salary. Although the size of the electorate was limited by a bewildering variety of property qualifications in many boroughs, it remained a costly proposition to canvass a constituency, bring the voters to the polls, and in some cases feed and house them. Outright bribery was not uncommon in many an old borough whose poorer voters looked on the bribe as a kind of income. The fact that the vote was a public one made indirect pressure an obvious possibility, but Tocqueville noted the fearlessness with which the electors announced their choices. He was equally struck by the intense interest that such a "saturnalia of English liberty" aroused even among those members of the community who lacked any direct voice in determining the outcome.

Although Parliament gave direction to the kingdom and created law, most Britons experienced the full impact of government only at the local level, where the United Kingdom's more than 100 counties and 16,000 parishes remained worlds of their own. A Justice of the Peace in his county was far more imposing than a distant M.P. sitting at Westminster. Britain was less centralized than contemporary France, and since 1689 the unpaid Justices of the Peace had indeed been local sovereigns. The new factory towns were often in the grip of similar oligarchs, but extragovernmental turnpike trusts and local improvement commissions were attempting to cope with the problems created by rapid industrialization and urban growth. They, rather than the gentlemen J.P.'s, foreshadowed the future pattern of local government.[3]

Even as Tocqueville looked on some provincial cities as harbingers of the future, he viewed others as relics of the past. The university towns of Oxford and Cambridge, for example, seemed both architecturally and academically to be arrested in the Middle Ages. Latin and Greek were the chief subjects taught there, and the exact sciences had gained only indifferent entry into the curriculum. England's two universities were surprisingly small. Oxford had only 1,500 students in attendance, and these were on vacation half the year. Many of the fellows who administered Oxford's constituent colleges did almost no work. Their liberty was limited only by the ancient tradition that they not marry (in emulation,

---

[3]K. B. Smellie, *A History of Local Government* (4th ed., 1968).

perhaps, of their monastic predecessors). Oxford and Cambridge no longer served as refuges for impecunious scholars, and tuition costs were high. In addition to educating Anglican clergymen, the universities served as finishing schools for young gentlemen, most of whom seemed more preoccupied with drinking, gambling, and rowing than with preparing for examinations. The lower levels of England's educational system were as diverse and uncentralized as its local government. The efforts of thousands of private elementary and grammar schools, charity schools, and Sunday schools, most set up under religious auspices, had produced a society in which a majority of the people could read and write. As of 1841, two-thirds of English bridegrooms and half of English brides could sign their names rather than an X on the marriage register, and the proportion of the illiterate was continuing to decline. The parishes of Scotland were obligated by law to provide for salaried schoolmasters, and the rate of literacy there was somewhat higher.

The other provincial cities visited by Tocqueville reflected the staggering industrial changes that were transforming Britain into the workshop of the world. Manchester was the center of the cotton textile industry. It had been built haphazardly, and the workers' hovels seemed carelessly scattered amid "the huge palaces of industry," the cotton mills that converted ever larger quantities of American cotton into fabrics and thread. Women and children made up three-quarters of Manchester's working force, which included some 60,000 Irish immigrants, many of whom lived in damp, unsanitary cellars. Paved streets and an efficient sewage system were still largely on the drawing boards. It was Manchester, more than any other city, that was to inspire Karl Marx and Friedrich Engels with their ideas on the inevitability of class conflict in a capitalistic society. Tocqueville's reactions were more ambivalent. "From this foul drain," he wrote, "the greatest stream of human industry flows out to fertilize the whole world." Birmingham, a center for the manufacture of iron, steel, and copper, seemed healthier, if only because the gulf between workers and their masters was much less noticeable. And Liverpool, the little fishing village that had grown into a great port on the profits of the slave and cotton trades, was described by Tocqueville as "beautiful." He was deeply impressed also by the ability of Liverpool's highly efficient shipbuilders to underbid French competitors despite the 33 percent tariff imposed on British builders by the French government. The city's leaders showed daring and imagination by planning a mile-and-a-half long railway tunnel under the community so that the port area might be connected more directly with manufacturing cities such as Birmingham and Manchester.

Thus Tocqueville discovered numerous paradoxes in the England of the 1830s. Despite a restricted political system, there *was* freedom of religion, speech, and the press (although cheap newspapers remained handicapped by expensive stamp duties). In theory, there was equality before the law, although in actuality it tended to be vitiated by distinctions in wealth. The central government coexisted with an unsystematic hodgepodge of local governments; yet both were restrained by judicial checks and balances. The English justly prided themselves on their individuality, but Tocqueville was quick to note that they (like Americans) were far more likely than continentals to found clubs and associations to further scientific, political, and business pursuits, or simply for recreation. Despite its apparent complacency, political stagnation, and oligarchical rule, England was boiling with intellectual excitement. "In olden times," noted one of Tocqueville's hosts, "the English thought that everything about their constitution was perfect, both advantages and abuses. Today everybody is looking for what needs mending. Sometimes it is one thing, sometimes another, but the process never stops." Perhaps this spirit of innovation, Tocqueville concluded, would enable the British to amend their political structure so that they would adjust peacefully to the democratic wave that (sometimes fearfully and sometimes hopefully) he foresaw sweeping across the world; thus they would escape the revolutionary violence that had already swept over his own country. Tocqueville's prognosis was to prove accurate, but in 1830 the future looked cloudy at best.

The Demand for Constitutional Reform

The year 1830 witnessed changes on both sides of the Channel: in France another revolution, a relatively bloodless one replacing Charles X, the last of the Bourbons, with Louis Philippe of the house of Orléans, the "bourgeois king"; in England the succession of King William IV after the death of his brother, George IV. By English law, the royal death was followed by a dissolution of Parliament and the holding of a new general election. In this election the subject of reform received a great deal of attention.

　For almost a century and a half the mechanism of Britain's constitutional structure had remained unaltered. The counties and boroughs of England, Wales, and (since 1707) Scotland were represented in the House of Commons by the same number of members as at the time of William and Mary — despite the growth and migration of the population. Each borough retained its own particular tradition for choosing its representatives. "Pocket boroughs" voted at the beck and call of their wealthy patrons; corporation boroughs were in the careful hands of a coterie of town fathers; in "Scot and Lot" constituencies, the vote went to resident householders; in a handful of democratic boroughs such as Preston, the entire adult male population possessed the vote. The borough franchise was a matter of local "liberty" and custom rather than of parliamentary statute. The English county franchise, on the other hand, was somewhat more uniform; since 1432 each forty-shilling freeholder (the owner of land worth that much in annual rental) had had the vote. By the early nineteenth century this provision would have created virtual universal manhood suffrage in the counties if the vast majority had been freeholders. But most were leaseholders or tenants or day laborers and thus excluded from the franchise.

This diverse system had come under repeated attack during the later years of the eighteenth century. Some reformers argued simply that the democratic element of the "mixed" British constitution, the House of Commons, ought to be made more democratic and more directly and justly representative of the population, while the aristocratic and monarchical elements represented by the House of Lords and the king should be allowed to retain their due influence on the government. A reform bill embodying significant changes in borough representation and franchise requirements came fairly close to success during the 1780s. The outbreak of the French Revolution in 1789 led to more extreme proposals; men such as Thomas Paine, Joseph Priestley, and William Godwin demanded not only that the House of Commons should be democratized but that the House of Lords and the crown should ultimately be abolished. Thomas Paine argued that "as there is but one species of man, there can be but one element of human power; and that element is man himself. Monarchy, aristocracy, and democracy are but creatures of the imagination; and a thousand such may be contrived as well as three."

The French Revolution briefly inflamed the British reform spirit, only to quench it thereafter. All reform became associated with the guillotine and the Reign of Terror and, when Britain and France went to war in 1793, reaction set in. An embattled island, standing at times alone against the Napoleonic colossus, seemed to require political stability rather than change. Thus, the social consequences of the inventions and industrial processes that literally altered the British landscape and contributed greatly to the ultimate military triumph of 1815 remained unreflected in the country's political structure. By 1820, however, reform was once again in the air, and political Radicals, moderate Whigs, and ambitious industrialists all clamored in diverse ways for a fundamental change in the political system.

The practical problem was, of course, that if a far-reaching political shift were to come about, it had to take place (barring revolution) inside Parliament itself. In other words, in a large number of cases, M.P.'s would have to vote themselves out of power. This dilemma helps to explain as readily as any appeal to abstract principle why men who were willing to reform the criminal code, to alter ancient tariffs, and even to ease the political lot of religious minorities proved reluctant to tackle a measure of general political reform. Yet if nothing were done, there was the intermittent fear that the patience of the unenfranchised (especially in the rapidly expanding industrial cities) might become exhausted, and that the nineteenth century, like the seventeenth, would prove to be revolutionary in British history.

One of the factors that helps to account for the ultimate timing of the Great Reform Bill was the breakup during the later 1820s of the ruling Tory party. It is a historical commonplace that political parties in the eighteenth century did not function as they do today; that government then was not party government; and that the situation in Parliament was complicated by the existence of family connections, of true indepen-

dents, and of men who for reasons of patronage or habit always supported
the cabinet nominated by the king. Yet the terms *Whig* and *Tory* were
used by eighteenth-century politicians and can be traced as far back as
the 1670s. There were Whig and Tory tendencies on particular political
issues, such as those dealing with the civil rights of Protestant dissenters
and the practical power of the king. During the long prime ministership
of William Pitt the Younger (1784–1801 and 1804–1806), a revived Tory
party came to dominate Parliament. Opposition to the French Revolution and resistance to any tampering with time-honored English institutions became the Tory *raison d'être*. During the prime ministership of
Lord Liverpool (1812–1827), the party first basked in the reflected triumph of Waterloo but later had to face the problem of dealing with the
symptoms of postwar economic distress. The "Peterloo Massacre" and
the Six Acts of 1819 seemed to demonstrate that the Tory government
was better at curbing than at appeasing dissent.

　During the 1820s the government was enlivened with fresh faces in
the cabinet. A Whig revival was squelched, but a shift in policy took
place. Lord Liverpool remained as prime minister, but in 1822 George
Canning replaced Viscount Castlereagh as foreign secretary and Tory
leader of the House of Commons. Canning held no brief for parliamentary reform, yet he was convinced that it could be avoided only if his
party could win a reputation for being less repressive and more willing to
see merit in change. The Combination Acts, which had outlawed the organization of trade unions, were partially repealed. A capriciously enforced criminal law that permitted capital punishment for more than 200
different crimes was simplified and made less harsh. The first steps were
taken to rationalize and lower tariffs on imports.

　Not even the deaths of both Liverpool and Canning in 1827 and the
selection in 1828 of that old warrior and Tory stalwart, the duke of
Wellington, as the country's prime minister could stem the tide of reform. The duke acquiesced in the formal repeal of two (inconsistently enforced) pillars of the ancient order, the century-and-a-half-old Test and
Corporation Acts, which barred religious dissenters from public office.
Emancipating Protestant dissenters proved relatively easy, but opening
the doors of Parliament to Catholics caused a furor and became one of the
issues that eventually broke up the Tory party. Faced with deep division
in England and a threat of civil war in Ireland unless Roman Catholics
were granted the right to sit in Parliament, Wellington finally gave way.
So at length did King George IV, who nonetheless feared that he was
thereby violating his coronation oath to maintain the authority of the
Church of England. The "Catholic Emancipation" act was therefore cou-
pled with a political "reform" bill raising Irish franchise requirements in
order to exclude all Catholic voters who were not well-to-do.

　In retrospect, the repeal of the Test and Corporation Acts and
Catholic emancipation appear as milestones along the road to complete
religious toleration in England. Yet, from the point of view of the Tory
party of 1829, they were most unfortunate, for the party was now split

three ways. One division was made up of Canningites, many of whom had been excluded from Wellington's cabinet in 1828. At the other extreme were the ultra-Tories, who felt certain that in his treatment of the Catholic question the duke had betrayed the principles of his party. In the middle now were Wellington and Sir Robert Peel (1788–1850), who had won his reputation as a politically orthodox chief secretary for Ireland and as a cautiously reform-minded home secretary. In a sense the ultra-Tories were right. Their principles had been betrayed, for one of these principles had long involved the support of the Anglican Church as the one true church and therefore as the sole church whose members should possess full political privileges. Another underlying assumption of the party was that the time-tested fabric of the state was inviolable. Yet now that the need for change had been recognized in Ireland, could fundamental political reform in England be long denied? Wellington refused to bow to such reasoning. He remained in office, adamant against further reform, while his party disintegrated around him.

The breakup of the Tory party in Parliament during the later 1820s gave the Whig opposition a new lease on life. The role of the Whigs in Parliament during the previous half century is reflected in the career of Lord Grey (1764–1845), the man who was to become the unexpected government leader at one of the most significant turning points in British history. By 1830, Lord Grey had been a member of Parliament, first in the Commons and then the Lords, for forty-four years. He had entered the lower house as a precocious young man of twenty-two and had participated in the debates on parliamentary reform during the 1780s and early 1790s as a Foxite Whig. But then came the French Revolution and, tarred by the brush of Jacobinism, reform ceased to be an issue of practical politics. Grey, like many another Whig magnate, retired to his country estate and visited Parliament only on occasion. He continued to pay lip service to a program featuring parliamentary reform, financial retrenchment, relief for Protestant dissenters, and the abolition of slavery in the British Empire; but for thirty years the cause of parliamentary reform remained a principle rather than a policy.

During the 1820s political reform was seriously debated again. M.P.'s were introducing reform bills into Parliament, and Radicals both inside and outside Parliament were advocating extreme changes in Britain's constitutional structure. Lord Grey was no extremist. He agreed with the eighteenth-century viewpoint that a voice in politics belonged primarily to men of property, but in defining property he included London merchants and Manchester manufacturers, as well as landed aristocrats and country gentlemen. Then, too, Whigs like Lord Grey could never completely forget that their party had been born of change, indeed of a revolution, even if it had been the relatively bloodless and respectable revolution of 1688. The comparably bloodless and respectable French Revolution of 1830 provided Lord Grey and other advocates of reform with an additional incentive to seek political change in Britain.

The Great Reform Bill

The death of George IV and the new general election were to give Lord Grey his chance, even though the results of the election of 1830 were far from conclusive. In only a minority of seats was there an electoral contest, and it was by no means immediately clear that the duke of Wellington and Toryism had been repudiated. Riots by farm laborers in southeastern England and unrest in manufacturing districts helped inspire calls for political reform in the new Parliament, however. When, in November 1830, Wellington defiantly denied the need for any change in the constitution of the nation, Whigs and the Radicals were aroused, and even some moderate Tories were upset. Two weeks later the House of Commons voted down a government finance bill, and Wellington resigned. King William thereupon called on Lord Grey to form a ministry. Thus, at the age of sixty-six, Grey found himself prime minister. The Whigs, strengthened by the alliance of moderate Tories, were back in power. Radicals outside Parliament were clamoring for reform. Reform was ceasing to be a theory; it had become an opportunity to find new and lasting strength for a party that had spent the greater part of fifty years in the political wilderness.[4]

In March 1831 Lord John Russell (1792–1878)[5] introduced into the House of Commons a reform bill to disenfranchise dozens of small boroughs, to enfranchise numerous large ones, and to make uniform the property qualifications of borough voters. Four important forces were now to become involved: the Radicals outside Parliament, for whom the bill might not go far enough; the House of Commons, for which it might go too far; the House of Lords, for which it was certain to seem dangerously revolutionary; and King William IV, who was not opposed to a degree of reform on principle but who preferred that nobody become agitated about anything.

Grey was confronted with the problem of convincing the politically active groups outside Parliament that the bill went far enough to suit them. At first the activists were unsure. They sought universal manhood suffrage and a secret ballot, and the bill obviously provided neither. But once the Tories began to attack the bill as a dangerously radical

---

[4]Michael George Brock, *The Great Reform Bill* (1973), provides a readable and reliable account. William H. Maehl, Jr., ed., *The Reform Bill of 1832* (1967), surveys causes and consequences as interpreted by several historians. In *Lord Grey: 1764–1845* (1990), E. A. Smith offers an informative life of the prime minister. Grey's rivals are assessed in Elizabeth Longford, *Wellington: Pillar of State* (1973), and in Norman Gash, *Sir Robert Peel: The Life of Sir Robert Peel After 1830* (1972). In *Whiggery and Reform, 1830–1841: The Politics of Government* (1990), Ian Newbould provides a helpful overview of the Whig decade.

[5]Grey's original cabinet consisted of ten peers and only three commoners. Russell was one of the three. His title was an honorary one, given to him as the younger son of a duke; Russell himself had been elected to the Commons.

Whig Prime Ministers of the 1830s Earl Grey (left) presided over the Reform Bill struggle of 1831–32, and Viscount Melbourne (right) headed the government, with but a brief interruption, from 1834 to 1841. He served as a guide to the youthful Queen Victoria, and he is shown in the robes that he wore at her coronation (1838). *(The Granger Collection)*

measure — which, by depriving old boroughs of their right to representation, would confiscate private property without compensation, would transfer political power to the urban population, and would lead to the destruction of the monarchy — the Radicals became convinced that the measure was worth the fight. For Lord Grey and his Whig colleagues the measure was a final one that would "remove at once, and for ever, all rational grounds for complaint from the minds of the intelligent and independent portion of the community"; for the Radicals it was merely a first step, a necessary prerequisite for the reforms they championed concerning the currency, the tariff, and local government.

The Whigs and the Radicals thus had little in common, but for the moment this was forgotten as groups such as Thomas Attwood's Birmingham-centered Political Union of the Lower and Middle Classes of the People and Francis Place's London-centered National Political Union began to agitate in favor of the bill. "Nothing [is] talked of, thought of, dreamt of," wrote a contemporary diarist, "but Reform. Every creature one meets asks, What is said Now? How will it go? What is the last news? What do you think? and so it is from morning till night, in the streets, in the clubs, and in the private houses." On the night of March 22, the bill came to its second reading and, with the House of Commons crowded with more members than had ever before crammed themselves within its walls, the crucial vote came at 3:00 A.M. on the following day. The bill passed by a majority of one (302 to 301).

A one-vote majority was hardly sufficient for a bill that, although approved in principle, had still to be taken up clause by clause in the House of Commons and to be pushed through the House of Lords. A Commons defeat of one such clause a week later caused Lord Grey to advise the king to dissolve Parliament and ask for new elections. The subsequent election of 1831 was, in contrast to previous general elections, a referendum on a single issue: whether "the bill, the whole bill, and nothing but the bill" should be approved. Many M.P.'s were elected without opposition, but in virtually every contested election, the victory went to the reformers. This became apparent in July, when a new reform bill introduced by Lord John Russell passed its second reading in the House of Commons by a vote of 367 to 231. It was subject to delays in committee — where it was voted on clause by clause — but in October did reach the House of Lords. After a five-day debate, the Lords defeated the bill, 199 to 158. The result was a sense of outrage in the nation's cities. Two London newspapers appeared with black borders as a symbol of mourning. The council of Birmingham's Political Union discussed the formation of a national guard and the arming of the people. Nottingham Castle, the property of the duke of Newcastle, was destroyed by political arsonists, and late in the month the city of Bristol was taken over and held for several days by a rioting and pillaging mob.

In December 1831 Lord Grey's ministry tried again. For a third time it introduced a reform bill with provisions substantially as before. Again it passed the House of Commons, and in April 1832 the principle of the bill, with the help of Tory "waverers," was also approved, 184 to 175, by the House of Lords. When the upper chamber began, however, to hack the details of the bill to pieces in committee, Lord Grey, on the basis of the precedent set by Queen Anne's action in 1712, requested that the king either create fifty additional peers to provide a Whig majority or else accept the government's resignation. William suggested that the creation of twenty peers might be satisfactory but that fifty was too many. He therefore accepted Grey's resignation and called upon the duke of Wellington to form a ministry again. Once more there were rumblings of revolution. Radical leaders urged their followers to stage a run on the banks and to refuse to pay taxes until Wellington resigned. After a week Wellington did resign, for by 1832 it had become impossible to remain prime minister of England in the face of an obviously hostile House of Commons and an even more hostile public outside its doors.

With great reluctance William IV asked Grey to resume his office, and with even greater reluctance he agreed to appoint enough new peers to assure approval of the bill. At that moment, the battle was over. The Lords did not wish to be swamped, and they went on to approve the bill with little further ado. Wellington himself, out of a sense of duty to his monarch, abstained. On June 7, 1832, the bill received the royal assent and became the law of the land. The crisis had passed, but bitter recriminations were exchanged by both sides. Even as the Tories blamed the Whigs for arousing public agitation outside Parliament, the Whigs indignantly retorted that they had saved the country from the revolution toward which Tory obstinancy was leading it. With the incorporation of nonlanded property owners into the electorate, the kingdom's political structure had been strengthened rather than weakened. Concession to sustained popular demand had proved the wisest policy for a governing aristocracy. Lord Grey, who continued to distrust Radicals and who remained in every sense an aristocrat, found to his own surprise that he had become a popular hero. The passing of the bill was everywhere greeted with the ringing of church bells, with illuminations and banquets, and Lord Grey, on a journey to the north of England, found his carriage repeatedly stopped and himself acclaimed. He could not understand it, he confided to an acquaintance: "My speeches were uniformly and strongly conservative in the true sense of the word."

Significance and Aftermath

The significance of the Reform Bill of 1832 lies only partly in its provisions. Indeed, the student who reads its clauses today may well concur with Lord Grey's assessment of the measure's conservative nature. In England and Wales there was a redistribution of seats: fifty-six boroughs, including one uninhabited cow pasture, were deprived of their two M.P.'s; thirty additional small boroughs lost one of their two members; twenty-two new two-member boroughs and twenty new one-member boroughs were created; and sixty-five additional seats were distributed among the English counties. Although metropolitan London and the industrializing Midlands and north were to be better represented than before, numerous anomalies remained, and the pocket borough, the seat under the virtual control of a particular landed magnate, did not disappear completely.

In the boroughs the right to vote was uniformly granted to all male[6] urban householders who either owned a house worth at least ten pounds a year or paid rent of ten pounds a year or more. About one-fourth to one-third of the houses in an average borough fell into this category, and rents in London were so high that almost all genuine householders were enfranchised. In the counties the vote was extended to men who held property on lease as well as to freeholders. This was a step toward universal suffrage that at the same time tended to increase the electoral influence of landlords over their tenants, because all voting continued to be by public declaration rather than by secret ballot.

One of the most important innovations made by the act was the imposition of a uniform borough franchise. This meant fewer voters in the more democratic boroughs, but the total electorate increased by some 50

---

[6]By tradition, the pre-1832 parliamentary franchise had been exercised by men only, but women had not been formally barred from the vote by statute law, and in the eighteenth century a few women householders had participated in parliamentary elections by proxy. Some women also participated in local government at the parish level, both as voters and as office-holders.

percent. One Englishman in five was now eligible to vote, and some 620,000 voters in England (and 814,000 in the British Isles as a whole) were registered at the general election of 1835.[7] Moreover, as the population rose and as prosperity increased, the number of ten-pound householders in the electorate would grow accordingly, even without further legislative change. From the duke of Wellington's point of view, the harm had been done. "The revolution is made," he declared in 1833; "that is to say, power is transferred from one class of society, the gentlemen of England professing the faith of the Church of England, to another class of society, the shopkeepers being dissenters from the church, many of them being Socinians [Unitarians], others atheists." Such a judgment was premature, to say the least. Landed gentlemen continued to dominate Parliament during the generation that followed.

It had been the purpose of Grey's ministry to remedy abuses and not to establish democracy in Britain. The Reform Bill can be looked back on as a significant step toward democracy, however, because it led directly and inevitably to an overhaul of English local government, because it materially weakened the position of both the monarch and the House of Lords, and because of the manner in which it became law. The newly reformed House of Commons decisively reorganized town government in the Municipal Corporations Act of 1835. This "postscript to the Reform Bills" dissolved 200 old corporations and set up in their place 179 municipal boroughs, each with a mayor and a fixed number of popularly elected town councillors who in turn chose a third of their number to be aldermen. Many a self-perpetuating small oligarchy, whose chief interest may well have been to choose two members of Parliament rather than to govern a town, was thus replaced by a council chosen by and responsible to all the ratepayers of the community. Many of the new municipal councils were indeed dominated by Protestant Nonconformists rather than by Anglicans. Their jurisdiction extended primarily over police and gaslight service, whereas sewers, street paving, and water supply often remained in private hands or under the jurisdiction of independent improvement commissioners. Yet, as in the case of the Reform Bill itself, uniformity of procedure replaced an often less equitable diversity, and in the course of the century the new municipal corporations tended to absorb functions still remaining in private hands.

The Reform Bill's effect on the monarchy was even more immediate. It proved once again that, in case of crisis, the crown could no longer hold

---

[7]A separate reform act for Scotland, hastily drawn up and little debated, had an even more dramatic effect. The electorate increased from 4,000 to 64,000, and seats hitherto controlled by tiny self-perpetuating oligarchies became dynamic centers of political activity. Before 1832, Scotland's forty-five M.P.'s usually supported the government of the day, which in turn delegated Scottish affairs to one or more prominent Scottish aristocrats. Only after 1832 did many Scots truly become involved in the parliamentary and national party system. See William Ferguson, *Scotland 1689 to the Present* (1968), Chapters 9 and 10, and G. C. Hutchinson, *A Political History of Scotland, 1832–1924* (1986).

out against the wishes of a cabinet representing a majority in the House of Commons. King William IV was not powerless, and on the question of the creation of peers he had resisted, but eventually he gave way just as his brother George IV had capitulated on the issue of Catholic emancipation three years before. In the course of fifty years the Hanoverian monarchs had been deprived not of their theoretical authority but of their practical ability to control the political life of the realm. The Economic Reform Act of 1782 had limited the number of patronage positions, and between 1815 and 1822 more than 2,000 sinecure positions in government had been abolished.

The very character of the Hanoverians contributed to their decline. The intermittent but ultimately permanent insanity of George III had necessarily limited that monarch's active role during his later years. His son, George IV, had succeeded him, first as regent in 1811 and then as king in 1820. George IV had certain amiable qualities as a human being and as a patron of the arts, but contemporaries seemed more aware of his quarrels with his wife, his numerous mistresses, his lavish life-style — and the fact that he was perpetually in debt. In an age in which the doings of crown prince, regent, and king were detailed in long reports, often accompanied by hostile caricatures, it is understandable that George IV came to be loathed by many middle-class Britons, whose attitudes toward private morality and businesslike efficiency were beginning to assume the mantle we call Victorian. To such people, the king seemed to be a wasteful, immoral nonentity. It is no wonder, then, that even the respectable *Times* of London should have published the most scathing of obituaries on the king's demise in 1830: "There never was an individual less regretted by his fellow countrymen than this deceased king. What eye has wept for him? What heart has heaved one sob of unmercenary sorrow?"

William IV rated only slightly higher in the eyes of many of his subjects. He had lived for many years with a popular actress, Dorothy Jordan, who had borne him ten illegitimate children, before he left her to marry his legal queen, Adelaide, at the age of fifty-seven. The *Spectator* took his death in 1837 very much in stride: "His late Majesty, though at times a jovial and, for a king, an honest man, was a weak, ignorant, commonplace sort of person." By the 1830s, the prestige of the British monarchy had clearly reached a low point. As an institution it had survived, but the widespread feeling of disrespect and even contempt toward George IV and William IV played a significant role in the decline of its political influence.

An even greater role was played by the crystallization of an increasingly disciplined two-party parliamentary system. In a Parliament composed of numerous small factions with no deep ideological issues dividing them and of many members who owed their jobs to royal favor, the king had much room to maneuver. With the party organization stronger and the party leader more clearly defined, the king had much less choice.

By enlarging the electorate, by imposing uniform franchise requirements, and by instituting a system of registering electors, the Reform Bill of 1832 encouraged not only the strengthening of the parliamentary party but also the beginning of a national party organization. The more clearly the House of Commons could be said to reflect the will of the British people, the less plausibly could a monarch oppose it in the name of the "true" interests of his subjects.

The bill had a comparable effect upon the House of Lords. The course of the struggle had demonstrated that in a showdown the House of Commons was the more powerful of the two chambers as well as the arena in which the more vital political personalities engaged in debate. The bill had also very much limited the influence that the peers could exercise as boroughmongers with numerous House of Commons seats at their disposal. Yet it would be an error to dismiss the peers as a dying breed. In 1760 there had been 182 hereditary English peers; by 1837 there were 365. As many traditional eighteenth-century sinecures were abolished, both monarchs and prime ministers had come to look upon the peerage as a suitable reward for political or other distinction. As a consequence, the House of Lords, which had feared being swamped in 1832, had in another sense already been swamped during the previous half century. Yet, if the scarcity value of the peerage had declined, peers continued to hold a majority of cabinet posts and to maintain great social prestige during the mid-Victorian years. Despite Wellington's fears, criticism of the House of Lords tended to abate for more than a generation.

At the same time that the Reform Bill had weakened the prestige of king, peers, and gentry, it had notably strengthened the position of the new custodians of commercial and industrial wealth. They now shared with old-line oligarchs the rule of the kingdom. The fundamental political imbalance caused by industrialization had been largely rectified, and it is no coincidence that within fourteen years of political reform, those bastions of Tory economic policy, the Corn Laws, were to be repealed or that, within another generation, liberal ideas, both in politics and trade, were to remodel yet further the economic and governmental structure of the British Isles.

Finally, it was the peaceful manner in which the bill was pushed through Parliament by the force of public opinion and extraparliamentary agitation that made the Reform Bill a landmark along the road to democracy. Perhaps the ultimate significance of the bill lies in the fact that it passed at all — and without revolution. It proved, as Peel and Wellington had rightly predicted, to be the first act of the play rather than the last; yet within a very short time it was accepted even by diehard Tories who had dreaded its passage. Some Radicals were soon to protest strongly that the measure had fallen woefully short of their hopes and that far too many ordinary working people remained excluded from political power at the national level. And yet the Reform Bill agitation had taught those Radicals, like the Whigs and the Tories, one crucial lesson that they were to apply repeatedly during the succeeding century. When the object was reform, it was possible in the last resort to gain fundamental change peacefully. Henceforth, whatever the grievance, political agitation appeared to be not merely a legitimate but also a practical way to achieve reform. The battle might be long and the opposition obdurate but, provided the grievance was real and enough people truly wanted change, a remedy by means of legislation rather than revolution was possible.

CHAPTER 2

The Railway Age

If we wish to understand both the economic foundations of the Britain that had successfully weathered the Reform Bill crisis and the forces of demographic and technological change that were molding a new society, a few statistics are in order.[1]

The People

The population of England, Wales, and Scotland in 1831 was 16,161,183 — more than twice what it had been seventy years earlier. Late in the eighteenth century, authorities still debated whether the population of the country was increasing or decreasing, but the first official census, in 1801, helped to make clear what every successive census confirmed — that despite considerable emigration the total population was on the rise. The annual birthrate remained high, approximately 35 per 1,000, while the death rate was substantially lower, approximately 22 per 1,000. By 1851 the population of England, Wales, and Scotland had swelled to 20,816,351 — with almost half the people aged twenty or younger and only one person in 14 older than sixty. By 1851 something else had happened as well. For the first time in the history of any large country, a majority of the population lived in towns and cities. Not until 1920 did the same situation prevail in the United States. The census of 1851 confirmed a type of migration — from farm to city — even more startling than that across the Atlantic. Of every 33 city dwellers in the Britain of

---

[1]An older but still highly useful compendium of information about the subjects treated in this chapter is J. H. Clapham, *An Economic History of Modern Britain*, I, *The Early Railway Age, 1820–1850* (2nd ed., 1930). More recent general accounts include S. G. Checkland, *The Rise of Industrial Society in England, 1815–1885* (1964); Sydney and Olive Checkland, *Industry and Ethos: Scotland 1832–1914* (1984); and Francois Crouzet, *The Victorian Economy* (1982). M. J. Daunton's *Progress and Poverty: An Economic and Social History of Britain 1700–1850* (1995) includes an up-to-date topical bibliography and numerous statistical tables. See also Harold Perkin, *The Origins of Modern English Society, 1780–1880* (1969); J. F. C. Harrison, *The Early Victorians: 1832–1851* (1971); and individual essays in F. M. L. Thompson, ed., *The Cambridge Social History of Britain: 1750–1950*, 3 vols. (1990).

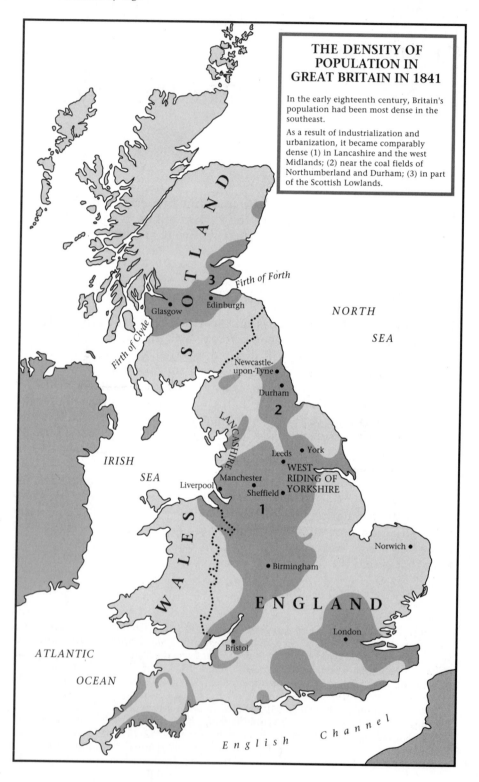

THE DENSITY OF POPULATION IN GREAT BRITAIN IN 1841

In the early eighteenth century, Britain's population had been most dense in the southeast.

As a result of industrialization and urbanization, it became comparably dense (1) in Lancashire and the west Midlands; (2) near the coal fields of Northumberland and Durham; (3) in part of the Scottish Lowlands.

1851, only 13 were city-born. The towns and cities, for the most part, were very new, very shoddy, and very crowded.

Earlier in the century Napoleon had taunted the English as being "a nation of shopkeepers," and many of them were still precisely that in the 1830s and 1840s. The large-scale cotton mill, the huge iron foundry, and the deep coal mine were portents of the future, but much manufacturing remained in the hands of small merchants or craftsmen with only a handful of employees. Agriculture also continued to play a highly significant role. For not only was one family in five still engaged almost solely in farming, but the rural scene included thousands of cobblers, blacksmiths, bricklayers, customer weavers, shopkeepers, and peddlers, who were part of a traditional rural life rather than representatives of an industrializing urban society.

More people lived in the countryside in 1851 than had lived on the entire island a century before. Much of the land was divided into large estates owned by wealthy aristocrats and country squires who rented the land on long or short lease to tenant farmers. The owner of a huge estate with a manor house and a deer park and a pack of foxhounds as well as dozens of servants continued to be the natural leader of his community.[2] Numerous new manor houses were indeed built during the early and mid-Victorian years, and others were enlarged. More than half the land leased to tenants involved farms of two hundred acres or more, considerably larger than the typical French or German farm of the nineteenth century. Vast estates were especially common in southeastern England, but in Wales, Yorkshire, and Scotland the family farm (held on long lease and operated without the help of regular outside labor) was widely known. For every family that owned or occupied land on long lease, there were two and a half families of hired laborers. Often engaged for a year at a time at annual hiring fairs, rural laborers remained the worst-fed and worst-housed group in British society. They generally had garden plots of their own to tend and nearby village alehouses in which to seek diversion, but their cash income remained minimal and their cottages were usually limited to two rooms and often lacked a fireplace.

By the 1830s, the common fields of earlier centuries had for the most part been divided and enclosed. Every farm owner or occupier could therefore decide which crops to plant. Although output per acre doubled between 1750 and 1850 and although the invention of a tile-making machine had made it cheaper to drain marshlands and to make other soils more productive, the overall pace of agricultural improvement remained slow. The planting of root crops had largely replaced the practice of leaving land fallow; but as good as turnips might be for the soil, they had

---

[2]See F. M. L. Thompson, *English Landed Society in the Nineteenth Century* (1963). G. E. Mingay has surveyed the subject briefly in *Rural Life in Victorian England* (1978) and more fully as the editor of a two-volume collection of essays by forty-six specialists in *The Victorian Countryside* (1981).

limited appeal as a diet staple. Agricultural chemistry was still in its infancy, and few machines had eased the farmer's toil. A steam-operated tractor proved to be an impractical luxury for most farmers. A mechanical thresher came into somewhat wider use during the 1830s, but its introduction had provoked widespread riots during a period of depression in 1829–1830. A practical reaper still lay in the future. The post-Napoleonic War agricultural depression had reduced farmers' income from the sale of wheat (in spite of protectionist Corn Laws) as well as of beef and dairy products. The 1830s brought recovery, however, as rents were adjusted downward and market prices leveled off. At the same time such prices continued to fluctuate sharply from year to year, the specter of overseas competition was drawing closer, and few individuals during these years regarded farming as the road to easy riches.

Industry and Banking

If Britain's "agricultural revolution" had been a gradual and often unsystematic development, can the same be said also of its much-vaunted Industrial Revolution? Certainly the term requires precise definition, for while there had been changes aplenty, no single British industry had undergone a complete technical revolution by 1830. The steam engine had been the most significant of a host of British inventions, and during the 1830s Charles Babbage (1792–1871) with his "Calculating Engine" laid the theoretical basis for the late twentieth-century computer. By the 1830s the factory system had become the accepted method of organization in the cotton industry; the more than fifty cotton mills of Manchester employed on the average more than 400 workers apiece, and a few employed over a thousand. Yet the cotton mills were still in many ways uncharacteristic. They gave work to at most one person in thirty, and at the very time that 60,000 steam-powered looms had been installed, there still remained 240,000 handloom weavers. There were a few large iron foundries, shipyards, and pottery manufacturers, but the small metal workshop remained typical in Birmingham, a city that was growing even more rapidly than Manchester. As a civic booster would boast in the 1860s, "Within a radius of thirty miles of Birmingham, nearly the whole hardware wants of the world are practically supplied."[3] Furthermore, the small retail shop remained the characteristic means of distribution, and in Glasgow (the most rapidly growing city in Scotland) Campbell's with its sixty-four employees was the closest approach to a department store. Many cities were engaged, however, in building or enlarging gigantic covered market halls in which scores of grocers, butchers, fishmongers, and sellers of housewares, clothes, and even toys would set up shop. Going to

---

[3]Cited in Leonore Davidoff and Catherine Hall, *Family Fortunes: Men and Women of the English Middle Class, 1780–1850* (1987), p. 248.

the market became a favorite Saturday night (payday) activity for working families. Such market halls served as precursors to the late twentieth-century shopping mall.[4]

Much manufacturing remained small-scale, in part because, at the time of the financial crash of 1720 known as the South Sea Bubble, Parliament had sharply discouraged the establishment of joint-stock companies. Such companies (or corporations) were used to conduct overseas trade and to operate canals — and, by the 1830s, railways — but individual ownership or partnership remained the customary mode of organization in industry. Factory owners found it difficult, therefore, to raise large sums of capital, because they did not possess the legal privilege of limited liability. (Limited liability meant that an investor in a company that had gone bankrupt stood to lose only the sum of his investment; his other holdings were legally inviolate in the payment of creditors.) Although the "Bubble Act" was repealed in 1825 and joint-stock companies were generally legalized in 1844, widespread doubts about the ethics of limited liability lingered, and not until Lowe's Act of 1856 was the right of limited liability generally accepted.

It is fallacious to speak of the process of industrialization as if it took place in a vacuum. A sizable urban population requires a sufficient food supply. A growing industrial society requires a sound currency and banking system. By the early nineteenth century Britain had both. The Bank of England, founded in 1694, had become a financial Rock of Gibraltar. It had successfully weathered the financial crises of the Napoleonic Wars. From 1797 until 1819 it had suspended the automatic exchange of its currency for gold on demand, but with the resumption of specie payment in the latter year, the British pound had become increasingly wedded to the gold standard. Peel's Bank Charter Act of 1844 indeed strengthened both the adherence of the Bank of England to the gold standard and its dominance in the issuing of currency. Hitherto, the expanding number of country banks had had the privilege of issuing currency outside the London metropolitan area. The Act of 1844 forbade newly chartered banks (except in Scotland) to issue their own currency, but it was not until the early twentieth century that the country had a single currency system. By this time, to be sure, the system of writing "cheques" had come to replace many of the transactions that had been settled by the transfer of currency a hundred years before. The banking system was accompanied by a growing number of insurance companies and by a variety of stock and commodity exchanges. These in turn were joined by banks such as the one founded by Nathan Mayer Rothschild (1777–1836), the German-Jewish immigrant who helped invent the international capital market; he financed governments in Europe and Latin America by selling bonds underwritten in London. Most such institutions were clustered near the

---

[4]See James Schmiechen and Kenneth Carls, *The British Market Hall: A Social and Architectural History* (1999).

Bank of England in "the City" (the original walled city of London), making finance one of London's major activities and bankers some of its wealthiest citizens.

Transportation

Transportation became an important adjunct to the process of industrialization, because mass production is clearly unprofitable if the reduction in cost is offset by the expense of moving the product to its potential customers. The traditional modes of transportation — the navigable rivers, the coastal seas, and the network of usually badly kept roads and footpaths — had become unsatisfactory to many eighteenth-century Britons. In the latter part of that century the traditional system was supplemented by the building of turnpikes and canals. Good roads made it possible to travel by coach from London to Edinburgh in forty-four hours, but coaches and horses were unsuitable for moving bulky merchandise. Heavy goods went by water, a fact that served as an incentive for the construction of canals to supplement the navigable river system. In 1763 a canal was opened between Manchester and Liverpool; during the eighty years that followed, a 2,500-mile canal network was completed. Transportation costs on canals were only one-quarter to one-half as high as the cost of road carriage, but canal boats remained narrow and the traffic was slow. The boats, pulled by horses, moved at an average speed of only two and a half miles an hour.

The New Era   The stage coach (1832) gives way to the coal-fired steam train (1852). *(Mary Evans Picture Library)*

During the 1820s and 1830s this slow evolution of transportation facilities underwent a dramatic shift — the development of what Americans call the "railroad" and Britons the "railway." Its early history shows the railway to be, like Watt's steam engine of the 1770s, a by-product of the coal industry. Short stretches of track were built to enable coal carts to be pulled along railed tracks by men or horses from colliery to riverside dock. During the Napoleonic Wars, the increasing expense of horses and fodder provided a new incentive for the development of alternative means of pulling the carts. Permanent steam engines that pulled the carts by means of cables were one possibility. Another was a mobile steam engine or locomotive that could pull a train of carts. In 1821 Thomas Gray published his *Observations on a General Iron Railway or Land Steam Conveyance; to supersede the Necessity of Horses in all Public Vehicles; showing its vast Superiority in every respect, over all the present Pitiful Methods of Conveyance by Turnpike Roads, Canals, and Coasting-Traders;* but before Gray's wordy prediction could be realized, a dependable iron rail and a reliable steam locomotive had to be invented. George Stephenson (1781–1848), a self-educated mining engineer, and his son Robert (1803–1859) played highly significant roles in the development of both. In 1825 the Stockton & Darlington line opened, the world's first public railway to carry goods other than coal with the aid of a steam locomotive. In 1830, with even greater fanfare, the Liverpool & Manchester Railway was inaugurated. Stephenson's *Rocket* pulled a passenger train at speeds as high as thirty-five miles an hour. "You can't imagine," wrote one lyrical passenger, "how strange it seemed to be journeying on thus, without any visible cause of progress other than the magical machine, with its flying white breath and rhythmical unvarying pace." That the "magical machine" was a potential monster as well was made clear on the same occasion when William Huskisson, the former president of the Board of Trade, failed to get out of the path of an onrushing locomotive on an adjoining track and was killed.

With the popular and financial success of the Liverpool & Manchester Railway assured, a period of intense, ambitious, and sometimes ruinous railway speculation began. Initially railway companies resembled turnpike trusts, and only in the late 1830s did it become clear that the companies would monopolize transportation on the tracks they built rather than open the roads to every individual carriage as turnpikes did. Whatever the cost in human lives, business reputations, and personal fortunes, by 1850 the "railway mania" had brought about a revolution in transportation:

Year	Miles of line	Number of passengers	Total capital invested
1842	1,857	18,453,504	(1843) £ 65,530,792
1846	3,036	43,790,983	126,296,369
1850	6,621	72,854,422	240,270,745

By 1844 even Parliament had come to realize that what was taking shape was not a series of local improvements but a new national transportation system. And that was indeed the long-term goal of speculators such as George Hudson, the one-time linen draper and mayor of York who came to be known as "the railway king." During the 1840s Hudson succeeded in negotiating dozens of amalgamations and creating the London & Midlands railway system, a model for other big systems to follow. Unlike other major countries (including the United States, in which Congress subsidized railroads with huge land grants), the initial British railway system was built almost solely with private capital; but in 1844 Parliament began the process of regulation. Laws required that there should be at least one train a day on each line in both directions. It should travel on the average (stops included) at least twelve miles an hour. Some seats were to be made available at a cost of no more than a penny a mile. Children under three were to be carried free and those under twelve at half-fare.

The basic English railway network was complete by 1850, although branch lines were to triple the total mileage in the course of the next half century. The economic consequences were monumental. The turnpike and canal building booms stopped. Coaches ceased to ply the English roads, and posthouses decayed. Many of the turnpike trusts were dissolved, and road building did not again become a national concern until the coming of the automobile in the twentieth century. The canals remained, and some continued to serve as useful subsidiary means of transportation for bulky goods like coal, but no new ones were built. The railways helped to create a vast expansion in the production of iron: 650,000 tons were manufactured in 1830 and two million tons in 1848. A comparable expansion of coal production, from twenty-one million tons in 1826 to forty-four million tons in 1846, was similarly stimulated by the railway. Coal production was to grow yet further in subsequent decades as the number of British miners increased from 100,000 in 1830 to over a million in the early twentieth century. Accompanying the lengthening lines of track from the late 1840s on were the soon-familiar telegraph poles and wires that by 1852 connected all major British cities.

Railway construction inspired a generation of civil engineers such as Isambard Kingdom Brunel (1806–1859) to design majestic iron bridges and long tunnels.[5] It also provided a new source of employment. During the 1840s as many as 200,000 men, many of them Irish immigrants, worked on rail construction gangs. By the end of the century, one English

---

[5]L. T. C. Rolt is the author of both *Isambard Kingdom Brunel: A Biography* (1957), and *George and Robert Stephenson: The Railway Revolution* (1962). The social impact is the subject of Michael Freeman, *Railways and the Victorian Imagination* (1999). See also Jack Simmons and Gordon Biddle, eds., *The Oxford Companion to British Railway History* (1997) and Roy Church, *The History of the British Coal Industry*, Vol. 3 [1830–1913] (1986).

GOING TO THE EPSOM RACE BY TRAIN

First Class

Second Class

Third Class

The Three Classes The early Victorian railway gave graphic expression to the notion that society was divided into precisely three classes — even if members of all three classes were traveling to the same horse race. *(From the* Illustrated London News, *1847)* workingman in twenty was in some fashion permanently "working on the railway." Such jobs were relatively well paid, but they could be dangerous: during the 1880s some 300 railway men died each year because of accidents, and five times that number were injured. At the same time, the railway cut the cost of transportation of many goods to only a fraction of what it had been before. A national market sprang up for building materials like bricks, glass, and roofing slate. Cattlemen, who since medieval times had driven their cattle from Devon, Hereford, and Scotland to East Anglia for fattening and then to London for market, now shipped the animals direct by rail. Milk for the metropolitan areas could be sent by morning milk train from thirty or forty miles away.

The railway transformed Great Britain into a single time zone; from 1842 on, all clocks were to abide by "Greenwich mean time" as determined by the Royal Naval Observatory there. In similar fashion, the railway revolutionized the operations of the post office in the form of the "penny post." In 1840, it implemented inventor Rowland Hill's idea that mailers should purchase and affix postage stamps prior to sending letters to any portion of the kingdom for a penny. The railway also made possible the national distribution of London newspapers. It stimulated architects to design more than 9,000 railway stations, some of them enormous Victorian Gothic palaces. Even provincial stations could boast ornate waiting rooms.

The social effects of the coming of the railway were equally significant. The average middle-class resident of eighteenth-century Birmingham had not visited London in an entire lifetime, even though it was only a hundred miles away. By 1850 rail travel for almost all classes had ceased to be a novelty; the railway brought English people from various regions and ranks of society into temporary communion, at the same time that it divided them, like the inhabitants of Plato's *Republic,* into precisely three classes. Initially, second-class passengers bought candles at news stalls for night travel, and third-class passengers rode in open trucks, but the Act of 1844 insisted that even the humblest travelers be protected from the rain. Evangelical moralists were inspired to compare life's pilgrimage to a railway journey:

> The line to Heaven by us is made,
> With heavenly truth the rails are laid;
> From Earth to Heaven the line extends
> And in eternal life it ends.

The railway also affected the everyday English language, as people began to speak of "getting up steam" and "blowing off steam" and to reckon distances in hours and minutes rather than in miles. Finally, the railway came to represent the most obvious example of human progress, and Alfred Lord Tennyson urged: "Let the great world spin forever down the ringing grooves of change." The poet laureate had apparently not taken a close look at the T-shaped rails on which his railway carriage sped.

Working Conditions

In many a survey of British history, the 1820s, 1830s, and 1840s have been summed up not as years of dynamic progress — when the economy grew at a faster rate than ever before or since — but as years of suffering and deprivation, as that "bleak age" in which the "evils of the Industrial Revolution" made themselves manifest.[6] It has become almost a twentieth-century truism that the early-nineteenth-century factory owner ground the faces of his workers in the dust, and evidence substantiating the pitiful conditions under which many a British worker labored during these years is indeed plentiful. Parliamentary blue books, those huge ponderous volumes that record in stenographic detail the hearings held and the conclusions reached by royal commissions and select committees investigating mines and factories, bear witness that hours were long and times hard. Samuel Coulson testified to one parliamentary committee in 1832 that in "brisk time" his children were expected to be in the cotton mills by 3:00 A.M. and to work until 10:00 P.M. with no more than an hour in all for mealtime breaks. In ordinary times they worked from 6:00 A.M. to 8:30 P.M. six days a week for a total weekly wage of three shillings. Other women and children were reported as having to crawl half-naked through the narrow shafts of ill-ventilated mines. Apprentice bricklayers might have fourteen-hour days and expect punishment with the strap if they tarried. Chimney sweeps were expected to climb up and down narrow chimneys even though their elbows and knees were rubbed raw; they might not wash for months at a time and never go to school at all. Sir Edwin Chadwick's Commission on the Sanitary Condition of the Labouring Population (1842) found that thousands of workers in Liverpool and Manchester lived in unventilated cellars, and although the row houses that had been built on every neighboring hillside provided a modicum of shelter, they often lacked paved streets, sewers, or garbage collectors. The average diet was often limited to bread, tea, sugar, and beer, supplemented with potatoes, cheese, turnips, beans, and cabbage. Among unskilled and semi-skilled working families, meat (mostly in the form of pork or bacon) was often reserved for the prime family breadwinner rather than for his wife or children. Every few years a period of "distress," or economic

---

[6]The more pessimistic point of view is presented in such works as J. L. and Barbara Hammond, *The Age of the Chartists, 1832–1854* (1930); and E. J. Hobsbawm, *Labouring Men* (1964); the more optimistic, by T. S. Ashton in *The Industrial Revolution, 1760–1830* (rev. ed., 1962); R. M. Hartwell, *The Industrial Revolution and Economic Growth* (1971); and Clark Nardinelli, *Child Labor and the Industrial Revolution* (1990). Phyllis Deane provides a studiously balanced assessment in *The First Industrial Revolution* (2nd ed., 1981). See also Peter Mathias, *The First Industrial Nation* (2nd ed., 1983). P. A. M. Taylor, ed., *The Industrial Revolution in Britain: Triumph or Disaster?* (2nd ed., 1970), samples the arguments of both optimists and pessimists.

depression, would occur, in which large numbers of workers were thrown out on the streets without jobs or even garden plots to call their own.

The reports make harrowing reading, but it may well be questioned whether the evils were necessarily the products of industrialization. It is clear that the process of economic change necessitated a severe readjustment for many rural family members. Although voluntary, the move to the city meant a breakup of old social ties, at least a temporary end to the security of status that a village provided, and acceptance of the work discipline imposed by the steam-driven machine and the factory whistle. Some industrialists encouraged their factory employees to see themselves as members of an extended family, which the owners governed in a spirit of moral paternalism. Whether the factory system meant actual impoverishment or a fall in real wages has been seriously questioned by most twentieth-century economic historians. It is demonstrable, moreover, that the groups that fared worst during these decades were not the workers in factory towns but rural laborers and the 240,000 handloom weavers, victims of "automation" during the 1830s and 1840s who found it difficult to change occupation in their mature years. It was not the population of industrializing England that experienced famine in the 1840s but the people of largely agricultural Ireland. An unindustrialized England could hardly have coped with a population that doubled in the course of the first half of the ninteenth century. Even at their worst, the slums of Manchester never approached the squalor of the slums of Bombay or Calcutta in unindustrialized India.

Long hours, low wages, the apprenticeship of children at the age of seven, and the insecurity brought by poor harvests and disease were hardly nineteenth-century novelties. Indeed, the very parliamentary reports that provide so much grist for the modern social historian's mill stressed the most extreme examples of misery and cruelty and may themselves be interpreted less as evidence of new evils than as the quickening of a social conscience often absent one hundred years earlier. "Whatever the merits of the preindustrial world may have been," concludes one present-day scholar, "they were enjoyed by a deplorably small proportion of those born into it."

The gains in productivity brought about by the new industries were not necessarily immediately passed on to those who worked in them, in part because of the expenses of the Napoleonic Wars and in part because the profits of industry were being plowed back into business. Such profits provided an important source of capital, and a high degree of reinvestment helps account for the relatively rapid rate of economic growth during the early and middle years of the nineteenth century. It was thus the consumer of cotton cloth rather than the spinner or weaver who profited most immediately from the lower costs made possible by the new machinery. Ultimately all members of society, whether they worked in the new industries and railways or not, benefited from the decline in the cost of producing goods and the cost of moving both goods and people.

For all its manifold imperfections, therefore, the process of industrialization provided solutions as well as problems. It created the prospect for the first time in human history that a majority of ordinary people — rather than a favored few — might spend their days at activities other than menial toil and live at a material level far above mere subsistence. Even by the 1830s and 1840s it had become clear that the answer to city sewage problems lay less in a state of mind than in the mass production of inexpensive iron pipes, and that the problem of disease could be solved in part by wearing cheap, washable cotton shirts and underwear and using soap. Only an industrialized nation could afford the luxury of sending its children to school rather than to the farm or factory. The self-confident nineteenth-century merchant breaking into new markets, the mill owner enlarging his factory, the mine operator digging ever deeper shafts, and the iron-master constructing his foundries — each saw himself not only as the seeker of a personal fortune but also as an individual who was developing his country and pushing back the threat of destitution. At least as much as the Whig politicians who had revamped the eighteenth-century constitution, they felt themselves to be the heralds of an age of improvement. On such grounds they had sought and partially won a place in society and a share in molding their country's future.

CHAPTER 3

The Curious Years
of Laissez-Faire

Although the 1830s and 1840s may justly be described as years of dynamic expansion symbolized by the coming of the railway, this growth was intermittent. The age also included years of distress — falling profits, falling wages, mass unemployment, and concomitant political unrest. As this chapter will demonstrate, depending on which aspect of the age we emphasize, we may look on these years as the surprisingly complacent "age of Melbourne" or as an era of virulent social discontent — as manifested by Chartists and Corn Law reformers — or as the years of laissez-faire. Inasmuch as public professions and political realities did not always coincide, we may justifiably call them "the curious years of laissez-faire."

Whigs and Tories

Some of the reformers of 1832 had hoped that a rejuvenated House of Commons would supplant the spirit of party with a spirit of disinterested public service. Yet by 1835 it was clear that the effect of the act had been to strengthen rather than weaken party loyalty. A Whig government was in power, although its continuance rested on a de facto alliance with Radicals and with the Irish followers of Daniel O'Connell (1775–1847), the hero of the Catholic emancipation struggle of 1829. Across the House of Commons aisle sat a revivified Tory opposition headed by Sir Robert Peel. Just as the Whigs of the 1830s were a traditional party of opposition adapting themselves to the role of government, so the Tories were a traditional party of government adapting themselves to the role of opposition. The purpose of the Carlton Club, organized in 1832, and of a variety of new local Conservative and Constitutional associations, was to encourage all sympathetic and eligible voters to register and to make the period of opposition as brief as possible.[1]

---

[1]Norman Gash, *Reaction and Reconstruction in English Politics, 1832–1852* (1965), provides an enlightening analysis of party politics of this era. Gash is also the author of *Politics in the Age of Peel* (1953) and of a magisterial two-volume biography of the statesman (1961, 1972), as well as of a brief one-volume version entitled simply *Peel* (1976).

On many political issues, Whig and Tory attitudes overlapped, but there were distinct differences as well. Few country gentlemen and almost none of the Anglican clergy supported the Whigs, who found adherents among a large number of city merchants and religious dissenters. Consequently, the Whigs showed greater willingness than the Tories to curb the privileges of the Anglican Church and to examine such novel political notions as the secret ballot. The Tories (or *Conservatives*, the term that Peel preferred) accepted the Reform Act as a *fait accompli* but saw their primary task as that of preserving what remained of the nation's constitutional foundations — the monarchy, the House of Lords, and the Church of England. Although Peel did not exclude the rectification of abuses when found, his professed purpose was "to preserve law, order, property and morality. . . ."

The Whig government, headed until 1834 by Lord Grey and thereafter by Lord Melbourne, had been responsible for, or had acquiesced in, a number of significant measures immediately after 1832: the abolition of slavery and the Factory Act of 1833, the new Poor Law Act of 1834, and what became the Municipal Corporations Act of 1835. But Lord Grey's retirement and other resignations from the cabinet in 1834 had so weakened the Whig government, in King William's opinion, that he dismissed it from office, the last example of such royal initiative in British history. Sir Robert Peel became prime minister and, since his followers were clearly in a minority in the House of Commons, he soon asked for a new general election.

The Tories gained 100 seats in the election of 1835, but they were still a minority, and Lord Melbourne returned as prime minister. Under his somewhat languid guidance, the Whig government passed several measures to limit the remaining political privileges of the Church of England, to reform the criminal law, and to increase national grants to (largely religiously supported) elementary schools. Otherwise, it tended to rest on its reform laurels. Melbourne himself was a worldly and tolerant aristocrat for whom the ultimate end of government was "to prevent crime and preserve contracts." Like most Whigs, he was distrustful in equal measure of despotism and democracy, and although he occasionally supported particular reforms, he was too conscious of the frailties of human nature to have much confidence in their efficacy. Melbourne's majority was eroded still further in the general election of 1837 — only 24 in a House of Commons of 658 members — and the weaknesses of his administration were scathingly satirized by a Tory rhymester:

> To promise, pause, prepare, postpone
> And end by letting things alone
> In short to earn the people's pay
> By doing nothing every day.

Although Melbourne gradually lost popular and parliamentary support, he successfully won the affection of the young Queen Victoria (1819–1901) who, as the nearest heir to William IV, ascended to the throne at the age of eighteen on her uncle's death in 1837. Melbourne served her as a political mentor and as the father she had lost years before. By 1839 she had become a confirmed Whig. When Melbourne resigned that year after a near-defeat in the House of Commons, Sir Robert Peel, the Tory leader, demanded that as prospective prime minister he be permitted to choose new ladies of the bedchamber for Victoria. The queen was still too influential politically, Peel felt, for all her confidantes to be from the opposition party. Victoria interpreted the request as a reflection on the standards of morality of her associates at court, and she refused. Peel thereupon declined to form a government, and Melbourne demonstrated notable political skills in hanging on for two additional years as prime minister.[2]

The parliamentary rivalry of Whigs and Tories during the Melbourne years was only distantly related to the founding of two of the century's most significant extraparliamentary protest movements, the Chartists and the Anti–Corn Law League. Although both the Chartist movement, largely working-class in membership, and the distinctively middle-class Anti–Corn Law League were most immediately a response to the economic depression of 1837–1839, they continued to play a significant role in British history for another decade.

The Chartists

The roots of Chartism lay both in the eighteenth-century tradition of political radicalism and in the world of London trade unions, organizations of skilled artisans seeking to preserve their traditional work practices. The clubs were generally small and localized, and although some became politically active during the 1832 Reform Bill crisis, they had not attempted to join forces as a single national labor federation.[3]

Indeed, those who publicly sought to promote the interests of the lower ranks of society looked to the past as much as to the future. William Cobbett (1763–1835), a prolific pamphleteer, saw the factory system as the archenemy that commanded "the common people to stoop in abject submission to the few." He was a Radical in his opposition to pensions and sinecures for the rich, tithes for the Anglican clergy, and taxes to pay for a standing army. In his detestation of commerce and urban

---

[2]David Cecil, *Melbourne* (1955) remains a classic biography, illuminating both the man and his world. L.G. Mitchell's excellent *Lord Melbourne, 1779–1848* (1997) takes into account more recent research.

[3]In *Chartism* (1973), J. T. Ward emphasizes both the antecedents and the diversity of the movement, as well as the failings of many of its leaders. In *The Chartists* (1984), Dorothy Thompson argues that the supporters of the movement constituted a unified working class that demonstrated "a whole alternative culture and lifestyle." Other relevant studies include J. F. C. Harrison, *Robert Owen and the Owenites in Britain and America* (1969); Donald Read and Evie Glasgow, *Feargus O'Connor* (1961); and Joel Wiener, *William Lovett* (1989), and Iorwerth Prothero, *Radical Artisans in England and France, 1830–1870* (1997).

growth and in his lament for the apparent decay of rural life and paternalistic landlords he was a Tory.

Robert Owen (1771–1858), generally regarded as the father of British socialism, also had conservative tendencies. By temperament he was as much an egalitarian aristocrat as a democrat. His early years were spent as a cotton manufacturer in Scotland. Owen was more interested in education than in profits, and he made an industrial showplace of his mills at New Lanark. He provided his workers with schools and houses and presided over his model community as a benevolent despot. He became convinced that the solution for the problem of intermittent unemployment and for the evils of industrial competition generally was the creation in rural areas of model communities in which all members would labor in concord at those tasks that best suited them.

> Community does all possess
> That can to man be given;
> Community is happiness,
> Community is heaven.

So sang the Owenite workers. In contrast to later Marxist socialists, Owen preached class cooperation rather than class struggle between employer and employee. Idle landlords, soldiers, and priests, on the other hand, were dismissed as nonproductive parasites who had no place in the ideal society.

In the course of a long life, Owen became involved in a variety of schemes, such as the abortive utopian community in the United States at New Harmony, Indiana. It was on his return to England in the early 1830s that he inspired the formation of a national trade union movement, the Grand National Consolidated Trades Union (1834), whose objective was to unite the working classes in a decisive but peaceful struggle to inaugurate the Owenite millennium. The union's purpose was not simply "to obtain some paltry rise or prevent some paltry reduction in wages," but by means of cooperative production and sales to establish "for the productive classes a complete dominion over the fruits of their own industry." The Grand National began to collapse the very year it was organized. Major trade unions such as the builders, potters, spinners, and clothiers refused to join, and new factory workers tended to hold themselves aloof. Employers, moreover, resisted its objectives with lockouts and strike breaking. That same year the government showed its suspicion of all unions when it supported the prosecution of the leaders of the Friendly Society of Agricultural Laborers at Tolpuddle in Dorset on the technical ground that they had administered unlawful oaths. Six of the "Tolpuddle martyrs" were transported to Australia.

Although most of Owen's specific projects failed, the spirit behind them did not. The cooperative ideal, at least on the retail level, bore new fruit in Rochdale in 1844. There twenty-eight Lancashire weavers began a successful cooperative grocery store and later a cooperative shoe factory and textile mill. The Rochdale Society, like Robert Owen, aimed both at moral elevation and at material comfort. "The objects of this Society," ran the Rochdale prospectus, "are the moral and intellectual advancement of its members. It provides them with groceries, butcher's meat, drapery goods, clothes, and clogs." Retail shops based on the cooperative principle proved far more successful than factories so organized, and by 1862 there were 450 such societies with 90,000 members. Equally important was the founding and growth of Friendly Societies such as the Odd Fellows and the Foresters whose purpose it was to gather small weekly savings in order to protect workers, and potentially their widows and orphans, against the contingencies of sickness and death. By 1847 such societies had a million and a half members.

Owen had never been particularly interested in political action, but the failure of the Grand National Consolidated Trades Union and the onset of the depression of 1837 revived the interest of many working-class leaders in a political solution to their problems. By that summer, 50,000 workers were either out of work or on short time in Manchester alone. The poor harvests and business failures of the late 1830s affected human emotions and imaginations as well and brought to the fore what came to be called the "Condition of England" question. Friedrich Engels (1820–1895), the youthful German-born Manchester manufacturer, deplored the lot of the laborer in his *The Condition of the Working Class in England in 1844*. Thomas Carlyle (1795–1881), the Scottish-born social critic, sought in vain for a hero to save his society. He deplored the materialism of his age and the failure of Britain's complacent rulers to be more concerned with the welfare of the poor. In the process he also denounced such concepts as progress, liberalism, and democracy with the intensity of an Old Testament prophet. Benjamin Disraeli (1804–1881), the youthful novelist and Tory M.P., popularized in *Sybil* (1845) the notion that England was divided into "two nations": the rich and the poor.

By 1837 a number of radical leaders had become persuaded that the Reform Bill of 1832 had not done nearly enough to alter the political structure of the country and that neither aristocrats nor factory owners and merchants were suitable parliamentary representatives for unenfranchised laborers. The head of the London Workingmen's Association, William Lovett (1800–1877), in consultation with Francis Place and a number of Radical M.P.'s, therefore drew up a People's Charter. It set forth six goals: (1) universal manhood suffrage, (2) annual elections for Parliament, (3) voting by secret ballot, (4) equal electoral districts, (5) abolition of property qualifications for members of Parliament, and (6) payment of members of Parliament. Most Chartists were confirmed believers in Parliament, but they demanded a completely democratized Commons and declared: "The House of Commons is the People's House, and *there* our opinions should be stated, *there* our rights ought to be advocated, *there* we ought to be represented or we are SERFS."

At an enormous meeting in Birmingham in August 1838, the Charter was officially adopted by delegates from all parts of the country. It was at Birmingham also that the voice of Feargus O'Connor (1796–1855) began to dominate Chartist proceedings. O'Connor had a paradoxical background for the leader of an English popular movement. He was a Protestant Irish landlord whose family claimed descent from the eleventh-century "high kings of Ireland." In his thirties, O'Connor set out to establish himself as a political Radical and as a supporter of Irish nationalism. He served in Parliament from 1832 until 1835, when he was unseated for lacking a sufficient amount of property. He then turned to English reform movements and sought in Chartism an alliance of Irish peasants and English workers against what seemed to be their joint oppressors. His bombastic manner and eloquent oratory appealed to large groups of overworked, poorly educated, and hungry people, and in his newspaper, the *Northern Star,* which boasted the then astonishing circulation of 50,000 copies a week, he called for a "holy and irresistible crusade" against the government in power. O'Connor represented the militant side of Chartism as did George Julian Harney, who habitually wore a red cap of liberty and who in 1839 sent thrills of horror up aristocratic spines by predicting: "Before the end of the year the people shall have universal suffrage or death."

More moderate Chartists were put off by the tactics of O'Connor and Harney, but the militants clearly won converts, and during the winter of 1838–1839 the movement gained momentum. Torchlight meetings were held throughout England for the purpose of electing representatives to a giant London convention in 1839 that was to prepare a petition to Parliament. Although agreed on the Charter itself, the London convention soon split on the question of what to do if the Charter were rejected. Some delegates wanted the Chartist convention to become a permanent "anti-Parliament"; others suggested a "national holiday" (a general strike); still others hinted at the use of physical force.

The Charter petition was introduced to the House of Commons in June 1839. It bore 1,280,000 signatures, but after a cursory debate the House, in effect, rejected the Charter by a vote of 235 to 46. As a consequence, the London convention broke up in confusion. A number of riots during the following autumn and winter and a clash in Newport, Monmouthshire, in which twenty people were killed, led to the arrest of at least 500 Chartist leaders, including Lovett and O'Connor. O'Connor, dubbed "the Lion of Freedom" by his more ardent followers, continued to edit the *Northern Star* from jail, but for the moment the movement lacked centralized direction, and an upturn in the economy weakened its hold on many workers. When, however, depression returned with a vengeance in 1841 and 1842, Chartism revived. A permanent National Charter Association was established, with centralized leadership and machinery for collecting a regular subscription of a penny a week per member. In May 1842 another monster petition, this time bearing more than 3,300,000 signatures, was presented to the House of Commons. It, too, was resoundingly rejected, 287 to 59.

Chartism, like so many workers' movements, was a child of bad times, and when prosperity returned in 1843, social protest began to subside. Moreover, the Charter had little or no upper-class support, and Parliament never really took it seriously. As Thomas Babington Macaulay (1800–1859), the Whig historian and M.P., put it in 1842, universal suffrage would be "fatal to the purposes for which government exists" and was "utterly incompatible with the existence of civilization." The goal of constitutional government was to provide a legal framework within which public issues might be reasonably discussed and resolved. An illiterate or ill-educated populace that gained political domination, he declared, would necessarily fall prey to demagogues. The result would be either anarchy or the mass confiscation of property, and the consequence would be not the alleviation but the deterioration of the lot of the poor.

The Chartists' only hope was to win sufficient popular support in a time of crisis to intimidate if not to convince the government. Yet, even at the height of Chartist agitation, many workers remained aloof. The movement was stronger in the North of England and in the Midlands, especially in centers of decaying industry and in medium-sized industrial towns, than in London. Yet a working class that included such disparate elements as factory operatives, handloom weavers, domestic nailmakers, and self-educated artisans tended to show far greater loyalty to occupation and locality than to the abstract concept of class. Chartism was weakened not merely by its failures to gain upper-class support and to solidify its ranks, but by a persistent vagueness about the economic means by which the weak were to become powerful and the poor were to become rich. Thus one Chartist orator assured his listeners: "If a man ask what I mean by universal suffrage, I mean to say that every working man in the land has a right to a good coat on his back, a good hat on his head, a good roof for the shelter of his household." Somehow political democracy was to produce fair shares for all; yet few Chartists were socialists in the sense that they wished to overturn the capitalist organization of industry. It is true that O'Connor, who once compared the unfortunate effects of machinery on workers' lives to the effects of the coming of the railway on the lives of horses, dreamed at times of the restoration of a rural utopia, but many Chartists remained incipient capitalists. As one critic told a gathering of laborers: "Denounce the middle classes as you may, there is not a man among you worth a half-penny a week that is not anxious to elevate himself among them." Analogously, like middle-class men, they sought to be the prime family bread-winners; women were expected to be partners at home rather than rivals at the workplace.[4]

The last gasp of Chartism came in 1848. Inspired by political revolution in France, Italy, and Germany, and galvanized into action by another downturn in the economy, a new convention gathered signatures for a third giant petition and decided to form itself into a national assembly on the French model if the Charter were rejected. The government took

---

[4]See, e.g., Anna Clark, *The Struggle for the Breeches: Gender and the Making of the British Working Class* (1995).

The Last Great Chartist Demonstration (1848) This is the oldest known photograph of a mass protest demonstration. *(Reproduced by gracious permission of Her Majesty the Queen)*

formidable precautions. Almost every London gentleman was created a special constable in order to handle the crowd that was expected to march upon the houses of Parliament. The gathering was not as large as predicted, if only because of the steady rain, a familiar handicap for all outdoor demonstrations in England. Feargus O'Connor, who had resumed leadership in the movement, was ordered to stop the march, and he did so. The petitions were transported to Parliament in three hansom cabs while everyone else went home.

The third Charter, which did no better in the House of Commons than the previous two, came to be looked upon as something of a fiasco. The almost two million valid signatures would seem to have shown impressive popular support, but because O'Connor had extravagantly claimed five million signatures, the smaller number was deemed insignificant. Renewed prosperity caused Chartism as an organized movement to peter out permanently during the next three years. It was to be remembered, however, as the first great national protest movement in British history, and it helped popularize the concept — however misleading — that there existed a single "working class." One may contend, moreover, that the meetings, the demonstrations, and other activities connected with the movement gave meaning to the lives of many Chartists. Like the analogous Populist movement in the late-nineteenth-century United States, Chartism frightened the respectable middle and upper classes and subsequently fell victim to prosperity; but the essential reforms advocated by each were to be enacted at different times under different auspices. Within only three-quarters of a century, five of the charter's six points — annual elections to Parliament being the sole exception — were to become part of the British constitution.

The Corn Law Reformers

The other major protest movement to which the depression of 1837–1839 gave rise was the Anti–Corn Law League.[5] During the Napoleonic Wars, English landlords and farmers had been encouraged to raise all the grain they could. Once the war was over, however, they were faced with the problem of a grain surplus. The government, sympathetic to their interests, sought to protect them against foreign competition with the Corn Laws of 1815, which barred foreign imports until the domestic price was so high as to threaten famine at home. The Corn Laws did not and could not prevent sharp ups and downs in the domestic price of grain. When an abundant harvest provided a supply greater than the effective public demand, the price would go down, Corn Laws notwithstanding. Yet the Corn Laws became the rock on which Tory economic policy rested. They were justified as a necessary protection for English landed society and the kingdom's national security.

The Corn Laws served a second vital function. Britain had been left by the Napoleonic Wars with what contemporaries justly regarded as a critical financial problem. In the course of the 1980s and 1990s Americans became understandably concerned about the size of a rapidly growing national debt, but that debt never approximated in scope that of early nineteenth-century Britain. Whereas the total national debt of the United States today is equal to less than two-thirds of the gross national product of any given year, that of Britain during the 1820s was two and a half times as great as its GNP. And whereas interest payments on the U.S. national debt absorbed less than 15 percent of the annual federal budget at the turn of the twenty-first century, they absorbed more than 50 percent of the annual British budget during the 1820s and dipped only slowly thereafter. Because much of the government's income was derived from customs and excise duties, and because imports of food were slowly increasing, the Corn Laws served as an important source of revenue as well as a means of agricultural protection.

Beset by the economic depression of 1837–1839 and disillusioned with an aristocratic Whig government whose taste for reform had waned, a group of Manchester industrialists headed by George Wilson (1808–1870) and Richard Cobden (1804–1865) concluded that their own economic salvation, as well as the political salvation of middle-class

---

[5]To understand the significance of the Corn Laws it is important to realize that *corn* in British usage refers to all grains — wheat, oats, barley — and not merely to American *maize*.

radicals, lay in the abolition of the Corn Laws. "The English people cannot be made to take up more than one question at a time with enthusiasm," confided Cobden, and the new league decided to concentrate on the "total and immediate" repeal of the Corn Laws as that issue. League leaders hoped to attract the support of all those who resented the privileges and entrenched influence in national life enjoyed by the aristocracy — even after 1832 — for to them the Corn Laws had become "the symbol of aristocratic misrule."

The Anti–Corn Law League was in one sense the outcome of the teachings of the classical economists. Adam Smith in his *Wealth of Nations* had concluded that the economic prosperity of individuals and nations was best advanced if each worked at that task for which he or she was best suited. As early as the 1830s it seemed clear to some Britons that their land had been designed by God for the role of an industrial power that exported its surplus manufactures in exchange for the raw materials and foodstuffs of other lands. In hindering that development, the Corn Laws appeared to contradict the will of Providence.

It would be a mistake to see the work of the league as that of a group of detached economists. The association was rather the best-organized pressure group Britain had ever known, and it broke precedent by seeking to persuade not merely the traditional governing class but also the unenfranchised masses. It was a highly effective lobby that appealed as much to human emotions as to material interests and whose speakers cited the Bible as often as they quoted economic statistics. The league appealed to the manufacturer: repeal the Corn Laws and your workers will have cheaper food and will therefore put less pressure on you for higher wages. Moreover, the countries from which the food will be imported will then have the means to buy English manufactured goods. The league appealed to the workers: repeal the Corn Laws and the cost of your bread will go down. The day of "the Big Loaf" will be at hand, and you will be assured of more regular employment. The league even attempted, if not very successfully, to appeal to the farmer: the Corn Laws keep the rents you pay your landlords at artificially high levels. Repeal the Corn Laws and your rents will fall. The league appealed to the humanitarian: the age of mercantilism has brought wars as nations squabble over trade advantage. The Corn Laws are the last great bastion of mercantilism. Repeal the Corn Laws and the result will be free trade for the English people. As other nations follow England's lead, the economic causes of war will disappear. An era of international fellowship will be at hand. Or to phrase it yet more simply: repeal the Corn Laws and the result will be world peace.

Although the league was increasingly successful in raising money from wealthy manufacturers and in campaigning with tracts, lectures, tea parties, and bazaars (at which free-trade handkerchiefs, bread plates, and teapots were sold), for the moment its influence on the country was more widespread than its influence on Parliament. As late as 1840 an anti–Corn Law resolution was defeated 300 to 177 in the House of

Robert Peel   The Conservative prime minister (1841–46) promoted financial reform. *(Mansell/Time)*

Richard Cobden   A photograph of Britain's prime champion of "Free Trade." *(Bettmann/Corbis)*

Commons; and by 1841 the league became convinced that, if it were to achieve economic reform, it would have to participate actively in politics. It organized registration drives to ensure that all eligible free traders were on the poll books, and on occasion it put up its own candidates. When the Whigs came out in support of a lower fixed rate on corn imports in 1841, the league threw its support to the Whigs rather than the Tories in the general election of that year. The results were disappointing. Individual free traders — Richard Cobden most importantly — gained seats in the House of Commons; but a revived Tory party under Robert Peel's leadership took over with an apparently solid seventy-eight-vote majority. The league's drive continued, and Cobden's disciple, John Bright (1811–1889), a Quaker manufacturer from Rochdale, added his eloquent voice to Cobden's own. But the parliamentary repeal of the Corn Laws seemed just as far away as ever.[6]

Peel and Repeal

Peel's ministry (1841–1846) proved more helpful to the free traders than they had expected. Sir Robert Peel, who after the debacle of 1832 had

---

[6]See Norman McCord, *The Anti–Corn Law League, 1838–1846* (1958); Donald Read, *Cobden and Bright: A Victorian Political Partnership* (1967); and Nicholas C. Edsall, *Richard Cobden: Independent Radical* (1986).

gained stature during his years in opposition as an exponent of responsible and restrained criticism, had molded a potent political force in his revived Tory party. Peel himself was not a "popular" leader. He was reserved and kept his own counsel, "an iceberg with a slight thaw on the surface." He was, however, not nearly so satisfied with a policy of simply preserving the status quo as many of his party would have preferred. The son of a successful textile printer, Peel was the type of hardworking administrator the Manchester industrialists appreciated. As prime minister, Peel felt it his duty to read all foreign dispatches, to keep up a steady correspondence with Queen Victoria and Prince Albert, to hold numerous private interviews, to superintend all patronage both in the Civil Service and the Anglican Church, to prepare for debates, to spend eight hours a day for 118 days a year in the House of Commons, and to "write with his own hand to every person of note who chooses to write to him." Peel embodied what came to be known as the Victorian "gospel of work."

In the budget of 1842 Sir Robert introduced far-reaching reforms that were ultimately to make the repeal of the Corn Laws easier. Hoping to overcome a succession of Whig deficits, he reintroduced the income tax as a significant source of government revenue. This Napoleonic War expedient had been abolished in 1817. Peel reintroduced it at a fixed rate of seven pence on the pound (slightly less than 3 percent), but he exempted all but those with relatively high incomes (£150 or more per year) from liability to pay the tax. At the same time he sponsored a general reduction in protective tariffs for 750 of some 1,200 itemized articles. With the aid of his equally hardworking colleague, William Ewart Gladstone (1809–1898), who served first as vice-president and then as president of the Board of Trade, some 430 articles, including imported raw cotton, were struck off the customs altogether, and in 1845 all remaining taxes on exports were ended. The British fiscal system was being streamlined in a way suitable to a highly industrialized nation.

As the years of his ministry went on, Peel became increasingly equivocal on the subject of the Corn Laws. Although the country had recovered from the economic depression of the early 1840s, the defenders of the Corn Laws found it difficult to answer the argument that their stand favored high food prices. Many free traders began to pin their hopes on Peel's public conversion to their cause, for they admired him far more as a statesman than they did Lord John Russell, who after 1841 had taken over the leadership of the Whigs from Lord Melbourne and who in 1845 announced his conversion to complete free trade.

The Irish Famine

The industrialists were not disappointed, for Peel's own conversion to free trade came during the winter of 1845–1846 when famine struck Ireland. In the course of the previous century, at least half of the Irish people had become accustomed to a diet consisting of a single staple: the potato. Meat might be a once-a-month treat, but day after day, three times a day, many of the Irish ate salted, boiled potatoes. The potato had been introduced into Ireland by 1600 from its South American home, but it was not until the later eighteenth century that — especially in the western counties — it came to predominate over the dairy and grain products that had till then provided Ireland's staple foods and exports. An increasing number of acres was devoted to raising potatoes, a crop with numerous advantages. It could be stored easily and made edible simply by boiling. It was easy to grow and less likely to be stolen, burned, or trampled than wheat or rye. It grew in the hills as well as on the plains. Most significantly, it fed a family on less than half as much land as wheat required. Until the 1820s the monotony of the potato was offset by its abundance. An average laborer was expected to consume ten to twenty pounds of potatoes a day, and together with milk this provided more than sufficient calories and vitamins, even by twentieth-century dietetic standards.

The potato may well have been a major cause of the rapid growth in the Irish population that began during the eighteenth century. From

Searching for Potatoes in a Stubble Field   This picture dates from December 1846, the second winter of the great Irish Famine.
(Hulton Deutsch Collection)

approximately four million people in 1780 it increased to over eight million by 1840, not counting the tens of thousands who emigrated in the interim to England or across the Atlantic. One explanation that has been offered for the rising fertility rate is that women engaged in cultivating potatoes breast-fed their babies for a shorter time and therefore became pregnant more often. At the same time, the landholding system did nothing to encourage either thrift or late marriage. Most Irish tenants lacked both the means and the incentive to improve their property, and as soon as sons reached manhood, they would receive portions of their father's holdings on which to start potato patches of their own. The great danger for a population so completely dependent on a single crop was that, for reasons of weather or disease, the crop might fail, and there was no substitute source of food. Because potatoes could not be stored for more than a year, the surplus of one year could not make up for the scarcity of the next. And because Ireland was a largely rural society, many counties lacked an organized food trade or even the custom of using money.

By 1830, regional failures of the potato crop in Ireland had become dangerously frequent, but it was not until 1845–1848 that a potato blight ruined almost the entire crop. The disease was caused by a fungus for which the scientists of the day could find no remedy. In the words of Lord John Russell, the result was "a famine of the thirteenth century acting upon a population of the nineteenth." Almost a million people died directly or indirectly of starvation; the young contracted dysentery; the old, typhus. During the ten years after 1845, at least a million and a half more sought refuge abroad. Many fled to England and Scotland; and more Irish people than ever before sought material salvation in the New World.

Although successive British governments failed to avert famine, the potato failure convinced Peel that, at the very least, all barriers to the importation of food to the United Kingdom should be ended. In November 1845 he proposed that the Corn Laws be suspended. In May 1846 he persuaded the House of Commons to end them completely, and with the aid of the duke of Wellington, he obtained the concurrence of the House of Lords. In the process he split his party, for while the opposition Whigs voted almost solidly for repeal, a majority of Tories believed that Peel had broken his political promises and betrayed the cause of the English farmer. Of his party, 112 voted with Peel, but 231 voted against him. Within a month of repeal, Peel's ministry was defeated, and Lord John Russell replaced him as prime minister.

Peel had sacrificed his party and his career to repeal the Corn Laws, but his actions did little to save Ireland. A generation of Irish nationalists became convinced, indeed, that the Irish famine had been a deliberate plot on the part of the English government to rid the world of the Irish. "The Almighty . . . sent the potato blight," declared John Mitchel, "but the English created the Famine." Not until the mid-twentieth century did a group of revisionist Irish historians conclude that the truth was not so simple.[7]

The almost one million Irish who died in the Great Famine were less the victims of a plot than of a government that lacked both the experience and the administrative machinery to handle such a crisis and of a political theory that did not consider relief to be one of the proper functions of government. "A government," conceded *The Economist*, "may remove all impediments which interfere to prevent the people from providing for themselves, but beyond that they can do little." Peel did arrange for an emergency shipment of American maize, or "Indian corn," and in 1847 the government headed by his successor subsidized a system of soup kitchens that fed as many as three million people a day. For the most part, however, Lord John Russell preferred to rely on the operations of the Poor Law, which a Whig government had introduced into Ireland less than ten years before. Russell both exaggerated the wealth and distrusted the character of Irish landlords; he was so eager to compel them to assume their paternal responsibilities, indeed, that he lost sight of the plight of their tenants. If people were hungry and out of work, the local Poor-Law guardians were expected to supply them with relief money in exchange for their labor on public works or in the poorhouse. Local storekeepers and merchants would import foreign grain, which the starving might purchase with their relief funds. According to the assumptions of classical economists, the system should have worked. What Russell and other English government leaders overlooked was that rural Ireland almost totally lacked the highly developed network of merchants, shops, and roads that they took for granted in England. Even the emergency shipments of American corn did little for people who did not know how to grind the grain and bake the bread. The British Exchequer ultimately paid half the cost of famine relief. The cost of the remainder was met by Irish Poor-Law rate payers and by the fund-raising drives launched by private British and American charitable groups such as the Quakers.

All these humanitarian efforts helped, but they did not prevent the Irish famine any more than did the repeal of the Corn Laws by act of Parliament. Corn Law repeal did, however, leave a lasting mark on the economic, political, and social scene of nineteenth-century England. Some modern experts have their doubts as to whether the repeal of the Corn Laws produced the decades of prosperity into which the country moved, but contemporaries were by and large willing to give the credit to the Anti–Corn Law League. Even British agriculture did not suffer greatly, at

---

[7]R. D. Edwards and T. D. Williams, eds., *The Great Famine: Studies in Irish History, 1845–1852* (1956). In *The Great Hunger* (1963), Cecil Woodham-Smith focuses on the plight of the victims. In *The Great Irish Famine* (1989), Cormac Ó Gráda provides a judicious and concise summary of modern scholarship. The events have been placed in a broader context in Ó Gráda's *Ireland: A New Economic History, 1780–1939* (1994). In a review essay in *Victorian Studies* 39 (Winter 1996), Sean Connolly surveys recent historical debate on the subject. See also John Prest, *Lord John Russell* (1972).

least for a generation, and the doctrine of free trade came to be defined by a nineteenth-century professor of economics as "a truth like those of physical science, [resting] on the solid basis of established fact."

Politically, the repeal of the Corn Laws determined the shape, or shapelessness, of British politics for the next two decades. The Protectionist Tories were condemned to minority status, and for a time the Peelite Tories became a separate third party. The Whigs, with no clear issue to hold them together, tended to disintegrate into factions, and the relatively clear-cut two-party system that had emerged from the Reform Bill struggle broke down. In other respects, Peel's actions had proved helpful. One of his chief motives in repealing the Corn Laws had been to heal the conflict between two of the most influential groups in the kingdom — the landowners and the factory owners. When in 1850 Sir Robert died, he may have left a shattered Conservative party, but he bequeathed a far more important legacy — a united land. At the close of the year of his death the *Annual Register* could report that "the domestic affairs of the British nation presented a tranquil and, with partial exceptions, a cheering aspect."

The Trend Toward Laissez-Faire

The obvious success of the Anti–Corn Law League in 1846, in contrast to the short-term failure of the Chartists, has contributed to one of the more persistent of historical oversimplifications: that the middle years of the nineteenth century marked the high-water mark of laissez-faire capitalism. In capsule form the thesis goes something like this:

During the sixteenth, seventeenth, and early eighteenth centuries the nations of Europe were under the sway of the doctrine of mercantilism. This doctrine encouraged national governments to regulate imports and exports, to aid the development and undertake the government of colonies, and to regulate the quality of manufactured goods and supervise the conditions under which these goods were made, all in order to further the economic interests of the nation and its people as a whole. Then in the eighteenth century came a group of "enlightened thinkers," the Physiocrats in France and Adam Smith in Scotland, to argue that mercantilism was mistaken and to suggest that a nation would prosper most not by enacting a mass of restrictive legislation regulating the procedures of manufacture and the terms of trade but by leaving economic affairs alone. Do away with restrictions; allow the government to confine itself essentially to the role of police constable; let it keep order at home and defend the nation against enemies abroad; and permit the law of supply and demand to operate freely. If individuals were allowed to follow their own self-interest, then, as if by an invisible hand, in the very act of following their own self-interest they would promote the interests of their country as well. Let every nation engage in those economic activities for which its climate, its natural resources, and the skills of its people best fit it. This was Adam Smith's prescription for the economic ills of his age: laissez-faire. As far as possible, leave things alone.

According to the thesis, Britons did not immediately begin to heed the wisdom of Adam Smith — it was especially difficult to do so in the midst of the Napoleonic Wars — but in the course of half a century, Smith's ideas and those of like-minded classical economists came to be widely accepted. Thus, at the very time that the Great Reform Bill was overhauling the political structure of the realm, economic reformers were abolishing the remnants of mercantilistic legislation and promoting the adoption of laissez-faire. The great triumph of laissez-faire came with the repeal of the Corn Laws in 1846. Britain continued to be guided by laissez-faire until the twentieth century when, as a result of world wars, socialist ideas, and other factors, it developed into the welfare state of the post-1945 era.

Although it remains a vast oversimplification, the thesis summarized above has a degree of validity. The phrase *laissez-faire*, it must be remembered, tends to be used interchangeably for government policy toward at least two distinct concerns: the commercial relationship between one country and another, and the relationship between workers and employers within the same country. Adam Smith was interested primarily in doing away with, or at least reducing, the numerous unreasonable — and therefore, to him, unnatural — restrictions of his day on international commerce. He was less concerned with the relationship between capital and labor, if for no other reason than that in eighteenth-century Britain a good deal of practical laissez-faire already existed in this area, even if it had not yet received theoretical justification. The Elizabethan apprenticeship laws were still in the statute book, and the local Justices of the Peace retained the power to set wage limits and price limits; but such laws were enforced only sporadically and were not always applicable to conditions in the new factory towns.

Two economists of the late eighteenth and early nineteenth centuries gave added sanction to the belief that government ought not to interfere in the relationship between capital and labor. Thomas Malthus reached the pessimistic conclusion that the human population had an inherent tendency to outrun the food supply and that government intervention in the form, say, of setting minimum wages would simply encourage working families to have more children. He admitted that state interference might relieve poverty in the short run, but in the long run the average standard of living would not improve substantially above the subsistence level. David Ricardo, with his so-called Iron Law of Wages, reached a similarly dreary conclusion. There was, he saw, only so much money to go around. If one group of workers, either by unionization or by means of government aid, were granted more, the result would be merely that some other group would end up with less. Once again, laissez-faire appeared to be the best answer.

In any event, by 1813 the remnants of the Elizabethan apprenticeship laws had been repealed, and one barrier (if a largely theoretical one) against workers and employers making their own employment arrangements was removed. The question of whether labor unions did or did not meet the test of laissez-faire remained open. On the one hand, it was argued that a group of workers acting together to force wages up was violating natural economic law — this was the logic of the Combination Acts of 1799, which prohibited labor unions. Yet one could equally argue that true laissez-faire consisted of letting both workers and their employers do what came naturally, and if organizing labor unions came naturally, then perhaps true laissez-faire implied that the government ought not to interfere. On that basis the Combination Acts were made much less rigorous in the mid-1820s, but for the next half century the question of whether or not the actions of a labor union might be ruled a conspiracy under English common law remained unsettled. At the same time lawyers had come to look on society less in terms of groups than in terms of free and responsible individuals who made solemn agreements with one another. It was the task of the courts to uphold the principle of freedom of contract.

If there were some indications of a trend toward laissez-faire in domestic labor relations, then that trend was far more marked in the field of foreign commerce. The actions of Pitt in the 1780s and of Huskisson in the 1820s were continued by Peel and Gladstone in the 1840s, and the great triumph of the Anti–Corn Law League in 1846 was succeeded in 1849 by the repeal of the last of the Navigation Acts, the statutes that had regulated with which countries and in whose ships British merchants might trade. A few years later, even Britain's coastal trade was opened to foreign vessels. It was, to be sure, not theory alone that destroyed those remnants of seventeenth-century mercantilism, but the fact that in the 1840s most British manufacturers and shippers were more efficient than their rivals.

To this extent the thesis that laissez-faire triumphed in nineteenth-century Britain is accurate.[8] It is accurate in another way as well. Almost every organized political group in Britain in the first half of the century believed in it. Certainly all parties denounced the evils of big government, although by continental standards Britain's central government in 1830 was absurdly small. Whereas France's minister of the interior alone had direct authority over 200,000 employees scattered throughout his country, all of Britain's ministers together employed scarcely 21,000 people. Nine thousand of these, however, were the hated customs officials, who swarmed the land inspecting every tea seller and tobacconist eight times a year and who laid down exacting regulations for everything from the brewing of spirits to the manufacture of glass and paper.

Most Whigs by this time had been sufficiently "enlightened" by the classical economists to regard government intervention in the economy

---

[8]In *Free Trade and Liberal England, 1846–1946* (1997), Anthony Howe reminds us to how significant a degree the doctrine of free trade was to impress several generations of Victorians as the key to political liberation and social progress.

as intrinsically wrong. The Radicals from the start had been suspicious of the central government as the entrenched home of the aristocracy; they regarded state control as simply an excuse for paying lazy aristocrats to do nothing and the Home Office as a den of police spies. The Tories by tradition were less ready to accept the ideas of the classical economists, and Samuel Taylor Coleridge, the Romantic poet, observed with disdain that the laissez-faire economists were prepared to dig up the charcoal foundations of the Greek temple at Ephesus in order to provide fuel for their steam engine. The Tories boasted of their greater concern with matters spiritual and their more paternal interest in the welfare of the factory worker, but in practice they, too, were opposed to the expansion of the central government. They expected to maintain their paternalism through voluntary associations or through such pillars of Tory influence as the parish vestry or the Justices of the Peace who continued to dominate county government.[9] It would seem, therefore, that, in theory as well as in practice, laissez-faire characterized the mood of the time. "The course of modern legislation," concluded a parliamentary committee in 1851, "seems to have been gradually to remove restrictions on the power which everyone has in the disposal of his property, and to remove those fetters on commercial freedom which long prevailed in this country."

The Trend Toward State Intervention

Despite all the evidence to support the thesis that the Britain of the second quarter of the nineteenth century was a land of laissez-faire, the fact remains that the powers of the central government were on the increase between 1833 and 1854. A central government that had rarely touched the lives of ordinary individuals and that had shown little direct concern for their well-being became directly involved with their working conditions, their health, and, to some extent, their education. The reasons for this curious development in the teeth of the most sacred professions of the major political parties must be sought in the growing conviction among the better-off that the filth, disease, and human suffering to be found in Britain's towns was an evil that could and should be alleviated by the only agency strong enough to act — the central government.

The two groups that did the most during the first half of the nineteenth century to promote government intervention in social conditions were the Evangelicals and the Utilitarians. The Evangelicals were those persons within the eighteenth-century Church of England who came to believe that the forms of worship and the theological interests of their Church had lost touch with the daily life of the common people. Christianity ought to inspire, they felt, not only a personal devotion to religious worship but also a personal involvement in the way people lived.

---

[9]In *Paternalism in Early Victorian England* (1979), David Roberts examines both the meaning of the idea and how it was applied.

John Wesley's Methodists had in time broken off from the Anglican Church, but many who were equally imbued with a sense of evangelical mission remained within the fold. It was their efforts, allied with those of members of the Nonconformist denominations, that had spearheaded the antislavery crusade of the early nineteenth century and had succeeded in freeing some seven hundred thousand black slaves (most of whom lived in the West Indies). The method was an act of Parliament that in 1833 appropriated £20 million as compensation to the former slaveholders. By the standards of the time, this was a huge sum, one and a half times as much as the entire British military budget for that year.

The antislavery movement helped to forge a new instrument in British domestic politics — the weapon of organized moral indignation. It was this spirit that drove men such as Lord Ashley (1801–1885)[10] to insist, despite all economic theories, that Parliament legislate protection for children who worked in factories and mines, for chimney sweeps, and for the insane. "What is morally wrong," he declared, "can never be politically right." This appeal to evangelical morality, to faith expressed through good works, may well have been the single most potent force behind nineteenth-century social reform.[11]

What was needed, however, was not only moral indignation, which tended to peter out in ineffective sermons and newspaper editorials, but a comprehensive theory of government responsibility and a systematic awareness of the problems of public administration. These were provided by the Utilitarians, a small group of well-educated people who followed the ideas of Jeremy Bentham (1748–1832), that "most celebrated and influential teacher of the age." Bentham was an extraordinary man with an astonishing variety of interests. He tried to simplify the English language; he proposed a league of nations; and he coined the word *international* as well as words like *maximize* and *minimize*. He was one of the chief founders of the University of London, a completely secular institution that in the 1820s broke the centuries-old monopoly on English university education held by Oxford and Cambridge. When Bentham died, he was one of the first men deliberately to leave his body to science; his mummified form resides to this day in the entrance hall of University College, London.

Bentham, like Adam Smith, was a man of the age of reason, and the object of his lifetime was to put the institutions of his day to a simple

---

[10]After 1851, the seventh earl of Shaftesbury.

[11]Excellent book-length treatments of the subject of this section and the next are Ursula R. Q. Henriques, *Before the Welfare State: Social Administration in Early Industrial Britain* (1979), and Oliver MacDonagh, *Early Victorian Government, 1830–70* (1977). Also helpful are G. Kitson Clark, *The Making of Victorian England* (1962), and David Roberts "The Utilitarian Conscience," in *The Conscience of the Victorian State*, ed. by Peter Marsh (1979). Relevant biographies include Geoffrey B. A. M. Finlayson, *The Seventh Earl of Shaftesbury* (1981), and Anthony Brundage, *England's "Prussian Minister": Edwin Chadwick and the Politics of Government Growth, 1832–1854* (1988).

test: is it useful? Bentham cared little whether institutions were traditional; he cared even less whether they had ancient religious sanction; he did not believe in natural rights any more than in natural duties. The only test was the utilitarian test: how useful is it? And for Bentham those institutions were useful that promoted the greatest happiness of the greatest number of people. He was not concerned with the happiness of nations because he did not believe in nations except insofar as they were aggregations of individuals — in that sense Bentham was, like Adam Smith, an individualist.

To a far greater degree than Adam Smith, however, Bentham argued for an *artificial* rather than a *natural* identity of interests. He maintained that human beings, in following their own interests, promote the interests of their fellows only if the laws of their society are so arranged that their self-regarding actions will be channeled in the direction of the common good. A pickpocket may decide that his own self-interest lies in seeking out people in the marketplace and picking their pockets, but his doing so will hardly promote the greatest happiness of the greatest number. If, however, society has set up a well-enforced law against pickpocketing and the pickpocket feels almost certain that he will be caught and sent to jail for a year, then he will hardly be following his own self-interest in picking pockets. His self-interest may instead dictate entering a different profession, one that will more readily promote the greatest happiness of the greatest number.

Bentham used the same criterion in determining types of punishment. The only legitimate object of punishment, he contended, was to deter, not to exert vengeance or to impose penitence. The ideal punishment, therefore, would be a sentence just harsh enough to deter the pickpocket. A harsher punishment — the death penalty, for example — might in fact have the opposite effect, for a jury, regarding the legal penalty as too severe for a mere pickpocket, might decide to acquit him altogether; the criminal counting on such an attitude would not be deterred from crime.

Although Bentham had no love of bureaucracy for its own sake, it is clear that his doctrine of "the artificial identity of interests" might require a great deal of government intervention. Bentham was a writer, not a lecturer or a parliamentary reformer, but he built up a circle of associates, men such as Sir Edwin Chadwick (1800–1890) and John Stuart Mill (1806–1873) who applied his criteria of reasonableness to a great many institutions. The Benthamite method, as employed by the ambitious and at times autocratic Chadwick, was to identify a problem and to bring pressure on Parliament or the ministry to appoint a select committee or royal commission to explore it. The committee or commission would then hold hearings and draft a statute to reform the abuses found. The statute would often require the creation of a new department of government which had authority to lay down uniform regulations and to appoint a force of inspectors to see to it that local authorities carried out the provisions of the law.

Bentham and Mill were heirs of the eighteenth-century Enlightenment, hoping to subject a complex world to the rule of reason. In contrast, the Evangelicals were representative of the Romantic approach to life; they appealed to the emotions rather than to the intellect. By the time that Victoria had ascended the throne, Romantic authors such as John Keats, Percy Bysshe Shelley, and Sir Walter Scott were dead. The Romantic movement, however, was still very evident in the turbulent paintings of J. M. W. Turner (1775–1851), in neo-Gothic architecture, on the Victorian stage, and in many of the novels of Charles Dickens (1809–1870), who peopled with memorable characters a child's world writ large, "bewildering, full of terrors, inexplicable rejection, pathetic loyalties and lost loves, apparently senseless cruelties and unexpected benevolences." Dickens's own family life was a troubled one, and his ideal society is made up of families whose personal happiness has been restored and of characters, such as Scrooge of *A Christmas Carol* (1843), who have undergone a profound change of heart. The Romantic movement was also exemplified in the popular orators of the day, who might be found behind the pulpit of a Nonconformist chapel, but who were just as likely to be found in a public lecture hall expounding the evils of drunkenness, African slavery, or the Corn Laws.[12]

The Victorian Regulatory State

Although their underlying motivations differed widely, Evangelicals and Utilitarians joined forces on numerous occasions in the 1830s and 1840s in the interests of social reform. The process got under way in 1832 when a parliamentary select committee headed by Michael Sadler, a Tory Radical, first publicized the appalling extent of child labor in unhealthful cotton mills. This led to a more thorough investigation the following year headed by two good Benthamites, Edwin Chadwick and Southwood Smith. The royal commission report confirmed the existence of the long hours worked by factory children, the physical fatigue engendered, and the lack of education from which such children suffered. The Factory Act of 1833, based on the commission's report, provided that no child under nine should be allowed to work in textile factories (eighteenth-century pauper children had usually been put to work by the time they were seven); that children between nine and thirteen work no more than eight hours a day and receive a minimum of three hours of schooling per day; and that adolescents between thirteen and eighteen work no more than twelve hours a day. Most important of all, four factory inspectors were to be appointed to enforce the law. Thus an all-important precedent was set. Unlike the Factory Acts of 1802 and 1819, which had remained virtual

---

[12]See, for example, G. S. R. Kitson Clark, "The Romantic Element, 1830 to 1850," in *Studies in Social History,* ed. by J. H. Plumb (1955), and Norman and Jeanne MacKenzie, *Dickens: A Life* (New York, 1979).

Letting Children Down a Coal Mine   Illustrations like this one persuaded Parliament in 1842 to pass the Mines Act that prohibited such work. *(Bettmann/Corbis)*

dead letters, the enforcement of the statute was not to be left in the hands of the local magistrates, who ordinarily felt no need to set foot in such establishments.

If there was to be supervision of the textile mills, then government regulation of the mining industry could not be far behind, and years of agitation by Lord Ashley led to the appointment of a Royal Commission on Mines in 1840. The commission compiled a three-volume indictment of the horrors of the mines — foul air, danger of explosions, long hours, and immorality. More successful in arousing public opinion than the statistics were the pictures of seminude women and bedraggled children pulling coal carts on their hands and knees along three-foot-high mine shafts. The Mines Act of 1842, which passed the House of Commons with only sixteen dissenting votes, prohibited the employment in mines of all women and of all boys under thirteen and, at Chadwick's suggestion, made provision for government inspectors. The pressure of coal-mine owners in the House of Lords reduced the minimum age for boys to ten, and the act did little for adult male miners. However, the large number of accidents in the mines — 765 of 200,000 active miners lost their lives in 1849 — led to the Mine Inspection Act of 1850, which brought conditions underground for all miners under some degree of central government supervision.

So far, government regulation had been limited to specific industries, but as early as 1830 Lord Ashley began to fight for a general ten-hour bill, a law to limit the work of all women and young people in factories to no more than ten hours a day.[13] Although Ashley was himself a Tory, the bill received more support from Whigs than from Tories, but it was repeatedly defeated. Only in 1847, a time of depression in which manufacturers found it difficult to argue that the machines had to be kept busy continuously, did the bill pass. Although the bill did not apply to adult male workers, it affected them as well, because in many factories it was impractical to have different shifts for the two sexes. By the late 1840s, indeed, the sixty-hour week had become commonplace in English factories. Men worked Mondays through Fridays from 7:00 A.M. to 7:00 P.M., with an hour and a half off for meals, and on Saturdays from 7:00 A.M. to 2:00 P.M., with half an hour off for meals.

A far more difficult problem to which the Benthamites sought to find a solution was the Poor Law. The problem of rural pauperism had been endemic in England, and ever since Elizabethan times it had been the responsibility of each parish to provide a refuge of last resort to paupers and to the ill, aged, and insane of the community. The success with which this task was accomplished varied greatly among Britain's thousands of parishes, for in the eighteenth century there was no central supervision of their efforts. A fateful change in the Poor-Law administration had begun in 1795 when the Berkshire magistrates at Speenhamland had ordered the overseers of the poor not only to provide "outdoor relief" (outside the poorhouse) to the unemployed but also to supplement the wages of employed rural laborers whenever the price of the standard loaf of bread exceeded a shilling. The "Speenhamland system" seemed humanitarian but it had unhappy results. Widely adopted throughout southern England by the 1830s, it helped keep agricultural wages low and forced many a hitherto independent worker into poor relief. Landlords had no incentive to raise wages because they knew that the wages of their workers would be supplemented from the poor rates. Rural pauperism seemed to demoralize the farm laborer, while the steadily increasing poor rates were felt by many a taxpaper to be an insufferable burden.

Successive parliamentary committees found the Poor Law wanting, but until 1833 no one in Westminster could figure out a way of persuading the parishes to carry out a uniform, enlightened policy of poor relief. The royal commission of that year, dominated by Chadwick and by Nassau Senior, the economist, came up with a solution in the spirit of Utilitarian economics. The parishes of a particular area were to be

---

[13]Such regulatory legislation involved adult women but not adult men for two overlapping reasons: (1) In Victorian law, women were not seen as altogether free agents who were able to contract for their own labor without state protection; (2) it was widely believed that women's work outside the home posed a danger to society that required intervention by government. See, e.g., Carolyn Malone, "Gendered Discourses and the Making of Protective Labor Legislation in England, 1830–1914," *Journal of British Studies* (April, 1998).

amalgamated into district boards managed by elected Poor-Law guardians, who were to establish workhouses, forbid "outdoor relief" to all able-bodied workers, expand provision for pauper education, and provide improved care for the aged and the ill. The district boards were to be under the supervision of a central board of three Poor-Law commissioners who would issue uniform regulations and supervise their enforcement. The recommendation received a mixed reception in 1834; but, in the hope that the new program would prove less costly than the old relief system, the report was translated into law.

Of all the social reforms of the 1830s and 1840s, the Poor Law of 1834 remains historically the most controversial. It was only three years after its passage that Charles Dickens first wrote about little Oliver Twist, who was sent by the Poor-Law guardians to a dismal workhouse to subsist on "three meals of gruel a day, with an onion twice a week, and half a roll on Sundays." The *Times* of London, a Tory journal, printed this fictional tale as it did many supposedly true stories of floggings, filth, and squalor in workhouses. The *Times* especially denounced the workhouse test, according to which no able-bodied person could gain relief except in the workhouse. In keeping with the doctrine of the classical economists, workhouse life was deliberately to be made less attractive than any private employment; thus the laborer would have every incentive to seek the latter. Deep resentment of this aspect of the new Poor Law led to riots in several parts of the country and did much to inspire the Chartist movement. The *Times* conceded that the monetary cost of Poor-Law operations had been reduced from an average of £6,700,000 a year (1825–1834) to about £4,500,000 a year (1834–1843), but it judged appalling the resulting human suffering. Although the verdict of the *Times* has been echoed by many historians, recent scholars have become more judicious in placing into its historical setting an act that was intended to promote economy, rationality, and morality. It is clear that the workhouses set up under the act were at least as clean and comfortable as the homes of the average English laborers of the day. The Poor-Law commissioners authorized a sufficiently nutritious diet and forbade corporal punishment of adults. In practice they were compelled to leave a great deal of independence to the locally elected boards of guardians — many of them dominated by the landed gentry — and they found the workhouse test impossible to enforce. During the depression year of 1839–1840, 86 percent of all relief recipients, including the ill and the aged, therefore received "outdoor relief" after all.

Doubtless the commissioners were unduly rigid in insisting on psychological discomforts, such as silence at mealtimes, and unduly fearful that workhouse conditions might prove superior to those outside. Whatever its limitations, the Poor Law of 1834 did ensure central supervision for local poor relief; under the energetic administration of Sir Edwin Chadwick, a general upgrading of institutions caring for the poorest groups in British society was accomplished. Moreover, the machinery of the Poor Law became the means by which the central government became involved in such matters as health and sanitation in the new industrial towns.[14]

Medical men in Liverpool and Manchester had long connected the spread of cholera with the lack of proper sewage facilities; but it was only when Chadwick, using his authority as one of the Poor-Law commissioners, investigated the situation in detail that widespread public attention was directed to the problem. In his classic *Report on the Sanitary Condition of the Labouring Population of Great Britain* (1842), Chadwick compiled a grim record of undrained streets, impure water, and crowded, unventilated tenements, all of which he saw closely related to the prevalence of crime, disease, and immorality. Chadwick's long-range goals were that every town would set up a single sanitation authority, that water would be piped into every house, and that every urban street would be paved. His report led to the appointment of a royal commission and to the creation of a Health of Towns Association, which rivaled the Anti–Corn Law League as a pressure group. The establishment of local boards of health supervised by a national board of health seemed to many the only appropriate solution; but numerous municipal corporations, private water companies, and similar vested interests feared that their powers would be curtailed. Local taxpayers were concerned that a national board of health would order expensive improvements for which they would have to pay. The controversy over the issue of centralization caused the question to hang fire for several years, but the threat of a new cholera epidemic induced Parliament in 1848 to establish a national Board of Health, with both Chadwick and Ashley as members. It was given the power to confirm the appointment and dismissal of local surveyors and health officers. In 1853 the Board of Health made vaccination against smallpox compulsory for all children.

Other examples of the unwitting "administrative revolution" of the 1830s and 1840s may be cited: a commissioner was appointed to confirm the constitutions of savings banks and friendly societies (1833); a central inspectorate for prisons was created in 1835; an inspectorate for asylums for the mentally ill was set up in 1842; a Merchant Marine Commission to regulate conditions on merchant vessels was established in 1854; and a Charity Commission to supervise private philanthropy was created in the same year. As the *Times* observed in 1850, "the solicitude of the public and the government for the physical and moral well-being of every class of the labouring population . . . is one of the most humane and distinguishing characteristics of the present time."

---

[14]The complexities of the passage and the administration of the Poor Law of 1834 are examined by Anthony Brundage, *The Making of the New Poor Law* (1978); Derek Fraser, ed., *The New Poor Law in the Nineteenth Century* (1976); and Anne Digby, *Pauper Palaces* (1978). In *The Idea of Poverty* (1983), Gertrude Himmelfarb places the act of 1834 in the context of a half century of debate about how "to rescue the poor from the fate of pauperism."

The Church and Education

A related question on which Utilitarians and Evangelicals could see eye to eye was the condition of the Church of England. It seemed obvious to both groups that the old Church was in dire need of reform. There were enormous, and irrational, differences between the incomes received by ecclesiastical peers and the pittances paid to many a parish vicar. More-over, many English people were still legally required to pay tithes (in the-ory, one-tenth of their income, to be paid in money or goods) to support clerical salaries, and they were similarly subject to church rates for the repair of parish churches. Such obligations were only sporadically en-forced, however, and the precise financial practice tended to vary as greatly from parish to parish as had the franchise requirements before the Great Reform Bill. Yet the archbishops of Canterbury and York still lived as feudal overlords, attended by huge retinues and dispensing lavish hos-pitality. The bishops in the House of Lords had not endeared themselves to reform-minded Utilitarians by their almost unanimous opposition to political reform. The widespread practice of absenteeism and pluralism and the obvious failure of the Church to adapt itself to the needs of the growing industrial towns were trenchantly criticized by Evangelicals. In their eyes, the tradition-bound High Church had become the high-and-dry Church.

In order to correct some of these irregularities, Peel initiated in 1835 — and Melbourne's Whig ministry made permanent in 1836 — an Ecclesiastical Commission made up of Anglican bishops, laymen, and cabinet ministers to end abuses in the Church and to reduce the anom-alies of wealth among the various bishoprics and parishes. A Tithes Com-mutation Act (1836) ended the practice that still compelled numerous farmers to supply their local clergyman with payments in the form of grain. A secular registrar's office was set up in 1838 to take over the tradi-tional role of the Anglican parish in recording births, deaths, and mar-riages. It became as legal to be married in a registrar's office or in a desig-nated Nonconformist chapel as in a parish church. In the name of utilitarianism and in the face of the protests of many of its leaders, the Church of England, that most ancient of the country's institutions, was to be reconditioned and modernized.[15]

Some members of the Church of England responded far more will-ingly to another kind of reform — that of the spirit. There began at Ox-ford during the 1830s a revival of High-Church beliefs that resembled the ideas advanced by Archbishop Laud in the seventeenth century. This

---

[15]Owen Chadwick's magisterial two volumes, *The Victorian Church* (1966, 1970), provide a reliable and sympathetic account of the secular and theological problems faced by the Church of England. Michael R. Watts surveys the role of the non-Anglican Protestants in *The Dissenters*, Vol. 2: *The Expansion of Evangelical Nonconformity, 1791–1859* (1995). In *Newman and His Age* (1990), Sheridan Gilley places in context one of the most signifi-cant religious figures of the Victorian era.

so-called Oxford Movement engaged the attention of many upper- and middle-class English more fully than did many of the social-reform movements of the era. The leading force in the movement was John Henry Newman (1801–1890), a young Anglican divine at Oxford whose eloquent sermons and polished prose writings once again made High-Church Anglicanism a vital creed. Newman emphasized the independence of the Church and frowned on the kind of toadying to the secular world demonstrated by one bishop of London, who apologized in the House of Lords for taking a stand on a particular issue at variance with that of the statesman who had recommended his appointment.

Newman stressed the idea that the Anglican Ecclesia was not just another Protestant church but one whose faith and doctrine were rooted in the undivided Church of medieval Catholicism; the Anglican Ecclesia differed from the Church of Rome only in denying obedience to the pope. The leaders of the Oxford Movement emphasized vestments and ceremonials in the Catholic tradition and steadfastly opposed the philosophical assumptions of the eighteenth-century Enlightenment that the kingdom of heaven might be hoped for on earth. Newman and his colleagues attracted a number of able followers; but when in 1841 in Tract #90 he attempted to reconcile completely the Thirty-nine Articles of the Church of England with the creed of the Church of Rome, he raised a furor. Most of the High-Church party did not wish for an actual reunion with Rome, but Newman himself could find no halfway point between atheism and Roman Catholicism and was admitted to the Church of Rome in 1845. He spent the remaining forty-five years of an often difficult life adhering to his adopted faith, thereby adding intellectual distinction to a church that most of the English tended to identify with the poor and often illiterate Irish. Despite the loss of Newman, the revived High-Church party remained a significant force that emphasized authority, tradition, and a more dignified and ceremonial form of worship. It also inspired the revival of religious orders within the Church of England for the first time since Henry VIII had closed the monasteries in the 1530s.

Although religion was a significant factor in promoting some of the social-reform movements of the age, its role in one particular field, that of education, was essentially divisive. Britain in the 1830s, unlike many continental nations, had no national system of education. Its primary schools had grown up largely under religious auspices, especially that of the Anglican National Society in England and the Presbyterian Church in Scotland. Most English schools were run on the monitorial system, by which adult teachers instructed the older children, who in turn taught and supervised the younger. Rote learning and a complex system of rewards and punishments were the norm. Although education was neither compulsory nor free, a majority of children between the ages of six and twelve were receiving some training in reading, writing, and arithmetic, as well as in Bible study. According to one early Victorian estimate, the average working-class child spent more than four years at school and the average middle-class child six years. Yet Utilitarian and other reformers

A Ragged School   Charitable schools for very poor children during the early nineteenth century were often given that name. This engraving shows a classroom supervised by John Pounds (1766–1839), a founder of the Ragged School movement. *(The Granger Collection)*

agreed that the elementary schools of England and (to a lesser degree) Scotland were grossly deficient and their teachers poorly trained. Dr. James Kay (1804–1877),[16] Assistant Poor-Law Commissioner, became the most eloquent advocate of educational reform during this period; he cited as an example of incompetence the teacher who had ordered for his classroom two globes, one for each hemisphere. A national system of education with tax-supported district schools inspected by the central government and offering nondenominational religious education had been proposed to Parliament as early as 1820. The Church of England was up in arms at such a suggestion, and during the 1830s it showed itself

---

[16]After 1849, Sir James Kay-Shuttleworth. The subject is briskly introduced by Eric Midwinter in *Nineteenth-Century Education* (1970), and more fully in John Hurt, *Education in Evolution: Church, State, Society, and Popular Education, 1800–1870* (1971) and in *Elementary Schooling and the Working Classes* (1979). In *Literacy and the Industrial Revolution* (1975), E. G. West calls attention to the rapid expansion of small private elementary schools decades before a national school system was set up in 1870.

equally averse to any attempt by the government to supervise its role as national educator. From 1833 on, the Church was willing to accept an annual subsidy from the national government to aid school building, but the decision by the Whig ministry in 1839 to set up a committee on education within the government and to appoint two inspectors to oversee government grants raised a new furor. On this issue the Church was supported by almost the entire Tory party, for the issue of religion remained a party issue in a manner in which the Factory and Mines Acts were not. The Church wanted no interference with the religious instruction its schools provided, while the Nonconformists wanted no national subsidy to Anglican schools. All that the ministry could secure was a Committee on Education with two school inspectors and Kay as secretary. Thus, as of 1850 the state had in a very tentative fashion assumed responsibility for educating its people; yet none of the reformers was satisfied with the manner in which the question had been resolved.

By 1850 two important precedents had been established in Britain: (1) the government might interfere in economic affairs in order to protect the individual citizen; and (2) the national government might supervise local government in order to assure administrative efficiency. These precedents had been established in the face of a prevalent government philosophy that accepted most of the dictates of laissez-faire. The paradox is explicable on the basis that the politically influential public opinion of the times did recognize a need for social betterment and was aware of the inadequacies of local government. All parties were fearful of centralization, and only the Utilitarians viewed a national bureaucracy with any degree of favor. But partly on the basis of Benthamite ideas and partly on the basis of what one critic called "presumptuous empiricism," a somewhat ramshackle Victorian administrative state had in fact been set up. All social ills had scarcely been remedied, but the Benthamite *Westminster Review* could take comfort in 1853 in the thought that "We are receding fast from the barbarism of former times and as a community we are awakening to a far stronger and more general sense of the claims and dues of all classes. We are beginning to estimate our objects and possessions more according to rational principles." At the very time that Britain was proclaiming the decisive victory of laissez-faire in international commerce, it had taken a series of giant strides in the direction of state intervention at home.

CHAPTER 4

Lord Palmerston's World

The Britain that occupied itself with railway building and political and social reform during the second quarter of the nineteenth century was often equally involved with affairs on the other side of the English Channel and beyond the seas. Britain was one of the five members of the Concert of Europe, which had emerged from the Congress of Vienna in 1815. Although that congress was often to be criticized for the manner in which it reaffirmed monarchical government on the continent and quashed the nationalistic aspirations of various European peoples, it did prove the prelude to ninety-nine years without a conflict comparable to the Napoleonic Wars. It provided a pattern for avoiding war by leaving none of the Great Powers (Britain, France, Russia, Prussia, and Austria) with a sense of overriding grievance and by giving new sanction to the concept of a balance of power. No single power was to be allowed to dominate the continent, and no power was to annex territory or strengthen its military influence without gaining the approval or acquiescence of its fellows. Treaties were not to be broken lightly, and whenever a threat to the general peace arose, the Concert powers were to participate in negotiations to settle disputes peacefully. The relative success of the resulting balance of power during the half century after 1815 rested not least of all on the fact that no permanent or rigid system of alliances divided the Great Powers.[1]

Britain's Place in the World

In looking back on the nineteenth century, a number of historians have dubbed it the *Pax Britannica*. The comparison to the *Pax Romana* of eighteen hundred years before is both instructive and misleading. Britain's influence operated over a much wider area than did Rome's at

---

[1]Comprehensive surveys of British foreign policy include Kenneth Bourne, *The Foreign Policy of Victorian England, 1830–1902* (1970), and Paul Hayes, *The Nineteenth Century, 1815–1880* (1975), a volume in the Modern British Foreign Policy series. In *"Pax Britannica"?: British Foreign Policy, 1789–1914* (1988), Muriel Chamberlain has provided a helpful brief overview. Paul W. Schroeder's *The Transformation of European Politics, 1763–1848* (1994) magisterially places the subject in a broad international setting.

its height, and Britain's role as an effective and often decisive mediator depended largely on factors other than force of arms. There was Britain's unique sense of security within an island bastion that even Napoleon had failed to storm. There was its ability, demonstrated repeatedly during the early decades of the nineteenth century, to combine domestic liberty with order and to achieve reform without revolution. Its constitutional monarchy was the idol of continental liberals, and its economic successes caused even the most reactionary of European powers to sit up and take notice. British shipping increased from 2,500,000 to 4,000,000 tons between 1827 and 1848. By 1850, more than half of all the merchant ships in the world flew the British flag, and more than a third of all international trade involved British interests. London was generally acknowledged as the world's financial center. Britain had served as "the paymaster of Europe" during the Napoleonic Wars, and during the postwar years even major powers such as Austria and Russia habitually floated loans in London.

The preeminence of Britain depended rather less on the fact that it laid claim to the world's largest overseas colonial empire, because during the 1830s and 1840s this empire seemed at times a dubious advantage.[2] At a time when tariff barriers were falling, when navigation acts were being abolished, when the principle of free trade was triumphing, the eighteenth-century mercantilistic justifications for colonies had largely ceased to matter. If foreigners could trade with Canada and Australia and even with India[3] on the same terms as British merchants could, what were colonies other than expensive encumbrances? Money had to be spent to govern, police, and protect them, but what did they provide in return? Such at least was the classic liberal argument.

It was not in the colonies that Britain invested the greatest amount of money. Before 1850 almost two-thirds of British overseas capital investment flowed to continental Europe and almost one-third to the United States and South America. Many more emigrants from the United Kingdom went to the United States than to all the colonies put together. Of over 2,200,000 emigrants between 1830 and 1850, some 1,346,000 sailed to the United States. Thus most English statesmen of the day became more involved with what has been called "the empire of free trade," the acquisition of new trading outlets, than with the expense of obtaining political control over additional subject territories.

---

[2]Helpful brief introductions to the British empire of the early and mid-Victorian eras may be found in Ronald Hyam, *Britain's Imperial Century, 1815–1914: A Study of Empire and Expansion* (2nd ed., 1993), and in John P. Halstead, *The Second British Empire: Trade, Philanthropy, and Good Government, 1820–1890* (1983). The connections between the classical economists and the evolution of Britain's influence are traced in Bernard Semmel, *The Rise of Free Trade Imperialism* (1970). The most recent broad overview has been provided by P. J. Cain and A. G. Hopkins in *British Imperialism: Innovation and Expansion, 1688–1914* (1993).

[3]Chapter 6 provides a fuller discussion of India during the 1830s and 1840s.

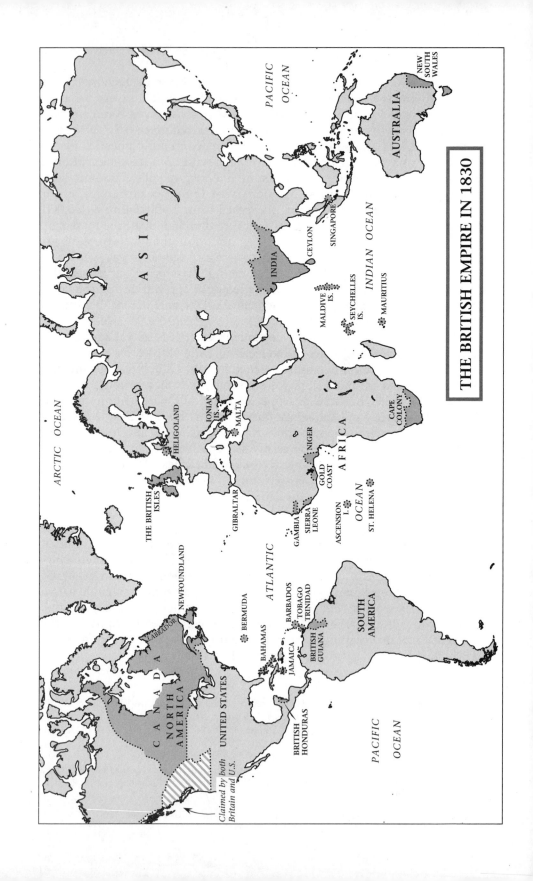

THE BRITISH EMPIRE IN 1830

PACIFIC
OCEAN

NEW
SOUTH
WALES

AUSTRALIA

INDIAN OCEAN

SINGAPORE

CEYLON

INDIA

ASIA

MALDIVE
IS.

SEYCHELLES
IS.

MAURITIUS

ARCTIC OCEAN

HELIGOLAND

IONIAN
IS.

MALTA

AFRICA

NIGER

CAPE
COLONY

THE BRITISH
ISLES

GIBRALTAR

GOLD
COAST

GAMBIA

SIERRA
LEONE

ASCENSION
I.

ST. HELENA

OCEAN

NEWFOUNDLAND

LABRADOR

BERMUDA

ATLANTIC

BAHAMAS

BARBADOS
TOBAGO
TRINIDAD

JAMAICA

BRITISH
GUIANA

SOUTH
AMERICA

CANADA

NORTH
AMERICA

UNITED STATES

BRITISH
HONDURAS

PACIFIC
OCEAN

*Claimed by both
Britain and U.S.*

At the same time that the classical economists encouraged a policy by which Britain would divest itself, for both moral and financial reasons, of most of its colonies, a group of "colonial reformers" such as Edward Gibbon Wakefield (1796–1862) and Lord Durham (1792–1840) believed that their country would be concerned for many years to come with its settlement colonies. They saw a program of systematic overseas colonization as a way of dealing with commercial overproduction and social tensions at home. In the 1830s, Canada's population was just beginning to expand westward beyond the St. Lawrence River valley and the Great Lakes. Australia was becoming the homeland of an increasing number of voluntary emigrants from the British Isles as well as of tens of thousands of British convicts — some 162,000 in all between 1788 and 1868 — who were transported there for a jail term followed by permanent exile in lieu of punishment at home. At a time when a journey to Australia might cost as much as the annual income of an English farm laborer, government subsidies derived from the sale of Australian land helped hundreds of thousands of emigrants from the British Isles to begin a new life down under. In New Zealand, the British army was compelled to intervene in 1837 in order to keep the peace between the native Maoris and recently arrived British settlers.[4] The colonial reformers did not expect Canada, the several Australian colonies, and New Zealand to sever all ties with the mother country. Once self-government had been granted to these lands, they expected family connections and bonds of sentiment to provide a continuing community of interest between them and the mother country.

When a rebellion broke out in Canada in 1837, it was not surprising that the Melbourne ministry should have appointed as high commissioner of British North America a colonial reformer, Lord Durham, to survey the situation. The rebellion itself was soon crushed, but the subsequent report, published in 1839, provided a pattern for dominion status and self-government within the British sphere. Durham suggested that Canadian ministers be made responsible to the colonial legislature rather than to the royal governor for all domestic affairs. The recommendation was not immediately adopted, but it was put into practice during the governorship of Lord Elgin (1847–1854), Durham's son-in-law. From Canada the idea spread, so that by 1872 most of the English-speaking areas of the empire had achieved a form of responsible domestic self-government.

The Pax Britannica rested largely on economic and political foundations, but Britain's military strength should not be discounted. Although Britain's army was reduced to minimal size after the Napoleonic Wars

[4]The Maoris had first settled the hitherto uninhabited islands in the eleventh century, and their hunter-gardener fortified-village economy continued to coexist with that of the British settlers even after the Treaty of Waitangi (1840) in which Maori chieftains ceded "governorship" but not full sovereignty to the British. See James Belich, *Making Peoples: A History of the New Zealanders from Polynesian Settlement to the End of the Nineteenth Century* (1997).

and although Britain ranked fourth among the Great Powers in population, the British navy remained the unchallenged "mistress of the seas" at least until the 1840s, when France began a two-decades-long large-scale naval-building program. The British navy not only was a force to be reckoned with by every continental power but also acted as a kind of international police force. It suppressed pirates in the Mediterranean Sea and the Indian Ocean and patrolled the coastal waters of West Africa seeking to intercept illegal slave traders. It also served merchant vessels of all lands by charting the world's oceans and publishing maps.

The Foreign Policy of Palmerston

The man most closely identified with the course of British foreign policy during the early Victorian era was Lord Palmerston, the ex-Tory who joined Grey's ministry in 1830 and served as foreign secretary from 1830 to 1834, from 1835 to 1841, and again from 1846 to 1851.[5] Palmerston's career was to illustrate the tension that was felt by many nineteenth-century Britons when they viewed the continent. Intermittently, they were aware that the preservation of continental peace required cooperation with the Great Powers of the continent: Russia, Austria, and Prussia as well as France. Thus, at times Palmerston stressed quiet diplomacy and the preservation of good relations among Europe's Big Five. At other times they thought, and Palmerston spoke, of a Europe hopelessly divided into two antagonistic camps — the liberal West (Britain and France, and at times Spain and Portugal) facing the reactionary East (Russia, Prussia, and Austria). Britons therefore sympathized with movements of liberal nationalism in central and eastern Europe and risked the danger that such movements might overturn the Vienna territorial settlement of 1815 and bring a renewal of European war. They ignored the possibility that if the "Holy Alliance" of the Eastern powers broke up, the rivalry of Russia versus Prussia or Austria might endanger world peace. Sympathy with continental liberalism was to lead Palmerston into policies that would be described in the mid-twentieth century as "brinksmanship," although Palmerston insisted that he was simply a friend "of free institutions" and not a promoter of revolutions. There was an additional complication: both Britain and France were liberal constitutional monarchies, at least after 1830, but France — as few Britons of the generation of Wellington were likely to forget — was also England's traditional national enemy, and where one Napoleon had come to power might not another claim his place? Whatever Palmerston's policies, few people questioned his superb qualifications for the post. He wrote and

---

[5]Because Lord Palmerston held an Irish rather than an English peerage, he was eligible to seek election for an English constituency, and he had served in the House of Commons ever since 1807. Jasper Ridley has provided a comprehensive biography in *Lord Palmerston* (1970).

Lord Palmerston (1784–1865)   The photograph was taken during the early 1860s when the veteran statesman served as prime minister. *(Hulton Deutsch Collection)*

spoke French fluently; he knew Spanish, Italian, and Portuguese as well. He was familiar with every person in his department. He personally read all dispatches from abroad, and he replied to a great many in his own elegant hand.

It was as peacemaker rather than as wielder of the "big stick" that Palmerston dealt with the first major crisis that he faced — revolution in Belgium. Since the Vienna peace settlement, Belgium had been attached to the Dutch monarchy as a bulwark against French expansion. A declaration of independence by a provisional Belgian government late in 1830 was a clear violation of the Vienna treaty. The king of the Netherlands would have welcomed Prussian intervention on his behalf, but the Belgian insurgents gave him no time; and Palmerston, in order to forestall foreign intervention, recommended to a Big Five conference in London the establishment of an independent Belgium.

After a great deal of hard bargaining — Palmerston attended seventy meetings on the Belgian question — Prussia, Russia, Austria, and France agreed with Britain on a protocol establishing an independent Belgium as a permanently neutral state under an international guarantee. Palmerston had the satisfaction of installing on the new Belgian throne Leopold of Saxe-Coburg, a German prince and uncle of the young Victoria, by then heir-apparent to the English throne. Although the protocol was ratified by the Great Powers in 1832, the Dutch king did not resign himself to the inevitable until Anglo-French forces intervened militarily and forced the Dutch out of Antwerp by a joint bombardment of the city. By gaining the reluctant acquiescence of the Eastern powers and sealing the bargain with a binational show of force, Palmerston thus maintained the European peace while installing a liberal constitutional monarch on the Belgian throne.

At the same time that the Belgian question was being settled without war, new threats to the European peace were arising elsewhere. Western liberal opinion was angered by the harsh Russian repression of the Polish revolutionaries of 1830 and by the similar repression in various German and Italian states. In 1832 the situation was complicated by a new threat to the balance of power in the Middle East where, as the Greek revolution of the 1820s had demonstrated, Russia, Britain, and France had potentially conflicting interests of commerce, strategy, and prestige. This time the Ottoman Empire, that proverbial sick man of Europe, faced a new revolt by one of its provinces. Mohammed Ali, a Balkan adventurer who had become pasha of Egypt, was warring against the sultan in Constantinople in order to gain complete control of the whole empire, which still rimmed the eastern third of the Mediterranean Sea. The French were sympathetic to Mohammed Ali, while the Russians, who once had sought to defeat — and ultimately to partition — the Ottoman Empire, now preferred influence to conquest and came to the sultan's aid. Mohammed Ali's territorial gains were confined to Syria. As Russian influence increased in Constantinople, so also did Palmerston's fears that Turkey would become a Russian satellite. "The Russian Ambassador becomes chief Cabinet Minister of the Sultan," Palmerston complained — but for the moment there was little he could do about the matter.

In 1839, however, the battle between Mohammed Ali and the Ottoman sultan again erupted. Palmerston, who saw the Mediterranean as an increasingly important British trade route even before the Suez Canal seemed a likely engineering project, hoped to maintain the peace and to promote his country's interests by "neutralizing" the Middle East, in much the same manner as he had neutralized Belgium. In order to forestall the French influence standing behind Mohammed Ali and to weaken Russian influence over the Ottoman sultan, he proposed a joint guarantee of Turkish integrity by all the Great Powers on condition that Turkey close the Dardanelles to all warships in any conflict in which Turkey was a neutral.

Palmerston succeeded in winning the support of the Russian tsar, Nicholas I, by joining the Russians in aiding the sultan against Mohammed Ali. The Austrians and the Prussians also concurred, but the French, angered by Britain's high-handed action, did not. Palmerston held his ground, however, and war between the two countries seemed imminent in 1840, until the French backed down and accepted the general settlement. Palmerston's "big stick" tactics, based on British economic and naval strength, appeared again to have been justified, and the tsar was so pleased with the new, if temporary, Anglo-Russian diplomatic alignment that he proposed a permanent alliance between the two countries. His offer was politely turned down, but he did make a formal state visit to Britain in 1844.

Anglo-American and Anglo-Chinese Relations

In the meantime, in 1841 the Tories, under Peel, had replaced the Whig ministry of Lord Melbourne, and Lord Palmerston had given way to Lord Aberdeen (1784–1860) as foreign secretary. Aberdeen's diplomacy was noted more for sobriety than for flamboyance, and his methods were probably better suited than Palmerston's for resolving a number of difficulties that had arisen between Britain and the United States. A period of friendly relations between the two nations after the War of 1812 had been followed by new discord. Overt American aid to the Canadian rebels of 1837 had led British troops to retaliate by seizing the American ship *Caroline* and sending it ablaze over Niagara Falls. Canadians and Maine backwoodsmen carried on a form of undeclared guerrilla war over the unsettled Maine-Canadian border, and the United States and Britain had also clashed over the British navy's right to search vessels suspected of carrying slaves.[6] Feelings between the two countries had been exacerbated by American resentment of British wealth and power at the same time that British tourists such as Charles Dickens found "a general lack of civilization" on the western side of the Atlantic. When several American states defaulted on their debts as a result of the depression of 1837, British investors were furious. The American eagle, observed *Punch*, was a predatory bird "extremely fatal to the large species of goose called the creditor."

Concession, rather than Palmerstonian bellicosity, was the tone of Aberdeen's handling of the American crisis. In 1842, the border conflict between Maine and Canada was resolved by a treaty that awarded approximately three-fifths of the disputed territory to Maine and two-fifths to Canada. The British also provided what was interpreted in the United States as a belated apology for the *Caroline* incident, and the United States promised anew to cooperate with Britain's efforts to curb the illegal international slave trade.

Two years later Great Britain remained patient when James K. Polk won his bid for the presidency of the United States on an "All of Texas, All of Oregon" platform. The American annexation of the entire Oregon territory would have deprived Canada of any outlet on the Pacific. Although the British navy was put on a war footing, the London *Times*

---

[6]H. C. Allen, *Great Britain and the United States: A History of Anglo-American Relations, 1783–1952* (1954), places the events in context.

urged the policy that ultimately prevailed in Whitehall: "We are two peoples, but we are of one family. We have fought, but we have been reconciled." British commercial interests were opposed to war, and once President Polk had become involved in a comparable dispute with Mexico, he decided to give way. A treaty of 1846 provided that the 49th parallel, the boundary between Canada and the United States from the Great Lakes to the Rocky Mountains, should be extended to the Pacific Coast — except for Vancouver Island, which remained Canadian — and war between the two countries was once again averted.

At the same time that Lord Aberdeen had been calming the Anglo-American diplomatic storms, he was involved in a somewhat different type of trouble with China. There he went along with Palmerstonian tactics. British merchants had for decades been eager for greater trading concessions from the empire of China, which had long looked with disdain on the "Western barbarians" from Europe. A disagreement between the Chinese authorities and a group of British merchants, some of whom had been illegally importing opium into China from India in exchange for Chinese tea, led in 1839 to the so-called Opium War. The British government insisted that a legitimate desire to suppress the trade in drugs did not justify the Chinese authorities in imprisoning British merchants and insulting the Queen's representative. A British fleet bombarded Canton, and British troops took Shanghai and entered the Yangtse Valley. By the Treaty of Nanking (1842), the Chinese were forced to open Shanghai and Canton to foreign merchants and to pay the claims of British traders whose goods had been seized. The island of Hong Kong, then "a mountainous, desolate-looking place with only a few fishermen's huts to be seen," was ceded outright to the British. Along with Singapore, another almost uninhabited island at the foot of the Malay peninsula that the adventurous Sir Stamford Raffles had secured for Britain back in 1824, it became one of Britain's two chief outposts in East Asia. The Chinese customs service was reorganized under British auspices. The Treaty of Nanking also ceded the legal privilege of extraterritoriality — exemption from Chinese legal jurisdiction — to most foreigners; in Chinese eyes it marked the beginning of a century of humiliation for China. In British eyes, it marked the widening of "the empire of free trade," the area in which British merchants and all others might trade without constraint.

Palmerston Again

In 1846, with the fall of the Peel ministry and Russell's assumption of the prime ministership, Palmerston returned to the foreign office. He had long sought to encourage peaceful internal reform within the continental monarchies as an antidote to violence, and the revolutions that broke out all over Europe in 1848 lent weight to his admonitions. Palmerston's prime purpose in 1848, however, was to preserve the European balance of power and to avoid a general war. France had once again become a radical republic, and Palmerston was eager to prevent a continental attack upon France as well as to stop any expansionist drive eastward by the new republic. Especially touchy was the situation in Italy. Here the Kingdom of Sardinia sought to take advantage of the apparent breakup of the Austrian empire in order to wrest the Italian provinces of Lombardy and Venetia from Austrian rule and create a unified Italian state. Palmerston, like most Britons, was sympathetic to the political unification of Italy if the process could take place peacefully but he feared that French intervention on behalf of the Italians would touch off a general European war. British diplomatic intervention did work to restore peace between Austria and Sardinia in 1849, but at the price of antagonizing Austria.

The Pax Britannica involved not only the forwarding of British commercial interests throughout the world and the use of diplomatic pressure to encourage the growth of constitutional government while preventing war. It also involved more than a touch of bombast in idealistic dress. Palmerston's unquestioned belief in the moral righteousness of all that was English and in the obvious superiority of the English constitutional system antagonized the Great Powers and relegated some of the less powerful states of Europe and Asia to an avowedly inferior status. Declared Palmerston in 1850:

> These half-civilized governments all require a dressing every eight or ten years to keep them in order. Their minds are too shallow to receive an impression that will last longer than some such period and warning is of little use. They care little for words, and they must not only see the stick but actually feel it on their shoulders before they yield to that only argument which to them brings conviction, the *argumentum baculinum*.

Palmerston's attitude is well illustrated by the Don Pacifico incident of 1850, which involved Greece, a kingdom set up under the protection of Britain, France, and Russia in the 1820s. During the decades that followed, Palmerston had taken a highly avuncular attitude toward Greece and had not hesitated to chide the new nation about many minor and not so minor matters: brigandage on the Greek roads; day-to-day policy administration; Greek tardiness in paying the interest due on its national debt; the failure of the Greek king to make sufficient apology to the Turkish ambassador after having insulted him at a court ball. He had also been keenly alive to the rival influence of the French. In 1847, the Athens home of Don Pacifico, a moneylender of Portuguese-Jewish ancestry, was pillaged by a Greek mob. The Greek government eventually made partial compensation, but Don Pacifico was unsatisfied and appealed directly to Palmerston with a detailed list of his claims. He had been born in Gibraltar, Don Pacifico pointed out, and was therefore by law a British subject. Palmerston saw the incident as another example of Greek skullduggery and endorsed every one of Don Pacifico's claims, including the £27,000 value he put on some Portuguese bonds destroyed in the fire.

Palmerston asked the Greek government for appropriate compensation for Don Pacifico. When it hesitated, he ordered a British squadron of fourteen ships under Admiral Sir William Parker to proceed to Greek waters. On January 17, 1850, Parker and the English minister to Greece sent an ultimatum to the Greek government. Receiving no reply within twenty-four hours, the British admiral proclaimed a blockade of Greece and seized several Greek ships. France and Russia complained about Britain's unilateral action. But since a British fleet held the command of the seas, the Greeks had no choice but to submit to Palmerston's demands.

The French government, which had sought to mediate the dispute, was furious and recalled its ambassador from London. Queen Victoria and Prince Albert were equally upset. The queen had long been at odds with Palmerston over his policies and his method of conducting diplomacy. As she had become accustomed to the role of queen, she increasingly resented the number of occasions on which the foreign secretary took action without her knowledge. Moreover, as her husband trained her to read the foreign dispatches assiduously, she became convinced that Palmerston was at heart a wild revolutionary hostile to her continental fellow monarchs.[7] And this time, Palmerston did indeed appear to have gone too far. A Conservative motion of censure passed the House of Lords by a vote of 169 to 132 and Russell's ministry seemed on the verge of defeat.

One of Palmerston's supporters thereupon introduced a resolution supporting the foreign secretary's policies as "calculated to maintain the honour and dignity of this country," and the House of Commons was launched on a full-dress, five-day foreign policy debate in which every major public figure participated. Gladstone for one criticized Palmerston's foreign policy for being motivated by a "spirit of interference." It was preferable, he thought, for a British foreign secretary to heed "the general sentiment of the civilised world" rather than to challenge all comers like a medieval knight at a tournament.

Palmerston defended his handling of the Don Pacifico case specifically and of foreign affairs generally in an eloquent five-hour oration. He denied that the British Goliath had bullied Greece: "Does the smallness of a country justify the magnitude of its evil acts?" It was said, Palmerston went on, that the claimants against the Greek government were unimportant people, "as if because a man was poor he might be . . . tortured with impunity, as if a man who was born in Scotland might be robbed without redress, or, because a man is of the Jewish persuasion, he is fair game for any outrage." In a final flurry, he summed up the moral foundations of the Pax Britannica, its reason for being, and the foreign policies that sustained it:

> We have shown that liberty is compatible with order; that individual freedom is reconcilable with obedience to the law. . . . I contend that we have not in our foreign policy done anything to forfeit the confidence of

---

[7]See Brian Connell, ed., *Regina vs. Palmerston* (1961).

the country. . . . I therefore fearlessly challenge the verdict which this House . . . is to give on the question now brought before it . . . whether, as the Roman, in days of old, held himself free from indignity, when he could say *Civis Romanus sum* [I am a Roman citizen]; so also a British subject, in whatever land he may be, shall feel confident that the watchful eye and the strong arm of England will protect him against injustice and wrong.

Palmerston carried the day. The motion supporting his policies was approved by a vote of 310 to 264 in the House of Commons and by a less specific but perhaps even larger majority by the ordinary Briton in the street — or, as Palmerston liked to call him, "the man in the omnibus with the umbrella." For many such people, Palmerston seemed John Bull incarnate, and for them British honor and universal justice were, after all, identical.

PART TWO

THE MID-VICTORIAN YEARS

1851 to 1873

LONDON'S REGENT'S PARK IN THE 1860S
(*The Granger Collection*)

CHAPTER 5

Prosperity, Propriety, and Progress

Like ancient Gaul, the reign of Queen Victoria may conveniently be divided into three parts. And the mid-Victorian period, which commenced symbolically with the opening of the Great Exhibition of 1851 and ended with the onset of the "great depression" of 1873, may readily be studied as a unit. For most Britons, these two decades were, in contrast with the previous age, years of prosperity and of relative social harmony during which both talk and consciousness of class division abated. It was an age in which underlying assumptions about the necessity for a high degree of individualism at home, free trade abroad, and progress in human affairs were accepted by most with uncritical, almost religious, conviction. Many Britons, but never all, therefore experienced a pleasing sense of self-confidence and complacency.[1]

The Age of Prosperity

Terms such as *prosperity, stability,* and *complacency* are necessarily relative, but in contrast to the age that had gone before, they are appropriate enough. A British observer of 1848, looking back upon the agitation of the Chartists, the triumph of the Corn Law reformers, and the social legislation resulting from the royal commission reports on factories and mines, might well have predicted that an even more noteworthy age of political and social reform was in the immediate offing. Yet the mid-Victorian years were to see no such remarkable examples of political

---

[1]The most up-to-date one-volume account of the era is K. Theodore Hoppen, *The Mid-Victorian Generation, 1846–1886* (1998), but Geoffrey Best, *Mid-Victorian Britain, 1851–1875* (1971), remains a useful introduction to the social structure, J. H. Clapham, *Free Trade and Steel, 1850–1886* (1932), to the economy, and W. L. Burn, *The Age of Equipoise* (1964), to the ideological assumptions. F. M. L. Thompson, *The Rise of Respectable Society: A Social History of Victorian Britain, 1830–1900* (1988), surveys attitudes toward marriage, children, work, and play; and Asa Briggs, *Victorian People* (1955), provides personality sketches of influential mid-Victorians. The symbol of the new era is assessed in Jeffrey A. Auerbach, *The Great Exhibition of 1851: A Nation on Display* (1999).

agitation; nor was the landed aristocracy, whose bell had presumably tolled in 1846, to disappear from the social or economic scene.

Thus, at the same time that industrialization had come to be accepted as a way of life and the predominance of an urban civilization assured, it was becoming clear that the economic revolution would bring not social confusion and bloodshed, nor even an easily discernible "triumph of the middle classes," but instead a far more gradual and peaceful readjustment of social groups amidst a widespread survival of habits, occupations, and institutions from earlier centuries. In politics, these mid-Victorian years were a lull, an "age of equipoise" between the political storms of the first half of the century and the more drastic changes still to come.

A vivid symbol both of Victorian material progress and of the sense of self-satisfaction to which it gave rise was the Great Exhibition of the Works of Industry of All Nations, which opened in London in May 1851. There had been a few similar exhibitions on a small scale in France, but this was the first true world's fair. Britain, as the workshop of the world, was clearly the appropriate host country. The central building of the exhibition was the Crystal Palace, in essence a gigantic greenhouse made of iron and glass, over 1,800 feet long and more than 400 feet wide — the largest enclosed space on the entire globe. Its ceiling was high enough to find room for several of the tallest elm trees in Hyde Park, sparrows and all. The chief inspirer of the exhibition, the queen's husband, Prince Albert, saw its purpose as a presentation of "a true test and a living picture of the point of development at which the whole of mankind has arrived . . . and a new starting point, from which all nations will be able to direct their further exertions." With this in mind, the exhibition displayed the wonders of the new industrial world. The United States exhibited a sewing machine. The French demonstrated a new medal-making machine that could produce fifty million medals in a single week. A British company set up an electric telegraph office with a direct connection to Edinburgh. The world's first international photographic competition was held to celebrate another technological marvel of the previous decade. More than half of the thirteen thousand exhibitors were British, and they displayed not only the latest textile machinery and a railway locomotive generating the power of a thousand horses but also such ingenious contraptions as "an alarm bedstead, causing a person to arise [quite literally] at any given hour" and the British equivalent of an automatic baseball pitching machine, "a cricket catapulta, for propelling the ball in the absence of a first-rate bowler."

Perhaps the greatest tribute to mid-Victorian economic efficiency was the fact that the exhibition had been planned and the Crystal Palace erected within a single year and that on the opening day, May 1, all exhibitors but the Russians were ready. Hundreds of thousands of people were on hand to greet Victoria and Albert, who delivered the opening speech; the archbishop of Canterbury, who pronounced the opening prayer; and the duke of Wellington, who delivered neither speech nor prayer but who was cheered by the people merely for having managed to survive to see it at all. The hero of Waterloo and the temporary villain of 1832 had become the great national hero of his generation, and he was able to render his country a final service on the occasion of the Great Exhibition. When Queen Victoria asked the duke's advice as to how best to deal with the nuisance of sparrows within the great glass building, his reply was succinct: "Try sparrow hawks, Ma'am."

It was clearly a grand day for a great many English people. One observer, the daughter of an aristocratic Whig landlord who had married the owner of one of Britain's largest iron foundries, marveled at how "all this pomp and panoply were called together to do honour to the industry of millions, whose toils, erst scorned upon, seemed suddenly ennobled." In the course of the next several months the exhibition was to attract six million visitors, and its profits were to be used to erect nearby in the years that followed a complex of scientific and educational institutions including the Natural History Museum and what was to become the Victoria and Albert Museum. The purpose of the exhibition, to be sure, was not merely to exhibit British industrial superiority but to proclaim to all foreign visitors the gospel of free trade and universal peace and the glories of the British constitution.

As the next two decades were to demonstrate, these lessons were not learned by all. Universal peace was soon to be broken by the Crimean War; and the French across the Channel, instead of adopting the British constitution, were about to proclaim another Napoleon as emperor. But the inept war against Russia was to end without unduly disrupting domestic prosperity and tranquility, and Napoleon III was to prove most of the time a respectable bourgeois emperor and not a dangerous firebrand. Thus to some degree the hopes of 1851 would pervade the whole era and, as Macaulay wrote, "1851 would long be remembered as a singularly happy year of peace, plenty, good feeling, innocent pleasure and national glory."

Available statistics confirmed a pervasive sense of progress and prosperity. Annual coal-production figures rose from 65 million tons to 125 million between 1854 and 1874, and the production of pig iron kept pace. In 1856 Henry Bessemer announced the development of the first process for making steel inexpensively, and a few years later William Siemens introduced the new open-hearth method of producing high-tensile steel; by the 1870s the age of iron was rapidly giving way to the era of steel. Precision toolmaking had come to be a major British industry, and the manufacture of interchangeable standard parts and the use of machine tools that could adjust measurements to a thousandth of an inch had become commonplace. The steam engines that Boulton and Watt had turned out by hand in the 1780s were being mass-produced by 1860.

The railways continued to be a major user of metals both at home and abroad. A network of 6,621 miles of track in 1850 expanded to over 16,000 miles by 1873, and the number of passengers per year increased from 64 million to 455 million. Aside from the continued trend toward amalgamating small railway companies, however, there was relatively little technical innovation during these years. Enclosed carriages had replaced third-class coaches open to the weather and to flying sparks from the locomotive; but British travelers continued to prefer their trains cut into compartments like a succession of stagecoaches, rather than to be exposed to fellow passengers en masse, as in an experimental American "coach" train imported from Detroit.

During the 1850s the Yankee clippers and other American vessels rivaled British merchant vessels in speed and number, but the American Civil War ended the competition. As a result, shipbuilding boomed in Britain. Despite conservative doubts about the ability of iron to float, the steam-powered iron ship came into its own in Britain's navy and in its merchant fleet. Steamships comprised but 5 percent of British merchant shipping in 1850, and only 33 percent by 1874, but by then the building of steamships had permanently outdistanced that of sailing vessels. Glasgow and its Clydeside suburbs had become the world's shipbuilding capital, and 60 percent of all ocean-going steamships flew the British flag.

The boom in the shipbuilding and shipping industries went hand in hand with an expansion of trade. Whereas the market value of British exports had increased only 14 percent between 1817 and 1842, it jumped during the next twenty-five-year period by 282 percent. Ever-increasing quantities of coal, iron, steel, machinery, and textiles were leaving British ports, while correspondingly larger quantities of raw cotton, raw wool, wheat, and timber were entering them. Britain exported not only the products of industry but also money. As recently as 1815, British investments abroad had been virtually balanced by foreign investments in Britain. By the 1850s, however, a net total of £264 million had been invested overseas, and two decades later the amount had jumped to £1,058 million. British investors were helping to build railroads all over the world — in Russia, Spain, Switzerland, Denmark, Turkey, Brazil, and the United States, as well as in India and other British colonies. British companies were to own and operate the railways of Argentina until after World War II. In 1857, British investors held £80 million in American railroad securities, and at least one British director headed each of nineteen European railway companies. The use of British funds often meant the employment of British iron, steel, and locomotives as well as British contractors and even laborers to do the work. In the meantime, British companies manufactured most of the copper and the "India rubber" insulation that increasingly enabled Europeans of the 1850s and 1860s to communicate instantaneously by means of electrical telegraph; during these same years, other British companies laid cable lines on the ocean floors to link Europe telegraphically with the Americas and with parts of Asia. Business competition was keen, and although the era was familiar with bankruptcies as well as success stories, new techniques were used, new markets were entered, and many an old partnership was transformed into a corporation. A nation of shopkeepers was increasingly becoming also a nation of shareholders. For England and Scotland the mid-Victorian

The *Great Eastern*   Designed by Isambard Kingdom Brunel and launched in 1858, the *Great Eastern* was the largest steam-powered passenger vessel that had ever been built. *(The Granger Collection)*

years constituted "the classic era of the expanding, competitive, capitalist economy."

Perhaps most surprising of all, the 1850s and 1860s remained prosperous years for agriculture. Those landlords who had steadfastly fought against the repeal of the Corn Laws and who had predicted that repeal would spell disaster seemed, for the moment, to have been proved wrong. Imported grain did indeed play an increasingly significant role in the English diet. In 1850 only a quarter of the grain consumed had been imported; two decades later the proportion had doubled. With a growing population, however, this change still left a large market for British farmers, and until 1872 the total acreage under cultivation continued to increase. Landlords emphasized scientific farming in the form of more efficient estate management and the use of new fertilizers and agricultural techniques (such as the steam-powered plow). The rural social structure (made up of landed gentry, tenant farmers, and landless laborers) was not altering significantly, however, and an 1871 survey showed that half the acreage of England was owned by 7,400 individuals. Unpaid Justices of the Peace still dominated local government in the rural areas. Yet during the mid-Victorian years most farmers prospered, and the earnings of farm laborers also rose significantly, especially in areas in which industry competed for their services. In many parts of the country their lot remained a meager one, however, and the medieval duel between poacher and gamekeeper had not yet ended.

Agricultural prosperity should not be attributed exclusively to profits derived directly from the land. "All that can be said about land," explains Lady Bracknell in Oscar Wilde's *The Importance of Being Earnest,* is that "it gives one position, and prevents one from keeping it up." Land conferred social status, but its financial value lay less in farm produce than in the coal or iron that might be found beneath it, the sale of rights-of-way to the railways that might traverse it, or the rents from the houses that might be built on top of it. Never had such real estate development opportunities been so plentiful as in the middle years of the nineteenth century.

The Victorian City

This rosy pattern of economic growth, at the average rate of 3.2 percent per year between 1850 and 1873, was stimulated in part by the continuing growth of the British population. Although tens of thousands still emigrated each year, the net population of England, Wales, and Scotland increased from 20,817,000 to 26,072,000 between 1851 and 1871. (Only in Ireland did emigration and the other social effects of the Great Famine initiate a gradual population decline.) This growing population was increasingly concentrated in large cities. In 1801, only one city —London — had claimed a population of over 100,000. By 1841 there were six; by 1871, sixteen; and by 1901, thirty. By 1851, the population of metropolitan London had passed the two million mark and, by 1871, the three million mark. Railways enabled people to work in one neighborhood and to live in another; they were supplemented, in the case of London, by hundreds of horse-drawn omnibuses and (beginning in 1862) by the world's first underground railway system.[2]

There is a fascinating paradox about the Victorian city. Contemporaries as well as more recent historians condemned the city for its filth, its smoke, and the wretchedness of its slums. Roden Noel summed up a widespread reaction when he wrote in 1872:

---

[2]H. J. Dyos and Michael Wolff, eds., *The Victorian City: Images and Realities* (2 vols., 1973), a lavishly illustrated collection of essays, provides an excellent introduction to the subject. See also Francis Sheppard, *London 1808–1870: The Infernal Wen* (1971); Donald J. Olson, *The Growth of Victorian London* (1976) and *The City as a Work of Art* (1986); and Gary S. Messinger, *Manchester in the Victorian Age* (1985). A major concern of city-dwellers is taken up by Anthony S. Wohl, *The Eternal Slum* (1977), John Burnett, *A Social History of Housing, 1815–1970* (1978), and M. J. Daunton, *House and Home in the Victorian City: Working-Class Housing, 1850–1914* (1983). In *People's Parks: The Design and Development of Victorian Parks in Britain* (1991), Hazel Conway focuses on a largely novel urban amenity.

This huge black whirlpool of the city sucks,
And swallows, and encroaches evermore
On vernal field, pure air, and wholesome heaven —
A vast dim province, ever under cloud,
O'er whose immeasurable unloveliness
His own foul breath broods sinister, like Fate

Yet even if the infant death rate was twice as high in London as in many rural areas and even if, in Disraeli's words, the river Thames was "a Stygian pool reeking with ineffable and intolerable horrors," the migrants continued to pour in by the tens of thousands. Whereas industry had attracted newcomers to cities like Manchester and Leeds, the appeal of London — the center of commerce, finance, and government — was more varied. To many of those drawn there, the city meant "the

London Bridge During Rush Hour   The metropolis as seen during the early 1870s by the French engraver Gustave Doré. *(The Granger Collection)*

contagion of numbers, the sense of something going on, the theatres and the music halls, the brightly lighted streets and busy crowds." It meant the bustle of the tens of thousands of streetsellers, scavengers, sweepers, rat killers, street musicians, beggars, and thieves who, like the working-class pubs and the gentlemen's clubs, lent variety and vitality to the greatest metropolis on earth.

What seems reasonably clear is that the third quarter of the nineteenth century brought a slow but significant rise in real wages for both the *average* worker and the *average* member of the middle classes. Although averages may conceal the existence of sizable groups of unskilled workers whose conditions did not improve, it is generally agreed that purchasing power increased by a third during the mid-Victorian generation. Many a middle-class shopkeeper could now afford a comfortable suburban home with antimacassars on the solid upholstered furniture, an aspidistra in the front hall, paintings and engravings on the walls, and a piano for the daughters of the house to play. Many a worker could begin to hope for continuing improvement rather than to fear that things would get worse. The building industry, still divided

London Tenement Houses   Doré's engraving depicts the dingy backyards of the London poor.

among hundreds of small contractors and little affected by new techniques, was succeeding in housing millions of new town dwellers at improved standards of comfort, while philanthropists such as Angela Burdett-Coutts (1814–1906) sponsored model housing estates for working-class families. Yet other philanthropists sought to mitigate urban squalor by encouraging Victorian city fathers to leave space for public parks, intended to serve not as places of amusement for the idle few but as recreation facilities for the laboring many. In Manchester, Liverpool, and Glasgow, municipal boards of health began to cope successfully with sanitation and water-supply problems: in 1847 less than a quarter of the houses of Manchester had running water; by 1876 the number had risen to four-fifths. During these same years London's Metropolitan Board of Works built a 283-mile network of drains and sewers, and the "vast and shapeless city which Dickens knew — fog-bound and fever-haunted, brooding over its dark, mysterious river" was converted "into the imperial capital, of Whitehall, the Thames Embankment, and South Kensington."

Many mid-Victorians attributed their prosperity to two doctrines stressed by the classical economists: free trade and the gold standard. The kingdom had embraced both, and Great Britain, it appeared, was being suitably rewarded by Divine Providence for its economic orthodoxy. Perhaps the cause-and-effect relationship was not quite so simple, but the end of tariff barriers did minimize earlier drags on economic growth. Other factors also contributed to prosperity: Britain's lead in technology, the willingness of business leaders to take risks, and their confidence in an efficient government. To some degree, the mid-Victorians were reaping the harvest sown by their ancestors, and many of them were imbued with a corresponding sense of achievement.

Victorian Morality

It is always difficult to sum up the atmosphere of an age, especially if, like the mid-Victorian, it lies little more than a century in the past and is documented by an immense profusion of books and journals, pictures, buildings, and pieces of furniture. Clearly, not all Victorians thought or acted alike. Yet it may be possible to postulate some reasonably valid generalizations about Victorianism. It is perhaps easier for us to do this than for historians writing in the 1920s, when writers such as Lytton Strachey wittily debunked what they condemned as Victorian prudery, hypocrisy, and stuffiness. *Victorian* remains for us a synonym for *old-fashioned* when referring to attitudes toward sex, but in the course of the past half century, we have become more appreciative (and even envious) of Victorian political ideals and Victorian successes in decreasing the crime rate. We have come to regard pieces of Victorian furniture as valuable antiques (as long as they are small enough to fit into our houses), and even in the United States many a Victorian building has been designated and preserved as an architectural landmark.[3]

In any event, it is wiser, if more difficult, to try to understand Victorianism than to ridicule it, especially if we view it less as a universally congenial or universally practiced moral and social code than as a set of ideals about efficiency and thrift, seriousness of character, respectability, and self-help to which the Victorians themselves often failed to adhere. Still, they tried. The maxim "Honesty is the best policy" was to serve not merely as a slogan but as an accepted and demonstrable truth. In the business world, it was by the profession (and often the practice) of such virtues that a merchant or an industrialist justified his role in society. Although a minority might engage in embezzlement or fraud, most mid-century British business proprietors were known more for their reliability than for sharp trading. Bankruptcy had come to be regarded not merely as a financial but also as a moral disgrace.

Morality in government was given similar, perhaps even greater, stress, and it may well be that the institution of a nonpolitical Civil Service was "the one great political invention in nineteenth-century England." The eighteenth-century political machine had been oiled with influence and patronage, but many sinecure positions had been abolished during the first third of the century; under Benthamite influence there was much talk as to how the national government might be made yet more efficient and competent. It was at the request of Gladstone, then Chancellor of the Exchequer, that a report was prepared in 1853 that recommended the open competitive examination as the ideal route toward government service, a method first used to recruit officials serving the East India Company.

Accordingly, the Civil Service was to be divided by 1870 into an "intellectual grade" of decision-making posts and a "mechanical grade" of copying clerks and others. Promotion was to be based not on political pressure or seniority, but only on merit. This did not mean the democratization of government service, although some expressed fear that the less quick-witted scions of aristocratic families might fare badly in the examinations. In practice, successful applicants for the "intellectual-grade" positions were the products of upper-class English public schools like Eton and Harrow and of Oxford and Cambridge universities. The introduction by Gladstone of the independent auditing of Exchequer

---

[3]Victorian morality is one of several topics taken up in the books by Asa Briggs, W. L. Burn, F. M. L. Thompson, and Geoffrey Best referred to earlier, as well as by G. Kitson Clark in *The Making of Victorian England* (1962). Walter Houghton's *The Victorian Frame of Mind* (1957), an excellent introduction to what literate Victorians thought and took for granted, may be supplemented with David Newsome, *The Victorian World Picture* (1997). G. M. Young's *Victorian England: Portrait of an Age* (1936) is at once brilliant and allusive; an annotated edition was prepared by G. Kitson Clark (1977). Also helpful are two thought-provoking collections of essays by Gertrude Himmelfarb, *Marriage and Morals Among the Victorians* (1986) and *The Demoralization of Society: From Victorian Virtues to Modern Values* (1994), and T. C. Smout, ed., *Victorian Values* (1992).

accounts gave added support to a growing demand for governmental honesty, which was being equally stressed in municipal administration and in the conduct of parliamentary elections. Between 1847 and 1866, the House of Commons unseated more than a hundred new members for electoral corruption.

Emphasis on morality was similarly, if at times less happily, characteristic of the Victorian taste in art, architecture, and music. The most popular paintings were large, realistic, and sentimental, and they were painted by artists whose personal morality was beyond cavil. Thus John Ruskin, the influential art critic, deliberately burned the "pornographic watercolors" produced by J. M. W. Turner, his favorite painter, in order to protect Turner's posthumous reputation. The most widely reproduced painting of the 1850s, Holman Hunt's *The Light of the World*, was a deeply religious picture depicting Christ standing in a doorway with lantern in hand. Morality was given similar stress in music: hundreds of new hymns were composed, and four and a half million copies of *Hymns: Ancient and Modern* were sold during the first seven years after the book's publication in 1861. Victorian domesticity and sentiment were reflected in the immense popularity of the German-born Felix Mendelssohn, the queen's favorite composer. Although few nineteenth-century British composers won an international reputation, and

The St. Pancras Hotel Designed by Gilbert Scott to adjoin a major London railway station, it was completed in 1863. It symbolizes both Victorian Gothic architecture at its zenith and the prosperity of the 1860s. *(National Monuments Record)*

continentals tended to look upon the island as "unmusical," numerous foreign musicians found it worthwhile to tour Great Britain. The land also blossomed with thousands of amateur choral societies.

In architecture it was Augustus Welby Pugin (1812–1852), a Roman Catholic by conversion, who deliberately popularized Victorian "Gothic" as a style more religiously inspired than the classical Georgian. By agreeing, after a disastrous fire in 1833, to have the houses of Parliament at Westminster rebuilt in this style, the government gave the Gothic revival its official approval.[4] Victorians delighted in immense, ornate railway stations and town halls, some Gothic and others in eclectic combinations of almost every style known to architectural history — Byzantine, Romanesque, Tudor, and Renaissance. The results were, from an eighteenth-century point of view, aesthetically confusing and ill-proportioned. Oddly enough, while Victorian architecture was indulging in ornamental variety and liberating itself from the rigid dictates of Georgian "good taste," it made little use of the new materials provided by industrial technology. Except for the iron and glass used in the Crystal Palace, Victorian buildings remained immense monuments to the stonemason and bricklayer.

Perhaps the most widely remembered element of Victorianism is its deliberate de-emphasis of sex. Ideally, sex was never to be referred to in conversation or in print, and one Victorian critic regarded Charles Dickens's greatest merit as the fact that "in forty works or more you will not find a phrase which a mother need withhold from her grown daughter." For Charles Dickens's contemporary, Anthony Trollope (1815–1882), the purpose of a novel was "to instruct in morals while it amuses," to teach "that truth prevails while falsehood fails; that a girl will be loved as she is pure, and sweet, and unselfish; that a man will be honoured as he is true, and honest, and brave of heart; that things meanly done are ugly and odious, and things nobly done beautiful and gracious." (It is fair to add that many characters in Trollope's novels display greater psychological complexity than such axioms would suggest.) But purity was indeed the standard for a lady, and continence became at least the professed ideal for a gentleman, who in the sexual as in the business world was expected to postpone immediate gratification for ultimate domestic and financial benefit. To be named in a divorce suit equaled bankruptcy as a source of social disgrace.

Although the reproduction of the species became the only publicly avowed justification for sexual relations, indirect evidence suggests that many Victorian couples found private pleasure as well. In any event, the praise of domestic family life came to be sung more loudly than ever

---

[4]Robert Furneaux Jordan, *Victorian Architecture* (1966), provides a fascinating illustrated introduction. In "The Victorians, the Historians, and the Idea of Modernism" (*American Historical Review*, April 1988), James Schmiechen reminds us of the purposes Victorians expected their buildings to serve.

before in British history. The Victorian family was a patriarchal one in which a wife was in no sense her husband's legal equal. Ideally, however, she was supposed to be "the Angel of the House" who served as the exemplar of morality and the arbiter of proper behavior. She was expected to beautify both herself and the home over whose operations she presided. Her most highly esteemed role was that of mother. Families were large, and the average wife spent "about fifteen years in a state of pregnancy and in nursing a child for the first year of its life." In such households it was almost a necessity that "little children should be seen and not heard," for the alternative was bedlam. It was the home, in any event, that Victorians felt to be the center of moral virtue and a refuge against the barbarism of the outside world.[5]

Although men were thus expected to dominate the "public sphere" and women the "private sphere" of life, many lower-class women worked for pay and many middle-class women were active outside the home in a variety of charitable enterprises. A reversal of roles was hardly unknown, moreover. As Trollope observed in one of his novels, *The Belton Estate*, according to theory "the wife is to bend herself in loving submission before her husband," but in most marriages the stronger personality took the lead, "whether clothed in petticoats, or in coat, waistcoat, and trousers."

Victorian prudery could lead to such absurdities as the separation of the works of male and female authors on library shelves and the use of euphemisms such as "limbs" for "legs." It was in the "Victorian" United States, to be sure, rather than in England that a British visitor discovered the "limbs" of a grand piano in a girls' school decently clad in little frilled trousers. Certainly it was Victorianism that helped give the word *immoral* the connotation it retains — that of defying sexual convention rather than of practicing fraudulent bookkeeping or telling lies or beating children. The fact that not all Victorians found it possible to live up to so rigid a sexual code is suggested both by the existence of a flourishing trade in illicit pornography and by the prevalence of prostitution. One London street was described in the 1850s as "the Western counterpart of an Eastern slave market."

The question of the origins of the admirable as well as the hypocritical elements in the Victorian social code is a disputed one. Two factors

---

[5]The roles played by Victorian women were determined in part by law, in part by social convention and gender ideology, and to a considerable degree by social class. Joan Perkin's *Victorian Women* (1993) provides a helpful overview, and the following books throw light on different aspects of the subject: Joan Perkin, *Women and Marriage in Nineteenth-Century England* (1989); Sheila Fletcher, *Victorian Girls: Lord Lyttelton's Daughters* (1997); M. Jeanne Peterson, *Family, Love, and Work in the Lives of Victorian Gentlewomen* (1989); Martha Vicinus, *Independent Women: Work and Community for Single Women, 1850–1920* (1985); Deborah Gorham, *The Victorian Girl and the Feminine Ideal* (1982); Kathryn Hughes, *The Victorian Governess* (1993); Patricia Branca, *Silent Sisterhood: Middle-Class Women in the Victorian Home* (1975); Lee Holcombe, *Women and Property* (1983); and Judith Walkowitz, *Prostitution and Victorian Society* (1980).

must first be recalled: Victorian morality was not exclusively British (counterparts in attitude could obviously be found in the France of the Second Empire, in the United States of Lincoln's and Louisa May Alcott's day, and in tsarist Russia), and the roots of Victorian morality can be traced back at least half a century before the accession of Victoria in 1837. Some significant "Puritan" elements necessarily have an even longer history. It was in 1818 that Thomas Bowdler, a well-to-do physician and part-time social reformer, added a new verb to the language, *bowdlerize,* by editing the *Family Shakespeare,* "in which nothing is added to the original text; but those words and expressions are omitted which cannot with propriety be read aloud in a family." The same parliamentary act of 1843 that made it easier for new theaters to be opened reaffirmed the authority of the lord chamberlain to forbid the presentation of stage plays in London "whenever he shall be of the opinion that it is fitting for the preservation of good Manners, Decorum, or of the public Peace to do so."

A principal root of Victorianism was the evangelical religious revival, which continued unabated until the middle decades of the century. Until the 1850s, the growth of church membership increased more rapidly than did the total population. An enormous amount of enthusiasm and hard work went into bringing the message of religion to those groups in society who had been overlooked in the rapidly growing cities or forgotten during the previous century. Church and chapel building[6] expanded at an unprecedented rate. The number of Congregationalist chapels increased three and a half times between 1801 and 1851; the number of Baptist meeting places multiplied fourfold; and the number of Methodist halls multiplied more than fourteen times during these same years. Evangelicals led over a third of the ministers and their congregations out of the Presbyterian Church of Scotland in "the Disruption of 1843." They formed a disestablished Free Church, with its own schools, chapels, and seminaries — a sign of religious vitality as well as of discord. In both England and Scotland there was also a Roman Catholic revival, encouraged by Irish immigration and by such noted converts as Newman and Henry Edward Manning (1808–1892); the latter headed the revived Roman Catholic hierarchy in England for a generation. The Anglican Church grew less rapidly but, invigorated in spirit by the Oxford Movement and reformed in administration by the Ecclesiastical Commission set up in 1836, it remained dominant in the countryside and by the 1850s had found ways to adapt its parish boundaries to the new industrial towns. Revival meetings on the American model proved popular among many Nonconformists, and the evangelically minded "Low Church" remained a prominent facet of Anglicanism.

---

[6]The places of worship of the Nonconformist denominations in Britain are usually referred to as "chapels."

The unique religious census of 1851 revealed that in a land of almost 18 million people, there had been 11 million church visits on Census Sunday. Because as many as a third of these visits had been made by persons who attended more than one service, Victorians were less impressed than the twenty-first-century student may be. Indeed, they were appalled to discover that at least five million of their largely lower-class compatriots (who had not the excuse of youth or age or illness) had failed to enter either church or chapel. Although the vast majority of England's people might in some general sense be defined as Anglican — after all, 85 percent of all weddings were performed by clergymen of the Church of England — Anglicans were shocked to learn that almost half the actual Census Sunday worshippers were not members of the established Church.

Many railway station waiting rooms were furnished with reading stands to which were chained Bibles for passengers to consult while changing trains — if only because, for many Victorians, the Bible remained from first page to last the revealed Word of God. Heaven and hell were as certain as the sun in the sky, and the Last Judgment was as real as a businessman's weekly balance sheet. The Bible provided the most comprehensive system of thought and code of ethics available, and the church or chapel furnished the introduction to music, literature, philosophy, and history. In the words of G. M. Young:

> Evangelicalism had imposed on society, even on classes which were indifferent to its religious basis and unaffected by its economic appeal, its code of Sabbath observance, responsibility, and philanthropy; of discipline in the home, regularity in affairs; it had created a most effective technique of agitation, of private persuasion and social persecution.

The evangelical revival was only one factor contributing to the creation of Victorianism. The Victorian unbeliever appears to have been possessed by as strong a sense of duty as was the professing Christian, with a moral code not outwardly distinguishable from that of the churchgoer. For a Utilitarian like John Stuart Mill, being good for good's sake was obviously as powerful a motive as being good for God's sake. Thus "good behavior" was the result not only of religious teaching or fear of the police on earth or punishment in the next world, but also of the pressures of social conformity and the hope, stemming from the Age of Enlightenment, that human beings, when left to their own devices, were fundamentally well-intentioned. As Dickens's David Copperfield put it, "We can all do some good if we will."

The Victorian code was obviously a response to the needs of an emerging industrial society and the consciousness that civilization provided a thin veneer at best for humanity's antisocial tendencies. It stressed the virtues of duty and industry because absenteeism and idleness were dangerous relics of the past. The emphasis on thrift was a reaction to the still-popular attitude of "Eat, drink, and be merry" and take no heed for the morrow. The creed of self-help was a virtue preached most earnestly to those who were not necessarily in a position to practice it. "Character" was a highly acclaimed ideal because rowdyism and drunkenness, despite the efforts of a growing army of largely Nonconformist temperance reformers, were still widespread. Seen as a set of ideals rather than as the attribute of a whole society, Victorianism becomes more understandable. Its snobbery reflected the impact of new classes wishing to secure a position in the traditional hierarchy. Its hypocrisy resulted from the attempt to lay claim to standards of conduct that proved too hard to maintain consistently. Its prudery was the byproduct of a battle for decency by a people many of whom were just emerging into civilized society.

The Cult of Respectability

One of the fascinating elements of Victorianism was the process by which the middle-class virtues of self-improvement, perseverance, thrift, duty, and character came to influence, or to be adopted independently by, other classes in society. This transformation was most obvious in the royal family. The rakish sons of George III gave way to Queen Victoria and Prince Albert.[7] Their marriage was based as much on love and mutual devotion as on convenience of state, and by the 1850s the royal family, with its nine children, had become the model family of the land. Mistresses, all-night gambling, and wild extravagance had yielded to propriety and respectability. The story is told of the Victorian playgoer who went to see a performance of *Oedipus Rex*, in which the hero murders his father, unwittingly marries his mother, and then blinds himself while his mother commits suicide. Murmured the playgoer as he emerged: "How different from the home life of our own dear Queen!"

Victoria's resolve, "I will be good!" — pronounced when she first learned of her royal destiny — was in harmony with her age. Prince Albert, who was not yet twenty-one at the time of his marriage to the queen, surpassed even his wife, the duke of Wellington concluded, as "a great stickler for morality." The prince added a touch of Germanic thoroughness to the court, which did not always make him popular, but it at least coincided with the Victorian emphasis on the virtue of industry. Albert streamlined the haphazardly run royal household. He vigorously supported scientific research and education, and he proved to be a reform-minded chancellor of Cambridge University. Albert much preferred the company of authors, scientists, and social reformers to that of aristocrats

---

[7]Elizabeth Longford's *Queen Victoria: Born to Succeed* (1965) is both scholarly and entertaining. Cecil Woodham-Smith's *Queen Victoria, 1819–1861* (1972), equally readable but more detailed, takes the story up to Albert's death. See also Stanley Weintraub's acerbic *Victoria: An Intimate Biography* (1987) as well as Daphne Bennett's life of Albert, *King Without a Crown* (1977) and Stanley Weintraub's *Prince Albert* (1998).

Queen Victoria, Prince Albert, and Their First Five Children   The royal family was romanticized as the nation's model family in this 1846 painting by Franz Winterhalter. *(Hulton Deutsch Collection)*

whose main preoccupation was horse racing. Queen Victoria was less intellectual and, as a consequence perhaps, more popular.

Prince Albert's death in 1861 was a shock from which Victoria never completely recovered. Although her state of mourning exemplified what has been called "the Victorian celebration of death," her refusal to take part in any of the public ceremonies expected of the monarch threatened to become permanent and caused her popularity to decline for more than a decade. Behind the scenes, it is true, the queen maintained her conscientious concern for government business, and she remained, and remains, the prototype of most aspects of Victorianism.

At least in their public behavior, aristocrats were almost as much influenced by Victorian morality as was the monarchy. Lord Melbourne, who was named co-respondent in a divorce suit while prime minister (he was found innocent), and Lord Palmerston, who fathered several children by Lady Cowper (who eventually became Lady Palmerston), were relics of a passing age. "Publish and be damned," the duke of Wellington had once exclaimed when threatened with the exposure of his indiscretions; but by the 1850s such a Regency attitude was in eclipse. In the words of G. K. Chesterton, "The great lords yielded on prudery as they had yielded on free trade." People in high society became both more responsible and more sober, and it was no longer true that "one-third of the gentlemen at least were always drunk." The change may well have benefited not merely their souls but also their pocketbooks and their life expectancy.

Not only had such "middle-class morality" changed the tone of upper-class society; it was influencing members of the working classes as well. The 1850s, for example, saw the beginnings of respectable trade unionism in England. The Amalgamated Society of Engineers (1851) and the Amalgamated Society of Carpenters and Joiners were typical "New Model" unions. They sought not to transform society but to profit from it. They disliked strikes, and they believed in thrift, temperance, and steady habits and in building up large insurance funds. Their professed object was to do nothing "illegally or indiscreetly, but on all occasions to perform the greatest amount of benefit to ourselves, without injury to others." Such unions were generally limited to workers with special skills, but the mid-Victorian economic boom encouraged trade unionism also among coal miners and, for a time, even agricultural laborers. In 1868 was held the first annual meeting of the Trades Union Congress, a national confederation of British labor unions that foreshadowed in both scope and attitude the American Federation of Labor, organized in the 1880s.

The New Model unions did much to disarm earlier middle-class distrust of trade unions. Although the mid-Victorian years witnessed a number of divisive strikes — such as the one by London building workers in 1859 — many Victorian employers were becoming accustomed to negotiating union contracts. For some years trade union funds were regarded as protected by the Friendly Societies Act of 1855. This statute did much to foster self-help among an increasing number of male workers — lower middle class, skilled, and semi-skilled — by placing the mantle of government protection over the funds of voluntary societies. By 1874 Friendly Societies providing sickness and death benefits had well over two million members, and other voluntary organizations enrolled millions more. The registrar of the Friendly Societies, a Mr. Stephenson, had become a kind of universal Dutch uncle to the worthy laboring man.

> Mr. Stephenson [reported one official] is as it were a minister of self-help to the whole of the industrious classes. The first penny deposited by a school child in a penny savings bank finds its way probably to a trustee savings bank, the rules of which are certified by Mr. Stephenson. When the boy begins to work for himself, if he has forethought and prudence, he very likely opens his own account, although still a minor, with a Savings Bank; toward the end of his apprenticeship he joins a benefit club or Odd Fellows lodge, certified by the same hand in a different capacity. If he desires to improve his hand he enters a Scientific or Literary institution, the rules of which have probably passed equally through the registrar's hand. If he becomes a member of a Trade Society, he learns that the only legal security for the funds is to be obtained by certification through the same hand. If he marry and have a family to provide for, he will seek to cheapen his living by entering a Co-operative Store, whose rules have received the same Registrar's sanction. As his capital accumu-

lates, and he aspires to the possession of a house of his own, he subscribes to a Benefit Building Society, still certified by the same authority. On the other hand, if he has difficulties to pass through, the Loan Society, certified by the same person, will frequently have proved his first resource, perhaps a fatal one. And if he has remained satisfied with the low rate of interest of the Post Office Savings Bank [set up in 1861], he knows, or should know, that in case of dispute it is still Mr. Stephenson who will be the arbitrator. Thus, at every step in life, he will have been met by the authority of the same person, who has been for him, as it were, the embodiment of the goodwill and protection of the State, in all that goes beyond police, the poor law, justice, and the school.[8]

For as many as a third of Britain's people, the dread of having to seek relief from the Poor Law was greater than the prospect of investing funds in savings banks or borrowing from building and loan societies; but for many Victorian artisans and shopkeepers, *Self-Help* was more than the title of a best-selling book by Samuel Smiles; it was a reality as well as a credo. In recent years some historians of Victorian Britain have tended to describe middle-class humanitarian and educational reformers as deliberately imposing on their poorer brethren a form of "social control" in order to make them more industrious, more obedient, and more docile. Yet it seems clear that those workers who sought respectability by devoting leisure hours to self-improvement, who were able to support a wife who could be spared from the need to work outside the home, who saved their pennies in order to pay their children's school fees and eventually to buy a house of their own, and who heeded temperance reformers by staying sober were doing so in order to feel and be more independent rather than more subservient.[9]

Associated with the spread of Victorianism to the poorer classes of British society was a growing sense of law-mindedness. Genuine obedience and deference to the law had not always been a notable English trait, and even in the 1850s and 1860s occasional election riots and scattered Protestant-Catholic street battles shook towns with sizable communities of Irish immigrants.[10] Yet there was less violence than during earlier decades, and by the 1850s even working-class leaders had begun to take pride in their ability to assemble large crowds without disorder. When Queen Victoria visited Birmingham in 1858, self-satisfaction was expressed in the enormous crowds "who behaved as well in the streets as could any assemblage of the aristocracy at a Queen's Drawing Room."

---

[8]David C. Douglas, ed., *English Historical Documents*, XII, Part I: 1830–1874 (1956).

[9]See, for example, Trygve Tholfsen, *Working Class Radicalism in Mid-Victorian England* (1977), and Margot Finn, *After Chartism: Class and Nationalism in English Radical Politics, 1848–1874* (1993).

[10]See Donald C. Richter, *Riotous Victorians* (1981); Walter L. Arnstein, *Protestant Versus Catholic in Mid-Victorian England* (1982); and Frank Neal, *Sectarian Violence: The Liverpool Experience, 1819–1914* (1988).

Why did lawlessness decrease? There was a broadening social consensus that condemned criminal behavior. Bodies of uniformed policemen in both cities and the countryside provided an increasingly visible deterrent. The spread of gas lighting to illuminate city streets at night also promoted a sense of public security. As early as 1839, one observer found it possible to walk from one end of London to the other without molestation, a feat deemed impossible half a century before. The decline in crime was accompanied by a decrease in the severity of punishment. Whereas, during the 1780s, more than 500 people had been executed in London (then a considerably smaller city), during the 1860s capital punishment was reserved for no more than 22. Use of the pillory and the public flogging of civilians had ended in the 1820s, and the flogging of soldiers in peacetime was formally abolished in 1868. During that same year the last public hanging took place at Tyburn. Thus ended one of the traditional, if dubious, sources of public amusement and edification. During the 1820s, public lotteries were abolished, and during the 1830s cockfighting, bull-baiting, and bearbaiting — the last-named sport actually subsidized by the government in the days of Queen Elizabeth I —were all made illegal.

Amateur and professional football and cricket would in due course take the place of public spectacles like hangings, and the music hall was already becoming an increasingly popular form of amusement for all classes. Its rough-and-tumble humor, its lusty singing, and its emphasis on drinking and on audience participation were often indecorous. Yet it was a far cry from the brutality of many earlier forms of entertainment.

The Victorian Gentleman

The social structure of mid-Victorian England is often described as one in which the middle classes had somehow triumphed over the upper classes. This view is far too simple. It may be more appropriate to see the change as one in which both aristocrats and members of the middle class were transformed into gentlemen, a status of respectability that was generally taken on by their wives and children as well. It might be difficult to define the word *gentleman,* conceded Anthony Trollope, but he was certain that "any one would know what it meant." To be descended from an old aristocratic family clearly gave one a head start. To lay claim to a coat of arms was an asset, as was the prospective ownership of a large estate, but membership in a profession such as the law or the clergy (or medicine or architecture) was equally likely to confer gentlemanly status, especially if one had been imbued with the notions of chivalry revived by Sir Walter Scott and echoed by Alfred Lord Tennyson.[11]

---

[11]This last is the theme emphasized by Mark Girouard in *The Return to Camelot: Chivalry and the English Gentleman* (1981). In *Manners, Morals and Class in England, 1774–1858* (1994), Marjorie Morgan analyzes the way in which conduct and etiquette books helped to fashion Victorians who sought the status of gentleman or lady.

It was not necessary to have gone to Oxford or Cambridge to be a gentleman, but it obviously helped. Both of the old universities increased in size during the middle years of the nineteenth century. But the increase of the combined entering class from 700 men a year in the early years of the century to 1,600 men in 1880 reflected the increase in total population more than growth in the ratio of young men educated at a university. Even if one did not attend a university, it was most desirable to attend a public school. Eton, Harrow, Rugby, Winchester, and almost a hundred similar but less-well-known boarding schools were public only in the sense that education there was not by private tutor and involved the company of boys from other walks of life and from different parts of the country. A landowner's son might well encounter the son of an industrialist who had made good, but he was increasingly less likely to encounter the genuinely poor boy for whom a proportion of scholarships had been reserved in earlier centuries.

Some English public schools had long histories; but in the eighteenth century they had, according to Dr. Bowdler, become best known as "nurseries of vice." Thomas Arnold (1795–1842), who became headmaster of Rugby in 1828, renewed the confidence of an increasing number of middle-class parents in the value of a public-school education. "What we must look for," Arnold explained, "is first, religious and moral principle; secondly, gentlemanly conduct; thirdly, intellectual ability." Rugby also came to stress organized athletics. Although modern languages and the natural sciences were taught at Rugby, as well as the classics, to a surprising degree Greek and Latin continued to dominate both the public-school and the university curricula. Admittedly, they would not get you far in a strictly utilitarian sense, but the assumption was that you were already somewhere when you took them up.[12]

Arnold and other reformers sought to curb flogging and bullying with a system of guided student self-government. Because boys were enrolled as young as eight or nine, public schools encouraged both self-discipline and independence from immediate family ties. Their most important product was "the character of an English gentleman," but in a very real sense they also trained the administrators of Victorian England and the Victorian empire. It was public-school gentlemen who were given the greatest encouragement to compete for the decision-making grades of the Civil Service. It was such gentlemen whom army reformers sought to fill the ranks of that service's commissioned officers. It was this same class of public-school graduates — comparable in training and outlook to the "guardians" of Plato's *Republic* — who went to India and Africa and elsewhere to take up posts in the imperial Civil Service. Schoolboy friendships influenced many a political appointment in later

---

[12]Thomas Hughes's mid-Victorian best-seller, *Tom Brown's Schooldays* (1857), spread the fame of Arnold's Rugby. See also Michael McCrum, *Thomas Arnold, Headmaster* (1990), and J. R. de S. Honey, *Tom Brown's Universe* (1977).

life, and old-school-tie-ism became one of the marks of the established Victorian order.

Although even the reformed public schools were still tainted by brutality and often limited in intellectual scope, the genus *Victorian gentleman* did include intellectuals as well. Architects, civil and mechanical engineers, lawyers, and physicians elevated their professions by setting up permanent organizations to establish standards and gain prestige.[13] The mid-Victorian world produced a considerable number of sober, well-written journals of opinion such as the *Edinburgh Review* (1802), the *Westminster Review* (1828), and the *Saturday Review* (1858). Although not aristocrats by birth, men such as the historian Macaulay, economist and political scientist John Stuart Mill, and editor and social observer Walter Bagehot all belonged to that privileged class of Victorian intellectuals who had the money and the leisure to read and write for such journals. They possessed the self-confidence and social prestige not only to reflect their age but to criticize it.

At the root of the mid-Victorian way of life lay a paradox. On the one hand, laissez-faire was implicit in the outlook of the age, not perhaps to the extent that the more dogmatic classical economists would have wished, but to a large degree nonetheless. Ultimately, it was the law of supply and demand that was expected to promote the competition that in turn would produce the maximum number of goods and thus benefit society. The chief function of government was therefore a highly restricted one: to see to it that the rules of the games were observed; to prevent frauds and enforce contracts; but not to enter the game itself. The true progress of a business — and of a nation — was expected to be the result of individual initiative and individual self-help. This idea pervades not only Mill's *On Liberty* (1859) but also that even more widely sold book published in the same year, *Self-Help*. Its ebullient author, Samuel Smiles, assured his earnest reader:

> Englishmen feel that they are free, not merely because they live under those free institutions which they have laboriously built up, but because each member of the society has to a greater or less extent got the root of the matter within himself.

If, however, economic and social life was a scramble of individuals each out for his own good, then what held society together? The bond, Smiles believed, lay in a common set of moral standards, in "the unfettered energetic actions of persons, together with the uniform subjection of all to the national code of Duty."[14]

---

[13]W. J. Reader analyzes this process in *Professional Men: The Rise of the Professional Classes in Nineteenth-Century England* (1966), while M. Jeanne Peterson focuses on one significant example in *The Medical Profession in Mid-Victorian London* (1978).

[14]The manner in which the tenets of the commercial and industrial economy were reconciled with a (predominantly Christian) framework of morality is the subject of G. R. Searle, *Morality and the Market in Victorian Britain* (1998).

In an age marked by a high degree of economic prosperity and social stability, in which the creed of progress was exemplified daily in the material world, many people came to view the world with a high degree of complacency, and the country's leaders showed little inclination to tamper with its political institutions. Neither Lord Aberdeen, the Peelite who headed a coalition ministry (1852–1855), nor Lord Palmerston, the Whig who with a brief interruption served as prime minister during the decade that followed, was a domestic reformer by inclination. In some ways the period was retrogressive. Edwin Chadwick, the eager social reformer, was forced off the Board of Health in 1854, and four years later the entire office was abolished. "We prefer to take our chance of cholera and the rest, rather than to be bullied into health," declared *The Times*. A contemporary observer, Walter Bagehot, found the English people of the early 1860s "politically contented as well as politically deferential. . . . A man can hardly get an audience if he wishes to complain of anything." Lord Palmerston typified such complacency about government-sponsored social and political reform when he was asked at the opening of the 1864 session of Parliament to describe his party's program. He mused for a moment and then answered, "Oh, there is really nothing to be done. We cannot go on adding to the Statute Book ad infinitum. Perhaps we may have a little law reform, or bankruptcy reform; but we cannot go on legislating forever."

The Critics of Victorianism

It would be a mistake, however, to see complacency as the hallmark of the age, for some Victorians could be as self-critical as others were self-confident. Thomas Carlyle continued to strike out against the "cash nexus" and "Mammon worship" of his age, and he branded his society as one in which materialistic mediocrity dominated, a society lacking heroes. John Ruskin (1819–1900) shared Carlyle's distrust of a competitive industrial society, founded on free enterprise and machine production. He was repelled alike by the artistic shoddiness that he saw as the product of industrial civilization and by the continued prevalence of poverty. "The first duty of the state," he believed, "is to see that every child born therein shall be well housed, clothed, fed, and educated, till it attains years of discretion." Concern for the welfare of the lower classes was also expressed by such avowed "Christian Socialists" as Charles Kingsley (1819–1875) and F. D. Maurice (1805–1872), moralists inspired by their religious beliefs to persuade the state to use its power to improve society.

Other critics accepted the basis of Victorian society while yet opposing some of its fruits. Matthew Arnold (1822–1888), the author of *Culture and Anarchy* (1869), appealed to his contemporaries to seek quality rather than quantity in life. He saw the English aristocracy as still "barbarians," the lower classes as still brutalized by the struggle for existence, and the middle classes as no more than "Philistines," narrow and prejudiced in outlook, handicapped by a "defective type of religion," "a stunted sense of beauty," and "a low standard of life."

> Your middle-class man thinks it the highest pitch of development and civilization when his letters are carried twelve times a day from Islington to Camberwell . . . and if railway trains run to and from them every quarter of an hour. He thinks it is nothing that the trains only carry him from an illiberal, dismal life at Islington to an illiberal, dismal life at Camberwell; and the letters only tell him that such is the life there.

Matthew Arnold was a freethinker, unconvinced by religious dogma but appreciative of religious moral teaching and of the literary splendor of the Bible. He was at the furthest end of the spectrum of a growing number of religious liberals or "Broad Churchmen." Although prepared to find something of value in every variety of Christian thought, they found contradictions in Christianity as defined in its traditional creeds, and they agreed that the "higher criticism" of the Bible made popular by German scholars had cast great doubt on many of its details. The book *Essays and Reviews*, published in 1860, was representative of such questioning of religious dogma. The authors, mostly Anglican clergymen, were criticized as heretics both by High Churchmen like Bishop Samuel Wilberforce (1805–1873) and Low Churchmen like Lord Shaftesbury, the most eminent of evangelical laymen.

It may seem curious to cite Charles Darwin (1809–1882) as one of the critics of Victorianism, because in background and character — and perhaps even in bearded appearance — he seems so very Victorian himself. Yet his own work did as much as that of any other man to raise doubts about the religious and philosophical underpinnings of Victorian thought. In one respect, it is true, Darwin — like Isaac Newton almost two centuries earlier — came less at the beginning of a process than toward the end. He summed things up. Darwin confined himself primarily to a single science, biology; yet as Newton had influenced a great many people who were neither physicists nor mathematicians, so Darwin was to influence a great many people who were not biologists. In the case of Darwin as in that of Newton, some of the most far-reaching implications were drawn not by the masters themselves but by their more militant disciples.

Newton's key concept was that of a mechanical universe, a universe running year in, year out, in accordance with precise mathematical formulas that human beings had discovered or could discover. Darwin's significance lay in confirming the idea of evolution in the natural world — eternal change rather than eternal stability. Although the concept of biological evolution can be traced back to Anaximander among the ancient Greek philosophers, the prevailing doctrine until the early nineteenth century was the Aristotelian and scholastic belief in a fixed number of species, each fulfilling its appointed role in nature and each created in Biblical fashion at a precise point in time a few thousand years before.

During the early nineteenth century, the doctrine of evolution had, however, made headway in a variety of fields. Geologists such as Charles Lyell (1797–1875) concluded that the forces of wind and water had gradually been altering the shape of the earth for a very long time. The discovery of fossils seemed to indicate that the age of the earth should be measured in terms of millions rather than thousands of years, and the accepted Biblical chronology was thereby overturned. Although Philip Gosse suggested that God had planted the fossils in the rocks to test man's faith, other Victorians rebelled at the idea of such a deception, dismissing it as decidedly unsporting on God's part. Jean-Baptiste Lamarck, the French naturalist, had put forward a theory of biological evolution six decades earlier. He was unable, however, to assemble persuasive evidence to buttress his claims.

Darwin succeeded where Lamarck had failed by providing for the first time an immense accumulation of data that supported the evolutionary hypothesis and by suggesting a plausible mechanism by which

Charles Darwin (1809–1882) and Thomas Henry Huxley (1825–1895)   Seen here are the reclusive author of *On the Origin of Species by Means of Natural Selection* (1859) and the militant advocate of the theory who came to be known as "Darwin's Bulldog." These caricatures were drawn for the Victorian weekly *Vanity Fair* in 1871. *(Vanity Fair, 1871)*

evolution had taken place: the natural selection of random variations. Over a period of twenty-five years, Darwin gathered geographical, geological, biological, and embryological evidence, which he then put together to make the argument that the entire animal kingdom had evolved from a few simple forms (or only one). His thesis was no longer merely a possible hypothesis but the most plausible manner of accounting for the assembled data. In proposing natural selection as the mechanism of organic change, Darwin in effect applied Malthusian theory to the whole natural world. In any given generation, more organisms are born than can support themselves. No two organisms are identical. The organisms best fitted for their environment survive in the struggle for existence and become the parents of the next generation. Small changes can accumulate from generation to generation and thereby make possible, in the course of millions of years, even the development of brand-new species — like that of humankind.

Upon its publication in 1859, the *Origin of Species* became the topic of much debate among scientists and laymen alike. An older generation of biologists found troublesome Darwin's challenge to the doctrine that species were permanently fixed. Even more worried were religious thinkers who considered Darwin's ideas a defiance of God's Word. At a debate sponsored by the British Association for the Advancement of Science in 1860, Bishop Samuel Wilberforce criticized the theory of evolution as an absurdity. Turning to Thomas Henry Huxley (1825–1895), who was to become Darwin's most cogent and forceful advocate, the bishop "begged to know, was it through his grandfather or his grandmother that he claimed his descent from a monkey?" Huxley quietly replied that he was present at the meeting in the interests of science and that thus far he had heard nothing to invalidate Darwin's ideas. He for one, he added, would not be ashamed to have a monkey for an ancestor; but he would be "ashamed to be connected with a man who used great gifts to obscure the truth."[15]

The British Association debate was only one episode in the ongoing controversy over the ultimate role of formal religion in Victorian life. Although the eighteenth century had known atheists and deists — usually among the upper classes — the early nineteenth century had seen a reaction against deism and against attempts to remove the emotional and the miraculous from religion. Many nineteenth-century Britons read their Bible faithfully and believed in it literally. Some had been affected by the "higher criticism" of the Bible practiced on the continent. Others had become aware of the conclusions of anthropologists on the variety of

---

[15]William Irvine, *Apes, Angels, and Victorians* (1955). See also Peter Brent, *Charles Darwin: A Man of Enlarged Curiosity* (1981); Peter J. Bowler, *Charles Darwin: The Man and His Influence* (1992); and John Greene, *Science, Ideology and World View: Essays in the History of Evolutionary Ideas* (1981). In *Huxley: The Devil's Disciple* (1994) and *Huxley: Evolution's High Priest* (1997), Adrian Desmond reminds us of Huxley's all-important role in raising the prestige of science among mid- and late Victorians.

contradictory beliefs concerning religion to be found in different parts of the world. But for many good Victorians, Darwin seemed to be by far the most severe threat to religion and the established order of things. The essential question was posed by Disraeli in 1864: "Is man an ape or an angel?" Like Disraeli, these Victorians aligned themselves on the side of the angels.

Other mid-Victorians, however, felt less certain. Darwin seemed to indicate — and in *The Descent of Man* (1871) to demonstrate — that human beings were as much a product of evolution as any other plant or animal. Yet the Darwinian thesis was a hard one to stomach: what of the human soul? What place was there for a divine design in a world that was the result of the amoral and mechanical interplay of random variations that had made some individual organisms more likely to survive than their rivals?

Some Victorians turned their backs on science and sought refuge in religious fundamentalism. Others, as devoted to the pursuit of scientific truth as to their religious upbringing, sought a compromise that might harmonize Darwinian evolution with Christian teaching. That some of the attempts to fashion such intellectual syntheses proved convincing is demonstrated by the fact that when Darwin died in 1882, he, like Isaac Newton, was buried in Westminster Abbey. For a good many Victorians, the conflux of the higher criticism and Darwinism meant a spiritually painful adjustment to a world in which there was room for neither God nor dogma. Huxley himself coined the word *agnosticism* as the only appropriate attitude for those who "confess themselves to be hopelessly ignorant concerning a variety of matters about which metaphysicians and theologians . . . dogmatize with the utmost confidence."

Darwin's theories came to play an influential role not only in biology and religion but also in the social sciences. Men such as Herbert Spencer (1820–1903) in England and Andrew Carnegie in the United States — thinkers often referred to as Social Darwinists — emphasized one particular part of Darwin's theory, that evolution was a struggle for survival in which only the fittest survived. As applied to economics, it meant the ceaseless struggle of the individual entrepreneur in which only the aggressive prospered. For Herbert Spencer, Darwinism simply reinforced earlier predilections toward laissez-faire in the economic world. Spencer was as doubtful as Malthus had been that human beings could overturn economic law. In the later years of the nineteenth century, other so-called Social Darwinists emphasized not so much individual as national or racial struggle. For such men, war provided the human analogy to the animal struggle for survival. Thus the Franco-Prussian War of 1870–1871 seemed to demonstrate that the German "race" was superior to the French "race," just as the Opium War of 1839–1842 had demonstrated the white "race" to be superior to the yellow "race." The word *race* came to be used in a clearly contradictory manner, and the subject continued to preoccupy a significant number of late-nineteenth-century thinkers and writers.

Not all social scientists drew the same implications from Darwinism. Some saw the logical inconsistency in applying the idea of struggle for existence to individuals in one instance, to nations in another, and to races based on skin color in a third. Some biologists contended that natural history afforded numerous examples of animal species that survived by means of mutual aid rather than competition. Still others, including Thomas Huxley himself, maintained that the pattern the scientist had found in nature did not necessarily have to serve as a pattern for human cultural development. Even if human biological evolution was the product of millions of years of variation and struggle for existence, cultural evolution represented the triumph of the human mind over so-called natural processes. Hence, in Huxley's view, Social Darwinists like Spencer had mistaken the evolution of ethics for the ethics of evolution.

If Social Darwinism and its various tributaries merely illustrated anew the danger of making a discovery in one science apply to every other branch of knowledge, this caveat does not undermine Darwin's long-range significance. The doctrine of biological evolution has come not merely to be accepted but also to be taken for granted by most educated people. The doctrine of natural selection has also largely stood the test of time, although twentieth-century geneticists are far better informed on the causes and workings of the "chance variations" — or mutations — and the genetic DNA recombinations that play so important a role in modern evolutionary theory.

In one sense Darwin was a critic of his age; in another he gave support to one of the chief credos of his times. If the implications of his ideas cast doubt on Victorian religion and the concept of a static universe, at least they seemed to sustain Darwin's hope that "as natural selection works solely by and for the good of each being, all corporal and mental environments will tend to progress toward perfection." The thought contains an unacknowledged value judgment — for the success of an organism in adapting to a particular environment says nothing about the intrinsic value of that environment. But the conclusion helped to reconcile the Victorians to Darwin. If the world was, indeed, in a constant state of flux, this was for most a sign that the present was better than the past and that the future would be better still.

CHAPTER 6

War Drums Sound Afar

The Vienna settlement held firm for forty years, from 1815 to 1854. There were international squabbles, ideological tensions, and domestic revolutions; but, by and large, the Great Powers showed surprising restraint, respect for treaties, a reluctance to become tied down by inflexible alliances, and a willingness to cooperate against any threat to the balance of power. Although sympathetic to the forces of liberal nationalism on the European continent, Lord Palmerston did his best in 1848–1849 to prevent the revolutions that had broken out in France, in Spain, and in many Italian and German states from leading to international war.

During the third quarter of the nineteenth century, as first France under Napoleon III and then Prussia under Bismarck sought a revision of earlier territorial boundaries, the Vienna system began to break down. Within less than two decades, six wars were fought: the Crimean War, the Austro-Sardinian War, the American Civil War, and the three wars of German unification. Britain was to be affected directly by the first and indirectly by the rest. Although Palmerston was to survive for the greater part of this turbulent period, his position was no longer that of foreign secretary. In 1851 he failed to consult either his colleagues or Queen Victoria before giving British approval to the coup d'état that made Napoleon president of France for life and emperor a year later. He was therefore asked to resign. His fall was hailed on the continent as the triumph of counterrevolution, but in reality British foreign policy underwent little change. Lord John Russell, who became foreign secretary late in 1852, defined that policy in words that would have received his predecessor's full endorsement:

> We are connected, and have been for more than a century, with the general system of Europe, and any territorial increase of one Power, any aggrandisement which disturbs the general balance of power in Europe, although it might not immediately lead to war, could not be a matter of indifference to this country and would, no doubt, be the subject of conference, and might ultimately, if that balance were seriously threatened, lead to war.

The Crimean War

The implied threat — that England might go to war in order to maintain the balance of power — was within two years put to the test. The cabinet that became increasingly involved in the events leading up to the Crimean War was the Whig-Peelite coalition of 1852, which had a Peelite, Lord Aberdeen, as prime minister, Russell as foreign secretary, and Palmerston in the unaccustomed role of home secretary.[1] The war has been variously explained as the result of the ambitions of Napoleon III, of British economic interests in Turkey, and of the diplomatic machinations of either Lord Palmerston or Viscount Stratford de Redcliffe, the British ambassador in Constantinople. The conflict may more realistically be seen as part of a century-long rivalry between Russia and the Ottoman Empire. In the long run the Russians hoped to take over Constantinople and to establish a naval outpost on the Mediterranean Sea. In the short run, they sought recognition of their right to serve as the protectors of the Eastern Orthodox Christian subjects of the Moslem sultan. Britain, France, and Austria were equally determined to halt the expansion of Russian influence into the Balkans and the Middle East. They wanted to maintain for the Dardanelles the status of neutrality that had been agreed on by the major powers in 1840 and that, in effect, blocked Russian expansion into the Mediterranean. The Ottoman Turks soon learned that no matter how irresponsibly they acted, France and Britain would feel obliged to back them up. In May 1853, diplomatic relations between Turkey and Russia were broken. Part of the British navy was sent to the northern Aegean Sea as a peace-keeping force. Russian troops thereupon occupied the principalities of Moldavia and Wallachia (modern Rumania). An attempt by the Great Powers to meet at Vienna and settle the issue by compromise was unsuccessful. The Turks refused to acknowledge Russia's special role as protector of Ottoman Christians, and the Russians were equally stubborn in their insistence. In October 1853, the sultan announced that Turkey would go to war if the Russians did not evacuate the principalities within two weeks. The tsar refused, and war began. Late in November, the inept Russian Black Sea fleet sank an even more inefficient Turkish flotilla at Sinope; four thousand Turkish seamen died.

---

[1]See two books by J. B. Conacher, *The Aberdeen Coalition, 1852–1855* (1968) and *Britain and the Crimea, 1855–56: Problems of War and Peace* (1987), as well as Olive Anderson, *A Liberal State at War* (1967). Norman Rich provides a scholarly modern overview in *Why the Crimean War?* (1985). Kingsley Martin, *The Triumph of Lord Palmerston* (1924), focuses on British public opinion. Paul W. Schroeder, *Austria, Great Britain, and the Crimean War* (1972), stresses the role of Palmerston's "war party." Cecil Woodham-Smith deals with the fighting in *The Reason Why* (1954) and with some of the consequences in *Florence Nightingale* (1951). In *Florence Nightingale: Reputation and Power* (1982), F. B. Smith provides a critical reappraisal of the work of the medical reformer.

The "massacre of Sinope" aroused British public opinion as no event in recent memory had done. During the following months, latent Russophobia came to the surface. "Our statesmen," wrote the London *Globe* after Sinope, "have been too much in the habit of transacting business with Russia as if Russia were accessible to the ordinary motives of the rest of the European family." Added the London *Chronicle* shortly thereafter: "We shall draw the sword, if draw we must, not only to preserve the independence of an ally, but to humble the ambition and thwart the machinations of a despot whose intolerable pretensions have made him the enemy of all civilized nations!" Alone among Europe's Great Powers, Russia retained the institution of serfdom. At the invitation of Austria, Russian troops had bloodily suppressed the Hungarian revolution of 1848–1849. The Russian military push toward Constantinople was viewed as a prelude to even vaster territorial ambitions that included a threat to British India. Urged on by jingoistic newspapers and Palmerston's insistence that his colleagues take a strong stand, Britain and France drifted into war. Their fleets entered the Black Sea, and both nations insisted that Russia confine its naval forces to the Crimean port of Sebastopol. The Russians refused, and Britain and France declared war in March 1854.

The war proved to be a limited one, partly because the expected Russian push on Constantinople did not materialize. Indeed, in the fall of 1854 the Russian government decided to evacuate the disputed principalities. In

The Crimean War   A contemporary illustration of the Battle of Balaclava (October 1854) shows the British light cavalry attacking Russian guns. *(Bettmann/Corbis)*

the meantime, grandiose British and French speculations about a possible march on Moscow were quickly subordinated to the attainment of a more limited objective: the invasion of the Crimea and the capture of the chief Russian naval base in the Black Sea, Sebastopol, "the eye tooth of the Bear which must be drawn." In late summer an expeditionary force of French and British troops — supplemented by Turkish and later by Sardinian contingents — landed on the peninsula, but there was so much confusion that by the time the armies were ready to attack Sebastopol, the port had been reinforced. A long siege ensued, and as the winter and spring of 1855 wore on, with no sign of victory, the British public became notably less obsessed with fear of Russia. War critics, such as Richard Cobden, the free-trade leader, began to wonder whey their country had ever entered "a war in which we have a despot for an enemy, a despot for an ally, and a despot for a client."

As fear of Russia waned, dissatisfaction increased with the manner in which the Aberdeen ministry was managing the British war effort. Military correspondents pointed out in damning dispatches that the whole Crimean operation was being bungled. Individual British soldiers demonstrated their heroism at several battles, but, as in the notorious Charge of the Light Brigade at Balaclava, it was clear that the high command had blundered. Elderly but inexperienced generals who had not seen battle since Waterloo were revealing the weaknesses of a system in which most officers purchased their commissions, thus often disbarring abler soldiers who lacked wealth or aristocratic connections. British commanders in the Crimea regarded officers who had fought in Indian frontier wars as social inferiors and therefore failed to make use of their skills. Events soon confirmed that the nation was ill-prepared to send such an army to wage a European war hundreds of miles from its home base.

Organizational confusion resulted in a lack of adequate food, supplies, and transportation and the failure to provide proper care for the sick and wounded. Cholera was to prove a greater killer than gunfire. When the Aberdeen cabinet ignored the growing demand for a full-scale investigation into the government's handling of the war, it was defeated in the House of Commons by the overwhelming vote of 305 to 148, and in February 1855 Palmerston replaced Aberdeen as prime minister. "We turned out the Quaker and put in the pugilist," was a contemporary reaction to the event. Palmerston was clearly the more effective prime minister if only because, unlike most of his colleagues, he was a genuinely popular public figure. His appeal — like Canning's a generation before — transcended party lines, and he was the first English statesman deliberately to ingratiate himself with all shades of newspaper opinion.

While Parliament appointed a select committee to investigate the conduct of the war, and Florence Nightingale (1820–1910) and her volunteer nurses tended Britain's sick and wounded soldiers, Lord Palmerston strengthened his position within the government. The fall of Sebastopol in September 1855 enhanced his reputation still further and made it possible to end the war. Palmerston was willing to continue the

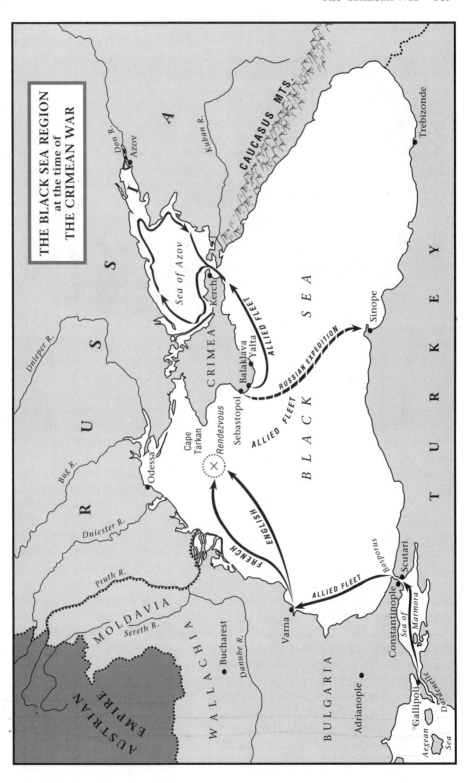

THE BLACK SEA REGION
at the time of
THE CRIMEAN WAR

Florence Nightingale (1820–1910)   The strong-willed "Lady with the Lamp" — here shown at Scutari, the Crimean War hospital — was the founder of modern nursing. *(Hulton Deutsch Collection)*

fighting, but Napoleon III announced that he was not, and because there were three times as many French troops in the Crimea as British, the emperor's attitude was necessarily influential. By then a British fleet in the Baltic Sea was successfully blockading St. Petersburg, the Russian capital, and the new tsar, Alexander II, was eager to bring the war to a close. Because Russian forces had inflicted several resounding defeats on the Turks in the Caucasus, he could sue for peace without complete humiliation. By the time land operations ceased in March 1856, almost a third of Britain's 56,000-man expeditionary force was dead. Almost 2,000 were killed on the battle field. An additional 16,000 succumbed to wounds and to disease. 9,000 more were wounded but survived the war.

Although the actual fighting had been inconclusive, the war produced a number of significant consequences, both at home and abroad. The temporary outcry in Britain against aristocratic incompetence (especially in the army) soon subsided, but a few permanent reforms resulted: the War Department was reorganized and at last separated from the Colonial Office. A new army medical school was begun that accepted the use of chloroform, new surgical techniques, and the modern nursing profession as fashioned by Florence Nightingale. The Treaty of Paris, which ended the war in March 1856, weakened Russian power in the Balkans by forcing the tsar to cede territory near the mouth of the Danube to the Turks. Russia was similarly compelled to acknowledge that it had no special authority as protector of Greek Orthodox Christians, thereby permitting the development of an autonomous Rumania and Serbia outside the immediate sphere of Russian influence. Russia agreed to neutralize the Black Sea by ceasing to maintain or establish along its coast "military-maritime arsenals." Russian power in Europe, which after 1848 had reached a nineteenth-century high point, was never to be so great again until the twentieth century. In the meantime, the Turkish Empire had been preserved, and the Ottoman sultan was admitted formally into the Concert of Europe, which was reconstituted in 1856 when Austria and Prussia, neither of which had participated militarily in the Crimean War, both took part in the peace conference.

Although the concept of a Concert of Europe had apparently been restored, during the years that followed, European governments were to show less national self-restraint, respect for treaties, or cooperation than they had during the previous forty years; and in Britain, once the war was over, people felt little desire to become further embroiled in continental affairs. Despite his association with an aggressive foreign policy, Palmerston himself remained popular, but he, too, seemed leery of undue involvement with the continent. When asked to aid the advocates of a project to build a tunnel under the English Channel, his reply was to the point: "What! You pretend to ask us to contribute to a work the object of which is to shorten a distance which we find already too short?"

During the 1850s, the French built a large fleet of steam-powered ironclad ships, and in 1859 rumors swept the country that Napoleon III, Britain's ally in the Crimea, was emulating his uncle and preparing to invade England. Palmerston's government strengthened fortifications along the Channel coast, and patriotic fervor prompted tens of thousands of landed gentlemen, shopkeepers, and clerks to join a "volunteer corps" in their neighborhood and to practice soldiering on weekends. More than 700 corps were set up in the course of the next two years. Such soldiers were never put to the test of battle, but the Palmerston government did take a very immediate interest in the struggle then going on for the unification of Italy. Many prominent Englishmen were pro-Italian as they had been pro-Hellene in the 1820s. Italian exiles such as Giuseppe Mazzini had long carried on their political agitation from London; and Count Camillo Cavour, prime minister of the Kingdom of Sardinia after 1851, made Britain his parliamentary model. When the war of 1859, which pitted Sardinia and France against Austria, forced Austria to cede Lombardy (the central section of northern Italy) to Sardinia, most Britons sympathized. When Napoleon III decided at this point to halt the process of Italian unification and to annex Nice and Savoy (hitherto part of Sardinia) as his reward for aiding Cavour, the British press was horrified. It completely approved, however, of the manner in which Cavour sponsored plebiscites to enable the inhabitants of central Italy — including three of the four states ruled directly by the pope — to demonstrate their wish to join a united Italy.[2] When Giuseppe Garibaldi launched his romantic

---

[2]See C. T. McIntire, *England Against the Papacy, 1858–1861* (1983).

expedition to bring Sicily and southern Italy into a united Italian kingdom, the British foreign secretary declared that the Italians had good reason to take up arms against their oppressors. Rather than censure Victor Emmanuel, the king of Sardinia and the prospective constitutional monarch of a unified Italy, Lord John Russell preferred to speak of "the gratifying prospect of a people building up the edifice of their liberties."

The statement was warmly applauded in the British Isles and won for Britain a wide popularity in Italy, for none of the other Great Powers supported Italian unification so strongly. Queen Victoria, who sympathized with the Austrian emperor and who would have preferred a more neutral stance, privately referred to Russell and Palmerston as "those two dreadful old men." The substantial unification of Italy nonetheless became an accomplished fact, and British support was not least among the factors that made it possible.

American Division and German Unification

The next major conflict that involved British interests was the American Civil War.[3] British public opinion had long been hostile to slavery; but because President Lincoln indicated in the spring of 1861 that the purpose of the suppression of the rebellion of the Southern states was to restore the Union rather than to abolish slavery, there was widespread public sympathy with a Southern government led by "gentlemen" and firmly committed to free trade. The Confederacy seemed to have as much right to rebel against the United States as the Greeks had to revolt against Turkey, the Italians against Austria, or for that matter the thirteen American colonies against Great Britain. Many Britons were horrified, moreover, at the prospective cost in blood and treasure of a Northern reconquest of the South. Although the British recognition of Southern belligerency in May 1861 was regarded by Northerners as an unfriendly act, it merely took cognizance of a state of affairs that Lincoln himself had previously acknowledged in proclaiming a blockade of the Southern ports.

The British government never did extend recognition to the Confederacy as an independent nation, but the *Trent* affair in the autumn of 1861 brought Great Britain and the United States to the brink of war. The captain of a Northern vessel had stopped the *Trent*, a British ship en route from Havana to England, and had kidnapped James M. Mason and John Slidell, two Confederate representatives on their way to London. The North applauded the act, but Britain looked upon it as an affront to its neutrality and a violation of freedom of the seas. The British army in Canada was quickly reinforced, and Palmerston's government sent an

---

[3]Brian Jenkins provides a highly detailed account in *Britain and the War for the Union,* 2 vols. (1974, 1980).

ultimatum demanding an apology and the release of Mason and Slidell within seven days. In his last official act before his unexpected death in December 1861, Prince Albert modified the belligerent tone of this dispatch. In turn, President Lincoln ordered the release of the two Southerners. The crisis subsided, but Anglo-American relations were repeatedly strained by the Confederate use both of blockade runners and of commerce raiders, such as the *Alabama*, that had been built in British shipyards. As long as such vessels were not armed in British waters, explained Russell, the British government could not legally prevent their construction. The argument was somewhat specious, because once the United States had taken a firm stand against this laissez-faire position, the British government solved the problem (in 1863) by purchasing from the shipbuilders a number of the vessels ordered by the Confederates.

The hopes of the Confederacy long rested on the prospect that a cotton famine would provide the economic lever that would force Britain and France to intervene on its behalf. By 1862 there was indeed great distress in Lancashire as numerous Manchester cotton mills shut down. The government arranged for subsidies to the local poor rates and for special public works projects. It never thought of entering the war, however, for the sake of cotton. Rather, it encouraged the development of substitute sources of the raw material in Egypt and India. After Lincoln's Emancipation Proclamation, British public opinion gradually turned against the Southern cause; although Anglo-American relations continued to be shadowed by the "*Alabama* claims," the danger of war died down.

It can be argued in retrospect that the cardinal blunder committed by the makers of British foreign policy in the 1860s was to permit — at times, indeed, to encourage — the unification of Germany under Prussian leadership. Palmerston was admittedly unhappy about the war between Denmark and an Austro-Prussian coalition in 1864, but intervention by Britain would have required the cooperation of France. The British were far too suspicious of Napoleon III's own territorial ambitions in Belgium and the Rhineland to rely on him. Thus Palmerston's somewhat hasty promise to aid the Danes remained unfulfilled. Flaunting the "big stick" in northern Europe in 1864 was not so easy as it had been in Greece in 1850, if only because the British navy could not by itself halt the Prussian army.

Even after its lightning-like victory over Austria in 1866 had again demonstrated the military prowess of the Prussian army, most British statesmen remained more fearful of France than of Prussia. The fact that the Franco-Prussian War of 1870–1871 was apparently begun by France evoked much sympathy for Prussia. Bismarck himself might be distrusted, but even the realization that the war was transferring the role of dominant continental power from France to the new German empire did not raise undue British fears. As one prominent English editor put it, France was "a nation that always hated us," while Germany was "a nation that never hated us." Queen Victoria, whose eldest daughter had married the Prussian crown prince, saw the German cause as that "of civilization, of liberty, of order, and of unity." By the time the war ended, British sympathy had begun to shift to defeated France; but the British government was provided with at least one satisfaction. Both sides heeded its warning that if either power invaded neutral Belgium, Britain would aid the other. The Belgian frontier remained unimpaired. A less pleasant consequence of the war was Russia's unilateral decision to abrogate the restrictions on the use of its navy in the Black Sea which had been imposed at Paris in 1856. The British government made the best of a situation it could not rectify alone by refusing to recognize the change until an international conference in London had signed a protocol declaring that nations could not unilaterally denounce treaties without threatening the system of international law. Russian acknowledgment of the principle of international law was then followed by the international recognition of the political reality, Russia's right to return its warships to the Black Sea. After 1871 British statesmen had reason to look at the world with considerably less confidence than Palmerston had done a generation before. Although the next forty years proved to be decades of peace for western and central Europe, Britain's moral, economic, and political position in the world had altered materially. It now had to share predominance with a new, vigorous, and ambitious German Empire.

The Sepoy Mutiny

During the 1850s and 1860s war drums sounded not only in Europe and North America but also in distant India, where decade by decade the sphere of British influence had increased, although the number of British citizens involved remained, by any reckoning, extraordinarily small.[4] The original focus of British trade with India had been the East India Company, which since the passage of Pitt's India Act in 1784 had shared power with a government-approved Board of Control in London whose president was after 1812 always a member of the cabinet. For the time being, the company remained a body that "maintained armies and retailed tea"; but in 1813 it lost its chartered monopoly of British trade with India. For a while it retained its monopoly of the China trade, but in 1833 it was ordered to bring all its commercial business to an end. As compensation, the proprietors received an annuity of £630,000 charged against India's territorial revenues.

---

[4]Geoffrey Moorhouse has provided a vivid brief introduction to British rule in India in *India Britannica* (1983). More detailed appraisals are provided by Sir Penderel Moon, *The British Conquest and Dominion of India* (1989), and Francis Hutchins, *The Illusion of Permanence: British Imperialism in India* (1967). The life and work of British administrators on the scene is readably described in Philip Woodruff, *The Man Who Ruled India* (2 vols., 1954), and that of the administrators back in London in Eric Stokes, *The English Utilitarians and India* (1959), and in Clive Dewey, *Anglo-Indian Attitudes: The Mind of the Indian Civil Service* (1994).

During the 1830s and 1840s the sphere of direct British rule in India continued to expand until by 1850 it included almost two-thirds of the subcontinent. The rest remained in the hands of independent princes who acknowledged Britain as the paramount power in India and were bound by treaties. Theoretically, the Mogul emperor at Delhi still governed this vast realm, with the East India Company serving as his agent, but his practical significance had become nil. From the British point of view, these were years of reform in India; indeed, the best British governors-general and their lieutenants went to India less to gain wealth than to win reputations as benevolent despots. Reform to them necessarily implied westernization — which generally meant the introduction of English institutions and English forms of land-ownership. Reform also meant the gradual establishment of an unprecedented degree of law and order over much of India. Traditional Hindu customs such as *thuggee, suttee,* and female infanticide were formally abolished. *Thuggee,* the Hindu word from which the English word *thug* is derived, involved murder and plunder by professional robbers and highwaymen who justified their activities in religious terms but who made peaceful commerce along many Indian roads all but impossible. *Suttee* meant that a faithful Hindu widow threw herself on her husband's funeral pyre. The custom had not been universal, but as late as 1844, one chieftain's funeral led to the death of ten wives and three hundred concubines.

Westernization included installing a competitive Civil Service system that actually preceded the establishment of a similar system in Great Britain itself. If for the moment there was no emphasis on self-government in India, there was at least great emphasis on good government. Indians were theoretically eligible to compete for Civil Service posts during the nineteenth century; however, only a handful succeeded in being appointed "district commissioner," the ruler of an area as large as four English counties amalgamated. For one thing, they had to become fluent in English, which was instituted as the language of the educated in what had always been a multilingual geographical area. On the Victorian premise that "a single shelf of a good European library was worth the whole native literature of India and Arabia," all government-funded education was to be in English. Such an education, to be sure, enabled young Indians to read in the original the works of John Locke, Thomas Jefferson, and John Stuart Mill.

Reform also increasingly came to mean great public works programs: the building of roads and harbors, telegraph lines that by 1870 were to link Calcutta to London, a colony-wide postal service, and immense irrigation projects such as the 900-mile canal between the Ganges and Jumna rivers completed in 1854 in order to bring water to 1,500,000 acres of semi-desert land. During the same decade, a network of railway lines was introduced, which was state-owned or state-aided and in part state-operated. A system of 2,500 miles as of 1863 would grow to 16,000 miles by 1890 and to 32,000 miles by 1910. These improvements, paid for by revenue collected in India or by bond issues, helped to make meaningful

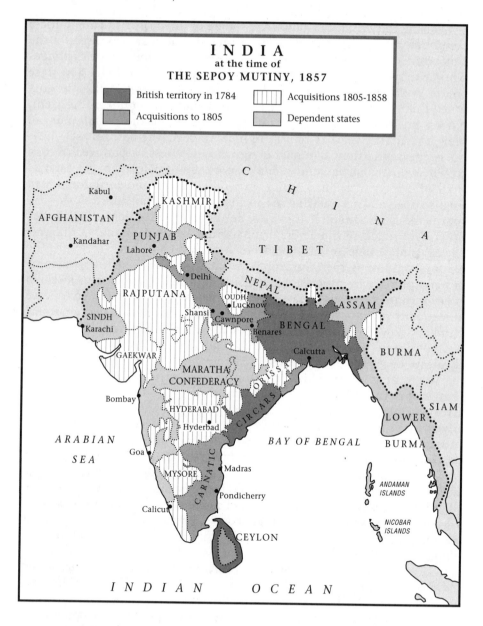

INDIA
at the time of
THE SEPOY MUTINY, 1857

British territory in 1784   Acquisitions 1805-1858

Acquisitions to 1805   Dependent states

the vast new free-trade area that the subcontinent represented. Not surprisingly, most Britons had come to take great pride in their Indian empire. That Indian trade was valuable to Britain none would have denied, but the Indian trade was now open to the merchants of other lands as well, and the reforms seemed to benefit the Indians most of all.

Many a native Indian came to see these same reforms in a different light, however. Eighteenth-century British rule of India had been marked by outright exploitation in a way in which nineteenth-century rule was not, but it had involved much less foreign interference in Indian politics, social life, and religion. The British governing class made no secret of its assumption of cultural and intellectual superiority, and socially it preferred to remain aloof. The "guardians" as a class, while often highly respected and credited with a sense of justice, were little loved. Indians were admitted to the lower branches of the Indian Civil Service and permitted to dominate the lower ranks of the Indian army, but otherwise their influence in governing their own lands steadily declined.

A systematic British effort to remold India necessarily implied interference with Indian religion. While European missionaries, who trooped to India in increasing numbers in the early decades of the nineteenth century, looked forward to the gradual supplanting of Hinduism by Christianity, faithful Hindus — as well as Moslems and Sikhs — not unnaturally feared what they interpreted as forcible Christianization. Irrigation canals might bring a greater abundance of food, but they might equally damage the sacred Ganges; and the subordination of native languages might undermine religious ritual. Similarly, the British reform of Bengal land law might simplify and rationalize land-ownership, but it clashed with traditions centuries old. The supplanting of village custom by complex legal procedures did not necessarily benefit the average Indian villager any more than the commercialization of agriculture, with its emphasis on cash crops for export (such as cotton, jute, indigo, and grain), increased the general sense of economic security. Unhappily, as the nineteenth century proceeded, the Malthusian dilemma continually reasserted itself in India. The advantages of an increase in the efficiency of agriculture and the bringing of additional acres under cultivation were counterbalanced by a growing population, and the standard of living of the average Indian villager rose little above subsistence level. Reform was obviously a two-edged sword, and differing judgments over the desirability of British reforms produced the Sepoy Mutiny of 1857.[5]

The Indian army of the day was made up predominantly of Sepoys (natives) who outnumbered British soldiers by a ratio of almost six to one (230,000 to 40,000). Complaints among the Sepoys that Hindu caste privileges were being ignored and that sacred customs were being violated rose to fever pitch in January 1857 when the rumor swept numerous Sepoy regiments in the Bengal that the grease used for the cartridges of the newly introduced Enfield rifle was made of the fat of cows and pigs. Because a soldier had to bite a cartridge before inserting it into his rifle, the religious scruples of both Hindus (against the killing of cows) and Moslems (against the eating of pork) were being disregarded. The rumors had some basis in fact, and the reassurances of British regimental officers were dismissed as lies. Rumbles of revolt and numerous courts-martial of

---

[5]In *The Great Mutiny: India 1857* (1978), Christopher Hibbert relies on contemporary accounts to tell a grim story. Thomas Metcalf takes up the consequences in *The Aftermath of Revolt: India, 1857–1870* (1965). See also, by the same author, *Ideologies of the Raj* (1994).

Sepoys led in May to a mutiny by three regiments, who shot their British officers and marched on Delhi, where they killed all the English men, women, and children they could find and pledged their allegiance to the old Mogul emperor.

Although most British commanders were blindly confident in the loyalty of their native troops and refused to disarm them, a similar rebellion occurred at Jhansi. Sepoys captured Cawnpore and besieged Lucknow. Then the tide turned. Late in 1857, a British force relieved Lucknow and recaptured Delhi. The mutinous Sepoys found themselves unable to take advantage of their overwhelming numbers. As a British relief force advanced up the Ganges valley with reinforcements, it countered massacre with massacre as a fit punishment for rebellion; although "Clemency" Canning, the new governor-general, helped to stop indiscriminate revenge, the mutiny stirred up a great deal of racial hatred. By early 1858 the mutiny as such was over, although sporadic fighting continued in parts of north-central India for two more years.

The British were to look on the struggle as no more than an army revolt, but some modern Indian nationalists have seized on the mutiny as the first significant example of armed Indian national rebellion against British rule. To see the mutiny purely in military terms ignores the complicity of numerous Indian civilians and the widespread distrust of British "reform" measures. It also ignores such symbolic gestures as the attempted restoration of the Delhi emperor. Conversely, to see the mutiny as national in scope is to ignore the fact that most of southern

The Sepoy Mutiny   A contemporary engraving shows the mutineers attacking the British force at Cawnpore (1857). *(Bettmann/Corbis)*

and western India remained unaffected by the rebellion. Many Indian princes and most Indian villagers remained untouched by modern notions of nationalism, and a majority either stayed loyal to or acquiesced in British rule even when it seemed in grave danger.

The mutiny marked a turning point in a number of respects. In 1858 the power of the East India Company was ended, and the British crown took over direct command of both the Indian army and the Indian government. The president of the Board of Control became the secretary of state for India (still with a seat in the cabinet) and the governor-general became the viceroy. The ratio of British contingents in the Indian army was increased, and the artillery was confined to the control of British troops. Although an extensive revision of the penal code was introduced after 1860, post-mutiny viceroys were less reform-minded than their predecessors. They continued to encourage public works such as railways, but the government hesitated to interfere further with social and religious customs. Private British investment in Indian industry became sizable for the first time during the 1860s and 1870s, and those portions of the colony prospered that specialized in the export of cotton and wheat. A late-nineteenth-century revival of orthodox Hinduism — hostile alike to Moslem and British ideas — provided new discouragement, however, for those British reformers who hoped that the slow infiltration of Western culture would cause Indians to give up their age-old "superstitions" and "prejudices." Standards of government efficiency remained remarkably high, but British administrators, military officers, and women "memsahibs" from Britain strongly discouraged interracial mixing or marriages, and the gulf between the rulers and the ruled tended to widen. An exception to this generalization was made up of Eurasians (later known as Anglo-Indians), the tens of thousands of families formed by the union of British men (many of them soldiers) and Indian women and their decendants. They remained staunchly loyal to British rule, and to an increasing degree they ran the postal and telegraph services, the railways, and the customs and excise offices of mid- and late-nineteenth-century India. In the meantime, the British populace back home, briefly stirred by the excitement of the great mutiny, rapidly lost interest in Indian affairs, and parliamentary debates involving India rarely attracted much interest.

The Mid-Victorian Empire

In this respect, India resembled the other parts of the mid-century British Empire. Trade continued to matter more than political control, and the settlement colonies often seemed a bother, an expense, and even a bore. "These wretched colonies. They are a millstone around our necks," Disraeli confided to a colleague in 1852. As Charles Dilke, a Liberal M.P. and pamphleteer, put it in 1868, why should "Dorsetshire agriculture labourers pay the cost of defending New Zealand colonists in Maori Wars"?

After all, he added, in what proved to be a curiously unprophetic analogy: "It is not likely nowadays that our colonies would, for any long stretch of time, engage to aid us in our purely European wars. Australia would scarcely feel herself deeply interested in the guarantee of Luxembourg, nor Canada in the affairs of Serbia." The same attitude prevailed among cabinet members. On one occasion when Lord Palmerston found it difficult to persuade a suitable colleague to become colonial secretary, he finally expostulated to one of the Colonial Office's career officials: "Well, I'll take the office myself. Just come upstairs and show me on the map where these damned places are."

It was in this atmosphere of studied neglect that the Australian provinces, New Zealand, and Canada achieved domestic autonomy. When the British North America Act of 1867 united Quebec, Ontario, and the Maritime Provinces (and, prospectively, the western provinces) to form the federal, self-governing Dominion of Canada, it received as much attention in the House of Commons "as if it were a private Bill uniting two or three English parishes." Yet the statute, which promised "peace, order and good government" to the new federation, was to serve as Canada's constitution until 1982.

In the long run, this relative lack of interest in formal political control, although combined with a continued insistence on opening and keeping open a worldwide market for British goods, helps to explain much that might otherwise remain mysterious in both the nineteenth-century growth and the twentieth-century decline of the British Empire. Colonization was seen by most Britons as essentially temporary and justifiable ultimately only in moral terms. Anthony Trollope, the novelist, provided this typically mid-Victorian appraisal:

> We are called upon to rule them [the colonies] — as far as we do rule them, not for our glory, but for their happiness. If we keep them, we should keep them — not because they are gems in our diadem, not in order that we may boast that the sun never sets on our dependencies, but because by keeping them we may assist them in developing their own resources. And when we part with them, as part with them we shall, let us do so with neither smothered jealousy nor open hostility, but with a proud feeling that we are sending a son out into the world able to take his place among men.

CHAPTER 7

The Reform Bill of 1867: Causes and Consequences

In politics, if not in other matters, the relative complacency of the 1850s and the 1860s came to an end in 1867. The rumblings that led to the political reform act of 1867 had been discernible for a number of years, but as long as Lord Palmerston lived and remained prime minister, his prestige and his conviction that the Reform Bill of 1832 had achieved as near-perfect a constitution as was humanly possible discouraged any tampering with the English political system.

Prelude to Reform

It was at the very end of the period of apparent placidity that Walter Bagehot wrote his classic account of the English constitution.[1] Although this witty guide to the practices and assumptions of mid-Victorian politicians has become hallowed by tradition for the twentieth-century student, *The English Constitution* impressed many of its early readers as the work of an iconoclast. Bagehot's main theme was that the practice of national government in England had ceased to correspond to the still widely held eighteenth-century theory that Britain's constitution was a balanced combination of monarchy, aristocracy, and democracy in the form of the crown, the House of Lords, and the House of Commons. This was no longer true, contended Bagehot, for "a republic has insinuated itself beneath the folds of a Monarchy." The queen retained significant "dignified" functions, but her practical or "efficient" functions while a ministry was in power were now limited to "the right to be consulted, the right to encourage and the right to warn." Her "efficient" power to choose among possible prime ministers was limited to those occasions

---

[1]Walter Bagehot's *The English Constitution* (1963) was first published in 1867. In *The Victorian Constitution: Conventions, Usages, and Contingencies* (1979), G. H. L. LeMay follows in Bagehot's footsteps. See also Gary W. Cox, *The Efficient Secret: The Cabinet and the Development of Political Parties in Victorian England* (1987).

when no party held a majority of House of Commons seats or when that party lacked an obvious leader. The House of Lords similarly retained significant dignified functions and provided the alternative of a worship of nobility to a worship of money. In practice the Lords were now, however, a secondary chamber that could at most revise or delay the actions of the House of Commons.

The House of Commons itself was seen by Bagehot less as a legislative chamber than as the public forum in which both sides of any issue could be aired and as the body that determined how long a prime minister remained in office. In the period between 1846 and 1868, with no single disciplined political party possessing an overall majority and the House of Commons divided into Whigs and Tories, Peelites and Radicals, and, at times, an autonomous Irish party, the tenure of a prime minister and his ministry was indeed often at the mercy of a vote of no confidence on a relatively trivial issue. Even if the House of Commons could not directly select the prime minister, it could and did choose to dismiss him on numerous occasions — six times between 1850 and 1860. The relative weakness of party organization made this in many ways the golden age of the private member of Parliament. In the eighteenth century, many members had been controlled by patronage exercised by the crown or by wealthy peers; later in the nineteenth century, they were increasingly to come under strong party discipline. For the moment, however, their independence was at its height.

The most important governmental institution, Bagehot insisted, was one for which eighteenth-century political theory left no room: the cabinet. The key to mid-nineteenth-century government, in Bagehot's estimation, was not the separation but the unification of powers, manifest in the cabinet, which represented "a hyphen which joins, a buckle which fastens, the legislative part of the state to the executive part of the state." The cabinet was responsible to the House of Commons, but it could at will, by asking the monarch to call a general election, appeal to the electorate against that house. Acting in the name of the monarch, members of the cabinet headed the various executive departments of state and had to defend their departments against the criticism of a Parliament of which they themselves were members.

In the sense that they favored such government by discussion — as well as a high degree of freedom of speech, press, religion, and enterprise at home and abroad — most English politicians of the mid-century era were liberals; but few were democrats who looked forward to an age of universal manhood or adult suffrage. The country seemed content, and the mass of the unenfranchised populace appeared satisfied. "Not only," wrote Bagehot, "does the nation endure a parliamentary government, which it would not do if Parliament were immoderate, but it likes parliamentary government. A sense of satisfaction permeates the country because most of the country feels it has got the precise thing that suits it."

At the very time that Bagehot was writing, evidence was beginning to accumulate that some groups in British society were not so satisfied with the status quo. The collapse of Chartism had led to a gradual revival of the earlier Radical alliance of employers, employees, and independent artisans and shopkeepers against the titled aristocrats and squires who, for the most part, were still running the country. The latter were identified both with special privilege and with what was still deemed the excessive cost of government. Although John Stuart Mill was the philosopher of this Radical movement, John Bright was its more typical leader. Bright was a Quaker who looked forward to a new franchise reform bill that would give the vote to all urban householders. Such a bill was the hope of the Reform Union of 1864, a national association that was essentially middle class in origin.

Although an M.P. since 1845, Bright had yet to be asked to join a cabinet. Thus far, indeed, no Nonconformist had ever been a member of any British cabinet. The man to whom Bright turned as the politician most likely to spearhead another bout of political reform was William Ewart Gladstone, the ex-Peelite who in 1859 had joined Palmerston's Whig ministry as Chancellor of the Exchequer. The new chancellor had followed Peel out of the Tory party over the Corn Law fight. His sympathy with Palmerston's pro-Italian policy proved a further bar to a reunion with his one-time colleagues. So did his continuing distrust of Peel's severest critic, Benjamin Disraeli.[2] His cabinet position gave Gladstone the opportunity to complete the work he had begun in Peel's ministry almost two decades before: the elimination not only of every protective tariff but, as far as possible, every revenue tariff as well. He inspired the reciprocal trade agreement negotiated by Richard Cobden with France in 1860. With the budget of 1860, Gladstone eliminated all tariffs whatsoever on 371 articles, leaving only 48 items on which a revenue tariff was collected.

It was as Chancellor of the Exchequer that Gladstone for the first time became a popular hero. His bill to eliminate the excise tax on paper

---

[2] In recent years there have appeared numerous valuable biographies of both men. H. C. G. Matthew's sympathetic *Gladstone* (1996) draws on the multi-volume Gladstone diaries of which the author served as chief editor. Roy Jenkins' *Gladstone* (1995) is also comprehensive and sympathetic. E. J. Feuchtwanger's briefer *Gladstone* (1975) focuses on politics, and Peter Stansky's yet briefer *Gladstone: A Progress in Politics* (1979) concentrates on a key episodes. Richard Shannon's two-volume *Gladstone* (1982, 1999) is far more critical; it emphasizes how "very odd and idiosyncratic" a Liberal the long-time party leader was. Robert Blake's *Disraeli* (1966) is both comprehensive and judicious. Of the briefer biographies, Richard W. Davis's *Disraeli* (1976) is shrewd and acerbic; T. A. Jenkins' *Disraeli and Victorian Conservatism* (1996) focuses on politics, and Paul Smith's *Disraeli: A Brief Life* (1996) demonstrates how Disraeli's romantic novels illuminate his career. Sarah Bradford's *Disraeli* (1982) provides a highly credible sketch of the Conservative leader's personality, while Stanley Weintraub's *Disraeli* (1994) is a yet fuller attempt to provide an "intimate biography."

was hailed by Radicals as a move toward a cheap press catering to the working-class reader. He was indignant when the House of Lords vetoed the bill, and in 1861 he reintroduced his measure to end the paper tax. This time, however, he added the provision to a consolidated budget that passed the House of Commons as a single appropriation bill rather than as one of a series. The House of Lords reluctantly accepted the new consolidated budget bill and was thus precluded from exercising a veto on individual money bills thereafter. To vote down the entire budget would necessarily produce a constitutional conflict. Despite Palmerston's misgivings, Gladstone also kept defense expenditures down and took advantage of growing national prosperity to cut the income tax rate from 4 percent to 2 percent over the course of five years.

With free trade confirmed and a high degree of financial responsibility assured, Gladstone slowly became converted to the cause of parliamentary reform. In the course of a debate in 1864, he declared that "every man who is not presumably incapacitated by some consideration of personal unfitness or political danger, is morally entitled to come within the pale of the constitution." Although the suffrage was not a natural right, it was in Gladstone's estimation a privilege that responsible workingmen had earned by their "self-command, self-control, respect for order, patience under suffering, confidence in the law and respect for superiors." Palmerston cautioned his colleague that it was not the business of cabinet members to invite agitation, and the University of Oxford decided, in the general election of 1865, that Gladstone's views on both the suffrage and the possibility of the disestablishment of the Anglican Church in Ireland were not to its liking. He was defeated at Oxford, only to contest successfully a seat in the "popular constituency" of South Lancashire. He had come to be a hero of the masses, and he in turn reciprocated their regard.

The general election of 1865 was yet another personal triumph for Palmerston, but before the new Parliament assembled, that doughty statesman had died at the age of eighty. Russell — who was now in the House of Lords — became prime minister and Gladstone the leader of the majority in the House of Commons. The death of Palmerston provided a new opportunity for reformers; so also did the victory of the Union forces in the American Civil War. The American republic, with its political democracy, its equality of opportunity, and its freedom from an established church, had long appealed to British Radicals. Now that it had survived its ordeal of battle and had, in the bargain, rid itself of the darkest blot upon its escutcheon, African-American slavery, it served as a renewed inspiration. "The great triumph of the Republic," wrote John Bright, "is the event of our age and future ages will confess it."[3]

---

[3]The developments outlined here are discussed in detail in J. R. Vincent, *The Formation of the British Liberal Party, 1857–1868* (2nd ed., 1977) and in Eugenio F. Biagini, *Liberty, Retrenchment and Reform: Popular Liberalism in the Age of Gladstone, 1860–1880* (1992). See also the biographies of John Bright by George Macaulay Trevelyan (1913) and Keith Robbins (1979).

The Reform Bills

In the spring of 1866 Gladstone introduced a reform bill to give the franchise to borough residents who occupied premises worth more than seven pounds a year in rent and thus to enfranchise some 300,000 town artisans.[4] Opinion within Gladstone's own party was strongly divided. For conservatives — both Whigs and Tories — the chief danger the bill posed was not that the aristocracy would lose its remaining influence but that educated Britons would be swamped by the ill-educated. The government since 1832 had satisfactorily reflected the various interests of the country. Why change it? The way to elevate the working classes was not to grant them the franchise en masse but to reserve it as a prize that tens of thousands had already earned since 1832 by thrift and self-improvement. "Reform" was all too likely to place political leadership in the hands of only the mediocre. The average M.P. would become the bound delegate rather than the independent representative of his constituency. Further franchise reform might lead to a war on property and advance the cause of socialism.

Whereas conservative Whigs voiced their fears about democracy, Gladstone contended that the purpose of the measure was not to establish democracy but simply to enfranchise an element of the population that was as entitled to direct representation as the wealthy financiers and manufacturers. With the Whigs divided, the bill barely squeaked through the House of Commons and almost immediately became bogged down in committee. In June of 1866 Lord Russell resigned, and the queen asked the Tory Lord Derby (1799–1869) once again to form a government. As they had briefly in 1852 and 1858–1859, Derby became prime minister and Benjamin Disraeli became Chancellor of the Exchequer and leader of the House of Commons.

The continued existence of the Tory party since 1846 was itself something of a tour de force, because as early as 1852 it had dropped from its platform the key issue of agricultural protection that had separated it from its erstwhile leader, Robert Peel, in 1846. The Tories were divided from Lord Palmerston less by doctrine than by their retention of a separate organization. Lord Derby, the leader of the party from 1846 to 1868, was a shrewd aristocrat, whose policy of patient opposition while waiting for the majority coalition (supported by Whigs, Radicals, and Peelites) to break up, enabled him to become prime minister on three separate occasions. When in office, he believed in moderate reform. Disraeli, the leader of the party in the House of Commons since the late 1840s, had been in his early political life both a Tory and a Radical, an unusual but not unknown combination. His "Young England" movement had looked

---

[4]Francis Barrymore Smith, *The Making of the Second Reform Bill* (1966), and Maurice Cowling, *1867: Disraeli, Gladstone and Revolution: The Passing of the Second Reform Bill* (1967), deal fully with the events of 1866 and 1867. Angus Hawkin, *British Party Politics, 1852–1886* (1998), places these events within a broader context.

***Punch* Salutes Disraeli**
The Conservative leader has persuaded the House of Commons to pass a major political reform bill. Gladstone is seen coming in second. *(Reproduced by permission of* Punch *May 25, 1867)*

back to an idealized patriarchal rural England in which paternalistic landlords had earned the faithful service of devoted farmers and servants and only the money-grubbing middle-class merchants or industrialists played the role of villains. In 1866, however, Disraeli (like Derby) approached the question of reform less as a Tory Radical than as a flexible Conservative. Both Derby and Disraeli thought the opportunity to benefit the party too good to be lost. Reform was sure to come. Why not let the Tories gain the credit?

An economic downturn in the fall of 1866 and an exceptionally poor harvest had temporarily produced large-scale unemployment and high prices; and, as in 1832, they provided an immediate economic motive for political change. Important, too was the legal decision of *Hornby* v. *Close* (1866), which declared that trade unions were unlawful societies in restraint of trade and that their funds were therefore not entitled to the protection of the Friendly Societies Act of 1855. This decision brought into the reform battle many skilled workers who had previously been lukewarm, and a turbulent and unlawful demonstration in London's Hyde Park indicated that popular feeling had been aroused.

In order to introduce in 1867 a bill more comprehensive than Gladstone's of the previous year, Disraeli and Derby had first to persuade their colleagues. They eventually won the approval of most of the cabinet, but they had to introduce an incredibly complex scheme in order to satisfy those Conservatives who were appalled at the idea of being engulfed by democracy. The bill that Disraeli finally patched together extended the franchise to all urban rate-payers but gave a second (or sometimes third or fourth) vote to all university graduates, to owners of government bonds or savings bank deposits of fifty pounds or more, to members of learned professions, and so on. Thus the concept of "household suffrage" was to be qualified by a series of "fancy franchises," designed to protect quality from the consequences of quantity.

Once the bill was subjected to clause-by-clause debate and amendment, it was changed almost beyond recognition. The bill that emerged in June 1867 was a composite that none of the participants would have begun to envisage two years or even one year earlier.[5] Although Disraeli denied to the last his intention of bringing about democracy, the result was far more democratic than either Disraeli or his opponents had originally wanted. In the United Kingdom as a whole, the registered electorate increased from 1,359,000 to 2,455,000 voters. In England alone the number of county voters increased by 44 percent, the number of borough voters by 124 percent. Only in Ireland, whose relatively small electorate had been doubled already by the separate Irish Reform Act of 1850, did the act of 1867 have little impact.

The immediate political implication of the enfranchisement of this host of workingmen, clerks, and shopkeepers proved to be smaller than might have been expected, one reason being that the redistribution of seats that accompanied the bill was much less far-reaching than the franchise reform. Many small boroughs remained, and even after 1867 at least forty seats continued under the immediate influence of landed aristocrats. Moreover, workingmen continued to vote representatives of the old-line parties into office rather than to organize their own political groups. Nonetheless, as Lord Derby conceded, the country had taken "a leap in the dark."

For Disraeli, the passage of the bill constituted a major parliamentary triumph, and when Lord Derby resigned the prime ministership for reasons of ill health early in 1868, Disraeli took his place. It was the summit of a lifelong ambition for a man who had always impressed many of his colleagues as a maverick. He was born a Jew at a time (1804) when Jews did not yet possess the full rights of English citizenship; and, although baptized an Anglican at the age of twelve and henceforth a faithful member of the Church of England, Disraeli retained great pride in his ancestry. His youthful dandyism, his flamboyance, his success as a novelist, and his caustic wit all set him apart from the average Tory M.P.; but sheer parliamentary ability at length won him the respect of his colleagues, and so in 1868 — with a helpful push from both Derby and Queen Victoria — he attained the prime ministership at last.

---

[5]One amendment (by John Stuart Mill) that did not pass would have enfranchised women property-owners on the same terms as men. The debate did help launch the women's suffrage movement, however. (See Chapter 11.)

The new prime minister was not destined to hold his office long, for the Tories were still a minority in the House of Commons; with a new reform bill on the statute book, a new general election was necessarily in the offing. At the moment when Disraeli first became undisputed leader of the Tory, or Conservative, party, William Ewart Gladstone succeeded Earl Russell as head of the coalition of Whigs, Radicals, and Peelites who were henceforth universally to be known as Liberals. Gladstone had not emerged too well from the confused debates on the Reform Bill of 1867, but his stature rose anew in 1868 when he sought to reunite his followers by making the disestablishment of the Irish Church a central issue of British politics. The general election of November 1868 saw both the Liberal and the Conservative parties better organized than their predecessors had been in previous contests. Each was headed by a dynamic new leader and each was separated from the other by specific issues. The victory was a personal triumph for Gladstone and gave his Liberal party a majority of 112 seats. John Stuart Mill summed up the results as a brief dialogue:

> Disraeli (to the working classes): I have given you the franchise.
> The Working Classes: Thank you Mr. Gladstone.

The new prime minister had himself overcome nearly as many obstacles on the road to the prime ministership as had Disraeli. Gladstone's father was a Scottish businessman who had settled in the thriving port city of Liverpool; this was a background far different from the landed aristocratic heritage of Melbourne, Palmerston, and Russell. Gladstone did, however, receive an orthodox education at Eton and Oxford at a time when the central doctrine taught there was that "the world never moves except in the wrong direction." He grew up in a devout Anglican family, and in his youth he was deeply tempted to become a clergyman. Gladstone finally decided that he could serve his Church better in Parliament than in the pulpit. The religious element in his personality can hardly be overestimated, for liberalism to Gladstone meant not so much the political recognition of the natural rights of man as preached by the advocates of the Enlightenment as the final acknowledgment by man of the common fatherhood of God. A year after Disraeli had briefly (in his words) "climbed to the top of the greasy pole," Gladstone confided to his diary, "I ascend a steepening path with a burden ever gathering weight. The Almighty seems to sustain and spare me for some purpose of his own, deeply unworthy as I know myself to be. Glory be to his name."

Gladstone's path to the prime ministership was almost the antithesis of that followed by Disraeli. While Disraeli had started out a Radical and moved toward Toryism, Gladstone was first elected to Parliament as an unbending Tory and ended his political career a Radical. It was his youthful eloquence at Oxford in opposing the Great Reform Bill that had led the duke of Newcastle to offer him the seat for a small pocket borough that had escaped disenfranchisement in the bill. Gladstone's initial electoral triumph was thus less a tribute to his oratorical powers than to the influence of his patron. His path along the road to liberalism has already been traced — as Peelite, as financial reformer, and as advocate of European liberal nationalism in Italy and elsewhere — and it was as a reformer that he began his own first ministry.

The First Gladstone Ministry

The Liberal ministry of 1868–1874 was at once one of the strongest and most reform-minded of the nineteenth century. Yet many of the legislative and administrative reforms it sponsored were very much within the earlier Whig and Radical traditions. The longstanding Whig support of religious liberty was closely involved with the first great issue that Gladstone tackled — the disestablishment of the Anglican Church within Ireland. This cause easily met the prime minister's criteria for a worthy reform: (1) It was ripe for solution and had substantial public pressure for change behind it. (2) It was a matter of justice. For Gladstone all great political decisions were ultimately moral decisions; and although Gladstone was as staunch a churchman as ever, he had come to look on the Anglican Church in Ireland not as a support for true religion but as a handicap. The fact that all the Irish were legally compelled to contribute directly or indirectly to the financial support of a religious organization to which but one in eight adhered tended to sully the moral position of the Church and to make yet more difficult the reconciliation of the Irish to British rule. Gladstone candidly confessed that his stand was at variance with his views of the 1830s. Then he had firmly advocated the privileged legal position of the established Church. Then, too, he had shared with many Britons the hope, now proved vain, that the Irish would at length desert the Roman Catholicism of their fathers.

The struggle over disestablishment took up the greater part of the 1869 parliamentary session. The Conservatives objected that the step not only broke with a tradition centuries old but also represented in a very literal sense an attack on the property rights of the Church. Gladstone, at the height of his parliamentary form, piloted the measure through the House of Commons and, less directly, through the House of Lords. The Anglican Church in Ireland was consequently deprived of a third of its revenues (some of which were applied to help education and agriculture) and was turned into a voluntary self-governing religious body. Ireland was no longer to have an "official" church.

Many of the reform measures of the ministry were concerned with increasing the efficiency of the government itself. The merit-based Civil Service system, whose beginnings in England Gladstone had encouraged sixteen years earlier as Chancellor of the Exchequer, was extended in 1870 to almost all government departments. Edward Cardwell (1813–1886), Gladstone's secretary for war and, like Gladstone, an ex-Peelite, occupied himself with the reform of the army. He improved the lot of the common soldier by eliminating flogging as a peacetime punishment and by permitting short-term enlistments (six years on active service and six years in the reserve). Cardwell also introduced a degree of streamlining into the upper echelons, where the commander-in-chief (at the time the duke of Cambridge, a cousin of Queen Victoria) was subordinated to the secretary for war. The most controversial proposal proved to be the abolition of the purchase of army commissions. It was the swift Prussian triumph over France in 1870–1871 that gave weight to the views of egalitarian reformers who condemned bought commissions as barriers to the natural rise of talent; and when the Lords refused to pass a bill to end the practice, the queen was prevailed upon to end commission purchase by royal warrant. Hugh Childers (1827–1896) steered a similar course in the now predominantly iron-clad Royal Navy. He reduced waste in the Royal Dockyards, and he reformed the system of promotion and retirement in order to remove "dead wood" from the navy's officer corps.

Similar reforms were introduced into the English judicial system, which, of all nineteenth-century European legal systems, had evolved with only the smallest alteration from its medieval foundations. The prevailing structure was a highly confusing one, with an overlapping of courts, some administering common law and others equity law. Moreover, there was no system of appeal, and the three common-law courts retained unlimited jurisdiction over all cases. The Judicature Act of 1873 fused the common-law and equity courts and established a single national court system in which the Queen's Bench, the Common Pleas, and the Exchequer courts were retained as separate divisions with specified jurisdictions. The court system, as in the United States, was to have three levels: a court of original jurisdiction, a court of appeal, and a supreme court, the House of Lords. (Since 1844, ordinary peers had not participated in the judicial functions of the House of Lords; these were instead exercised by a group of law lords appointed for life.)

The Secret Ballot Act of 1872 was also in part a measure of administrative reform. The open ballot had long been advocated in England as a standard of manly courage; a voter, it was felt, should proudly avow his political convictions. Many reformers had wondered, however, whether the open ballot did not do more to encourage bribery than to promote manliness, and the act of 1872 was patterned upon measures successfully applied in the Australian colonies. Its actual impact on the outcome of British elections turned out to be far less significant than reformers had expected.

In one sense the most important act of the first Gladstone ministry was one with which the prime minister himself was only indirectly concerned, the Education Act of 1870, which was steered through Parliament by William Edward Forster (1818–1886). Since the 1830s, England's network of private (predominantly Church of England) schools had received aid via grants from the national Exchequer to help pay for new school buildings and, somewhat later, to help pay teacher salaries as well. The size of such grants had depended on the number of school pupils who passed a series of standardized examinations in the "three

THE THREE R's; OR, BETTER LATE THAN NEVER.

Right Hon. W. E. Forster (Chairman of Board). "Well, my little people, we have been gravely and earnestly considering whether
you may learn to read. I am happy to tell you that, subject to a variety of restrictions, conscience clauses, and the
consent of your vestries—*you may!*"

National Education   This cartoon from *Punch,* March 26, 1870, shows William
Edward Forster, the member of Gladstone's cabinet who piloted the Education
Act of 1870 through Parliament, explaining to the children of England that they
were now to be educated at state expense. *(Reproduced by permission of* Punch)

Rs." Significant pockets of illiteracy remained, however, and the Reform
Act of 1867 gave added weight to the argument that an increasingly democratic electorate required a broader education. Forster's key problem remained that of finding an acceptable role for organized religion. By 1870
most Nonconformists wanted a national school system under secular
auspices. The Anglican Church, however, hoped to retain its predominant influence. Like most controversial statutes, the new Education Act
satisfied neither side. It authorized the election of local school boards
that were given the power to levy rates (school taxes), build schools, and
hire teachers wherever there was an insufficient number of private
schools. Anglicans resented the fact that religious education in the new
board schools was to be nondenominational. Nonconformists objected
strongly to the manner in which the national government continued at
the same time to subsidize Anglican and other religious schools. In 1880
elementary school attendance was made compulsory, and in 1891 all
school fees were abolished. Some working-class parents were troubled by
the manner in which school-attendance officers and government-appointed teachers now intruded on their lives and those of children on
whose earnings the family had come to rely. A majority of parents

THE DECLINE OF ILLITERACY IN VICTORIAN ENGLAND
(as measured at five-year intervals by the percentage of brides and bridegrooms unable to sign their names at registrars' offices)

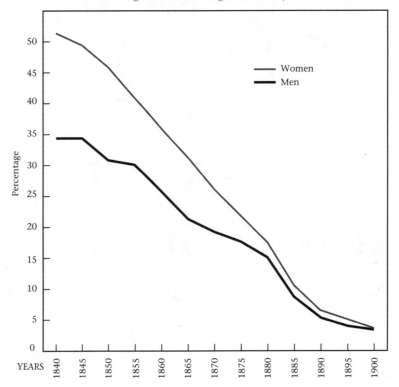

Adapted from E. G. West, "Literacy and the Industrial Revolution," *Economic History Review* (August 1978), p. 380.

supported the new schools, however, and most children adapted to and benefited from the environment of disciplined learning that those schools provided.[6] A separate Education Act (1872) for Scotland set up a similar system of elective school boards there. Coordinated by a Scottish Educational Committee, they took over all the schools previously operated by the several wings of the Presbyterian Church, built many new ones, and agreed on 45 minutes of religious education per day. In the meantime, an 1871 act had ended all religious restrictions on students attending the traditionally Anglican universities of Oxford and Cambridge.

In the short run, no legislative solution could be found for what, in Gladstone's eyes, was the most ticklish domestic difficulty that he faced — the position of the monarchy in a democracy. Gladstone's ministry coincided with a marked republican movement in England.

---

[6]J. S. Hurt, *Elementary Schooling and the Working Classes, 1860–1918* (1979). See also Jonathan Rose, "Willingly to School: The Working-Class Response to Elementary Education in Britain, 1875–1914," *Journal of British Studies* (April, 1993).

Retrenchment-minded M.P.'s were growing restive under the steady stream of demands to vote funds to enable the queen's children to set up housekeeping; and Sir Charles Dilke (1843–1911), a Liberal M.P., launched an inquiry into the queen's own finances. Joseph Chamberlain (1836–1914), head of the National Education League for free secular schools and soon to be elected Radical mayor of Birmingham, was telling cheering crowds that, in England as in France, a republic was inevitable.

The trouble was, Gladstone privately admitted, that "the Queen is invisible, and the Prince of Wales is not respected." Since the death of Prince Albert in 1861, the now middle-aged Victoria had been "the widow of Windsor." She was as assiduous as ever in perusing state documents and in discussing the merits of prospective Anglican bishops; but she had almost ceased to attend to her ceremonial duties, and she hardly ever set foot in London. Because Gladstone was not a republican and revered the crown as an institution, he repeatedly tried to make Victoria

The Rivals   The magnetic William Ewart Gladstone (left), Liberal prime minister, 1868–1874, 1880–1885, 1886, and 1892–1894; and the imperturbable Benjamin Disraeli, earl of Beaconsfield, Conservative prime minister, 1868 and 1874–1880. Both portraits were painted during the late 1870s by John Everett Millais. *(National Portrait Gallery, London)*

understand that it was for her own good to make occasional public appearances. Edward, the Prince of Wales, had become an idle if amiable young man who had just been named as co-respondent in a divorce suit. (He was found not guilty.) In order to tie Ireland more closely to Britain and to give the prince something useful to do, Gladstone wished to appoint him to the position of Irish viceroy, a largely ceremonial post.

The queen either could not or would not understand. She had a typically Hanoverian dislike of entrusting her son and heir with even a semblance of political power; she therefore refused to name Edward as viceroy. Similarly, she refused one year to delay her summer vacation by a mere two days in order to prorogue Parliament in person. "Do *pet* the Queen a little," Mrs. Gladstone had once advised her husband; but the art that Disraeli possessed in overabundant measure Gladstone possessed not at all. Disraeli sought the company of women and gloried in it. It was part of his nature to heap on flattery with a trowel, a trait that Gladstone thought hypocritical. Gladstone was invariably polite to Victoria, as even the queen conceded; but, she added: "The trouble with Mr. Gladstone is that he always addresses me as if I were a public meeting."

As things turned out, the monarchy survived not only Gladstone's failure to mollify the queen but also the substantial series of domestic reforms that his ministry enacted before it was ended by the Conservative victory in the general election of 1874, an election that found the two-party tradition more vital than ever. Gladstone's resignation from the Liberal party leadership a year later in order to devote himself to theology seemed to presage the end of his political career. But circumstance and an apparently inexhaustible fund of personal energy were soon to dictate a revival of the Gladstone–Disraeli duel. First as rival chancellors of the Exchequer, then as rival leaders of the House of Commons, and finally as rival prime ministers, the two men had come to dominate the British political world.

Notable as the Gladstonian reforms had been, they had almost all remained within the nineteenth-century Liberal tradition of gradually removing the religious, economic, and political barriers that prevented men of varied creeds and classes from exercising their individual talents in order to improve themselves and their society. As the third quarter of the century drew to a close, the essential bastions of Victorianism still held firm: respectability; a government of aristocrats and gentlemen now influenced not only by middle-class merchants and manufacturers but also by industrious working people; a prosperity that seemed to rest largely on the tenets of laissez-faire economics combined with a collective sense of duty; and a Britannia that ruled the waves and many a dominion beyond. The last quarter of the century was to bring an end to the boom in the form of the paradoxical "great depression"; and the apparent certainties to the mid-Victorian world were to be subjected to searching reexamination.

PART THREE

THE LATE-VICTORIAN YEARS

1873 to 1900

QUEEN VICTORIA'S DIAMOND JUBILEE PROCESSION
OF 1897 CROSSES THE THAMES
(The Granger Collection)

CHAPTER 8

Disraeli and Gladstone

For purposes of convenience, we shall consider the last three decades of the nineteenth century as a distinctive unit. Such a classification, like most historical subdivisions, is open to argument. It may be contended, with some justification, that the 1880s were in fact a notable decade of transition — especially in Anglo-Irish relations, in British attitudes toward empire, and in the transformation of political beliefs regarding the proper role of the government in the national economy. It may also be argued that the last decade and a half of the queen's reign was not typically Victorian at all — that, for example, neither Oscar Wilde nor George Bernard Shaw was, in a literary as opposed to a strictly chronological sense, a Victorian playwright. Yet, aside from the feeling of unity provided by Queen Victoria's longevity and the influence that continued to be wielded by Disraeli and Gladstone until their deaths, the period does have a common economic backdrop; it was the age of the "great depression."[1]

The Curious "Great Depression"

When Americans encounter the term *great depression*, they are most likely to think of the period following the stock market crash of 1929, when for a number of years all the indices of economic prosperity went wrong: the rate of unemployment soared; the number of bank failures climbed; the total production of goods and services fell; the average standard of living declined. It was not until the beginning of the Second World War that most of these indices returned to their 1929 levels; and some, such as stock market price averages, did not do so until many years afterward.

Britain's "great depression" of 1873–1896 resembled the U.S. economic collapse of the 1930s only in part, but enough late-nineteenth-century economic indicators headed downward — prices fell, profit

---

[1]The "great depression" is considered in W. W. Rostow, *British Economy of the 19th Century* (1948), in S. B. Saul, *The Myth of the Great Depression, 1873–1896* (1969), and in Sidney Pollard, *Britain's Prime and Britain's Decline: The British Economy, 1870–1914* (1989). Also relevant are Herman Ausubel, *The Late Victorians* (1955), and Charles Wilson, "Economy and Society in Late Victorian Britain," *Economic History Review*, 2nd ser., XVIII (August 1965).

margins fell, interest rates fell, agriculture declined — to prompt grave disquiet among many influential Victorians. They began to write and publish such pamphlets as *Protection and Bad Times* (1879) and *The Trade Depression: Its Causes and Its Remedies* (1885), and they secured the appointment of royal commissions to inquire into the farm depression and the depression in trade and industry.

The plight of the agriculturist is most often cited in support of this concept of a late-Victorian "great depression." The 1870s were marked by a series of bad harvests, climaxed by that of 1879, the worst in a century. Bad harvests, as such, were hardly a novelty. What was unusual about the 1870s was that the farmer was not compensated for smaller crops by higher prices. Prices stayed low, primarily because cheap transportation rates and a rapid expansion of grain production in the American Midwest and to a lesser extent in the Russian Ukraine now made it possible to ship wheat and barley into England more cheaply than to grow the grain there. Whereas in 1860 it had cost 25 cents to ship a bushel of grain from New York to Liverpool, by 1886 large steam-powered freighters charged only five cents. The result was the increasing dependence of Britain on imported food. The decision to rely on food imports had, of course, been implicit in the repeal of the Corn Laws of 1846. Although wheat imports had in fact grown steadily after 1846, several European and American wars and the continuance, for a time, of high transportation costs had kept up the price of grain so that the English farmer could compete successfully with imported food. As late as 1868, 80 percent of all food consumed in the United Kingdom was produced at home. During the late nineteenth century that percentage dropped steadily, as fast, cheap freighters brought in American wheat and, after 1878, refrigerated meat, as well as tropical fruits from the Mediterranean and tea from India and China.

The result is often spoken of as "the collapse of British agriculture." The phrase, although vivid, is not altogether accurate. It does fit the wheat farmers of southern England, for wheat acreage declined by 50 percent during these thirty years, and land devoted to all cereals declined by at least 25 percent. It is also suitable insofar as it reflects a time when contracting income made it difficult for landlords to invest money in land, buildings, and drainage that would have enabled their tenants to farm more efficiently. And as long as the government was unwilling to protect the farmer with tariff barriers against American wheat — and the doctrine of free trade had taken root too strongly to permit it to do so — the agriculturist had to adapt somehow. Many landlords did so by turning their croplands into pasturelands; cattle raisers found themselves in a much less precarious position than wheat farmers. They, too, had to face foreign competition; but low grain prices reduced their own costs and, as the standard of living rose, they helped satisfy the rising demand for fresh meat together with the American, Argentinian, and Australian beef raisers. Still other landlords sought economic salvation by catering to the growing demand for vegetables, fruits, and dairy products from a population that by 1900 was three-quarters urban.

Late-Victorian Agriculture   The lot of the farm laborer remained a bleak one. The meeting in a Northamptonshire village (1872) shown in the picture was called to organize a farm laborers' union. The attempt did not succeed. *(Mary Evans Picture Library)*

Many farmers survived, but the "great depression" in agriculture undermined the economic foundations of nineteenth-century aristocrats at the same time that changes in local government were diminishing their traditional local political influence. Agriculture, which had provided 17.4 percent of the total national income in 1870, provided only 6.7 percent in 1913. Although many landlords and farmers did adjust to the new situation, England had ceased to exemplify progressive farming by the early twentieth century. Countries such as Denmark and the Netherlands, in which a healthy agriculture was a matter of national survival, adapted with greater success.

Many an English businessman also thought of the late nineteenth century in terms of economic depression because the prices he received for his products were falling at a fairly steady rate. His profit margins were also falling, and the dividend income from his investments was similarly on the decline. Because a prolonged period of deflation has not occurred among industrialized nations in the twentieth century, we may find the phenomenon difficult to understand. It was, however, a development not limited to Britain but equally evident in the United States and continental Europe. The era of deflation has been attributed to two related developments: (1) At a time when more and more nations were adhering to the gold standard, the available supply of that metal was not keeping pace with the growing volume of commerce. (2) Industry was becoming steadily more productive, and, given the keen competition among manufacturers, both wholesale and retail prices tended to fall. However comforting to the consumer with a steady job or the possessor of large bankholdings, deflation was a dreaded monster to the investor in search of high earnings and to the debtor in search of "cheap money" (as in the United States, where the "Greenbackers" of the 1870s and the "free silverites" of the 1890s urged their particular inflationary panaceas).

If the price deflation was in many ways a worldwide phenomenon, another late-Victorian tendency was peculiarly British: Britain's years as the "workshop of the world" were drawing to a close. By 1900, two newer industrial powers, Germany and the United States, had surpassed Great Britain in annual steel production and in several other manufactures.

The causes of Britain's relative decline are manifold. For one thing, Britain, having adopted the industrial process earliest, had too much money invested in older machinery. British cotton manufacturers, for example, found it less worthwhile to invest in automatic looms than did American manufacturers who were just starting out. There was the fact, increasingly bemoaned in late-Victorian Britain, that private companies were not establishing their own research laboratories and that technical education generally seemed to be neglected. The fruitful marriage of academic science and industrial technology that was characteristic of Germany seemed absent in Britain. Individual Britons had not ceased to be inventive. Michael Faraday (1791–1867), who perfected the first dynamo, and James Clerk Maxwell (1831–1879), who founded the Cavendish Laboratory at Cambridge, laid the theoretical foundations for the practical utilization of electricity. Sir Charles Parsons invented the steam turbine in the 1880s, and the unsung J. W. Swan deserves as much as Thomas Edison to be called the inventor of the electric lightbulb. Yet electric power stations spread far more rapidly in the United States than in Britain where, until World War I, electricity was used primarily for lighting. Similarly, two English cousins, Gilchrist Thomas and Percy Gilchrist, perfected the process of making steel out of phosphoric iron, but it was the mines of Germany and France that benefited most. Another Englishman, William Henry Perkin, discovered during the 1850s that chemical dyes could be derived more cheaply and efficiently from coal tar than from vegetation; yet it was in Germany that the chemical-dye industry took root.

PERCENTAGE OF WORLD'S MANUFACTURING CAPACITY

	1870	1906–1910
Britain	31.8	14.7
United States	23.3	35.3
Germany	13.2	15.9

From R. C. K. Ensor, *England, 1870–1914* (1936).

The industrial consequences of the "great depression" for Britain must be seen in perspective. Britain's decline as an industrial leader was relative rather than absolute. Decade by decade, British steel production increased, but that of Germany and the United States increased at a more rapid rate. Such a relative decline was in one sense inevitable. Once other countries had entered upon full-scale industrialization, it was to be expected that those with a larger population and a greater number of natural resources would ultimately overtake Britain. By the late nineteenth century, Germany had twice the population of Britain, and the United States, with plentiful supplies of coal and far more iron and waterpower, had two and a half times as many people. As early as the 1840s, the *Economist* had warned that the "superiority of the United States to England is ultimately as certain as the next eclipse."

The fact remains, however, that Great Britain was becoming a less flexible industrial society. Ernest E. Williams, in *Made in Germany*, a bestseller of 1896, attributed Germany's growing industrial and commercial strength in part to the help its businessmen were receiving from the state in the form of protective tariffs, to the high standard of technical education at home, and to the aid given by the consular services abroad. Equally important, Williams believed, was the spirit of enterprise displayed by German exporters. They were willing salesmen, eager to please their customers and to adapt their products to fit their customers' needs. Germany's industrial growth, he concluded, ought to be looked upon by the English less as a threat than as a bracing challenge.

Perhaps Victorians had never become completely persuaded of the values of an enterprising capitalist society. Certainly by the closing decades of the nineteenth century their temporary pride in Britain's industrial supremacy had faded. The enterprising capitalist was often looked upon less as the creator of wealth and as the provider of new employment opportunities than as the exploiter of workers, the destroyer of old crafts, and the despoiler of the countryside. Successful industrialists preferred their sons to become gentlemen instead, and gentlemen preferred their sons to become lawyers or civil servants or colonial administrators rather than captains of industry.[2]

Many British businessmen therefore came to view their fading industrial supremacy more as a cause for uneasiness than as a reason for giving up tried and true ways — and, in certain activities, Britain did indeed meet successfully the late-nineteenth-century German and American

---

[2]Martin J. Wiener, *English Culture and the Decline of the Industrial Spirit, 1850–1980* (1981), provides an illuminating analysis of a complex subject that remains a matter of dispute among historians. Walter L. Arnstein, "The Survival of the Victorian Aristocracy," *The Rich, The Well-Born, and The Powerful,* ed. by F. C. Jaher (1973), explores aspects of the same subject more briefly. W. D. Rubenstein's *Capitalism, Culture and Economic Decline in Britain, 1750–1990* (1993) seeks to counter Wiener's thesis. In *Britain's Prime and Britain's Decline* (1989), Sidney Pollard reminds us that during the late-Victorian years Britain's "was still the richest and most productive economy in Europe."

challenge. In the year 1900, 62 percent of the world's merchant shipping tonnage was built in British shipyards, as compared with 14 percent in American, 9 percent in German, and less than 1 percent in Japanese yards. Britain also remained the leading nation in volume of imports and exports — even if, among exports, textiles were becoming less important and machinery and raw coal more so. Britain also maintained the world's largest merchant fleet; in 1913, as in 1870, about one-third of all oceanic trade was done in British ships, thereby adding highly significant "invisible exports" to the visible exports that helped to pay for food and raw materials. Banking was seen as far more prestigious than industry, and in London "the City" remained the acknowledged center of international finance, the site of the world's largest banks and insurance companies.

The "great depression" may well have spurred many individual entrepreneurs and partnerships to transform their concerns into limited-liability companies. Such corporations had become commonplace in commerce and banking by the mid-Victorian years, but it was only in the late nineteenth century that the typical cotton factory or iron foundry became a limited-liability company. A good many remained private corporations, whose stock was held largely by members of the same family, rather than public corporations whose shares were traded in the stock market. Even on the eve of the First World War, the family firm was still far more characteristic of Britain (and France) than it was of the United States or Germany.

Some of these businesses sought to meet the challenge of the "great depression" by amalgamating, both vertically and horizontally. Vertical amalgamation had as its aim, as in the case of the steel mills, the monopolistic control of the entire process of production from the mining of the ore to the processing and delivery of the manufactured product. There was a drive in this direction, from 1894 to 1902 especially, among steel manufacturers, shipbuilders, and armaments makers. Horizontal amalga-

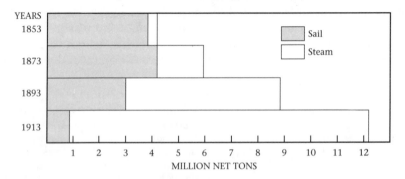

FROM SAIL TO STEAM: U.K. MERCHANT TONNAGE
(Steam overtakes sail construction in 1870.)

Adapted from R. R. Sellman, *Modern British Economic and Social History: A Practical Guide,* 3rd ed. (1972).

mation involved the attempt to undercut or buy out all competing firms. The closest British counterpart in this respect to the Standard Oil Company of the late nineteenth century in the United States was the Salt Union, which by 1888 monopolized 90 percent of British salt production. In textile dyeing, cement making, tobacco manufacturing, and a few other industries, the late 1890s were, as in the United States, an era of horizontal amalgamation in which oligopoly, the control of a particular industry by a few great firms, became commonplace. Yet the drive in that direction never went so far in England as in the United States; consequently, "trust busting" never became a vital political issue.

One reason why the term *great depression* impresses some economists as an inadequate term for the economic trends of the late nineteenth century is that one significant economic indicator — the rate of unemployment — did not increase notably. It was in the year 1888 that the word *unemployment*, defined as the inability of a person to find a job through no fault of his own, first entered the dictionary, but except for particular years, the average rate of unemployment during the final decades of the century differed little from the average rate for the mid-Victorian decades of prosperity. (Nineteenth-century governments did not attempt to estimate national unemployment statistics, so historians must rely on the records kept by trade unions. They reported an average of 5 percent for their members.)

Furthermore, the average employed worker's standard of living definitely improved during the years of the "great depression." His money wages rose little, if at all, but he and his family paid less than before for food, clothing, and shelter. Consumer-oriented industries such as those producing soap and chocolates grew at a prodigious rate, and local outlets of national chains of grocery, shoe, clothing, and chemist shops (drugstores) blossomed in every British city and town. The benefits of mass distribution as well as increased industrial productivity came to the average working-class family in the form of reduced prices. Real wages rose on the average of 2 percent a year at a time when leisure hours also increased. The sixty-hour week had been normal in 1870; the fifty-four-hour week was typical by 1900. The standard of living rose most obviously with respect to food. Wrote an observer in 1899: "The sort of man who had bread and cheese for his dinner forty years ago now demands a chop." As the cost of tea and sugar continued to fall, these staples became commonplace in the British diet, and neighborhood "fish and chips" shops multiplied. An increasing number of working-class families set aside a few pennies a week in savings banks and in the insurance policies against death and sickness provided by Friendly Societies, while others continued to resort to the local pawnbroker as a reliable if expensive source of emergency funds.[3] The "average worker" remains as

---

[3]Paul Johnson, *Saving and Spending: The Working-Class Economy in Britain, 1870–1939* (1986).

hypothetical an entity in the late nineteenth century as at any other time, and talk of such an average conceals the existence of vast pockets of poverty to which late-Victorian reformers were at pains to call attention. Nonetheless, the "great depression" proved to be a period of relative industrial peace and of social satisfaction for many workers. In assessing the political, social, and imperial changes of the late-Victorian period, the paradoxical facets of the "great depression" should be kept in mind. They clarify much that might otherwise remain puzzling.

Liberals and Conservatives

"When I am ill," wrote Sir William Harcourt, "I am in bed. When I am not, I am in the House of Commons." Harcourt (1827–1904), the M.P., cabinet member, and (for two years) leader of the Liberal party, reflected an absorption with politics common to many Victorian gentlemen.[4] It was, moreover, an attitude increasingly congenial to large numbers of British citizens who were not gentlemen in the generally accepted sense. The Reform Act of 1867 had officially recognized their right to have a direct voice in politics. This interest was reflected in the newspapers of the day.

As Walter Bagehot put it in the 1860s, the newspapers "give a precedent and a dignity to the political world which they do not give to any other. The literary world, the scientific world, the philosophic world not only are not comparable in dignity to the political world, but in comparison are hardly worlds at all." The newspapers of the 1860s and 1870s had been freed from the stamp taxes that during the first half of the nineteenth century curtailed popular journalism; the steam press had made possible their rapid duplication. An increasing number of lower-class English people were reading (often less than respectable) Sunday newspapers, but very few were as yet daily newspaper readers, and a daily circulation of 200,000 copies, which London's *Daily Telegraph* attained in the 1870s, was still regarded as an exception. The influential *Times* of London could boast of a reading public of only 50,000 a day, and the more important provincial papers such as the *Yorkshire Post*, the *Birmingham Post*, the *Manchester Guardian*, and the *Scotsman* of Edinburgh were selling 25,000 to 40,000 copies a day.

---

[4]Of recent surveys of late-Victorian Britain, E. J. Feuchtwanger, *Democracy and Empire: Britain, 1865–1914* (1985), is strongest on political history, and Donald Read, *The Age of Urban Democracy: England 1868–1914*, rev. ed. (1994), on social history. Even after more than six decades, Sir Robert Ensor's *England, 1870–1914* (1936) retains great value. H. J. Hanham, *Elections and Party Management: Politics in the Time of Disraeli and Gladstone* (1959; with new introduction, 1978), and Richard Shannon, *The Age of Disraeli, 1868–1881: The Rise of Tory Democracy* (1992), illuminate the political world outside Parliament, and Martin Pugh, *The Making of Modern British Politics, 1867–1939* (1982), throws helpful light on topics that historians have debated.

London papers were first and foremost concerned with politics, and even provincial papers devoted closely printed pages to stenographic reports of parliamentary debates. While political leaders sought to use the press to guide public opinion, journalists in turn came to see themselves as the conscience of the party whose cause they extolled and the press as a privileged "Fourth Estate" of the realm.[5] A seat in the House of Commons understandably represented the summit of ambition to many a Victorian. Parliament, in the public estimation, not only brought status and provided the nation's preeminent public forum, but it also decided important matters. Finally, Parliament provided excitement, and a parliamentary debater was judged not only by what he said but also by how he said it. Professional football and cricket leagues were still in their infancy, but the sport of politics was keenly followed and widely reported in the press.

The competitive character of politics was particularly noticeable at a time when the confusion of parties of the 1850s had come to an end. Representatives of the two major parties confronted each other day after day from opposite benches in the House of Commons, and from 1867 to 1875 the dynamic team captains themselves, Gladstone and Disraeli, sat barely two sword-lengths apart on opposite sides of the speaker's table. In some American presidential campaigns, the rival candidates have scarcely met one another, much less listened to one another's opinions; but neither Gladstone nor Disraeli could escape the verbal shafts of his rival. When on one occasion Disraeli complained that Gladstone had become "intoxicated by the exuberance of his own verbosity," his description, however self-interested, was based on first-hand observation.

Both parties were of necessity coalitions, but after the Reform Bill of 1867 the political independence of an individual member of Parliament increasingly came to be circumscribed by party organization. The dominance of Gladstone and Disraeli spurred a greater degree of party loyalty. A member who had been elected in 1868 on the basis of a pledge to support Gladstone's leadership was presumably impelled to support his chosen leader on most issues. Until the 1860s, political parties tended to be seen primarily as parliamentary rather than as national organizations, but the Reform Act of 1867 encouraged more centralized efforts to promote voter registration and to provide a list of suitable candidates to those constituencies that lacked suitable local prospects. (There was no law compelling a Member of Parliament to come from or to live in his constituency.) Although the Reform Club (Liberal) and the Carlton Club (Conservative) dated back to the 1830s, not until the 1870s did both parties set up real national headquarters in London (usually headed by the party's chief whip in the House of Commons) to coordinate

[5]See Stephen Koss, *The Rise and Fall of the Political Press in Britain: The Nineteenth Century* (1981); and, more generally, George Boyce et al., *Newspaper History from the Seventeenth Century to the Present Day* (1979).

general-election campaigns. Any attempt by such national organizations to influence party policy remained suspect, however.

The Reform Act of 1867 also prompted the growth of constituency organizations in order to attract the new working-class voters. The first prominent example of this sort was the "Birmingham caucus" set up by Joseph Chamberlain and Francis Schnadhorst. The Liberals of Birmingham had a particular incentive for building a party machine, because the Reform Bill gave the city a third member while leaving each voter with the right to vote for only two candidates. The purpose of this provision — added to the bill at the behest of the House of Lords — had been to permit the Conservatives to concentrate their votes in order to elect at least one member out of three. Careful organization on a ward-by-ward basis by the Birmingham Liberals enabled them to instruct their adherents in such a manner that they divided their votes almost equally among three Liberal candidates, thereby foiling the intent of the 1867 proviso. The "Birmingham caucus" came to have ambivalent connotations for those who feared that democracy would mean American-style political-machine and political-boss control in Britain. (The word *caucus* illustrates the element of Americanization. It is by origin an American Indian word that was taken over to describe particular types of congressional meetings. Its pejorative use as a synonym for leadership of local mass political organizations is peculiarly English.)

Although all Birmingham voters possessed the right to help choose the caucus, or leadership, of their constituency party organization, in practice most of them did not bother to attend party meetings, and such leadership remained in the hands of those who were interested. Consequently, a relative handful of party workers came to choose nominees in Birmingham and elsewhere, and primary elections did not become part of the British political tradition.

If the independence of an individual M.P. was restrained by the growth of a strong local organization, then it was similarly curbed by the increasing influence of particular pressure groups that required candidates to take a stand before they received the organization's verbal or monetary support. In the case of the Liberals, such organizations included the Liberation Society (whose purpose was to disestablish the Church of England in England itself), the United Kingdom Alliance (the leading temperance organization, whose aim was to limit pub hours and permit individual communities, by means of "local veto," to bar the sale of intoxicating beverages), and the National Education League (which sought free, compulsory, nonsectarian schools). Most of the adherents of these organizations were religious Nonconformists, and the Liberal party was increasingly dependent on the Nonconformist vote. What was novel in the late nineteenth century was the increasing number of Nonconformists who were themselves elected M.P.'s. There had been only twenty-three in 1833, ten of them Unitarians. By 1868 their number had risen to fifty-five and in 1880 there were eighty-five, all but one of them Liberals. Politically sophisticated Unitarians and Quakers continued to be elected at a ratio far higher than their number in the nation at large would have warranted. In contrast, Methodists and Baptists, most of whom ranked lower in wealth and social status, tended to lag behind.

Religion also helps to account for the fact that the enlarged post-1867 electorate in Wales and Scotland was drawn more to the Liberal than to the Conservative party. Welsh voters believed that Liberals were more likely to bring about the disestablishment of the Anglican Church in Wales as they had done in Ireland. In Scotland, after the religious Disruption of 1843, "Free Church" voters became staunch Liberal supporters in reaction to Conservative landlords who harassed the newly created "Free Church" congregations. The Liberal party was also somewhat more successful in attracting the vote of the self-conscious workingman. When two men of distinct laborer origin, Thomas Burt and Alexander MacDonald, were elected to Parliament in 1874, they both took their seats on the Liberal benches, the first of an increasing number of "Lib-Labs."

The Conservative party, as the 1870s began, was still largely in the hands of a coalition of landed oligarchs. Although Disraeli, in preparation for the election of 1874, encouraged efforts to register voters and to strengthen constituency party organizations, he continued to rely primarily on the local influence of the party's traditional leaders. Those leaders had long felt that they represented not a class but the whole agricultural community of landlords, tenant farmers, and laborers. Disraeli once observed captiously that the English aristocracy most resembled "the old Hellenic race; excelling in athletic sports, speaking no other language than their own, and never reading." More typical, however, was his comment on another occasion:

> The proper leaders of the people are the gentlemen of England. If they are not the leaders of the people, I do not see why there should be gentlemen. . . . If it be true that we are on the eve of troublous times, if it indeed be necessary that changes should take place in this country, let them be effected by those who ought to be the leaders in all political and social changes.

Yet the Conservatives were also familiar with pressure groups. Just as Nonconformists tended to vote Liberal, so the Church Defence Institution (an advocate of the traditional role and privileges of the Anglican Church) supported the Conservatives. As temperance advocates adhered to the Liberal ranks and succeeded in bringing about in 1872 the passage of a restrictive licensing bill, so the brewing industry and pubkeepers generally became Conservatives. In the early 1870s, the strength of the party still rested in the rural areas where the lord of the manor held sway, but, before the end of the century, the Conservative hold on the rural voter was to weaken and its hold on the urban industrialist and the suburban white-collar worker was to increase.

Although an analysis of their makeup and organization helps to clarify the role of political parties in late-Victorian England, it does not by itself explain why the Conservatives were victorious in 1874 and why the

Liberals returned in triumph in 1880. The Liberal defeat in 1874 was a tribute to Disraeli's skill in revamping his party and in creating the impression of a positive program. His new conservatism, as outlined in a speech at London's Crystal Palace in 1872, rested on three bases: social reform, the monarchy, and the empire. The Conservative party was, in his opinion, more suited than the Liberal for promoting public health and better housing for the working classes. Disraeli's program of paternalistic social reform — "Tory democracy" — harked back to his youthful insistence that the Tory aristocrat, not the liberal industrial plutocrat or doctrinaire classical economist, was the true friend of the worker, and that the Conservative party could successfully bridge social class divisions.

Secondly, Disraeli sought to focus on the monarchy once again as the symbol of national unity. This revival of an old Tory tradition seemed an appropriate countermove against the temporary flurry of republican sentiment. Finally, there was the empire. The Liberals, argued Disraeli, had looked upon the empire in far too penny-pinching a manner. They had discounted it as an unnecessary expense, ignoring the ties of sentiment that still united Canadians, Australians, New Zealanders, and South Africans of British descent with the mother country. They had failed to appreciate the significance of India for Britain's international power and influence.

Gladstone's Liberal party suffered in 1874 not only from this rejuvenated Tory platform but also from its own success in introducing reform legislation. Disraeli not unjustly compared the Liberal front bench to a range of "exhausted volcanoes." One difficulty with even a successful reform program is that it alienates as often as it satisfies. Many Britons resented the Liberals' pro-temperance legislation. "I have been borne down in a torrent of gin and beer," lamented Gladstone, when news of his defeat came. Perhaps as important had been the electoral abstention of many Nonconformists in whose eyes the Education Act of 1870 had provided too great a subsidy to the Church of England. As a result, the Conservatives held a majority of eighty-three in Great Britain alone and an overall majority of at least forty-eight in the United Kingdom Parliament, where both the Liberals and a distinct Irish Home Rule party now sat on the opposition benches.

The Disraeli Ministry of 1874–1880

For Disraeli, the election of 1874 was the political climax of his career. For the first time since the early 1840s, the Conservatives had again become the majority party. The election was in a very real sense his personal victory. Yet victory had come in some ways too late. Disraeli was already seventy years old. His wife had died a year before, and for the aging M.P. the loss was a great one. He was increasingly crippled by gout, and he no longer possessed the energy of his earlier days.

In many ways the most constructive aspect of Disraeli's ministry of 1874–1880 was his social reform program, piloted through the House of Commons by his able home secretary, Sir Richard Assheton Cross (1823–1914). A Trade Union Act of 1875 gave complete government sanction to such union activities as peaceful picketing; it went considerably further in this direction than Gladstone's Act of 1871 had done. An Artisans' Dwellings Act, also passed in 1875, empowered local authorities for the first time to condemn, demolish, and reconstruct whole areas of city slums. A Sale of Food and Drugs Act of the same year banned all ingredients "injurious to health" and remained the fundamental statute on the subject for half a century. Part of the same program was the Public Health Act of 1875, a consolidating measure that armed British municipalities with the authority to impose proper water, sewage, and drainage facilities. Three years later Britain's network of local prisons was nationalized; the national Exchequer was henceforth to pay for their upkeep, and a uniform system of penal discipline was to be applied.

Yet other acts of social legislation were passed during Disraeli's ministry, but the prime minister and his cabinet became absorbed primarily with foreign affairs.[6] Convinced that continental diplomats had ignored British interests, Disraeli deliberately launched a more "forward" policy. His skillful coup in 1875 secured for England the shares in the Suez Canal that the bankrupt khedive of Egypt felt compelled to sell. The Suez Canal had been completed by a French company in 1869 and had become Britain's "lifeline to India." More British ships used the canal than those of any other nation; Britain therefore had particular concern for the canal's protection. But the timing of Disraeli's coup had less to do with British ambition than with the khedive's mishandling of his own finances. Faced with bankruptcy, he needed money in a hurry; and the £4 million purchase price had to be secured so quickly that it was impossible to obtain immediate parliamentary consent. Disraeli thereupon borrowed the money from his banker friends, the Rothschilds, until such time as Parliament could and did consent to purchase the shares and appropriate the required sum.

A comparable stroke — although a more controversial one — was the prime minister's Royal Titles Bill, which added to Victoria's titles that of "Empress of India." The new empress was delighted; in terms of status she could now hold her own with the German, Austrian, and Russian emperors, and those Indians who until 1858 had been accustomed to an emperor at Delhi now possessed a visible substitute. Yet many Liberals

---

[6]The "Eastern Question" of the 1870s is taken up in A. J. P. Taylor, *The Struggle for Mastery in Europe, 1848–1918* (1954); and in such specialized studies as Richard T. Shannon, *Gladstone and the Bulgarian Agitation of 1876* (2nd ed., 1975); Ann Pottinger Saab, *Gladstone, Bulgaria, and the Working Classes, 1856–1878* (1991); and Richard Millman, *Britain and the Eastern Question, 1875–1878* (1979).

"New Crowns for Old Ones!"   Disraeli, as Aladdin, offers Victoria the title "Empress of India." *(Reproduced by permission of* Punch, *1876)*

and some Conservatives initially looked upon the title of "empress" as essentially un-English and not quite proper.

Although Britain's naval strength remained unchallenged in 1874, Disraeli considered his country's situation vis-à-vis the continental powers as dangerously isolated. France was still in the process of recovering from the Franco-Prussian War, and its new government, the Third Republic, did not yet seem securely established. Spain was racked by civil war and played no role in European affairs commensurate with its population. The central and eastern part of Europe was, however, dominated by three great autocratic monarchies, the new German Empire (with Bismarck as chancellor), the Austro-Hungarian Empire, and the Russian Empire. These powers were joined in a Three Emperors' League that harked back to the post-Vienna Holy Alliance. A major theme underlying Disraeli's foreign policy was his attempt to disrupt the league.

Of the three great monarchies, Russia, as in the 1850s, seemed most antagonistic to British interests. When Disraeli came to power in 1874, Anglo-Russian relations, cemented as they were by a marriage between Victoria's second son and Tsar Alexander's only daughter, were friendly; but the perennial "Eastern Question" was soon to bring the two countries once again close to war. The gradual, if sporadic, process of Turkish decline as a Balkan and Near Eastern power was still going on, and although Disraeli's absorption with Near Eastern affairs is sometimes attributed to his "oriental" background, less mystical explanations fit the facts more easily. The "nonoriental" Palmerston had been equally involved with Near Eastern affairs in the 1840s, and the equally "nonoriental" Aberdeen had found his government implicated in the Crimean War in 1854.

It was a revolt in 1876 in Bosnia, one of Turkey's Slavic provinces, that touched off a series of wars and internal upheavals within the Turkish Empire that almost immediately involved the Great Powers. For a time, Disraeli's government had no fixed policy. When, however, the prime minister gratuitously dismissed as "coffee house babble" the reports — afterwards confirmed — that Turkish troops had systematically murdered 12,000 Bulgarian men, women, and children, Gladstone was inspired to reenter the political arena. The former prime minister had resigned the Liberal leadership in 1875; and partly because his rival no longer occupied his traditional front bench seat in the House of Commons, Disraeli had thought it safe in 1876 to move to the House of Lords as earl of Beaconsfield. The "Bulgarian atrocities" and Disraeli's apparently cynical reaction were too much for a man who viewed foreign affairs as well as economic ones from a moral position; and Gladstone eloquently challenged the proposition that Britain's chief interest lay in the territorial preservation of an immoral and non-Christian Turkey rather than in the succor of fellow Christians oppressed by the sultan. Gladstone's campaign of pamphlets, mass meetings, and petitions mobilized Nonconformist voters anew on behalf of this Liberal cause.

Public sympathy veered toward Turkey in 1877. After the Turkish government had rejected a series of Russian demands for domestic reform, Russia had declared war. Traditional fears of Russian aggression revived in Britain as the tsar's troops advanced toward Constantinople. Victoria wanted immediate war against Russia and asked that the government "be bold" and "rally round the Sovereign and country." In the music halls, they were singing:

> We don't want to fight
> But, by Jingo, if we do
> We've got the men
> We've got the arms
> We've got the money too!

Disraeli was clearly sympathetic, but his cabinet was divided, and when he at last authorized the British fleet to enter the Dardanelles, it was Abdul Hamid, the new Ottoman sultan, who urged the British to go slowly. The arrival of a British squadron, he warned, might bring on the very event Disraeli most wished to prevent — the Russian seizure of Constantinople.

For in the meantime Turkey had sued for peace. In the Treaty of San Stefano, Russia and Turkey agreed that Russia should obtain Bessarabia; that the autonomous states of Serbia, Rumania, and Montenegro should be completely independent of Turkey; and that a large new Bulgaria should be created under Russian protection. Both Britain and Austria were outraged. They had been ignored as Russia extended its influence deep into the Balkans and all the way to the Mediterranean Sea; the tsar had flagrantly breached the tradition that major boundary changes should involve all the Great Powers of Europe. The result was the Congress of Berlin (1878), the most significant diplomatic gathering since Vienna in 1815. For the first time a British prime minister attended an international diplomatic conference in person — as did his new foreign secretary, the marquess of Salisbury (1830–1903) — and for the first time in over two centuries such a gathering was not conducted exclusively in the French language. Disraeli, who spoke French with a strong accent, was persuaded to use his native English.

Disraeli and Salisbury returned from Berlin claiming to have brought back "Peace with Honour." They had agreed to a decline in Turkish power, but they had succeeded in reducing the influence in the Balkans that the Russians had apparently won at San Stefano. The proposed Russian satellite kingdom of Bulgaria was split into three small states with various degrees of autonomy, and Austria was granted the right to occupy but not to annex Bosnia-Herzegovina. As subsequent events proved, Disraeli had not succeeded in breaking up the Three Emperors' League, but he had once again placed Britain at the center of the European diplomatic stage. Britain, in addition to influencing the ultimate settlement, obtained the Turkish island of Cyprus for a naval base in the eastern Mediterranean. Although Liberals quarreled with the substance of his diplomatic triumph, Disraeli was for the moment a national hero, and a general election in 1878 might well have returned an even more strongly Conservative House of Commons. The date of election was put off, however, and, by the time it came, public opinion had changed markedly.

Events in South Africa and Afghanistan were largely responsible. Lord Carnarvon, who had supervised the creation of the autonomous Dominion of Canada in 1867, looked forward to creating under British auspices a similar Union of South Africa, made up of the two English coastal colonies (Cape Colony and Natal) and the two inland republics (Transvaal and the Orange Free State) inhabited by Boers, the descendants of the original Dutch settlers of South Africa. It was Lord Carnarvon's hope that a greater degree of British control would ease the perpetually strained relations between the Boers and the neighboring Zulus. The Boers, although they had agreed in theory to outlaw slavery, continued to practice it, and they both feared and hated the Zulus. It was the Zulu threat that caused the Boers to acquiesce for the moment in the British annexation of the Transvaal in 1877. An ultimatum to the Zulus, sent by the British high commissioner in South Africa in defiance of instructions from London, committed British troops to a full-fledged Zulu war. The war proved the mettle of the 40,000 skilled spearthrowers who constituted the Zulu army. It also led to the massacre of the inhabitants of a British fort and a prolonged military campaign. By the summer of 1879, the Zulu army had been destroyed, but the war had proved costly both in men and in money and was extremely unpopular in England.

Equally disagreeable things were happening to the English in India. The British viceroy had long been fearful of the Russian advance into central Asia, which seemed to pose an eventual threat to India. In the 1870s, the focus of this threat was Afghanistan, whose amir preferred a policy of neutrality rather than becoming the satellite of either Russia or Britain. In order to forestall the Russians, however, the British insisted on the amir's acceptance of a British military mission. When he refused, the British army invaded the country and dictated a treaty ceding military control over the Afghan passes to Britain and accepting British control over Afghan foreign policy. Just as the British were celebrating their military success, a group of Afghan army mutineers in Kabul massacred the new British minister and his entire entourage. The war then began all over again, and once again the British press began to question the price of imperial glory.

Britain's international discomforts gave Gladstone the opportunity for a political return. He was far too emotionally involved not to speak out against Disraeli and his policies and far too energetic to stay in political retirement. As a young man he had thought nothing of walking thirty miles a day. Even at the age of seventy, which he attained in 1879, his favorite exercises were still walking and felling trees on his estate at Hawarden near Liverpool. When Gladstone was invited to stand as the Liberal candidate for the Scottish county of Midlothian, he was provided with a welcome opportunity to attack six years of "Beaconsfieldism." The "Midlothian campaign" of the autumn of 1879 and the winter of 1880, a long series of formal public addresses punctuated by a score of brief, whistle-stop speeches, marked the final conversion of the Tory of the 1830s into the popular democrat of the 1880s, the G.O.M. (Grand Old Man) of the late-Victorian world.

Gladstone lacked the tact to get along with the queen or even with his colleagues as easily as Disraeli did. He could, however, impress those colleagues with his intellect, his energy, and his impassioned parliamentary orations, and, unlike his Tory rival, he could electrify a crowd. Canning had for a time been a popular hero, and so had Palmerston; but never in the nineteenth century did an English statesman manage to embody the aspirations and gain the respect and admiration of millions of his people as did Gladstone at the time of the Midlothian campaign.

His opponents, who regarded the proper site for a public speech to be the floor of the House of Commons and not an open-air arena, ridiculed him as a demagogue. Gladstone's public appeals were indeed unorthodox, but he never condescended to his audience, and he appealed less to the self-interest of the masses than to their self-respect. Both privately and publicly, he looked upon "the people" as a high tribunal to whom he was presenting a legal case. The voters were to him a great jury of intelligent men who were concerned with political issues and who looked upon the casting of a vote, as did Gladstone himself, as a profound moral act.

In the speeches that comprised the Midlothian campaign, Gladstone stressed many subjects, but time and again he harked back to his main theme: in foreign relations, Britain should neither act unilaterally nor attempt to dominate others. Rather, Britain should neutralize the selfish

"The Colossus of Words"
The Colossus of Rhodes
was one of the Seven
Wonders of the Ancient
World. This *Punch*
cartoon shows Gladstone
at the time of the
Midlothian campaign
of 1879. *(Reproduced by
permission of* Punch*)*

aims of immoral governments by adhering to international law. (A case
in point had been the agreement of Gladstone's government in 1871 to
refer the "*Alabama* claims" quarrel with the United States to a five-
nation arbitration tribunal meeting in Geneva.) The small nations of Europe would then look to Britain as a guide as they pursued orderly and
constitutional freedom. Britain should support their aspirations, as it had
in Belgium and Italy, and not treat them as pawns, as Disraeli had done in
the Balkans. Disraeli saw his prime duty as that of advancing British interests and upholding British honor by whatever means were available.
For Gladstone, words such as *interest* and *honor* were meaningless if
they were not reconcilable with underlying moral principles, with the
cause of humanity, justice, civilization, and religion.

Gladstone's eloquent indictment of Disraeli, combined with Chamberlain's organizing talents on the constituency level and the agricultural
and industrial depression of the later 1870s, resulted in a Liberal landslide in the general election of 1880. In the new House of Commons, 347
Liberals overshadowed 240 Conservatives and 65 Irish Home Rulers. Disraeli retired from the prime ministership; a year later, having completed
his twelfth novel — *Endymion*, the story of a young man who grows up
to be prime minister of England — he was dead.

At the time of the Liberal triumph, the leadership of the party was still formally in the hands of the marquess of Hartington, and Victoria would have much preferred him to Gladstone. "I never could take Mr. Gladstone . . . as my minister again," she had written privately in 1879, "for I never COULD have the slightest particle of confidence in Mr. Gladstone after his violent, mischievous, and dangerous conduct for the last three years." But as Hartington soon made plain to her, the queen had no choice. It was clearly Gladstone who embodied the Liberal party and Gladstone who had won the election.

Gladstone's Second Ministry (1880–1885)

Gladstone's second ministry was to be so bogged down by frustrations abroad and at home that it is easy to miss its real accomplishments. Although the Liberal slogan continued to be "Peace, Retrenchment, and Reform," the Liberal party in 1880 lacked any pressing or agreed-upon reform program. The election had, after all, been fought primarily on the issue of foreign policy. The ministry did, nonetheless, produce a series of notable legislative reforms. The Corrupt Practices Act of 1883 proved more significant than any other single measure in curbing electoral dishonesty. A series of acts did much to improve the position of English and Scottish tenant farmers. They were granted the right to claim compensation for the improvements they made on their lands and the right to guard their crops against the hares that had been protected in order to be hunted for pleasure by aristocrats. The legal transfer of land, often subject to entail and to century-long leases, was made much easier.

The single most important legislative action of the second Gladstone ministry was the passage of the Reform Bill of 1884, the act that, in effect, extended to the county voter the franchise that the act of 1867 had extended to the urban voter. Passage increased the total electorate from 3,150,000 to 5,700,000 and in the counties alone almost tripled the number of voters. Although the result was not in theory universal manhood suffrage, the vast majority of adult males now possessed the vote. The only men permanently excluded were those who did not own or rent a home of their own — such as bachelors who lived with their parents or servants and laborers who lived in their master's house. Others were often deterred from voting by rigid residence and registration requirements.

The Reform Bill of 1884 did not elicit the kind of ideological debate that the Reform Bill of 1867 had produced. Some Britons might still have doubts about the theoretical virtues of political democracy, but it had ceased to be practical politics to debate the issue. The fact that the bill was not accompanied by a Redistribution Bill caused it initially to be rejected by the House of Lords, and for a few weeks in 1884 it appeared as if a major battle between the houses was in the offing. Then, partly as a result of Queen Victoria's influence, a bipartisan committee was set up to work out an acceptable reapportionment act. This act did much to bring about the Chartist ideal of equal electoral districts. Although a few exceptions remained, it was the single-member district that now became standard in place of the traditional two-member borough or county. The act consequently altered the fundamental basis on which the English theory of representation had rested for about a thousand years. It was no longer the community that an M.P. represented — it was now the individual.

The Reform Act of 1884 helped to complete the transition in both party machinery and party appeal that the Reform Act of 1867 had begun. It increased the role of party political organizations outside Parliament. The growth of the Birmingham caucus has been noted above. It was from an association of such local constituency organizations that Joseph Chamberlain in 1877 fashioned the National Liberal Federation. Relations between that organization and the party leadership in Parliament were not always smooth, especially since the general attitude of the National Liberal Federation was more radical than that of the more Whiggish party leadership. Similarly, in the wake of the Conservative defeat of 1880, a youthful Tory, Lord Randolph Churchill (1849–1895), took over the National Union of Conservative Associations and transformed it into a vehicle to unite the various Conservative constituency organizations, thus giving the party rank and file a sense of participation they had formerly lacked. Both party organizations were to hold annual conferences from then on.

Although Churchill claimed to have taken over the mantle of "Tory Democracy" from Disraeli, it was not to the workers that the Conservatives of the 1880s appealed most strongly. "The Conservative party have done more for the working classes in five years than the Liberals have done in fifty," declared Alexander MacDonald, the working-class M.P., in 1879; but it is noteworthy that he remained a Liberal. The new converts to Conservatism were generally the suburban householders and the inhabitants of the more prosperous city districts. They were white-collar workers — clerks, teachers, and shopkeepers — whose income might not be higher than that of the factory worker but whose status aspirations were.[7] For the alteration of the theoretical basis of representation from community to individual coincided with a change in the old communities. In the old-style borough, the community leaders had lived side by side with the people they influenced and, as in the country districts, regarded the interests of employer and employee as essentially one. In the sprawling industrial city, on the other hand, there was a growing pattern of residential segregation by class and income. The more prosperous tended to become faithful Conservative supporters, while the less prosperous became for the time being rather less regular Liberal supporters.

During the same decade, the increase in the rural electorate as well as legislation favoring the tenant farmer caused a profound change in the

---

[7]James Cornford, "The Transformation of Conservatism," *Victorian Studies VII* (September 1963).

country areas. The shires had been traditionally in the hands of Tory squires who exercised great influence over their tenants. The influence had much declined by 1885; and in the general election of that year, in which many industrial cities first provided a Conservative majority, many rural boroughs for the first time voted Liberal.

The reforms of the second Gladstone ministry, real as they were, tended to be overshadowed in the public press by a series of domestic and foreign frustrations. An especially plaguing problem for Gladstone was the case of Charles Bradlaugh (1833–1891), a notorious atheist and advocate of birth control, who was not permitted by the House of Commons to take the required parliamentary oath and who was thereby prevented from taking the seat for which the electors of the borough of Northampton had chosen him in 1880. His case aroused a flood of emotional oratory and testified to the continued significance in the Britain of the 1880s of organized religion and the Victorian canons of respectability. Gladstone found it distasteful to defend the constitutional rights of a man whose atheistic convictions he found abhorrent; but when it proved impossible to defer the matter to the courts, he supported the Affirmation Bill of 1883 in one of his most eloquent speeches. The bill would have granted Bradlaugh and all other M.P.'s the right to affirm, rather than to swear on the Bible, their loyalty to the crown; but public opinion was too hostile at the time to permit the bill to pass. Bradlaugh, whose Northampton constituents repeatedly elected him, was finally admitted to the House of Commons in 1886, and he secured the passage of a permanent Affirmation Bill in 1888. Thus Parliament, which had been opened to Roman Catholics in the 1820s and to professing Jews in the 1850s, was thrown open to avowed atheists in the 1880s.[8]

Although issues of foreign policy had helped Gladstone win the election of 1880, the same issues were equally responsible for the decline of his popularity by 1885. In Afghanistan, it is true, the situation was satisfactorily resolved. British troops were evacuated, but in return for a subsidy and a guarantee against foreign aggression, the reigning amir permitted Britain to supervise Afghanistan's foreign relations. Things went less well in South Africa. There Gladstone had promised to end the annexation of the Transvaal if elected. When disagreement in the new Liberal government delayed a settlement, the Boers went on the offensive and defeated a small British contingent at Majuba Hill in February 1881. Gladstone had to choose between fighting for an annexation in which he did not believe and making peace, thereby conceding to force of arms what he seemingly had refused to concede to reason. He decided to make peace, despite the fact that his decision was interpreted as an affront to British honor and a justification of Boer arrogance.

It was at the other end of Africa, however, where Gladstone had his greatest trouble. Egypt, in which Disraeli's purchase of the Suez Canal

---

[8]Walter L. Arnstein, *The Bradlaugh Case* (1965; new ed., 1984).

shares had involved Britain, proved to be the location of both the ministry's greatest military victory and its most stinging defeat. The khedive's extravagance had led in 1878 to the setting up of an Anglo-French control board to supervise Egyptian finances. This led to an outburst of Egyptian nationalism under one Colonel Arabi, who resented not only the British and the French but also the Turkish advisers who dominated the khedive's court (Egypt was still nominally a part of the Ottoman Empire). Negotiations for a joint Anglo-French intervention collapsed; and when in 1882 Colonel Arabi's forces staged a coup d'état that resulted in the death of fifty Europeans in Alexandria, the British government intervened alone. Its navy shelled Alexandria; and in a model military maneuver, it collected and landed a 16,000-troop army that, after a long night march, completely defeated Colonel Arabi's forces. Against his better judgment, Gladstone decided on the temporary occupation of Egypt. Clearly a good deal of governmental and economic rebuilding was in order there, and the prime minister did not believe he could leave that task in the hands of either the Egyptians or another European power.

In order to simplify the administration of Egypt, the British government decided to relinquish all Egyptian territorial claims to the area south of Egypt: the Sudan. General Charles "Chinese" Gordon, a soldier-adventurer, was summoned to superintend the evacuation of the scattered Egyptian forces in the Sudan. He decided, instead, to make a stand to keep Khartoum and the Nile Valley in Anglo-Egyptian hands in the face of the fanatical Sudanese Mahdi (or "messiah") and his followers. The British cabinet opposed the step but delayed — against local advice — in authorizing a relief expedition up the Nile to bring back General Gordon. A force was finally authorized and sent, but it arrived at Khartoum only on January 28, 1885, two days after the city had been stormed and General Gordon killed. No single event of his career made Gladstone more unpopular. He had tried in his fashion to adhere to the moral foreign policy he had outlined in the Midlothian campaign, but good intentions were not always sufficient and events did not always oblige.

The general election of 1885 was thus fought in the face of a foreign policy record about which Britons had at best mixed feelings. The greatest accomplishment in foreign affairs of Gladstone's second ministry — the occupation of Egypt — was paradoxically one that Gladstone looked forward to terminating as soon as possible. The years had, however, brought some significant legislative changes at home, most notably the Reform Act of 1884 and the accompanying Redistribution Act. These same years, finally, had brought a revival of the perennial Irish question; and it was Ireland rather than political reform acts or military maneuvers in distant lands that dominated British politics in the 1880s. Disraeli's death had brought the long parliamentary duel of Disraeli and Gladstone to a close, but Ireland was to add one last chapter to Gladstone's long career.

CHAPTER 9

The Irish Question

The Irish question is almost as old as English history itself. It is rooted in geography and in the fact that, from the days of Henry II on, the rulers of a larger and more populous England claimed authority over many or all of the inhabitants of their smaller island neighbor — if only to stop them from allying themselves with England's continental enemies.

The Nineteenth-Century Background

Many Victorian Englishmen recognized that the treatment their forebears had meted out to the Irish had often been unjust and cruel and that the Irish had been dealt with in the past as a conquered people. But this they felt was no longer true in the nineteenth century. The Irish now had their proper share of representation in the Parliament of the United Kingdom. The religion of so many of them, Roman Catholicism, was no longer a bar to their economic or political advancement. Their merchants were no longer discriminated against economically, as they admittedly had been in the eighteenth century. Like the English, they were helped by state-supported schools and public health legislation; if in dire need, they too could resort to the Poor Law. The Irish, many English people concluded, had acquired both the privilege and the glory of constituting a part of the worldwide British Empire.[1]

Therefore, when Irish nationalists compared their lot to that of Greeks under Turkish rule or Italians under Austrian rule, most of the English failed to grasp the analogy. Nationalism admittedly remains a concept very difficult to define: distinct geographical boundaries, a common religion, and a common language are often cited as significant

---

[1]Alan O'Day's *Irish Home Rule 1867–1921* (1998) provides a comprehensive and helpful modern overview, as do the essays that make up W. E. Vaughan, ed., *A New History of Ireland VI: Ireland Under the Union II, 1870–1921* (1996). Two older books that retain great value are Nicholas Mansergh, *The Irish Question, 1840–1921* (3rd ed., 1975), and F. S. L. Lyons, *Ireland Since the Famine* (rev. ed., 1973). K. Theodore Hoppen, *Elections, Politics, and Society in Ireland, 1832–1885* (1984), emphasizes the local rather than the "national" concerns of a majority of the Irish during the nineteenth century. The changing nature of the nationalist movement is charted by Robert Kee in *The Green Flag* (1972) and by D. George Boyce in *Nationalism in Ireland* (3rd ed., 1995).

attributes of nationalism; yet there are nations, such as the Swiss, that defy all three. Ultimately, the most potent source of nationalism is simply a state of mind, a widespread feeling on the part of a group of people that they constitute a separate nationality and therefore deserve to be a separate nation. What some nineteenth-century Irishmen defined as loyalty to nationality, a nineteenth-century Englishman might, with equal consistency, regard as treason to that more comprehensive focus of loyalty, the United Kingdom, or that yet broader and more heterogeneous entity, the British Empire. Most inhabitants of nineteenth-century Ireland were too pragmatic — and usually too absorbed in the day-to-day tasks of earning a subsistence living — to expect the establishment of an independent Irish nation. A few revolutionary Young Irelanders had that hope in the 1840s; so did the revolutionary Fenians of the 1860s. Some of the Fenians were emigrants to the United States who fought on the Union side in the American Civil War in order to gain the military experience to fight the real enemy, England. But their "invasion" of Canada in 1866 proved abortive; and their attempt to establish an Irish republic in 1867 failed to evoke any widespread support among the Irish peasantry.

Most Irish leaders, men such as Daniel O'Connell in the 1830s and 1840s and Isaac Butt in the 1870s, sought not independence but less fanciful objectives: to put pressure on Parliament to pass legislation that would ameliorate social and economic conditions within Ireland and, eventually, to achieve for Ireland domestic self-government within the British Empire. British political leaders, admittedly, were more prone to deal with Irish grievances when they were expressed in violent form than when voiced more calmly. The 1850s and 1860s, the years after the Great Famine, turned out to be a relatively peaceful period in Anglo-Irish relations, however, even if Irish prosperity was the result of the manner in which starvation and mass emigration had reduced the population and thus increased the relative supply of food. "Free trade" was expected to benefit the Irish economy as much as the British and, except for statutes making it easier to transfer the legal titles to Irish land, Parliament made no attempt at this time to interfere with traditional landlord-tenant relations. Gladstone's attention to the Irish question was characteristically first attracted by the Fenian "outrages" that marred this peaceful era. Although Gladstone recognized more readily than his fellow politicians the reality of Irish nationalism, his purpose was not to encourage it but to reconcile the Irish to the continuation of the United Kingdom. It was his hope that the disestablishment of the Anglican Church in Ireland in 1869 and an Irish Land Act in 1870 to aid tenant farmers would complete his "mission to pacify Ireland."

This hope was soon shattered, because in some respects both disestablishment and the land act spurred rather than dampened Irish national aspirations. A Fenian revolution might be out of the question, but a constitutional movement advocating Home Rule won increasing electoral support. Few landlords were attracted, but their political influence had increasingly been challenged by that of the Roman Catholic clergy. A growing number of priests were willing to support Home Rule candidates, especially those pledged to promote their church's role in Irish education. Of 105 M.P.'s elected in Ireland in 1874, some 59 called themselves neither Liberals nor Conservatives but Home Rulers.

The phrase "Home Rule" had been coined by Isaac Butt (1813–1879), the Protestant Dublin lawyer who headed the group. His aim was to establish a parliament in Dublin in which Irishmen could control all domestic affairs while leaving imperial defense and foreign policy in the hands of the British Parliament at Westminster. Butt hoped that Britons repelled by the possibility of repealing the Act of Union of 1801 would find Home Rule a more palatable alternative. An autonomous Irish parliament, he pointed out, would be more successful than the current arrangement in protecting Ireland against revolutionary tendencies. Despite Butt's electoral success in 1874, he made little headway in converting either of the major parties to his program; nor did the mass of the Irish peasantry — most of them still ineligible to vote because they did not meet property requirements — see Home Rule as a solution to their day-to-day economic concerns.

Those concerns were multiplied by the agricultural depression of the later 1870s. A combination of bad harvests and competition from grain imported from the United States caused Irish farm prices to plummet. Rents that had seemed fair earlier in the decade now seemed exorbitant; evictions for nonpayment became ever more common. In predominantly agricultural Ireland, there were few factory jobs to take up the slack. A more immediate solution to the farm problem seemed to lie in the Irish Land League, an organization founded in 1879 by Michael Davitt, an ex-Fenian. Its slogan was "the Land for the People" and its purpose was to marshal the power of the tenant farmers against the landlords.

The Rise of Parnell

In the meantime, the economic depression and the apparent failure of Butt's attempts at gentle persuasion had brought to the forefront within the Home Rule ranks a young man named Charles Stewart Parnell (1846–1891), who decided that far more extreme measures were needed. In 1877 he displaced Butt as president of the Home Rule Federation of Great Britain. Although he was himself an Irish landlord and distrustful of Davitt's more radical proposals, Parnell gave his blessing to the Irish Land League and was elected its president as well. The economic and political movements were thus joined, and the Home Rulers gained a mass following in Ireland.[2]

---

[2]The most comprehensive modern biography is F. S. L. Lyons, *Parnell* (1977), but see also Paul Bew's more concise *C. S. Parnell* (1980) and D. George Boyce and Alan O'Day, eds., *Parnell in Perspective* (1991). Parnell and his era are also illuminated by Conor Cruise O'Brien, *Parnell and His Party, 1880–1890* (1957), by Emmet Larkin, *The Roman Catholic*

The Uncrowned King of Ireland   Charles Stewart Parnell (1846–1891) addresses a group of admiring followers from a hotel window. *(Hulton Deutsch Collection)*

At Westminster the Irish "third party" was beginning to attract more attention by reason of Parnell's brilliance in the art of political obstructionism. Although brief earlier examples are known, it was not until the late 1870s that any group in the House of Commons had ever so deliberately taken advantage of parliamentary rules of order to snarl parliamentary business. A policy of obstruction won the Irish Home Rulers no popularity but made it impossible to ignore them any longer. Moreover, Parnell's third party had money: a highly significant factor in financing both the Land League and the Home Rule party in Westminster was the generosity of the Irish-Americans in the United States. A generation had gone by since the Great Famine, and enough of them had made good in the new world to enable them to do much for their compatriots back home.

The Disraeli ministry of 1874–1880 made no significant attempt to deal with Irish grievances; but when Gladstone returned as prime minister in 1880, it appeared for a while as if the situation would improve.

Church and the Creation of the Modern Irish State, 1878–1886 (1975), and by Alan O'Day, *The English Face of Irish Nationalism* (1977). Several modern scholars have come to see late-Victorian Irish landlords less as cruel exploiters than as victims of the same changes in world agriculture that afflicted their English counterparts. See, e.g., Barbara Solow, *The Land Question and the Irish Economy, 1870–1903* (1971), and W. E. Vaughan, *Landlords and Tenants in Mid-Victorian Ireland* (1994).

Gladstone did, after all, have a reputation as a friend of Irish causes, and he and the Home Rulers had sat together on the opposition benches. The new Gladstone ministry let lapse the most recent of many temporary "coercion acts" — statutes that sought to deal with Irish violence by suspending the writ of habeas corpus in Ireland — and it sponsored a bill to have the government pay compensation to evicted Irish tenants. The bill passed the House of Commons only to be vetoed by the House of Lords. The result was renewed Land League agitation in Ireland on behalf of evicted tenants. Although the league did not publicly advocate violence, the burning of hayricks, the maiming of cattle, and the firing of shotgun blasts at houses during the night often followed in the wake of its agitation. Moreover, the league advocated a system of social ostracism in which anyone who purchased a farm from which the previous tenant had been unjustly evicted would be totally ignored by his neighbors. They would not talk to him, buy from him, or sell to him. He was to be treated, in Parnell's words, like "a leper of old." The first victim of this policy was the agent of a large landowner in County Mayo, one Captain Charles Boycott, who thereby unintentionally added a new word to the English language. At Westminster, in the meantime, the Irish renewed their filibustering tactics, which reached their height in January 1881 when the Parnellites kept the House of Commons in session for an unprecedented forty-one hours in order to prevent a vote on a bill dealing with Ireland. Only then did the Speaker take it upon himself to set aside the rules and stop the debate.

The Gladstone ministry met the problem of violence in Ireland and obstruction in Westminster by a characteristic combination of sticks and carrots. The sticks consisted of a new "coercion act" early in 1881 and a change of parliamentary regulations late in 1882 that made it much easier to shut off debate in the face of deliberate filibustering. The major carrot was the Irish Land Act of 1881, an epic piece of legislation that was piloted through the House of Commons by Gladstone himself. The statute granted to the Irish tenant farmers the "three Fs" they had long demanded: fair rent, free sale, and fixity of tenure. The Act of 1881, once the machinery for its enforcement could be set up, proved far more effective than any previous efforts by the government to alter landlord-tenant relations. It set down the principle that tenants were to be treated as virtual co-owners of the acres that they rented from their landlords. Such a break with laissez-faire doctrine was one that late-Victorian Liberals were often more willing to make when dealing with troubled Ireland than with England. (A similar exception was to be made for farmers in the Scottish Highlands in the Crofters Holdings Act of 1886).

As often happens when agitation arouses human passions, a particular act of legislation did not at once calm the storm. The autumn of 1881 brought new violence in Ireland; this in turn caused the government to outlaw the Land League and to place Parnell and his leading lieutenants under arrest in Kilmainham jail. Just when matters looked worst, both sides began to compromise. In April 1882, Gladstone and Parnell reached an understanding by which the government was to release the Irish leaders and appropriate money to pay the arrears in rent of 100,000 Irish tenants. Parnell in turn promised henceforth to cooperate with the Liberal government to end crime and disorder. Many Britons were outraged by this so-called Kilmainham Treaty, which seemed to represent the appeasement of an arch-revolutionary. But Gladstone's canons of political morality included a pragmatic ability to forgive and forget; and Parnell, although suspected of being the devil incarnate by many Britons, was ultimately more a constitutionalist than a revolutionary. Yet Parnell impressed even his own supporters as a somewhat aloof and mysterious man. The haziness of his ultimate aims and the enigmatic nature of his character enabled him to do what no Irish leader since O'Connell had accomplished — to unite, if only temporarily, revolutionaries and moderates on behalf of the cause of Home Rule.

It was by one of those quirks of irony that seem to bedevil Anglo-Irish history that only four days after Parnell's release, the new chief secretary for Ireland, Lord Frederick Cavendish, and an associate were murdered in Phoenix Park, Dublin. Parnell himself was outraged and denounced the murder in a manifesto. The assassins were eventually identified as members of The Invincibles, a secret murder club that flourished on the extremes of the Irish nationalist movement. Although the murder, which led to still another coercion act, necessarily marred what may be termed "the Spirit of Kilmainham," the atmosphere of cooperation did not disappear altogether during the next three years. Occasional acts of violence continued, and the Parnellites opposed the Liberal government in a number of instances, but affairs did not again reach the fever pitch of 1879–1882.

The Parnellites had not, of course, forgotten that their ultimate aim was Home Rule. Thus far, no major English political leader had been converted to the idea; but in 1882 Gladstone surprised the House of Commons by indicating that he was not opposed to Irish Home Rule in principle but thought the project impracticable. By the spring of 1885, the second Gladstone ministry had been damaged by the death of Gordon at Khartoum, and its cabinet was split on a growing number of issues. Gladstone almost welcomed a House of Commons defeat on a budget provision as an excuse to resign. A new general election had to await the redrawing of electoral boundary lines and the preparation of new electoral registers made necessary by the Reform Act of 1884 and the Redistribution of Seats Act of 1885. The new Conservative leader, the marquess of Salisbury, agreed therefore to head a minority caretaker government for the time being.

During the previous years a number of Irish M.P.'s had drawn closer to the Conservatives as fellow opponents to the Gladstone ministry, and rising Conservative leaders such as Randolph Churchill began to play with the idea of a genuine Irish-Tory alliance. The Salisbury government permitted the most recent coercion act to lapse, and the new Conservative viceroy in Ireland hinted that a Conservative government might approve some form of Home Rule. Irish M.P.'s began to hope that it might be 1867 all over again. The Conservatives would introduce a reform bill, the Liberals would broaden it, and the Irish would benefit. With this expectation in mind, two days before the general election, Parnell issued a manifesto asking all Irishmen in England to vote Conservative.

The results of the election of November 1885 were ironic: Liberals, 335; Conservatives, 249; Irish Home Rulers, 86. In one sense the election was a triumph for Gladstone. Although the Liberals had lost numerous urban seats, they had made gains in the rural areas that almost compensated for their losses. At the end of his second ministry, Gladstone clearly retained far more popular support than he had at the end of his first ministry in 1874. In a still more obvious sense, the election was a triumph for Parnell. In the 1880 Parliament he had never been able to count on the full-fledged support of more than 44 Irish M.P.'s; now 85 out of 103 Irish members were pledged personally to him.[3] He was indeed "the uncrowned King of Ireland." There was, however, a further irony: whereas neither major party could now govern without Irish support, the Conservatives did not have enough M.P.'s to command a working majority, even with Irish support. The practical grounds for a Tory-Irish alliance had collapsed.

The First Home Rule Bill

Before the new Parliament assembled in January, an indiscreet revelation by one of Gladstone's sons made it clear that Gladstone definitely had been converted to Home Rule. Whatever temptations the Conservative government might have had to deal with the problem now disappeared, and the Parnellites flocked en masse to the Gladstone banner they had scorned only two months before. Late in January, the Liberals and Irish combined to defeat the Conservatives in the new Parliament. Salisbury resigned, and Gladstone at the age of seventy-six became prime minister for the third time. Some critics at the time and some historians subsequently accused Gladstone of gross expediency, of allying himself with the Irish Home Rulers because he needed Irish votes to govern.[4] This judgment fails to take into account the fact that no one was more aware than the new prime minister that, although his conversion to Home Rule might gain him Irish support, it might equally well split his own party in the process. Much more influential in the slow formation of Gladstone's

---

[3] The 86th represented an English constituency, Liverpool.

[4] A modern version of this interpretation may be found in A. B. Cooke and John Vincent, *The Governing Passion: Cabinet Government and Party Politics in Britain, 1885–86* (1974). In *Liberal Politics in the Age of Gladstone and Rosebery* (1972), D. A. Hamer agrees that Gladstone hoped that his Home Rule policy would ultimately prove a focus of party unity. In *Parliamentary Politics and the Home Rule Crisis* (1988), W. C. Lubenow demonstrates how in the short run Gladstone failed.

opinion had been the election results in Ireland. The populace, a majority of whose adult males were for the first time enfranchised, had overwhelmingly demonstrated its desire for Home Rule. This popular pressure helped to convince him that the Irish question was a moral issue that deserved his complete support.

In April, Gladstone introduced a bill to create in Dublin a separate parliament and executive to handle Irish domestic affairs. The Parliament at Westminster, in which the Irish would no longer be directly represented, would continue to have control of foreign policy (including trade agreements), defense, and the coinage. The bill aroused in England the kind of popular and parliamentary excitement not known since 1832. In June 1886, the decisive vote came: the proposed statute was defeated, 343 to 313. A number of factors help to explain this result. For one, Parnell was still, in the minds of many Britons, a criminal and hardly the man to be entrusted with the government of Ireland. The bill thus seemed to be a reward for lawless behavior. Secondly, the proposal was in some ways too sudden. Gladstone, despite a number of masterful orations, found himself unable to convince two of his most important colleagues, the marquess of Hartington (the head of the Whig wing of the party) and Joseph Chamberlain (on all other subjects the leading radical of his party and, in the minds of many Liberals, the logical successor to Gladstone). It is a tribute to Gladstone's inspired parliamentary leadership that on the vital division he managed to retain the support of 227 of his sorely perplexed Liberal followers; 93, including Hartington and Chamberlain, voted against him.

There are still other reasons for the defeat of Home Rule. It went against what may be called the spirit of the age in Britain. In fact, if not in name, it appeared to repeal the Act of Union of 1801. It therefore revived ancient fears that Britain's enemies might someday use Ireland as a military base. It was necessarily opposed by all ardent advocates of imperialism. At a time when the British Empire appeared to be both expanding and strengthening its links, Home Rule implied imperial disintegration. Finally, there was the question of Ulster. Parnell himself was a Protestant, but the Irish Home Rule party was predominantly Roman Catholic, and Catholicism, the church of the Irish peasantry, had become part of the fabric of militant Irish nationalism. Irish Protestants — a majority in northeastern Ireland — reacted with an equally militant "unionism." Although some opponents of Home Rule did not hesitate to stir religious passions for political purposes, the religious and cultural divisions within Ireland proved to be all too real.

In the summer of 1886, Gladstone appealed to the electorate to reverse the verdict of Parliament in a new general election. Unlike the election of the previous year, there were now four parties in the field: Conservatives, Irish Home Rulers, Gladstonian Liberals, and Liberal Unionists (the followers of Hartington and Chamberlain who opposed the repeal of "union" with Ireland and who set up their own party organization). There was no doubt as to how the nation felt. The results were bleak for

Gladstone: 316 Conservatives; 78 Liberal Unionists; 191 Liberals; 85 Irish Home Rulers. For the moment, clearly, Home Rule was dead and the Liberal party was divided in much the same fashion as the Tories had been split over the repeal of the Corn Laws in 1846.

More, however, was involved in the breakup of the Liberal party. For some right-wing Whigs in the party, the Home Rule crisis was simply the occasion to cut a tie they had found increasingly uncomfortable. Their departure might not deprive the party of all its mass support, but it did sever its connection with most aristocratic landlords and with a majority of its wealthy members in general. A majority of Liberal peers also broke with Gladstone, thereby helping to transform the House of Lords into a more or less permanent organ of the Conservative party. The Whiggish Liberal Unionists led by Hartington drifted increasingly toward a permanent alliance with the Conservatives, just as many Peelites of the 1850s had drifted toward Liberalism.

Chamberlain's defection was even more important.[5] As a Radical who supported a sweeping program of free secular education, land reform, the disestablishment of the Church of England, universal manhood suffrage, and the payment of salaries to Members of Parliament, he seemed to be part of the wave of the future and much more at home in a Liberal party shorn of Whig support than in Salisbury's Conservative party. Clearly this was at first Chamberlain's view as well. He was an ambitious but practical politician. He decided to wait for Gladstone's retirement. Then he would return, replace the unpopular Home Rule plank with his own plan for greater Irish self-government at the county level, reunite the Liberal party, and lead it in a genuinely radical direction. The one factor that Chamberlain did not count on was the incredible longevity of William Ewart Gladstone.

To become leader of the opposition at the age of seventy-seven was at best a discouraging prospect, but Gladstone set himself to the task of remaining in politics until he could convince his compatriots that justice to Ireland was not treason to England but a moral obligation and that only by concession could the two peoples be reconciled. So long as the "Grand Old Man" remained in politics and kept the Irish issue alive, Chamberlain found it impossible to return to the Liberal fold; instead he eventually discovered his guiding star in imperialism and drifted toward conservatism. In the meantime, the party split continued to widen. Henry Labouchere, a Gladstonian Liberal, went so far as to compare Chamberlain's behavior to that of Judas Iscariot. Historical analogies, Labouchere conceded, were seldom exact, but "Judas had some good points about him. It is true that he betrayed his Master, but he did not

---

[5]Peter Marsh, *Joseph Chamberlain: Entrepreneur in Politics* (1994), is a comprehensive and reliable modern biography of the man who has been called "the most famous and influential British politician who never reached 10 Downing Street." See also Dennis Judd, *Radical Joe* (1977).

afterwards stump Judea and appear on platforms surrounded by scribes and Pharisees."

As the Liberal party disintegrated, Salisbury's Conservative ministry (1886–1892) ruled Ireland with a firm hand. It was willing to make concessions in some areas, but against Home Rule it was adamant. Salisbury looked with sympathy on proposals to aid Irish tenant farmers in purchasing their own land; the first of several Conservative land purchase acts had been passed in 1885. Such legislation may not have aided the Irish farm laborer or promoted the efficiency of Irish agriculture, but it did much to end the era of absentee landlords and to transform Ireland into a land of small family farmers.

Salisbury's government was for the time being unwilling to include Ireland in the County Councils Act of 1888, a significant part of the late-Victorian democratization of Britain. The administrative and judicial duties and powers wielded for centuries by appointed justices of the peace — as well as powers involving health and highways for which ad hoc local authorities had been set up earlier in the century — were now taken over by elected bodies. Women, if unmarried and otherwise eligible, were given the right to vote for both county and borough councillors. The act was particularly significant for London, which was created as a separate county (including both the original small borough of London and the many neighboring boroughs that by 1888 constituted a metropolitan area of over three million people). This democratization of local government undercut still further the squirarchical tradition of England's rural areas, although habits of deference tended to last longer than the economic and political institutions that had given rise to them.[6] Although analogous to American political life, such democratization differed significantly with prevailing continental practice, both in republican France and in imperial Germany.

The operation of the County Councils Act was not to be extended to Ireland until 1898. In the meantime a new period of unrest had begun. Renewed evictions in Ireland in 1886 had been followed by a radical Irish Plan of Campaign, which urged Irish tenants to unite in defiance of their landlords and to pay only those rents they considered fair. The number of evictions increased, and violence was more widespread than at any time since 1882. The new chief secretary for Ireland, Salisbury's nephew, Arthur Balfour (1848–1930), forced through Parliament a drastic new Crimes Act. Although Balfour attempted to be fair in his dealings with landlords and tenants, his prime goal was to end disorder. In this he

---

[6]Salisbury's pragmatic conservatism is the subject of Peter Marsh's revealing book, *The Discipline of Popular Government: Lord Salisbury's Domestic Statecraft, 1881–1902* (1978). Two major new biographies, Andrew Roberts's *Salisbury: Victorian Titan* (1999) and David Steele's *Salisbury: A Political Biography* (1999), also credit the late-Victorian prime minister with enormous skill in attracting a democratic electorate to conservatism. By contrast, Richard Shannon, *The Age of Salisbury, 1881–1902* (1996), contends that Conservative political successes took place in spite of, rather than because of, Salisbury's leadership.

had considerable success, but his rule gained him the hatred of many of the Irish.

The year 1889 brought a break in the clouds for Gladstone and Parnell. Twenty-four months earlier, at the very time that Balfour had been piloting his Crimes Act through the House of Commons, a series of articles had appeared in the *Times* entitled "Parnellism and Crime." One of these articles included a facsimile letter, apparently written by Parnell a few days after the Phoenix Park murders of 1882, condoning those crimes. Parnell at once denounced the document as a forgery, but because he failed to bring suit, he was not generally believed. When other so-called secret letters were produced in 1888, Parnell asked for an independent investigation, and the government acceded to the appointment of a special commission of three judges. The commission investigated the matter in some detail and questioned at length one Richard Pigott, an Irish journalist, who, through an intermediary, had sold the letters to the *Times.* In the witness box, Pigott broke down and admitted that he himself had forged the letters. He fled to Spain, posted a full confession, and, before he could be arrested in Madrid, committed suicide. The revelation was a sensation; and Parnell, for so long a villain in the English press, suddenly became the underdog hero, the victim of deceit and trickery. Keeping in mind the unpopularity of Balfour's rule in Ireland and the government's steady loss of seats at by-elections, there can be little doubt that a general election late in 1889 or early in 1890 would have resulted in a decisive pro–Home Rule majority.

But the Irish question was not to be solved so easily; as usual it was dogged with bad luck, tragedy, and the quirks of individual personalities. Before 1890 had ended, a Captain William O'Shea had won a divorce suit against his wife, Katherine, in which Parnell was named as co-respondent. There was no defense; Parnell, it seemed, had for ten years deceived O'Shea by living illegally with his wife. The revelation came as a terrible shock to Nonconformist sentiment in England, and Parnell was in due course denounced by the Roman Catholic clergy of Ireland as well. The true story of the affair makes Parnell seem as much victim as villain. Mrs. O'Shea had lived apart from her husband for many years before she met Parnell, but she had kept up the pretense of the married state to please her wealthy great-aunt who was her (and O'Shea's) main source of financial support. Thus there had been no divorce and no remarriage, and for ten years Parnell and Kitty O'Shea had for practical purposes lived as man and wife (with O'Shea's full knowledge) and had had three children. This unusual arrangement lasted as long as the great-aunt lived. When she died in 1889 at the age of ninety-seven, O'Shea offered his wife a private divorce for £20,000; only when she could not produce the money (because the will was being contested) did O'Shea sue for a public divorce and name Parnell as his wife's lover.

Whatever judgment may be passed on Parnell's private life, it was clearly in the public interest of his party that he should retire, at least for the time being, from its leadership. This he refused to do, and when

Gladstone indicated that he could not continue the Irish-Liberal alliance in such circumstances, the Parnellites split. A majority backed Gladstone, but Parnell fought stubbornly on, bitingly denouncing his erstwhile allies while contesting by-election seats. Anti-Parnell Home Rulers now battled (and defeated) pro-Parnell Home Rulers. Not a robust man to begin with, Parnell wore himself out and died in October 1891, less than a year after the divorce case judgment. Parnell left a troubled heritage to his erstwhile political followers, but his memory inspired the generation of poets, novelists, and playwrights who constituted the Irish cultural revival of the 1890s and the early twentieth century. On the day of Parnell's death, William Butler Yeats (1865–1939) wrote:[7]

> Mourn — and then onward, there is no returning
> He guides ye from the tomb;
> His memory now is a tall pillar, burning
> Before us in the gloom!

The Second Home Rule Bill

The Liberal party, shorn of most of its Whig landlords and of its Birmingham Radicals and apparently permanently allied with the Irish nationalists, had become more than ever the party of "the Celtic Fringe." At Newcastle in 1891, it embraced a radical program including Church disestablishment in Wales and Scotland, local veto on liquor sales, the end of the few remaining plural franchises, and extensive land-law reform. Many of these proposals were in line with earlier Liberal traditions, although a new if vague promise to limit legally the hours of labor for adult workingmen was not.

The Liberals, with their controversial and faintly welfare-state creed, in alliance with their Irish Nationalist allies, won a majority in the general election in 1892. The results (Liberals, 273; Irish Home Rulers, 81; Conservatives, 269; Liberal Unionists, 46; Independent Labourite, 1) were not overwhelming and not nearly so favorable as they might have been before the Parnell divorce case, but they were sufficient to make William Ewart Gladstone prime minister for the fourth time at the age of eighty-two.

This time Gladstone actually pushed a Home Rule bill through the House of Commons. Unlike the 1886 proposal, this measure was accepted by the Commons not merely as a principle but as an involved scheme of government, of which each clause had been debated in detail. The bill was in most respects similar to that of 1886, except that it called for some Irish M.P.'s to be retained at Westminster for the purpose of vot-

---

[7]Reprinted with the permission of Scribner, a Division of Simon & Schuster from *The Collected Poems of W. B. Yeats, Revised Second Edition*, edited by Richard J. Finneran. Copyright © 1957 by Macmillan Publishing Company.

William Ewart Gladstone Introduces the Second Home Rule Bill into the House of Commons (1893)   *(Hulton Deutsch Collection)*

ing on matters of Irish or imperial concern. Although beset by increasing blindness and deafness, Gladstone still retained his keen mind and his passionate eloquence, and the final passage of the bill after eighty-five sittings was in every sense a personal triumph for him.

Yet it was a vain triumph, for the House of Lords (in which the Liberals since 1886 had been a small minority) rejected the measure, 419 to 41, after a scornfully brief debate. His colleagues did not wish to fight a general election on the issue of the House of Lords — largely because they were dubious of victory — and in March 1894, after a stinging lecture to the upper House warning it that its days were numbered, Gladstone retired from the prime ministership and soon afterward from the House of Commons in which he had sat for sixty-two years.

Gladstone's influence transcended his island home,[8] and not the least of his disciples was an American, Woodrow Wilson. Although Wilson's public career was to be much shorter, the two men resembled one another in their moral approach to politics, in their attitude toward international affairs, and in the antagonism they evoked in some of their fellow politicians. There is a close parallel also in the great disappointment that marked the close of their careers: Gladstone on Irish Home Rule, Wilson on American entry into the League of Nations, both battling vainly against what they could only look upon as the blindness of their people. For the defeat of the second Home Rule Bill had not resolved the Irish question; it had merely, Gladstone felt certain, postponed it. Critics felt

---

[8]Robert Kelley, *The Transatlantic Persuasion* (1969).

equally certain that the implantation of a federal system in the constitution of the United Kingdom would not work. We cannot be sure who was right, because the experiment was not tried.

Gladstone lived on for another four years. He even emerged from retirement in 1896 in his eighty-seventh year to denounce before a mass audience in Liverpool the massacre of Armenians in the Turkish Empire. He spoke with the same passionate eloquence with which he had opposed the Bulgarian massacres of the 1870s, Neapolitan misgovernment in the 1850s, and, for that matter, the Great Reform Bill back at Oxford in 1831.

Gladstone was a born parliamentarian and, although particular measures he sponsored and actions he took are as open to criticism as those of any other statesman, few now deny his role as the embodiment of Victorian morality and conscientious public service. Arthur Balfour, himself a future prime minister and long-time admiring opponent of the Grand Old Man, observed at the time of his death in 1898 that, of all the political leaders of the century, it had been Gladstone above all who had raised in the public estimation the whole level of British politics. He had helped to turn an aristocratic debating society into a national forum that wrestled with great moral questions, questions that were not limited to Ireland and Great Britain but that encompassed the entire world.

CHAPTER 10

The High Tide of Empire

Judging by its effect upon the British party structure and by the incredible number of hours of parliamentary time devoted to it, the single most important issue in late-Victorian British history was the Irish question, with all its various ramifications. As Prime Minister Salisbury complained in 1887, "Torn in two by a controversy which almost threatens her existence," England "cannot . . . interfere with any decisive action abroad." Yet curiously enough, it was during these same thirty years, when public attention was continually focused on the 32,000-square-mile island next door with its five million people, that Britain acquired as colonies or protectorates some 750,000 square miles with twenty million people in Asia and the South Pacific, and approximately 4,400,000 square miles with sixty million people in Africa![1]

The Causes of Imperialism

These sweeping additions to the existing empire, made up largely of Canada, Australia, New Zealand, and India, have caused some historians to speak of the lands acquired after 1870 as the third British Empire in contrast to the first (pre-1783) and the second (1783–1870). The mid-Victorian years had witnessed notable lack of public interest in imperial expansion. The eventual independence of the settlement colonies had been looked upon as inevitable; and although most Britons acknowledged the

---

[1]See Andrew Porter, ed., *The Oxford History of the British Empire: The Nineteenth Century* (1999). *The Empire-Commonwealth, 1870–1919* (1959), Vol. III of *The Cambridge History of the British Empire,* remains a classic account. Colin C. Eldridge, *Victorian Imperialism* (1978), summarizes the debates among historians on theories of empire-building and on motives. A. P. Thornton, *The Imperial Idea and Its Enemies* (1959), and Bernard Semmel, *Imperialism and Social Reform* (1960), provide revealing studies of imperial attitudes. C. J. Lowe, *The Reluctant Imperialists, 1870–1902* (1968), emphasizes diplomatic implications, and Margaret Strobel, *European Women and the Second British Empire* (1991), calls attention to both the passive and the active roles played by women in the colonial enterprise. In *Tools of Empire* (1981), Daniel R. Headrick provides a useful reminder of how steamships, rifles, and quinine made European expansion possible. Lance E. Davis and Robert Huttenback, *Mammon and the Pursuit of Empire: The Political Economy of British Imperialism, 1860–1912* (1986), constitutes the most comprehensive attempt to answer the difficult question of whether or not empire "paid."

value of India, they saw the encouragement of trade rather than the acquisition of territory as their prime purpose overseas. The most highly regarded colonial administrator was invariably the one who cost the home government the least money, required the fewest troops, and involved Britain in the smallest number of diplomatic entanglements. To a large degree, these attitudes persisted well into the 1880s. Disraeli's "forward" policy had resulted in the electoral rebuff of 1880; and although few British citizens of the day were literally "Little Englanders" who wished to end all of Britain's imperial ties, a majority were clearly consolidationists, rather than expansionists, and preferred to develop the empire that already existed rather than to acquire new responsibilities in Asia and Africa. As late as 1883, a British textbook on colonies took it for granted that "the policy of England discourages any increase of territory in tropical countries already occupied by native races."

Yet this attitude changed rapidly until for a time in the 1890s the leaders of both parties, Salisbury for the Conservatives and Rosebery (Gladstone's successor as prime minister) for the Liberals, had become expansionists in outlook. The traditional explanation for this so-called "new imperialism" is a trio of economic requirements: markets, raw materials, and areas in which surplus funds might be invested. Such a rationale for territorial aggrandizement on the part of the major European powers was first elaborated in 1902 by the British journalist and political theorist, John A. Hobson. Hobson's economic explanation, with special emphasis on the need of capitalists for investment opportunities overseas, was used by Vladimir Lenin in 1916 in his *Imperialism: The Highest Stage of Capitalism.* The industrialized capitalist nations, according to Lenin, had been able artificially to prolong their existence and stave off the economic collapse and the social revolution that Marx had predicted by investing surplus funds overseas and exploiting native labor.

The fact that Lenin became the founder of the revolutionary Soviet Union spread the influence of the so-called Hobson-Lenin thesis and helped persuade the leaders of Third World nations that private foreign investment must be synonymous with colonialism; but modern research has made clear its fallaciousness as an explanation for late-nineteenth-century imperialism. Although a few individuals made fortunes in underdeveloped areas, these lands usually lacked the necessary "social overhead facilities" — roads, railways, harbors, docks, dams, power plants, and schools — to secure a high return on the original investment. For most investors, such lands were too risky. Not surprisingly, then, British capitalists preferred to put money into advanced industrialized or semi-industrialized countries such as the United States, Germany, and Argentina, even though such lands were not part of the empire. Of that minority share of British capital that did go to the empire, more was invested before 1914 in Australia and New Zealand alone — with their tiny but hardly "exploited" populations — than in all of India and Africa put together.

This conclusion does not deny that particular British merchants, shippers, and even bankers sought and occasionally found profits in Africa. Yet the desire to amass wealth is a motive almost as old as man himself. Why, then, should merchants seek territorial and political domination in the late nineteenth century when earlier they had been satisfied with an "open door" for trading opportunities? One explanation is that, whereas in the middle years of the century the Great Powers seemed to be following the British lead in the direction of international free trade, by the 1880s this process had been completely reversed. The United States led the way with the protectionist Morrill Tariff of 1861. Germany and Austria-Hungary followed suit in the 1870s and France in 1892. In a world divided by rising tariff barriers, colonies began to regain some of the value they had possessed in an age of mercantilism. It came to be argued that Britain should occupy territories whose current commercial value was small if those territories might otherwise fall within the protective tariff sphere of another power. As the "great depression" ground on, such arguments were more and more often heard. When H. M. Stanley, the man who presumed to find David Livingstone, the great missionary-explorer, suggested to the British government in the 1870s that it undertake the economic development of the Congo, the government declined. By 1895, however, that attitude had altered. It *was* the government's business, declared Prime Minister Salisbury, "to make smooth the paths of British commerce . . . for the application of British capital, at a time when . . . other outlets for the commercial energies of our race are being gradually closed."

The levying of protective tariffs by the industrial powers of Europe and by the United States was but one aspect of a more fundamental political change that was instrumental in fostering the new imperialism — the emergence of the new and militant German Empire as economically and politically the most powerful nation on the continent. As a result of the Franco-Prussian War, the balance of power in Europe had been decisively altered and Britain's relative position seriously weakened. Germany's fear of French revenge after 1871 had led to the development on the part of Bismarck of a series of alliances with Austria-Hungary and with the newly united Italian kingdom, as well as the Three Emperors' League that tied Germany to Russia and Austria. Although Anglo-German relations remained for the most part friendly, Britain (like France) was isolated from the continental network of alliances. International relations on the continent were becoming fixed in a relatively rigid pattern, a state of affairs that helps to explain the new quest for colonies on the part of the major powers. The only areas that remained for diplomatic maneuver were now outside Europe, and France, Italy, Russia, and Germany all turned their eyes to Africa or Asia. But in each case the mainspring of their imperial expansion rested in Europe. "My map of Africa," Bismarck explained in 1888, "lies in Europe. Here is Russia and here lies France. That is my map of Africa." In other words, many leaders of the major powers judged the "scramble for Africa" on the basis of whether it aided or injured their relative strategic and political position in Europe. Such diplomatic considerations played at least as significant a role in bringing on the new imperialism as did specific economic interests.

Once the scramble for Africa had started in the early 1880s, the surprise is that, though it caused occasional war scares, it did not lead to a general war between the Great Powers. The map of the Dark Continent was painted a hodgepodge of bright imperial colors within little more than a decade; yet the powers generally abided by the ground rules for African aggrandizement laid down at the Conference of Berlin in 1884–1885.[2]

Although the thoughts of statesmen may have been largely on the European balance of power, a host of other motives inspired individual imperialists. Not the least of these was that of "civilizing" the native races. The Anglican Church Missionary Society had been active in Africa since the beginning of the century, and most Nonconformist denominations had established their missions as well. It was missionaries such as Livingstone who had long been urging that it was the white man's duty to bring civilization and Christianity to Africa. They discovered to their horror in the 1850s that, while British example and the British naval patrol had virtually ended the slave trade in West Africa, this iniquitous practice still flourished in East Africa. There the sultan of Zanzibar protected the Arab vendors of human flesh who dominated the East African coastal trade. It was as a result of British pressure that the sultan reluctantly restricted the East African slave trade, which ended altogether in 1876. But slavery remained, and it was not until shocked public opinion and missionary zeal pressured the British government into establishing a protectorate over Zanzibar in 1895 that the institution of slavery was finally abolished there. Only at the Brussels Conference of 1889–1890 did the other powers grant the British navy the authority to stamp out the slave trade in the Red Sea and the Indian Ocean, and only European administration caused slavery itself largely to disappear in the interior of Africa.[3]

Although H. M. Stanley once estimated that if Christianity were able to teach the natives of the Congo no more than to cover their nakedness with a single Sunday-go-to-meeting dress apiece, this alone would create a market for "320,000,000 yards of Manchester cotton cloth," missionary pressure alone was rarely sufficient to bring direct government intervention. When the state did intervene, however, the missionaries were a significant humanitarian group reminding the British government that native peoples deserved protection, that they should not be exploited through forced labor, that they should be considered as equal before the

---

[2]No power was to declare a new protectorate without giving due notice to the others or without making some pretense of occupying the area. Disputes were to be settled by arbitration. The subject is explored in Thomas Pakenham, *The Scramble for Africa, 1876–1912* (1991), as well as in Vol. VI (1985) of the *Cambridge History of Africa* and in Ronald Robinson et al., *Africa and the Victorians* (1961).

[3]Suzanne Miers, *Britain and the Ending of the Slave Trade* (1975).

law, and that whenever possible their customary forms of landholding and tribal government (although not of religion) should be preserved.

Most Britons took for granted that Europeans in general and Anglo-Saxons in particular had evolved further in the direction of civilization than had people of all other colors. That widespread sense of racial superiority could give rise to both arrogance and cruelty and was often to earn the white man the hatred of those not "blessed" with the same color of skin.[4] Yet, as Rudyard Kipling suggested in "The White Man's Burden" (1899), the conviction that such superiority involved an obligation as well as an advantage motivated thousands of Britons to toil and suffer in remote parts of the earth:

> Take up the White Man's burden —
>   Send forth the best ye breed —
> Go bind your sons to exile
>   To serve your captives' need;
> To wait in heavy harness,
>   On fluttered folk and wild —
> Your new-caught, sullen peoples,
>   Half-devil and half-child.

Although in the early twenty-first century old-style imperialism or colonialism may be condemned outright, it is important to understand that the late-nineteenth-century imperialistic spirit included a considerable element of Peace Corps–style idealism.

Still another component of late-nineteenth-century imperialism was its popularity with the newly enfranchised masses; at least one historian has maintained that the electorate that emerged from the Reform Bills of 1867 and 1884 was less inclined to take a penny-pinching attitude toward colonies than the industrious middle-class voter of the previous generation. The high tide of imperialism coincided with the rise of the popular press, and the daily papers often made imperialism a romantic subject. It was, after all, a newspaper that sponsored Stanley's hunt for Livingstone. The empire-building urge was inspired also by the works of H. Rider Haggard (*King Solomon's Mines*, for example), Kipling's tales of India, and the ninety novels addressed by G. A. Henty to the youthful English reader. Henty's hero was almost invariably a typical product of England's public schools:

> a good specimen of the class by which Britain has been built up, her colonies formed, and her battlefields won — a class in point of energy, fearlessness, the spirit of adventure, and a readiness to face and overcome all difficulties, unmatched in the world.

---

[4]The "new orthodoxy" of feminist and anticolonialist writings has been assessed in Elazar Barkan, "Post-Anti-Colonial Histories: Representing the Other in Imperial Britain," *Journal of British Studies* (April 1994). At the same time, Paul Crook has undermined the belief in the influence of Social Darwinism or "biological determinism" on empire building. See "Historical Monkey Business: The Myth of a Darwinized British Imperial Discourse," *History* (Oct. 1999).

Writings such as these helped to mold the popular attitude toward the glories of empire "played out against a gaudy backdrop of tropical forests, and great sluggish rivers, and empty plains, and sand, and terrible mountain passes."[5]

Clearly a great many late-Victorian Britons took a vicarious satisfaction in painting the map red, even if they had no personal wealth to gain thereby and even if the particular aim achieved — such as planting a flag in the middle of the Sahara Desert — was of no conceivable economic value to anyone. Still it would be dangerous to overstress the point. Imperialism might win elections; but to the despair of politicians, the public proved all too fickle, and imperialism might equally well lose elections, as it did in 1880 and was again to do in 1906.

Imperialism in Action

Although the conquest of nonwhite peoples implied an element of paternalism as well as the use of force, it did not at first involve any attempt to build up systems of self-government along the lines employed in the older settlement colonies. Even when British rule — whether direct or indirect — was paternalistic, it also tended to be despotic. An appropriate example is Egypt, where a khedive, his Egyptian ministers, and a legislature constituted the visible government. More important than any of them, however, was Sir Evelyn Baring (later Lord Cromer, 1841–1917), who served as British consul-general and high commissioner from 1883 to 1907. It was Cromer who insisted on such Western notions as balancing the budget, who encouraged the building of the first Aswan Dam, and who battled against "the three C's — the Courbash, the Corvee, and Corruption." The *courbash,* the strip of hippopotamus hide with which peasants had been flogged for millennia in order to make them work, was outlawed. The *corvee,* the unpaid compulsory labor by which peasants were forced to clear the mud from the irrigation canals, was largely replaced by a system of wages and free labor. Cromer did not claim to have eliminated the third C, *corruption,* altogether, but he felt sure that it "was greatly diminished."

There is little doubt that Cromer's rule marked a kind of golden age for the Egyptian peasant. Benevolence did not, however, make the British popular. They could be arrogant; they could be unjust; they were foreigners both in culture and religion, and their continued presence eventually excited among the former ruling classes a strong spirit of nationalism. Moreover, the advantages of economic progress were largely counterbalanced by a rapid growth of population, which doubled between 1882 and 1922.

---

[5]D. G. Creighton, "The Victorian and the Empire," *The Making of English History,* ed. by Robert L. Schuyler and Herman Ausubel (1950).

It is important to note, however, that both in Egypt and in many other regions of the empire, British rule rested less on periodic displays of force than on the widespread acquiescence of the native population. Leonard Woolf (1880–1969), later to become a noted writer and professed anti-imperialist, recalled his youthful tenure in the British civil service in Ceylon (as Sri Lanka was then known):

> Ceylon in 1906 was the exact opposite of a "police state." There were very few police and outside Columbo and Kandy not a single soldier. From the point of law and order nothing could have been more danger- ously precarious than the Pearl Fishery camp, a temporary town of 30,000 or 40,000 men many of whom were habitual criminals . . . but we four civil servants never even thought about the possibility of our not be- ing able to maintain law and order. And we were quite right.[6]

In both Ceylon and India, the British raj was looked upon almost in fam- ily terms: the English civil administrator was regarded as a father who might behave unaccountably but who was disinterested and not lining his pockets by commercial speculations. As Woolf confirms, the typical British civil servant regarded local businessmen as social inferiors and would not even admit them to his clubs.

Paradoxically, during the very years in which the British Empire was growing to its largest size and being bound more closely by the wonders of technology — ocean liners, railways, and the telegraph — a process be- gun earlier of loosening the ties of empire was proceeding apace. Respon- sible government had been granted to most of the Canadian and Aus- tralian provinces and New Zealand in the 1850s and to Cape Colony in 1872. Although permanent British army garrisons had been withdrawn from Canada and Australia by 1871, all of the settlement colonies re- mained conscious of their dependence on the Royal Navy, and in 1887 some of the Australian states agreed to pay a small annual subsidy to help support the imperial fleet in Australian waters. It was the potential threat of Germany (which occupied part of New Guinea in 1884) as well as a growing awareness of the advantages of dealing in common with such questions as intra-Australian tariff barriers and immigration policy that led the autonomous Australian states to emulate Canada and form a federal Dominion of Australia in 1900. The proposed constitution, an amalgam of the British form of cabinet responsibility and the American form of two-chamber federalism, was prepared by a constitutional con- vention of Australians but made operative by act of Parliament at West- minster. Although theoretically the Parliament in Westminster might still legislate for the dominions, in practice this power had fallen into disuse. "Influence and advice" remained, as did the Judicial Committee of the Privy Council, which since its reform in the 1830s had served as a supreme court for British subjects throughout the empire. Yet even in

---

[6]Leonard Woolf, *Growing: An Autobiography of the Years 1904–1911* (1962).

foreign affairs, dominion governments now expected representation on British delegations negotiating commercial treaties affecting their interests. The dominions "already stand to us," observed one Liberal M.P., "in the virtual relation of friendly allied states speaking our tongue."

The same years that saw a continued growth in the self-governing dominions also witnessed the first stirrings of nationalist revolt in India and the beginnings of Western-style representative institutions in that land. In the wake of the Sepoy Mutiny of 1857, the Indian Civil Service, although not antagonistic to economic growth, had become in some ways less liberal and reform-minded. The vast majority of Indians remained agricultural villagers, but a sizable commercial class was growing in the late nineteenth century, and certain Indian industries during the 1880s were aided by a 10 to 15 percent tariff. By 1914 India could boast one of the world's five largest cotton textile industries, one of the two largest jute industries, the third largest railway network, and a sizable coal-mining industry. Foreign trade figures went up accordingly:

Year	Exports (in millions of pounds)	Imports (in millions of pounds)
1834	8	4.5
1870	53	33.5
1910	137	86.0

Commercial and agricultural expansion was accompanied by a comparable growth of population, which rose from 100 million in 1700 to 150 million in 1850 to 283 million in 1901. Despite a runaway population and the fact that occasional famines took millions of lives, India probably did experience a period of genuine economic improvement in the nineteenth century. Agricultural output per man-hour and per acre were both up, and — keeping in mind that millions of Indians lived at a point barely above subsistence level — the average standard of living may have increased slightly as well.

The Indian Civil Service continued to be highly efficient and merited its reputation for incorruptibility. Public protestations notwithstanding, the upper branches of that service remained almost totally closed to native Indians; and, although an act of 1861 provided the bare beginnings of advisory legislative councils for provincial governors, the theme of British rule continued to be one of benevolent despotism. In the early 1880s Lord Ripon, the British viceroy nominated by Gladstone, initiated a program of local elective bodies, not so much to improve the administration as to provide "a measure of political and popular education." In 1892, Indian representation in the provincial councils was expanded.

By 1892 some Indians had come to conclude, however, that they had far too small a role in the government of their own nation. The word *nation* is instructive because India, although a civilization and at various times an *empire*, became a nation — to the extent that it did so — only as a consequence of British rule. The Indian nationalism exemplified after 1885 by the annual meetings of the Indian National Congress was essentially, and ironically, a product of the British raj. It was the British who brought political unification and a common language for the increasing number of educated Indians. Indian nationalism necessarily was fostered by cheap postage rates, printing presses, and the railway that facilitated national assemblies. The nationalist leaders were members of a small but growing class of lawyers, businessmen, and teachers, many of whom found inspiration in the writings of John Locke and Thomas Jefferson and in the lives of Mazzini of Italy, Kossuth of Hungary, and Parnell of Ireland. Most early Indian nationalists, although irritated by the arrogance and sense of racial superiority manifested by the British in India, were advocates of liberal parliamentary methods; only slowly, in the face of specific insults, did they come to realize that they would have to unite as a militant, Western-style pressure group in order to gain recognition. One such affront was a change in the rules for the Indian Civil Service examinations in 1877 that made Indian candidates even less likely to be appointed. Another was the largely successful protest by the English in India against a bill in 1883 that would have made it possible for Europeans to be tried before Indian judges.

Not all Indian nationalists were Western-oriented, for in the late nineteenth century there was a widespread revival of Hindu religious thought.

> Once more [said the Swami Vivekanada in 1897] the world must be conquered by India. This is the great ideal before us. Let them come and flood the land with their armies, never mind. Up, India, and conquer the world with your spirituality! Spirituality must conquer the West. Where are the men ready to go out to every country of the world with the messages of the great sages of India?

Although such Indian spirituality was to find a greater welcome in the West in the 1960s than in the 1890s, the apostles of this Hindu renaissance gave Indian nationalism a heightened fervor and emotional strength. It had another effect as well: it increasingly caused Indian Moslems to desert the National Congress. The followers of Mohammed feared that if India attained autonomy under outspoken Hindu auspices, they might become a maligned minority; the result was the establishment by 1906 of a separate Moslem League as a rival to the Indian National Congress. Thus were laid the foundations of the division that in 1947 led to the partition of the subcontinent into secular (but largely Hindu) India and Moslem Pakistan.

Although the late nineteenth century saw the beginnings of Indian nationalism and of representative government on the local level, India remained in the minds of most English people the most precious jewel of the British Empire, one constantly growing in value and luster. The autonomous Indian princely states were no longer subject to annexation, but adjacent areas still were. The northwest frontier was secured by the Afghan War of 1879, and Baluchistan was annexed. Farther east, the greater part of Burma was added to the coastal areas already under British rule and was henceforth governed as part of British India. In the judgment of Lord Curzon, India's diligent viceroy from 1898 to 1905, the British Empire remained "the greatest instrument for good the world has ever seen."[7]

The high tide of late-Victorian imperialism can be discussed in terms of impersonal forces, yet it must always be recalled that the initiative in both economic and political expansion was taken by individuals who were on the scene — men such as Sir George Goldie (1846–1925) in West Africa, Sir Harry Johnston (1858–1927) in East Africa, and preeminently by Cecil John Rhodes (1853–1902) in South Africa. No person managed more successfully than Rhodes to combine the down-to-earth practicality and the starry-eyed idealism that constituted the late-nineteenth-century imperialistic spirit. He was the younger son of an Anglican clergyman and came to South Africa from England in 1870 for reasons of health. Apparently the climate was satisfactory, for he thrived both physically and economically. Diamonds were first discovered in South Africa in 1870; Rhodes proved to be a shrewd businessman who, by buying up the claims of discouraged miners whose capital had been exhausted, succeeded by 1886 in making himself director of a ten-million-dollar mining company paying dividends of 25 percent a year. By 1888 he monopolized 90 percent of the world's diamond output. Then he went into the gold-mining business in the Transvaal with similar success. By 1890, he had an income of five million dollars a year. (In order to translate that figure into the relative values of a century later, multiply by at least fifty.)

Rhodes was always interested in far more than money. In a document he wrote when only twenty-four years of age, he declared it to be his life's purpose to work "for the furtherance of the British Empire, for the bringing of the whole civilized world under British rule, for the recovery of the United States, for the making of the Anglo-Saxon race into an empire." By 1890 he had the wealth to make at least a part of that dream a reality. He entered politics and became the prime minister of Cape Colony, one of the two South African lands in British possession, although even there a majority of the white population consisted of Boers rather than Britons. To the north lay the two Boer republics, Transvaal and the Orange Free State, again virtually independent since 1881, although Britain continued to claim a vague and disputed suzerainty. Beyond lay a vast area, still largely unexplored, in which Portuguese, Germans, and others seemed to

---

[7]See David Gilmour, *Curzon* (1994).

be dangerously interested. Rhodes's ultimate dream was to bring under British control a strip of territory extending all the way from South Africa to Egypt, so that a Cape-to-Cairo railway might be built. Rhodes was influential in having Britain in 1885 declare a protectorate over Bechuanaland. He then inspired the creation of the South Africa Company to explore and develop the area beyond. It was this company that, on the basis of a very dubious treaty made with a local native chieftain, began the development and settlement of the lands that until 1980 were to be known as Rhodesia (and today as Zimbabwe, Zambia, and Malawi).

Rhodes's plans did not always meet with the full backing of the government in London. Gladstone, whose fourth ministry had been dominated by his unsuccessful attempt to extend Home Rule to Ireland, never became converted to the exuberant empire building of the 1890s. "There is a wild and irrational spirit abroad," he lamented. Lord Rosebery, his successor as Liberal prime minister, was, however, a professed imperialist. His brief ministry (1894–1895) is best remembered, to be sure, not for its exploits abroad or at home but for the fact that the prime minister's horse won the Derby two years in succession. The feat did not endear Rosebery to a Nonconformist Liberal electorate that frowned on both horse racing and gambling.

The Role of Joseph Chamberlain

The general election of 1895 brought back into power a strong coalition of Conservatives and Liberal Unionists. The Liberal Unionists by this time had become almost completely swallowed up by the Conservatives, although the alliance tended to use the word *Unionist*, and the term *Conservative* fell into disfavor for two decades. This amalgamation was symbolized by the entry of Joseph Chamberlain, the ex-Radical, into Salisbury's cabinet as colonial secretary. Imperialism was the cry of the hour, and the new secretary became one of its staunchest champions. The British, he had become convinced, were "the greatest of the governing races the world has ever seen" and were "predestined" by their defects as well as their virtues "to spread over the habitable globe." To critics who accused him of forsaking his earlier cause of social reform, Chamberlain replied that only a strong empire could provide prosperity for the working people back home.

In the new colonial secretary, the empire builders in Africa found a statesman who not only approved of their projects but also advocated that the government directly promote colonial development by building railways and ports, setting up schools of tropical agriculture and medicine, guaranteeing loans, and stimulating capital investment in every corner of the empire. Chamberlain immediately speeded plans to acquire Uganda as a protectorate. All that this territory in east-central Africa needed, he said, was what his own city of Birmingham already had — "an

Joseph Chamberlain (1836–1914)   The municipal reformer and political radical became the most ardent prophet of empire. *(Reproduced by courtesy of the Trustees of the British Museum)*

improvement scheme." Late in 1895, however, both Rhodes and Chamberlain found their plans for African expansion thwarted by some stubborn Dutchmen, the Boers of the Orange Free State and the Transvaal.

The struggle for South African supremacy was in a sense the result of geological accident; the Boers, by occupation conservative patriarchal farmers, in their flight from British control happened to settle on the Rand, the site of some of the richest gold and diamond deposits in the world. From the 1880s on, miners from all over the world swarmed into the Transvaal and soon made Johannesburg one of the world's great boom towns. There many of the newcomers prospered.[8] Their taxes helped to transform the Transvaal from a poverty-stricken, backward farming state into a rich and growing community. On one subject, however, the Boers under President Paul Kruger were adamant: they would admit the *Uitlanders* ("foreigners"), they would tax them, but they would not grant them rights of citizenship. Increasingly, the Uitlanders complained, and by 1894–1895 a revolt was brewing. Cecil Rhodes encouraged it, and his lieutenant, Dr. Leander Starr Jameson, prepared a force of soldiers in the employ of the South Africa Company to be ready to march to the assis-

---

[8]See Geoffrey Wheatcroft, *The Randlords: The Men Who Made South Africa* (1985).

tance of the Johannesburg revolutionaries. Plans went awry and the revolt collapsed; but late in December 1895 Jameson marched anyway, only to have his tiny band defeated and captured by the Boers.

Although the British government immediately denied any responsibility for the raid, it appeared to the world as a gross violation of international law by Britain. Chamberlain, who was certainly aware of Jameson's plans beforehand, escaped immediate censure; but Cecil Rhodes was forced to resign as prime minister of Cape Colony. He had affronted the Boers, and they continued to be a highly important segment of the white population of Cape Colony as well as the dominant group in the Transvaal. The Jameson Raid also had international repercussions. It emphasized anew Britain's diplomatic isolation in the world at large.

In the decade before the Jameson Raid, Great Britain had looked to Germany for friendship. With the French alienated by the British occupation of Egypt and with the Russians continuing their pressure in the Near East and on the Indian frontier, Britain had naturally drifted closer to the Triple Alliance of Germany, Austria-Hungary, and Italy. Salisbury's secret Mediterranean Agreement in 1887 with Austria and Italy constituted a virtual *entente* with the Triple Alliance; and the treaty of 1890, in which the British granted to Germany the small but strategic island of Heligoland in the North Sea in exchange for German concessions in East Africa, was seen as solid proof of Anglo-German friendship. After the dismissal of Bismarck in 1890, however, Germany was governed by men increasingly eager to demonstrate in the colonial and military arena that Germany had indeed become the "great power" heralded by its population and industrial might. Nothing showed the ebbing of Anglo-German understanding more clearly or evoked so strong a sense of resentment in England as the telegram that the German emperor, William II, sent to President Kruger after the collapse of the Jameson Raid. He congratulated Kruger on having preserved the independence of his country "without appealing to the help of friendly powers." The implication seemed clear: Germany was prepared to go to war against Britain in South Africa.

Inasmuch as the embarrassment of the Jameson Raid coincided with an acrimonious dispute between Britain and the United States over the boundary between Venezuela and British Guiana, Britain did seem, for the moment at least, to be diplomatically isolated. So it was all the more desirable, thought Joseph Chamberlain, to emphasize the ties of empire. This was done in 1897 with the Diamond Jubilee, the imperial celebration of the sixtieth anniversary of Queen Victoria's accession to the throne. From all over the world came the prime ministers, sultans, and chieftains — black, white, and yellow — to pay homage to the Great White Queen. A similar celebration, the Golden Jubilee, had taken place a decade before, but the Diamond Jubilee, at once romantic and bellicose, was if anything even less restrained. Chamberlain hoped to utilize the jubilee to take the first steps toward imperial federation, a joint customs union and defense union of the colonies that would ultimately be followed by the creation of an imperial parliament. Few of the colonial leaders were interested, and as long as Britain adhered to a policy of free trade, it was impossible to create any practical plan of imperial tariff preference. Chamberlain had to be satisfied with a poor substitute: the meeting at intervals of the various colonial prime ministers. Out of these gatherings evolved one institution of the old empire that has endured into the twenty-first century — the regular meetings of the Commonwealth prime ministers.

In the meantime Chamberlain committed his government to military expansion in two parts of Africa. British troops were sent into northern Nigeria, where they defeated the Ashanti warriors, freed the land from the slave trade, and made it safe for commerce. Several thousand miles to the east, the British commander of the Egyptian army, Sir Herbert Kitchener, was encouraged to reverse Gladstone's policy and reenter the Sudan, an area long claimed by Egypt. There General Gordon had been killed a decade before, and there the Mahdi's successor and his dervishes still held sway. Kitchener's force slowly made its way southward along the Nile valley, building a railway as it went. At Omdurman, Kitchener's Anglo-Egyptian army of 20,000 men met a dervish army almost three times its size. Modern artillery and rifle fire, supplemented by one of military history's last great cavalry charges — in which a young subaltern named Winston Churchill took part — overwhelmed the dervishes, who had more spears than rifles. Kitchener's army went on to reoccupy Khartoum and thereby to avenge Gordon. Still farther upstream the British encountered a small French-Sudanese force under Colonel Jean-Baptiste Marchand, which had made an extraordinary three-thousand-mile journey through trackless jungles, endless deserts, and brackish swamps to plant the French tricolor at Fashoda. Imperial emotions were so highly charged that for several months it appeared likely that the Fashoda affair would lead to war between France and Britain. But eventually France conceded the British claims to the Sudan, claims that Britain technically shared with Egypt; both the Union Jack and the Egyptian flag were raised. In return Britain acknowledged all French claims to the Sahara and other disputed parts of equatorial Africa.

The Boer War

Kitchener's triumph at Khartoum brought the Cape-to-Cairo railway another step closer, but the Boers still refused to acknowledge the "manifest destiny" of English imperialism in Africa. Britons and Boers were in a state of cold war. The Boers began to arm feverishly, and after his triumphant reelection as president of the Transvaal in 1898, President Kruger assumed dictatorial powers that ended any possibility of a peaceful compromise between the Uitlanders and the Boers. "There is no way out of the political troubles of South Africa except reform in the Transvaal or war," wrote Sir Alfred Milner (1854–1925), the new British high commissioner in South Africa. And reform, he went on, did not seem to be in the

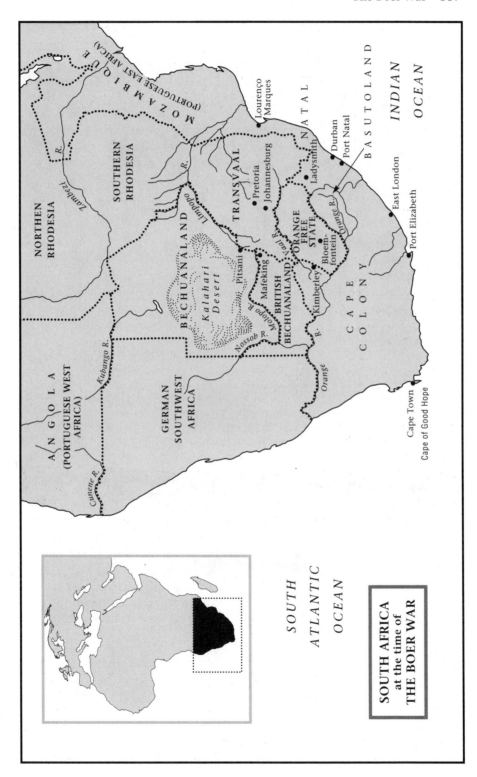

SOUTH AFRICA
at the time of
THE BOER WAR

A Boer War Battle   Under Boer fire, a British cavalry force crosses the Tugela River in February 1900 in order to relieve the besieged city of Ladysmith. *(Bettmann/Corbis)*

offing; British citizens in the Transvaal were being treated like helots. After the murder of an English laborer, twenty thousand Uitlanders petitioned the British government for help. Although an excellent administrator, Milner had little faith in the ultimately fruitless diplomatic negotiations he carried on about possible reforms in the Transvaal. The step that finally resulted in war was not, however, a British ultimatum to the Boers but a Boer demand in October 1899 that the British withdraw their troops and stop interfering in Transvaal domestic affairs. The British rejected the ultimatum, and war began.[9]

The European world looked upon the Boer War as a fight between a pygmy (Kruger's Transvaal and the neighboring Orange Free State) and an imperial giant. Yet the war was more than a defensive one for the Boers. Kruger himself clearly sought to lead a united South Africa under native Dutch auspices and throw the British out altogether. In England, the war made good copy, for much of the expanded newspaper-reading public was in a jingoistic mood.

The first months of the war did not, however, follow the path to imperial glory expected by the readers of the yellow press. The Boers invaded Cape Colony and Natal, inflicted ignominious defeats on the British, and besieged the towns of Kimberley, Ladysmith, and Mafeking.

---

[9]Thomas Pakenham, *The Boer War* (1979), deals with all aspects of the conflict. Byron Farwell, *The Great Anglo-Boer War* (1976), focuses on the military campaigns.

These initial victories should not have surprised anybody, because the Boer army was twice the size of the British force on hand and because it possessed excellent German-made rifles and machine guns.

Back in England, public opinion quickly began to sober. Calls for volunteers received a ready response, and the other self-governing colonies offered contingents of troops. They saw the Boer War as an example of the mother country's championship of overseas nationals and responded accordingly. By late winter in 1900 the tide of war had turned. Ladysmith and Kimberley had been relieved, and General Frederick Roberts had begun an invasion of the Orange Free State and the Transvaal. On May 31 Roberts' forces triumphantly entered Johannesburg; five days later they occupied Pretoria, the Transvaal capital, and freed 3,000 British prisoners of war. President Kruger fled into exile. In the meantime, the relief of Mafeking, which had been heroically defended for 217 days by a force under Colonel Robert Baden-Powell, led to wild rejoicing in London. The result was both a new word in the language — *mafficking* (meaning "to celebrate boisterously") — and the inspiration for the subsequent British and later worldwide Boy Scout movement.

The war seemed to be over. The Orange Free State and then the Transvaal were formally annexed by Britain, and in November Lord Salisbury's Conservative government and its imperialistic policies received a strong endorsement in the so-called Khaki election. The Liberal party had been split by the war into Liberal Imperialists (such as Rosebery, Herbert Asquith, and Sir Edward Grey), who supported the conflict, and pro-Boers (such as John Morley and the youthful David Lloyd George), who regarded it as morally insupportable. Not long after the general election and after General Roberts and many of the British had sailed for home, it became clear that the war was not in fact over at all. Small Boer contingents kept up a guerrilla war for another year and a half. Only by systematically denuding parts of the country of its farms and livestock and by gathering more than 100,000 of the non-combatants into "concentration camps" did Kitchener, who had succeeded Roberts, finally bring the war to an end with the Peace of Vereeniging of May 1902.

By then the spirit of complacent self-righteousness and romantic glory with which the imperialism of the 1890s had imbued some Englishmen had passed its crest. The Boer War had been too bloody, too costly, and too cruel; 6,000 British troops had died in battle, 16,000 more perished of wounds and disease, and 23,000 had been wounded. Seven thousand Boers had died in battle, and perhaps 20,000 more had succumbed to disease in the camps; more than 10,000 black Africans — laborers, drivers, guides, and servants — had also fallen victim. The use of concentration camps, denounced in the House of Commons as "methods of barbarism" by Sir Henry Campbell-Bannerman, the new Liberal leader, prompted a mood of self-questioning in Britain. The Transvaal and the Orange Free State were indeed annexed to the empire, but the high tide of imperialistic enthusiasm proved in some respects an aberration that did not permanently halt the evolution of empire into commonwealth, the voluntary association of self-governing states anticipated by Victorian Liberals earlier in the century.

By then, too, Queen Victoria was dead. In her old age she had grown to welcome the public occasions she had long avoided. Although she was revered more as a symbol than as an active component of the British constitution, she had not lost all political power. As late as 1892 she successfully vetoed one of Gladstone's choices for a cabinet post, and in 1894, faced with a choice of several plausible Liberals, she picked Rosebery as Gladstone's successor as prime minister. To the last she remained conscientiously dutiful, if not always wise. She took great pride in her country and her empire, and she supported the government staunchly in its conduct of the Boer War. During Christmas of 1900 she had gone as usual to her palace at Osborne on the Isle of Wight. There she celebrated the official advent of the twentieth century. Three weeks later, after a brief illness, she died in the presence of many members of her large family, including her eldest grandson, Emperor William II of Germany. Her reign of almost sixty-four years, the longest in British history, was over. "We feel," said A. J. Balfour, the Conservative leader of the House of Commons, "that the end of a great epoch has come upon us." In fact it had, for her death represented, symbolically at least, the conclusion of a century during which Great Britain's international prestige and influence had reached their zenith.

CHAPTER 11

Society and
Social Reform

At the same time that late-Victorian Britain was being shaken by the struggle for Irish nationalism and alternately exhilarated and dismayed by the expansion of empire, it was experiencing a number of other changes. There were technical changes in industry and communications, a less noticeable transformation in the social structure, and a gradual but significant alteration in the attitude of the average Briton toward the role that government should play in the affairs of the individual. There was an increasingly widespread acceptance of the idea that poverty, unemployment, and ignorance were neither inevitable nor necessarily the personal fault of the victims, but rather the consequence of particular social arrangements that demanded the attention of the leaders of government. These new impulses in late-Victorian Britain must be examined with care if the more obvious political and social changes of the twentieth century are to be understood in their proper historical context.[1]

Technological Advances

The most easily observable changes were technological. As the railway and the telegraph had revolutionized the first two-thirds of the nineteenth century, so the telephone helped to transform the last third. Whereas the average Briton posted four times as many letters per year in 1887 as in 1837, he now had an excuse to write less often. At the same time, the typewriter was beginning to alter business office methods,

---

[1] J. F. C. Harrison, *Late Victorian Britain, 1875–1901* (1990), and José Harris, *The Penguin Social History of Britain 1870–1914* (1995), provide excellent syntheses of many of the subjects taken up in this chapter. The works by Read, Ensor, and Ausubel cited in Chapter 8 also remain relevant. Rosalind Mitchison takes up vital statistics in *British Population Change Since 1860* (1977). Anthony Wohl, *Endangered Lives: Public Health in Victorian England* (1983), charts both improvements and setbacks. For other aspects of the late-Victorian experience, see Colin Holmes, *John Bull's Island: Immigration and British Society, 1871–1971* (1988), and Richard Holt, *Sport and the British: A Modern History* (1989).

The Triumph of Technology   The horse-drawn omnibus gives way to the electric streetcar (London, 1903). *(Hulton Deutsch Collection)*

mark an end to the age-old occupation of copyist, and downgrade the value of good penmanship. The 1880s brought the tricycle — then an adult vehicle rather than a children's toy — and the next decade the even speedier, if less stable, bicycle. The wealthy had long used horses and carriages, but never before had members of the lower classes been able to afford their own means of conveyance. The 1880s also marked the onset of the age of electricity. By the end of the century, most cities boasted their own central power stations, and gas lights both in the streets and in the wealthier private homes gradually gave way to the incandescent bulb. Even working-class families could afford the gas-cookers that simplified the process of providing home-cooked meals. By the end of the century, the electric streetcar was replacing the horse-drawn omnibus as the chief mode of municipal transportation. By 1900 the hand-wound gramophone was becoming popular, and the first successful experiments with motion pictures had taken place. The automobile run by a gasoline-driven internal combustion engine had also been invented, but its possibilities were not yet foreseen. Until 1896 an automobile in Britain had to be preceded on the street by a man waving a red flag and was forbidden to exceed a speed of four miles an hour.

A Bicycle Built for Five   A late-Victorian invention that even lower-class families could afford. *(The Granger Collection)*

The Social Structure

Although such technological changes were obvious to the generation experiencing them, certain equally significant changes in the social structure were less immediately visible. For one thing, more people lived longer. The death rate, which had remained fairly steady during the first three-quarters of the century, began to decline dramatically during the last quarter:

DEATH RATES (PER 1,000)

Years	Male	Female
1846–1850	24.1	22.6
1871–1875	23.3	20.7
1896–1900	18.8	16.6

Public-health measures and improved nutrition were largely responsible. Pure water was now widely available, and most cities had installed reasonably effective sewage systems. Smallpox vaccination and the isolation of victims of infectious diseases had become standard practice. Infant mortality remained high, but smallpox had been largely eliminated, and after the 1860s there were no further cholera epidemics. An improved diet and somewhat improved housing and working conditions made people more resistant to infectious diseases, and the number of deaths from tuberculosis (the leading killer of young adults), typhus, typhoid fever, and scarlet fever were all on the decline. The use of anesthetics (from the late 1840s on) and of antiseptic techniques (pioneered in the 1860s by Dr. Joseph Lister of the University of Glasgow) eased the pain and greatly improved the chances of survival for patients undergoing surgery. Many infectious diseases remained, however, that could be cured neither by the the prestigious physicians of London's Harley Street nor by the overworked general practitioners who attended the poor at workhouse infirmaries. Many such infirmaries were being transformed into state hospitals to complement the country's voluntary hospitals.

The result of a falling death rate would have been a dramatic rise in the population had it not been for two compensating factors. One was emigration: during the later decades of the nineteenth century, a continuing stream of migrants sought their fortunes in the United States, Canada, Australia, New Zealand, and to a lesser extent, South Africa and South America. Over 1.5 million left the British Isles during the 1870s, 2.5 million during the 1880s, and another 2 million during the 1890s. In part, this outflow was balanced by immigration. The Irish continued to flock to England and Scotland; and throughout the century, Britain served as a refuge for small groups of continental exiles, as it had for Flemings in the sixteenth century and for French Huguenots in the seventeenth. Between 1870 and 1914 some 120,000 Jewish refugees from Eastern Europe found a new home in Britain, especially in London's East End, where many of them became tailors and seamstresses, while others became retail traders. Two of the largest retail chains in twentieth-century Britain, Burton's tailoring shops and Marks and Spencer's clothing and food shops, were to be founded by such immigrant entrepreneurs.

The other compensating factor was a falling birthrate; men and women were marrying later and having fewer children. Whereas the average married woman of the 1860s had had six children, her granddaughter four decades later had only three. Although the decline in the birthrate was evident in all classes, it affected most rapidly the business and professional groups who, by the turn of the century, often had no more than two children per family. One reason for this decline was the growing availability of contraceptive knowledge; perhaps more significant was the desire to make use of it. The very availability of new consumer comforts and conveniences provided an additional incentive for having a smaller family. A greater number of benefits could be bestowed on children if there were not so many of them. By the early twentieth century women further down in the social scale were reporting similar motivations:

Among the working-classes, people who desire to "get on" are house-proud and like to be well-dressed and enjoy pleasure; small families are the rule. . . . Young wives will not be tied down by small children; they wish to dress, walk out and amuse themselves more than of old. The reduction has not occurred among the lowest and poorest class, who can neither afford to buy, or will not trouble to use, preventatives. . . . To the lowest classes . . . children are a good investment as they cost little to rear and become a source of income at thirteen years of age. To the better class of people children are an anxiety and expense, and it is this class that resorts freely to preventative measures.[2]

The decline in the size of middle-class families had other implications. Houses and rooms no longer needed to be so large, and fewer domestic servants were required per household. Domestics had traditionally been drawn from the countryside, the daughters of tenant farmers and farm laborers. As agriculture declined, so did the number of farm girls. As late as 1880 one out of every six English and Welsh workers was in domestic service; thereafter that ratio began to decline. Inasmuch as the birthrate and the death rate were both going down, the overall population of the United Kingdom — except for Ireland — continued to increase at a steady pace. In 1871 there had been 22.5 million people in England and Wales. Three decades later there were 32.5 million, a larger proportion of them adults and a smaller proportion dependent children.

The Status of Women

No step did more for the emancipation of the middle-class woman than the reduction in the size of her family. By the late nineteenth century, a series of overlapping but diverse movements seeking to expand the rights of women under law, in politics, in education, and in the economy were also well under way. Queen Victoria herself was no admirer of the emancipated female, and in 1870 she had privately insisted that she was "anxious to enlist everyone who can speak or write to join in checking this mad, wicked folly of 'Woman's Rights,' with all its attendant horrors." She could not, however, halt the Divorce Act of 1857, or the Married Women's Property Acts of 1870 and 1882, or the opening of Civil Service posts to women — such as that of post office supervisor in 1873 and factory inspector in 1893. Nor could the queen stem the drive for women's suffrage that John Stuart Mill had helped to launch in 1867 in the House of Commons. Unmarried women householders had been granted the municipal franchise in 1869 and the school board franchise in 1870. In the

---

[2]Cited in Wally Seccombe, "Starting to Stop: Working-Class Fertility Decline in Britain," *Past & Present* 126 (Feb. 1990), p. 186. In a revisionist work, *Fertility, Class and Gender in Britain 1860–1940* (1996), Simon Szreter argues that historians, in explaining the decline in the birthrate, have tended to exaggerate the importance of contraception and to underestimate the significance of sexual abstinence.

years that followed, many women were elected as school board members and as Poor Law Union guardians. They were given the right to vote for county councillors in 1888. The Local Government Act of 1894 not only made both single and married women eligible to vote for district and parish councillors but also gave them the right to stand for election. Only Parliament remained beyond their direct influence.[3] Yet even Parliament could be swayed, so Josephine Butler (1828–1906) and her Ladies' National Association demonstrated when they secured the repeal in 1886 of a two-decade-old system requiring the compulsory sanitary inspection of prostitutes in cities adjoining large army bases in England and Ireland. The system had not merely curtailed the liberty of lower-class women but had also enshrined into law the double standard of sexual morality.[4]

A third or more of lower-class women had worked full-time outside the home for money wages throughout the early- and mid-Victorian years, and during the decades that followed they constituted three workers out of four in the new ready-made clothing industry. It was the growing number of middle-class women who were expected to serve as "the angel of the hearth" while their husbands dealt with the outside world:

> Man for the field and woman for the hearth,
> Man for the sword and for the needle she;
> Man with the head, and woman with the heart;
> Man to command, and woman to obey,
> All else confusion.

So had Tennyson epitomized the Victorian doctrine of "separate spheres" for the two sexes. So sharp a distinction in assigned roles had at no time completely reflected Victorian reality, and it was blunted further during the century's final decades. An increasing number of single middle-class women became not only governesses but also nurses, elementary school teachers, and school administrators (a group growing both in number and in prestige). By the onset of the twentieth century, numerous female clerks, secretaries, and typists had found a place in business offices; the 1861 census recorded only 279, the 1911 census, 125,000. In 1894 the Society of Women Journalists was founded. At the same time, virtually all

---

[3]In recent years these topics have been explored in a large number of books: Philippa Levine, *Victorian Feminism, 1850–1900* (1986); Lee Holcombe, *Victorian Ladies at Work* (1973); Olive Banks, *Faces of Feminism* (1981); Patricia Hollis, *Ladies Elect: Women in English Local Government, 1865–1914* (1987); David Rubinstein, *Before the Suffragettes: Women's Emancipation in the 1890s* (1986); Pat Jalland, *Women, Marriage, and Politics, 1860–1914* (1987); Kathleen E. McCrone, *Playing the Game: Sport and the Physical Emancipation of English Women, 1870–1914* (1988). In *Sex and Suffrage in Britain, 1860–1914* (1987), Susan Kingsley Kent contends that late-Victorian suffragists sought a total transformation of the position of women in society and an ultimate overthrow of the institution of marriage. The evidence provided in books such as Barbara Caine, *Victorian Feminists* (1992), throws doubt on that thesis.

[4]Judith R. Walkowitz, *Prostitution and Victorian Society: Women, Class, and the State* (1980).

men in business and the professions and all respectable workingmen continued to look on a wife working for money wages outside the home as an embarrassment, as a reflection on their manly ability to serve as the family breadwinner.

During these same years, educational doors were opening, however, as secondary schools for girls multiplied. Both Oxford and Cambridge added women's colleges in the 1870s, and the University of London began to award degrees on an equal basis in 1878. The four Scottish universities began to admit women in 1892. Instrumental in bringing a comparable emancipation in female clothing was the growing popularity of bicycling and of other forms of athletics not only in the form of riding, hunting, and rowing but also of archery, golf, croquet, and lawn tennis. "So much of our success depends on quickness of movement and suppleness of body," explained Lady Milner, a staunch advocate of women cricketers, "that I may be pardoned for pointing out that if we are steelbound and whale-bound throughout, the free use of our limbs which the game demands is rendered impossible."

Religion and Leisure

The increasing popularity of sports for both sexes helped to change the way Britons spent their Sundays.[5] Although church attendance was still growing, by the end of the century it was no longer keeping up with the rise of population. A survey of 1902 showed that only one out of five Londoners was in church on an average Sunday, a far smaller percentage than that revealed by the Religious Census of 1851. The type of family prayers described by Tocqueville in the 1830s was characteristic of fewer households. The sale of religious books was declining and, conversely, that of novels and works of history rising.

The intellectual questioning of the Bible evoked by "higher criticism" and by Darwinism had opened a breach between Christian doctrine and the beliefs of many educated men and women. Some Anglican parishioners were inspired but others were alienated by an increasing tendency toward ritualism on the part of their clergymen; in the use of candles, ornate vestments, and ceremony, and in the stress on the sacrament of communion, Anglican services resembled more and more those of Roman Catholicism. A significant number of late Victorians were attracted by spiritualism — the attempt at séances to communicate with the dead — as a substitute or complementary religion. Yet other late Victorians revived the ancient cult of astrology. The agricultural depression reduced the income of rural parsons, and fewer university graduates entered the ministry. A majority of the English continued to be baptized, married, and buried under the auspices of the Church of England and to

---

[5]The process is explained in Hugh McLeod, *Religion and Society in England, 1850–1914* (1996).

attend its Sunday schools, but in other respects its influence had subtly begun to wane.

The Nonconformist chapels remained strong, but they, too, were growing less quickly than the population. Many an able young man of lower-class origin who earlier in the century had been drawn to the Methodist ministry was now drawn to a secular career. He might become a trade-union leader or enter politics or, now that so many legal and educational barriers had been lifted, perhaps even enter a profession; and he or his children might, at least for social reasons, actually join the Church of England. The sharp mid-Victorian social and political distinction between church and chapel was thus beginning to blur; but particular measures involving pub licensing or the role of religion in education did, at least temporarily, resharpen the distinction; and in Wales, Nonconformity remained closely allied with a revived spirit of Welsh nationality.

By the 1890s there was also a widespread hedonistic reaction against the strict ethical code of Victorianism. The American-born James McNeill Whistler insisted that art had no relation to morality — he defiantly labeled a portrait of his mother an *Arrangement in Grey and Black* — and writers such as Max Beerbohm and artists such as Aubrey Beardsley professed pride in the supposed decadence of this *fin-de-siècle* decade. Fears of such societal "moral degeneration" were fueled by the widely publicized trial and subsequent imprisonment of the playwright Oscar Wilde for homosexual practices.[6] Even more sanguine observers were in agreement that "A New Spirit of Pleasure is abroad amongst us." It was typified in several ways by the Prince of Wales, the future King Edward VII, who became the leader of London's fashionable high society, a world his mother neither approved nor understood. It meant horse racing, golf, tennis, and polo by day and restaurants and theaters by night. Edward VII is often credited with inventing the country house "weekend" as a peculiarly British institution.

A relative increase in leisure time combined with urbanization and ready access to railroads helps explain the rapid growth of spectator sports during the final decades of the century. Although cricket remained largely middle class and upper class in appeal, association football (soccer) brought more than a million predominantly working-class spectators to the stadiums each winter Saturday afternoon. By 1900 every major city could boast its own professional team, and the leading players had come to be better known than Members of Parliament. The ablest were chosen for national teams to represent England, Wales, Scotland, and Ireland. All manner of present-day British athletic traditions had their origins during the mid- and late-Victorian years: the first British Open golf championship (1860); the Marquess of Queensberry rules for boxing (1867); the Football Association Cup (1871); the county cricket championship (1873); and at Wimbledon (near London) the first world tennis

---

[6]See, e.g., Richard Ellmann, *Oscar Wilde* (1987), and Michael S. Foldy, *The Trials of Oscar Wilde: Deviance, Morality, and Late-Victorian Society* (1997).

championships for men (1877) and women (1884). It was more the cult of amateur athletics at British public schools than it was memories of ancient Greece that motivated a Frenchman, Baron Pierre de Coubertin, to revive the Olympic games in Athens in 1896.

The discovery was made in the 1890s not only that the lower classes had a widespread interest in organized athletics, in gambling, in music hall performances, and in seaside holidays, but also that they constituted a great untapped market of daily newspaper readers. The mid-Victorian papers, although not always as respectable in content as their format might indicate, had appealed primarily to the gentleman. Working-class readers might buy an occasional Sunday paper and had within their price range a great variety of penny serial novels and printed street ballads that dealt with those three universal and timeless best-sellers: sex, crime, and violence. The man who united the respectable Victorian daily with the pulp literature of the street ballad to create the modern mass-circulation newspaper was Alfred Harmsworth (1865–1922), a youthful, poorly educated barrister's son who in 1896 founded the *Daily Mail* as a halfpenny morning paper. The *Daily Mail* combined a simplified presentation of old-style news with "human interest" stories, jokes, gossip, and prize competitions to attract an increasing number of readers and, not surprisingly, an increasing number of advertisers. Within three years, the *Daily Mail* had a circulation of half a million copies. Newspapers had become big business; and although Lord Salisbury dismissed the *Daily Mail* as "written by office-boys for office-boys," Harmsworth's shrewdness won him a fortune, a peerage (as Lord Northcliffe), and the flattery of emulation by his fellow press barons, who by the early twentieth century dominated the British newspaper scene.

The Decline of Laissez-Faire

Perhaps the most significant late-Victorian transformation was one of social and political attitudes, specifically, a strong current of opposition to the prevailing laissez-faire preconceptions of most mid-Victorian economists. Laissez-faire was never as all-inclusive as popular stereotype would have it, but it was dominant. Individual enterprise seemed to be the key to both high production and general prosperity; and the occasions on which the state might intervene were carefully circumscribed. Political philosophers such as Herbert Spencer (1830–1903) continued to portray government as innately both authoritarian and incompetent, but an increasing number of social critics called on the government to play a more decisive role in alleviating the social evils that they saw all around them.[7]

---

[7]Late-Victorian attitudes as to how best to deal with the poor are sympathetically assessed in Gertrude Himmelfarb, *Poverty and Compassion: The Moral Imagination of the Late Victorians* (1991). Different facets of late-Victorian socialism and trade-union activity are

Those who decried Victorian Liberal economics most loudly were avowed socialists. Utopian socialism had been professed by Robert Owen half a century earlier, and Christian socialism had been advocated by Charles Kingsley and others a generation earlier. But it had then died out, and only in the 1880s did organized socialism reappear in the British Isles. Karl Marx, strangely enough, had little to do with the English socialist revival. London was his home in exile for three decades, but he always remained a foreigner there, and no English translation of *Das Kapital* was attempted until some years after his death in 1883. Yet most of the factual data for his interpretation of history and his moral condemnation of capitalism were gleaned from British publications during daily sessions in the British Museum, the country's largest library. Some years ago a prospective biographer of Karl Marx went up to the oldest attendant in the reading room and asked him whether he remembered a bespectacled and bearded little man who used to sit every day at seat G7. After a bit of thought, the attendant said: "Ah yes, sir, I remember: a Mr. Marx it was, wasn't it? He came in every day like clockwork for years, and then one day he didn't come in, and no one's ever heard of him since."

The story may be apocryphal but it illustrates how elusive a role the godfather of Soviet and Chinese communism was to play in the modern British socialist tradition. The first professed Marxist socialist was an ex-Tory businessman and journalist, H. M. Hyndman (1842–1921), who in the 1880s peddled his weekly paper *Justice* at a penny a copy and preached class revolution while dressed in top hat and frock coat. He wrote a popularization of Marx's ideas entitled *A Textbook of Democracy: England for All* and founded a small group of devotees who came to be known as the Social Democratic Federation. Since Hyndman neglected to mention Marx's name in his book, Marx promptly disowned him and thus excommunicated the first Marxist party in England.

As significant as Hyndman's difficulties with his spiritual godfather was his conversion to the socialist cause of William Morris (1834–1896), a man of much greater talents than Hyndman himself. Morris had led an artistic reaction against the absence of design in mid-Victorian furniture and carpeting, and he helped to inspire the Arts and Crafts movement. He sought to empty the Victorian parlor of its litter of manufactured knickknacks. "Have nothing in your homes," he advised, "which you do not know to be useful or believe to be beautiful." Morris's socialism was less concerned with material gain for the working population than with a somewhat utopian readjustment of society that would make all people happy and self-reliant in their work. He hoped to return to an idealized

---

examined by Henry Pelling in *The Origins of the Labour Party, 1880–1900* (2nd ed., 1966) and *A History of British Trade Unionism* (4th ed., 1987); by Norman and Jeanne MacKenzie in *The First Fabians* (1977); by E. H. Hunt in *British Labour History, 1815–1914* (1981); by Patrick Joyce in *Work, Society, and Politics: The Culture of the Factory in Late Victorian England* (1980); and by Alan Fox in *History and Heritage: The Social Origins of the British Industrial Relations System* (1985).

rural world of individual medieval craftsmanship, which he believed the Industrial Revolution had destroyed. Morris cooperated with Hyndman for three years and then they split, mostly because Morris was not fundamentally in accord with Marx's vision of "scientific socialism." "I do not know what Marx's theory of value is," Morris burst out on one occasion, "and I'm damned if I want to know."

More influential than either Hyndman or Morris was the Fabian Society, a small group of intellectuals including George Bernard Shaw, the aspiring playwright, Graham Wallas, the son of an evangelical clergyman, Sidney Webb, the scholarly son of a London accountant, and his wife Beatrice (Potter) Webb, the daughter of a well-to-do manufacturer. Like most nineteenth-century socialists, the Fabians tended to dwell more on the evils of the capitalism of the present than on the details of the socialist utopia of the future. The Webbs agreed with Hyndman in their definition of socialism — "It is an organized attempt to substitute ordered cooperation for existence for the present anarchical competition for existence" — but they were far apart on tactics. Hyndman's small band of followers looked forward ardently to the day of proletarian revolution, and they were half fearful that such capitalist concessions as an eight-hour working day would delay the coming of class war. The Fabians, on the other hand, wanted to use existing government machinery to forward the cause of economic equality by legislating against poverty and by bringing all major industries under the control of a democratically

Sidney and Beatrice Webb   These photographs were taken in 1891, shortly before their marriage and at the start of their half-century-long collaboration as Fabian socialists and historians of trade unionism and local government. *(Passfield Papers, Harvard University Press)*

elected government. They sought no revolution; rather, they wished to permeate the existing parties and organizations and gradually to wear down the opposition, just as the Roman general Fabius Cunctator in the third century B.C. had worn down the onslaught of Hannibal and eventually defeated him. Ultimately, the Fabians had greater faith in the wisdom of the trained expert than in the intelligence of the mass electorate, and, in the words of one hostile critic, they "expected, by cautious and indeed almost imperceptible degrees, eventually to achieve a beatific state of intolerable bureaucracy."

The most widely read late-nineteenth-century socialist was a Lancashire journalist named Robert Blatchford, whose *Merrie England* (1894) explained in simple, good-humored language that society as it was then constituted was unjust. It sold over a million copies. Although not even Blatchford converted the mass of workers to socialism, socialist groups like the Fabians gathered useful collections of economic statistics on income distribution in society and on the operation of the Poor Law. The Fabians, who were instrumental in founding the world-renowned London School of Economics, in this respect followed in the footsteps of Benthamites like Edwin Chadwick. They were not afraid of using humor as a weapon. One of their favorite tactics was to try to show that socialism, far from being a radical foreign innovation, was already a successful English institution. Wrote Sidney Webb in 1889:

> The practical man, oblivious or contemptuous of any theory of the general principles of social organization, has been forced, by the necessities of the time, into an ever-deepening collective channel. Socialism, of course, he still rejects or despises. The individualist town councillor will walk along the municipal pavement, lit by municipal light and cleansed by municipal brooms with municipal water, and seeing, by the municipal clock in the municipal market, that he is too early to meet his children coming home from the municipal school, hard by the county lunatic asylum and the municipal hospital, will use the national telegraph system to tell them not to walk through the municipal park, but to come by the municipal tramway, to meet him in the municipal reading-room, by the municipal museum, art gallery, and library, where he intends to consult some of the national publications in order to prepare his next speech in the municipal town hall in favour of the nationalization of canals and the increase of Government control over the railway system. "Socialism, sir," he will say; "don't waste the time of a practical man by your fantastic absurdities. Self-help, Sir, individual self-help, that's what has made our city what it is."[8]

Webb's parable was a shrewd one, for the late nineteenth century saw a notable expansion in the social duties undertaken by urban municipalities. It was under the mayoralty (1873–1876) of Joseph Chamberlain, for example, that Birmingham took over the private gas and water works and demolished over forty acres of slums in order to build model homes for

---

[8]Cited in D. C. Somervell, *English Thought in the Nineteenth Century* (1929).

workers. In the 1880s Birmingham took the lead in providing municipal electric lighting and in operating the street railways. Successive acts of Parliament had ended most limitations on the powers of municipal councils, and thereafter they were permitted to put out bond issues to pay for long-term capital improvements. By 1900 the new London County Council had come to epitomize progressive municipal administration in matters of education, health, and housing. Although Chamberlain accepted "gas-and-water socialism" as a description for the kind of work he had pioneered in Birmingham, he preferred to compare his city to a large corporation. "The leading idea of the English system of municipal government," he explained, "may be that of a joint-stock or cooperative enterprise in which every citizen is a shareholder, and of which the dividends are receivable in the improved health and the increase in the comfort and happiness of the community."

More immediately influential than professed socialists or reluctant municipal officers swept along by the course of events in helping to change the prevailing attitude toward government intervention in the economy were a host of pamphleteers, politicians, socially conscious clergymen, and secular social reformers. Highly significant was Henry George, an American whose panacea for poverty was the elimination of all taxes except a single tax on the "unearned increment" in the value of land; his book *Progress and Poverty* was a best-seller in England throughout the 1880s. Although not a socialist, George helped to undermine the doctrine of laissez-faire by his insistence that poverty was a man-made evil. In a very real sense, poverty was rediscovered in late-Victorian England. The upper-middle-class manufacturers who had moved to the suburbs a generation before were sharply reminded that at least three out of ten English people still lived close to the subsistence level. Andrew Mearns's pamphlet *The Bitter Cry of Outcast London* led to a Royal Commission on the Housing of the Working Classes (1884), which included such luminaries as Sir Charles Dilke, the Prince of Wales, Lord Salisbury, and the theologically conservative but socially radical Roman Catholic prelate, Cardinal Manning. Another royal commission called attention to the plight of the "sweated workers," men and women who worked not in factories but at home. There they produced cheap clothing, shoes, and furniture under extraordinarily unhealthful and unregulated conditions. In 1889 Charles Booth published the first of eighteen exhaustive volumes on the *Life and Labour of the People of London.* Booth's work and B. Seebohm Rowntree's comparable study of the city of York (1901) are pioneer examples of detailed sociological investigation.

The implication of all such studies was that economic suffering could and must be cured by human action. Not all reformers, however, were agreed on the means. Numerous private charitable organizations continued to expend huge sums to assist the unfortunate, and thousands of middle-class ladies became home visitors who sought to teach working-class women how to become better mothers, cooks, and housekeepers. In

A Well-Dressed Boy   The advertisement appeared in a Glasgow newspaper in 1884. The photograph (1900) suggests that not all late-Victorian lads could afford such elegance. *(The Bailie,* May 28, 1884/*Graham Collection, Mitchell Library, Glasgow; Graham Collection, Mitchell Library, Glasgow)*

1878 after years of evangelical mission work in the East End of London, "General" William Booth, a Methodist clergyman, founded the Salvation Army to provide succor and, if possible, a new start for the down-and-outers at the bottom of the English social ladder. Six years later, anxious not only to relieve symptoms but also to remove causes, another Anglican clergyman, Canon Samuel Barnett, founded Toynbee Hall, the prototype of subsequent settlement houses throughout the world. Barnett's plan was to settle a colony of social workers, preferably university graduates, among the poor and thereby try to bridge the chasm of class indifference and ignorance and offer an opportunity for intellectual and material improvement.

In some ways it may seem surprising that what Beatrice Webb called "the humanitarian upsurge of the eighties" should have taken place at a time when the standard of living was rising and the number of people relying on the Poor Law was continuing to decline. The explanation lies partly in the sense of uncertainty and insecurity that the "great depression" had fostered among many English people; but economic motivation was only half the story. The desire to save the bodies as well as the souls of those groups in society who had not shared in the general rise of living standards proved to be a powerful motive for many earnest people who had either forsaken orthodox religion and sought secular substitutes or felt that, as clergymen, their Christian faith required them to relieve suffering in the world around them. The notable improvement in the condition of the working classes in late-Victorian England did not keep pace with humanitarian conceptions of what that position should be.

Social Reform and Politics

The workers who were members of trade unions were not at first particularly attracted by the social creed of either socialists or social reformers. The prosperous sixties had been climaxed by a burst of union organizing, and the total membership in the Trades Union Congress (TUC) grew from 114,000 to 735,000 between 1868 and 1873. The next fifteen years were to prove less favorable to union growth, and TUC membership first declined sharply and then began to grow again at a much slower pace. For the most part, the TUC continued to represent unions of skilled craftsmen who were essentially satisfied with the capitalistic organization of industry, provided that they could negotiate with their employers stable and formal contracts safeguarding their wages and work practices. They generally preferred negotiation to strikes, they often voted Liberal, and most saw little need to have Parliament legislate on hours and wages.

Some of the new unions of the late 1880s and 1890s were, however, of a different social and political complexion. These were usually made up of less skilled and less highly paid workers. Their leaders were far more class conscious, more favorable toward strikes, more distrustful of the goodwill of their employers, and therefore more intent on parliamentary action. One of the first such unions was the London Dock Workers. Traditionally, the London docker had been exposed to all the vagaries of laissez-faire economics; there was no continuity of employment, and a host of men competed daily for whatever work was available. In 1889 the dock workers demanded a minimum wage of six pence an hour (twelve and a half cents in terms of the American dollar of that day), at least four hours of work at a time, and extra pay for overtime. When their demands were refused, they struck, and for five weeks the port of London was virtually closed to all traffic. The strike caused hardships for many Londoners, not least of all for the strikers themselves; but eventually a committee of citizens, including the aged Cardinal Manning, succeeded in bringing about a settlement. The dockers, beneficiaries of the financial aid and sympathy of many middle-class Londoners, won their six pence an hour and most of their other demands.

The success of the dock strike provided a stimulus for other new unions among office clerks, teachers, and shop assistants (retail clerks), some of whom worked an incredible eighty-six hours a week. Such

James Keir Hardie (1856–1915)   The Scottish coal miner and labor leader wore his cloth cap even in the House of Commons. *(Hulton Deutsch Collection)*

organizations and a revived miners' union caused the TUC membership to rise from 750,000 in 1887 to over 1,500,000 by 1892. It also inspired the idea that workers should have representatives of their own in Parliament rather than vote for Liberals or Conservatives. The first such representative was Keir Hardie, a Scottish miner who was elected in 1892 and who astonished the House of Commons by entering the chamber wearing a cloth cap and a tweed jacket rather than the traditional top hat and frock coat. In 1893, under Hardie's influence, an organization known as the Independent Labour party was set up. It was the first "popular" political party founded by socialists in Britain, and it derived its strength from trade unions and Nonconformist chapels. Yet for the moment its popularity too was open to question, for it could boast but a single Member of Parliament. In the general election of 1895, all of its twenty-eight candidates were defeated, including Hardie himself. Imperialist excitement largely explains the election returns of 1895, but during the Boer War plans were laid to create a real labor party that could win votes. Three elements — socialist intellectuals (especially the Fabians), the trade unions, and Hardie's Independent Labour party — met to organize a Labour Representation Committee for the purpose of seeking the nomination and election of labor candidates to Parliament. That committee was to become the nucleus of the twentieth-century British Labour party.

Although no significant separate labor party was to arrive in the House of Commons until 1906, the two major parties were both affected by the gradual shift of sentiment in favor of a greater degree of government intervention in the economic scene. Yet traditional Liberal political philosophy exalted not social welfare but individual freedom from archaic legal and economic shackles. A veteran of many of those earlier conflicts, John Bright, expressed the opinion in 1883 that no political issues remained on which great conflicts were likely to arise.

Still, at this very time, the opinion was obviously gaining weight that the economy of an industrialized country produced problems for which the answers of traditional liberalism were insufficient. The highly touted "freedom of contract" that all adult laborers enjoyed might well be illusory when factories employed thousands of men. Either such workers would organize — and both large unions and employer associations might require government regulation — or else they might demand the setting of minimum standards by the government. Nor could "natural" monopolies such as telegraph and telephone companies, railways, and electric power companies be treated by the state as if they were small shopkeepers. Finally, the Liberals faced the paradox that the electorate that emerged from the extension of the franchise in 1867 and 1884 might wish to use its vote for purposes opposed to earlier liberalism.

Some pragmatic Liberals began to shift their outlook. John Morley, a member of Gladstone's last cabinet, illustrated such a change of attitude with his comments on Britain's housing problem in 1883: "I am beginning to doubt whether it is possible to grapple with this enormous mass of evil in our society by merely private, voluntary, and philanthropic effort. I believe we shall have to bring to bear the collective force of the whole community, shortly called the State, in order to remedy things against which our social conscience is at last beginning to revolt." It was in this spirit that the Liberals sponsored the Irish Land Acts of 1870 and 1881, and they hesitantly began the regulation of the labor of adult men (rather than merely women and children) in the Employers' Liability Act of 1880, which permitted an employee to sue his employer for compensation for industrial accidents, even if a fellow employee was technically at fault. By 1891 the Liberals were even tentatively advocating a mandatory eight-hour workday. It was a Liberal Chancellor of the Exchequer, Sir William Harcourt, who in the budget of 1894 introduced, in regard to "death duties" (inheritance taxes), the principle of a graduated tax, the key to all future efforts to redistribute wealth. Liberals found comfort in the teachings of a new generation of idealistic philosophers such as Oxford's Thomas Hill Green, who wanted the state to create "positive freedoms" for its citizens. Some of them also heeded economists such as Henry Sidgwick, who gave new emphasis to the distinction that John Stuart Mill had made between the *production* of wealth, which society ought to leave alone, and the *distribution* of wealth, which society might well regulate. Sidgwick noted that not all individuals could look after themselves, that some types of state intervention (such as compulsory education) actually encouraged individual self-help rather than hindered it, and that in particular cases social needs must take precedence over private profit.

The Conservatives had fewer doctrinal difficulties in opposing the tenets of laissez-faire than did the Liberals. They did face a practical difficulty, however: to an increasing degree, they constituted the party not only of large landowners but also of big business proprietors, the very people whose property would have to be taxed more heavily if the goals of the social reformers were to be attained. Yet Disraeli's paternalistic ideal of "Tory Democracy" was never completely forgotten in the decades that followed his death, and the irrepressible Joseph Chamberlain added a new dose of the same tonic to political conservatism.

Although the Irish issue and Gladstone's longevity had pushed Chamberlain into an alignment with the Conservatives, his absorption with imperial problems never overshadowed totally his interest in municipal and national social reform and his willingness to break with old-style assumptions. The question of the hour, Chamberlain had declared in 1885, was, "What ransom will property pay for the security which it enjoys?" Noting in 1891 that one out of every four English people over sixty was on poor relief, Chamberlain became the first important British statesman to advocate a system of government-sponsored old-age pensions. As minister in a largely Conservative cabinet, Chamberlain helped to pass the Workmen's Compensation Act of 1897, which made it compulsory for employers to pay the costs of industrial accidents and thus greatly strengthened the Employers' Liability Act of 1880.

For a time in the 1890s public preoccupation with social reform gave way to preoccupation with empire, but the ideological shift that was to cause Britain to establish the fundamentals of a welfare state in the early years of the twentieth century had already taken place. In the words of one historian, "The Poor had become Labour and Labour had become the People, a power which could not be ignored." Declared Sir William Harcourt, a Liberal, in 1889: "We are all Socialists now." The analysis was succinct but misleading. Harcourt's thought was more moderately expressed by the Conservative prime minister, Lord Salisbury, when he concluded that in many areas "the policy of laissez-faire can no longer be pursued without disaster to the State."

PART FOUR

THE EARLY TWENTIETH CENTURY

1900 to 1924

WORLD WAR I
A wounded Canadian soldier is carried from the battlefield.
(The Granger Collection)

The Rocky Road to the Welfare State

The years before 1914 were long nostalgically remembered by aging survivors as an era of peace, dignity, and stability, a time when European influence and European values were dominant throughout the world and, most prominently, an epoch that knew nothing of world wars or cold wars or "Star Wars." The age did have some of these qualities, and we are not wholly wrong if we visualize it in terms of an Edwardian upper class dancing the "Ascot Gavotte" in *My Fair Lady* fashion. Yet contemporary Britons were as likely to see themselves living in the dawn of a new age as in the Indian summer of an old. In the field of social reform, the transformation of attitudes that had taken place in the late-Victorian years was to lead in the early years of the new century to a body of laws and institutions that by 1914 had laid the foundations of the welfare state. Those foundations were put in place against a background of social and ideological unrest, and they were as much the product of the accident of personalities and events as of premeditated calculation.[1]

Edwardian Prosperity

A significant backdrop for social and political change was provided by the paradoxical period of "Edwardian prosperity." Just as historical accident had identified the later part of Victoria's reign with the curious "great depression," so it was to identify the reign of her son Edward VII (1901–1910) with a period of economic boom. The association is not

---

[1]The 1900–1914 domestic scene is dealt with in the books by Feuchtwanger, Read, Ensor, and Pugh (cited in Chapter 8). Two helpful collections of essays are Alan O'Day, ed., *The Edwardian Age: Conflict and Stability, 1900–1914* (1979), and Donald Read, ed., *Edwardian England* (1982). Peter Rowland has chronicled the history of *The Last Liberal Governments, 1905–1915* (2 vols., 1968, 1971); George L. Bernstein has summed up the prevailing political ethos in *Liberalism and Liberal Politics in Edwardian England* (1986); and Bentley Gilbert, in *The Evolution of National Insurance in Great Britain* (1966), has provided the most penetrating study of the formulation of the social reform measures of the era. In *London 1900: The Imperial Metropolis* (1999), Jonathan Schneer describes the buildings, the people, and the attitudes.

Three Kings   Seated, in a photograph taken in 1906, is King Edward VII (1901–1910). To his right stands his son and successor, King George V (1910–1936), to his left his grandson, King Edward VIII (1936), who after his abdication became the Duke of Windsor. *(Bettmann/Corbis)*

altogether specious. Whereas Queen Victoria had conveyed the image of the rather formidable and moralistic mother (and grandmother) of her people, Edward gave the impression of the genial uncle who enjoyed life and who wanted his people to enjoy life also. He delighted in good food and good drink, and if only because he preferred men to books and women to either, he came to be known (privately) as "Edward the Caresser."

Most of the economic statistics of the first fifteen years of the twentieth century substantiate the widespread impression of prosperity. In contrast to the last decades of Victoria's reign, prices were rising rather than declining and so were the margins of business profit. Agriculture remained in the doldrums, but the decline had been halted, and cattle-raisers who fed their herds on imported grains were doing well. The value of exports (discounting inflation) grew by one-third; as late as 1913, Britain produced 27 percent of the world's exports of manufactured articles. American and German competition were still increasing, and Britain's relative economic position continued to decline — but if Britain was no longer the world's workshop, it was at least "its warehouseman, its banker, and its commission agent." Britain remained by far the world's greatest shipbuilder and maintained the largest merchant marine. Although an Italian, Guglielmo Marconi, invented radio, it was in his mother's Britain that he carried on his experiments, and it was the British who first put radio to practical use as a method of keeping in touch with ships at sea. Contributing notably to the atmosphere of prosperity was a rapid growth in British investments overseas. They had outdistanced foreign investments within Britain by £764 million back in 1872; that amount had risen to £2,431 million in 1902 and £3,568 million by 1912.

The period of Edwardian prosperity, although real enough for many British merchants and corporations, rested at least in part on unstable foundations. The upsurge of financial investment abroad, where a better monetary return could be expected, tended to discourage investment in industry at home. This in turn contributed to a noticeable rise in the rate of obsolescence in many British industries in comparison with those of the Americans and the Germans. United States cotton mills had adopted the latest ring-spinning machinery, but the Lancashire cotton firms continued to rely on early-nineteenth-century mules. Coal-cutting machines were becoming prominent in the United States, whereas the English mine owner continued to rely almost solely on hand labor. Yet coal mining — in almost 3,000 separate, and often separately owned, mines — was more important than ever in the British economy, and the annual production of coal in 1910 (more than 260 million tons) was more than twice what it had been in 1870. The export of coal had become one of the most significant ways in which Britain paid for its imports. There was still plenty of coal underground, but mine shafts had to be sunk ever deeper and coal seams often slanted at sharp angles that made it difficult to use machinery. The result was that productivity per miner, which had been steadily rising during the nineteenth century, was now on the decline. In 1881 the annual output per man had been 403 tons; because miners worked shorter hours, in 1901 it was 340 tons, in 1911, 309 tons. Company profits dwindled, and the wages paid to miners stagnated. It is not surprising, then, that the coal industry gave rise to more legislation between 1906 and 1914 than any other, that a decade and a half later it inspired the only general strike in British history, and that in 1946 it became the first major British industry to be nationalized.

The most paradoxical aspect of Edwardian prosperity was that, unlike the middle and later years of Victoria's reign, wages only barely kept pace with rising prices, and real wages for a majority of British workers did not rise at all. The average worker may have labored shorter hours and may have enjoyed a few more social services, but the income of many working-class families appeared to stand still at a time when other groups in society were apparently prospering. The failure of real wages to rise proved a potent stimulus to overseas emigration, and between 1900 and 1914 more than 4.5 million people left the British Isles, an all-time high. In contrast to their nineteenth-century predecessors, a majority of them (56 percent) settled in Canada and other dominions of the British Empire; this fact was a source of deep satisfaction to imperial federationists such as Joseph Chamberlain.

The reasons why real wages were no longer increasing are complex, but a few may be suggested. Complacent management was slow to replace obsolete machinery and thus delayed a rise in productivity. Laborers resisted technological change and accepted all too readily the doctrine that there was only so much work to go around (and that if one did more work, there would be less for one's mates); this attitude similarly discouraged a rise in productivity. The terms of trade, moreover, had altered so that the cost of imports was rising more quickly than the value of exports. Whatever the precise causes, the failure of wages to keep up with profits (or even with prices) evoked among members of the upper and middle classes an aura of prosperity even as it evoked among many laborers either the desire to emigrate or the incentive to join trade unions. By the end of the decade, the phenomenon had helped to inspire a widespread atmosphere of social unrest.

Although it was no longer exclusively landed in its economic interests, a class of gentlemen and ladies remained at the top of the British social ladder, and for them life in Edwardian England could be very comfortable indeed. Despite the complaint of one lady about "domestic servants now so difficult to get, and so exacting when found," many country estates still boasted large staffs whose function it was to provide "ordered luxury and plenty of punctual meals and silent service" for the master and his wife, their children, and a great host of guests. In London there were full-time nannies to care for the children, and during the Lon-

"A Quiet Sunday in Our Village"   *Punch* appraises the automobile age (1906). *(Reproduced by permission of* Punch)

don "season" there was a glittering round of teas, luncheons, dinners, and formal dances. Horse-drawn hansom cabs clattered along London streets; and although the first gasoline-driven omnibuses entered London transit service in 1905, the family-owned automobile remained a noisy luxury. The rich man's car, as it sped along unpaved streets, frightened the casual passerby and covered him with dust on a dry day and water on a rainy one; it seemed a visible symbol of arrogant wealth. At the very time that many gentlemen were becoming more conscious of social problems, they often unwittingly aggravated class feeling.

"Ladies were ladies in those days," recalls Darwin's granddaughter in her revealing account of a late-Victorian and Edwardian girlhood.[2] Ladies did not do things themselves. They told other people what to do and how to do it. The author's Aunt Etty never made a pot of tea in her life. She never traveled in a cab or in a train without her maid. She never sewed on a button or mailed a letter, and she never put on a shawl or answered a doorbell except on those rare occasions when no maid was immediately at hand.

If life was luxurious for the upper class, it remained reasonably comfortable (if somewhat stereotyped) in middle-class suburbia, where families lived in semidetached houses along quiet residential streets, and children played with scooters, tricycles, and hoops on the walks lining manicured, fenced-in gardens. Here too there was considerable entertaining — amateur dramatics, music, and tennis. Yet the middle class was by no means rich. Forty-four of the forty-five million people who lived in the British Isles in 1911 still had an income of less than $15 a week (in 1911 dollars). Many of the lower-middle-class clerks and teachers, anxious to preserve their social status, were troubled by the stagnation of real wages; some of them also became increasingly fearful of the additional taxes required to pay for battleships and for novel social services.

The lower rungs of the social ladder were occupied by artisans and wage laborers for whose families life remained materially simple and often bleak. Their world consisted of the endless, ignoble acres of narrow two- and three-story rowhouses with their multitude of chimney pots that made up metropolitan London and the industrial cities of the Midlands. The English were slow to take to apartments and much preferred a house, however small or dingy. Although only a minority of working-class families were in any sense on the edge of starvation, diets remained plain, and prolonged illness, unemployment, or old age could push most families below the poverty line. The average work week was still fifty-four hours, and only Saturday afternoons and Sundays were exempt from labor. Working-class neighborhoods might boast numerous pubs and shops as well as bookmakers, music halls, and an increasing number of

---

[2]Gwen Raverat, *Period Piece* (1960).

silent cinemas. Paid vacations were still unknown, however, and few working-class families had occasion to venture far beyond the neighborhoods in which they lived or worked.[3]

The Cultural Revival

If the glittering brilliance of Edwardian society was largely limited to the privileged few, this did not make it any less real. It was connected, moreover, with a remarkable revival in music and drama. With the partial exception of the self-styled "Glasgow Boys," an enterprising group of turn-of-the-century Scottish painters, most British artists were content hesitantly to follow the lead of the French along the road to impressionism and cubism; but English composers, for the first time since Purcell in the seventeenth century, played a distinct role in European music. Sir Arthur Sullivan (1842–1900) had aspired to serious composition, but he remains best remembered for the delightfully satirical operettas he wrote in collaboration with W. S. Gilbert (1836–1911). Sir Edward Elgar (1857–1934), in contrast, with his major symphonies, concertos, and oratorios, became a distinguished late-Romantic composer, and one of his *Pomp and Circumstance* marches, *Land of Hope and Glory*, was adopted as virtually a second national anthem. Its mood of heroic nostalgia was also to inspire the graduates at innumerable American high school and college commencement ceremonies. Frederick Delius (1862–1934), who was born in Bradford and spent much of his life near Paris, composed a number of impressionistic tone poems in a highly personal style. Ralph Vaughan Williams (1872–1958), who was to become one of the great symphonic composers of the twentieth century, began during the Edwardian years to incorporate long-neglected English folk tunes into his music.[4]

The plays of Arthur Pinero (1855–1934) and Henry Arthur Jones (1851–1929), influenced by Henrik Ibsen, had introduced to the England of the 1880s and 1890s the notion that the theater should not only provide entertainment but also deal realistically with current social problems. The Edwardian era saw still other British playwrights at the height of their powers. Whereas James Barrie (1860–1937) tended toward sentiment and whimsey (as in *Peter Pan*) and Somerset Maugham (1872–1966) was a master of the comedy of manners, John Galsworthy (1867–1933) and George Bernard Shaw (1856–1950) were more concerned with

---

[3]Standish Meacham provides a sensitive description and assessment in *A Life Apart: The English Working Class, 1890–1914* (1977). See also that illuminating compound of autobiography and social history, Robert Roberts, *The Classic Slum: Salford Life in the First Quarter of the Century* (1971), and a book based in large part on oral history, Carl Chinn's *They Worked All Their Lives: Women of the Urban Poor in England, 1880–1939* (1988).

[4]Boris Ford, ed., *Early 20th Century Britain: The Cambridge Cultural History* (1989), includes chapters on music, literature, and drama, as well as the visual arts, architecture, and design.

the social problems of the age. Galsworthy's *Strife* (1909) was an attack on prevailing relations between capital and labor, and his *Justice* (1910) criticized prison conditions. For many twentieth-century playgoers, the Irish-born Shaw ranked second only to Shakespeare among dramatists writing in English, and by 1918 he had become the single best-known writer in the world. He saw the theatre as an arena in which he might conduct amusing debates on the great issues of the day, and he proved both willing and eager to thrust his dramatic stiletto into every established institution, be it private property (as in *Major Barbara*) or class relations (as in *Pygmalion*) or militarism (as in *Arms and the Man*). He was ever the enemy of pretense and hypocrisy, and he succeeded in both entertaining and puzzling his upper- and upper-middle-class audiences. "One really doesn't quite know what to think," was the reaction of a typical Edwardian playgoer.

The revival in drama was matched by a revival in fiction. Joseph Conrad (1857–1924), Polish by birth and English by adoption, added subtle psychological analysis to tales pitting man against nature in distant lands. Arnold Bennett (1867–1931) was more typical in his concern with life in provincial industrial towns, as reflected in novels such as *Old Wives' Tale* and *Clayhanger*. Galsworthy began his masterly multivolume study of British upper-class life, *The Forsyte Saga*, with *The Man of Property* (1906). Most representative of the widespread early-twentieth-century attitude that, although serious social problems existed, they could be solved by a combination of popular education and remedial legislation was H. G. Wells (1866–1946). He wrote a prodigious number of works of science fiction, such as *The First Men in the Moon* (1901), as well as realistic novels and political manifestos such as *Mankind in the Making* (1903) and *A Modern Utopia* (1905); their purpose was to provide a blueprint by which science and education would completely remake society. Less hopeful of social progress but no less articulate were Hilaire Belloc (1870–1953) and G. K. Chesterton (1874–1936). The former a Roman Catholic by birth, the latter by conversion, both sought their utopias in the Middle Ages rather than in the twentieth century. However discordant their voices, the Edwardians lacked neither the energy nor the skill to bring a sense of intellectual ferment to their society.[5]

The Conservative Decline (1900–1905)

The government in power when the new century began was that of Lord Salisbury, who, although in no sense a Conservative diehard, was still very much part of a tradition harking back to William Cecil, Salisbury's sixteenth-century forebear — a tradition combining the life of a landed aristocrat with a career of public service. A peer as prime minister had

---

[5]A lively appraisal is provided by Samuel Hynes in *The Edwardian Turn of Mind* (1968).

come to seem anachronistic to many Britons, however, and Salisbury proved to be the last. His final ministry was dominated by Joseph Chamberlain; but the latter was by this time far more involved with schemes of imperial federation than with new programs of social reform. Salisbury's coalition of Conservatives and Liberal Unionists — the two did not finally and officially coalesce until 1912 — had received a strong vote of confidence in the "khaki election" of 1900, called in the wake of the Boer War victories. The governing coalition held 402 seats in the House of Commons and the opposition Liberals and Irish Home Rulers only 248 between them. The Liberal party, moreover, was still sorely divided between "Liberal imperialists" and "pro-Boers."

When Salisbury retired from the prime ministership because of ill health in 1902, the most obviously qualified successor was Joseph Chamberlain; but he was not really trusted by his political colleagues, and he made no serious fight for the position. The prime ministership was thereupon inherited by the longtime Conservative leader of the House of Commons, Salisbury's nephew Arthur James Balfour (1848–1930). Balfour was a genial fifty-five-year-old bachelor, a brilliant and charming conversationalist who possessed shrewd political insight and whose writings gave him some claim for consideration as a professional philosopher. Yet philosophical detachment was not the most useful talent for a twentieth-century political leader; and Balfour, as things turned out, presided over three successive years in which his party lost political strength, a process climaxed by the overwhelming Liberal triumph and Conservative defeat of January 1906.

That Liberal triumph was far less the result of the development of a positive Liberal program than of a capitalization on the political errors committed, often for the worthiest of motives, by Balfour's ministry. The first of these was the Education Act of 1902. Its main objective, that of raising educational standards in England and Wales, was beyond dispute. The means used for that end proved highly controversial, however. The locally elected school boards established by the Forster Education Act of 1870 were abolished as too small for the purpose; and the national primary-education system was put into the hands of the elected county and borough councils. At a time when elementary schooling had become universal but when at most only one fourteen-year-old in ten was still in the classroom, such councils were also authorized to set up their own tax-supported secondary schools. The number of students in such secondary institutions consequently increased from 94,000 in 1905 to 200,000 in 1914.

The controversial aspect of the act was that it authorized the new educational authorities to give grants to voluntary Church-affiliated schools (mostly Anglican) in order to raise the salaries of their teachers and limit the size of their classes to the level of the state schools. Because at the time the act was passed more children went to such "voluntary" schools (3,000,000) than to "board" schools (2,600,000), this meant that in many districts a child of Nonconformist parents was required to attend a school in which he might be taught Anglican doctrine and urged to attend Anglican services.

The Nonconformists had objected to the principle of tax grants to Church schools in 1870; now they were doubly outraged because the subsidy to religion was to come from locally raised "rates" (real estate taxes). Under the direction of a Baptist minister, John Clifford, they protested against this threat to "that divinest gift to man; the right to the free, unfettered and full use of his inmost soul," and they organized a Passive Resisters' League pledged to withhold taxes intended for Church schools. The league became so influential, especially in Wales, that Balfour's ministry felt compelled to pass special enforcement legislation. The Education Bill, its beneficial provisions overlooked, reconverted many a straying Liberal Unionist to the political faith of his fathers.

The Licensing Act of 1904 had a similar result. Temperance advocates, as convinced as ever that the prohibition of alcohol should take precedence over all other reform measures, had been cheered by a House of Lords ruling that pub licenses were limited for one year at a time and might therefore be revoked by municipal authorities. The act delegated authority over pubs instead to Justices of the Peace meeting in quarter sessions and levied a tax on brewers designed to compensate pub owners whose licenses had been taken away. In the long run, the act served to reduce the number of pubs without penalizing their owners, but in the short run the measure was denounced by temperance advocates as "a brewer's bill" intended to endow "the devilish trade." The Licensing Act thus won the Liberals additional recruits.

In the meantime the Conservative party had been split on an issue far more explosive than alcohol. Joseph Chamberlain, the man who in 1886 had divided the Liberal party by refusing to follow Gladstone on Irish Home Rule, in 1903 resigned from the cabinet and divided the Conservative party by publicly advocating tariff reform. After half a century of free trade, he wanted Britain to return to protection. His reasoning was simple enough. Let Britain set up a tariff wall taxing all imports, including food. Then let the government knock holes in the wall to admit food and manufactures from the colonies at a lower rate of duty. The result would be a customs union covering a quarter of the globe and 400 million people. Just as the German *Zollverein* of the 1830s had led to the German Empire of the 1870s, so, Chamberlain argued, the British customs union would in due course lead to a politically united empire. In the meantime, the extra revenue the government would acquire from the tariffs could be used for social reforms such as old-age pensions.

Chamberlain soon won over many members of his party; but a significant number, including the duke of Devonshire, the man who as marquess of Hartington had joined Chamberlain's secession from the Liberals, did not go along. Balfour vainly sought to steer a middle course. The country as a whole seemed unready to turn its back on free trade, an action that Sir Henry Campbell-Bannerman, the Liberal party leader, compared to "disputing the law of gravitation." "I don't think they will vote for Protection," explained Chamberlain's own brother Arthur, "because I can't think they will be so silly as to ask the government to tax the food they eat, the clothes they wear and the commodities they use, on the promise of the politicians that their wages will rise."

There, indeed, lay the crux of the matter. No matter how eloquently Chamberlain sang the praises of tariff protection and imperial federation, he found it difficult to deny that the most immediate result of tariff reform would be more expensive food. Thus Chamberlain's Tariff Reform League was soon countered by a Free Food League; and during the election campaign, Herbert Asquith, the former Liberal home secretary, stalked Chamberlain from town to town rebutting his arguments and contrasting, by means of placards and actual loaves of bread, the "Big Loaf" of free trade with the "Little Loaf" of protection. Chamberlain did not really expect to convert the country immediately. What he hoped was that the Liberals would briefly take over, that they would demonstrate their inability to govern, and that a Conservative party by then pledged to tariff protection would thereupon replace them. Balfour, although he did not take sides on the question of tariff reform, had similar expectations of Liberal incompetence. He therefore resigned in December 1905 without first calling for a general election. Perhaps, he thought, the divided Liberals might find it impossible even to construct a cabinet.

The Liberal Revival (1905–1908)

Conservative expectations were confounded. Henry Campbell-Bannerman was named prime minister by King Edward VII, and he soon put together one of the ablest cabinets in British history, one-third of them fellow Scots. Campbell-Bannerman had impressed most of his colleagues as a rather lackluster figure, but behind the scenes he had done much to heal the split in Liberal ranks created by the Boer War. He was a millionaire who had inherited his fortune from his father, a Glasgow warehouseman, and the second half of his hyphenated name from a maternal uncle who had deeded him a life interest in a large landed estate. Campbell-Bannerman had held office in all of Gladstone's ministries and had represented the same Scottish borough since 1868. He was similarly constant in his personal habits, but in politics he welcomed innovation. His appointment as prime minister transformed his manner from one of ineffectuality into one of decision and authority, and he had no fear that the more flamboyant or more articulate members of his cabinet would overshadow him.[6]

These included Herbert Asquith, Chancellor of the Exchequer; Sir Edward Grey, foreign secretary; and R. B. Haldane, secretary for war. The Liberal leader in the Lords, the marquess of Ripon, had the distinction of having served in the same cabinet as Palmerston and of being the son of a

---

[6]John Wilson, *CB: A Life of Sir Henry Campbell-Bannerman* (1973).

man who had been an M.P. with Fox. Herbert Gladstone, the youngest son of a distinguished father, was appointed home secretary, and David Lloyd George, a dynamic Welshman, was named president of the Board of Trade. Another young M.P., Winston Churchill, who had switched from his father's Conservative party on the issue of tariff protection, joined the ministry as under secretary for colonies; he was to join the cabinet proper two and a half years later. The most remarkable of Campbell-Bannerman's appointments at the time seemed to be that of John Burns as president of the Local Government Board. A one-time member of Hyndman's Social Democratic Federation and a leader of the London dock strike of 1889, Burns was the first manual laborer ever to enter a British cabinet. Paradoxically enough, he proved far less radical a political innovator than did several of his upper-middle-class colleagues.

As soon as the cabinet had been firmly installed, Campbell-Bannerman asked the king to dissolve Parliament and call for new elections. The brief campaign concentrated on the Education Act, the Licensing Act, and the tariff issue. The subject of imperialism also emerged in the form of "Chinese slavery": had the Conservative government been right to sanction the importation into South Africa of 46,000 Chinese to work under conditions of semislavery in South Africa's gold and diamond mines? To the Liberals this smacked too much of the concept that labor was a commodity.

While the significance of election billboards featuring sinister Chinese faces may not have been clear to every voter, most other issues were; and the election results were equally straightforward. The Liberals won by a landslide: Liberals, 401; Irish Nationalists, 83; Labour party, 29; Conservatives, 132; Liberal Unionists, 25. The popular vote margin was not nearly so decisive (3.15 million votes for the first three parties and 2.5 million for the remaining two); but it, too, was unmistakable. The Liberals had captured every seat in Wales, four-fifths of all the Scottish seats, and, for the first time since 1880, a clear majority of English seats as well. The Parliament of 1906 included at least 300 new M.P.'s. It was, in some ways, the first truly middle-class Parliament in English history, made up to a large extent of lawyers, journalists, and teachers, all of whom worked for a living and many of whom were extremely sympathetic to the idea that Members of Parliament should be paid. The Liberal contingent included only a minority (one in three) who had attended a public school. Never since the Parliaments of Oliver Cromwell had so many Nonconformists sat in the House of Commons.

One election result that caused considerable public comment was the arrival on the parliamentary scene of a separate Labour party of twenty-nine members. True, they dutifully hired the traditional top hats for the occasion, but their appearance as professed working-class representatives was a novelty. Labor's success at the polls was not only a reflection of the hard work done by the Labour Representation Committee but also the result of the Taff-Vale decision by the House of Lords in 1901, which decreed that an employer could sue a labor union for property damage caused by an individual member of that union. The decision seemed to threaten the funds and throw into question the legal status of trade unions, and many a worker decided, for the first time, that since Balfour's Conservative government appeared unwilling to reverse the judicial verdict by legislation, a distinct Labour party was needed.

A less advertised explanation for the presence of Labour M.P.'s in 1906 was a secret compact in 1903 between Herbert Gladstone, then chief Liberal whip, and Ramsay MacDonald, the secretary of the Labour Representation Committee. They agreed that, in a certain number of constituencies, Labourites and Liberals would not compete with each other and thereby risk a Conservative victory. The compact aided both parties in 1906 and provided the Labourites with at least sixteen of the twenty-nine seats they won that year. The Labourites could not afford, of course, to publicize an arrangement that seemed to make them no more than a Liberal appendage.

The new Liberal ministry soon set to work. It had no prepared social program; but its supporters included many impatient, reform-minded idealists, and it was conscious of the presence of the new band of Labourites, ready to criticize as too tame every projected reform. In imperial policy, the ministry was Gladstonian in outlook. At the fifth Colonial Conference of Prime Ministers (1907), it happily accepted the substitution of the term *dominion* for *colony* when referring to self-governing parts of the empire. In South Africa, Campbell-Bannerman — who had shown strong sympathy for the "pro-Boers" of his party a few years before — brought to an end the importation of Chinese laborers and insisted on the rapid establishment of autonomy in both the Transvaal and the Orange River Colony. Conservatives protested, but ex-Boer generals such as Louis Botha and Jan Christian Smuts cooperated willingly. A constitutional convention in 1908 among representatives of the four South African colonies led in 1909 to the establishment of the Union of South Africa to take its place with the other dominions as an autonomous member of the British imperial family.

The successful reconciliation of Briton and Boer after so many years of conflict was for some decades regarded as a triumph of British liberalism, but the long-term consequences were far more ambiguous. If only because the Boer War was not followed by a wave of immigrants from Britain, the spirit of Paul Kruger proved stronger than that of Campbell-Bannerman. Neither Briton nor Boer concerned himself at the time with the legal status of the native black population. In the Treaty of Vereeniging, which had ended the Boer War, the British government had indeed specifically pledged itself not to enfranchise black Africans until white South Africans had regained self-government. A Labour party motion to give such Africans the vote on terms of equality with the British and Boer population was consequently little heeded and easily defeated. The new Union of South Africa Parliament made no attempt to enfranchise even literate black Africans, and in the Natives Land Act (1913) it laid the foundation stone of the policy of racial *apartheid* that was to characterize South African life from the late 1940s until the late 1980s.

In India, the new Liberal ministry turned away from the paternalism represented by the viceroyalty of Lord Curzon and returned to a policy of cautiously developing the machinery for self-government. "We have had imposed upon us by the unlucky prowess of our ancestors," wrote John Morley, the secretary of state for India, "the task of ruling a vast number of millions of alien dependents." It was his hope to win the support of the more moderate leaders of educated and nationalistically inclined Indian middle classes, who had been convinced by British defeats in the Boer War and Russian defeats in the Russo-Japanese War that neither Britons nor white men generally were imbued with the innate superiority they had so often assumed. The reforms put into effect by the Liberals in 1909 did much to reconcile the Indian National Congress leaders for the moment. Henceforth, there was to be at least one Indian in the viceroy's cabinet and two in the secretary of state's Advisory Council in London. The provincial and central legislative councils were enlarged to include a greater number of elected members.

Extremists like B. G. Tilak, who sought immediate independence and were willing to use terroristic methods to obtain it, lost support for the

The Rulers of India A model "benevolent despot," the viceroy, Lord Curzon, and his Chicago-born wife ride in state during a procession in Delhi (1903). *(Reproduced by permission of the British Library)*

time being; and when King George V visited India in 1911 to assume the emperorship formally and receive the homage of Indian princes, he was hailed by hundreds of thousands of Indians. A step taken by the king-emperor that was popular with the Indians, although resented by many English civil servants, was to move the capital of British rule from sophisticated Calcutta to historic Delhi. There a British architect, Sir Edwin Lutyens, planned the handsome public buildings, the wide avenues, and the circular colonnades of New Delhi that were to serve first the British raj and, after World War II, the rulers of the new Republic of India.

Back at home, the Conservatives quickly rallied in defeat. Joseph Chamberlain, whose native Birmingham had remained loyal to him despite the Liberal landslide elsewhere, was ready to replace Balfour as leader on a platform of "tariff reform"; but on July 11, 1906, three days after the city of Birmingham celebrated Chamberlain's seventieth birthday with extraordinary enthusiasm, that difficult political warrior was struck down by a paralytic stroke. Although he lingered on until 1914, his political career had come to an abrupt end. Arthur James Balfour thus remained the leader of the opposition, and a year later he decided to embrace the doctrine of tariff protection as his own.

By then he had also learned to use the House of Lords as a means of blocking Liberal bills that the Conservatives could not stop in the House of Commons. The traditional upper chamber — in which the Liberals were a small minority and which had not rejected a single measure during the previous ten years of Conservative rule — was now used as an adjunct of the Conservative party. In 1906 the Lords vetoed an Education Bill to relieve English and Welsh Nonconformists of their objections to the 1902 act. All further attempts to amend the religious provisions of that bill proved equally unavailing. Another bill, to end plural voting by persons who owned property in more than one constituency and had the right to vote in each, was similarly thrown out by the Lords. In 1907 two bills to expand the rights of Scottish tenant farmers were turned down. The same fate befell a 1908 Licensing Act by which the Liberals hoped within a few years to close 32,000 pubs, one-third of the country's establishments serving alcoholic beverages.

Campbell-Bannerman was outraged. It was all very well for the House of Lords to argue that, on issues that had not been publicly debated, the peers should serve as a delaying chamber that gave public opinion time to make itself felt. But the country had just expressed its opinion on measures such as the Education Act of 1902 by electing an overwhelming majority of Liberals. He moved a resolution that the power of the House of Lords be so restricted by law "as to secure that within the limits of a single Parliament the final decision of the Commons should prevail." The House of Commons approved the resolution by a vote of 432 to 147, but for the moment the prime minister refrained from carrying the fight to the House of Lords. To appeal to the country in a new general election so soon again seemed undesirable, and even risky, and for two years the issue of the House of Lords hung fire.

The House of Lords in any event did not block a number of measures likely to be of special appeal to workingmen, a group of voters many Conservatives sought to win, or rewin, to their side. Thus the Trade Disputes Act of 1906 overturned the Taff-Vale decision of 1901 and freed unions (unlike corporations) from all legal suits involving their members' activities. This statute, passed at a time when only one worker in ten had joined a trade union, was to remain in force even after more than half the labor force had become unionized. Whereas in other industrialized nations, employer-employee relations were to be subject to a code of legal regulations, in Britain trade unions became essentially immune to restraint by law.[7] In 1906 English and Welsh schools were authorized to provide hot lunches for schoolchildren; soon thereafter they were given the task of providing regular medical examinations for all schoolchildren and with setting up school clinics as well. In 1908 an eight-hour day for miners was established by law. For the first time since the repeal of the Elizabethan Apprenticeship Statutes, the hours worked by adult males were brought under governmental supervision. At the Board of Trade, David Lloyd George established a reputation for constructive statesmanship by sponsoring the first census of industrial production in Britain and by codifying merchant shipping legislation and reforming patent law. Lloyd George went on successfully to mediate a railway and shipyard strike and to supersede the chaos of private dock companies along the Thames with a single Port of London authority, in effect a measure of nationalization. In the meantime, Herbert Asquith at the Exchequer had introduced a novel old-age-pension scheme into the 1908 budget. Virtually all British and Irish citizens seventy or older with a weekly income of ten shillings ($2.50 in 1908 dollars) or less were to be entitled to a weekly pension of five shillings ($1.25) from the government. The sums were small, even by 1908 standards, but a scheme that immediately benefited one million citizens set a major precedent. For the first time, the obligation of society to take care of its elderly citizens was accepted by the state as a matter of right rather than of charity.

Asquith, Churchill, and Lloyd George

By the time the old-age-pension scheme had become law in 1908, Campbell-Bannerman was dead. His logical successor as prime minister, in the eyes of both King Edward VII and of Liberal M.P.'s, was Herbert Henry Asquith (1852–1928), a Yorkshireman of Nonconformist origins who had won plaudits at Oxford but who had then worked for several years as an obscure London lawyer commuting each night to a small house in Hampstead, where he kept chickens in his back garden. He was elected to Parliament in 1886, became a cabinet minister six years later, and, three years after the death of his first wife, married Margot Tennant, a star in

---

[7]See Henry Phelps Brown, *The Origins of Trade Union Power* (1984).

the firmament of literate upper-class London society. His pro-government stand at the time of the Boer War had alienated many Liberals; but those wounds had healed by 1908, and Asquith had won a deserved reputation as a parliamentary debater and as Chancellor of the Exchequer. He never became a popular hero, perhaps because he lacked the imaginative flair that Britain's greatest prime ministers have all possessed. He did, however, have the ability to manage men; and he was so able an orator and could support a case with such lawyerlike precision and conviction that his predecessor nicknamed him "The Sledgehammer." At one public meeting Asquith spoke eloquently for an hour in support of the government's Licensing Bill. He reinforced his case with reams of facts and strings of statistics. When an admiring listener came up to him afterwards and asked whether she might have his notes as a souvenir, he handed her a scrap of paper on which were scrawled three words: "Too many pubs."

Asquith's prime ministership began in April 1908 and was to be the longest continuous prime ministership since Lord Liverpool's a century before, but an eight-and-a-half-year tenure seemed at the time a most unlikely prospect. An economic recession had raised unemployment figures to close to 10 percent. The government was losing by-elections right and left, and the tariff reformers were winning new converts. Conservative strategists felt increasingly confident that a new general election would return their party to power with a comfortable majority. Under the circumstances, Asquith was fully prepared to listen to cabinet members who were willing to look for ways to implement the "new liberalism" espoused by sociologists such as Leonard T. Hobhouse and publicists such as J. A. Hobson. Both sought to curb the power of corporate wealth and to enlarge the role of government while retaining the traditional Liberal concern with individual liberty and remaining suspicious of a tendency toward dictatorial bureaucracy in doctrinaire socialism.[8]

The two cabinet members most eager to revive the government's sagging fortunes by experimenting with novel reforms were David Lloyd George, who now became Chancellor of the Exchequer, and Winston Churchill, who replaced Lloyd George as president of the Board of Trade. As a grandson of the eighth duke of Marlborough, Churchill had had no youthful contact with lower-class life and was regarded by his erstwhile Conservative colleagues as a turncoat. But Churchill shared with Lloyd George a restless urge to seek out and apply new ideas, and in 1909 he discovered and pushed two far-reaching concepts.[9] One of these was sug-

---

[8]Such ideas are assessed by Michael Freeden, *The New Liberalism* (1978), and Peter Clarke, *Liberals and Social Democrats* (1978).

[9]The period and the men are brought alive in biographies such as Stephen Koss's exemplary *Asquith* (1976) and Roy Jenkins's elegant *Asquith: Portrait of a Man and an Era* (1964); in John Grigg's evocative *Lloyd George: The People's Champion, 1902–1911* (1978), the second volume of a multivolume series, and in Bentley Gilbert's more skeptical *David Lloyd*

Two Liberal Social Reformers The youthful Winston Churchill (1904) and the dynamic David Lloyd George (1910). *(Hulton Deutsch Collection)*

gested to him by a young journalist and amateur sociologist named William Beveridge (1879–1963), who in 1909 published a book entitled *Unemployment*. Beveridge met Churchill at one of the many dinners Beatrice and Sidney Webb gave for intellectuals and politicians and convinced him that the government should sponsor a network of Labour Exchanges, offices where the unemployed might register for jobs and where employers might make known their needs. Churchill pushed a measure calling for such a network through Parliament in 1909 and appointed Beveridge the first director of Labour Exchanges. The new offices could not create employment as such, but they could spare people the daily drudgery of walking the streets in search of work. Employers were similarly benefited. The Labour Exchanges were a still-novel example of government offices whose purpose was not to tax people or sell them things — such as the post office — but to promote their welfare. They were also the necessary prelude to an even bolder measure, for which Churchill was also primarily responsible — the establishment of a scheme of unemployment insurance.

Churchill's other proposal dealt with the regulation of the "sweated" trades. A royal commission two decades earlier had deplored the fate of

George: A Political Life — the first two volumes (1987, 1992) carry the story to 1916. The best brief life is Chris Wrigley, *Lloyd George* (1992). For Churchill, see Volume II (1967) of the eight-volume biography begun by Randolph Churchill and completed by Martin Gilbert (1965–1988). Henry Pelling's *Winston Churchill* (2nd ed., 1989) provides a more compact overview. See also Paul Addison, *Churchill on the Home Front, 1900–1955* (1992).

this new generation of domestic workers, but successive governments had hesitated to tackle the regulation of subcontracted work done, not in factories or workshops, but in the cellars or garrets of private homes. In 1906, however, a Sweated Trades Exhibition, sponsored by the liberal *Daily News,* called attention anew to the fact that the fine clothes worn by a middle- or upper-class woman might well have been stitched by starving wretches slaving sixteen hours a day in East End cellars for less than a penny an hour. Churchill's Trade Boards Act of 1909 established government commissions for the tailoring, paper box, lace, and chain trades to set minimum wages and maximum hours.

In the meantime the new Chancellor of the Exchequer had not been idle at his post. Lloyd George, the orphaned son of a Welsh village schoolmaster, had been raised by a shoemaker uncle and was a genuine "man of the people" in a sense that Churchill could not be. He rose in politics as the champion of Welsh Nonconformity, although in fact he had little religious faith, and as the symbol of militant teetotalism, although in private he enjoyed his glass of champagne. Lloyd George possessed the voice and the magnetic personality to sweep an audience into an emotional frenzy. He outraged his Conservative opponents from the start by his public radicalism; yet in private negotiation he could be an adept mediator and a mollifying persuader. It was Lloyd George's radicalism, however, that was most apparent in the renowned "People's Budget" of 1909.

Lloyd George had a number of purposes in constructing his budget. One was to raise £16 million in order to build additional warships and to pay for old-age pensions and other social services. "This is a War Budget," he emphasized. "It is for raising money to wage an implacable war against poverty and squalidness." Second, he saw the budget as a means of translating into action a longstanding Liberal campaign promise to deal with selfish Conservative landlords. Third, he saw the budget as a way to capture the attention of the electorate through a dramatic measure of reform: the budget altered the British tax system. The income tax was turned into the single most important source of government revenue, and a new "super tax" to be paid by the very wealthy established the concept of progressive taxation for income as it had earlier been established for inheritance. Moreover, death duties were raised as high as 25 percent for those leaving estates of over a million pounds. A new tax on gasoline and automobiles was introduced for road-paving purposes. Most controversial of all were taxes on land — a 20 percent levy on the unearned increment of land value (to be paid whenever real estate changed hands) and a small duty on the capital value of undeveloped lands and minerals. It was these last taxes that raised the greatest outcry, if only because they required a precise valuation of all the landholdings in the country.[10] The Conservatives in the House of Commons resisted the budget every step of the way; but

---

[10]The most controversial tax, that on the unearned increment of land, proved to cost more to administer than it contributed in revenue. It was later repealed.

after seventy sittings and 554 divisions, it was passed in November 1909 by a vote of 379 to 149. Three and a half weeks later the House of Lords overwhelmingly rejected the budget, 350 to 75.

The Revolt of the Peers

It has sometimes been argued that Lloyd George introduced the budget of 1909 with the purpose of goading the Lords into vetoing the measure. This seems unlikely, if only because Asquith, who supported his Chancellor of the Exchequer all the way, did not think the House of Lords would do anything so obviously unconstitutional. To deprive the government of revenue was tantamount to voting it out of office. Never since the Glorious Revolution had the House of Lords laid claim to such a power, and not since Gladstone introduced the consolidated annual budget of 1861 had the upper house tampered with any revenue measure. By 1909, however, Conservatives had become deeply fearful of the threat to their purses and of the manner in which Lloyd George's brand of "socialism" undermined their own panacea of "tariff reform" and at the same time threatened the future of the British Empire. They therefore failed to heed the possible political consequences. Dozens of peers who had scarcely set foot in the House of Lords before now appeared to cast their votes.

Once the prospect of a House of Lords veto loomed, Lloyd George was happy enough to goad the peers on. "The peers may decree a revolution," he declared, "but the people will direct it. If they begin, issues will be raised that they little dream of. . . . It will be asked why 500 ordinary men, chosen accidentally from among the unemployed, should override the judgment — the deliberate judgment — of millions of people." Immediately after the unprecedented veto, Prime Minister Asquith moved and carried in the House of Commons a resolution declaring the peers' action "a breach of the Constitution and a usurpation of the rights of the Commons." Shortly thereafter he asked the king to dissolve Parliament. A new general election was called to resolve the conflict of "the Peers against the People."

The key issue was the budget, but the future role of the House of Lords was involved as well, and Lloyd George continued to speak scornfully of the qualifications for the upper house. "No testimonials are required. There are no credentials. They do not even need a medical certificate. They need not be sound, either in body or in mind. They only require a certificate of birth, just to prove that they are the first of the litter. You would not choose a spaniel on these principles." The Conservatives, in turn, charged the Liberals with a "conspiracy" to substitute single-chamber government for Britain's traditional system and renewed their championship of Chamberlain's policy of tariff reform.

The results were disappointing to both major parties: Liberals, 275; Conservatives, 273; Irish Nationalists, 82; Labour party, 40. In one sense the Liberal position had been upheld. The parties that wished to limit the power of the House of Lords — the Liberals and the Irish and the Labourites — together had a large majority. Yet it was clear that Asquith's Liberals could no longer act alone; they were now dependent on the support of the smaller parties. The only way to assure Irish cooperation for the budget was to promise a new push for Irish Home Rule. The only way to assure Labour support was to sponsor additional laws favored by trade unions. The Conservatives, who had staged a remarkable recovery, were even more frustrated by their inability to regain office.

The government's immediate project was to enact the controversial Lloyd George budget. With Irish help, it easily passed the Commons, and a considerably chastened House of Lords accepted it without a division after a single day's debate. Willingness to accept a "People's Budget" was not sufficient, however, to stave off constitutional retribution, for the House of Commons quickly passed a Parliament Bill to limit the powers of the House of Lords permanently. Henceforth, the upper house might delay money bills (including budgets) for at most one month. Other bills were to be limited to a delay of two years and to become law without the approval of the Lords provided that three successive sessions of the Commons had passed the same measure. Finally, the bill required a general election at least every five years rather than every seven years.

The question of the hour became whether the House of Lords would acquiesce in its demotion to second-class status or whether it would fight. Many peers suddenly became interested in alternate schemes of reform that would have retained the power of the House of Lords but modified its structure: to restrict the right to vote to certain peers only; to add a number of peers for life to the hereditary peers. No such proposals came to fruition.

A number of Liberal and Conservative leaders were disposed to seek a compromise solution to the constitutional dilemma, however, and their opportunity came in the summer of 1910. Edward VII had died unexpectedly in April; the new king, George V, called on the leaders of the two major parties to advance the national interest by coming up with a mutually acceptable compromise. A consequent series of secret conferences came close to resolving the crisis. Provisional agreement was reached on a procedure for settling disputes between the two houses that would have involved joint sittings for most disputed bills and popular referenda for constitutional changes. The conferences were going so well, in fact, that Lloyd George, switching from the role of radical agitator to persuasive manipulator of power, proposed a Liberal-Conservative coalition ministry in which Asquith would move to the House of Lords and continue as prime minister while Balfour would lead the House of Commons. In return for Conservative support for their social reforms, the Liberals would accept a Conservative proposal for compulsory military service (in emulation of Switzerland) and promise to consider tariff reform. Ultimately, both the attempt to evolve a compromise plan for dealing with the House of Lords and Lloyd George's surprising coalition proposal proved abortive. Balfour was too fearful that his party would lose its iden-

didn't work

tity, and the Liberals were too worried that such a coalition would destroy any chance of Home Rule for Ireland.

When the conference broke down and the House of Lords defeated the Parliament Bill, Asquith advised the king to dissolve Parliament and call another election, the second within the year. The specific issue presented to the electorate was whether the House of Lords was to be permanently curbed or not. If the Liberal ministry were to be returned to power, the king promised to create — if necessary — a sufficient number of peers to ensure the passage of the Parliament Bill by the House of Lords. This was an eventuality King George V wished desperately to avoid, but he felt that he had no constitutional alternative. For the moment, however, the king's promise was kept secret.

The second election proved in many respects a replica of the first. For the Liberals the crucial problem was the necessity of curbing the authority of the House of Lords; for the Conservatives it was the danger of Home Rule for Ireland, which seemed sure to follow. The Labour party had its own interests — specifically the Osborne Judgment of 1909 in which the House of Lords (meaning the law lords acting as supreme court) had held illegal the manner in which the trade unions had used the dues of their members to support political candidates and to provide an income to M.P.'s sponsored by unions. As a result, the party was left with virtually no funds, and several Labour M.P.'s were in dire straits. There is considerable evidence that, although such issues very much concerned the politicians at Westminster, the average voter was becoming apathetic. A number of seats changed hands, but the overall results of the election of December 1910 were almost identical to those of the previous January: Liberals, 272; Conservatives, 272; Irish Nationalists, 84; Labour party, 42.

According to the traditional rules of politics, the Conservatives should now have conceded the battle. But they refused to recognize the reality of their defeat. They did not know that the king had already given Asquith a pledge to create enough peers to end their control of the House of Lords. Many of them felt the Liberals were somehow cheating by relying for their majority on two such splinter groups as the Labour party and the Irish Nationalists. Certain Conservatives, convinced that their leaders — A. J. Balfour in the Commons and Lord Lansdowne in the Lords — were not providing sufficiently vigorous party leadership, hoped that continued resistance to the Parliament Bill would necessitate yet a third general election.

"The House of Lords," Lloyd George had observed in 1908, "is not the watchdog of the Constitution; it is Mr. Balfour's poodle."[11] Now the

---

[11]Roy Jenkins's *Mr. Balfour's Poodle* (1954) is a comprehensive and readable account of the whole constitutional crisis of 1909–1911. For the "ditchers," see Gregory D. Phillips, *The Diehards: Aristocratic Society and Politics in Edwardian England* (1979). For the pre-war Conservative ethos generally, see Frans Coetzee, *For Party or Country: Nationalism and the Dilemmas of Popular Conservatism in Edwardian England* (1990).

poodle began to bite its erstwhile master, as a group of Conservatives appeared who ignored Balfour's advice and preferred if necessary "to die in the last ditch." The "Ditchers," under the eighty-eight-year-old Lord Halsbury, stood firm against the "Hedgers," who preferred the retention by the House of Lords of a suspensive veto to being swamped by 400 new peers.

The Ditchers did not really believe that Asquith would dare to recommend the mass creation of peers; but the prime minister was serious and had secretly prepared a list that included some of Britain's most prominent scholars and writers. The crisis reached its climax when the Ditchers emasculated the Parliament Bill with amendments. Asquith privately informed the Conservative leaders that he would ask the king to fulfill his promise unless the amendments were dropped; but when he rose in the House of Commons to move the rejection of those amendments, outraged Conservative M.P.'s greeted his motion with a chorus of shouts, catcalls, and denunciations. For the first time in British history, a House of Commons refused to let a prime minister speak, and after half an hour of tumult the Speaker suspended the sitting. Balfour had earlier counseled the Conservative peers simply to abstain and let the Liberal peers pass the controversial bill; but as the Ditchers remained adamant, he now felt forced to ask some Conservatives to vote for the measure they despised. The final vote took place during a mid-August heat wave. On August 9, the Greenwich Observatory thermometer reached 100 degrees — the highest temperature ever recorded in Great Britain — and the temperature inside the Lords' chamber seemed even hotter. The outcome was uncertain until the last moment, but in the end the bill passed, 131 to 114. Every Liberal peer had been mustered, and eventually the Liberals were joined by thirty-seven Unionists peers, the two archbishops, and eleven bishops. The Ditchers had been defeated, and no mass creation of peers would take place.

The Twentieth-Century Constitution

The Parliament Act of 1911 had an important effect upon both the nation's constitution and all of its political parties. It belongs with the Reform Acts of 1832, 1867, and 1884 as a key measure that helped to make Britain a political democracy. The statute made a matter of law what had long been a matter of practice, the preeminence of the House of Commons; yet despite the fears of many Conservatives, it did not lead to the total abolition of the traditional two-chamber structure of the government. The House of Lords retained its power to amend, its power to delay, and its role as a reservoir of cabinet members.

The constitutional crisis had also shown once again that if the monarch were to remain above politics, he would have to abide by the decisions of a cabinet that possessed the confidence of a parliamentary majority. So long as such a majority existed, the monarch retained in practice three rights only — "the right to be consulted, the right to encourage, the right to warn." Half a century before, Walter Bagehot had so defined the limits of monarchical authority, but George V was the first English king to have read Bagehot or to think of himself as a constitutional and limited monarch who reigned but did not rule.[12] The change has been aptly described:

> In the eighteenth century the prime minister got his importance from the fact that he was the only person in the realm who had the right of constant access to the monarch; today the monarch gets his importance from the fact that he is the only person in the realm who has the right of constant access to the prime minister.

With the passage of the Parliament Act and the decision made during the same year to pay all members of Parliament £400 annually, all but one of the Chartist demands of the 1830s and 1840s had been substantially enacted into law. Even the last, annual elections, had been tried in 1910; but neither M.P.'s nor the electorate saw great value in repeating that experiment. The House of Commons of 1911 was made up much less of individually independent members than of members pledged to support their party. As a result, it was no longer so much the House of Commons that controlled the cabinet as it was the cabinet that now controlled the Commons. Admittedly, ministers still had to justify their policies to members of their own party, but, provided that party controlled a majority of seats, the possibility of the House of Commons voting "no confidence" in a ministry had now almost disappeared. The odium of party disloyalty was too great an electoral handicap. Thus by 1911 the real check on a ministry was not the House of Commons but the electorate, which could and did exercise its power firmly but intermittently.

The prime minister of 1911 remained in theory no more than first among equals; the concept of collective cabinet responsibility remained. But insofar as the prime minister had a dominant voice in choosing and placing his colleagues, he obviously approached the powers of an American president; and insofar as he was not only chief executive but by definition leader of the majority in the legislature, his authority was often more effective than that of an American president. Some prime ministers saw their role primarily as chairman of the board and initiated little. Others saw themselves as leaders of the nation in all but ceremonial matters, which should appropriately be left in the hands of a monarch who symbolized national unity and historical continuity.

The Parliament Act of 1911 had immediate as well as long-range political repercussions. In the Conservative party the irate Ditchers launched

---

[12]Harold Nicolson, *King George V* (1952), and Kenneth Rose, *King George V* (1984). See also Frank Hardie, *The Political Influence of the British Monarchy, 1868–1952* (1970).

a "B.M.G." campaign: Balfour Must Go. Always the somewhat detached philosopher, Balfour refused to combat the movement, and in November 1911 he resigned as party leader. As matters turned out, his political career was far from over. His successor was Andrew Bonar Law (1858–1923), a Member of Parliament for eleven years who had been born in Canada and raised in Scotland and who had never held cabinet office. Although he appeared to be a morose and solitary man, Law also demonstrated shrewd political skills in successfully holding his divided party together. Under his leadership, however, the mood of frustrated militancy that had become apparent in Conservative ranks grew yet stronger.

The Liberals, in turn, had to satisfy the Labourites and the Irish Nationalists with whose cooperation they had chastised and chastened the House of Lords. With Lloyd George still Chancellor of the Exchequer and Winston Churchill now home secretary, the ministry introduced a bill calling for two precedent-breaking social reforms: national health insurance and unemployment insurance. Both proposals were in part the consequence of the Poor Law Commission Report of 1909, which was published after four years of hearings. Both the Majority and Minority Reports recommended extensive changes in the operations of the 1834 Poor Law. The Minority Report, written by the Webbs, indeed proposed the scrapping of the Poor Law concept altogether in favor of separate government-sponsored social services dealing with illness, unemployment, and old age. The old workhouse, whose conditions were by definition to be worse than those the lowest-paid wage-earner could afford, was to give way to "the national minimum" below which no citizen was to be allowed to fall. Neither set of recommendations was, for the time being, put into effect. For the moment, the Poor Law was not abolished, but it was increasingly being supplemented by new state services, which (unlike the Poor Law) did not designate recipients as second-class citizens.

In setting up a national health service, Lloyd George was much influenced by the successful operation of a similar scheme in Germany. Because a host of voluntary societies already provided members of the working class with sickness and death benefits, Lloyd George decided to incorporate these societies into a national scheme that would apply to all workers who earned less than £160 ($800) a year. Each employee would contribute fourpence a week, each employer threepence, and the national government twopence. In return the employee would obtain free medical care from the doctor on whose panel he or she was enrolled and weekly sick pay when out of work because of illness. The act passed Parliament with relatively little difficulty, although there was great opposition for a time from the employers of domestic servants and from the British Medical Association. The doctors were soon won over by the fact that the government was prepared to pay them more per panel patient than voluntary societies had ever done. The act applied almost immediately to fourteen million people, one-third of the population, and in due course became the basis for the far more comprehensive National Health Service established in 1948.

The other part of the National Insurance Act of 1911 provided the national program of unemployment insurance. In contrast to old-age pensions and health insurance, Britain was in this matter blazing a new trail rather than following the example of Germany, and the project was seen at the time as "a risky adventure into the unknown." For the moment it was limited to some 2,250,000 workers in the construction, engineering, shipbuilding, and vehicle-building industries. The unemployment insurance fund was created by equal contributions from employer, employee, and the state. In return, an insured worker who lost a job could expect a weekly payment of seven shillings ($1.75 in 1911 dollars) for up to fifteen weeks a year. Although the contributory principle at the time bitterly split the small Labour party — Ramsay MacDonald favored it and Philip Snowden wished all expenses to come from the national Exchequer — the principle of dividing costs among employer, employee, and state was to become the pattern for most future welfare state programs.

The National Insurance Act of 1911 proved to be the last major social reform enacted by the Liberal government, but it did place in the statute book a number of minor measures as well. The Osborne Judgment of 1909 was partially repealed by a Trades Disputes Act of 1913, which provided that trade unions might collect money for political purposes if their members approved, if they placed it in a separate fund, and if they gave each member the option of "contracting out." Shop assistants, a class of workers who lacked union organization and who were often greatly exploited, were given a compulsory half-day off in addition to Sunday; thus arose the longtime British custom of an "early closing day" (not necessarily Saturday) for all stores. Another Liberal measure, one more in line with nineteenth-century tradition, was the Welsh Disestablishment Bill of 1912. The purpose of the bill was to deprive the Church of England of its special privileges and some of the property in Wales, where its adherents numbered no more than one-quarter of the population. The measure passed the Commons but was halted in the Lords until 1920. Along with the University of Wales, chartered in 1893 (as a federation of three constituent university colleges), the measure gave formal recognition to a reviving sense of cultural Welsh identity.

Suffragettes and Syndicalists

By 1912 the dynamism of reform was exhausted. The Liberal party had taken a series of giant strides along the road to the welfare state, but much of the party remained middle class in leadership and Victorian in inclination and viewed such social reform legislation with considerable misgivings; nor did the measures seem to arouse great political enthusiasm among their intended lower-class beneficiaries. Moreover, the time and energy of the Liberal cabinet was increasingly involved with efforts to preserve law and order in the face of a growing number of civil disobedience campaigns. The catcalls and clamor that had greeted Asquith in the House of Commons during the debate on the Parliament Bill seemed to herald an era of militancy and even violence in which at times all precepts of Victorian respectability and moderation were thrown to the winds. Beneath a surface stability, the "Revolt of the Peers" was followed by comparable revolts by suffragettes, syndicalist union leaders, and Irish Ulstermen — until these domestic tempests were suddenly submerged within that far greater and more frightful storm of violence called world war.[13]

In some ways the most sensational difficulty confronting the Liberal government was how to deal with the tactics of the suffragettes, who demanded complete political equality for both sexes. The movement for women's suffrage dated back to the 1860s and had won a number of successes at the level of local government. The Women's Social and Political Union, founded in 1903 by Emmeline Pankhurst (1857–1928), the widow of a Manchester doctor who was a one-time member of Keir Hardie's Independent Labour party, soon broke with earlier methods of petitioning and pamphleteering. By 1908 a clear distinction had grown up between the constitutionalist "suffragists," the National Union of Women's Suffrage Societies headed by Millicent Garrett Fawcett (1847–1929), and the militant "suffragettes" led by Mrs. Pankhurst and her daughters, Christabel and Sylvia. The suffragists were far more numerous, but the suffragettes dominated the newspaper headlines.

In 1905 the militants began a regular program of interrupting Liberal speakers with the cry "Votes for Women!" All Liberals were heckled — those who openly supported women's suffrage, such as Sir Edward Grey and Lloyd George, and those who were hostile, such as Asquith. The heckling was limited to Liberals on the grounds that, as long as the Liberals constituted the government, they alone could provide women's suffrage. The political difficulty faced by the Liberals was that, as long as the vote was still granted on the basis of the ownership or rental of property, then to give the vote to women would mean enfranchising only a minority (women property-owners), who would in all likelihood proceed to vote Conservative. The alternative was a bill to enfranchise all adults equally, but for this there was little popular pressure. Between 1907 and 1913 several bills enfranchising women received approval in principle in the House of Commons, but none was enacted into law.

In 1912, after the failure of one such measure, the tactics of the suffragettes grew more violent. They broke the windows in No. 10 Downing

---

[13]Although weak at analysis, George Dangerfield is excellent at evoking the prewar atmosphere in *The Strange Death of Liberal England* (1935). In *The Edwardian Crisis, 1901–1914* (1996), David Powell provides a judicious if more prosaic look at the same topics. For the suffragette movement, Roger Fulford's *Votes for Women* (1957) remains a helpful overview. Amid a plethora of more recent books on the subject, Andrew Rosen, *Rise Up, Women!* (1974), David Morgan, *Suffragists and Liberals* (1975), Sandra Holton, *Feminism and Democracy: Women's Suffrage and Reform Politics in Britain, 1900–1918* (1986), and Lisa Tickner, *The Spectacle of Women: Imagery of the Suffrage Campaign, 1907–1914* (1988), stand out.

Broken Glass On March 1, 1912, hundreds of militant suffragettes descended on the West End of London wielding hammers and stones in order to break the windows of scores of elegant shops and department stores. Emmeline Pankhurst and 120 other women were arrested. The illustration is by a contemporary artist. *(Bettman/Corbis)*

Street and embarked on an orgy of window smashing in London's shopping districts. "The argument of broken glass is the most valuable argument in modern politics," explained Mrs. Pankhurst. They chained themselves to railings in Parliament Square. They dropped acid into mail boxes. They slashed pictures in public art galleries. From her Paris hideout, Christabel Pankhurst began in 1912 a campaign of arson. Empty houses in different parts of the country were burned; so were several churches, a school, and a railway station. When arrested and jailed, many suffragettes would go on hunger strikes; and the government, anxious not to have them die in jail, employed controversial methods of forced feeding.

Although such aggressive tactics initially gave new life to the cause of women's suffrage and helped the passage in 1907 of an act removing all doubt as to the eligibility of women to serve as town and county councillors, eventually the extremist strategy impeded that cause. It gave rise, indeed, to an influential counterpressure group, the National League for Opposing Woman Suffrage, headed by the imperialist Lord Cromer and the novelists Mrs. Humphrey Ward and Violet Markham, who dismissed the cause of female suffrage as a frivolous distraction from more important national concerns. Yet it remained *the* cause — a badge of equality rather than the means to any particular end — for the most militant suffragettes, such as the young woman who courted, and found, martyrdom on Derby Day in 1913 by throwing herself in front of the king's horse.

Ultimately, such militancy contradicted the professed purpose of the movement, because exercise of the vote presupposes the rule of free persuasion. As the leading suffragist, Millicent Garrett Fawcett, pointed out,

> The House of Commons, with all its faults, stands for order against anarchy, for justice against brutality, and to overcome it and to invite others to overcome it by brute force . . . was in my opinion the act either of a mad woman or a dastard. . . . It is not by such weapons as these that we stand to win.[14]

Yet the suffragette leaders continued to proclaim by word and deed that the way to get results was by violent action. "The militants will rejoice when victory comes," wrote Christabel Pankhurst, "and yet, mixed with joy, will be regret that the most glorious chapter in women's history is closed and the militant fight over — over, when so many have not yet known the exaltation, the rapture of battle."

If the combative suffragettes were a nuisance to the government, then the mass labor strikes of 1911 and 1912 were a threat to the entire economy of the country. Here too a mood of violence and frustration was evident —frustration with the failure of some wages to keep up with rising prices, irritation with the peaceful and seemingly ineffectual methods of the Labour party. For the time being, a number of trade-union leaders preferred direct action to parliamentary pressure. Some of them, men such as Tom Mann of the engineers and A. J. Cook of the miners, became convinced syndicalists. They saw the trade union not as a pressure group but as a potential unit of government. They saw the class struggle as a war that should be fought with a series of militant strikes, all leading up to the general strike that would bring the capitalist parliamentary system to an end and somehow bring into being a syndicalist utopia. Orthodox socialists distrusted the syndicalists, and most of the trade-union members did not fully understand the ultimate aims of their leaders. They did prove, however, increasingly sympathetic to the appeal to violence. Whether the motive for strikes was wages or forced unionization of unorganized workers or sympathy with the grievances of other laborers mattered little. Often, indeed, strikes began in defiance of the national union leadership.

In 1910 a strike of Lancashire cotton workers, which began over a question involving the duties of one man, idled 120,000 workers. A strike by a handful of South Wales miners who were dissatisfied with the rate of pay on a particular seam of coal resulted in a sympathy walkout by 30,000 miners. A seamen's strike in Liverpool during the summer of 1911 led to rioting. The army was called in; strikers stoned the troops and burned trains; two men were killed and two hundred wounded. During the same summer Britain experienced its first general railway strike. Late

---

[14]Cited in Leslie Parker Hume, *The National Union of Women's Suffrage Societies, 1897–1914* (1985), p. 51.

in the year, a weavers' strike idled 126,000 workers for a month, and in March 1912 a general miners' strike involved 850,000 men. This particular dispute was finally settled by an act of Parliament setting up district conferences to decide on minimum wages along lines the government had proposed before the strike began. Later in 1912 a dock strike began on the technical issue of whether one particular foreman had the right to work as a regular union hand. The strike evoked little public sympathy and collapsed after six weeks. The year 1913 saw the organization of a "Triple Alliance" of miners, railway men, and transport workers. The three unions agreed to coordinate their tactics and to plan for a possible general strike late in 1914.

Although some of these strikes were successful in winning specific gains, others were not. Still others demonstrated the unwieldiness of a strike involving hundreds of thousands of men in settling fairly technical contract details. The union leaders often lacked both the freedom and the flexibility to bargain effectively. The strikes did, however, strengthen a sense of working-class consciousness and, because the rate of unemployment was low, they went hand in hand with a steady growth of union membership. Between 1910 and 1914 membership in unions affiliated with the Trades Union Congress (and almost all now were) increased from 2.3 million to 4 million.

Ireland Again

Of all the pre–World War I revolts, it was the Irish question that by 1914 represented the greatest threat to parliamentary government and that brought Britain closer to genuine civil war than it had been at any time since the early eighteenth century. The issue had slumbered since Gladstone's second Home Rule Bill had been defeated by the House of Lords in 1893. The Irish Nationalist party had remained strong in Parliament and, under the leadership of John Redmond (1856–1918), it waited patiently for the day when the Liberals would be powerful enough to overawe the House of Lords. In 1911 that day seemed at hand; and during the parliamentary session following the passage of the act curbing the upper house, Asquith introduced, and the House of Commons approved, a Home Rule Bill. The Lords refused to pass it, but they could delay it for only two years. It was clear to all that in 1914 Home Rule would automatically become law.

By 1914, the chief stumbling block to Home Rule was no longer opposition in Great Britain but opposition in Ireland. The non-Catholic majority in parts of Ulster, the counties of northeastern Ireland, adamantly objected to the prospect of being deprived by Parliament of full citizenship in the United Kingdom. A fanatical Irish lawyer named Edward Carson (1854–1935) organized an Ulster Unionist Council that proclaimed a provisional government in case Home Rule became law. On his knees in Belfast's city hall he signed an Ulster Covenant — in emulation of the

Scots Covenant of 1637 — binding himself to use "all means which may be found necessary to defeat the present conspiracy to set up a Home Rule Parliament in Ireland." Almost half a million Ulstermen signed the document. Unauthorized military drilling began. It took the Liberal government some time to realize that if Home Rule were to become a reality for all of Ireland, it might have to be imposed by armed force. The Conservative party, moreover, was encouraging rather than discouraging talk of violence and military resistance in Ulster. "There are things stronger than Parliamentary majorities," declared the party's leader, Bonar Law. "I can imagine no length of resistance to which Ulster can go in which I should not be prepared to support them."

By the spring of 1914 the Liberal government began to toy with a plan permitting the Ulster counties to "contract out" of Home Rule for a period of six years. For Redmond this concession was too much; for Carson it was not enough. Then the government decided on a show of force, only to be met with the most serious of all challenges to political authority — the threat of mutiny within the army. Several officers resigned their commissions rather than be faced with the possibility of having to fight the Ulster loyalists. Britain's government appeared paralyzed in coping with what the *Times* (London) defined as "the greatest crisis in the history of the British race."[15]

Irish nationalists in the South now began to emulate the Ulster volunteers in the North. Both sides smuggled in arms from abroad and, although Home Rule was to become law in September 1914, its detailed implementation remained in doubt during the spring and summer of that year. Violence continued to flare in Ireland as a conference of party leaders sought a compromise solution. Carson demanded the permanent exclusion of Ulster from an autonomous Ireland. Redmond, his authority among Irish Nationalists already weakened by his attempts to cooperate loyally with the Liberal government, felt unable to consent to permanent partition. As yet another conference session broke up in deadlock and the members rose to go, the foreign secretary announced that he had just received bad news — the text of an ultimatum that the Austrian government had sent to Serbia the day before. The specter of a general European war suddenly darkened the conference chamber.

Thus the rocky road toward the welfare state and toward the reinterpretation of nineteenth-century liberalism came into sudden conjunction with the road to war. The "revolts" of the peers, the women, the workers, and the Irish (the last involving an extraordinary degree of scorn for the parliamentary process by the Conservative party leadership) were all to be overshadowed by the conflagration of the next four years. They reflected nonetheless a widespread resentment of authority and a deliberate flouting of accepted mores and canons of respectability by large num-

---

[15]Cited in Powell, *Edwardian Crisis.*

bers of British citizens. Yet in the midst of these disturbances, in an unsystematic trial-and-error manner, the Liberal government had instituted a series of far-reaching social reforms. Their potential scope and implications were not fully appreciated at the time, and even their immediate benefits tended to be downgraded. Yet in the decades that followed, these acts of legislation were to have a far greater impact on the daily lives of millions of Britons than did either the surface glitter and stability of upper-class Edwardian society or the often irrational revolts against authority that seem at first glance to have dominated the domestic scene before World War I.

CHAPTER 13

The Roundabout Road to War

In retrospect, 1914 remains preeminent as a demarcation point, as the year that saw the beginning of the First World War, the war that was to destroy the "old order" in Europe, the war that was to topple four empires, bring death to nine million people and injury to twenty-two million others, and cause untold misery and destruction. Its long-range consequences were to include the rise of totalitarian dictatorships in Europe, the awakening of militant nationalism in Asia and Africa, the Second World War, and the Cold War. To call the war of 1914–1918 the "First" World War is technically misleading. Eighteenth-century conflicts such as the War of the Spanish Succession, the War of the Austrian Succession, and the American Revolution had all been fought on at least three continents as well as on the high seas. It was the lapse of a century since the last world war — the Napoleonic — and the achievement in the meantime of an unprecedented potential for military destruction that caused Europeans of 1914 to look upon their world war as unique.[1]

The circumstances that led to World War I have been analyzed and disputed by more than three generations of historians; and although this chapter concentrates on Britain's role, the wider problem of causation cannot be avoided. There is much about the immediate causes of the war, such as the assassination of Austrian Archduke Franz Ferdinand, that partakes of the fortuitous. Yet the decisions made by the chancellories of

---

[1]The causes of World War I are discussed in thousands of books. Luigi Albertini provides the most detailed account based on the fullest use of government archives in *The Origins of the War of 1914* (3 vols., 1952–1957). Excellent one-volume introductions have been provided by Laurence Lafore, *The Long Fuse* (1965), which goes back to the nineteenth-century roots, and by James Joll, *The Origins of the First World War* (1984), which pays particular attention to the "unspoken assumptions" of the major decision makers. Zara S. Steiner, *Britain and the Origins of the First World War* (1977), judiciously assesses the manner in which Britain became involved. Different aspects of the story are illuminated by George W. Monger, *The End of Isolation: British Foreign Policy, 1900–1907* (1963); S. R. Williamson, Jr., *The Politics of Grand Strategy: Britain and France Prepare for War, 1904–1914* (1969); F. H. Hinsley, ed., *British Foreign Policy Under Sir Edward Grey* (1977); Paul M. Kennedy, *The Rise of the Anglo-German Antagonism, 1860–1914* (1980); and Peter Padfield, *The Great Naval Race* (1974).

the Great Powers during the last days of July and the first days of August 1914 can be explained only in the light of assumptions and preconceptions that went back in some cases half a decade, in others half a century. Britain's ultimate entry involved elements — such as concern with the Low Countries and with the European balance of power — that went back half a millennium.

The Web of Diplomacy

As recently as the 1890s, Britain had seemed relatively aloof from the power blocs into which continental Europe was organizing itself. The extent of such isolation can easily be exaggerated, however. Britain's interest in the Near East, shown in 1878 at the Congress of Berlin, its cooperation with the Great Powers on the Egyptian Debt Commission, and the secret Mediterranean Agreement with Austria and Italy in the 1880s all demonstrate Britain's involvement with the continent. Every diplomat prefers to be a free agent, but at times the pressure of national security seems to dictate a more or less binding alliance with another power. It was fear of French military revenge (a fear made plausible by Germany's forcible takeover of Alsace-Lorraine in 1871) that prompted Bismarck's Triple Alliance with Austria (1879) and Italy (1882). It was a French desire to escape diplomatic isolation and a suspicion, shared by Russia, of British ambitions overseas that prompted the Franco-Russian Alliance of 1894. The wish to be free from binding commitments in unforeseen circumstances prompted British statesmen to avoid such alliances until a number of events in the later 1890s led in due course to a reappraisal.

What G. M. Young called "that passionate jealousy of England which for a generation was the most widely diffused emotion in Europe" was brought home to Britons by a variety of incidents: the Venezuela Boundary Dispute of 1895, which aroused widespread anti-British sentiment in the United States; the telegram sent by Emperor William II to President Kruger at the time of the Jameson Raid; the Fashoda incident, which brought France and Britain to the brink of war; and, finally, the Boer War. Each demonstrated anew the perils of diplomatic isolation.

In 1901 Joseph Chamberlain grasped the bull by the horns and publicly proposed an alliance with Germany (and, if possible, with the United States as well) as the most logical step for Britain to take in view of its longstanding rivalry with France and Russia. His suggestion was but the latest of a number of approaches in such a direction. Bismarck had hoped to attach Britain to his Triple Alliance in the 1880s but had been unable to overcome Britain's fears that any such alliance would commit it to support Austrian ambitions in the Balkans. In 1901 it was the German government that hesitated to agree to any arrangements that did not involve Britain's complete adherence to their Triple Alliance. It did not wish to provoke unnecessary antagonism toward Germany on the part of Russia, Britain's perennial rival in the Near East and along the Indian frontier. Later historians were to criticize Bismarck's successors for antagonizing first Russia, the world's greatest land empire, and then Britain, the world's greatest sea empire. Yet German diplomats remained confident in 1901 that Britain's conflicts with Russia and France were too deep-rooted to make possible any diplomatic outcome other than an ultimate British adherence to Germany's Triple Alliance on German terms.

That the attitude of the British public had undergone a fundamental change was shown by the relatively cool reception that Chamberlain's proposal of an Anglo-German entente received in British newspapers. There had been too many examples of German hostility in Africa and in the Near East, where German diplomats and a German military mission had supplanted their British counterparts in Constantinople. German opinion might well have proved equally hostile, for nowhere on the continent did envy of Britain stir more breasts than in Germany. The emperor was representative of many of his subjects in his frequently expressed feeling that German industrial and military power had thus far failed to elicit the worldwide respect and recognition they merited. Germany had been expanding its markets throughout the world with little difficulty, but Britain retained the largest colonial empire and possessed the mightiest navy; London remained the financial capital of the world; and an occasion such as Victoria's Diamond Jubilee conveyed an impression of romantic glory that William's Berlin could not match. It was this sense of psychological rather than any specific material frustration that caused German publicist Friedrich Naumann to declare in 1900: "If there is anything certain in the history of the world, it is the future outbreak of a world war, i.e., a war fought by those who seek to deliver themselves from England."

A consciousness of diplomatic isolation and an awareness that an alliance with Germany was impractical led Britain in the course of the early years of the twentieth century to resolve various overseas anxieties that from time to time had threatened war with France and Russia. The very first break with diplomatic isolation, however, came not in the form of an understanding with a European nation but in the form of an alliance with a country that a generation before would not have been regarded as a power at all, much less a great one — Japan. The last years of the nineteenth century had brought a disintegration of the Open Door trading policy that Britain had fostered in China. As a result of the Opium War of 1839–1842 and the Treaty of Tientsin of 1859, major Chinese ports had been opened to the commerce not only of Britain but also of the major continental nations and the United States. Yet for a long time British trade was preponderant and, partly as a consequence, Japan, Russia, Germany, and France during the 1890s all began to seek more permanent concessions (involving railroad building and mining) and to look forward to the eventual division of all China into foreign "spheres of influence." The British, although deploring the tendency, joined in it by securing what was in effect a sphere of influence over the Yangtse valley.

The alliance with Britain in 1902 was welcomed by the Japanese in that **B. allies w/ Japan** Britain, unlike Russia, France, and Germany, had not sought to deprive Japan of the spoils of its military victory over China in 1895. Britain had, moreover, been the first European power to give up its claims of extraterritoriality in Japan. The treaty provided for mutual aid if either nation were attacked in the Far East by two other powers. By thus engaging in advance to take military action under circumstances not precisely foreseen at the time the treaty was signed, Britain was clearly embarking along a new diplomatic path. The immediate result was to enable the British government to feel more secure about its interests in the Far East and thus to withdraw most of its naval forces from the area. For Japan the treaty was an assurance that if war were to break out between Russia and Japan over Manchuria, Russia's ally France would be deterred from entering on the tsar's side.

The Russo-Japanese War of 1904–1905 fulfilled this expectation. It also had two other results that were ultimately less helpful to British interests:

1. By defeating the world's largest land power, the Japanese demonstrated to nonwhite peoples throughout Asia that European overlordship rested more on temporary technological advantage than on innate racial superiority. No other single event may have done more to awaken the hopes of Asian nationalists under Western domination.

2. By frustrating Russia's ambitions in the Far East, the war rekindled Russian ambitions in the Balkans, thereby making more likely a conflict with Austria that might well involve all Europe.

At the very time that the British government was successfully mending diplomatic fences in the Orient, it embarked on a similar endeavor with the United States. The Venezuela Boundary Dispute of 1895 was settled by arbitration, essentially to British satisfaction, and the government sought to forestall any future quarrels that might injure Anglo-American relations. Unlike other European powers, Britain remained friendly to the United States during the Spanish-American War; and in the Hay-Pauncefote Treaty of 1901, the Salisbury government gave up all claims to a share in an American-built Panama Canal. The following year, when the Venezuelan dictator, Cipriano Castro, defaulted on debt payments, British ships joined German ships in a naval blockade of Caracas; but, unlike the German ships, they withdrew in deference to American protests that such an action violated the Monroe Doctrine. A year later the British representative on an international commission to resolve a long-slumbering dispute concerning the boundary between Alaska and British Columbia bent over backward to side with the American and against the Canadian position.[2]

The ultimate justification for such a pro-American policy was the belief that the fundamental interests of the two countries were broadly

---

[2]Bradford Perkins, *The Great Rapprochement: England and the United States, 1895–1914* (1968).

the same and that theirs was a "special relationship" that should not be marred by minor irritants. No formal alliance resulted, but at least one United States senator spoke of an *entente cordiale* between the two countries as early as 1898. A few years later the British naval squadron was withdrawn from the Caribbean Sea, leaving it essentially an American lake, and by the time World War I broke out in 1914, the two countries could look back on almost two decades of friendly relations.

The Triple Entente

In the search for friends in a diplomatically uncertain world, it was apparent that eventually Great Britain would have to choose between Germany and France. Although to many Britons France remained the historic national enemy and to many of the French Britain remained "perfidious Albion," diplomats in both countries were prepared to reexamine old assumptions. For a man such as French Foreign Minister Delcassé, fear of Germany in Europe took precedence over fear of Britain in Africa; in 1900 he commenced a deliberate policy of reconciliation. In his English counterpart, Lord Lansdowne, he found a receptive spirit who arranged in 1903 for a state visit to France by King Edward VII. This was a task the monarch found most congenial for, unlike his mother, he had always been a Francophile. The royal visitor's initial reception in Paris was cold. "The French don't like us," remarked a worried aide. "Why should they?" replied the king, bowing and smiling unperturbedly from his carriage. He made numerous public appearances and everywhere made graceful and tactful speeches in French about his friendship with and admiration for his hosts. By the end of his visit a notable change of attitude had come about, and Parisian crowds were shouting "Vive notre roi!"[3]

King Edward's visit paved the way for the Anglo-French Entente of 1904. In return for acknowledging Britain's paramount role in Egypt, France received a similar British recognition of its position in Morocco, a state that like China and the Ottoman Empire seemed to be on the verge of disintegration. After long negotiation, other disputes, ranging the world from Madagascar to Siam and from the islands of the South Pacific to the Newfoundland fisheries, were resolved in similarly amicable fashion. Although Delcassé's ultimate hope was that the entente would align Britain diplomatically with France, this was not Lansdowne's expectation. He viewed the treaty as a settling of old differences — comparable to the Heligoland Treaty with Germany (1890) and the Hay-Pauncefote Treaty (1901) with the United States — and not as a step toward an Anglo-French alliance. That the entente could lead, however, in the direction of alliance was made clear the following year, when Emperor William II of Germany challenged the

---

[3]The story is told in Christopher Hibbert, *The Royal Victorians: King Edward VII, His Family and Friends* (1976), pp. 292–294. See also Sir Philip Magnus, *King Edward VII* (1964), and Giles St. Aubyn, *Edward VII: Prince and King* (1979).

King Edward VII Enters Paris   On his 1903 state visit, he is accompanied by
French president Loubet. *(Topham)*

French right to establish a protectorate over Morocco by making a flamboyant visit to the port of Tangier. He succeeded in forcing the resignation of
Delcassé as foreign minister and compelled the French to let the future of
Morocco be determined by an international conference at Algeciras, Spain.
The Germans hoped that their diplomatic initiative would once again drive
a wedge between Britain and France, but in this expectation they were disappointed; for Britain gave France strong diplomatic support, and the new
entente was materially strengthened.

By the time the Algeciras conference met in 1906, Balfour's Conservative government had fallen and Lansdowne's post as foreign secretary
had been taken over by the Liberal Sir Edward Grey (1862–1933), who
was to hold it for the next ten fateful years. Grey also looked upon the entente with France more as the settlement of past differences than as the
prelude to a firm alliance, and he repeatedly explained to the French that
no British government could undertake a binding commitment to
France. Parliament would not accept such an agreement. Impressed by
the Morocco crisis of 1905–1906, Grey did, however, come to look on

Germany as Europe's greatest potential troublemaker; he foresaw the possibility that Britain might find it necessary someday to ally herself with France in a war against Germany. If such a war should ever come about, Grey believed that Britain should have the option either to aid France or to stand aside. Should the decision be to help France, such aid would be meaningful only if French and British generals had held secret conversations to discuss methods of military cooperation. Such confidential discussions began in 1906. They were intended as no more than the means to several possible ends, but they created in some English minds the impression that Britain was in effect allied with France, and they undoubtedly encouraged the French to believe that, in a showdown with Germany, Britain would side with its Channel neighbor.

Once Britain was diplomatically associated with France, it was only a matter of time before expediency dictated a settlement of international differences with France's continental ally, Russia. The rivalry between Britain and Russia in the Middle East, on the Indian frontier, and in the Far East had been even more unremitting than the comparable conflicts with France; but prolonged negotiations led to the Anglo-Russian Convention of 1907. The convention eased Britain's fears for the safety of the Indian frontier by recognizing its right to determine the foreign policy of Afghanistan and resolved another conflict by dividing Persia into a large Russian sphere of influence in the north, a smaller British sphere of influence in the south, and a neutral zone in between. Although some diplomats henceforth spoke of a Triple Entente of Britain, France, and Russia to counterbalance the Triple Alliance of Germany, Austria-Hungary, and Italy, Grey himself disliked the phrase. The convention with Russia impressed him as a resolution of old disputes rather than a promise of future cooperation. And, indeed, the sense of common culture and shared political aspirations that some Britons felt for France could much less readily be extended to an aristocratic Russia that had crushed the Revolution of 1905 and remained the prime example of European despotism. When Edward VII embarked on a state visit to St. Petersburg in 1908, several Labour Members of Parliament protested against the idea of His Majesty "hobnobbing with bloodstained creatures." Although the king was his usual gracious self and dutifully danced the "Merry Widow Waltz" with the tsarina, the pre-1914 tie between Britain and Russia never became more than a polite formality.

Anglo-German Rivalry

While Sir Edward Grey at the foreign office was very much involved with the various diplomatic crises that beset early-twentieth-century Europe, most Britons tended to be more concerned with domestic affairs. The one issue of foreign policy that did, however, awaken their interest and that more than any other convinced them that Germany had become the greatest potential threat to their security was Anglo-German naval rivalry.

H.M.S. *Dreadnought* (1907) The first battleship of the new era. *(The Granger Collection)*

In the late nineteenth century, Admiral Alfred von Tirpitz had persuaded the kaiser's government that only if Germany built a large navy could it make its diplomatic weight felt and safeguard its links with its new colonies in Africa and the South Pacific. If Admiral Tirpitz expected the British government to permit its navy to be overtaken in size and fire power, he reckoned without Sir John Fisher (1841–1920), the fiery and energetic First Sea Lord from 1904 to 1910 and from 1914 to 1915.[4] On one occasion even King Edward VII felt forced to remonstrate with the admiral: "Will you kindly leave off shaking your fist in my face?"

Confronted by the German naval menace, Fisher argued that Britain's navy should be reorganized and rebuilt. Rather than having British squadrons spread throughout the world, he believed that most of the fleet should be concentrated in the North Sea to meet any threat from Germany. A new naval base was established at Scapa Flow in the Orkney Islands north of Scotland. From there the navy could intercept a German fleet steaming out into the North Sea or attempting to pass through the English Channel. Fisher ruthlessly scrapped hundreds of outmoded naval vessels and secretly planned the *Dreadnought,* the prototype of the twentieth-century battleship that was to dominate the seas until World War II. A number of successively improved iron battleships had been built during the late nineteenth century, and British expenditures on the navy had edged upward from the late 1880s

---

[4]See Ruddock F. Mackay, *Fisher of Silverstone* (1974), and Robert K. Massey, *Dreadnought: Britain, Germany, and the Coming of the Great War* (1991).

on; but the *Dreadnought* surpassed all its predecessors. Its ten twelve-inch guns possessed more than twice the firing power of earlier ironclads; its steam turbines improved its speed; and it could be adapted to run on oil instead of coal. In the years after 1911 almost all new British naval vessels used oil.

It was obvious that if the Germans wished to stay in the naval race, they, too, would have to build dreadnoughts. This decision, in turn, would force them to widen the Kiel Canal, the German water artery between the Baltic and the North Seas. In the meantime the new Liberal government temporarily halted the Fisher program of building four dreadnoughts a year and initiated attempts to reach an agreement with Germany placing a ceiling on the size of both navies. But Emperor William II made it clear that he "did not wish good relations at the expense of the fleet." A sudden realization in the winter of 1908 that Admiral Tirpitz's shipbuilding plans would enable Germany to overtake Britain in the number of dreadnoughts within two years caused alarm, first in a divided Liberal cabinet and then in the British press. Public pressure eventually forced the government to begin laying the keels of eight great battleships rather than the four initially planned. "We want eight and we won't wait," went the contemporary music hall refrain.

This is how the naval race progressed over the next few years:

NUMBER OF DREADNOUGHTS IN OPERATION

Year	Britain	Germany
1910	5	2
1911	8	4
1912	12	7
1913	15	10
1914	18	13

By 1914 France and the United States each possessed eight comparable battleships, and Japan five. Back in 1905 Liberals had criticized the Conservative government for the extravagant size of the annual naval budget. The Liberal naval budget of 1913–1914 was almost 60 percent larger.

The navy necessarily retained a different meaning for Britain than for Germany. Britain by 1914 was so dependent on imported food that to lose control of the seas would mean starvation. Moreover, a German navy large enough to control the Channel would allow the German army to capture London. Yet no degree of British naval superiority could ever enable a British army to capture Berlin, for in 1911 the German army (including trained reserves) comprised 4,800,000 men. The comparable British force was confined to 380,000 men. Although the Anglo-German naval rivalry was clearly a factor that exacerbated relations between the two countries, it is difficult to see how the men responsible for British national security could have responded to the German challenge except

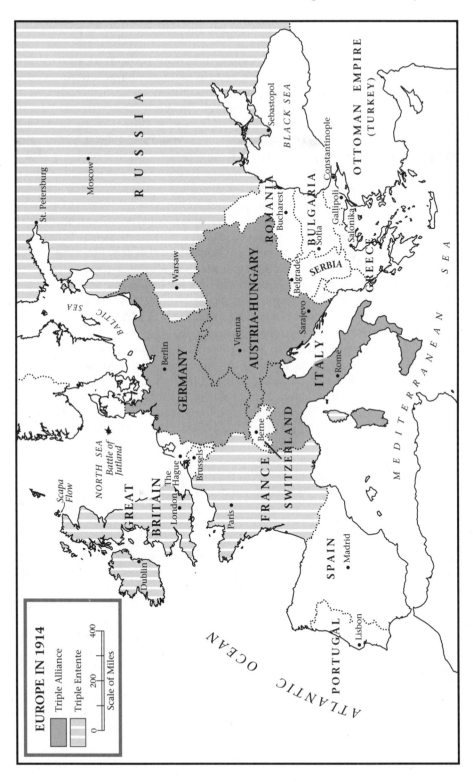

EUROPE IN 1914

Triple Alliance

Triple Entente

Scale of Miles

0   200   400

by seeking a program of naval limitation and, failing that, by persevering in their own naval building program.

Although some leaders of British public opinion were tempted from time to time to emulate the large conscript armies characteristic of continental nations for half a century, the principle of voluntary recruitment was retained during the decades before World War I. The relatively small British army was reorganized during these years, however, by Secretary of War Richard Burdon Haldane (1856–1928)[5] in order to make it a more efficient fighting force. For the first time a general staff was set up along Prussian lines and a Military Intelligence Branch was associated with it. An expeditionary force of six infantry divisions (with associated artillery and cavalry contingents capable of rapid mobilization) was set up to be sent to the continent if necessary. The older, locally organized militia and volunteer forces were replaced by a fourteen-division Territorial Army to take over home defense in wartime. Officer's Training Corps programs were established in most public schools, designed to produce tens of thousands of commissioned officers for modern war. In 1911 the Royal Flying Corps was founded to assist the army in reconnaissance work, and that same year a little-noted measure, the Official Secrets Act, reversed traditional judicial procedures by making it necessary for anyone accused of attempting to transmit secret military information to a foreign state to prove his innocence. Mass conscription had not been adopted, but Britain was adapting its military forces with reasonable efficiency for the possible demands of twentieth-century warfare.

Every so often an international crisis would upstage domestic concerns in the newspaper headlines. The Bosnian crisis of 1908 was one example; on that occasion Austria weakened Russian prestige in the Balkans by proclaiming the full annexation of Bosnia-Herzegovina, the Turkish territory it had been occupying since 1878. Another crisis captured the headlines in 1911 when the German gunboat *Panther* appeared off the coast of Morocco at Agadir in an effort to reassert and dramatize German influence in North Africa. Lloyd George gave public expression to the concern of his country: "Britain should at all hazards maintain her place and prestige among the Great Powers, and if a situation were to be forced upon us in which peace could only be preserved by sacrifice of the great and beneficent position that Britain had won by centuries of heroism and achievement — then I say emphatically that peace at such a price would be a humiliation intolerable for a great country like ours to endure." These ringing phrases sounded more like Palmerston at his most bellicose than like a former "pro-Boer" Liberal who belonged to the pacifist wing of his party. But times had changed and so had Lloyd George. Each international crisis seemed to elicit greater tension and excitement.

---

[5]He was created Viscount Haldane in 1911.

Sometimes World War I is seen as the inevitable result of two increasingly rigid alliance systems meeting in inevitable head-on collision. Yet neither the Triple Alliance nor the Triple Entente was ever as rigid or stable as it seemed at the height of a temporary and often deliberately manufactured crisis. No state could ever be totally assured of the support of its supposed allies. No nation ever wished to break all ties with states in the other camp. Nor, in one very real sense, could they; for the monarchs of pre-1914 were almost all related. There was good reason to call Queen Victoria "the Grandmother of Europe" (see p. 484).

Emperor William II of Germany, who in his earlier days had written dutiful "Dear Grandmama" letters to Victoria, continued during the early years of the twentieth century to write similarly personal letters to his cousin, Nicholas II of Russia. He would write in English, addressing the tsar as "Dearest Nicky" and signing the letters "Your affectionate friend Willy." Envy of his uncle, Edward VII, who regarded William as the *enfant terrible* of Europe, did not prevent him from wearing his scarlet British field marshal's uniform and proudly taking his place of honor in the imposing monarchical funeral cortege that followed his uncle's coffin through the streets of London in May 1910. Torn like so many other Germans between feelings of envy and admiration for Britain, William for once was satisfied that his assigned role at the funeral befitted his station, and he wrote to Berlin from Windsor Castle: "I am proud to call this place my home and to be a member of this royal family."

Stronger even than links of monarchy were ties of trade and finance. International commerce was increasing everywhere; and although German competition aroused grave alarm among some British business leaders, it never caused as much general concern as did German naval competition. When in the summer of 1914 Britain agreed not to hamper the building of a projected Berlin-to-Baghdad railway, it acknowledged the fact that Germany had peacefully supplanted Britain as the major foreign economic influence in Turkey. Furthermore, Britain was Germany's best customer, while Russia was Germany's single most important supplier of food and raw materials. During the years 1912–1914, as Germany (if only for budgetary reasons) apparently came to accept the impossibility of surpassing British naval power, Anglo-German diplomatic relations improved. Both countries cooperated in limiting the scope of the Balkan Wars of 1912–1913, and by June 1914 one leading German diplomat spoke of the "pleasant cordiality of Anglo-German relations." World War I was far less the inevitable outcome of economic rivalries or of inflexible alliances than the result of mediocre statesmanship and the subordination of true national interest to ephemeral notions of national prestige.

The Lamps Go Out

The assassination of the Austrian crown prince in Sarajevo on June 28, 1914, alerted the chancelleries of Europe to the probability of another international crisis; but the absence of an immediate diplomatic reaction by Austria gave the political atmosphere a deceptive calm. Two weeks after the assassination, Lloyd George could assure an audience that the international sky had never looked bluer. Behind the scenes, however, the Austrians were planning to make use of the assassination to crush their pesky southern neighbor, Serbia, once and for all; the assassin had been a young Bosnian who hoped to make Austrian-controlled Bosnia part of a greater Serbia. Having obtained the promise of full support from their German ally, the Austrians on July 23 issued a forty-eight-hour ultimatum to Serbia demanding the suppression in Serbia of all anti-Austrian publications, the punishment of all teachers who spoke out against Habsburg rule in Bosnia, and the admission of Austrian officials to enforce Serbian compliance with these demands. The Serbian government, which had known of the assassination plot, provided an unexpectedly conciliatory reply. The Serbs accepted all the Austrian demands except the one regarding the entry of Austrian officials into Serbia and even on this point agreed to refer the matter to the international court at the Hague. Austria, however, pronounced the Serbian reply to be unsatisfactory and on July 28 declared war; a day later its guns began shelling Belgrade.

Russia's reaction to Austro-Hungarian aggression in the Balkans was immediate and decisive — it declared first a partial and then a general mobilization of its army. In the meantime Sir Edward Grey desperately sought to reconvene the London Conference that had satisfactorily resolved the Balkan Wars of the year before. Germany, insisting that the conflict concerned only Austria and Serbia, turned down the invitation. In the face of what appeared to be Germany's refusal to prevent a wider war, Grey asked both France and Germany to respect Belgian neutrality. France agreed, Germany was noncommittal. By July 30, the German civilian government did indeed belatedly caution Austria to go slow; but its advice was secretly superseded by Count Helmuth von Moltke, the chief of the German general staff, who urged Austria to mobilize against Russia and promised unconditional German aid. By the summer of 1914 the German general staff had clearly convinced itself that a general European war was inevitable in the near future and that the relative military position of Germany and Austria-Hungary was as favorable then as it was ever likely to be. The German general staff was in no sense responsible for the assassination of the Austrian archduke nor was it directly involved in the preparation of the Austrian ultimatum; but once the occasion for war arose, it seized the opportunity in the form of a preemptive strike. Neither the weak-willed German emperor nor his civilian chancellor could make a stand for good sense.

Military timetables dictated the scenario that then unfolded. The German war plan against France and Russia required an immediate push to Paris, which was expected to fall within six weeks. Once France had been knocked out of the war, the full might of the German army could be turned against the larger but more slowly assembling Russian forces. After ultimatums demanding an immediate halt to Russian mobilization and an immediate promise of French neutrality were not answered to German satisfaction, Germany declared war on Russia and began its attack in the west.

The British cabinet, its peace efforts unavailing, was painfully divided on the subject of whether to aid France in case of German attack. A majority of members of the Liberal cabinet was initially averse to intervention. London bankers, fearful that war would "break down the whole system of credit with London as its center," pleaded with the government to remain neutral. At the same time the French ambassador frantically begged for aid, and ill-informed members of the cabinet suddenly became aware of the extent of the government's secret military conversations with France. Not only had the generals been preparing a plan for sending a British Expeditionary Force to France, but the admirals had in effect allotted the Mediterranean Sea to the French fleet and the English Channel to the British. If a German fleet were now to steam down the English Channel to shell unprotected French ports, could Britain justify a position of standing aside?

Although the First Lord of the Admiralty, Winston Churchill, placed the navy on a precautionary war footing, Asquith's cabinet was still undecided on August 3, when Grey addressed an expectant House of Commons. Speaking slowly but with evident emotion, Grey asked the House to approach the crisis from the point of view of "British interests, British honor, and British obligations." He related the history of the military conversations with France but made clear that no secret engagement restricted Britain's choice of action. Yet Grey urged that Britain must take a stand "against the unmeasured aggrandizement of any power whatsoever."

> I ask the House [Grey went on] from the point of view of British interests to consider what may be at stake. If France is beaten to her knees . . . if Belgium fell under the same dominating influence and then Holland and then Denmark . . . if, in a crisis like this, we run away from these obligations of honor and interest as regards the Belgian Treaty . . . I do not believe for a moment that, at the end of this war, even if we stood aside, we should be able to undo what had happened, in the course of the war, to prevent the whole of the West of Europe opposite us from falling under the domination of a single power . . . and we should, I believe, sacrifice our respect and good name and reputation before the world and should not escape the most serious and grave economic consequences.

Grey won the support of the House of Commons and, after he sat down, first Bonar Law, on behalf of the Conservatives, and then, in a signal act of courage, John Redmond, on behalf of the Irish Nationalists, announced their support. Only Ramsay MacDonald, the head of the Labour party, dissented; but even he soon proved to be part of a minority within his own small party.

By the time Grey spoke, the German government had asked for the right to cross Belgium; but Belgium's King Albert, on the grounds of his country's permanent neutralization by international agreement, refused his consent and requested British diplomatic support. On the morning of August 4 news came that a German invasion of Belgium had nonetheless begun. The British government mobilized its army and sent an ultimatum asking the Germans to withdraw from Belgium by 12:00 P.M. No reply was received, and at midnight of August 4, 1914, Britain found itself at war with Germany.

The German invasion of Belgium, a country whose neutrality Britain had guaranteed in 1839, resolved the cabinet's dilemma. Although two members of the cabinet resigned, Germany's violation of an international agreement enabled the British government to enter the war with a substantially unified populace staunchly behind it. It might have been difficult to persuade the British public on grounds of self-interest alone, but the issue of Belgium now added the all-important moral factor to the decision.

Because it was clear in both London and Berlin that Britain's entry into the war was directly tied to Germany's invasion of neutral Belgium, the question necessarily arises: Why did the kaiser's government make what appears in retrospect a monumental blunder? The answer is that the German war plan for the west, the Schlieffen Plan, left no alternative. Only by speeding through Belgium could the German army hope to capture Paris in six weeks. Moreover, although German generals were fully aware that British participation would necessarily follow, the significance of the British military contribution was discounted in advance. Britain's army was after all, in Emperor William II's words, "contemptibly small."

Although anticipated by the German generals, the British declaration of war infuriated the German populace. The immediate origins of the war of 1914 had nothing to do with a direct Anglo-German rivalry, for no outstanding issue between the two countries was remotely worth a war; but once Britain declared war, England became immediately the most hated of Germany's enemies. Britain's action was attributed to a selfish envy of Germany's successes as a trading nation; it was also denounced as an act of treason to the "Nordic race." The deity was therefore called upon to punish the perfidy — "Gott Strafe England!" The kaiser's own explanation of the origin of the war was simplistic. "To think," he lamented, "that George and Nicky should have played me false! If my grandmother had been alive she would never have allowed it."

Whatever the immediate chain of events and the last-minute soul searchings, Britain's decision to enter the war followed logically from the historic British preoccupations with the independence of Belgium — a significant factor as early as the onset of the Hundred Years' War with France in 1337 — and with the fear of a Europe dominated by a single power, whether it be the Spain of Philip II, the France of Napoleon I, or the Germany of William II or his successors. Whatever may be said for some members of the London populace, who — like their counterparts in Berlin, Vienna, Paris, and St. Petersburg — cheered the onset of war as a release from peacetime tensions and as the opening bell of the ultimate athletic contest, Britain's governmental leaders were aware of the gravity of their decision.[6] An English publicist, Norman Angell, had vividly portrayed the horrors of war between industrialized nations in *The Great Illusion* (1910); and although other generals were more hopeful, Lord Kitchener, Britain's new secretary for war, predicted a conflict that would last at least three years. As the sky darkened on the night of August 4 and the time limit of Britain's ultimatum to Germany to halt the invasion of Belgium drew inexorably to an end, Sir Edward Grey stood by a Whitehall window. Sadly he turned to an aide standing at his side and spoke the words that were to become the epitaph of nineteenth-century Europe and the Victorian and Edwardian eras: "The lamps are going out all over Europe. We shall not see them lit again in our lifetime."

---

[6]Two youthful British historians have recently reopened the debate in lengthy books by arguing, among other things, not that Britain precipitated World War I directly but that Britain should have remained neutral and permitted the German Empire of William II to dominate the greater part of continental Europe. That such a decision would have saved many British lives in the short run is self-evident. That it would have preserved the British Empire indefinitely or led to a harmonious and peaceful "European Union" is far more doubtful. See Niall Ferguson, *The Pity of War* (1999), and John Charmley, *Splendid Isolation? Britain, the Balance of Power, and the Origins of the First World War* (1999).

CHAPTER 14

Britain and World War I

Once Britain had declared war on August 4, the contingency plans worked out with the French general staff were, with minor revisions, put into effect. Three divisions and, after brief hesitation, a fourth — 100,000 men in all — of the British Expeditionary Force under Field Marshall Sir John French were safely transported under naval cover across the Channel.

The Fighting Fronts (1914–1915)

By August 22 the British forces were taking their assigned place on the left sector of the French front. They had little opportunity to establish themselves, for rapidly advancing German troops had already captured or bypassed all Belgian fortifications. No sooner had the British forces crossed into Belgium than they began, together with their French allies, a general strategic retreat.

The main thrust of the German attack was still toward Paris, in accordance with the Schlieffen Plan, which came within an eyelash of succeeding. But at the Battle of the Marne, on the outskirts of Paris, the Allied forces (predominantly French), under General Joseph Joffre, held firm. During the second week of September, the German onslaught was halted and in some places pushed back. Frustrated in its attempt to reach Paris, the German army turned west toward the Channel and captured the Belgian ports of Zeebrugge and Ostend. But after heavy fighting at what came to be known as the first Battle of Ypres in October and November of 1914, the British managed to halt the German advance. Half the British regular army was destroyed, but a tiny corner of western Belgium was saved, and so were the vital French ports of Dunkirk, Calais, and Boulogne. By spring 1915 the war in the west had bogged down amidst hundreds of miles of trenches, barbed wire, and machine gun positions that stretched from Switzerland to the North Sea.[1]

---

[1]E. L. Woodward, *Great Britain and the War of 1914–1918* (1967), stresses military events, whereas J. M. Winter, *The Great War and the British People* (1986), emphasizes social change, as does Arthur Marwick, *The Deluge: British Society and the First World War*, 2nd

With the exception of a few generals, such as Lord Kitchener, neither the Allied nor the German leaders had expected such an impasse. Most generals and civilians were guided in their thinking by the wars of the mid-nineteenth century, which had been almost invariably quick and often decided by a single battle. The American Civil War, with its virtual four-year stalemate on the eastern front between Richmond and Washington, offered military food for thought of a different order, but European strategists had paid the American ordeal little heed.

A twentieth-century defense had stymied a nineteenth-century offense, and what most strategists had expected to be a swift surgical operation was turning into a slow bleeding to death. On both sides, the generals refused to acknowledge military reality. Instead, they excused the stalemate on the grounds that they lacked the men and guns to carry out the strategic doctrines in which they had been trained. They planned and hoped for a successful frontal breakthrough; but although they spent tens of thousands of lives and hundreds of thousands of artillery shells, they repeatedly failed. Battle was no longer the decisive factor. "Europe was locked in gigantic siege operations, in which victory would come by the attrition of manpower, industrial resources, food supplies, and morale, rather than by generalship."[2]

Although frustrated on land, Britain immediately put to use its naval superiority to drive Germany's merchant marine from the high seas and to enforce a strict blockade to prevent Germany and its allies from importing foodstuffs or munitions from abroad. In the meantime, isolated German warships were hunted down or forced to seek refuge in neutral ports, where their crews were interned, until the greater part of the German navy was blockaded in its home waters. The inability of the German government to send assistance to its overseas colonies resulted in their falling into Allied hands during the next few years, the one exception being German East Africa, where a small German force succeeded in holding out as long as the Fatherland did.

Early in 1915 the Allies made their major attempt to outflank the entire Western Front by attacking what seemed to be the weakest link among the Central Powers — Turkey. For decades the preservation of the Ottoman Empire had been a major object of British foreign policy. By

---

ed. (1991). Trevor Wilson's monumental *The Myriad Faces of War: Britain and the Great War, 1914–1918* (1986) adds the political dimension as well. Paul Fussell, in *The Great War and Modern Memory* (1975), and Samuel Hynes, in *A War Imagined: The First World War and English Culture* (1990), appraise the impact of the conflict on Britain's writers and (especially in the case of Hynes) its artists, musicians, and dramatists. More compact accounts may be found in the first three chapters of A. J. P. Taylor, *English History, 1914–1945* (1965), and in Chapters 2 and 3 of John Stevenson, *British Society, 1914–1945* (1984). The impact of the war on party politics is taken up in Cameron Hazelhurst, *Politicians at War, 1914–1915* (1971), and in John Turner, *British Politics and the Great War: Coalition and Conflict, 1915–1918* (1992), as well as in the biographies of Asquith, Lloyd George, and Churchill cited in Chapter 12.

[2]William B. Willcox, *Star of Empire* (1950), p. 322.

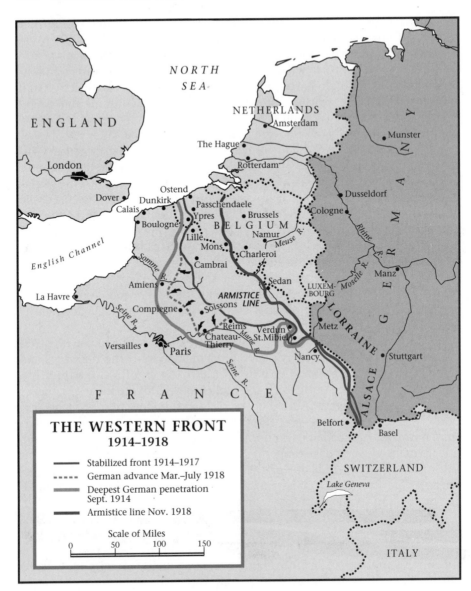

THE WESTERN FRONT
1914–1918

——— Stabilized front 1914–1917
----- German advance Mar.–July 1918
——— Deepest German penetration
Sept. 1914
——— Armistice line Nov. 1918

Scale of Miles

0   50   100   150

the turn of the twentieth century, this aim no longer loomed so large, and the Anglo-Russian Entente of 1907 necessarily made the defense of the Dardanelles against Russia a less pressing concern. This same entente had convinced the dominant forces in the Turkish government by 1914 that their salvation now lay with Germany. The Allied naval and land attack upon the Dardanelles thus had the paradoxical purpose of opening that waterway to Russia. The Russians were eager for closer military cooperation and easier communications with the Western powers and strongly favored the plan. Its chief defender in London was Winston

Churchill, the First Lord of the Admiralty, who had become aware sooner than most of his colleagues of the stalemate that lay ahead in France.

The operation was badly mismanaged. The British and French fleets, seeking to force their way through the straits, withdrew because of losses at the very time that the Turkish defenders were ready to give in. The Allies then decided to stage a land invasion instead. The first major amphibious operation of modern warfare, it involved the use of airplanes, submarines, landing craft, and radio communications. However, by the time that British, Australian, and New Zealand troops landed on the beaches of the Gallipoli peninsula in April of 1915, it had been so well fortified by the Turks that the Allied army found it impossible to storm the almost impregnable hilltop positions overlooking their small beachhead. Heavy fighting in Poland prevented the Russian armies from lending support; and after clinging to their beachhead for several months, the Allies were forced, in December 1915, to evacuate Gallipoli. Fifty-five thousand men were lost in a campaign that from the start had been strongly opposed by the French government and by the more conservative military leaders in Britain. Winston Churchill became the scapegoat for the debacle and lost his position as First Lord of the Admiralty.

The Home Front (1914–1915)

Within Britain itself, once war had begun, all the animosities that had troubled the immediate prewar domestic scene were subordinated to what Winston Churchill was to call "a higher principle of hatred." Trade unions called off pending strikes. Political parties agreed on an electoral truce. John Redmond, the Irish Nationalist leader, and Sir Edward Carson, the Ulster leader who had dallied with rebellion in the interest of preserving the Anglo-Irish union, both turned their energies to recruiting army volunteers. Suffragette leaders newly released from jail devoted themselves to winding bandages, organizing war relief, and asking young men why they were not at the front. All over the country, recruiting posters depicting the stern and imposing features of Lord Kitchener, secretary for war, bore the same message: "Your Country Needs You." "Oh, we don't want to lose you but we think you ought to go," went the words of one music hall ballad. For the time being, Britain insisted on preserving its volunteer-army tradition. As a result, "Kitchener's army was the closest thing to a true citizen army that Britain has ever produced. Without the support and enthusiasm of the majority of the population no administration could have secured nearly 2,500,000 men by purely voluntary methods in less than 17 months from the outbreak of the war."[3] Wrote Rupert Brooke in 1914:

---

[3]Peter Simkins, *Kitchener's Army: The Raising of the New Armies, 1914–1916* (1988), p. 326. See also R. J. Q. Adams and Philip P. Poirier, *The Conscription Controversy in Great Britain, 1900–1918* (1987).

> Now, God be thanked Who has matched us with His hour
> And caught our youth, and wakened us from sleeping.

Poets such as Brooke, who was to die in 1915 of blood poisoning aboard a Mediterranean troopship, welcomed the conflict as an antidote to prewar cynicism and as an opportunity to subordinate individual selfishness to the higher national good. A year into the war, H. G. Wells, the prophet of modern scientific progress, could still write: "England is today a cleaner, harder, brighter . . . and finer country than it was last August."

The immense changes that world war was to bring to the economy and political life of the nation were not at first appreciated. Some company managers, once the initial shock of war had worn off, thought in terms of business as usual and found solace in the thought that much German overseas trade would now fall into British hands. It soon turned out, however, that British industry had not the capacity to gear itself to full war production and at the same time continue its traditional role of exporter. Nor was the requisite shipping available. As a result, German and British markets in Canada and Latin America were largely taken over by businesses based in the United States. Japanese companies played a similar role in East Asia.

One major industry that felt the effects of war at once was the railways. In accordance with a standby measure dating back to 1871, they were immediately taken over by the government on a rental basis and for the first time operated as a single system. As overseas freight rates doubled and tripled in the early months of 1915 because of submarine damage, the government also took over refrigerator ships. Eventually all oceangoing vessels were placed under government control. Trade unions had, in the meantime, become increasingly disturbed by the way in which the labor shortage had caused the managements of the war industries to "dilute" union standards by recruiting lower-paid women workers and laborers from other industries. In reaction to the threat of labor unrest, the government utilized its powers under the comprehensive Defence of the Realm Act to obtain a trade-union conference agreement in which unions pledged to abandon the use of the strike in wartime, to accept government arbitration in all disputes, and to relax traditional union rules. In return the government promised that such concessions would not be used to depress wages, that the financial benefits of such union concessions would accrue to the state rather than to the employers, that the suspended rules would be restored when peace came, and that postwar preference in rehiring would be given to prewar employees.

The difficulties encountered by Local Armaments Committees, composed of employers, workers, and government representatives, in giving force to this agreement led to a more direct measure of government control: the Ministry of Munitions. It provided for the limitation of profits in war industries and also restricted the right of workers to move from one such industry to another. Such impositions of government control on labor and management alike did not curb all labor discontent — a major

World War I Recruiting Lord Kitchener and the "Women of Britain" gave the same advice. *(Imperial War Museum, London)*

It Was Heeded *(Hulton Deutsch Collection)*

strike in the Welsh coalfields broke out in July 1915 — but it did mark a notable and largely successful step in the mobilization of domestic resources for military purposes.

By the spring of 1915, just as the initial surge of patriotism had begun to fade on the industrial scene, so did the comparable truce in domestic politics. The Conservatives under Bonar Law became frustrated by their inability to influence policymaking directly. The war, moreover, was clearly not leading to any speedy victory. The first major reconstruction of the government, in May 1915, was precipitated by the resignation of the aging First Sea Lord, Admiral Fisher. Fisher had been restored to his former post in 1914 because his successor, Prince Louis of Battenberg, bore too German-sounding a name. Fisher and his civilian superior, Winston Churchill, found themselves continually at odds. Churchill favored the Gallipoli invasion while Fisher preferred a more dramatic venture that would have been even less likely to succeed: a landing of Russian troops under British naval protection on the Baltic coast near Berlin.

The apparent failure at Gallipoli prompted Fisher's resignation, and Bonar Law, the Conservative leader, took advantage of the situation to demand a change in the cabinet. The government now became a three-party coalition, and the general election scheduled for late 1915 was put off for the duration of the war. Asquith remained prime minister, but Bonar Law, Balfour, Carson, and other Conservatives now joined the cabinet. Lloyd George assumed the significant new post of minister of munitions, and Arthur Henderson joined the government as president of the Board of Education, the first member of the Labour party to gain cabinet office. John Redmond declined Asquith's comparable invitation to the Irish Nationalists. In the meantime, Winston Churchill was demoted to a minor office and soon left London for a winter in the trenches in France. Lord Haldane was similarly forced out of the cabinet; the creator of the British Expeditionary Force in France had become the victim of widespread newspaper criticism because in his youth he had received his higher education at a German university.

The Rise of Lloyd George

The grueling months of war stretched into years, and by the summer of 1916 victory seemed as distant as ever. July 1 proved to be the single deadliest day in all of British military history, as 100,000 British troops stormed German fortifications in the Battle of the Somme. Twenty thousand died, and 40,000 were wounded, many of them traumatized by what came to be known as "shell shock." Although the fighting continued through the summer and thereby assisted the stalwart French defense of Verdun further east, it ultimately cost the British army a total of 400,000 casualties without achieving a decisive change in the battle lines. Both in the United States and in Europe there was occasional talk of a compromise peace; but Germany would accept only a peace that recognized its military advances in the east and west. The Allied leaders, in turn, found it impossible to justify to their peoples a peace that preserved and strengthened the very Prussian militarism for whose destruction they were asking such enormous human sacrifice.

A prolonged war that brings no victory invariably injures the reputation of the government conducting it, and in the fall of 1916 two of Britain's press lords, Lord Northcliffe and Sir Max Aitken (the future Lord Beaverbrook), launched a newspaper campaign to replace Asquith as prime minister. He appeared too undramatic and too ineffectual to be an appropriate war leader. Much more fitting seemed David Lloyd George, the fiery Welsh orator whose popular reputation had been made by the "People's Budget" of 1909 and reinforced by his success as minister of munitions in setting an example of wartime mobilization and in overcoming a notorious shell shortage.[4] That there should have been a shortage of artillery ammunition was not surprising, considering that in three weeks of the Battle of the Somme the British army had fired more ammunition than it had during the entire three years of the Boer War. In the summer of 1916 Lord Kitchener was drowned while on his way to Russia in a warship that struck a German mine, and Lloyd George became secretary for war as well. In the autumn he proposed that a special four-man war cabinet be created to run the war, with himself in charge. After giving tentative approval to the plan, Asquith decided to reject it as an unconstitutional abdication of his own responsibilities. Lloyd George thereupon resigned, and Conservative members of the cabinet, also eager for new leadership, did likewise. Asquith consequently submitted his own resignation. King George V requested the Conservative leader, Bonar Law, to form a government; when the latter declined, Lloyd George was left as the logical choice. On December 7, 1916 he was offered the prime ministership and accepted the task.[5]

The erstwhile radical and pacifist, the scourge of dukes and terror of millionaires, thus became head of a coalition cabinet in which Conservatives predominated. Unwilling to accept subordinate office, both Asquith and Sir Edward Grey found themselves out of power. Asquith felt deeply hurt by this demotion; although he asked his followers to support the new prime minister, the official Liberal party became, in effect, an anti–Lloyd George faction. The party wounds opened by the manner and the consequences of Lloyd George's elevation to the prime ministership were never to heal completely and probably did more than any prewar event or historical force to propel one of Britain's major political parties along the road to disintegration.

---

[4]R. J. Q. Adams, *Arms and the Wizard: Lloyd George and the Ministry of Munitions* (1978).

[5]In *British Interparty Conferences: A Study of the Procedure of Conciliation in British Politics, 1867–1921* (1980), John D. Fair provides a succinct and persuasive account of this controversial episode.

"For King and Country" E. F. Skinner depicts a wartime plant manufacturing artillery shells that was operated predominantly by women. *(The Granger Collection)*

In 1916, admittedly, most Britons were more concerned with country than with party; if Lloyd George should indeed prove to be the man who could win the war, all else might be forgiven him. That he was imbued with driving energy, boundless self-confidence, and unshakable resolution became evident almost at once. He organized a small war cabinet along the lines he had previously proposed, and for the time being the House of Commons fell very much into eclipse. "The Wizard of Wales" seemed to personify, indeed, the "total war" that the conflict with Germany and its allies had become.

By the time Lloyd George became prime minister, much of the legislation converting Britain into a warfare state was already in the statute book. Railways and munitions plants were under government control, and the free market of peacetime capitalism had been drastically curbed. If Lloyd George never imposed on British labor the degree of compulsion that the law empowered him to decree, it was because he preferred to exert his own vast powers of persuasion. "When the house is on fire," he had insisted in 1916, "questions of procedure and precedence, of etiquette and time and division of labour must disappear." Such questions never did disappear altogether, and the last years of the conflict were filled with sporadic stoppages and "unofficial" strikes led by factory shop stewards. Such agitation was particularly common among workers in the shipyards and the engineering shops in and near Glasgow. At least some of their leaders hoped that the war would lead to a socialist revolution, and the area came to be known as "Red Clydeside."

For most civilian workers and their families, however, the full employment and opportunities to work overtime brought about by the war resulted in a rise in living standards relative to other groups in society. It also meant a 50 percent increase in the number of women in the paid work force. The number of domestic servants shrank rapidly, but large numbers of women served as nurses and as clerks in banks, post offices, and government offices, and, for the first time ever, as auxiliary soldiers and sailors, as police officers, and as omnibus and railway conductors, and in a host of other traditionally masculine preserves. By 1917 three out of every four workers in the munitions factories were women, thereby permitting male workers to be drafted into the army. According to the weekly *New Statesman,* such young women demonstrated their growing independence and self-confidence not only by wearing shorter skirts but also by "a keener appetite for experience and pleasure and a tendency . . . to protest against wrongs before they became 'intolerable.'"[6]

Women with young children were far less likely to join the paid work force, and by 1916, the national government was paying a monthly allowance to the wives and children of more than a million soldiers in the British army. Such allowances, collected by the wife at the local post office, often provided such families with a larger and more dependable source of income than had unskilled or unreliable husbands in peacetime.[7] Such family allowances help to explain why in 1918 London's school medical officers could report that fewer than half as many children were poorly nourished than was true before the war. The organized labor movement also gained from the war, as trade-union membership nearly doubled in five years (1914–1919) from a little over four million to almost eight million. A host of petty grievances, price inflation, a general sense of war fatigue, and the conviction that labor had been more severely restricted than had management all contributed, however, to a legacy of ill will that erupted in industrial strife as soon as the war was over.

Swollen wartime wage packets went hand in hand with shortages of consumer goods and with the increased taxes necessitated by the abrupt rise in government spending. The British wartime budget of 1917–1918 (£2.7 billion) was more than thirteen times as large as the peacetime budget of 1913–1914. The standard rate of income tax levied rose from about 6 percent in 1914 to 15 percent in 1915–1916, 25 percent in 1917–1918, and 30 percent during 1918–1921. Even that sum proved insufficient to pay for the war on a pay-as-you-go basis. Over the 1914–1920 period, the government did succeed in paying for some 44 percent of expenditures by current taxes, but the remainder had to come from borrowing. The cost of servicing a new national debt of £7 billion was to prove a heavy burden for postwar Chancellors of the Exchequer, although it is difficult to see how such a burden could have been avoided. Relative to

[6]Cited in Marwick, *The Deluge,* p. 134. See also Gail Braybon and Penny Summerfield, *Out of the Cage: Women's Experiences in Two World Wars* (1987).

[7]See Susan Pedersen, "Gender, Welfare, and Citizenship in Britain During the Great War," *American Historical Review* (Oct. 1990).

Britain's wealth and population, it was, moreover, no heavier than that which Britain's Napoleonic War government had left to its successors.

One area of regulation in which the government may well have lagged behind popular demand was in the control of prices. Where the rapid growth of munitions factories swamped the housing market, wartime rents shot up, and a Glasgow "rent strike" in 1915 prompted the imposition of national rent controls. During the first three years of the war, prices increased at the rate of some 25 percent a year, a totally novel experience for Britain's people, but only in 1917 did the government attempt to impose further price controls. By then, wheat, meat, tea, and sugar were all in short supply, and long queues stretched in front of every food store. Attempts to expand grain and potato production at home made up only in part for the losses imposed by German submarine warfare; and in early 1918 the government, in the person of Lord Rhondda, the minister of food, established rationing for meat, sugar, butter, and margarine. The system, which required each consumer to register with a particular retail store, proved generally equitable and caused the queues to disappear.

The complete mobilization of the economy that constituted total war at home was only a reflection of the manner in which new means of warfare were obliterating the traditional distinction between soldier and civilian. Sporadically from early 1915 on, fleets of as many as sixty zeppelins (lighter-than-air dirigibles) dropped bombs on London and other English cities. In 1917 airplanes supplemented zeppelins, and one German bomber raid resulted in the deaths of 120 school children in London's East End. The zeppelin raids were initially regarded by most English people more as a risky type of entertainment than as acts of war, but the bomber raids came to be viewed less as acts of war than as the random murder of women and children.

War on Sea and Land (1915–1917)

The same breaking down of traditional demarcation lines that was involved in the bombing of civilians was implied by the German decision in the spring of 1915 to embark on unrestricted submarine warfare. The German government defended the step as justifiable retaliation for the increasingly successful British naval blockade. Of the German fleet, only the submarines were still at sea; only submarines could break Britain's economic links with the outside world. International law provided that a warship encountering an unarmed merchant vessel should fire a warning shot across its bow, board the ship, and search for contraband, or military supplies intended for the enemy. If contraband were found, the vessel might be taken as prize or sunk, as long as provision was made for the crew. If no contraband were found, the merchantman was to be permitted to go on its way. Unrestricted submarine warfare meant that there was to be no warning shot, no search, and no provision for the crew or passengers — only a torpedo blast and a watery grave in the North Atlantic.

The German government argued, cogently enough, that a submarine could not act as if it were a battleship. Its effectiveness depended not on armament but on speed and surprise. The Allied reaction, and the reaction of most Americans, was that the military nature of the submarine did not excuse its violation of international law. In May 1915 the German sinking of the British luxury liner *Lusitania*, the largest passenger ship still at sea, resulted in the loss of more than a thousand civilian lives and prompted a much greater sense of outrage than did the deaths of thousands of soldiers in the trenches of northern France. The warnings of the American government were indeed so strong that the German government quietly ordered its submarine commanders to cease attacking passenger vessels for the time being.

In May 1916, while unrestricted submarine warfare was temporarily suspended, the greatest naval battle of the war, the Battle of Jutland, was fought. The main German fleet had remained in its home base, awaiting the gradual attrition of British naval strength. Seeking to speed the process, a small German squadron sailed into the North Sea to lure the lightly armed British cruiser fleet into the path of the main German dreadnought fleet. The Germans were not aware that heavily armed British battleships were in the same area, and the snare originally set for the English turned out to be a trap for the entire German High Seas Fleet. The stage seemed set for the greatest sea battle of all time, with more than 250 vessels of all sizes taking part. During the night, however, the German fleet succeeded in evading the British ships and managed to return to its home base at Kiel. The battle thus ended on a strangely inconclusive note, and the British commander, Admiral John Rushworth Jellicoe (1859–1935), was afterward much criticized for his inability to take advantage of this opportunity to destroy German naval strength. The accuracy of German naval guns turned out to be superior, however, and the British lost fifteen ships, the Germans eleven; more than 6,000 British sailors died in the engagement in contrast to 2,500 Germans. At the same time, the German fleet never ventured successfully again beyond its North Sea home waters, and British naval superiority remained unchallenged on the high seas, if not in the waters beneath.

The last proviso is important, for in the beginning of 1917 Germany renewed unrestricted submarine warfare. For a time one merchant ship in every four that left the British Isles was sunk, and the loss of shipping in April 1917 — 870,000 tons — was so severe that the prospect of starvation became a genuine one.[8] The same month (largely as a response to

---

[8]Back in April 1912, enormous shock had been caused by the sinking of the *Titanic*, the world's largest passenger ship, when on its maiden voyage across the Atlantic it hit an iceberg and two-thirds of its passengers and crew were drowned. In the course of April 1917, the British fleet lost the equivalent of more than eighteen *Titanics*.

unrestricted submarine warfare), the United States entered the war on the Allied side, and American naval cooperation, combined with the development of new weapons, such as the depth charge, and the revival of old methods, such as the convoy system, gradually brought the submarine menace under control. Nonetheless, the British merchant fleet was hard hit. Seven million tons of British shipping were lost during World War I — 38 percent of the prewar merchant fleet, the world's largest.

In the meantime, the war had still to be won. Lloyd George's government was committed to the idea of striking a knockout blow and never seriously considered the possibility of a negotiated peace. The only drawback to such a militant position was that no one had a plausible plan to win the war. The secret had not been found in the Dardanelles, nor had it been discovered in an equally ill-fated attempt to launch a Balkan invasion from Salonika in Greece. Nor did new allies necessarily provide the key. Italy, an erstwhile member of the Triple Alliance, had entered the war on the British-French side in May 1915, but the Austro-Italian front soon became as stalemated as the older Western Front. The entry of Rumania on the Allied side in August 1916 led only to the conquest of that Balkan country by the Central Powers. By the spring of 1917, Russia was engulfed by revolution; although the liberal Russian government that emerged from the February Revolution insisted on abiding by all the military and diplomatic pledges given by its tsarist predecessors, domestic disorder made Russia an ever less reliable ally. After the Bolsheviks had supplanted their liberal predecessors in the October Revolution, Russia ceased to be a combatant at all.

From the point of view of France and Britain, the loss of Russia was counterbalanced by the entrance of the United States. Even before the American declaration of war, Britain's military effort had become increasingly dependent on weapons purchased in the United States and on funds borrowed from private American investors.[9] Formal American involvement at first brought little help in terms of manpower. During the summer of 1917 the bulk of the British army remained immobilized on the Western Front; and for Field Marshal Sir Douglas Haig, who had replaced Sir John French in December 1915, it was the Western Front that retained paramount importance. The Pyrrhic victory of Verdun in 1916 had decimated the French forces, and by 1917 more than half of the Western Front was manned by British troops. For the first time since the Middle Ages, Britain had become a great land power. It was under Haig's leadership that the British summer offensive of 1917 was conducted. The results were just as disappointing and grisly as the Somme campaign of 1916 — a few muddy acres around Passchendaele in Belgium won at a cost of another 400,000 casualties. As Lloyd George saw it, his country could afford no more such triumphs. If the tank, a British invention,

---

[9]Kathleen Burk, *Britain, America, and the Sinews of War, 1914–1918* (1985), explains the complexities of the relationship.

had been used with greater tactical skill in 1916 and 1917, it might successfully have broken through barbed wire entanglements and crossed over trenches. Tanks were used effectively by the Allies in 1918, but it was to be German, rather than British, generals who twenty years later would exploit fully their potential power.

Much of the idealism that the war had first evoked had begun to erode by 1917 and 1918. A generation of Britain's finest young men was being sacrificed, and a mounting hatred of the consequences of war found expression in the literature of the period. For a man like H. G. Wells, initial idealism gave way to the eventual conclusion that the war itself, "that whirlwind of disaster," had become the enemy. Bertrand Russell lost his lectureship at Cambridge because of his pacifist views and was jailed "for statements likely to prejudice recruiting and discipline of His Majesty's forces." Writers such as Lytton Strachey and Aldous Huxley were conscientious objectors. Others, although serving in the armed forces, expressed their opposition in print. John Buchan, often remembered as a pro-imperialist writer, expressed his disillusionment in his autobiography: "I acquired a bitter detestation of war, less for its horrors than for its boredom and futility. . . . To speak of glory seemed a horrid impiety." It seems fair to conclude, however, that in the face of the grievous losses that many British families had undergone, a majority still took comfort in the thought that the costs that they had borne would be compensated, at least in part, by the prospect of a better life to come.[10]

In the short run, the war brought both new prosperity and respectability to agricultural laborers, many of them women. The Agricultural Wages Board, set up in 1917, guaranteed a national minimum wage and a fixed working week. At the same time, high taxes and a shortage of domestics were making traditional country house life difficult or impossible for the upper classes to maintain. Class lines were being blurred in business and politics as well as in the army. Wartime shortages and the growing popularity of ready-to-wear clothes encouraged Britons of all ranks to dress increasingly alike.

The Lloyd George ministry heeded the widespread feeling that the war should mark the beginning of a new world as well as the destruction of an old. In 1917 it appointed a minister of reconstruction to centralize postwar planning of industrial conditions, housing, public health, and transportation facilities.[11] In 1918 it asked Parliament to place on the statute book two major pieces of legislation that, in their way, constituted a climax to the prewar Liberal program. One was the Representation of the People Act of February 1918. Its authors wanted to assure the right to participate in politics to all of Britain's brave soldiers, and so the law

---

[10]See, e.g., Jay Winter, *Sites of Memory, Sites of Mourning: The Great War in European Cultural History* (1997).

[11]Paul Barton Johnson, *Land Fit for Heroes* (1968), judiciously appraises the ministry's ambitious goals and subsequent disillusionments.

eliminated property qualifications for male voters over the age of twenty-one. The concept of "household" suffrage, still partially retained in the Reform Act of 1884, gave way to individual suffrage, and the Chartist ideal of the 1840s was at last achieved. Women over thirty were similarly enfranchised. The age differential remained for a decade because of a lingering fear that English political life might be dominated by a female majority. In other respects men and women, for the first time in British history, became politically equal. Thus the aim that prewar suffragettes had been unable to achieve by violence was granted to women en masse as a reward for their patriotic support of the war effort. In the midst of that conflict, party politics no longer blocked an enfranchisement that a majority of prewar M.P.'s had already approved in principle.[12] The other major legislative measure was the Education Act of August 1918. Although it was never to be fully implemented during the interwar years, the act called for the establishing of state nursery schools for the very young, extending the compulsory age of schooling to fourteen, and increasing teachers' salaries and pensions. A comparable act for Scotland substituted elected county educational authorities supervised by a Scottish Education Department for the local school boards introduced back in 1872.

The End of the War

Much of this postwar planning took place at a time when the war was far from over. As 1918 began, Britain and France had lost their most important ally, Russia, and gained an equally important associate, the United States. The question of the moment was whether Germany would be able to rush to the Western Front the vast armies hitherto tied up in the east more quickly than the United States could speed its newly trained recruits across the North Atlantic. Before either eventuality had occurred on a large scale, President Woodrow Wilson of the United States had issued his Fourteen Points. The American preoccupation with spelling out the purposes of the war impelled the British government to issue its own statement of war aims. Britain's original aims of 1914, as expressed by Asquith, had been the recovery of Belgium, the security of France, the rights of small nations, and the destruction of Prussian military domination. However, for many Britons victory per se remained always the overriding, if inconclusive, purpose of the war; only in October 1917 did the British government commit itself to as specific a goal as the French recovery of Alsace-Lorraine.

The question of Allied war aims was muddied in the eyes of most Americans and many left-wing Britons when the revolutionary Soviet government released early in 1918 the texts of secret treaties that the tsarist government had signed in the course of the war with its Western Allies. The treaties assumed that after an Allied victory both the Ot-

---

[12]Martin Pugh clarifies the details in *Electoral Reform in War and Peace, 1906–1918* (1978).

toman and Habsburg empires would in all likelihood break up and that it was desirable to plan for the disposition of the territories involved. The treaties, despite the interpretations subsequently placed on them, were not the cause but the consequence of World War I; and some of their provisions were less signs of Allied greed than of mutual Allied distrust. The promise that Russia might at long last occupy Constantinople was agreed to by Britain in order to reassure the tsarist government that the Gallipoli invasion, if successful, would not entail the permanent British takeover of Turkey. The promise of part of the Austrian Tyrol to Italy was intended as an incentive to gain Italian support for the Allied side. The ultimate breakup of the Habsburg and Ottoman empires had less to do with secret treaties, moreover, than with the longstanding nationalistic ambitions of Czechs, Poles, Serbs, Rumanians, and Arabs and with the fact that both these empires chose the losing side in the war.

The Fourteen Points demonstrated the curious ambiguity that marked the American entry into the war. Wilson had long urged "peace without victory"; and the Fourteen Points of January 1918 implied that, even though the United States was now militarily associated with the anti-German side, Americans still saw themselves above the battle, fighting not for reasons of self-interest but in order "to make the world safe for democracy." Some historians have long argued that American entry into the war *was* a matter of self-interest — Wilson himself had said: "England is fighting our fight!" — but American war aims were not ordinarily expressed in this fashion. The British in general and Lloyd George in particular could sympathize with many of the Fourteen Points, such as the doctrine of national self-determination as a basis for changing the boundary lines of Europe and the establishment of a League of Nations, a proposal advocated for a number of years by influential Britons. But Westminster was far less certain than Wilson seemed to be that the war had been the result of secret diplomacy, and it could not accept Wilson's insistence upon "absolute freedom of navigation upon the seas, alike in peace and war." To accept this provision, Lloyd George pointed out, would mean that Britain would deprive itself of the right to enforce a naval blockade, one of its major war weapons against Germany. Equally unacceptable to much of western European opinion was the implication that Belgium and France deserved no compensation or reparations for the immense material and human damage done by the German invaders.

The German government answered the Fourteen Points with an all-out drive for total victory. In the east, Germany imposed the Treaty of Bucharest on Rumania and the Treaty of Brest-Litovsk on Russia. The purpose was to convert the Balkans and much of prewar European Russia into German satellite states. Then in March of 1918, with its Eastern Front secure, Germany launched its last great offensive of the war. A rapid advance was made in the Somme area, where the depleted British forces retreated in the face of superior German numbers; German guns with a seventy-mile range began to shell Paris. The threat of a breakthrough between the British and French forces impelled the western

Allies at last to entrust the strategic direction of the war in the west to one man, General Ferdinand Foch. A more drastic conscription act in Britain made every man between seventeen and fifty-five liable to compulsory military service, and 355,000 British reserves, who had been kept at home because of Lloyd George's fears of General Haig's intentions, were now sent to the continent. In April, the United States first took active part in the fighting and during the next three months more than 600,000 additional American troops crossed the Atlantic. The war effort was only briefly interrupted by the worldwide influenza epidemic that first swept through Britain in June and July and that in due course killed more than 150,000 people there.

During May and June the Germans succeeded in making small advances, but by July the tide had turned. The Allied side had now achieved technological superiority, and in August General Haig's forces, successfully using tanks, began a general offensive in the Somme region. The German forces slowly retreated along the whole Western Front, and by early September the German army chiefs informed their government that peace had to be made at once. The kaiser's government, which had scorned the Fourteen Points in January, now accepted them in October "as a basis for peace negotiations." The British cabinet issued a reminder that "the pronouncements of President Wilson were a statement of attitude made before the Brest-Litovsk Treaty [and] the enforcement of the

Armistice Day in London (1918)   *(Hulton Deutsch Collection)*

peace of Bucharest on Roumania. . . . They cannot, therefore, be understood as a full recitation of the conditions of peace."

In the meantime, the Austrians had suffered a major defeat on the Italian front, and an Allied advance from Salonika in Greece had pushed Bulgaria out of the war. A long-drawn-out British campaign against the Ottoman Empire in the Middle East, in the course of which Britain's Colonel T. E. Lawrence had roused the Arab tribes against their Turkish suzerains, reached a climax in October 1918 with the capture of Damascus. Now that British forces occupied large portions of Turkey's Middle Eastern territories, the Turkish government decided on October 31 to withdraw from the war. In Germany itself, more than four years of unremitting war effort had likewise taken their toll. The reconstruction of the government in October 1918 only fanned the fires of domestic discontent. In early November a naval mutiny began to spread inland; Emperor William II was forced to abdicate; and early on November 11 it was announced that representatives of the German government had agreed to terms that amounted to a virtual unconditional surrender.

More than five million Britons had served in the armed forces. Of these Britons, 723,000 lost their lives (88 percent as a result of battle) and 1,700,000 were wounded. Members of the upper and upper-middle classes had been particularly hard hit, and of the male graduates of the elite public schools and of Oxford and Cambridge universities who had served in the military, one in five lay dead. For the moment, all that the living could think of was that the ordeal was over at last. As the bells announced the armistice, London became "a sea of laughing, joking people" dancing and singing in the streets and on buses. The horrors of the past and the fears for the future evaporated for the moment in "a triumphant pandemonium."

CHAPTER 15

The Consequences of the Peace

The energies of the inhabitants of a country engaged in all-out war may be repeatedly buoyed up by the prospects of victory; but when the moment of victory arrives, the survivors may discover that the triumph is hollow and that the difficulties prompted by peace are more frustrating than the challenges posed by war. Thus the exultant Britons of Armistice Day 1918 soon encountered troubles that transformed victory for many of them into a tawdry, second-rate achievement. Their nation faced not only the difficulty of restoring a stable international order but also the perennial Irish question, the hazards of domestic reconstruction, the perils of economic boom and bust, and the uncertainties entailed by a political party structure undergoing a fundamental transformation.[1]

The Election of 1918

One of the first peacetime events was a new election, and on November 21, 1918, the voters went to the polls to replace a House of Commons that had been sitting for eight years. Lloyd George, now "the prime minister who won the war," dramatically sought a popular mandate for his coalition ministry and authority for himself to negotiate the peace abroad and begin the work of economic reconstruction at home. The

---

[1]Even after four decades, Charles Loch Mowat's *Britain Between the Wars, 1918–1940* (1955) remains the most comprehensive general survey. Briefer accounts may be found in the works by A. J. P. Taylor and John Stevenson cited in Chapter 14. A survey by two contemporaries, Robert Graves and Alan Hodge, *The Long Week-End: A Social History of Great Britain, 1918–1939* (1940), remains both readable and revealing. The interwar economy is taken up in Chapters 2 and 3 of Sidney Pollard, *The Development of the British Economy, 1914–1990* (1992). Kenneth Morgan's *Consensus and Disunity: The Lloyd George Coalition Government, 1918–1922* (1979) is revisionist in emphasizing the government's achievements rather than its failures. Helpful in explaining a major political transformation of the era are Ross McKibbin, *The Evolution of the Labour Party, 1910–1924* (1984), Stephen Graubard, *British Labor and the Russian Revolution, 1917–1924* (1956), and Maurice Cowling, *The Impact of Labour, 1920–1924* (1971).

wartime coalition government had included Liberals, Conservatives, and even Labourites, but not all these groups joined forces for the election. The Conservatives under Bonar Law continued to give loyal support to Lloyd George, but many prewar Liberals did not. The rift between Asquith and Lloyd George, first opened in 1916, had not been bridged, and in 1918 it deepened when Asquith asked for a Select Committee of Inquiry into a military incident on the Western Front and Lloyd George angrily denounced the request as "a conspiracy to overthrow the Government." In the resultant parliamentary division, the Liberal party split down the middle.

During the general election in November, Lloyd George granted certificates of political loyalty, popularly known as "coupons," to 150 Liberal candidates; Bonar Law saw to it that virtually none of these candidates faced Conservative opposition. The remnant of the Liberal party, still led by Asquith, ran a separate slate of candidates. So did the Labour party, which, strengthened by the rapid growth of trade-union membership and by the vast increase of the total electorate, for the first time nominated candidates in a majority of constituencies. It had adopted a new constitution, which converted what had been a federation of trade unions and socialist groups into a national party with local branches and individual members. The party's program — drafted in large part by Sidney Webb of the Fabian Society — became professedly socialist. The party deliberately distinguished itself from its prewar Liberal allies by calling for the "common ownership of the means of production." The war had confirmed the expectation of most Labourites that such industries as coal, railways, and power could be operated efficiently by the state, and the party advocated the expansion of nationalization in the interest of workers' welfare. The party also supported the old Fabian demand of "a national minimum" of social services and the distribution of surplus wealth — by means of a sharply progressive income tax and a capital levy — for the common good.

Although desirous of using their coalition to transcend prewar political bickering and labor strife, Lloyd George and his teammates spoke vaguely of their long-range social goals and more specifically of their immediate foreign-policy aims: to try Emperor William II for war crimes, to punish those guilty of atrocities, and to make Germany pay for the cost of the war "to the uttermost farthing."[2] As the campaign progressed, the prime minister's utterances, carefully attuned to the popular mood, became ever more extravagant. "Heaven only knows," he later confided, "what I would have had to promise them if the campaign had lasted a week longer." The Asquithian Liberals denounced the "rush election" as a deliberate attempt to crush all independent political opinion, and Asquith prided himself on remaining a Liberal "without prefix or suffix."

---

[2]A farthing (one-fourth of a penny) was the smallest English coin in circulation.

It may well be that the electorate was not as aroused by the election as the more flamboyant newspaper headlines of the time seemed to indicate. Only 57.6 percent of the eligible electorate, which now included six million newly enfranchised women, participated, and the result was an overwhelming triumph for the Lloyd George coalition. The voters chose 484 coalition members, 338 of them Conservatives; 48 additional Conservatives were elected as well. Aided by the provisions of the Reform Act of 1918, the Labour party managed to increase its popular vote since 1910 almost sixfold. The party elected only 59 M.P.'s, however. These sufficed to transform the Labour party, for the first time, into the largest opposition group, but its principal leaders — Ramsay MacDonald, Philip Snowden, and Arthur Henderson — were all defeated. Although the cooperation of their Conservative partners had enabled the Lloyd George Liberals to prosper, only 26 Asquith Liberals managed to survive the election, and the former prime minister was for the moment not among them. A similar upheaval overtook those longtime Liberal party allies, the Irish Nationalists. All but seven of them were defeated by the revolutionary Sinn Feiners ("Ourselves Alone" in Gaelic), who refused to take their seats at Westminster. The new House of Commons was thus a remarkably different body from its predecessor. Its host of new members included an unusually large number of company directors, but the chamber lacked the cohesion that the traditional nineteenth-century party system had provided. A *finis* had clearly been written to the prewar era, but the political shape of the new age seemed far from certain.

Lloyd George at Paris

One prewar Liberal who had escaped unscathed from war and general election was David Lloyd George. He set out for Paris to make the peace with the apparent support of a large majority of the populace.[3] The Paris Peace Conference of 1919 inevitably evoked recollections of a similar gathering at Vienna a little more than a century before. Once again a coalition in which Britain had played a leading role, on sea and land, had emerged victorious and had succeeded in preventing a single power from dominating the European continent. Once again representatives assembled from many lands; but the leaders of just a few, the Big Five in 1815 and the Big Three now (or the Big Four if one counted Italy), made all the major decisions.

The differences between the two peace settlements were as notable as the similarities. In 1815 tsarist Russia had been one of the victorious allies; in 1919 Communist Russia had withdrawn in defeat from a war it condemned as nothing more than a power struggle among capitalist states headed straight for inevitable revolution and destruction. In 1815

---

[3]The best modern account is provided by Michael J. Dockrill and J. Douglas Gould, *Peace Without Promise: Britain and the Peace Conferences, 1919–1923* (1981).

the defeated power, France, had helped to negotiate the peace. In 1919 the defeated power, Germany, was forced to accept the consensus reached by the victors. In 1815 the Big Five had all been European; in 1919 the Big Three included an all-important non-European power, the United States of America.

The Big Three among the victorious powers did not find it easy to reach a common accord at Paris, if only because they had drawn conflicting lessons from the years of war. The French, who had suffered most, whose soil had been the scene of the most severe fighting, and who had witnessed a generation of young men killed or crippled, drew but one lesson: Germany must never again be allowed to possess the power to invade France. At best, Germany should be again divided into several small states; at the very least, it should be deprived of the right to a standing army. A binding anti-German alliance uniting France, Britain, and the United States seemed to be the best guarantee of French security. In contrast, the United States, whose ratio of casualties to population had been only one-fiftieth as great as France's, had not fought consciously for material gain. Its cities had not been destroyed, nor had its people faced the prospect of starvation by submarine blockade. Consequently, it was willing to assist in the building of a new and better Europe but not to the extent of signing an entangling alliance. Ultimately, indeed, even the slight limitation on national sovereignty that membership in the new League of Nations would have entailed proved a stumbling block to the United States Senate.

Britain, whose cost in casualties had been half as great as France's but twenty-five times that of the United States, took a diplomatic stand somewhere between the other two. Britain had some overseas ambitions, and several erstwhile Ottoman territories and German colonies were in due course added to the British Empire as League of Nations mandates. In regard to Europe itself, however, the British approach resembled the American more closely than the French. Some of Britain's chief objectives — the defeat of Germany, the restoration of Belgian independence, the surrender of the German fleet, the abdication of William II — had all been achieved by the time the diplomats met at Paris. Britain, although it had not fought the war to break up the Austrian Empire, could sympathize with the Poles, Czechs, Serbs, and Rumanians, who had thrown off generations of German, Russian, and Magyar rule. Although Lloyd George did not have such high hopes for the League of Nations as Wilson did, he was quite willing to associate Britain with the new organization. (Lord Robert Cecil, a younger son of Prime Minister Salisbury who became the British representative to the League, was a convinced Wilsonian idealist.) Lloyd George was no more eager than Wilson to sign a binding military alliance with France. He was less fearful of the new German Republic than was France, and he soon came to realize that Germany could not be destroyed as a viable state and still be expected to pay huge reparations or buy British goods. Once Germany had accepted the peace terms, Lloyd George promised in March 1919, Britain would do

The Big Four at Paris (1919)   British Prime Minister David Lloyd George (far left) is seen here with Italian Prime Minister Vittorio Orlando, French Premier Georges Clemenceau, and U.S. President Woodrow Wilson. *(The Image Works)*

"everything possible to enable the German people to get on their legs again. We cannot both cripple her and expect her to pay."

The resultant treaty was necessarily a compromise, not sufficiently idealistic to please Wilson nor sufficiently attentive to the needs of French security to please Clemenceau. Even Lloyd George, once he returned to London, was criticized. "I think I did as well as might be expected," he replied, "seated as I was between Jesus Christ and Napoleon Bonaparte." The main territorial and disarmament provisions of the Treaty of Versailles with Germany were not as severe as a generation of critics inside and outside of Germany was to contend. The provisions for reparations payments *were* severe, but they ultimately proved to be both politically unenforceable and economically impractical; thus the coal that Germany had to export to Italy as a reparation payment deprived Britain of a former export market. In the course of the next decade Germany ended up paying only a small portion of the $33 billion reparations bill decided on in 1921.

One factor of instability promoted by the Paris Peace Settlement was the new and untried governments set up in eastern Europe. Old habits of obedience had been ended, and traditional channels of trade were blocked by new tariff walls. Yet the new boundaries reflected much more adequately than those of 1914 the national preferences of the people of Eastern Europe. A second and much greater factor of instability was that, whereas the Great Powers of 1815 had all participated in and substantially agreed on the settlement of Vienna, three of the big powers of 1919 were clearly not satisfied with the Paris Peace Settlement. The Italians, one of the victors, regarded themselves as denied their legitimate gains in the Adriatic. The absent Russians obviously hoped to bring within the boundaries of international communism all the lands that the tsars had controlled, and more besides. Finally, some Germans were soon to argue that international equity required the restoration of their fleet, their colonies, and at least some of their lands in eastern Europe, where a Polish "corridor" now separated East Prussia from the rest of Germany.

For the moment, neither Germany nor the Soviet Union had the power to change the settlement, and a long era of at least relative peace seemed a reasonable hope in the summer of 1919. A balance of power of sorts had returned to the continent of Europe, and British statesmen could once again afford to turn their attention to other matters. One of these was the British Empire, on which World War I had had a paradoxical effect. On the one hand, that empire had grown, so that a map of the world drawn in 1919 showed more areas than ever "painted red" in the traditional imperial sense. The new acquisitions admittedly were neither colonies nor protectorates but League of Nations mandates, a status midway between colony and international trusteeship, in that a specific mandatory power had practical control but owed ultimate responsibility to the new international organization. Although some Britons in 1918 and 1919 dreamed of vast new colonies in the Middle East, an obvious lack of will, money, and soldiers soon punctured such dreams. Three Arab states that had hitherto formed parts of the Ottoman Empire did, however, come under British rule as class A mandates (protectorates soon to gain independence): Palestine, Trans-Jordan (eventually the Kingdom of Jordan), and Mesopotamia (henceforth called Iraq). With German and Russian influence curtailed at a time when the area was becoming an increasingly significant supplier of oil for the world, the Middle East was now predominantly a British sphere of influence. In Africa, parts of former German Togoland and Kamerun (Cameroons) and all of German East Africa (Tanganyika) became class B mandates, in which the mandatory power, Britain, was granted "full powers of administration and legislation."

For the older British dominions and for India, the war had provided both an opportunity to demonstrate their loyalty to the mother country and an incentive to develop a new sense of separatism. The government in London might still have claimed in 1914 the technical right to involve all the dominions in war, but it could hardly have compelled their military aid. Yet tiny New Zealand sent 112,000 troops to fight overseas, almost as large a percentage of its total population as was recruited for the armed forces in the British Isles themselves; even larger contingents

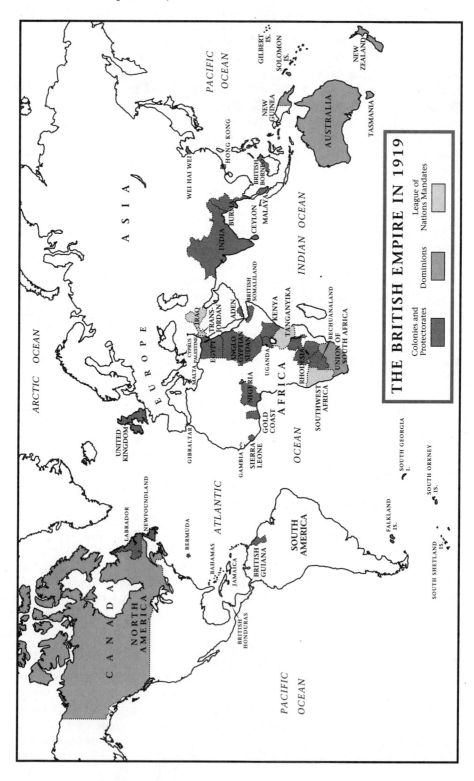

(representing a somewhat smaller percentage of the total population) were sent by Australia, Canada, and South Africa. Almost the entire professional Indian army (80,000 Europeans and 230,000 Indians) was immediately sent to Europe or the Middle East, and over a million Indians fought overseas before the war was over. The motives ranged from traditional loyalty by emigrant sons and outrage at German militarism to a desire (in India at least) to be rewarded with a greater degree of self-government.

War weariness at times sapped the spirit of imperial unity overseas, just as it encouraged political discord at home. Some South African Boers wished to take advantage of the conflict to regain their republican status; but other Boer leaders, such as Botha and Smuts, working in cooperation with South Africans of British origin, kept South Africa in the war. New Zealand and Canada adopted military conscription, in emulation of the mother country, although in Canada the issue opened up latent Anglo-French rivalry. French Canadians took comfort in the fact that the British Empire and France were, for once, allies, but they still opposed conscription if only because the French Third Republic was anticlerical rather than loyally Catholic. Australia, whose Labour party was much influenced by Irish immigrants, narrowly voted down conscription in two national referendums. In all other ways Australia cooperated loyally with the imperial war effort, and all the dominions, as well as India, found cause to take pride in the military exploits of their fighting men.

In India, the war impelled the British government to spell out its future intentions. Edwin Montagu, Secretary of State for India, did so in 1917 when he called for "the increasing association of Indians in every branch of the administration, and the gradual development of self-governing institutions, with a view to the progressive realization of responsible government in India as an integral part of the British Empire." The same spirit characterized the Montagu-Chelmsford Report of 1918, which in turn led to the Government of India Act of 1919. "Transferred" powers were henceforth to be exercised by ministries responsible to the elected provincial legislatures, and only "reserved" powers remained directly in the hands of British officials. Nationalist leaders were disappointed by the limited nature of the reforms and launched a civil-disobedience campaign against new anti-sedition acts that accompanied them. In Amritsar, General Reginald Dyer ordered his native troops to fire on an unauthorized assembly. The resulting "Amritsar Massacre" killed 379 people and wounded 1,200 others. Some Britons applauded the action as having averted a second Indian mutiny, but Asquith termed it "one of the worst outrages in the whole of our history." Dyer was ultimately dismissed from the service, and leaders of the Indian National Congress found new fuel to inflame the sometimes fitful nationalistic zeal of their people.

For a time in 1917 and 1918 an Imperial War Conference of Dominion Prime Ministers and representatives from India convened regularly in London. They generally met with Lloyd George's five-man war cabinet as an enlarged Imperial War Cabinet. Such wartime planning promised to revive Joseph Chamberlain's hope of a federal supergovernment for the British Empire, but the entry of the United States into the war and increasing interest in the prospective League of Nations eventually sidetracked such speculation.

Although the Imperial War Cabinet transformed itself into the British Empire Delegation at the Paris Peace Conference, Canada, Australia, New Zealand, South Africa, and India signed the peace treaties as if they were independent states, and afterward they gained independent membership in the League of Nations Assembly. Many Americans regarded this decision as an example of British duplicity in that it increased British representation; the multiple membership in the League was often cited by its opponents as a reason for steering clear of the venture. In fact, the initiative for separate representation had come from Canada; it was less a tribute to Lloyd George's Machiavellian cunning than a reflection of political embarrassment. Dominion status henceforth was to connote a high degree of foreign policy autonomy as well as of domestic independence. In this sense the First World War was a giant step toward the gradual transformation of the British Empire into what some in 1918 were beginning to call the British Commonwealth of Nations.[4]

A Solution for Ireland

As had happened so often before in British history, the most troublesome imperial problem provoked by war was the one next door in Ireland. While Redmond and his fellow Irish Nationalists had sought to rally their countrymen to the British cause as the only way of winning Home Rule without splitting their island, the revolutionary members of Sinn Fein preferred to take advantage of the war by accepting German aid, as some of their predecessors had once sought Spanish or French help. By the spring of 1916, little German support had been forthcoming and a majority of Sinn Fein leaders were in jail. A minority, however, succeeded in April 1916 in launching "the Easter Rebellion" in Dublin. For one of its romantic leaders, Patrick Pearse (1879–1916), blood shed in the national cause was "a cleansing and sanctifying thing." Those leaders declared Ireland to be a republic, but within a week the 1,600 rebels had been defeated. A majority of the Irish might have remained acquiescent had not the British government decided to execute fifteen of the ringleaders. Another leader, Eamon de Valera (1882–1975), an American citizen, escaped death, and he henceforth led the movement for complete independence. In the aftermath of the Easter Rebellion, Lloyd George secured from Redmond and Carson an agreement on a compromise plan by which Home Rule would have been implemented immediately (with Ulster excluded for the time being). Unionist opposition within the coalition

---

[4]Nicholas Mansergh, *The Commonwealth Experience* (1969), is a reliable guide to the twentieth-century evolution of empire into commonwealth.

cabinet killed this opportunity to resolve the question peacefully, and an Irish Convention that met in 1917–1918 also ended in disagreement. Some 200,000 Irishmen volunteered for service in the British army during World War I, but Irish hostility forced the cabinet to give up its plan to impose conscription on that portion of the British Isles. By the end of 1918, Redmond was dead and the "Time of Troubles" had begun.[5]

The general election of 1918 sealed the doom of Redmond's constitutionalist policy. The Sinn Feiners elected were pledged to sit in a parliament in Dublin but never in Westminster, and in January 1919 those not in jail or in hiding renewed their declaration of independence and attempted to set up their own parliament in Dublin and their own courts elsewhere in the country. The military wing of the Sinn Fein, the Irish Republican Army (I.R.A.), began a campaign of assassination and barracks burning designed to intimidate the Royal Irish Constabulary; in due course the British government sought to supplement the beleaguered Irish police with a specially recruited force of war veterans, the notorious "Black and Tans." No traditional rules of war restrained either the I.R.A. or the Black and Tans in their tactics of ambush, plunder, arson, and seizure of hostages. In the course of two years some 750 Irishmen and 700 British soldiers and police officers died.

In the middle of this sporadic civil war, the Parliament at Westminster replaced the Home Rule Act of 1914 — which had never been put into effect — with the Home Rule Act of 1920. This provided for two Irish parliaments, one for the twenty-six counties of the south, the other for the six Ulster counties of the north, with authority over all activities except defense, currency, and tariffs. These were to remain in the hands of the British Parliament, in which the Irish were to retain limited representation. The Northern Irish accepted the plan; thus the section of the island that had so long fought against the concept of Home Rule now paradoxically received it. The Sinn Feiners, on the other hand, rejected the plan as a political mockery and a criminal effort to partition the island. The Sinn Fein Dail (Parliament) claimed to be the government of all Ireland, and the civil war continued.

Sir Henry Wilson, chief of the Imperial General Staff, urged that the government must either "Go all out or get out." Lloyd George, although in part responsible for the civil war, ultimately preferred the latter alternative. The protracted fighting not only alienated public opinion in the United States and in the empire but also caused a similar sense of revulsion

---

[5]The story is told most fully in Nicholas Mansergh, *The Unresolved Question: The Anglo-Irish Settlement and Its Undoing, 1912–1972* (1991), and more briefly in the books by Lyons and Vaughan cited in Chapter 9. Robert Kee, *Ourselves Alone* (1972); D. G. Boyce, *Englishmen and Irish Troubles: British Public Opinion and the Making of Irish Policy, 1918–22* (1972); Charles Townshend, *The British Campaign in Ireland 1919–1921* (1975); Lord Longford, *Peace by Ordeal* (1972); and Sean Farrell Moran, *Patrick Pearse and the Politics of Redemption: The Mind of the Easter Rising, 1916* (1994), focus on different facets of the 1916–1923 era.

in England itself. A number of newspapers, the archbishop of Canterbury, and King George V all spoke in favor of a peaceful settlement.

Protracted negotiations in 1921 by Lloyd George and Sinn Fein representatives led to a treaty giving the new Irish Free State dominion status in the empire. Men such as Arthur Griffith and Michael Collins preferred the substance of complete independence to the letter, if only because a total military triumph was beyond their power. Reluctantly, they also acknowledged the right of the Northern Irish parliament to exempt itself from the new Irish Free State. Although the Dail ratified the treaty by a narrow margin, de Valera and the more radical Sinn Feiners denounced it as a betrayal, and the year that followed the withdrawal of British troops saw an outbreak of civil war among the Irish that was even more fierce and damaging than the fighting of the previous three years. Only after Collins had been killed in ambush and Griffith had died of heart failure did de Valera call off armed resistance. Ultimately, even he came to realize that the treaty of 1921 had given, at least to the twenty-six counties of southern Ireland, independence in fact, and that the remaining tenuous bonds between the Irish Free State and Britain — such as the required oath of loyalty to King George V — could be cut step by step in a constitutional fashion. Until a new "Time of Troubles" befell Northern Ireland in 1969, it was widely believed that the centuries-long Irish question had been resolved in 1922 by a combination of violence and compromise. Partition remained a stumbling block as did the privileged position of the Roman Catholic Church set forth in the Irish Constitution of 1937. Yet as feelings gradually mellowed, some of the Irish began to realize that, politically independent or not, they remained tied to Great Britain by economic interest, by language — because the attempt to replace English with Irish Gaelic as "the national language" did not succeed — and by a common heritage of legal and political institutions.

The Twenties: Economy and Society

The inhabitants of England and Scotland could not help being concerned with Irish affairs during the immediate postwar period, but they were even more engrossed with events on their own island. Although the government had promised returning veterans that it would "make Britain a fit country for heroes to live in" and had set up a separate Ministry of Reconstruction to provide schemes for government-aided housing and town planning, it looked forward with considerable foreboding to the sudden demobilization of millions of war veterans at a time when the specter of socialist revolution seemed to haunt the continent. The reconstruction proposals had assumed the existence of a stable economy and of the temporary continuation of wartime rationing and price controls. Instead, there was an immediate demand for a general relaxation of controls, and Britain was caught up for a year and a half in an unprecedented economic boom.

Returning veterans might not find "civvy street" paved with gold, but for the moment they had no difficulty locating jobs, because many large companies worked overtime filling orders for civilian goods and poured capital into plant expansion. The result was widespread inflation, which carried wholesale prices to 225 percent of their prewar level. Labor unions found their energies diverted from long-range goals of nationalization to the more immediate problem of keeping the pay packets of their members in line with rising prices. Strikes were epidemic — an average of 49 million working days a year were lost to strikes in 1919–1921, a figure more than twice that of even the most turbulent prewar year and ten times as high as any year in the 1930s, 1940s, or 1950s. In the midst of such militancy, a spirit of class consciousness impressed many observers as more evident than ever before in British history.

No sooner had both workers and employers become accustomed to the immediate postwar boom than in 1921 the bubble burst, and in the course of the next few years Britain's people became less concerned with labor strife than with long-term unemployment. Available statistics suggest that from 1883 to 1913 only one worker in twenty suffered from unemployment at any given time; but during the years 1921–1938 one in seven was likely to be looking for a job. Such economic waste was in part the by-product of the fact that during the 1920s, international trade did not return to pre–World War I levels. Three of Britain's most important nineteenth-century industries — coal mining, cotton manufacturing, and shipbuilding — all suffered dramatically as a result. The difficulty was alleviated only in part by the growth of newer consumer and service industries.

The economic slump of 1921 did not at first dim the hopes of all those who wanted the state permanently to play a more direct role in running the economy. It is true that the reorganized railways were restored to private ownership, and so — despite the pleas of mine union leaders and a majority of the government-appointed Sankey Commission — were the coal mines. The Housing and Town Planning Act of 1919 became the first of several statutes, however, that accepted the still novel assumption that the government might not only tear down slums but also build, own, and rent out both flats (apartments) and houses. The Industrial Courts Act of the same year permanently increased the power of the Ministry of Labour to mediate labor disputes. The slump of 1921, although it dampened labor militancy and brought about a downturn in union membership, was not necessarily followed by a decline in real wages. In many industries, prices fell more quickly than did wages among those who held on to their jobs. At the same time, the standard British factory work week declined from fifty-four hours to no more than forty-eight hours.

The most significant of the immediate postwar social-service measures proved to be the Unemployment Insurance Act of 1920, which extended the scope of the act of 1911 to include more than twelve million workers. Because the number of unemployed remained at a million or

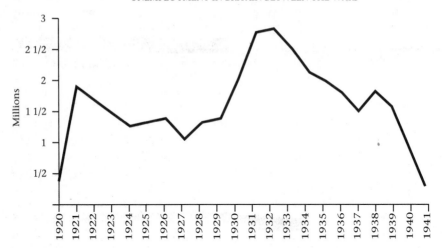

Annual averages based largely on B. R. Mitchell and Phyllis Deane, *Abstract of British Historical Statistics* (1962).

more from 1921 on, this statute became for many English people the most meaningful of all government welfare measures. Unemployment benefits made up an ever-increasing portion of the national budget. The £500,000 of benefits paid in 1913–1914 swelled to £53,000,000 in 1921–1922. The dole was to be the butt of many a wry joke during the 1920s and 1930s, and applicants expressed resentment at the "means test" they had to pass to remain eligible (from 1931 on) after their original half-year of benefits had expired. Yet unemployment relief remained an official acknowledgment that neither private charity nor the poorhouse could be the sole refuge for those out of work. They had a "right" to receive help, and those afflicted came to accept it as such.

The war, which gave rise to the postwar boom-and-bust cycle and which underlined Britain's decline from its unrivaled pre-1914 international trading position, also accentuated many long-slumbering social changes. Four years of war had blurred outward distinctions of class and sex. The mass consumption of ready-made clothing softened social differences in dress, and first the cinema and later the radio provided a common cultural experience for all elements of society. The lower-class deference that Walter Bagehot had discerned in the 1860s was far less evident in the 1920s, and the phrase "O let us . . . always know our proper stations" was reserved for anthologies of Victorian poetry. The Edwardian upper class had seen a pitifully large number of its sons killed in battle, and many an ancient estate fell victim to steeply increased inheritance taxes. During the years 1919–1921, some ten million acres of land were sold by Britain's aristocratic and gentry families; the result was an often dramatic transformation of country society. Those country squires who remained now had to rub shoulders in popular esteem not only with business leaders but also with movie stars and heroes of "the now all-important world of sport." The columnist and the gossip writer had found a niche in the newspaper world, and "society" was increasingly defined as "people worthy of a columnist's respectful attention."

Although the number of women factory workers declined sharply during the postwar years, unmarried middle-class women maintained a significant foothold in both business and the professions. The law that provided votes for women was followed by others admitting women to the courtroom as both lawyers and jurors; but the advocates of "equal pay for equal work" found business managers and union leaders less sympathetic than politicians. Once war veterans had returned to civilian life and unemployment levels had risen, trade unions sought a "family wage" for the male breadwinner and a return to the home for his wife. According to *Vogue,* even among women, "there are few who would not rather have the men than the men's jobs."[6] Many interwar feminists became more concerned with causes such as the health of mothers and the welfare of children than with enhancing the independence of women and opening new jobs to them. In national politics, women M.P.'s such as the Virginia-born Lady (Nancy) Astor, who was elected to the House of Commons in 1919, continued to be the exception rather than the rule. The female ideal of those who "thought modern" in the 1920s became the "flapper": the easygoing, sporty young woman with a boyish figure who wore short hair, short skirts, and flesh-colored stockings; who danced cheek-to-cheek; and who dispensed with chaperones.

Divorces were made easier to obtain, but the only legally accepted causes remained adultery and desertion; despite the fears of an older generation of moralists, the number granted in any given year during the 1920s remained below 5,000. It became fashionable to talk about the psychological theories of Sigmund Freud. Dr. Marie Stopes, who opened Britain's first birth-control clinic in 1921, gave new prominence and respectability to the use of contraceptive methods by married people; in 1930 the Anglican Church gave the practice its somewhat hesitant blessing. Old barriers were collapsing in the upper-class nursery as well. Children were no longer barred from eating or conversing or playing games with their parents until they had reached late adolescence. With the falling birthrate, children were in some cases enjoying a scarcity value they had hitherto lacked.

---

[6]See Deirdre Beddoe, *Back to Home and Duty: Women Between the Wars, 1918–1939* (1990), and Brian Harrison, *Prudent Revolutionaries: Portraits of British Feminists Between the Wars* (1987). The broader context is provided by Jane Lewis, *Women in England, 1870–1950: Sexual Divisions and Social Change* (1984), and Martin Pugh, *Women and the Women's Movement in Britain, 1914–1959* (1992).

The Careless Twenties   Four "flappers" perform the Charleston in a London stage review. *(Bettmann/Corbis)*

For most Britons, the decade came to be seen as less the "roaring" than the "careless" twenties. Though older standards did not disappear altogether, there was, in both literature and life, a change of attitude that the war had promoted. It was the attitude of somewhat cynical and superficially lighthearted disillusionment embodied in the phrase "Life's too short" and in the adjective *bittersweet*, which became the title of one of Noel Coward's popular musical comedies. The war had demonstrated that neither life nor property was sacred, and the postwar period provided an incentive to seek "psychological compensation" for social tensions in idle amusements. British railways reminded their customers that "Sunshine is Life" and invited the more affluent to take "the Blue Train" to the French and Italian Riviera. The fact that a good many Britons could afford to travel abroad and that most others managed to spend a week each year at a seaside resort such as Brighton or Blackpool reflected a reasonably high standard of living. Comfort as well as social satire could be derived from the fact that when the newspaper headlines screamed ENGLAND IN PERIL or CAN WE AVOID DISASTER? the reference was not to a new military or diplomatic catastrophe but to the results of a cricket match.

The Fall of Lloyd George

The economic slump that began in 1921 could only weaken the political position of the powerful coalition ministry that had governed Britain under Lloyd George's leadership since the general election of 1918. Not that the prime minister had become personally unpopular. He was still "the pilot who weathered the storm," and published reports stating that individuals he had recommended for knighthood and the peerage had paid large sums into his party war chest (£150,000 per barony) hurt his reputation little. Admittedly, he had been less successful than he wished in restoring Europe to perfect harmony. Although Vladimir Lenin was in the process of fashioning the Soviet Union as a totalitarian one-party state, Lloyd George had been quick to withdraw British troops from a Russia torn by civil war. They had first been sent there in 1918 in order to keep Allied war supplies out of the hands of the Germans after the Bolsheviks signed a separate peace with them, but before the end of 1919 the last British soldiers had been ordered home. In 1921 Lloyd George had even extended de facto recognition to the Soviet regime and signed a trade treaty. Yet the problem of German reparations and interallied war debts hampered the restoration of the prewar system of international trade. Anglo-French distrust added to the lack of international stability, Britain and France being the two great powers in the League of Nations. Britain went so far in 1922 as to offer France the diplomatic guarantee against Germany it had been demanding since 1919; but when the offer was not accompanied by a military convention that accorded with French wishes, the arrangement fell through. A war between Greece and Kemal Ataturk's new Turkish Republic was still going on in the Near East, and Lloyd George was widely, although perhaps unjustly, criticized for his handling of the "Chanak affair." He had warned the Turks not to attack the area of the Dardanelles occupied by British troops, pending a final peace settlement. He then discovered that the French and most of the dominion prime ministers were unwilling to pledge support if the stand led to war. As things turned out, Lloyd George's firmness paid off and led to a resolution of the Greco-Turkish war in the Treaty of Lausanne (1923), but many of Lloyd George's compatriots viewed his policy as unnecessarily militaristic.

Although most Conservative party leaders continued to favor the coalition arrangement, an increasing number of Conservative backbenchers did not. They feared the permanent eclipse of an independent Conservative party, even though many prewar Liberal-Conservative differences had disappeared and even though the rise of a professedly socialist Labour party seemed to dictate fusion with the Liberals. Moreover, Lloyd George's greatest diplomatic achievement, the Irish Treaty of December 1921, impressed many old-guard Tories as a sellout of their "unionist" principles. For a Conservative such as Lord Beaverbrook, the publisher of the influential *Daily Express*, Lloyd George's unwillingness to meet economic problems with a full-fledged program of tariff protection and imperial preference provided an adequate reason for wanting him out of office.

Ultimately, it was the decision by Bonar Law to support the back-bench revolt that led the Conservative party in 1922 to leave the coalition. The resignation of his chief cabinet ministers forced Lloyd George to resign as well, and the king asked Bonar Law to head the new, purely Conservative ministry. King George V fully expected to see the fifty-nine-year-old Lloyd George prime minister again — and so doubtless did Lloyd George himself — but matters worked out otherwise. Bonar Law's first decision was to ask the king to dissolve Parliament and call for new general elections on a platform that bore a close kinship to President Harding's "normalcy" in the United States: "tranquillity and freedom from adventures and commitments both at home and abroad."

Both Liberals and Conservatives stressed the danger of the Labour party's coming to power. That party in turn defended its socialist policy as one of bringing about "a more equitable distribution of the nation's wealth by constitutional means. This is neither Bolshevism nor Communism, but common sense and justice." The results of the election (5.5 million votes for the Conservatives, 4.2 million votes for Labour, 4.1 million votes for the Liberals) indicated that Britain's prewar pattern of two major parties and two minor parties had been replaced by a virtual three-party system. The Conservative popular vote plurality was, however, sufficient to give the Conservatives a decisive overall parliamentary majority: 347 Conservatives, 142 Labourites, and 117 Liberals (divided between 60 Asquith Liberals and 57 Lloyd George Liberals).

Bonar Law's ministry proved to be a short one, because the throat cancer that was to end his life in 1923 began to grow progressively worse during his term of office. Law did achieve one major foreign-policy settlement, which proved for the second time in two years how much Britain had come to make good relations with the United States a cornerstone of its foreign policy. Although Britain had emerged from World War I with its navy still the foremost in the world, naval officials soon came to realize that both finances and Anglo-American relations made the goal of naval parity preferable to a new naval race. Thus at the Washington Conference of 1921–1922, Britain, by accepting a 5–5–3–1.75–1.75 ratio of battleships with the United States, Japan, France, and Italy, respectively, quietly agreed to end over 200 years of naval supremacy. The same conference also replaced the Anglo-Japanese Alliance of 1902 with a more vaguely worded agreement involving the United States and France, as well as Japan and Britain, that guaranteed the status quo in East Asia. Japan had profited from its role as ally in World War I by usurping in China much of the influence formerly exerted by Germany and Russia, and the Washington Conference treaties facilitated the furthering of Japanese expansionist ambitions. But this result was not obvious to the other major powers at the time.

A still more notable example of British recognition of the political and financial importance World War I had bestowed on the United States was the signing of a war-debt agreement in January 1923. One of the economic heritages of the war was that Britain had become both a debtor and a creditor nation. Its European allies owed it $10.5 billion, the Germans owed it $7.2 billion in reparations, but the United Kingdom itself owed $4.25 billion to the United States. Although Lloyd George had initially advocated heavy reparations payments, his government soon came to realize that the immense burden of inter-European debt was proving an enormous obstacle to the restoration and growth of international trade. In the 1922 "Balfour Note," Britain sought to cut the Gordian knot by offering to cancel all Allied payments and German reparations payments if the United States would cancel all British debts as part of an international financial settlement. If the United States refused, Britain would ask of its allies only so much money as it had to pay to the United States.

Neither the French nor the Americans were sympathetic. The French argued that the United States should cancel all Allied debts as its contribution to a common cause to which France had committed more than its share of human lives; German reparations, on the other hand, were seen as a legitimate compensation for damage done and suffering incurred. The American government viewed France and Britain as debtors, not as allies in a common cause. "They hired the money, didn't they?" was President Coolidge's laconic reaction. The settlement reached in Washington by Stanley Baldwin, Chancellor of the Exchequer, provided for Britain to repay its debts to the United States over a sixty-two-year period at 3.5 percent interest. Americans regarded the terms as a generous concession, and for the moment the settlement aided Anglo-American relations and safe-guarded the British reputation for financial integrity. By 1931 Britain had repaid nearly $2 billion, a difficult task in the light of increasingly steep American tariff barriers. Initially, the settlement also raised Baldwin's prestige, but it was to be much criticized later when the United States concluded similar agreements with other European debtors on terms much less onerous than those imposed on Britain.

Bonar Law's retirement from the prime ministership in May 1923 forced King George V to name a successor, since the Conservative party had no obvious candidate. Lord Curzon (1859–1925), the former viceroy of India who since 1919 had served as foreign secretary, expected the call, but the nomination went instead to Stanley Baldwin — largely because, in Curzon's biting words, Baldwin possessed "the supreme and indispensible qualification of not being a peer." By 1923 it seemed no longer practical to most Britons to have a prime minister rule from the House of Lords, especially when the largest opposition party, the Labour party, was virtually unrepresented there. Baldwin (1867–1947), an M.P. since 1908, had reached cabinet rank only in 1921, and his critics found him unprepossessing in appearance and less than brilliant in intellect. He established, however, a reputation as a man of moral integrity, common sense, and good will; and his precepts of "Faith, Hope, Love, and Work" as the remedy for the ailments besetting Britain and the world were sufficiently characteristic of the attitudes of a majority of his fellow Britons to cause one writer to dub the 1920s and 1930s the "Baldwin Age" and another, the "Age of Illusion."

Stanley Baldwin's decision in the fall of 1923 to unite his party and to meet the continuing problem of mass unemployment on a platform of full-fledged tariff protection did not prove similarly in tune with the views of the voters. The unexpected election of December 1923 did attract wavering Conservative leaders back to their party's standard, but at the same time it revived a potent prewar political controversy. The issue that had reunited the Liberals back in 1905 sufficed to cause the Asquith and Lloyd George Liberals to wage a strong antiprotection campaign under a common banner in 1923. Labourites also opposed protective tariffs, but for them the remedy for unemployment lay not in tariffs but in socialism. The election results showed how a relatively small switch in popular votes in a few constituencies could completely alter the parliamentary picture. There were now 258 Conservative M.P.'s (formerly 346), 191 Labourites (formerly 142), and 158 Liberals (formerly 117).

The First Labour Government

Although Baldwin faced the new Parliament as prime minister, he resigned after a vote of "no confidence" by the combined Liberal-Labour opposition, and the king called upon Ramsay MacDonald, the leader of the Labour party, to form a new government. That a "revolutionary socialist" should be named prime minister seemed startling to many Britons, and few Labour leaders had really expected that their distant vision of a Labour government would become reality so soon. Asquith was begged by many to "save the country from the horrors of Socialism and Confiscation"; but a Conservative-Liberal coalition after an election fought on the issue of protection would have been as illogical as a Labourite-Liberal coalition. There was also a widespread realization that a Labour government dependent on Liberal support would give the supposedly revolutionary party a taste of power while preventing it from enacting truly revolutionary measures.

The Labour party of 1924 was, in any event, an amalgam of both moderate and radical trade-union leaders, socialist intellectuals, and recent converts from Liberalism who were attracted more by the party's humanitarianism and internationalism than by its socialism. Although leaders such as F. W. Jowett pungently criticized the "terrible tribute to Rent, Interest, and Profit" paid by the workers to "enrich mainly the class which has already more to spend than it can usefully spend," proponents such as Sidney Webb struck a different note. "For we must always remember," he observed in 1923, "that the founder of British socialism was not Karl Marx but Robert Owen, and that Robert Owen preached not class war but the ancient doctrine of human brotherhood."

Ramsay MacDonald (1866–1937), the new prime minister, was the illegitimate son of a poor Scotswoman. A long-term party worker, he had

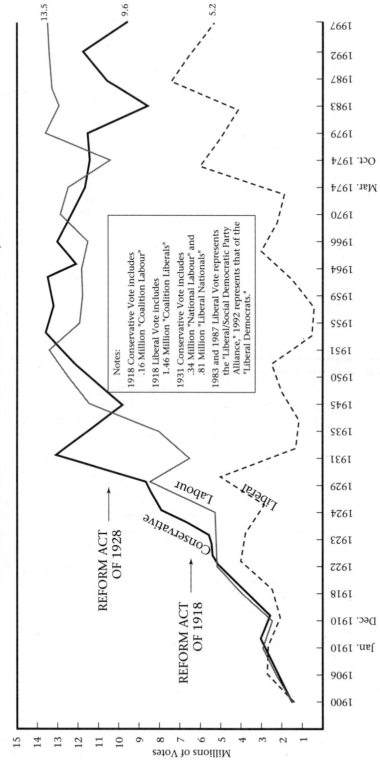

PARTY POPULAR VOTE IN GENERAL ELECTIONS, 1900–1992

Millions of Votes

15 14 13 12 11 10 9 8 7 6 5 4 3 2 1

13.5
9.6
5.2

1900 1906 Jan. 1910 Dec. 1910 1918 1922 1923 1924 1929 1931 1935 1945 1950 1951 1955 1959 1964 1966 1970 Mar. 1974 Oct. 1974 1979 1983 1987 1992 1997

REFORM ACT OF 1928

REFORM ACT OF 1918

Labour

Conservative

Liberal

Notes:

1918 Conservative Vote includes .16 Million "Coalition Labour"

1918 Liberal Vote includes 1.46 Million "Coalition Liberals"

1931 Conservative Vote includes .34 Million "National Labour" and .81 Million "Liberal Nationals"

1983 and 1987 Liberal Vote represents the "Liberal/Social Democratic Party Alliance," 1992 represents that of the "Liberal Democrats."

Adapted from David Butler and J. Freeman, *British Political Facts*, 2nd ed. (1968), and David Butler and Dennis Kavanagh, *The British General Election of 1997* (1997).

gained a great reputation for radicalism because of his opposition to World War I, but he proved in practice to be a political moderate as well as "the handsomest of all Prime Ministers"; and his new cabinet of twenty included not only trade-union members (five) but also former Liberals such as Lord Haldane. A minor furor was raised in the party's ranks by the question of whether the cabinet should wear formal dress to meet the king. Some did and others did not; the cabinet eventually bought three uniforms of formal court attire to be worn in turn by whichever cabinet members required them on specified occasions. "I could not help marvelling," noted J. R. Clynes, the new Lord Privy Seal, as he waited to be received by King George V, "at the strange turn of Fortune's wheel, which had brought MacDonald, the starveling clerk, Thomas, the engine-driver, Henderson, the foundry laborer and Clynes, the millhand, to this pinnacle."

The Labour government of 1924 disappointed the expectations of its more enthusiastic supporters, but it did succeed in taking over the governmental reins, and it did enact several social-welfare measures. It raised unemployment benefits, eased the conditions under which the elderly received their pensions, and enacted a new housing act that provided added government subsidies for the building of working-class houses under controlled rents. Under its provisions, more than half a million houses were built during the next decade. The government repealed certain wartime tariffs. It also widened the educational opportunities of working-class children by increasing the number of "free places" in secondary schools and providing university scholarships.

MacDonald was his own foreign secretary and did his best to advance the task of European reconciliation. America's Dawes Plan to extend and regularize German reparations payments — written largely by Josiah Stamp, the British expert on the Dawes Committee — led, as a result of MacDonald's skillful diplomacy, to the withdrawal of French forces from the German Ruhr, into which they had moved the year before to force German compliance. The result was an Anglo-French reconciliation and the laying of the groundwork for the readmission of Germany to the European diplomatic family. MacDonald gave full British support to the League of Nations and was the first British prime minister to attend in person its sessions in Geneva.

The Labour government's most controversial foreign policy innovation involved British relations with Russia. Although most Labour party adherents were becoming disappointed in their initial expectation that the Bolshevik Revolution would transform the erstwhile Russian Empire into a democratic socialist state rather than into a repressive despotism, they repeatedly insisted that the new Soviet government ought to be recognized and dealt with like any other legitimate power. They saw no contradiction between their championship of Russian rights on the international scene and their quick decision to bar the small new British Communist party from membership in the Labour party. "A Communist," wrote J. R. Clynes in 1924, "is no more a Left Wing member of the

The Red Scare (1924) A Unionist (Conservative) election poster for the November 1924 election shows Prime Minister Ramsay MacDonald turning toward the Russians. *(Hulton Deutsch Collection)*

Labour Party than an atheist is a Left Wing member of the Christian Church."

Despite the 1921 trade treaty, Anglo-Russian relations had remained uneasy, but as soon as the Labour government took office in 1924 it extended de jure recognition to the Soviet Union. Later that summer, after several months of negotiations, it also announced the signing of two treaties: first, a commercial agreement and, second, a treaty promising that in return for Russian consideration of the claims of British holders of tsarist bonds and former owners of property nationalized by Russia without compensation, the government would recommend to Parliament a British guarantee of a sizable loan to the USSR. The treaty, which required parliamentary ratification, was opposed by Conservatives and Liberals alike and might well have brought down the government. What actually did do so, however, was the Campbell case, the decision by the government to drop its prosecution of a Communist editor who had violated a statute of 1797 against incitement to mutiny by urging soldiers never to fire on fellow workers. Asquith's motion for a Select Committee of Inquiry was interpreted by MacDonald as an issue of confidence, and when the Labour government was defeated, he resigned from office. The result was the third general election in three years.

The Conservatives, who seized the opportunity to brand the Labourites as Bolsheviks, were given added ammunition when late in the election campaign the Zinoviev letter was published in the newspapers. Purportedly written by the secretary of the Communist International, the document urged ratification of the Anglo-Russian treaty as a necessary prelude to "the revolutionizing of the international and British proletariat," the spreading of Communist propaganda in Britain, and ultimate "armed insurrection." The genuineness of the Zinoviev letter was to be debated both in the 1920s and later, but a scholar who examined the surviving evidence has concluded that it was no forgery.[7] Certainly it reflected accurately the secret ambitions of the Soviet Union at that time. Most Labour party leaders blamed their defeat in the general election of November 1924 on the revelation of the secret letter. An analysis of the election returns demonstrates, however, that it was a sharp decline in the votes obtained by the Liberal party — the voice of studious moderation in the midst of the "Red Scare" — that determined the outcome. In contrast to the election of the year before, the Conservative popular vote increased by 2 million, but the Labour vote also increased by 1.2 million. The Liberal vote, however, declined by 1.2 million. The Labourites, who had benefited from the Conservative-Liberal split in many a three-cornered fight the previous year, could do so no longer, and for the next five years the government was in the hands of a decisive Conservative parliamentary majority: 415 Conservatives, 152 Labourites, and but 42 Liberals. The Liberal party, the victim of war and personalities as well as of changing social conditions, had ceased to be a major party, and Stanley Baldwin was back as the head of what he promised would be a "sane, commonsense Government, not carried away by revolutionary theories or hare-brained schemes."

---

[7]Christopher Andrew, *Her Majesty's Secret Service: The Making of the British Intelligence Community* (1985), pp. 301–316.

PART FIVE

THE SHADOW OF DEPRESSION AND WAR

1924 to 1956

WOMEN MARCHERS APPROACH LONDON (1934)
Women from all over Britain march to Hyde Park to
protest against a harsh new unemployment insurance act.
(Bettmann/Corbis)

CHAPTER 16

The False Dawn and the Great Depression

Stanley Baldwin's second ministry (1924–1929) provided many Britons of the day with the impression that the domestic political and economic reverberations set off by World War I had died down. The "spirit of Locarno" added a glow of reconciliation to the international horizon. Only in retrospect did it become clear that the dawn was a false one and that the economic dislocations created by war had only been patched and not mended. The resulting international Great Depression, by bringing Adolf Hitler and his national socialist movement to power in Germany, was to lead directly to another world war.[1]

Baldwin's cabinet included a number of notable personalities: two sons of Joseph Chamberlain, Austen as foreign minister and his half-brother Neville as minister of health, and Winston Churchill as Chancellor of the Exchequer. Churchill's return to the party he had left in 1904 symbolized the erosion that had been taking place within the Liberal ranks and the drift away from the Liberal camp toward either the Conservative right or the Labourite left. One of Churchill's first steps as Chancellor of the Exchequer was to prove highly controversial; he made the British pound once again freely exchangeable for gold at the prewar ratio of $4.86. The return to the gold standard had for some years been the dream of such English financiers as Montagu Norman, the influential governor of the Bank of England. It seemed at once the symbol of the revival of prewar economic and moral values and the step that would restore Britain's trade, prosperity, and prestige. The return to gold may well have helped restore such a spirit of confidence, but the rate of exchange tended to overvalue Britain's exports by 10 percent, thus magnifying the problems faced by the country's exporters. At the same time, the need to

---

[1]The books by Mowat, A. J. P. Taylor, Stevenson, and Graves and Hodge, cited in Chapter 15, are all relevant for this chapter as well. So is the book by Sidney Pollard, from which the economic statistics are derived. Noreen Branson and Margot Heinemann, *Britain in the Nineteen Thirties* (1971), emphasize the negative aspects of the era, whereas John Stevenson and Chris Cook, *The Slump: Society and Politics During the Great Depression* (1977), and Andrew Thorpe, *Britain in the 1930s: The Deceptive Decade* (1992), call attention to the positive.

maintain a sufficient gold reserve kept interest rates high and tended to discourage industrial investment. It was a little like putting on the brakes while going up hill. Although the unemployment rate was lower between 1925 and 1929 than it had been during the previous four years, Britain did not experience as dramatic an economic boom as did the United States during that same time.

The General Strike and After

The restoration of the gold standard may have provided the illusion that normalcy had been achieved, but the troubles of the coal industry led, in May 1926, to a highly abnormal event — the only general strike in British history. The coal industry had already undergone one damaging strike in 1921, when the mines had been returned to private ownership. At that time wages had been cut, but the miners had been allowed to keep the seven-hour day they had gained in 1919. For a time, special conditions, such as the decline in German coal production that resulted from the French occupation of the Ruhr in 1923, increased British coal exports. By 1925, however, the industry was again in the doldrums. For many purposes oil had proved to be the cheaper and cleaner fuel; overall coal demand was therefore down. British mines were lagging in technological innovation; many pits had closed; and 300,000 miners were out of work. The owners could see no way out but to reduce costs either by lowering wages again or by restoring the eight-hour day. Secretary A. J. Cook of the Miner's Federation responded with the battle cry: "Not a penny off the pay, not a minute on the day." A strike was averted in 1925 when the government appointed a royal commission under Herbert Samuel (1870–1963) to seek a solution while providing the mine owners with a subsidy to keep wages at the old rate.

The Samuel Commission reported the following March with various suggestions for increasing mine efficiency: these might make it possible to enable the industry to maintain wage levels, but they provided no solution for the immediate problem. Both sides remained obdurate. "It would be possible to say, without exaggeration," wrote Lord Birkenhead (a member of Baldwin's cabinet), "that the miners' leaders were the stupidest men in England if we had not had frequent occasions to meet the owners." On May 1, the day the temporary government subsidy ceased, the miners struck. They had been sufficiently shrewd to gain a pledge of support from the Trades Union Congress, and on May 4 a general strike began as well.

A sudden stillness descended upon the land. No trains moved, nor did trams or buses. No ordinary newspapers were printed. Silence reigned on the docks and in the steel mills. All construction work stopped, and no men reported for work at the electric power plants and gasworks. Yet the general strike of 1926 proved to be among labor disputes what the Revolution of 1688 had been among political revolutions — bloodless and peculiarly English. The mass of union members was indeed faithful

UNDER WHICH FLAG?

John Bull. "ONE OF THESE TWO FLAGS HAS GOT TO COME DOWN—AND IT WON'T
BE MINE."

**One View of the
General Strike**
*(Reproduced by
permission of* Punch,
May 12, 1926)

to the strike call, as much out of loyalty to their movement as out of a
sense of passionate conviction concerning the miners' case. The rest of
the public in turn remained loyal to the government without feeling fanatical resentment against the strikers. Indeed, for many the days of the
strike provided an unexpected and refreshing break with routine. Some
London office workers were put up in hotels while others took pride in
walking ten miles to work. Vacationing university students attempted to
load ships, and middle-aged businessmen realized childhood ambitions
by serving as locomotive engineers. Although police and strikers clashed
in Glasgow and a few other cities, there was no loss of life. In some parts
of the country, strikers played football matches with police officers. Winston Churchill edited a government newspaper, the *British Gazette,*
while the Trades Union Congress put out the *British Worker.* The only
source of news for most people was the radio, although wireless sets were
as yet owned by fewer than one family in four.

Despite the apparent success of the general strike, the leaders of the
Trades Union Congress soon became uncomfortable with its continuation. They now faced a dilemma that, when a comparable strike had been
threatened in 1919, Lloyd George had clearly outlined:

. . . you will defeat us. But if you do so have you weighed the consequences? The strike will be in defiance of the government of the country and by its very success will precipitate a constitutional crisis of the first importance. For, if a force arises in the state which is stronger than the state itself, then it must be ready to take on the functions of the state, or withdraw and accept the authority of the state. Gentlemen — have you considered, and if you have, are you ready?

A. J. Cook, a self-confessed "humble disciple of Lenin," might blithely declare, "I don't care a hang for any government, or army, or navy," but most Trades Union Congress leaders were loyal parliamentarians and had no wish to stage a revolution. They insisted, indeed, that the strike was only a sympathy strike and not a general strike at all. Thus, as soon as Herbert Samuel proposed that coal-industry negotiations be resumed and that there be no changes in miners' wages until the mine owners had adopted the money-saving provisions of his report, the TUC leaders called off the strike.

It had lasted nine days, and individual strikes went on for several days more; but Baldwin specifically urged employers not to take advantage of the return to work to secure wage reductions, and most railwaymen and others were soon back at work under their old conditions. Neither the Trades Union Congress leaders nor the prime minister, however, could prevail upon the miners. They were adamant and for six months refused any proposal that involved the slightest reduction in pay. Eventually the resentful miners straggled back to the mines essentially on the owners' terms, which included a return to the eight-hour day. They had lost £60 million in wages.

The following year, with Baldwin's acquiescence although not with his encouragement, a Trade Disputes Act was passed that outlawed general and sympathy strikes and that decreed that union members could be required to contribute to the Labour party only if they specifically indicated their wish to do so. Although the act was regarded as punitive by the Labour party, which pledged itself to repeal the measure as soon as it could (and did so in 1946), the legislation had little immediate practical effect. The general strike had cost the trade-union movement about a third of its financial reserves, however, and in the course of the year that followed about half a million members left the ranks of the union movement. In talks with employer representatives during the later 1920s, union leaders adopted a tone of responsible moderation. A sense of sharp social class division was giving way to an "informal corporate 'entente,'" which most of the time kept employers, employees, and government in balance. By then, too, an expanding class of professionals whose "ideal was based on trained expertise and selection by merit" was playing an increasingly influential role in Britain's social structure, and such men and women did not truly fit into any simple worker-versus-capitalist mold.[2]

---

[2]This point of view is supported in persuasive fashion and in comprehensive detail by Harold Perkin in *The Rise of Professional Society: England Since 1880* (1989). See especially Chapters 6 and 7.

Although a number of intellectuals were attracted to the cause of the political left by the general strike, most Britons were satisfied by Baldwin's goal of "one nation" divided neither by class nor by ideology. "I am opposed to Socialism," the prime minister declared, "but I have always endeavoured to make the Conservative party face left in its anti-Socialism." As minister of health, Neville Chamberlain introduced several measures of social reform that adhered closely to the philosophy his father had espoused as a left-wing Liberal in the 1880s. The Widows', Orphans', and Old Age Contributory Pensions Bill provided pensions at age sixty-five (rather than seventy) and a form of social security to all those — about half the population — covered by the National Health Insurance Act of 1911 and their families. Chamberlain's Local Government Act of 1929 abolished the century-old Poor-Law unions and transferred their responsibilities and others to the public assistance committees of the elected county and borough councils. The traditional source of income for these bodies, property taxes, was curtailed and in part replaced by "block grants" from the national treasury. The net effect of this change was to redistribute wealth from the richer counties to the poorer ones. The Electricity Act of 1926 gave a new public authority control over the national distribution of electricity generated in private or municipal plants, thereby creating a "national grid" that did much to enable Britain during the 1930s to catch up with the world's other leading industrial nations in the utilization of electricity.

The Central Electricity Board, a public board appointed by the minister of transport, was to serve as a model for post–World War II measures of nationalization; but other legislative measures of the second Baldwin ministry harked back to an earlier age. The Reform Act of 1928, which gave the vote to women on the same basis as men, was in some ways the climax of a process that had begun in 1832. The debate over the Prayer Book Bill of 1927 evoked an even earlier age, that of the Tudors, since its backers sought to gain parliamentary approval for a revised Book of Common Prayer. Slumbering evangelical passions were revived; the proposal was denounced as papistical and the measure was defeated. Although religious questions could still stir occasional excitement, a downward trend in church and chapel membership and attendance that had been precipitated by World War I continued more gradually during the interwar era. Thus, whereas 36 percent of the population of the city of York had worshiped on an average Sunday in 1901, only 18 percent did so in 1935. In the face of such erosion of religious commitment, the two main branches of Scottish Presbyterianism found it possible to reunite in 1928 and the three main branches of British Methodism to do so in 1932.

The Spirit of Locarno

The spirit of relative domestic tranquility that marked the later 1920s was echoed in international affairs. There MacDonald had done much

Off to the Polling Booth　The "flappers" voted for the first time in the general election of 1929. *(Hulton Deutsch Collection)*

during his brief prime ministership to ease old tensions. He went so far as to support the Geneva Protocol, which would have bound Britain automatically to go to war against any country the League of Nations declared to be an aggressor. This was a form of "blank check" that most Britons still found difficult to sign; and Austen Chamberlain, the new Conservative foreign secretary (1924–1929), therefore scuttled British support for the protocol. He was willing, however, to apply the principle of the protocol to one particular area, Germany's western frontier. Meeting in 1925 at the Swiss city of Locarno, representatives of Germany, France, Belgium, Poland, and Czechoslovakia solemnly pledged not to go to war with one another and to arbitrate all disputes. Great Britain and Italy specifically guaranteed Germany's western frontier; France, which had alliances with Poland and Czechoslovakia, did the same for the eastern borders. Consequently, Allied occupation troops were withdrawn from the German Rhineland and Germany was admitted to the League of Nations. Although the Locarno Treaty involved an element of wishful thinking (it deliberately ignored Germany's evasion of the disarmament clauses of the Treaty of Versailles), the "spirit of Locarno" was not wholly bogus. Germany faithfully paid its war reparations installments under the Dawes plan, and foreign ministers Stresemann of Germany, Briand of France, and Chamberlain of England conferred regularly and amicably at Geneva. Although specific disarmament proposals often foundered, Britain joined France, the United States, and twelve other powers in signing the euphoric (and unenforceable) Kellogg-Briand Pact of 1928, which "outlawed war as an instrument of national policy."

A comparable tranquility affected the British Empire during the later 1920s. The Imperial Conference of 1926, recognizing the changes brought by World War I, defined the self-governing dominions (such as Canada and Australia) as henceforth "autonomous Communities within the British Empire, equal in status . . . united by a common allegiance to the Crown, and freely associated as members of the British Commonwealth of Nations." The definition was given parliamentary sanction in the Statute of Westminster of 1931. Whatever troubles might still plague the world, that of world war seemed far in the distance by the end of the 1920s. As the novelist John Buchan remarked in 1929, "civilization has been saved, and, on the whole, the nations are once more a stable society."

The Second Labour Government

Secure in the conviction that the Conservative party had at least helped to save civilization, Baldwin called an election in 1929. The Conservatives offered the electorate the comforting if soporific slogan "Safety First," while the Labour party pledged "to end the capitalist dictatorship in which democracy finds everywhere its most insidious and most relentless foe." Under the leadership of Lloyd George, still the most eloquent speaker and most dynamic personality in British politics, an apparently reviving Liberal party offered fewer slogans and more precise proposals for coming to grips with such problems as the continued high level of unemployment. The Liberals suggested that industries of public concern be placed under public boards, that employer-worker councils be expanded, and that the Bank of England's credit powers, public works, and deliberate deficit financing be used by the government in order to assure true prosperity.

The election results were inevitably disappointing to the Liberals. They had gained two million popular votes since 1924, but they had won only 59 parliamentary seats. Stanley Baldwin's Conservatives retained 261, and Ramsay MacDonald's Labourites won 287 and emerged for the first time as the largest parliamentary party. MacDonald became prime minister for a second time, relying on Liberal support (or acquiescence) to stay in power.

The second Labour government was beset by the same misfortunes that were to cloud the reputation of the Hoover administration in the United States. Within a matter of months after its accession to office in May 1929, the government witnessed the stock market crash in the United States and the collapse of the international financial structure of the 1920s. American loans to Germany ceased; so, in due course, did

German reparations to France and Britain; and finally, to complete the circle, so did Allied repayments of war loans to the United States. All the economic statistics skidded steadily downhill; and if Britain's relative descent by 1932 was less precipitous than that of the United States, this was largely the consequence of not having experienced a comparable economic boom.

The total value of Britain's exports dropped by half between 1929 and 1932, and so did the production of iron and steel. Over three million tons of shipping were laid up, and shipbuilding came to a virtual standstill. J. H. Thomas, who had been appointed Lord Privy Seal in order to be "minister of employment," found his problems multiplying as unemployment figures soared: 1 million in June of 1929, 1.5 million in January of 1930, 2.5 million in December of 1930. By midsummer of 1932 almost one English family breadwinner in four (in Wales, one in three) was out of work, and almost 7 million people of a total population of 45 million subsisted solely on the dole.

The depression shattered the nineteenth-century assumption that markets would continue to expand along with a society's productive capacities. The defenders of laissez-faire capitalism were everywhere placed on the defensive; yet the attempts of a professedly socialist Labour government to deal with the depression proved as unavailing as those of the Republican Hoover administration in the United States. A new housing act, a compulsory seven-and-a-half-hour (rather than eight-hour) day in the mines, and an increased treasury grant to the overburdened Unemployment Insurance Fund proved mild palliatives at best. The failure of the MacDonald government to do more is explained partly by the fact that it was a minority government, partly by the fact that many Labour leaders, although socialists, shared most of the orthodox financial tenets of the time. Philip Snowden, Chancellor of the Exchequer, was as convinced as Herbert Hoover that the government's duty was, if at all possible, to balance its budget and to adhere to the gold standard as a bastion of financial integrity.

In the face of mounting economic crisis, ministerial unity began to dissolve. The youthful Sir Oswald Mosley (1896–1980) resigned from the cabinet on the grounds that the government was insufficiently dynamic to meet the problem of unemployment. Mosley, who had originally entered Parliament as a Conservative, resigned from the Labour party to form his own "New party" and eventually became the leader of the British Fascist Union. The Liberals were also split, and Conservative ranks were temporarily brought into disarray by the attempt of two press lords, Lords Beaverbrook and Rothermere, to found their own United Empire party on a platform of imperial protectionism.

The event that ultimately toppled the Labour government was the financial crisis precipitated in the summer of 1931 by an international run on the gold reserves of the Bank of England. Britain had seemed the financial Rock of Gibraltar until 1931. Since most of its private banks were organized into five nationwide amalgamations that could look for emergency support from the Bank of England, the country had undergone no rash of bank failures as had the United States. Because of its own loans to continental banks, however, the Bank of England was seriously affected by the failure of Austria's largest banking firm, the Creditanstalt, and by a host of bank failures in Germany.

Year	British wholesale prices	Percent unemployed	Index of industrial activity
1929	100.0	10.4	118.7
1930	87.5	16.1	107.4
1931	76.8	21.3	86.8
1932	74.9	22.1	81.1
1933	75.0	19.9	89.3

From Sidney Pollard, *The Development of the British Economy, 1914–1967* (2nd ed., 1969), p. 225.

The fact that the 1931 budget could not be completely balanced weakened foreign confidence in British financial stability; so did the prediction in July by a government-appointed committee headed by Sir George May that much bigger deficits were in the offing. The government was advised to make stringent economies (notably in unemployment insurance benefits) in order to balance the budget and restore foreign confidence in British financial stability. The Labour cabinet struggled for three weeks to find ways of cutting expenses. Substantial economies were agreed upon, but the ministry ultimately split on the necessity of slashing benefits to the unemployed. Living costs were declining, and MacDonald and Snowden insisted that such a reduction was necessary, but nine members of the cabinet refused to agree. That a Labour government should be responsible for deliberately injuring the interests of jobless laborers was an irony too poignant to be borne.

The National Government

MacDonald submitted his resignation, but King George V, after consulting the leaders of the other parties, asked him to head a new National government instead. It would be a temporary government of personalities — four Labourites, four Conservatives, and two Liberals —which would meet the financial crisis as a coalition, just as the coalition government of 1915 had faced the military crisis of World War I. Thereafter it would resign and normal party politics would resume. MacDonald agreed, but his decision was almost immediately denounced by the executive committee of the Labour party as a betrayal; two months later he and his colleagues in the National government were expelled from the party. MacDonald went down among his longtime compatriots as a traitor to his cause. The fictionalized account of his career — the novel (by

Howard Spring) and film *Fame is the Spur* — presents him as the boy from the bottom of the social ladder who had achieved high political office only to be corrupted by the desire to win the plaudits of Britain's high society. MacDonald saw himself, in contrast, as a man who had placed the welfare of his country above the well-being of his party, and it has been cogently argued that, keeping in mind the predominant economic assumptions of the time, a National government was the best possible solution.[3] Although MacDonald initially expected the coalition arrangement to provide only a brief political interlude after which he would rejoin the Labour party, the National government survived under Conservative domination until the decade's end.

Within a month, the new National government, having won a vote of confidence in the old Parliament, introduced a new budget and promptly went off the gold standard. The budget increased taxes and cut all government salaries (including those of teachers) and all unemployment benefits by 10 percent. A more rigorous "means test" sought to reduce the dole for any of the long-term unemployed who had alternate means of support. The budget was no surprise, but the decision to go off the gold standard was, to say the least, paradoxical. It was the result of a new run on the pound by foreign investors frightened by exaggerated reports of a naval mutiny in the Scottish port of Invergordon. With an "orthodox" government in power, the Bank of England assented to a step that only a month before it had regarded as revolutionary. Although it shocked foreign financial opinion, the decision no longer to exchange British currency for gold on demand made little difference in the short run but promoted economic recovery in the longer run. The international exchange value of the pound fell, but domestic prices were little affected. British exporters derived some benefit from the move, and after 1932 stock market prices began to improve as well. In 1933 the United States followed the British example by also abandoning the gold standard.

Widespread Conservative pressure caused the National government to call for a new election in October 1931 and to seek a vote of confidence from the electorate as a single coalition, somewhat as the Lloyd George government had done in 1918. It did not try to formulate a single program, and MacDonald simply asked for a "doctor's mandate" to diagnose and prescribe for the depression. The result was an overwhelming victory for the national slate: 556 (472 of whom were Conservatives) as against 56 for the Labour opposition. The popular-vote margin, 14.5 million to 6.6 million, was less overwhelming, but the election was still the most one-sided in British history. The parliamentary Labour party, now headed by George Lansbury (1859–1940), the only undefeated anti-MacDonald cabinet member, was angry and frustrated. The election all but destroyed what was left of the Liberal

---

[3]The best modern account may be found in Philip Williamson, *National Crisis and National Government: British Politics, the Economy and Empire, 1926–1932* (1992). See also David Marquand, *Ramsay MacDonald* (1977).

Stanley Baldwin and Ramsay MacDonald Seek an Answer to the Great Depression The leaders of the newly formed National government meet the press in August 1931. The picture was taken by Erich Salomon, pioneer "candid camera" press photographer. *(Erich Salomon/ Magnum Photos, Inc.)*

party. It had divided into three splinter groups, two of which supported the National government. That government obviously reflected the prevailing currents of British public opinion, but the lack of an effective alternate government or opposition party was to prove an element of weakness as well as strength.

In its Import Duties Act early in 1932 the National government proposed, as one method of curing the depression, that the United Kingdom return to the system of protective tariffs that had been abandoned during the 1840s. The first digressions from the policy of free trade had come with the "McKenna Duties" during the First World War; and those duties, largely retained during the 1920s, had given some protection to the automobile industry. Yet as late as 1930, 83 percent of all British imports had been completely duty free, and the decision to return to a policy of protection represented a major change of principle. Most of the Conservatives in the National government had long favored such a step, and Neville Chamberlain — as the new Chancellor of the Exchequer — took pride in the opportunity of introducing the bill his father had championed so long. Only the Labourite Philip Snowden and the Liberal party representatives in the cabinet objected, and they were permitted for the time being to dissent publicly, a temporary break in the century-and-a-half-old tradition of cabinet unanimity.

The act imposed tariffs ranging from 10 to 33⅓ percent of both industrial and agricultural imports, except for meat and wool. The bill enabled an Imperial Economic Conference at Ottawa, Canada, in August 1932 to approach the elder Chamberlain's ideal of an imperial customs union. By then, however, many of the economic prerequisites for Chamberlain's neo-mercantilistic views had vanished; no one could seriously envisage Great Britain as the industrialized heart of an empire in which the dominions served merely as sources of raw material. All the dominions had their own infant industries to protect, as did India, whose production of cotton cloth had almost eliminated a once giant market for English textiles. (Whereas three billion yards of cotton cloth had been exported to India back in 1913, less than 15 million went there in 1939.) Moreover, both Britain and the dominions had long-established trading relationships with other parts of the world. Yet the act and the conference did encourage a greater amount of trade within the Commonwealth. At the same time the relinquishment of the gold standard led to the development of the "sterling area": because most colonies and dominions kept their monetary reserves in London banks, it became easier to transact financial business within the Commonwealth than outside it. Most of the world's industralized nations became addicted to raising protective tariffs during the early 1930s, and Britons felt compelled to follow suit.

It has been a common tendency among historians to contrast the National government's policies in Britain unfavorably with Roosevelt's New Deal in the United States. The National government, it is said, sought to wait out the depression — or to put it more bluntly, "Millions were starving but the Tories did nothing" — while in the United States Roosevelt was seeking to combat the depression with dynamic if sometimes contradictory measures. It is true that in Britain, unlike the United States, many of the same political leaders remained in power under a new label. It is also true that Britain's National government never embarked on a full-fledged public works program based on deficit spending. But even in the United States the desirability of deliberate deficit spending as a means of countering depression came to be accepted by most politicians only in the 1940s and by most big business leaders only in the 1960s — by which time large-scale deficit spending had come to be associated with an increasing rate of wage and price inflation. Churchill's statement of 1929 that "very little additional employment and no permanent additional employment can, in fact, and as a general rule, be created by State borrowing and State expenditure" was still accepted by most economists in the 1930s.

This thesis was strongly challenged by the Liberal economist John Maynard Keynes (1883–1946) in his *General Theory of Employment, Interest, and Money* (1936), the fullest elaboration of views first expounded in the 1920s. Keynes disagreed that economists had no more control over the ups and downs of the economy than meteorologists had over the alternations of rain and sunshine. Economists could not only chart national growth and decline, but they could also advise the government how to stabilize the economy. Governments, he argued, should encourage deficit spending and low interest rates in time of depression, budget surpluses and high interest rates in times of inflationary boom. At first Keynes received an indifferent reception in Britain, if only because he alienated Conservatives by his emphasis on the role of government in business and Labourites by his defense of capitalism and the role of the individual.

Although the National government did not overtly subscribe to Keynes's views, its policies — tariff protection and removal of the gold standard — did imply considerable management of the economy. So did the farm subsidy and marketing acts, tightened stock market regulations, and new housing acts. Of the 4.5 million houses built in Britain between the wars, 1.4 million were built by public authorities and another 500,000 were constructed with the aid of government subsidies. One reason why the National government does not seem more closely comparable to the New Deal is that so many New Deal measures — such as old-age pensions and unemployment insurance — had been adopted by Britain before World War I. The proportion of the national income spent by British public authorities, local and national, rose steadily from 5.5 percent in 1913 to 13 percent in 1938. The accompanying table makes clear the expansion of social services by the 1930s.

SOCIAL SERVICES (IN MILLIONS OF £s)		
Payments made by the Government	1913–1914	1933–1934
Poor relief	16.5	47
Health insurance	14.5	32
Old-age pensions	10	58.5
Widows', etc., pensions	—	22.5
War pensions	—	44
Unemployment insurance	.5	88.5
TOTALS	41.5	292.5
Contributions levied on individuals*	1913–1914	1933–1934
Health insurance	17	26
Pensions	—	23
Unemployment insurance	2	39.5
TOTALS	19	88.5

Derived from Sidney Pollard, *The Development of the British Economy, 1914–1967* (2nd ed., 1969).
*The remainder of the expenditures were derived from regular taxation. The social services constituted almost 3/7 of the annual national budget in 1933–1934; 1/7 was devoted to defense expenditures and another 3/7 to interest payments on the national debt.

The Depression and British Society

The impact of economic conditions on human beings can never be measured by statistics alone. It is not true that the unemployed starved during the Great Depression or that "the Tories did nothing," but it remains true that the problem of unemployment during the 1920s and

1930s was ultimately resolved in Britain — as in the United States — only by war. Unemployment during the 1930s had a different meaning than it was to have during more recent decades because then only one married woman in ten worked full time outside her own home. Prolonged and unrelenting unemployment therefore put a lasting mark on those British workingmen who experienced it. It left a sense of frustration and futility; it caused a loss of skills and of self-respect, and sometimes triggered the onset of physical deterioration. A situation in which the breadwinner was perpetually out of work warped traditional family relationships. To keep one's sense of respectability while living on the dole meant a degree of penny-pinching that left room for none of the occasional luxuries that add spice to life.

The depression helped confirm a trend that was already well under way by the beginning of World War I, a reduction in the size of the average family. Whereas during the first decade of the century, more than 27 percent of all families included five children or more, during the 1930s fewer than ten families in a hundred were so large. The two-child family became the standard. A larger proportion of men and women were married than during the Victorian era, but the number of births per women of child-bearing age was only a third as great, and the number of children born to unmarried mothers reached an all-time low. At no time in British

The Hunger Marchers   In the depth of the Great Depression (1933), a group of protesters makes its way from a railway station to a mass rally in London's Hyde Park. *(Keystone/Hulton Getty/Archive Photos)*

history were there as many small, sober, and stable nuclear working-class families as in the Britain of the interwar era. Rather than encouraging a new outflow of emigrants, the depression paradoxically led to a reversal of this centuries-old trend. Canada, Australia, and the United States were similarly depression-ridden, and in the course of the decade some 650,000 more people moved into the United Kingdom (from Ireland, the dominions, and the continent) than moved out.

Faced with the specter of joblessness and (for a few years) a falling standard of living, the British worker proved remarkably moderate. Never in British history was the crime rate as low as during the interwar years. There were occasional "hunger marches" on London from as far away as Scotland and Wales, but only a small minority of the unemployed gave their political allegiance to either communism or fascism. At the same time, as long as they could rely on the dole, the out-of-work proved highly reluctant to move from areas in which jobs were scarce to those in which they were more plentiful or to switch from declining industries into growing ones.

Among university students and in certain intellectual circles, it became fashionable to become a Communist or fellow traveler, prepared mentally at least to overthrow society by force in the professed interest of the proletariat. The USSR became the Mecca of the Left in the 1930s, and British writers who did not speak Russian were taken on carefully conducted tours from which they emerged singing the praises of their hosts. They gloried in the economic efficiency promised by Stalin's five-year plans while studiously ignoring the evidence available even then that Stalin had "solved" the problem of unemployment by placing millions in slave labor camps, by spurring mass famine in the Ukraine, and by "purging" millions more — at least twelve million people in all. Beatrice and Sidney Webb returned from one such pilgrimage with a book, *Soviet Communism: A New Civilisation?* (1934). In the second edition they removed the question mark.[4] Eventually many such disciples became disillusioned, and Britain's Communist party never attracted more than a few thousand card-carrying members; it elected only a single M.P. in the course of the decade, and it never succeeded in winning the Labour party to the cause of a Popular Front against fascism. Yet secret subsidies from the Soviet Union enabled the party to maintain a large staff and its own newspaper and publishing house. It also succeeded in recruiting as spies for the Soviet Union men such as the remarkable Kim Philby, who was to work his way into the highest echelons of British intelligence during World War II and after. In contrast to the Soviet Union, the United States had been scorned by the British Left

---

[4]Paul Hollander, *Political Pilgrims: Travels of Western Intellectuals in the Soviet Union, China and Cuba 1928–1978* (1982), provides the most illuminating account of this often puzzling phenomenon. The aging Webbs may well have fallen victim to what has been called "the totalitarian temptation," a willingness to dispense with democratic methods and to permit authoritarian planners to impose an ideal society.

ever since the Sacco-Vanzetti case of the 1920s. Even Roosevelt's New Deal was often dismissed as a "fascist economy." One enterprising British publisher did borrow an American idea, however, in the form of the Left Book Club, which from 1936 on faithfully supplied its 50,000 members with nonfiction works flavored with Communist propaganda.

An alternative cure for the ills of society was offered by Sir Oswald Mosley's British Union of Fascists. In emulation of Mussolini and Hitler, they paraded in blackshirt uniforms, held theatrical floodlighted meetings, and in unison saluted their leader, "Hail Mosley!" The Fascists saw themselves as representatives of "Youth" and "Vigour" and spoke constantly of "Action" and "Getting Things Done." Mosley mercilessly taunted his former Labour allies who had resigned their governmental power in the face of the collapse of capitalism they had so long predicted. "What would you think," asked Mosley, "of a Salvation Army which took to its heels on the Day of Judgment?" Although the Union of Fascists had 20,000 members by 1934, their paramilitary organization, their overt anti-Semitism, and their bullying and violent tactics alienated most British opinion. "Mosley won't come to any good," predicted Stanley Baldwin in 1934, "and we need not bother about him." The government did bother about him to the extent of passing a Public Order Act in 1936 that outlawed the wearing of political uniforms, but otherwise Baldwin's prediction was borne out by events.

Numerous other fringe groups were active in the 1930s, each with its own particular panacea for the nation's ills. The Distributionists saw industrialization as the enemy and echoed the early nineteenth-century Luddites in their advocacy of peasant proprietorship and the wearing of handwoven clothes. The Social Credit party saw the bankers as the enemy, wore green shirts, and sought to raise consumer purchasing power by distributing what they called "the national dividend." Although such movements suggest a disillusionment with politics as usual during the 1930s, they all proved in the long run to be lost causes.

A desire to be socially conscious and an affinity for the Left were found among a generation of new poets and novelists such as W. H. Auden, Stephen Spender, and Christopher Isherwood. George Orwell explored British life during the depression in fact-based novels such as *The Road to Wigan Pier* (1937). Yet other tendencies persisted as well during the interwar era: the celebration of sex in the novels of D. H. Lawrence (1885–1930); the use of stream of consciousness and word play in the works of the Dublin-born James Joyce (1882–1941); and the concern with personal relationships and with both literary and artistic modernism shown by Virginia Woolf (1882–1941) and other members of that renowned, if often snobbish and self-indulgent, group of writers, artists, and thinkers centered since before World War I in London's Bloomsbury area. Woolf's *A Room of One's Own* (1929) was to inspire feminists of more recent times. Such Edwardian literary giants as Shaw, Wells, and Galsworthy also remained active well into the 1930s or beyond. More widely read than works by any of these authors (or in fact by any British author ever) were the detective stories and novels of Agatha Christie (1890–1976); by the time of the centenary of her birth more than two billion copies in more than 100 languages of these prototypically English tales had been sold.

Regarded as "neither art nor smart" by the intellectuals but far more influential than the serious novel among the working classes, the cinema came gradually to replace the music hall as the chief source of popular entertainment. Even laborers on the dole could afford to attend the movies once a week, and many a cinema became *the* town social center, providing youth clubs, prize contests, and a steady diet of Hollywood and homemade adventure, glamor, and music. Far more acceptable to intellectuals was the BBC, the British Broadcasting Corporation, begun in 1922 and established in 1927 in a form that was to persist for the next forty years. The BBC was a monopoly established under the auspices of the state but not subject to its day-to-day control. It received its income not from advertisers but from license fees paid by individual listeners to the Post Office. There were three million licenseholders by 1929, nine million by 1938. In the words of Sir John Reith, who directed the corporation from its founding until 1939, its governors "were not interested in the material welfare of the Corporation; their interest was in the intellectual and ethical welfare of the listeners." From the beginning the pattern of programming was established as a combination of classical music, discussion and variety programs, weather forecasts, a children's hour, Sunday services, and programs for schools. Its news reporters were expected to wear evening dress. The faithful manner in which broadcasters reported the statements of government and strike leaders alike during the general strike of 1926 gave it a reputation for impartiality in reporting the news that was to make it the symbol of factual integrity for millions of Europeans in occupied lands during World War II. In the late 1930s, the BBC also began regular television broadcasts, the first in the world.

The BBC is often credited with doing much to broaden the musical taste of the British public. The English revival of classical music that had begun at the turn of the century continued, along with more popular music. Ralph Vaughan Williams, William Walton, and Arnold Bax composed actively, and Benjamin Britten (1913–1976) embarked on a career that was to make him Britain's most renowned composer of operas and choral works during the post–World War II era. Sir Thomas Beecham (1879–1961) utilized his family medicine-pill fortune to found symphony orchestras. A division comparable to that between popular music and serious music existed in the world of journalism. Britain could boast a handful of serious and well-edited newspapers and reviews; others, such as the weekly *News of the World*, served primarily as a form of entertainment.[5]

---

[5]The best overview of the "mass media" is provided by D. L. LeMahieu, *A Culture for Democracy: Mass Communication and the Cultural Mind in Britain Between the Wars* (1988). See also Asa Briggs, *The BBC: The First Fifty Years* (1985), and Joseph McAleer, *Popular Reading and Publishing in Britain, 1914–1950* (1992).

Recovery

By 1935 Britain was clearly recovering from the Great Depression. The budget of the previous year had restored the cuts in unemployment benefits and most of the salary reductions imposed in 1931. The problem of unemployment remained serious in the depressed areas of Scotland, Wales, and northwest England, but the rest of the country was enjoying a mild boom. Government-boosted housing construction employed millions and aided other industries as well. The automobile and steel industries were flourishing. Sometime during the 1920s it had become cheaper to own and operate a car than to keep a live-in domestic servant, and by 1939 three million motor vehicles traveled Britain's roads. Members of working-class families were far more likely to be able to afford a motorcycle with a sidecar than an automobile, and British car manufacturers did not adopt all of America's labor-saving, mass-production techniques, but during the later 1930s the British automobile industry became for a time the second largest in the world.[6] The British aircraft industry also flourished.

Another relatively new business, the electrical appliance industry, helped to take up the slack of the older depressed businesses such as coal, textiles, and shipbuilding. The 730,000 electric power consumers of 1920 had grown to over 9 million by 1939, and many a British household had become accustomed to the same amenities — vacuum cleaners, refrigerators, and washing machines — as its American counterpart. As in most advanced industrial countries, the number of people employed in service trades ranging from amusements and barbering to dry cleaning and automobile maintenance was growing more quickly than those employed in manufacturing. The fact that productivity per worker rose 50 percent between 1913 and 1939 is, of course, one explanation for why the long-stagnating index of industrial production could begin to rise sharply in the mid-1930s without restoring full employment.

Even if Britain's export trade was not reviving quite so rapidly as its industrial production, the average Briton was benefiting from the fact that international terms of trade were once again shifting in Britain's favor. During the interwar era the cost of Britain's imports — mostly food and raw materials — was falling more rapidly than the cost of its exports. Thus it required in 1938 a volume of exports only 70 percent as high as that of 1914 to "buy" the same volume of imports. The shift in terms of trade and the overall rise in productivity help to explain why, for all but the chronically unemployed, the 1920s and 1930s provided a notable rise in the standard of living.

---

[6]Roy Church provides a brief overview in *The Rise and Decline of the British Motor Industry* (1994).

INDEX OF INDUSTRIAL
PRODUCTION IN U.K.
(1924 = 100)

1913	94.2
1920	102.3
1924	100.0
1929	117.3
1931	99.0
1935	130.8
1937	153.1

From Sidney Pollard, *The Development of the British Economy, 1914–
1967* (2nd ed., 1969), p. 96.

Although its critics continued to give it the same disparaging name, the capitalism that had survived the Great Depression was at best only a reasonable facsimile of its early-nineteenth-century prototype. Even those industries, transport services, and utilities that were not operated by public authorities were subjected to a considerable degree of regulation and, in the case of agriculture and housing, provided with sizable state subsidies. Subsidies designed to encourage new industry in areas worst hit by unemployment failed, however, to halt a tendency toward moving south. Back in the eighteenth and early nineteenth centuries, manufacturers had sought the coal mines and swiftly flowing rivers of England's north and northwest and of lowland Scotland. The new and growing industries of the interwar era, however, were no longer tied to ports or coalfields, and they tended to move once again to the southeast. London, whose growth Tudor commentators had found "monstrous" in the sixteenth century, grew more monstrous still in the 1930s.

Other tendencies were at work. The small, individually owned manufacturing concern had almost completely given way to the giant corporation, but the corporation in turn had also changed. The ownership of shares was increasingly far removed from the actual exercise of control, which was left in the hands of hired managers. Another tendency was the increasing domination of particular industries by combines and cartels such as the ICI (Imperial Chemical Industries) in chemicals and the Lever Combine in soap. Although as late as 1919 a government Committee on Trusts had deplored this movement toward monopoly, the government's attitude altered during the depression. In a fashion similar to Roosevelt's short-lived NRA (National Recovery Administration), the Macmillan Committee of 1931 encouraged "desirable amalgamations and reconstructions designed to eliminate waste and cheapen costs." Large concerns could provide economic stability as well as mass packaging and national advertising. They also cooperated with trade-union leaders to make the later 1930s one of the most harmonious eras in the history of

British industrial relations. Finally, they could, and increasingly did, encourage the process of industrial research and discovery. So did Cambridge University's Cavendish Laboratory, headed during the interwar years by Lord Rutherford (1871–1937), the scientist who helped make the laboratory a world center for pioneering research in nuclear physics. Other British scientists and technologists were instrumental in the development of television and radar and in the improvement of airplane engines.

Although the general movement in industry during the 1930s continued toward an oligarchical corporate structure, this tendency never went all the way. Large sectors of the economy remained unorganized; the individual entrepreneur still played a significant role on the retail level; and oligopolies often competed very strenuously with each other. In its modified form, the capitalist system in Britain proved far more flexible and adaptable than its depression-era critics had expected.

Left to their own devices, it is difficult to say how successful or unsuccessful Britain's business leaders or its National government would have been in guiding Great Britain into the 1940s. Unfortunately, economic affairs and domestic politics were not allowed to remain isolated from events abroad. By 1936 Britain faced a threat even greater than depression: the specter of German Hitlerism, Japanese expansion, and the coming of yet another world war.

CHAPTER 17

The Storm Gathers Anew

In 1918 many Britons had shared with President Woodrow Wilson the hope that World War I would indeed prove to be "the war to end war." In 1928 Britain had joined the major nations of the world, including the United States and Germany, in pledging forever to "outlaw war as an instrument of national policy." And yet in 1939 Britain found itself at war again, a war that was to involve every continent, almost every country of the world, and that was never to be concluded by a peace treaty comparable to that of Paris or Vienna. More than any other constellation of events, World War II and its aftershocks were to fashion the world known to the next two generations.[1]

The Rise of Totalitarianism

For Britain as for much of western and central Europe, the later 1920s seemed to bring an easing of international tensions and an alleviation of some of the grievances (such as reparations) that the Treaty of Versailles had left in the minds and pocketbooks of the German people. Although the League of Nations did not live up to the hopes of its founders, it was

---

[1]For many years, the single most influential version of the events leading up to World War II was Winston S. Churchill, *The Gathering Storm* (1948), Vol. 1 of his six-volume *History of the Second World War.* Laurence Lafore places the origins of the conflict in a broad historical context in *The End of Glory* (1970); so does Keith Eubank in *The Origins of World War II* (2nd ed., 1990). The unfolding of events is expertly narrated by D. Cameron Watt in *How the War Came* (1989). The foundations of the policy of appeasement are explored in Martin Gilbert, *The Roots of Appeasement* (1967). The policy is analyzed and found wanting in Martin Gilbert and Richard Gott, *The Appeasers* (1963), and more recently in Williamson Murray, *The Change in the European Balance of Power, 1938–1939: The Path to Ruin* (1984), and in R. J. Q. Adams, *British Politics and Foreign Policy in the Age of Appeasement, 1935–1939* (1993), a readable, compact overview. It is viewed with greater sympathy in the biographies of Neville Chamberlain by Keith Feiling (1946) and Iain Macleod (1960), as well as in Maurice Cowling, *The Impact of Hitler: British Politics and British Policy, 1933–1940* (1975), and in John Charmley, *Chamberlain and the Lost Peace* (1989). R. A. C. Parker provides a judicious appraisal in *Chamberlain and Appeasement* (1993). With the prime exception of A. J. P. Taylor, *The Origins of the Second World War* (1961), the causes of World War II have evoked much less revisionist controversy than did those of World War I. Divergent emphases are surveyed in both Keith Eubank, ed., *World War II: Roots and Causes* (2nd ed., 1992) and R. J. Q. Adams, ed., *British Appeasement and the Origins of World War II* (1994).

a going concern; and although the dream of worldwide disarmament proved chimerical, Europe was at least spared an arms race comparable to that of the pre–World War I decade.

This false dawn was swiftly obscured by two related developments of the new decade: worldwide economic depression and widespread repudiation of liberal democracy. The first, the Great Depression, with its hundreds of bank failures, its thousands of bankruptcies, its millions of unemployed, its millions more with reduced living standards, helped to swing the balance toward the second. Throughout the Western world, the response to the depression lay in economic nationalism, in building tariff barriers, and, more often than not, in curtailing political liberties.

The depression years accentuated the repudiation of the liberal democracy that had seemed to be the goal, if not the achievement, of most Europeans as recently as 1918. In Germany the extremist parties, the Communists and the National Socialists (Nazis), became increasingly popular, and a majority of the German people either supported or acquiesced in the takeover of political power by the Nazis and their leader, Adolf Hitler, in 1933. In him they found the self-appointed messiah who would save them from Communism and who, paradoxically, would at the same time imbue them with a new sense of collective pride in their nation and its ability to overcome the shame of military defeat and the perils of economic adversity. Hitler had long-range goals, but in working toward them he proved to be a brilliant opportunist. His demagogic speeches, with their message of racial superiority and their undertone of violence, caused ex-soldiers, students, and many others to feel themselves part of a national mission that transcended individual material self-interest. As a deeply impressed Lloyd George was to report of Hitler in 1936: "The old trust him; the young idolize him. It is not the admiration accorded to a popular Leader. It is the worship of a national hero who has saved his country from utter despondency and degradation." By then Germany, like Britain, was recovering from the economic depression. By then, too, the Nazis had eliminated by executive edict and by street terrorism all vestiges of parliamentary democracy and all internal political opposition.

Nationalism had once seemed an essentially liberal doctrine, and as recently as 1918 Woodrow Wilson had considered a Europe divided along lines of nationality to be fully compatible with a world made safe for democracy. But the nationalism that flourished during the 1930s in Germany and Italy and Japan was in every sense antipathetic to nineteenth-century democratic liberalism, with its emphasis on the legal rights of individuals. Marxist Communism was supposedly internationalist in outlook, but Hitler's Germany — with its leadership cult, its single legal party, its powerful secret police, its centralized economic planning, and its ever more powerful state apparatus — came in many ways to resemble the nation that was professedly its chief enemy: Stalin's Russia.

The Great Depression and the rise of fanatical nationalism changed the entire background of European diplomacy; but the makers of British foreign policy were slow to appreciate this fact. They came to realize only gradually that Germany's new rulers did not share their own assumption about the use of reason in politics, about the desirability of compromise, and about liberal democracy as the best form of government. The British were deflected from strong initiatives in foreign policy by domestic economic problems, by difficulties in concerting policy with erstwhile allies, and by widespread pacifism. "From 1918 to 1939," wrote R. H. Tawney, "the loathing of war was unquestionably the most powerful, the most general and the most constant of political emotions."

The policy resulting from these presuppositions is known as appeasement. After 1940 that word was to take on a derogatory, an almost treasonous connotation. This was not so in the 1930s. An appeaser then was merely someone who promoted peace. In any event, it may be a misleading use of hindsight to convey the impression that British foreign policymakers during the 1930s saw themselves as carrying out a single, always consistent policy. Rather, like most diplomats at most times, they were faced with specific difficulties on specific occasions. At times they may have been too sensitive to the feelings of the British electorate and more often than not they may have taken the easy way out, but even provisional judgment should be attempted only after the challenges they faced are reviewed and assessed.

In the Far East, Japan had as a result of World War I become the inheritor of European claims to spheres of influence in China. In 1931 Japan invaded Manchuria and transformed it into a puppet state. The League of Nations, on the basis of a report issued by an international commission headed by the English earl of Lytton, condemned the Japanese action but found it impossible to enforce its views. Neither Britain nor any other major power was prepared to wage war for the sake of Manchuria. Nor was the imposition of economic sanctions palatable at a time when they might aggravate the economic distress brought on by the depression. The only concrete result of the adoption of the Lytton Report by the League of Nations was Japan's decision to leave the League and to continue gradually to expand its economic and political influence over a divided China.

The policy of orderly retreat followed by Britain in the Far East was, to a degree, applied to India. There during the 1920s the leadership of the Indian National Congress fell into the hands of Mohandas K. Gandhi (1869–1948), a physically small and far from handsome man, who inspired millions of fellow Indians with his quest for spiritual renewal and his dream of national independence. He did much to transform the Congress from an urban debating society into a movement that transcended boundaries of caste and class and that attracted worldwide attention. Gandhi's minimum demand was dominion status. When the Simon Commission was sent to review Indian governmental arrangements eight years after the passage of the Government of India Act of 1919, Gandhi protested the failure to include native Indians on the commission with a

Mohandas Gandhi   The Indian nationalist leader and one of his aides lead a civil disobedience march in 1930. *(UPI/Bettmann Newsphotos/Corbis)*

campaign of civil disobedience, a boycott of English cloth imports, and a defiance of the government salt monopoly.[2]

Although Gandhi and other Indian leaders were arrested from time to time, they were also permitted to play a political role; Gandhi himself participated in 1931 in the second of three Round-Table Conferences that sought to draft a new Indian constitution. Life in London did not change Gandhi's habitual asceticism, and he wore his by then customary loincloth to a Buckingham Palace reception by King George. The two men chatted politely enough, but the monarch felt compelled to warn: "Remember, Mr. Gandhi, I won't have any attacks on my Empire!" Gandhi replied politely: "I must not be drawn into a political argument in Your Majesty's Palace after receiving Your Majesty's hospitality."

The Round-Table Conference could not reconcile all differences, if only because many Conservatives (such as Winston Churchill) were hostile to further concessions to Indian nationalism and because the Indian

---

[2]Judith M. Brown, *Modern India: The Origins of an Asian Democracy* (1985), provides a helpful introduction to Gandhi's world. Her biography, *Gandhi: Prisoner of Hope* (1990), portrays the man and his ideas. See also D. A. Low, *Britain and Indian Nationalism: The Imprint of Ambiguity, 1929–42* (1997).

representatives themselves were divided between Hindu and Moslem, Brahmin and "untouchable." The statute that finally resulted, the Government of India Act of 1935, did not give India dominion status; but except for reserve emergency powers retained by British governors, the eleven provinces of British (as opposed to princely) India became virtually self-governing. Matters of defense and foreign policy remained, however, firmly in the hands of the British-controlled national government. Although the Indian National Congress initially chose to boycott the new constitution, it subsequently relaxed its stand, and millions of Indians participated in what was becoming at least partly their government. Hitler once privately recommended to the British a different mode of dealing with Indian nationalism: "Shoot Gandhi, and if that does not suffice to reduce them to submission, shoot a dozen leading members of Congress; and if that does not suffice, shoot two hundred and so on until order is established. You will see how quickly they will collapse as soon as you make it clear that you mean business." No twentieth-century British government could reconcile such conduct with its principles; that is why it proved so susceptible to tactics of civil disobedience. The Government of India Act of 1935 thus remains a tribute to MacDonald's and Baldwin's diplomacy, a form of appeasement that was to receive less subsequent condemnation than did Britain's policy toward Germany.

In 1933, the year of his death, Lord Grey, the pre–World War I foreign secretary, declared hopefully: "The great security for peace at the present moment is that Germany is not armed and not in a position to go to war." Such security was soon to fade. Germany withdrew from the Disarmament Conference of 1933, resigned from the League of Nations that same year, and in 1935 announced that it would no longer abide by the disarmament provisions of the Treaty of Versailles. The building of an air force was in fact already under way, but now military conscription was reintroduced, and the army grew rapidly from 100,000 to more than 500,000 men.

The British and other Western governments protested, as did the Council of the League of Nations, but they took no meaningful steps to halt German rearmament. Some Britons found it all too easy to go along with Hitler's reasoning that, since his neighbors had not disarmed fully, he possessed the moral right to rearm. By signing a naval agreement with Germany in June 1935, permitting Germany to build battleships and submarines but limiting a German navy to 35 percent of British tonnage, Britain gave implicit recognition to Hitler's right to violate the peace treaty. Britons took comfort in the thought that the agreement saved them from a naval race comparable to that preceding World War I. Since Hitler was, in any case, giving preference to land and air rearmament and since the limits allowed by the treaty would keep his shipyards busy for many years, the treaty was scarcely a meaningful barrier to his ambitions. It did, however, erode still further the ideal of collective security against aggression.

When the next challenge to international peace came, Britain reacted more forcefully. Mussolini's invasion in the summer of 1935 of the independent African kingdom of Ethiopia was not a direct threat to Britain, but it impressed British opinion as a clear-cut moral issue. It seemed to be a flagrant violation of the sovereignty of an independent state, and British Foreign Secretary Sir Samuel Hoare (1880–1959) strongly urged collective League action against Italy. Such action was forthcoming in the form of financial sanctions, an embargo on all goods imported from Italy, and a partial embargo on goods exported to Italy. Sentiment hostile to international bullying was widespread in Britain, and for once the League of Nations seemed to be operating as intended.

The Election of 1935

It was while the Ethiopian crisis was still in the headlines that the general election of 1935 took place. The Labour party had strong hopes of regaining some of its pre-1931 stature. A new generation of leaders, Clement Attlee (1883–1967), Herbert Morrison (1888–1965), Stafford Cripps (1889–1952), and Ernest Bevin (1881–1951) among them, were moving to the fore. In the local elections of 1934, the Labour party under Morrison's leadership had gained control of the London County Council. Comparable victories had given it a majority in more boroughs and county councils than ever before. Although the party was agreed on the goal of peace and socialism, it still had its ideological left wing and right wing. Intellectuals such as Cripps talked at times about the possibility of armed revolution, but trade-union leaders such as Bevin supported "common sense" and parliamentary democracy under all circumstances. For four years the parliamentary party had been led by George Lansbury who, as a Christian pacifist, did not quite belong to either wing. At the party's 1935 conference, supporters of sanctions against Italy swamped advocates of the peace-at-any-price policy put forward by Lansbury. The latter was replaced by Clement Attlee, the experienced parliamentarian most acceptable to trade unionists.

It was the apparent popularity of its foreign policy stance and the widespread evidence of economic recovery that caused the National government to seek a new electoral mandate in November 1935. MacDonald had resigned as prime minister the previous June and had been replaced by his deputy, Stanley Baldwin. The government's program stressed additional steps to speed economic recovery, support for the League of Nations, and a program of rearmament to keep air parity with Germany and replace obsolescent ships. The Labourites and the Liberals found at least some of their ideological clothes stolen and, as the campaign proceeded, often accused Baldwin and Chancellor of the Exchequer Neville Chamberlain, who had increased the military budget, of being warmongers. Baldwin, in turn, sought to mollify the electorate with assurances that his government had no desire for rearmament on a large scale.

The election resulted in another overwhelming victory for the National government: 428 of its supporters (387 of them Conservatives) faced an opposition made up of 157 Labourites, 17 Liberals, and a handful of independents. The popular-vote margin was not nearly so decisive: there were 11.5 million government supporters (10.5 million of them Conservatives) compared with 8.3 million Labour supporters and 1.4 million who voted Liberal.

The question relating to Ethiopia that neither government nor opposition had truly asked during the general election was: what if economic sanctions proved insufficient? Would Britain, as the chief League military power, be willing to fight a war against Italy to prevent the absorption of Ethiopia? Sir Samuel Hoare thought not. "Keep us out of war," Baldwin had told him; "we are not ready for it." Because the French were even less eager to alienate Mussolini and drive him into the arms of Hitler, Hoare agreed on a plan suggested by Pierre Laval, the French prime minister, according to which Mussolini was to give up his plan of total conquest in favor of the cession of half of Ethiopia. When details of the Hoare-Laval plan leaked out to the press, British public opinion was appalled by this apparent betrayal of pre-election pledges. Baldwin's government felt compelled to repudiate Hoare, who resigned and was replaced as foreign secretary by Anthony Eden (1897–1977).

A victory had been won for principle but not for Ethiopia. While the League debated the imposition of further sanctions in the spring of 1936, Italy completed its military conquest. The sanctions imposed had not proved effective, if only because they did not include oil and could not be enforced on either Germany or the United States. In July 1936 the British government and the League decided therefore to end economic sanctions against Italy. Neville Chamberlain described them as "the very midsummer of madness." Although the sanctions had not helped Ethiopia, they had alienated Mussolini enough to push him into an alliance with Germany, and in November 1936 he and Hitler formed the Rome-Berlin Axis, which became a Rome-Berlin-Tokyo triangle a year later.

Whether the government was arming fast enough was debated by contemporaries (and continued to be debated by subsequent historians), but even as the Labour party opposition voted systematically against all expenditures on defense, the government *did* keep its pledge to rearm. The defense budget rose from £127 million in 1935 to £343 million in 1938 and £630 million in 1939. Aircraft production quadrupled during the same period. Yet even in 1938, German military expenditures were twice as high as those of Britain and France combined.

In the meantime, the British government quietly deplored Hitler's increasingly harsh treatment of German Jews, who in growing numbers sought to emigrate from a state that, step by step, was depriving them of their livelihoods, their property, and their citizenship. At a time when rates of unemployment remained high, no Western nation was eager to accept immigrants, but by the time that war began, Britain had admitted more than 60,000 Jewish refugees from Germany, a number larger than that taken in by any other country including the United States.[3]

The Abdication

In the year 1936 new storm signals from Germany were drowned out for many British citizens and for millions of others around the world by a royal drama.[4] In January 1936, only half a year after King George V and his wife Queen Mary had marked their Silver Jubilee amid popular adulation, the old king, the apparent embodiment of Victorian virtues, was dead. A state funeral followed, as did a new king, Edward VIII, who as Prince of Wales had often toured the empire and commonwealth and who had been built up by newspaper publicity as a glamorous personality, handsome, athletic, versatile.

The new king *was* unconventional: he flew to his accession council by airplane; he liked to spend his leisure time gardening in a grubby shirt or eating dinners with small groups of friends in London flats; he rarely attended church; he had a freely avowed interest in the welfare of the miners in depressed areas of Wales; he preferred to live in Fort Belvedere, a military lookout post built by George II, rather than in Buckingham Palace. Most curious of all, the king at age forty was still single, the most eligible bachelor in all Europe. All European and American newspaper readers soon learned a fact from which British newspaper proprietors tactfully shielded their readers until late in November 1936: the king was obsessively in love with Wallis Warfield Simpson, a commoner, an American, and a divorcée who in October 1936 had filed for a divorce from her second husband, Ernest Simpson, in order that she might marry Edward. Stanley Baldwin was deeply perturbed, as was the royal family and the Church of England. The king was its head. The archbishop of Canterbury was to preside over the king's coronation the following year, but the Church did not recognize the propriety of divorce.

Once the case broke in the British press, the story rapidly reached a climax. The king refused to put off a possible marriage until after his coronation. He played with the idea of a morganatic marriage in which Mrs. Simpson would not officially become queen. The king had his supporters: Lord Beaverbrook, Winston Churchill, and others who maintained that "the King's Happiness Comes First" or asked that "God Save the King from Mr. Baldwin." It was Baldwin who was prime minister, however, and he refused to introduce a bill making a morganatic marriage possible. The dominions that Edward served as monarch would not

---

[3]See Bernard Wasserstein, *Britain and the Jews of Europe, 1939–1945*, 2nd ed. (1999), pp. 6–7.

[4]Philip Ziegler, the author of *King Edward VIII: A Biography* (1990), is the first biographer to gain access to the Royal Archives. Frances Donaldson, *Edward VIII* (1974), provides a persuasive portrait of a troubled personality.

The Fruits of Abdication The former Wallis Warfield Simpson and the former King Edward VIII as portrayed shortly after their marriage in 1937 by one of the century's foremost photographers, Cecil Beaton. *(The Granger Collection)*

accept such a proposal, argued Baldwin, and neither would public opinion in Britain. "I believe I know what the people would tolerate and what they would not," he had confided to the king earlier, and he was probably right.

If the monarch had failed to accept the prime minister's advice, a constitutional tradition would have been broken, and the king would have had to find another cabinet capable of securing the support of a majority of the House of Commons. Failing that, a general election would have had to be fought on the issue of the king's private life. Edward did not wish to provoke a constitutional crisis of such dimensions, and on December 10 he abdicated the throne so that he could marry Mrs. Simpson. He was succeeded by his brother, the duke of York, as George VI. The new king had long lived in the shadow of his elder brother and was unduly modest about his own abilities. A model family man with a strong sense of duty, he served as a proper constitutional monarch during the fifteen years that followed.

Steps Toward War

Although the abdication crisis was clearly the biggest news story of the year if not of the decade, it was not the most significant. More fateful was Hitler's unilateral remilitarization of the German Rhineland. This was an obvious violation of both the Treaty of Versailles and the Treaty of Locarno, and Hitler had promised to uphold the latter only a year before. Had the French immediately intervened, Britain might have been compelled to provide support. But the French hesitated, and the British did not find the cause worth the risk of military conflict. "After all," observed one English diplomat about the Germans, "they are only going into their own back-garden." The fortification of Germany's western frontier, however, had other noteworthy military consequences. It confirmed Hitler's prescience among German army leaders, who had felt sure that the German bluff would be called, and it also made possible a subsequent German expansion eastward.

The year 1936 also brought the beginnings of the Spanish Civil War, a conflict between large units of the Spanish army, supported by the Catholic Church, who under General Francisco Franco, fought against the sorely divided government of the Spanish Republic, which had found itself unable to keep domestic order in the face of a growing number of church burnings, political murders, and violent strikes. To prevent the civil war from spreading, Britain joined twenty-six other nations — including Germany and Italy — in agreeing not to take sides. In Foreign Secretary Anthony Eden's words, the hope was to preserve "peace at almost any price." Both Mussolini and Hitler soon broke their word. Mussolini sent five army divisions to fight on Franco's side, and Hitler sent technicians and matériel to be tested under actual war conditions. The Republican government bought 1,000 planes, 900 tanks, and much other equipment from the Soviet Union and, as the war progressed, that government fell increasingly under (Soviet-directed) Communist influence. Although Britain supplied arms to neither side, some 2,700 British volunteers flocked southward to join others to fight and die (as one in five did) on the Republican side; yet others fought for Franco. The Spanish Civil War kindled ideological passions in Britain in the manner that the Greek war of independence had inflamed the imagination of Byron. No other event of the decade became so burning a cause.[5] In the process, some left-wing intellectuals endowed the Spanish Republic with virtues neither it nor any other human society could have possessed. In some ways the Spanish Civil War proved to be a preview of World War II; but the outcome, Franco's victory in 1939, turned out to be less useful to the cause of the Axis powers in World War II than either friend or foe anticipated in the 1930s.

The Road to Munich

In May 1937, shortly after King George VI's coronation, Stanley Baldwin resigned from the prime ministership because of ill health. The logical choice as his successor was Neville Chamberlain, who thus obtained the

---

[5]See Tom Buchanan, *Britain and the Spanish Civil War* (1997).

prize that had eluded his father and half-brother. Chamberlain had a deserved reputation as a highly competent administrator, and on most issues of domestic and foreign policy he and Baldwin had seen eye to eye. But whereas Baldwin had been a sociable man who shunned foreign affairs, Chamberlain was a man with few close friends who approached the European scene with courage and astonishing self-confidence. His immediate experience had been in domestic matters, but he soon in effect became his own foreign minister — especially after Eden's resignation from that post in February 1938 — and the foremost exponent of personal diplomacy in pre–World War II Europe.

Chamberlain faced his first major crisis when Germany annexed Austria in March 1938. The so-called Anschluss violated both the Treaty of Versailles and Hitler's pledges of only two years before. Britain and France did little except to agree to continue the talks between the general staffs of their armies, which had been resumed in 1936. In the course of the summer that followed, it became clear that the next trouble spot was to be Czechoslovakia, the nation in eastern Europe with the greatest affinity for Western democracy. Czechoslovakia contained within its borders — established at Paris in 1919 — more than three million German-speaking inhabitants (erstwhile subjects of the defunct Austro-Hungarian Empire), who were encouraged by Hitler's agents to demand complete autonomy within their state and the ultimate right of "reunion" with Germany.

Because German violence inside Czechoslovakia was likely to serve as an excuse for an invasion by German troops, because France was treaty-bound to protect Czech frontiers, and because Britain was equally bound to support France in case of war with Germany, Prime Minister Neville Chamberlain made it his special interest to seek a peaceful solution. Under Franco-British pressure, the Czechs offered the Sudeten Germans almost complete local autonomy; but for Hitler — who had ordered his generals to prepare for war by autumn — this was not enough. In mid-September Chamberlain flew to Berchtesgaden, Hitler's Bavarian mountain retreat, to hear from Hitler's own lips the demand that areas of Czechoslovakia in which Germans constituted more than 50 percent of the population be immediately incorporated into Germany.

Chamberlain, who peculiarly enough formed the impression on this occasion that Hitler "was a man who could be relied upon when he had given his word," returned to confer with the French and the Czech representatives. Only if the Czechs would accede to Hitler's dismemberment plans, the British and French representatives insisted, would the Western allies continue their support. The Czechs reluctantly acquiesced, and Chamberlain flew to Godesberg to meet Hitler a second time to announce Czech acceptance. Chamberlain discovered that Hitler had upped his price and demanded the Sudeten territories as of October 1 and not by means of the gradual transfer plan the Western allies had worked out. This was too much, even for Chamberlain, and he returned home. The Czech and French armies mobilized, as did the

British fleet, and the prime minister was in the midst of explaining to the House of Commons that the British people might soon find themselves at war when a message was handed to him asking him to join a four-power conference at Munich to discuss the situation once more. The only result of that conference between Hitler, Mussolini, Chamberlain, and Daladier (the French premier) was to postpone the German takeover of parts of the Sudetenland for ten days. Chamberlain and Hitler then went on to sign a joint declaration that there was to be no more war.

Chamberlain returned to London a conquering hero. Not since Disraeli had returned in triumph from the Congress of Berlin bearing "peace with honour" was an English statesman so universally acclaimed. For at the very brink of war, with German bombers presumably only hours away from London, he had returned with "peace in our time." Winston Churchill, who as an independent Conservative backbencher had for several years criticized the government's appeasement policy and the lagging pace of its rearmament efforts, was in a small but vocal minority when he described the Munich settlement as "a total and unmitigated defeat." As Churchill put it: "The German Dictator, instead of snatching his victuals from the table, has been content to have them served to him course by course. £1 was demanded at the pistol's point. When it was given, £2 was demanded at the pistol's point. Finally, the Dictator consented to take £1 17s. 6d."

The End of Appeasement

Chamberlain's temporary popularity soon faded, for, as might have been predicted, the Munich agreement precipitated the breakup of the Czechoslovak state, and in March 1939 German troops marched into Prague. The Czech treasury and the Czech armaments industry (the best in eastern Europe) were taken over by Hitler, and they did much to enhance Germany's power to wage war. The promises made by Hitler at Munich were broken within six months, as so many earlier commitments had been. In March 1939 even Neville Chamberlain came to realize that his hopes had been misplaced, and Britain began to speed up its preparations for war. In May military conscription was reintroduced — for the first time in British history in time of peace. Poland and Rumania, one or the other of which now seemed next on Hitler's list, were given guarantees of support by Britain.

Attempts were also made to forge an alliance with Communist Russia and thereby reconstruct the pre–World War I Triple Entente. The attempt failed, largely because Poland refused to concede to Russian troops the potential right to cross Polish territory to fight the Germans. In the light of post–World War II events, Polish misgivings are understandable. Agreement with Russia failed ultimately not only because of mutual distrust but because Hitler offered better terms. The Hitler-Stalin Non-

Neville Chamberlain
The prime minister returns in September 1938 from the second of his three summit conferences with Adolf Hitler, hoping to have secured "Peace in our Time." He is greeted by Lord Halifax, the foreign secretary (on the left). *(Bettman/Corbis)*

Aggression Pact, which surprised the world on August 24, 1939, secretly gave Communist Russia a free hand (for the moment) in all the lands of eastern Europe (Finland, the Baltic States, eastern Poland, and Bessarabia) that had been part of the Russian Empire in 1914. Britain held firm to its guarantee of Poland, however, and confirmed it with a treaty of mutual assistance on August 25. A last-minute German demand for a multitude of Polish territorial concessions had not even been officially communicated to the Polish government when German troops entered Polish territory and German planes began to rain bombs on Polish cities on September 1, 1939. Two days later Britain and France declared war on Germany. World War II had begun.

The policy of appeasement had failed, but the policy must not only be condemned but also understood. For a long time it had the approval of a great majority of the British people, if only because it had strong roots in British idealism. Many Britons had come to think in the 1920s that Germany had been badly treated at Versailles; Hitler exploited this feeling of guilt in the 1930s. Many Britons had come to think that World War I had been caused by an excessive absorption with ideas of national prestige. Was it not better to attempt in a businesslike fashion to bend over backward to resolve every plausible national grievance that might lead to war? And German grievances — in the Rhineland, in Austria, in the Sudetenland — were, after all, cleverly based on an old liberal doctrine, national self-determination. Hitler found it easy to speak in Wilsonian terms.

Neither Baldwin nor Chamberlain was a pacifist, and although their rearmament program permitted Germany to gain air superiority and did not proceed at the pace Churchill demanded, it was in tune with a public opinion that on the subject of weapon costs was probably even more cautious than the government's. Rearmament proceeded at a far more rapid rate than the official opposition might have permitted, had it been in power. The manner in which Czechs and anti-Nazi Germans were in effect handed over to Hitler was indeed callous; but a country that had suffered 2.5 million military casualties less than a generation before might readily see a new war as an even greater evil. Perhaps Chamberlain was disingenuous when he spoke of the Czechoslovakian dispute in September 1938 as "a quarrel in a far away country between people of whom we know nothing"; but his feelings may well have been shared by a majority of his countrymen, and they were evidently shared by the prime ministers of the Commonwealth, who almost invariably urged caution.

Of course the appeasers were caught in an illusion. Until 1939 they looked upon Nazi Germany as merely another state in the international balance of power, dictatorial at home but diplomatically sensible abroad. Hitler successfully maintained that illusion in official documents and in personal conversations with numerous private English visitors. They took satisfaction in his repeated assurances of a desire for peace, his decision to give English priority among foreign languages taught in German schools, and his apparent modesty when speaking of his own rise to eminence.

As a result, some of the appeasers began to confuse means with ends. Nazi racial policies, concentration camps, and violent speeches were explained away as products of the exuberance of a revolutionary movement that would diminish as soon as Hitler acquired the maturity that ideally accompanies power. Chamberlain's government used behind-the-scenes influence to encourage Britain's newspapers to support appeasement and to mute their criticism of the Nazi leader. Geoffrey Dawson, editor of the influential *Times* of London, needed no persuading. To him the harassment of independent church leaders within Germany and the use of German planes to bomb defenseless Spanish towns during the civil war were less signs of a rising totalitarian force upsetting the prevailing balance of power than obstacles to the desired Anglo-German rapprochement. It was to become clear in retrospect that the ragings in Hitler's book, *Mein Kampf*, were a more accurate indication of his ultimate ambitions than were his tea talks with visiting Englishmen. Although Hitler might prove flexible in tactics, he never forgot his ultimate goal of dominating all of eastern Europe even at the expected risk of war with the West.

Thus the appeasers placed too much faith in treaties, underestimated the rapidity of German rearmament, and initially felt too secure about their own ultimate ability to defend themselves. They took too much comfort in the thought that whatever else he was, Hitler was at least an anti-Communist — until that illusion, too, was shattered by the Stalin-Hitler Pact. (That pact, in similar fashion, shattered the illusions of many left-wing Labourites who had hoped to cooperate with the Communists in an anti-Fascist "popular front.")

Yet whatever their mistakes or illusions, the appeasers must be credited with a genuine desire to preserve the peace. It was indeed the very failure of the policy of appeasement that persuaded Britons and others that Hitler wanted war and that there was no alternative to military resistance. When war began in September 1939, there existed in Britain no desire for martial glory — as had stirred some hearts in 1914 — but only a strong sense that justice lay entirely on the British side and an absolute conviction that Hitler's Germany could be stopped only by force of arms.

CHAPTER 18

The Age of Churchill

For Britain, World War II resembled World War I in many ways. Both were fought against the same enemy, Germany and its allies, who occupied the center of the continent and relied upon vast initial superiority on land and upon submarine power at sea. In both wars Britain, France, Russia, and the United States fought together against their common enemy. In both wars Britain and its allies entered the conflict less well prepared than Germany and depended on both naval power and the gradual utilization of resources outside Europe to build up a power sufficient to defeat the enemy.

Yet the two world wars had vast differences. Japanese military ambitions in Asia and the South Pacific and extensive fighting in North Africa caused the Second World War to live up to its name more truly than the first. New techniques — especially the coordinated utilization of the airplane and the tank — caused the second conflict to be far more a war of movement than the first. Britain came closer to defeat in 1940–1941 than at any time in 1914–1918 but ultimately won an even more complete victory in 1945 than in 1918 — even if, like all twentieth-century military victories, it was a triumph tinged with tragedy.[1]

Of Germany's enemies, only Britain and its dependencies plus four of its dominions were involved in the Second World War from its first week to its last. Canada, Australia, and New Zealand loyally declared war on Germany in September 1939, as did South Africa (by a narrow parliamen-

---

[1]Churchill's six-volume *History of the Second World War* (1948–1954) remains in a class by itself. The story is told anew in Volume VI, *Finest Hour, 1939–1941* (1983), and Volume VII, *Road to Victory, 1941–1945* (1987), of Martin Gilbert's massive biography of Churchill. Gilbert has also provided a compendious one-volume summary of the eight-volume work, *Churchill: A Life* (1991). Henry Pelling has furnished both a somewhat shorter but reliable single-volume life, *Winston Churchill* (2nd ed., 1989), and a helpful overview, *Britain and the Second World War* (1970). In *Churchill: A Major New Assessment of His Life in Peace and War* (1993), Robert Blake and William Roger Louis have assembled twenty-nine topical papers by different authors. Gerhard L. Weinberg has provided the best general overview in *A World at Arms: A Global History of World War II* (1994). The Battle of Britain is taken up in Drew Middleton, *The Sky Suspended* (1962), and Hitler's invasion plans in Ronald Wheatley's *Operation Sea-Lion* (1958). The impact of war on domestic life is explored in Arthur Marwick, *The Home Front: The British and the Second World War* (1976); in Angus Calder, *The People's War: Britain, 1939 to 1945* (1969); and in Harold L. Smith, *Britain and the Second World War: A Social History* (1996).

tary margin). India, to the displeasure of the National Congress, was also declared to be at war. The Irish Free State (Eire) remained strictly neutral, thereby depriving the Royal Navy of the use of southern Irish ports. Some 60,000 Irishmen volunteered to serve in Britain's armed forces, however, and many thousands more worked in British factories.

As the war began, Neville Chamberlain was still prime minister, but he immediately called Winston Churchill to the post of First Lord of the Admiralty, the same position Churchill had held in 1914. "Winston is back" — the message was flashed from ship to ship. Because this one man, as statesman, strategist, diplomat, and orator, was to lead his people through defeat to triumph and because he was afterward, as historian, to chronicle that epic ordeal, it seems only fitting to write of Britain's involvement in World War II as "the Age of Churchill."

The "Phoney War"

The conflict began in a peculiar fashion. Britain and France went to war on behalf of Poland, but they were in no position to save it from destruction. Within three weeks, Hitler's *Blitzkrieg* ("lightning war") had overwhelmed the Polish army, whereupon Soviet Russia moved its troops westward to share in the partition of that unhappy land in a manner reminiscent of the eighteenth century. In the meantime the British held air-raid drills, supplied civilians with gas masks, and evacuated some two million people (most of them children) from cities such as London that seemed the probable targets of German bombers. The Emergency Powers (Defence) Act of September 1939 gave the government the authority it needed to control the civilian economy in the interests of war.

After the initial excitement produced by the declaration of war, there was a letdown. Although German submarines sank a number of British merchant vessels, Hitler's regime appeared to be in no mood to attack the West, and a certain leisureliness overtook the war effort. The number of men in uniform increased from half a million in the summer of 1939 to almost two million in the spring of 1940; but as of April 1940 a million people were still unemployed. Munitions factories were not yet producing at full capacity. No special attempt was made to stockpile fats, sugar, timber, oil, or iron ore, even though the requisite shipping was available.

Britain sent the promised four army divisions to France, and British and French general staffs coordinated strategy. But that strategy was the purely defensive one of awaiting a German assault behind the Maginot Line, a vast complex of tank traps, fixed artillery sites, subterranean railways, and living quarters, which paralleled the Franco-German border but failed to protect the Franco-Belgian border. Somehow the war was to be won by starving Germany into submission by economic blockade alone. Chamberlain privately questioned whether Germany had any intention of attacking the West at all; and a number of Britons, including Lloyd George, suggested that serious consideration be given to all

German peace proposals. This the government refused to do. Yet as the months dragged on, it did seem increasingly appropriate to call the war, as Americans were beginning to do, the "Phoney War."

War was indeed going on at sea; but on land and in the air there was a virtual standstill, and in England some of the evacuees began drifting back to their homes. Fighting *was* going on in northern Europe, where the Soviet Union took advantage of the Stalin-Hitler Pact to annex the three independent Baltic states of Lithuania, Latvia, and Estonia and to launch an attack on Finland. There was strong Anglo-French sympathy for the Finnish cause; and a projected Allied expeditionary force to Finland was thwarted only by the refusal of Norway and Denmark to permit its transit and by the fact that the Finns made peace with (and ceded territory to) Russia in March 1940.

The Phoney War ended suddenly on April 9, 1940. At dawn German naval units assaulted Copenhagen, Denmark, and all the major ports of Norway. Hitler's purpose was to prevent any Allied intervention in Scandinavia and to secure Germany's use of the iron-ore supplies of neutral Sweden. The German invasion showed extraordinary coordination of sea, land, and air forces. Denmark surrendered within five hours, but the Norwegians held out for several weeks. For a time a British expeditionary force hung on to outposts in central and northern Norway and at the same time managed to do much damage to the German surface navy. Half of the enemy's destroyers, three of its eight cruisers, and a battleship were destroyed. But German air superiority forced a British withdrawal.

Churchill Becomes Prime Minister

It was the debacle in Norway that led to one of the most dramatic debates in the history of the House of Commons. Although an electoral truce had been declared in September 1939, Chamberlain had not been able to form a true coalition government. Neither the Labour party nor the tiny remnant of the Liberal party was represented in his cabinet. The Labour party therefore had no hesitation early in May about introducing a motion of censure of the Chamberlain ministry. Liberals and independent Conservatives joined in. "The Government," declared Archibald Sinclair, the Liberal leader, "is giving us a one-shift war while the Germans are working a three-shift war."

The most scathing attack came from Leo Amery, a Conservative M.P. who had at one time been Chamberlain's cabinet colleague. What was needed, declared Amery, was a government willing to match the enemy in fighting spirit, in daring, in resolution, and in the thirst for victory. He climaxed his speech by quoting the words Oliver Cromwell had addressed three centuries before to the remnant of the Long Parliament: "You have sat too long here for any good you have been doing. Depart, I say, and let us have done with you. In the name of God, go." Chamberlain's government had been accustomed to a majority of 200 votes or more; but in the vote of confidence of May 8, more than 40 Conservatives voted with the opposition and an even greater number abstained. The government won the vote, 281 to 200, but the Labour party continued to refuse participation in a coalition government under Chamberlain's leadership; the prime minister's approval rating in the public opinion polls had plummeted from 68 percent in November 1939 to 33 percent in May 1940. On May 10, the very day on which Hitler attacked the Netherlands, Belgium, and France, Chamberlain resigned. George VI, after first considering naming Lord Halifax, the foreign secretary, asked Winston Churchill to form a new government.

Churchill was sixty-five and, until his return to the admiralty the year before, had not held cabinet office for a decade; yet he was the man for the hour. In a sense his whole life, beginning with his service as soldier-correspondent in Cuba, India, and Africa in the 1890s, had been a preparation for the part he was now to play. He had always been a controversial figure. "I have," he said, "derived continued benefit from criticism at all periods of my life, and I do not remember any time when I was ever short of it." His brilliance and energy had long been recognized but also distrusted. He had devoted the 1930s to warning his countrymen against the menace of Nazi Germany; as early as 1932 he had prophesied that Hitler's demands would "shake to their foundations every country in the world." He had also spent his years out of office chronicling the deeds of his distant ancestor, John Churchill, first duke of Marlborough, who had served as leader of a European coalition battling the threat to the peace of an earlier age, that of Louis XIV. The new prime minister was a democrat by conviction but an aristocrat by birth and training, and his self-confidence was never daunted by the fact that he happened to be in the minority at any given moment. In his sense of Britain's imperial mission, in his assurance that the struggle before him was one of good versus evil and that he was on the side of good, he personified the tradition of Cromwell, of Chatham, and of Pitt.

When he received the call from his sovereign to become Britain's wartime leader, Churchill was filled with a sense of quiet exhilaration. "I was conscious," he wrote later in his memoirs,

> of a profound sense of relief. At last I had the authority to give directions over the whole scene. I felt as if I were walking with destiny, and that all my past life had been but a preparation for this hour and for this trial. Ten years in the political wilderness had freed me from ordinary party antagonisms. My warnings over the last six years had been so numerous, so detailed, and were now so terribly vindicated, that no one could gainsay me. I could not be reproached either for making the war or with want of preparation for it. I thought I knew a good deal about it all, and I was sure I should not fail.[2]

Three days later he made his first appearance in the House of Commons as prime minister to outline his nation's problems and to define its aims.

---

[2]*The Gathering Storm*, p. 532.

"I have nothing to offer but blood, toil, tears, and sweat." Long months of struggle and suffering lay ahead. "You ask, What is our policy? I will say: It is to wage war, by sea, land, and air, with all our might . . . against a monstrous tyranny, never surpassed in the dark, lamentable catalogue of human crime. . . . You ask, What is our aim? I can answer in one word: Victory — victory at all costs, victory in spite of all terror; victory, however long and hard the road may be."

"He mobilized the English language and sent it into battle," President John F. Kennedy was to say of Churchill; and during the years that followed, radio enabled Churchill to become the inspiration not only of his own people but of millions of Europeans and Americans as well. For the moment, indeed, the English language was the most effective weapon Churchill had at hand. On the battlefield all his immediate hopes went awry. German armored battalions, supported by bombers and preceded by parachute units, conquered Holland in five days and Belgium in three weeks. By early June the German army was well inside France. This time there was no last stand at the Marne, for the Maginot Line had been outflanked and the Allied line broken. Italy's entry into the war on the German side prevented the use against Germany of French regiments stationed on the Italian border. On June 14, German troops entered Paris. Two days later, the last premier of the Third Republic was forced to resign, and his successor, the aged Marshal Pétain, signed an armistice with Germany according to which the German army, at French expense, was to occupy more than half of France, including the entire Atlantic coast, and to take over the French navy. Jersey and Guernsey, British islands in the English Channel off the coast of France, were occupied by German troops for the duration of the war.

Churchill had appealed to the Belgians to continue to resist. He had appealed to Italy to stay out of the war. He had appealed to the French — in the French language — to become citizens of a joint Anglo-French union, to turn the French fleet over to Britain, and to keep up the battle in France's North African possessions. None of these appeals was heeded. The only comfort the English could find in the events of May and June 1940 lay in "the miracle of Dunkirk." At that small French port, more than 338,000 Allied troops (224,000 of them British), surrounded on all sides by advancing German columns, were rescued by a motley flotilla of regular naval vessels, private yachts, trawlers, and motorboats. The success of this impromptu but superbly organized operation buoyed British spirits, even though it meant that 2,300 guns, 7,000 tons of ammunition, and 82,000 motor vehicles had been left to the enemy. Churchill freely admitted that Dunkirk was "a colossal military disaster. Wars are not won by evacuations."

The Battle of Britain

Hitler now bestrode the continent from the North Cape to the Pyrenees, and in his shadow Mussolini sought to make the Mediterranean an Italian lake. Britain stood alone. London had become the home of numerous exiled kings and queens and of men like Charles de Gaulle (undersecretary of war in the last government of the Third Republic), who attempted to rally the "free French." Britain had no ally left on the continent of Europe; it was subject to air attack from any point on the continent; and as in 1066 it was subject to the threat of invasion at once from Norway and from France.

Hitler, and many neutral observers, expected Britain to seek terms within a matter of weeks. But Churchill stood defiant. "We shall not flag or fail. We shall go on to the end. We shall fight in France, we shall fight on the seas and oceans, we shall fight with growing confidence and growing strength in the air, we shall defend our island whatever the cost may be, we shall fight on the beaches, we shall fight on the landing grounds, we shall fight in the fields and in the streets, we shall fight in the hills; we shall never surrender." The British, who had been rather unimaginative in anticipating the coming of war, showed themselves equally unimaginative in failing to acknowledge that they were beaten. Indeed, the consciousness that they were the last holdouts against a Europe dominated by Hitler evoked in many Britons a curious sense of elation.[3]

In the summer of 1940 Churchill took a number of desperate measures. He had British troops occupy Iceland in order to anticipate any German venture in that direction and to safeguard North Atlantic sea lanes. At his command, the British navy destroyed or damaged the French fleets anchored in Oran (in French Algeria) and Dakar (in French West Africa) in order to prevent them from falling into German hands. He sent men, guns, and tanks to Egypt (nominally independent since 1922) to hold the Suez Canal against an expected invasion from Italian Libya.

In the meantime, Hitler, wearying of British obstinacy, had given his general staff new secret orders. "Since England, in spite of her militarily hopeless position, shows no signs of coming to terms," he declared in mid-July, "I have decided to prepare a landing operation against England, and if necessary to carry it out. . . . The preparations for the entire operation must be completed by mid-August." Plans for what the Germans called "Operation Sea-Lion" were duly prepared, although Hitler's staff was handicapped by lack of time and by a relative lack of experience in mounting amphibious operations. The German High Command realized that a successful invasion of England required air superiority over the Channel, and the demands of Operation Sea-Lion led necessarily to the

---

[3]In biographies of Churchill, both John Charmley (1993) and Clive Ponting (1994) have argued that if Churchill had made a separate peace with Hitler in 1940, he could have saved both the British economy and the British Empire, but most historians remain persuaded that such revisionists misunderstand profoundly Hitler's personality, policies, and record of broken promises.

"Very Well, Alone"　Cartoon by David Low for the London *Evening Standard* (June 18, 1940). *(By permission of the Low Trustees and the* Evening Standard*)*

Battle of Britain, the attempt to gain such air superiority and trammel Britain into submission by airpower.

Day after day, night after night — as many as 1,800 on a single attack — German bombers and fighter escorts streamed across the Channel to bomb and strafe British factories, ports, and airfields — as well as numerous dummy airfields that successfully confused the Germans. Late in August, as a sign of impudence, British night bombers began to raid Berlin. Hitler was so enraged by this audacity that he ordered his pilots to pay less attention to vital military targets and to concentrate all efforts on the city of London itself. On September 7–8, German bombs succeeded in setting much of central London aflame; the raids continued without let-up for the next fifty-six nights. The underground (subway) stations that served as nightly air-raid shelters for the London populace did not prevent hundreds of people from being killed and thousands more from being wounded. (In the course of the war some 60,000 British civilians were to die as a result of air raids.) In the meantime, the alert had gone out along England's Channel coast that thousands of landing barges had been sighted in the ports of northern France. Invasion seemed imminent. All directional signs were removed from hundreds of roads in southern England in order to confuse the enemy. Members of the Home Guard took their places along the beaches to await the invader, often armed with weapons little more complicated than the wooden pikes with which Harold's men had faced William the Conqueror in 1066.

The War Comes Home, 1940 Children observe aerial dogfights from a trench dug in a hop field in Kent. *(Topham/The Image Works)*

The invasion never came. Hitler repeatedly postponed the date for a number of reasons, the most important of which may well have been the heroic resistance of the British air-fighter command. Outnumbered four to one, the intrepid Hurricane and Spitfire pilots downed two German planes for every one of their own that was destroyed. "Never in the field of human conflict," declared Churchill, "was so much owed by so many to so few." German air superiority over the Channel was not achieved, and an increasing number of German invasion transports and barges were sunk in port. Neither industrial production nor civilian morale had been damaged by air raids to the degree that German planners had anticipated. Londoners digging in the rubble after a severe air raid often found King George and his wife, Queen Elizabeth, on hand to commiserate or else a defiant Churchill puffing a cigar, his fingers formed in a "V for Victory" sign.

In mid-October, Hitler decided to postpone Operation Sea-Lion until the spring of 1941. He had experienced his first great military rebuff. Like the Battle of the Marne of September 1914 and the triumph over the Spanish Armada in 1588, the Battle of Britain of 1940 was a defensive victory. It halted the enemy in his tracks. It did not defeat him. But as did the victory over the Armada, so the Battle of Britain became a legend as well as a fact, one that helped to stiffen English resolve during the agonizing years of war that lay ahead, and thereby led to Germany's ultimate defeat.

The Battle of Britain in London   Winston Churchill inspects the ruins of the House of Commons chamber after its destruction by German bombs in May 1941. *(Kemsley Picture Service)*

The War Economy

To write the history of a war only in terms of barbarities and outrages or of courageous deeds and glowing words is necessarily a distortion of reality. Twentieth-century war was also a business that involved transforming a nation into one vast war-making machine. Such total mobilization transformed Britain during the winter and spring of 1940–1941. Ordinary politics were adjourned for the duration of the war, as Labourites and Liberals became part of a genuine coalition cabinet. Churchill's inner war cabinet of five, in which Churchill served not only as prime minister but also as minister of defense, included two Labourites — Clement Attlee, the leader of the Labour party, as deputy prime minister, and Ernest Bevin, for many years the general secretary of the Transport and General Workers Union and the outstanding trade unionist of the day, as minister of labor and national service. Another Labourite, Herbert Morrison, became successively minister of supply, home secretary, and minister of home security. Lord Beaverbrook, the politically independent press lord, took on the all-important job of minister of aircraft production. Under his auspices, British factories, which had produced 2,800 planes in 1938, built 20,000 in 1941 and 26,000 in 1943.

John Maynard Keynes became economic adviser to the treasury. With his help and that of other economists, a national system of material allocation, rationing, and price control was set up that put the entire economy under government direction — if not, except for the railways and the ports, under immediate government management. The right to conscript workers for munitions factories as well as for the armed forces was granted to the government by Parliament; some nine million men and women, one British citizen in five, were mobilized for the armed services, the auxiliary forces, and munitions work. The right to conscript for nonmilitary activities was exercised sparingly; but the British economy was mobilized to an extent not matched by Germany, Italy, or the USSR; and Churchill, although always subject to ultimate parliamentary control, became a dictator in all but name in his day-to-day conduct of the war.

World War II necessarily had an effect on "women's work" similar to that evoked by World War I, except that in 1941 the Churchill Coalition depended not solely on wartime patriotism but also on an element of compulsion: all women aged nineteen to fifty had to register at government

Wartime Rationing   A British woman puzzles over her family's nine ration books during World War II. *(Kurt Hutton/ Hulton Deutsch)*

employment agencies so that the Ministry of Labour might direct those considered suitable to do "essential work." Women between 19 and 30 also had to register for possible conscription into the women's army, navy, or air force auxiliary or the Women's Land Army (to work on farms). Only women taking care of children under age fourteen at home were totally exempt from such regulations. By 1943, as a result, some 1,500,000 more women were working at jobs in industry and transportation than had done so back in 1939. A comparable number held jobs in commerce, government, and the armed forces. Many trade-union leaders and employers were as reluctant as ever to admit women into traditional male preserves, but in most industries they did reach voluntary agreements to set aside peacetime rules for the time being.

Not only did the needs of war demand the continued growth of the iron, steel, and aluminum industries, but they also dictated an expansion of agriculture. Not since the Napoleonic Wars had the British farmer been given so great an incentive to grow crops. In the course of the war, the number of acres in the British Isles devoted to grains and potatoes increased from twelve to eighteen million, thus saving vital shipping space. Thousands of city folk devoted weekends to spading and weeding their "allotments." Even the moat of the Tower of London became a vegetable patch. The number of tractors on British farms tripled, and farm laborers received the greatest boost in income and status in their often dismal history.

The government was anxious not to alienate the labor movement and, except for one Welsh coal strike, World War II brought little of the industrial unrest that had marred the conflict of a generation before. Labor's belief in the justice of the war and the Labour party's important role in the government were in large part responsible. As had been the case during the previous war, the number of trade-union members grew sharply — from fewer than six million to more than eight million. (These included one million women in 1939, 2.2 million six years later.) The government did its best by means of rationing and price controls to stabilize the cost of living; by means of food subsidies, the official price index of daily necessities was kept steady from 1941 to 1945. Although real wages rose little if at all during the war, real earnings did rise in the sense that unemployment was now unknown and that overtime pay had become the rule. All major items of food, clothing, and furniture were rationed. All use of gasoline for civilian cars was banned, and the cost of a restaurant meal was limited to five shillings. Because of a shortage of newsprint, newspapers were restricted to four pages per issue. The only luxuries encouraged (although heavily taxed) were alcohol, tobacco, and the cinema. These presumably kept up civilian morale and absorbed excess spending power.

Wartime exigencies caused the national government to become involved in various health measures to an extent not known before. School meals became the general rule for rich and poor alike. Public nurseries helped working mothers, and cheap milk and vitamins were provided for children and expectant mothers. Factories were encouraged to provide doctors, nurses, and canteens. Deprived of their accustomed "sweets,"

British children could boast better teeth than ever before or since. The Ministry of Food deliberately sought to improve the British diet by curbing the use of fats and sugar while encouraging the consumption of green vegetables. Such measures, in spite of air raids, food shortages, overcrowding, and strains on medical facilities, undoubtedly brought an overall improvement in the health of British children. Whereas as recently as 1900, 154 of every thousand babies born in England and Wales had died during their first year, the number had declined to 56 by 1940 and was to fall to 30 by 1950. In Scotland, which had long lagged behind England in health standards, the improvement was even more noticeable.

In this wartime environment, class distinctions were submerged — air-raid shelters, emergency hospitals, and evacuation centers were made available to all; the rationing system played no favorites; and the tax system tended more than ever before to equalize incomes. In this same atmosphere, the coalition government began, even sooner than during the First World War, to plan for the postwar world. Lord (formerly Sir William) Beveridge (1879–1963), the veteran Liberal social reformer, compiled the Beveridge Report (1942), which envisaged a comprehensive public insurance system that would ensure for all Britons security from the cradle to the grave against all ills not of their own making. The report had been prepared under government auspices, and Churchill publicly supported the creation of a comprehensive national health service, but his Coalition Government made no attempt to enact the first Beveridge Report into law while the war was going on. It did formally approve the main provisions of a second Beveridge Report on unemployment. Keynesian methods were to be used in the future to secure the permanent reduction of unemployment to 3 percent or less of the British working force. In 1944, under the urging of a youthful Conservative minister, Richard Austen Butler (1902–1982), Parliament passed a major education act, which set the school-leaving age at fifteen (a goal achieved three years later) and secured the right of free secondary education for all.

Before any postwar utopia could be achieved, the war had to be won, and not least among the problems faced by the Churchill ministry was how to finance an economy in which fully half of the entire national output of goods and services was being devoted to the war effort. Initially, the expectation of the government had been that World War II would be paid for in the same fashion World War I had been — half by borrowing and half by increases in taxation. Upon Keynes's advice, the prime criterion of wartime financial policy became its success in counteracting the inflationary pressure being created by the disparity between rising wages and diminishing consumer goods. The basic income tax rate was raised to 42.5 percent in 1940 and to 50 percent in 1941. Many earlier tax exemptions were ended, and an excess-profits tax of 100 percent was slapped on all corporate earnings that exceeded prewar expectations. In 1943, at about the same time as in the United States, the "pay as you earn" withholding tax practice was introduced. Yet tax increases could not pay for the entire war effort, and the government channeled all savings either directly or indirectly (through banks) into the purchase of government bonds by prohibiting all ordinary capital investment.

The utilization of the taxes and savings of its own people was still not sufficient to finance the war. Nor did the borrowing of money from the dominions and other member countries of the sterling area (notably India and Egypt) fill the gap. The most vital outside source of war matériel was once again the United States; but when World War II began, the United States had made it far more difficult to purchase supplies than twenty-five years before. The neutrality legislation of the 1930s forbade private American corporations from lending money to European nations and private American vessels from shipping goods to war-torn Europe. All purchases had to be made on a cash-and-carry basis. Only after the fall of France in June 1940 did the American government, increasingly conscious of the threat to its own military security posed by a European continent dominated by Hitler's Germany, gradually relax such restrictions. Three months later, the United States exchanged fifty of its over-age destroyers for leases of military bases in British possessions in the Western Hemisphere.

In the meantime, large-scale British military purchases in the United States continued; but by the start of 1941 Britain's financial resources in the United States were exhausted. The country that during the Napoleonic Wars had been able to shoulder the financial burdens of successive coalitions and that during World War I had still, in effect, been able to finance its own war effort could no longer do so in World War II. The United States, under President Roosevelt's urging, responded in March 1941 with "An Act Further to Promote the Defense of the United States," popularly known as the Lend-Lease Act. The president promised "unqualified, immediate, all-out aid until total victory had been won." As Roosevelt phrased it in a homely analogy: if a neighbor's house is on fire, it is only right to lend him your garden hose.

The flow of Lend-Lease aid was slow at first, but before the war ended some $27 billion worth of goods had been sent eastward across the Atlantic. Although called "the most unsordid act" in diplomatic history and clearly essential to British military survival, the law also imposed onerous restrictions on British policy and ultimately involved some $6 billion of reverse Lend-Lease (from Britain to the United States), a sum that constituted as high a proportion of the British national income as Lend-Lease did of the American.

Despite the Lend-Lease Act, the United States in the spring of 1941 was still technically neutral, and its war production facilities were not yet geared for full-scale war. Britain remained the only major power actively resisting Axis expansion. The winter months had brought cheering news from Egypt, where a British force had chased an Italian army back into Italian Libya. Soon after, British troops to the south liberated one of the earliest of the lands conquered by the Axis powers — Ethiopia was restored to Emperor Haile Selassie.

The spring brought a reversal of fortune, however. German forces swept into the Balkans, and British efforts to make a last-ditch stand in mainland Greece or on the nearby island of Crete proved vain. Italian regiments in Libya were reinforced by German divisions under the command of General Erwin Rommel, soon to be known as "the Desert Fox." The ill-equipped British forces were driven back into Egypt, and only with difficulty could pro-British governments be kept in power in the Middle East. In the meantime, German bombing raids continued on a large scale. Plymouth, Liverpool, and Birmingham were all badly damaged; in London the chamber of the House of Commons was destroyed in May 1941, and for the next decade the Commons had to meet in the House of Lords' chamber.

Forging the Grand Alliance

Late in the spring, German air raids began to let up, and on June 22, 1941, Hitler launched his invasion of the Soviet Union. Apparently underestimating the extent of Russian resistance, he hoped in a few bold strokes to win the wheat of the Ukraine, the oil of the Caucasus, and the greater part of Russia's industrial resources as well as the *Lebensraum* (living space) he had long claimed as the right of the German people. Once he dominated the continent up to the Ural Mountains, he hoped that even Britain would have to come to terms and that no actual invasion of the island would prove necessary. Perhaps he expected to re-arouse the latent strength of anti-Communism in Britain. Although Germany succeeded in conquering those parts of the Soviet Union that produced 60 percent of its coal and steel and almost half its grain, ultimately Hitler's gamble failed. The Soviet army suffered millions of casualties and ceded tens of thousands of square miles of territory, but it did not disintegrate. Churchill immediately pledged his aid to the USSR. Staunch anti-Communist that he was, he saw Germany in 1941 as the far more immediate threat. It was German bombers, after all, that had been killing English civilians, and Germany that had deliberately set about invading its neighbors.

Thus, Hitler's invasion of Russia forged the first link in the "Grand Alliance" that was ultimately to win World War II. As Churchill put it publicly: "Any man or State who fights on against Nazidom will have our aid." He also remarked privately that if Hitler invaded hell it would be desirable to find something friendly to say about the devil. Churchill may have seen the formal twenty-year alliance he concluded in 1942 with Stalin in Moscow as a tactic of convenience, but many Britons came to view the Russian people through a romantic haze as their favorite allies — not merely courageous defenders of "Mother Russia" (as many doubtless were), but also dwellers in a socialist utopia. The British Aid to Russia Committee (headed by Clementine Churchill, the prime minister's wife) raised over £7 million in voluntary contributions, while the British government sent both weapons and equipment through Iran and by way of the hazardous Arctic Sea route to Murmansk.

Even before the United States and Britain had become actual military allies, Franklin D. Roosevelt and Winston Churchill became warm personal friends. Before the Second World War was over, Churchill was to hold nine meetings with the American president and to exchange 1,700 telegrams, telephone calls, and letters.[4] Their first meeting took place in August 1941 on a battleship off the Newfoundland coast. There the two statesmen composed the Atlantic Charter, a document setting forth Anglo-American war aims. It rejected any territorial aggrandizement for either Britain or the United States and affirmed the right of all peoples to choose their own form of government.

On December 7, 1941, Japan forged the second link in the Grand Alliance. Its surprise attack on Pearl Harbor, followed as it was by an American declaration of war against Japan, a German and Italian declaration of war against the United States, and a British declaration of war against Japan, was the true turning point of the war for Britain.

> No American will think it wrong of me [Churchill was to write] if I proclaim that to have the United States at our side was to me the greatest joy. . . . I do not pretend to have measured accurately the martial might of Japan, but now at this very moment I knew the United States was in the war, up to the neck and in to the death. So we had won after all! after Dunkirk; after the fall of France; after the horrible episode of Oran [the destruction of the French navy]; after the threat of invasion, when, apart from the Air and the Navy, we were an almost unarmed people; after the deadly struggle of the U-Boat War — the first Battle of the Atlantic, gained by a hand's breadth; after seventeen months of lonely fighting and nineteen months of my responsibility in dire stress, we had won the war. England would live; Britain would live; the Commonwealth of Nations and the Empire would live. . . . Once again in our long Island history we should emerge, however mauled or mutilated, safe and victorious. We should not be wiped out. Our history would not come to an end.[5]

Churchill immediately traveled to Washington, D.C., to confer with President Roosevelt and to address the American Congress. He did all in his power to buttress the links of Anglo-American understanding and often reminded his hearers that his mother had been American by birth and that he was therefore himself "an English-Speaking Union." Britain and the United States drafted a pact in the name of twenty-six "United Nations"; and their respective war efforts became so intertwined that Gen-

---

[4]The entire interchange has been published as *Churchill and Roosevelt: The Complete Correspondence*, ed. Warren Kimball, 3 vols. (1984). See also Joseph P. Lasch, *Roosevelt and Churchill, 1939–1941: The Partnership that Saved the West* (1976), and Warren Kimball, *Forged in War: Churchill, Roosevelt and the Second World War* (1996).

[5]*The Grand Alliance*, pp. 606–607.

eral George Marshall, the American army chief of staff, could describe their cooperation as "the most complete unification of military effort ever achieved by two allied nations."[6] Churchill also helped to convince the American leaders that the defeat of Germany should be given first priority.

The immediate post–Pearl Harbor military prospects did not, admittedly, look bright. In the Far East, Japan rapidly overran not only the American Philippines and hundreds of other small Pacific islands but also the Dutch East Indies, British Malaya and Singapore, and much of British Burma. For the first time since the American Revolution, a substantial portion of the British Empire fell into enemy hands. In the meantime, America's own wartime requirements took precedence over Britain's needs. German submarines in the North Atlantic sank ships far more rapidly than British and American shipyards could build them. During 1942 alone, 656 British ships (constituting 3.5 million tons) and 485 American vessels were sunk, thereby bringing on the most serious shipping crisis of the war. German troops were again advancing into Egypt and farther into Russia. Even a linkup in India between German and Japanese forces came to seem possible.

The Road to Victory

Throughout the year, however, American productive capacities were being built up and the American armed forces kept growing. In the autumn of 1942 came the military turning of the tide. The Axis powers had attained their greatest territorial extent, and almost simultaneously, in the Far East, in Russia, and in North Africa, the Allies began a counterattack. In November 1942 American Marines landed on the island of Guadalcanal; it was to become the first of many islands to be recaptured from the Japanese. By then the mammoth battle of Stalingrad was under way. When it ended in February 1943, the greater part of a German army had died or surrendered to the Russians and the remainder was retreating westward. In October 1942 the British Eighth Army under General Bernard (later Lord) Montgomery (1887–1976) halted General Rommel's forces at El Alamein, seventy miles west of Alexandria, Egypt, and began a victorious drive westward. In November 1942 Allied forces under General Dwight Eisenhower's command landed in Morocco and Algeria and

---

[6]This degree of cooperation is all the more surprising when one recalls how deep were the suspicions that had divided the United States from Britain during the interwar era. As recently as the 1920s, the U.S. navy had worked out theoretical plans for a possible war against Britain. During the 1920s many Americans had become persuaded that British propaganda had been primarily responsible for luring them into World War I. They pictured Britain as a land run by a decadent clique of aristocratic snobs who presided over a class-ridden social structure and a deplorable empire. See, e.g., John E. Moser, *Twisting the Lion's Tail: Anglophobia in the United States, 1921–1948* (1999).

began a drive that pushed all Axis forces in Africa into Tunisia and that, seven months later, in cooperation with Montgomery's Eighth Army, expelled them from Africa altogether. "Now this is not the end," proclaimed a jubilant Churchill on first hearing of the successful landings. "It is not even the beginning of the end. But it is, perhaps, the end of the beginning."[7]

It was in 1942 that the embattled Hitler regime embarked on the "Final Solution," its deliberate program of methodically exterminating the Jews of Europe. Although rumors had reached Britain by the end of the year, the British response, like the American, proved unimaginative. Britain had shown itself relatively hospitable to German Jewish refugees before the war, but once the war began it maintained severe restrictions on Jewish immigration to the Palestine mandate, a possible haven for those few Jews who did manage to escape from Nazi-occupied eastern Europe. It was fearful that the Arab states of the Middle East would join the Axis powers in the war. Nor was priority given to the bombing of the gas chambers, a step that might have slowed the process by which millions of Jews — as well as Poles, Russians, Gypsies, homosexuals, and invalids — were being put to death.

The British proved far more imaginative in other areas: in using counterintelligence to mislead the Germans about Allied military plans on crucial occasions; in developing both radar and defenses against it; in establishing a Special Operations Executive in 1940 to aid anti-German resistance movements in Norway, France, and elsewhere; and in embarking on the research that led to the development of the atomic bomb. In 1942 all British scientists involved in the last-named effort were sent to the United States to become part of the Manhattan Project team. Although a Scottish doctor, Alexander Fleming, had discovered the antibacterial properties of penicillin back in 1928, it was only during the war that the Australian-born professor of pathology at Oxford, Howard Florey, succeeded in producing on a mass scale the first of such antibiotic wonder drugs, initially in Britain and then in the United States. The greatest such British triumph was not to be revealed until the war had been over for a generation, the fact that early in the conflict, a group of British cryptographers had cracked the code by which German military commanders communicated with each other. The secrets revealed had to be used with enormous care in order not to alert the German High Command, but the code-breakers proved instrumental in preventing General Rommel's forces from reaching Cairo, in ultimately winning "the Battle of the Atlantic" against German submarines, and in deceiving the Germans about the location of the D-Day invasion. In the process, one of the leading members of the cryptography team, Alan

---

[7] In *Why the Allies Won* (1995), Richard Overy provides a thoughtful reassesssment of why the Axis powers were ultimately unable to hang on to the vast empire they had conquered by the summer of 1942.

Turing, pioneered the study of "artificial intelligence" and designed the first modern computer.[8]

The year 1943 brought a slow but steady Allied advance in the Mediterranean area and in Russia. Despite Russian urging, the Western Allies did not yet feel themselves in a position to launch a full-fledged second front in France; but in July, American, British, and Canadian units invaded Sicily. Their invasion of mainland Italy early in September was immediately followed by the overthrow of Mussolini and the signing of an armistice by a new Italian government. Unfortunately, Germany now treated its erstwhile ally as an occupied country, and powerful German resistance made the campaign up the Italian peninsula a costly one, reminiscent at times of the deadly trench warfare of World War I. Churchill pushed for an Allied attack on the Balkans as well, partly in order to prevent postwar domination of the entire area by the Soviet Union. In this case, he was overruled by the Americans who, by virtue of the greater wealth and manpower at their command, had of necessity become the senior partner in the Anglo-American partnership.

Some of Churchill's strategic proposals were to receive critical scrutiny in postwar memoirs, but the value of his role in planning grand strategy and sometimes tactics as well is generally conceded, as is his ever-present consciousness of the political probabilities of the postwar world. No permanent cleavage divided him from his generals, as had estranged Lloyd George from General Haig. Not that he hesitated to speak frankly to them at all times. For instance, when General Montgomery, the son of an Anglican vicar, boasted to Churchill, "I don't drink and I don't smoke and I am 100 percent fit," the prime minister retorted, "I *do* drink and I *do* smoke and I am 200 percent fit." Montgomery evoked great loyalty from his troops, but relations between him and his American counterparts were often strained: he impressed them as overcautious in planning campaigns at the same time that he liked to lecture them as if he were a Victorian schoolmaster admonishing somewhat backward students.

As 1944 began, almost all Allied planning was concentrated upon D-Day, the most massive and audacious amphibious invasion ever planned in military history. By then Allied bombers had become increasingly effective in disrupting the German industrial and transportation system; in the course of the war Britain's Bomber Command was to drop almost a million tons of bombs over Germany, mostly in nighttime raids, and in the process to lose 8,000 bombers and 46,000 airmen. By then, too, 1.5 million American troops had landed in Britain. There they introduced the joys of jitterbugging and gum chewing to the natives and flirted with the local women, 60,000 of whom were eventually to move to the United States as war brides. In the short run, the Americans impressed more

---

[8]See, for example, Anthony Cave Brown, *The Bodyguard of Lies*, 2 vols. (1975), and F. H. Hinsley, *British Intelligence in the Second World War* (abridged ed., 1993).

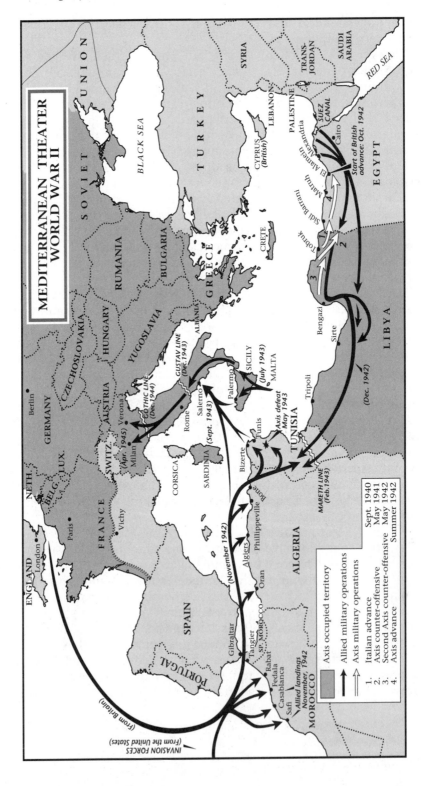

MEDITERRANEAN THEATER
WORLD WAR II

Axis occupied territory
Allied military operations
Axis military operations

1. Italian advance   Sept. 1940
2. Axis counter-offensive   May 1941
3. Second Axis counter-offensive May 1942
4. Axis advance   Summer 1942

jaundiced Britons as "overpaid, overfed, oversexed, and over here!"[9] The grand assault on Normandy began on June 6, in the form of an armada of 5,300 ships carrying 370,000 soldiers and sailors and supported by 11,000 airplanes. Although there were setbacks after the initial landings, by the end of July the Allied forces had broken out of Normandy and had encircled the greater part of one German army. By late August, Paris was liberated and Hitler's forces were everywhere on the retreat.

Germany seemed on the point of collapse. But as German defensive lines began to resemble those of the First World War, they stiffened; and in the autumn the Allied drive in Belgium and eastern France was halted. During these weeks of temporary stalemate, Londoners and other English people were exposed to a new threat, in some ways more unnerving than the nightly bomber raids of earlier years. These were the pilotless jet-propelled planes, the "buzz-bombs," which descended suddenly from the stratosphere and did considerable damage. Even after the launching pads in France of the short-range V-1 buzz-bombs had been captured, long-range V-2 rockets fired from the German Ruhr — more than 1,000 in all — continued to destroy and to disconcert for seven more months; they constituted "a sinister, eerie form of war."

In January 1945, a Big Three conference in the Crimea secured Russian agreement to a postwar international organization and Russian aid to the Far Eastern war, which was expected to continue for at least a year and a half after the war in Europe was over. Occupation zones for Germany were drawn up, and a government based on "free and unfettered elections" was promised for a reconstructed Poland, which was to cede its eastern lands to the Soviet Union and occupy former German territory instead.

A temporarily successful German counterattack in December — the Battle of the Bulge — had discouraged Allied strategists, and the sudden success of the Allies' late winter offensive came almost as a surprise. In March, Allied forces crossed the Rhine, and on May 7, 1945, with Hitler and Mussolini both dead, the German High Command conceded unconditional surrender. King George VI and his family — and Winston Churchill — waved to cheering crowds from the balcony of Buckingham Palace. The long-dimmed lights of Trafalgar Square and Piccadilly Circus gave way to floodlights as hundreds of thousands milled about in celebration of V-E Day.

For most of the British public, the war against Japan had always been of secondary importance, but the shift of men and matériel soon began; and by the time of V-J Day, less than three months later, over 650,000 British troops were engaged in the Pacific theater of war. Under the over-all command of Admiral Lord Louis Mountbatten (1900–1979), the British were especially active in Burma and Malaya and received the Japanese

---

[9]David Reynolds, *Rich Relations: The American Occupation of Britain 1942–45* (1995), throws light on all aspects of that societal encounter.

The Big Three at Teheran, November 1943   Stalin, Roosevelt, and Churchill.
(The Granger Collection)

surrenders in what before the war had been French Indo-China and the Dutch East Indies. The use of the atomic bomb in August 1945 obviated the full-scale invasion of the main Japanese islands that had long been thought necessary (with a projected casualty rate of more than a million soldiers) and thereby brought the East Asian war to a relatively speedy conclusion.

The effects of World War II on Britain were manifold: 357,000 Britons had been killed (30,000 of them merchant seamen, 60,000 of them civilian air-raid victims) and 600,000 more had been disabled. If the Second World War proved for Britain only one-half as deadly as the first, it was because British troops had not had to undergo four years and more of continuous full-scale land fighting. The closest analogies to the Sommes, Passchendaeles, and Verduns of the First World War were the battles of Leningrad, Moscow, and Stalingrad. Yet Britain's cities had been destroyed in a manner for which the earlier war provided no precedent. Port facilities and railways had deteriorated. Britain now had a national debt of over £25 billion and had become a debtor country for the first time in a century and a half. It remained dependent on the import of food and raw materials; yet most of the export industries with which it balanced accounts had been converted to military purposes, and the merchant marine, which provided "invisible earnings," was 30 percent smaller than it had been in 1938. The Pax Britannica was now a memory, and naval supremacy had been conceded to the United States.

The problems of the peace — the long-range economic dislocations, the nationalist upsurge in Asia and Africa, and, most notably, the Cold War that soon divided the members of the Grand Alliance — obscured so quickly the triumph of 1945 that its significance tends to be slighted. An Anglo-American alliance had been forged to bridge at last the schism that had divided the English-speaking peoples since 1775. A new and more comprehensive international organization, the United Nations, had been created. In spite of overwhelming odds, Britain had emerged from World War II as one of the Big Three just as it had been one of the Big Three at Paris and one of the Big Five at Vienna. Finally, in the battle between a totalitarian, fanatical, nationalistic ideology and that of liberal democracy, it was liberal democracy that had emerged triumphant once again. Certainly British stubbornness in 1940 had something to do with that outcome. The Battle of Britain and the symbol of defiance it produced in the person of Winston Churchill, the greatest of all English war ministers, deserve the honored place they have attained in the collective memory of the British people and of free people everywhere. Britain's perseverance in the face of overwhelming odds had its own effect upon the postwar world and, despite setbacks, helped for two decades to make the spirit of post–World War II Britain more hopeful and harmonious than the spirit of the 1920s and 1930s.

CHAPTER 19

Social Security and International Insecurity

To call 1945 an eventful year is an understatement. It marked the end of the Second World War against Germany and Japan. It saw the organization of the postwar United Nations at San Francisco. It brought death for Mussolini and Hitler, as well as for Franklin D. Roosevelt, eulogized by Churchill as "the greatest American friend we have ever known." It marked the explosion of the first atomic bomb and thus ushered in what, with mingled pride and terror, we call "the nuclear age." In 1945 the foundations were laid for the Cold War, whose temperature was to rise and fall many times during the decades that followed — until the collapse of the Soviet Union in the early 1990s. For Britain 1945 also signified a momentous general election, the first in a decade.

The election was to bring to fruition the welfare state whose essentials, a decade later, had ceased to be a matter of political controversy. Yet the same Labour and Conservative ministries that were to secure for the average British citizen a far higher degree of social security than had ever been known before were forced to steer the ship of state through international seas troubled by problems of postwar reconstruction, Cold War rivalries, and nationalist strivings in Asia and the Middle East.[1]

The General Election of 1945

Winston Churchill would have been happy to continue his coalition government until the war against Japan had been won, but the Labour and

---

[1]Events since 1945 may be followed in Kenneth O. Morgan, *The People's Peace: British History, 1945–1989* (1990), a book that emphasizes shifts in politics and the public mood; in Alan Sked and Chris Cook, *Post-War Britain: A Political History* (2nd ed., 1991); and in Arthur Marwick, *British Society Since 1945* (rev. ed., 1991). The immediate postwar period has been assessed sympathetically by Kenneth O. Morgan in *Labour in Power, 1945–1951* (1984) and by Henry Pelling in *The Labour Governments, 1945–51* (1984), a work that focuses on nationalization, the welfare state, and foreign policy. *Never Again: Britain 1945–1951* (1992) by Peter Hennessy is a popular history that relies in large part on interviews with survivors. Kenneth Harris, *Attlee* (1982), is a reliable biography. *The Welfare State in Britain Since 1945* (1993) by Rodney Lowe summarizes policies and policy debates about employment, social security, education, health, housing, and personal social services.

Liberal members of his government preferred not to wait. Churchill therefore formed an all-Conservative "caretaker" government in May, and elections were scheduled for July 5. In order to allow for servicemen's votes to be counted with the regular ballots, the actual tallying of the votes was held off until July 26. By that time Churchill was off at Potsdam to confer with Stalin and Harry S. Truman, the new president of the United States, in what proved to be the third and last of World War II's Big Three conferences. Churchill returned to London to hear the returns: Labourites, 394; Conservatives, 196; Liberals, 12; various minor groups and independents, 38. The swing in the popular vote was less dramatic but significant enough. Labour had advanced from 38 percent (in 1935) to 48 percent of the total popular vote. The Conservative share had declined from 54 percent to 40 percent.

As soon as the outcome of the election was clear, Churchill called at Buckingham Palace to tender his resignation as prime minister to the king. Hardly had he departed in his chauffeur-driven Rolls Royce than Clement Attlee drove up in his small family car to be named the new prime minister. Shortly thereafter Attlee set off for Potsdam to take his place as one of the Big Three.

The election results came as a dramatic surprise to most Britons and to most overseas newspaper readers as well. For Winston Churchill himself they were both a great shock and a sore disappointment. As he was to write in his *History of the Second World War*, "I acquired the chief power in the state, which henceforth I wielded in ever-growing measure for five years and three months of world war, at the end of which time, all our enemies having surrendered unconditionally or being about to do so, I was immediately dismissed by the British electorate from all further conduct of their affairs."[2] The conclusion is at once succinct and misleading. For Labour in 1945 did not specifically wage an anti-Churchill campaign. The Labourites were more than willing to acknowledge Churchill's great services as a war leader. One young Labour supporter, for example, shouted herself hoarse in Churchill's honor as he toured the city. "He's a marvel," she proclaimed, "and we owe him everything. But how old he looks! And how tired! What he wants is a good rest, and that is what we are going to give him."

The Labour party was looking ahead to the postwar years, when the chief concerns seemed likely to be domestic rather than foreign. And the Conservatives, contended the Labourites, had demonstrated during the 1930s their ineptitude in combating unemployment as well as in preventing war. Labour had set forth a more detailed electoral program and had maintained during the war a much better organized party machinery. Churchill, moreover, found the abrupt change from world statesman to party spokesman a difficult one. When in one broadcast he predicted that in order to establish socialism the Labour leaders would

---

[2]*The Gathering Storm*, p. 596.

Smiles of Victory The new Prime Minister Clement Attlee and his wife welcome the results of the general election of July 1945. *(Hulton Deutsch Collection)*

have to rely "on some form of Gestapo," Hitler's dreaded secret police, the charge redounded against him. Attlee, Morrison, and Bevin had, after all, been his trusted cabinet colleagues for half a decade, they had never revealed a cabinet secret, and their patriotism was beyond cavil.

For the Labour party July 26, 1945, was its one great historic moment. For the first time in British history — and for the first (and only) time among the major democratic nations — a professedly socialist party had won an overwhelming parliamentary majority. The election seemed to vindicate the pioneers who had organized the Labour Representation Committee in 1900 and to assuage the frustrations encountered by their successors of the 1930s, who had rebuilt the party after MacDonald's "betrayal."

A few farsighted Conservatives, however, were able to see a silver lining in the worst electoral disaster to befall them since 1906. The new government, they were aware, would not be able to concentrate solely on "building socialism." It would have to deal with all the problems of postwar reconstruction, both physical and economic, and it might prove more successful in asking for necessary working-class sacrifice than a Conservative government. It would likewise have to deal with the monumental international repercussions wrought by war, and it might more readily achieve national unity against Russian expansion, if that were to prove a major postwar problem.

Although pledged to establish a "Socialist Commonwealth," the Attlee ministry produced neither the shock nor the fear of complete social overturn that the first Labour cabinet of Ramsay MacDonald had briefly occasioned. Yet Labour M.P.'s did on one occasion jar the House of Commons by singing "The Red Flag" within the historic walls of Westminster Palace, and the background of the ministers gave some sanction to the party's claim to be "of the people." Eight of the thirty-seven ministers had at one time been coal miners; eleven had been active trade-union leaders. While Hugh Dalton (1887–1962), Chancellor of the Exchequer, and Sir Stafford Cripps, president of the Board of Trade, came from upper-middle-class backgrounds, Herbert Morrison, the leader of the House of Commons, was the son of a policeman and a housemaid and had grown up in a London slum. Ernest Bevin, who as foreign secretary soon became the number two man in the government, had similarly risen from extreme poverty, as had Aneurin Bevan, the new minister of health. Bevan (1899–1960) was to play in the Labour government of 1945 a role comparable to Lloyd George's in the Liberal government of 1906. Like Lloyd George, he was a Welshman and a spellbinding orator; none of the new ministers felt more conscious than he of having been the victim of social injustice, for his father had died early of a respiratory disease caught in the coal mines; and the gibes of no other Labour M.P. could so infuriate the Conservative opposition.

Attlee himself was of upper-middle-class background and had earned an Oxford degree. He had been drawn to the Labour party by his interest in social work and by the influence of the Webbs. No greater contrast to Churchill could have been imagined in physique or manner or oratorical power. "Mr. Attlee is a modest man," observed one of his aides to Churchill. Replied Churchill: "A modest man, but then he has so much to be modest about." Attlee possessed in fact a high degree of self-assurance, but he lacked all sense of political showmanship, and — in the words of one journalist — he "tucked his personality behind a pipe and left colleagues and public to make what they could of the smoke signals." Yet the man who had successfully led a difficult party for a decade was to guide an even more difficult cabinet with a quiet demeanor but a firm hand.

Nationalization and Social Security

For a generation the Labour party had pledged itself to nationalize the commanding heights of the British economy, and Attlee himself defined nationalization as Labour's most distinctive policy. The electoral triumph of 1945 gave the party the opportunity to pass the appropriate acts of Parliament. Nationalization meant that an industry or utility was to be operated by a public corporation such as the Tennessee Valley Authority in the United States and not directly by a government department. Former owners were to be compensated. Workers in nationalized industries retained the right to bargain collectively and the right to strike. Henceforth, however, the purpose of the enterprise was to be public service rather than private profit. The power of capitalist stockholders was to be curbed, and the ability of the government to counteract the ups and downs of the economy and to plan for the national welfare was to be enhanced.

The nationalization of the Bank of England in 1946 caused little visible change; the former governor was asked to stay on. Although originally a private institution, the bank had long exercised unique public responsibilities. The confirmation of its public status, analogous to that of the Federal Reserve System in the United States, comforted those Labourites who had blamed a bankers' plot for the downfall of the Labour ministry of 1929–1931.

The first important segment of the economy to be nationalized was the coal mines. Although coal remained the most important fuel source for both electric power stations and the heating of private homes, it had for decades been the most problem-afflicted of British industries. The easily accessible coal seams had long since been exhausted, and during much of the twentieth century the productivity of the mines had been declining. The industry, moreover, had the poorest record of labor relations, and the Miners' Union had long advocated nationalization. The act finally passed in 1946 provided that the more than 800 private coal companies, employing 765,000 workers, were to be replaced by a single National Coal Board appointed by the minister of fuel and power and consisting of nine representatives of the various functions within the industry (such as finance, technology, labor, and marketing). The board was to operate the mines subject to the general supervision of the ministry.

Another act of 1946 placed the greater part of a much smaller but rapidly expanding industry, aviation, in the hands of three (and ultimately two) public corporations. BOAC (British Overseas Airways Corporation) had been created by the Chamberlain government in 1939 but came into operation only in 1945. BEA (British European Airways) was set up in 1946.[3] The overseas cable system was nationalized during the same year; the domestic telegraph system had been part of the Post Office since 1870. In 1947 and 1948 followed the nationalization of the electricity and gas industries. The establishment of the Central Electricity Board in 1926 had been a giant step toward the goal reached by the act of 1947. The nationalized gas industry was left in the hands of twelve large autonomous regional boards. A much greater undertaking was the nationalization of inland transport. The consolidation of the four mainline railways left after the post–World War I amalgamations to form British Rail proved a fairly simple undertaking. Much more complicated was the nationalization of the hundreds of small trucking companies that had been feverishly competing with the railways since the 1920s. Inland transport also included docks and canals; in terms of number of employees (888,000) and monetary value, the nationalization of inland transport was the largest of all such undertakings by the Labour government.

---

[3]The two were combined in 1974 to form British Airways.

Even after the program of nationalization was complete, some 80 percent of the British economy remained in private hands, and the most surprising result of nationalization, for fervent advocates and diehard opponents alike, was how little difference the change made in the short run. Rational industrial planning may have been made easier, yet few long-range plans were instituted. The government expected nationalized enterprises to break even rather than to earn a profit, but the answers to related questions remained more elusive: How then were they to raise the capital to pay for the re-equipment and the modernization of war-worn railways? How was the nationalized but still inefficient coal industry to hold its own against alternative fuels and international competitors? How would nationalization affect the state of labor relations? Although miners may indirectly have been represented on the new National Coal Board, many of them soon came to look on that board as the old coal-mine owner writ large; it was "still the same bloomin' boss!" Even a staunch advocate of nationalization was forced to concede a decade later that the most notable failure of the government-controlled industries "has been their inability to evoke a new kind of response from the workers whom they employ."[4]

If the life of the average Briton was affected only indirectly by nationalization, it was touched far more immediately by the National Insurance and the National Health Service Acts of 1946, twin pillars of the postwar welfare state. The first act consolidated steps taken by various British governments since the late nineteenth century to assume responsibility for the general welfare by providing unemployment, sickness, and disability benefits; maternity and death benefits; and payments to retired persons, widows, and orphans. For the individual, all these benefits were to be secured by the weekly purchase of a single insurance stamp. In practice, the insurance fund thus accumulated had to be supplemented by grants from the national Exchequer. The National Insurance scheme and associated schemes of family allowances (paid to mothers with two children or more) and industrial injury benefits were both compulsory and universal and embodied much of the first wartime Beveridge Report. A National Assistance Board was instituted to provide for the relatively few who might still fall through the cracks of the welfare state. Although the resulting social insurance program was far more comprehensive than the prewar program, for the time being it represented a smaller percentage of total government expenditure in 1950 (11.3 percent) than in 1938 (13.6 percent). Payments to the unemployed had dominated the interwar social insurance expenditures, but large-scale unemployment was to be absent from Britain's postwar economy until the mid-1970s.

Initially more controversial than the National Insurance system was the National Health Service, which went into effect in 1948. It enabled all Britons, regardless of class or status or gender, to enjoy free medical

---

[4]William A. Robson, *Nationalised Industries and Public Ownership* (1960).

LET THE
TODDLER'S
FIRST
STEPS

-lead to the
WELFARE CENTRE

GET EXPERT ATTENTION AND ADVICE BEFORE AND AFTER BABY COMES
ADVICE ON FEEDING- MILK OR SPECIAL FOOD
TRAINED NURSES WHO LIKE CHILDREN
DO WHAT THE DOCTOR TELLS YOU

An Early National Health Service Poster   New parents are encouraged to make full use of state facilities. *(Courtesy of the National Health Service)*

and hospital care. Within a year, 95 percent of the population had enrolled itself on the panel of the doctor of their choice. The doctor, in turn, was paid by the Health Service from Exchequer funds on the basis of the number of patients on his or her panel (a maximum of 3,500, an average of 2,200). Many British doctors had experienced the panel system under the working-class health insurance act of 1911. The new service was far more comprehensive in that it included not only full-time working people but also the self-employed, the unemployed, and the dependent members of each family; it paid for the services of specialists as well as general practitioners; and it provided for the care of teeth and eyes as well as other medical care. The legislation also brought about the nationalization of most British hospitals.

Although the British Medical Association had long favored a comprehensive national health service, it became fearful of the prospect during the 1940s. Long months of negotiation were required before Minister of Health Bevan could work out a formula to which a majority of doctors were willing to accede. In due course, 97 percent of British doctors joined the National Health Service. Although it placed upper limits on their income, it freed them from the problem of financially delinquent patients. "The absence of any financial barrier between doctor and patient," observed one physician, "must make the doctor-patient relationship easier and more satisfactory."[5]

The new National Health Service was handicapped initially by a severe shortage of hospitals, equipment, and staff, but it soon became the single most popular measure enacted by the Labour government. Estimates of its cost, it is true, much exceeded government predictions, because the sudden availability of free medical care revealed an unexpectedly high pent-up demand for dentures and eyeglasses. Although the pace of hospital construction remained slow and although the challenge of providing appropriate compensation to doctors and nurses at a time of inflation and rising expectations remained a troublesome one, the number of doctors increased rapidly (from 36,500 in 1948 to 49,000 in 1958). As a consequence of the National Health Service, many working-class women, who before the war still relied on the neighborhood "granny" or the local "chemist" for most medical advice, now came to rely on the neighborhood general practitioner instead. It was he (or, more rarely, she) who was able to prescribe the new antibiotic drugs and vaccines that all but eliminated formerly widespread diseases such as tuberculosis, typhoid, diphtheria, and poliomyelitis. The infant mortality rate continued its steady twentieth-century descent — from 56 per 1,000 births in 1940 to 18 in 1970 and 7 in 1992. Life expectancy also continued to rise. By 1958, the average British man lived to sixty-nine, the average woman to seventy-four. The figures for 1998 were respectively seventy-four and seventy-nine.

The Labour government instituted other benefits such as a publicly supported legal aid service and a law permitting members of the public to sue the government. At the same time, it maintained the wartime subsidies paid to British farmers. It was far less successful, however, with the building of houses. The population had grown, but almost no new houses had been built during the war even as half a million houses had been destroyed by enemy air raids. Rigorous rent-control measures may have helped to counter inflationary pressures, but they provided no incentive to private builders. As a result, the number of houses constructed annually during the late 1940s — mostly by local government authorities — was only half as large as the number built annually during the 1930s.

Austerity

All the Labour government's plans of nationalization and socialist planning were increasingly handicapped and often overshadowed by the grave economic problems inherited from the Second World War. The underlying

---

[5]Harry Eckstein, *The English National Health Service* (1959).

problem — a gap in the balance of payments — was easy to describe but difficult to resolve. Britain's net annual income from overseas investments had decreased from £175 to £73 million since 1938, but the prices of necessary imports had increased fourfold. The immediate postwar years brought a worldwide shortage of the food and the raw materials Britain needed to import; their cost, therefore, had increased far more rapidly than the price of the manufactured goods that Britain was reconverting its industries to export. Thus the terms of trade, which had been favorable to Britain in the 1930s and had helped to raise living standards for all but the unemployed, were now unfavorable. A government poster showed Britain in housewifely terms as a woman at a shop counter who had ordered more goods than she could afford. Only by raising the value of exports 75 percent above their prewar levels could the nation right its international balance of payments.

During the war, the payment problem had been greatly eased by American Lend-Lease aid. But in August 1945 the United States abruptly ended Lend-Lease, and Britain was faced with the immediate necessity of paying in dollars even for goods already in the country or on the way. Americans justified the sudden halt of Lend-Lease on the basis that the war was over and that they now had to think of their own domestic needs. But reconversion to peacetime industry was only beginning in Britain, and the dimensions of the economic problem were only just becoming clear. A British delegation headed by Lord (formerly Sir John Maynard) Keynes went to Washington to seek a loan of $3.75 billion. Months of difficult negotiation followed, because few Americans were yet conscious of the complexities of postwar European economic reconstruction. "Not one dollar for Britain," declared one American congressman, "as long as they have got the Crown Jewels in London." In July 1946, with the support of the Truman administration, the loan was successfully pushed through Congress at the cost of fatally undermining Keynes's health and forcing the British delegation to accede to onerous restrictions. Only the rumbles of the Cold War — a Russian refusal to evacuate northern Iran and a plea by Joseph P. Kennedy, the former American ambassador to Britain, for aid to the United Kingdom as a bulwark against atheistic Communism — turned the tide of congressional opinion.

The American loan was at best a stopgap. Within nine months a billion dollars had been spent, but the imbalance in international payments was as great as ever. And Britons who had been looking forward to the easing of wartime restrictions were instead exposed to the full rigors of postwar austerity. In the summer of 1946, the Labour government felt compelled to introduce bread rationing, a step that, Churchill testily reminded the country, his own government had been able to avoid even during the most difficult months of submarine warfare. During the winter of 1946–1947, conditions reached their nadir. On a typical day in February, London's *Daily Telegraph* printed the following headlines:

BREAD RATION MAY BE CUT
PEERS HEAR REVIEW OF 1947 FOOD OUTLOOK
LESS BACON AND HOME MEAT
BEER SUPPLIES TO BE HALVED IMMEDIATELY
SNOW FALLS IN LONDON

The last headline proved for the moment the most portentous, for the worst winter weather in a century prevented the movement of coal to the factories and electric plants and worsened what was already a dire fuel shortage. Railways were disrupted; gas and electricity supplies were sharply cut. The snows of winter were followed by the floods of spring, which inundated croplands and killed thousands of head of cattle and a fifth of all sheep.

In 1947 and 1948, food rations were reduced well below the wartime average to thirteen ounces of meat, eight ounces of sugar, one quart of milk, and one egg per week per person. Bread became one of a maximum of three courses in a restaurant meal, and any customer who ordered bread with the main dish forfeited the right to dessert. The food shortage posed a peculiar dilemma for advertisers who sought to resume prewar traditions but found the demand for their products far exceeding the available supply. Our milk chocolate is wonderful, exulted one manufacturer, but unfortunately we

Sir Stafford Cripps
The Chancellor of the
Exchequer became a
symbol of post–World War
II austerity. *(Hulton
Deutsch Collection)*

"are only allowed the milk to make an extremely small quantity, so if you are lucky enough to get some, do save it for the children." For the most part, however, even children were forced to substitute carrots for prewar sweets, oranges, grapes, and bananas. The average housewife spent at least an hour a day waiting in a queue, clutching her various ration books and mentally juggling ration points as well as prices. Shortages were no longer explained on the basis of "Don't you know there's a war on?" Now the favorite phrase was: "All the best goes for export." The food shortage implied drabness rather than actual starvation, but in the summer of 1946 Prime Minister Attlee suggested that those British citizens who felt quixotically impelled to send food parcels to the continent — where some people were worse off — might do more good by simply eating less.

Various spectacular government efforts to solve the food problem met with indifferent success. A giant peanut-raising scheme in East Africa (part of the sterling area) failed to get off the ground. Nor was the government able to make some readily available whale meat a permanent part of the British diet. In 1947 the government imported large quantities of canned snoek, a tropical fish from South Africa, as a substitute for meat. Although the fish was given considerable publicity, with a ministerial snoek-tasting party and government-published recipes for "snoek piquante," snoek turned out to provide more food for cartoonists and music-hall comedians than for ordinary people. The trouble with snoek, as even one Labour minister conceded, was that it was "palatable, but rather dull." A few years later the large stocks of canned snoek which remained unsold were reduced in price, given new labels, and sold as "selected fish food for cats and kittens."

The food shortage was accompanied by a notable shortage of clothing. "We must *all* have new clothes," confided King George VI to Attlee in 1945; "my family is down to the lowest ebb." Clothes, like food, were rationed on a points system; and in 1947 when Princess Elizabeth, the heiress to the throne, was married to Lieutenant Philip Mountbatten, it was officially announced that for the occasion the princess had been given one hundred clothing coupons, bridesmaids twenty-three coupons each, and pages ten coupons each. The clothing shortage caused the new women's fashions of 1947 to become an issue of state. Few people objected to women looking more feminine; they were happy enough to see rounded shoulders and nipped-in waists replace the angular uniform look that women's clothing had taken on in wartime. But the fact that the "New Look" introduced by Paris designers involved a six- to eight-inch lengthening of skirts caused dismay at the Board of Trade. Material was already in short supply; now it would make fewer garments. Paris designers won out over government officials, however, and after an unavailing propaganda campaign, even the Board of Trade was forced to concede: "We cannot dictate to women the length of their skirts."[6]

---

[6]Harry Hopkins, *The New Look* (1964), remains an illuminating near-contemporary social history of the Britain of the 1940s and 1950s.

In 1947, after a brief postwar respite, the use of gasoline for civilian cars was entirely prohibited, and newspapers were restricted once more to four-page issues. Tobacco taxes were raised by 43 percent, and for some months a 75 percent import duty was placed on American films in order to discourage the consumption of two products that used up so much of the again-dwindling supply of dollars. The fuel shortage led to occasional factory shutdowns and to sporadic cuts in the electricity supply. As during the war, it was deemed unpatriotic to fill a bathtub with more than a few inches of water, and to turn on an electric heater in the summer was made a criminal offense. For a time, all right of foreign travel for nonbusiness or nonmilitary purposes was suspended.

The member of the Labour government who, first as president of the Board of Trade and from 1947 on as minister of economic affairs and Chancellor of the Exchequer, came to epitomize the spirit of austerity was Sir Stafford Cripps. He was lean in appearance and ascetic in habit, and his earliest ambition had been to be a churchman rather than a politician. His confidence in his own rightness made him a difficult colleague but an inspiring leader. One can detect admiration as well as criticism in Churchill's comment: "There, but for the grace of God, goes God." Thought too intellectual by some, Cripps was still the most successful of the Labour ministers in appealing to the better natures of his countrymen, for he sought to make them understand the restrictions of austerity as joint contributions to a national revival. Cripps, a left-wing party heretic during the 1930s, was willing and able to ask miners to work an extra half-hour a day and could address the Trades Union Congress in terms that David Ricardo would have understood. "There is only a certain sized cake," he told the union leaders, "and if a lot of people want a larger slice they can only get it by taking it from others."

In 1948 and 1949, the economic situation gradually began to improve, not least because the United States had come to realize that only substantial American assistance could truly revive the floundering European economies. The European Recovery Program, or Marshall Plan (named after U.S. Secretary of State George C. Marshall), came into effect in 1948 and did much to encourage European economic cooperation and to break the vicious circle of shortages in one sector of the economy that impeded the recovery of another. Britain received $2.7 billion in American aid between 1948 and 1951.[7]

Britain did have to undergo one last major "dollar crisis" in the summer of 1949, when an American recession depressed the flow of British exports. After a long delay for fear of incurring the stigma of fiscal irresponsibility, Cripps persuaded the Labour government in September 1949 to devalue the pound in terms of the dollar from $4.03 to $2.80. Other sterling area countries followed suit. As a result British goods

---

[7]The story is explained in full detail in Michael J. Hogan, *The Marshall Plan: America, Britain, and the Reconstruction of Western Europe, 1947–1952* (1987).

became cheaper in dollar countries, and American imports became more costly in the United Kingdom. The policy implied that the Labour government preferred to risk price and wage inflation over a revival of large-scale unemployment. The action illustrated two other phenomena as well: first, in the post-1945 world (at least until 1971), the American dollar (still tied in value to the price of gold) had largely taken the place of gold as the standard by which all other currencies were valued; and second, the British Treasury had come to regulate the financial transactions, domestic and international, of Britain's citizens to a far greater degree than ever before in time of peace. To that extent, a "Keynesian Revolution" in economic thinking had indeed taken place. Critics would argue later, to be sure, that the economic policies of the Labour government had bought short-term stability at the expense of long-term growth.

Not all Britons met the perils of adversity in the proverbial fashion of pulling in their belts, putting their shoulders to the wheel, making the best of a bad job, and keeping their upper lips stiff. The multitude of restrictions could not help but invite violations. In 1946 groups of squatters settled in expensive but unoccupied houses in central London, while others made homes of deserted army barracks. The squatters were evicted from the London homes, but the use of army barracks as emergency housing was eventually legalized. Black-marketeers were active, and the "spiv" enjoyed a temporary notoriety. He was the sort of man who smuggled liquor from France by motorboat, hijacked a truckload of chocolates, ferried illegal immigrants, engaged in unlawful currency exchanges, and often got away with his misdeeds. Twice as many criminal acts were recorded in 1948 as in 1937, and people spoke of a postwar crime wave. In similar fashion, some businessmen began to employ expense accounts as a method of evading taxes. Yet the majority of the population abided by a rationing system that was deemed onerous but equitable and that did, by and large, live up to the Labour government motto: "Fair shares for all."

Although the Attlee government inspired a high degree of political idealism, it did not inspire a new literary mood. More people than ever were reading books — the "paperback revolution" had been launched under the Penguin imprint — but the most notable literary luminaries of the time were prewar authors such as Evelyn Waugh, Graham Greene, Anthony Powell, and Elizabeth Bowen. They — and on a more popular level, authors such as Angela Thirkell — commemorated the passing of the old aristocracy or celebrated the resistance of old country families and other members of the upper-middle classes to engulfment by the values of "mass society." Even Labour party intellectuals had long held an ambivalent attitude toward these same masses: on the one hand they wished to identify with them; on the other, they wished to uplift them. It was more than coincidence that in 1946 the BBC introduced its "Third Programme," a broadcast service of serious music, high-level lectures, and discussion, which in practice appealed to at most 2 percent of the total listening audience.

The postwar English theater reacted against the naturalistic productions of the 1930s in favor of free-verse plays such as Christopher Fry's *The Lady's Not for Burning* (1949) and T. S. Eliot's *The Cocktail Party* (1949). Eliot, an American expatriate, had by this time become "perhaps the most influential highbrow on either side of the Atlantic, the focus of intellectual reaction against the new mass society." In the meantime, the English film industry underwent its own notable artistic, if not financial, renaissance and brought world renown to such actors as Laurence Olivier and Alec Guinness. And by the end of the decade, television, reintroduced by the BBC in 1946, seemed likely to replace the cinema as the mass entertainment of the future, just as the cinema had replaced the music hall.

Imperial Twilight: Asia and the Middle East

One accomplishment of the post–World War II Labour government likely to be permanently remembered is the voluntary granting of independence to India. World War II had imbued Indian National Congress leaders with a grim determination to bring their long and largely nonviolent drive for national independence to a triumphant conclusion. The decision of Churchill's wartime government to defer any decision on independence until after the war did little but add fuel to Indian discontent. The Labour victory in the British general election of 1945 was decisive in determining that the British Empire in India would end. The Labour party had long pledged itself to procure self-government for India, and Attlee himself had been a convert to such a policy ever since a visit to India in 1927. Post–World War II Britain might conceivably have thwarted Indian independence by military means, for most Indian soldiers in the Indian army had remained steadfastly loyal to their British officers throughout the war. Russian and American suspicions notwithstanding, the British lacked the desire, however, to cling by force to what would rapidly have become an economic liability. The two-centuries-old empire in India may have been partly won by force, but it had been held less by military power than by prestige and by widespread Indian acceptance. Once British prestige (and that of the West generally) had been dissipated by two world wars, the granting of independence was ultimately the only solution in keeping with Britain's own political ideals and institutions.

The question from July 1945 on was not whether, but how. Was independent India to be maintained as the single political unit that British rule had fashioned, or was it again to be divided, as so often in its history, along religious and linguistic lines? The Indian National Congress under Gandhi and Jawaharlal Nehru continued to agitate for complete unity, but Mohammed Ali Jinnah's Moslem League was stronger than ever and increasingly fearful that an independent India would fall under Hindu domination. In 1946 Jinnah briefly agreed to a federal India that controlled defense and foreign affairs but left the separate states otherwise self-governing. When Nehru then insisted on a stronger central parliament, Jinnah reneged and began to press openly and with increasing adamance in favor of a separate Moslem state, Pakistan.

The impasse was broken early in 1947 by Attlee's declaration that India would have independence by 1948 at the latest and by his appointment of Admiral Lord Mountbatten as viceroy to bring matters to fruition. A great-grandson of Queen Victoria as well as a World War II military hero, Mountbatten lived up to his reputation for speed and decisiveness as well as personal charm by working out — together with V. P. Menon, his secretary — a partition plan and then convincing not only Nehru and Jinnah and the autonomous Indian princes but also the Labour government and the Conservative opposition of its viability. The knowledge that the end of British rule was actually coming led to demoralization and uncertainty within the Indian civil and police services, and Mountbatten decided therefore to speed up the timetable yet further. The British Parliament passed the appropriate legislation without division, and August 15, 1947, was celebrated as Independence Day by Indians and Pakistanis alike.

The one aspect of the transfer of power that afterward evoked the greatest criticism was that insufficient provision had been made for the migration of Moslem minorities in India to Pakistan and of Hindu minorities in Pakistan to India. Although the leaders of both new states had

Nehru and Gandhi on the Eve of Indian Independence (1946)   *(UPI/Bettmann/ Corbis)*

promised protection to minorities, neither community felt safe, and amid sporadic rioting some 10.5 million people fled from one state to another. Gandhi's pleas for tolerance helped to limit the violence in Bengal, but more than half a million people perished in communal rioting on the subcontinent. And a year later Gandhi was himself assassinated by a fellow Hindu. Clearly, neither Hindu nor Moslem leaders had anticipated such violence on the part of their followers. Yet had the British sought to delay their departure, they might simply have become the victims of a renewed sense of distrust and — as happened to the Dutch in Indonesia and the French in Indo-China — the villains of an Indian civil war.

In the aftermath of independence, India, Pakistan, and nearby Ceylon (the future Sri Lanka) all agreed to remain members of the Commonwealth of Nations. Nehru even recommended Mountbatten as India's first governor-general. The status of a dominion was exchanged early in 1950 for that of a republic associated with the Commonwealth and recognizing the British monarch as "Head of the Commonwealth," a definition that stretched still further but did not sever completely the political ties that had so long bound Britain and India.

For neither India nor Pakistan did independence resolve the question of what kind of government policy would best encourage economic growth or most effectively sustain a food supply for an ever-burgeoning population. Inevitably also, independence dissipated the temporary bonds of unity that the common struggle against British rule had fashioned. With the revolt of Bangladesh (East Pakistan) in 1972, Pakistan split into two separate nations, and a supposedly secular India was increasingly riven by the sectarian strife that led in 1984 to the assassination of Nehru's daughter, prime minister Indira Gandhi, and in 1991 to the assassination of his grandson, former and would-be prime minister Rahjiv Gandhi. Despite political unrest and corruption, India remains at the outset of the twenty-first century the world's most populous democracy, and it largely retains the parliament, the independent judiciary, and the civil service system instituted by Britain. In a linguistically divided land, English remains the most accessible common language for India's educated minority.

Pakistan soon substituted a more authoritarian presidential system for its parliamentary structure but it, too, has retained some British institutions, as has Burma, which received its independence in January 1948 but which declined to keep any association with the Commonwealth. Although prompted by domestic economic difficulties as well as by long-standing political principles, and although marred by violence between Hindus and Moslems, Britain's peaceful transfer of power in India remains a remarkable example of enlightened statesmanship.[8]

---

[8]V. P. Menon, *The Transfer of Power in India* (1952); Michael Edwardes, *The Last Years of British India* (1963); B. N. Pandey, *The Break-Up of British India* (1969).

Such statesmanship was less evident in the Middle East, especially in Palestine, where the British had been dominant since their occupation of Jerusalem in 1918 and their assumption of a League of Nations mandate in 1919. The Balfour Declaration of 1917 had pledged the establishment of a national home for the Jewish people in Palestine. At the same moment when the British government was seeking to win the support of Jews throughout the world by this move, it was also encouraging an Arab national revival against the Ottoman Empire. Thus the immediate dictates of World War I diplomacy trapped successive British governments on the horns of a dilemma largely of their own making. Although the 1920s brought much economic progress to Palestine, clashes between the growing number of Jewish immigrants and the resident Arabs became ever more frequent during the interwar years. A British plan of partition was rejected by the Arabs in 1936, and a subsequent Arab rebellion was put down by force. In a 1939 White Paper, however, the British government announced its intention of creating a single independent state that would necessarily have become predominantly Arab in population. Jewish immigration would be limited to 1,500 people per month until 1944, when it was to be halted altogether. Although those restrictions were eased a little during the war, the policy appeared callous to the Jewish community in Palestine and to those few Jews who escaped Nazi clutches while the war was going on.

Tensions in Palestine itself eased somewhat during the Second World War, however, and in its aftermath men such as Ernest Bevin, foreign secretary in the Labour government, sought to maintain a British sphere of influence in the entire region. He hoped to promote social reform there and "to develop the Middle East as a producing area (in agriculture as well as in oil) to help our own economy and take the place of India."[9] This was a dream shared by few Egyptian or Arab leaders, and in Palestine Zionist leaders were far more concerned with working for the establishment of a self-governing Jewish state. It seemed imperative to provide a homeland for those Jewish refugees who had escaped the Nazi gas chambers, but the British government remained reluctant to alienate Arab opinion by again permitting unrestricted Jewish immigration. The desire to maintain oil concessions in the Middle East, fear for the safety of the Suez Canal, pro-Arab sentiment on the part of some officials, and a genuine sense of being a neutral party above the battle all influenced the formation of British policy. The administration of Palestine involved 100,000 British troops and cost the British Exchequer more than £100 million between 1945 and 1947. Bevin felt sure at first that he could resolve the dilemma; and both he and many other Britons were increasingly frustrated as Jewish terrorist groups attacked isolated groups of British military personnel and on one occasion blew up the largest hotel in Jerusalem. The deaths of British soldiers led to a number of anti-

---

[9]William Roger Louis, *The British Empire in the Middle East, 1945–1951* (1985).

Semitic outbursts within Britain and a resentment on the part of Bevin against a widespread pro-Zionist attitude in the United States. Because local Arabs proved equally uncooperative, Britain turned the matter over to the United Nations.

In 1947 the U.N. voted to partition the Palestine mandate in a manner that would have provided the Jewish population with an independent but territorially almost indefensible state. The Arab states refused to acknowledge the decision, and Britain abstained, announcing that it would end its Palestine mandate in 1948. Bevin's expectation was that, without British protection, the Jews would be driven into the sea and that only by withdrawing their army could the British prove how necessary their presence was. An Arab-Jewish war did break out in April 1948; but contrary to British anticipations, the beleaguered Jewish forces not only emerged victorious but upset the original boundaries established by the United Nations and forged a state with defensible frontiers. (The neighboring kingdom of Jordan occupied most of the remainder of what had been the Palestine mandate.) An independent state of Israel was proclaimed, and Chaim Weizmann, the naturalized British citizen (and chemist) who had helped to secure the Balfour Declaration, became the country's first president.

While Palestine proved in some ways to be the Labour government's "Irish Question," actual Anglo-Irish relations were for the time being more harmonious. In the course of the 1930s, the independent Irish Parliament had removed most of the links that still bound Ireland to Britain after the treaty of 1922. The parliamentary oath of loyalty to the British monarch was abolished; so was the post of governor-general and the right on the part of an Irish citizen to look to the British Privy Council as a final court of legal appeal. After 1937, when a new republican constitution was adopted by the Irish Free State, the only remaining link was that British diplomats continued to represent Ireland in those countries to which Ireland sent no envoys of its own. Ireland broke this last tie in 1948, and Britain in the Ireland Act of 1949 acknowledged that the Irish Republic had ceased to be part of "His Majesty's Dominions" but guaranteed to the Northern Irish that their section of the island would remain part of the United Kingdom as long as their autonomous parliament preferred such an arrangement. The Ireland Act also stated that although the Irish Republic was completely independent, its citizens were not to be treated in Britain as foreigners. They were to retain free access as visitors or immigrants and, if resident in the United Kingdom, the right to vote in British elections. The economies of the two nations remained as tightly intertwined as before.

The Cold War

Nationalism was one of the two forces that did most to determine the shape of the post-1945 world. The other was the Cold War between the

Soviet Union and the Western allies. In one sense, the Cold War was implicit in the very manner in which World War II had come about. Although the fact was little recognized at the time, World War II had ceased, from 1940 on, to be a war that the Western democracies could win in any absolute sense. By then they were badly outmatched, and of the big powers on the democratic side only Britain and potentially the United States remained. On the totalitarian side stood Germany, Italy, Japan, and Russia. If these four states could ever fully ally, the cause of Western democracy was lost. The only manner in which Britain and the United States could possibly defeat Germany and Japan was by means of Russian aid. Soviet Russia had disturbed much of Western opinion ever since the Communist revolution of 1917 by its state-run economy, its dictatorial government, and the manner in which it had purged millions of Soviet citizens. But in the years before World War II, Russia had not overtly attacked its neighbors. Germany *had* and was therefore seen as the stronger military power and as the more obvious threat to world peace.

The problem, however, was this. If the Western democracies could win the war only by allying themselves with one of the nondemocratic powers, then quite obviously the ultimate victory would strengthen the nondemocratic regime at the same time that it strengthened the democracies. In the long run this was exactly what happened. Germany and Japan were defeated, but in the process Russia filled the vacuum of power created in eastern Europe and (for a briefer time) in parts of eastern Asia. As a gigantic country boasting the world's largest army, it soon came to be acknowledged as one of the world's only two superpowers.

Admiration for Russian heroism in wartime prompted hopes in both Britain and the United States that the Grand Alliance might continue into the postwar years, and in 1944 and 1945 both governments did much to accede to Stalin's wishes. Thus they compelled some 2,700,000 anti-Soviet émigrés (many of whom had never fought on the German side) to return to a realm that condemned some to death and most others to long prison terms.[10] The hope of continued cooperation was soon shattered, however, and in the very process of formulating peace treaties for the nations involved in World War II, the foreign ministers of the Big Three found themselves increasingly at odds. Peace treaties were achieved for Italy, Finland, Hungary, Bulgaria, and Rumania in 1947, but Russia refused to sign the 1951 settlement with Japan.

No peace treaty at all was achieved for occupied Germany. Instead, the supposedly temporary zones of military occupation became fixed and eventually fortified boundaries — the American, British, and French zones of occupation being joined into the Federal Republic of (West) Germany in 1949. At the same time, the Soviet zone was transformed into a Soviet satellite called the German Democratic Republic. Although the Soviet Union had pledged itself to support "free elections" in Poland

---

[10]Nikolai Tolstoy, *The Secret Betrayal, 1944–1947* (1978).

and the other countries of eastern Europe, it became clear between 1945 and 1948 that the Soviet definition of the phrase differed greatly from the British or American. By a combination of force and fraud, coalition governments gave way to Communist party domination. With the passive or active assistance of the Red armies of occupation — whose initial ruthlessness had shocked Western observers — Poland, Hungary, Rumania, Bulgaria, and, for a time, Yugoslavia all became Soviet satellites.[11]

The one exception was Greece. Here Churchill, looking ahead more pragmatically than Roosevelt to the probabilities of the postwar world, had in 1944 struck an unofficial bargain with Stalin. If Russian influence was to predominate in Rumania, Hungary, and Bulgaria — and Churchill did not see how this could be prevented at a time when the Red Army was occupying these areas — then British influence should predominate in Greece and influence in Yugoslavia should be divided on a 50-50 basis. Reports of such an arrangement were anathema to liberal opinion in both Britain and the United States; but, as a result, British troops were sent to Greece in 1944 and helped its embattled government prevent a Communist takeover. In January 1945 Churchill sped to Athens in person to arrange a temporary truce and a national plebiscite.

The Labour government inherited the responsibility later that year, and although unhappy with the decision of the Greeks to restore their king, it continued British support. The only alternative appeared to be the complete Communist domination of the Balkans. Between 1944 and 1947, successive British governments spent £87 million on military and economic aid to Greece and forgave the Greeks another £46 million in war debts. As Bevin told a Labour party conference: "We cannot afford to lose our position in the Middle East; our navy, our shipping, a great deal of our motive power for our industry, in the shape of oil, are there. . . . The standard of life and the wages of the workmen of this country are dependent upon these things." The words might have been those of Palmerston; the only difficulty was that gunboat diplomacy was no longer sufficient to uphold British influence, and Britain's economic resources were sorely strained.

In 1946, the year in which Winston Churchill made famous the term "Iron Curtain" in a speech in Fulton, Missouri, some Americans began speaking of a "Cold War" between Britain and Russia in the Balkans and in Iran, in which the American role was that of bystander. For the

---

[11]Victor Rothwell, *Britain and the Cold War, 1941–1947* (1982), and Anne Deighton, *The Impossible Peace: Britain, the Division of Germany, and the Origins of the Cold War* (1990), clarify the oft-neglected British role. Alan Bullock's *Ernest Bevin, Foreign Secretary, 1945–1951* (1983) is of central importance. Various aspects of the story are explored in Hugh Thomas, *Armed Truce: The Beginnings of the Cold War, 1945–1946* (1987); Elizabeth Barker, *The British Between the Superpowers, 1945–50* (1984); D. Cameron Watt, *Succeeding John Bull: America in Britain's Place, 1900–1975* (1984); and William Roger Louis and Hedley Bull, eds., *The Special Relationship: Anglo-American Relations Since 1945* (1987).

The Liberation of Athens (1944)   As British forces enter the city, Greek civilians waving British and American flags celebrate their release from Nazi occupation. *(UPI/Bettmann/Corbis)*

moment at least, there was a pronounced American tendency toward bringing armies back home and limiting commitments abroad. For a time Bevin was almost as fearful of American isolationism as of Russian expansion. But in the spring of 1947 the British government convinced the United States that the United Kingdom could no longer provide the economic and military support necessary to ensure that Greece and its neighbor Turkey were kept out of the Russian sphere. The result was the Truman Doctrine, an American decision to take Britain's place in those two countries. Henceforth the United States was to be "the leader of the free world" in the "containment" of Soviet expansion, and Britain was forced by economic necessity to become a junior partner in the Western alliance.

Bevin was subject to severe criticism by left-wing members of his party who sought to explain away Stalin's actions in a manner analogous to the way some Conservatives had attempted to excuse Hitler's a decade before. Yet the most influential assessments of the actualities and potentialities of Soviet totalitarianism were the work of a disenchanted, independent British socialist, George Orwell (1903–1950), whose *Animal Farm* (1945) dramatized in allegorical form the idea that the Soviet Union represented a "revolution betrayed" and whose *Nineteen Eighty-Four* (1949) projected (if precautions were not taken) a totalitarian anti-utopia governed by "Big Brother" and by the practice of "doublethink."

The Labour government welcomed successive American efforts to strengthen western Europe. Thus Bevin hailed what became the Marshall Plan of 1948–1952 as a "lifeline to a sinking man." The program was not initially a Cold War measure, but the economic recovery it promoted did much to weaken the appeal of the large Communist parties of France and Italy. The Berlin airlift of 1948–1949 successfully repulsed a Russian attempt to drive the Western powers out of their outpost in that isolated and divided city. Also in 1948 a Communist coup toppled the government of Czechoslovakia: thus the most democratic of pre–World War II states in eastern Europe became the last to fall behind the Iron Curtain. In 1949, the Communist movement completed its takeover of China, and the Soviet Union successfully tested its own nuclear bomb. By then, many observers were predicting the imminent outbreak of World War III. As a result, during that same year and in large part at Bevin's initiative, Britain and the United States — along with Canada, France, Italy, and some of the smaller states of western Europe — created NATO, the North Atlantic Treaty Organization. For the first time in their history, both Britain and the United States entered into a long-term peacetime multipartner military alliance under a unified military command; its immediate purpose was to deter a possible Soviet invasion of western Europe. When in June 1950, with Soviet blessing, Communist North Korea invaded South Korea, Britain cooperated with the United States in combating — under U.N. auspices — this new onslaught. By this time, the Cold War was in full swing and the pattern of the postwar world had apparently been set.

The Elections of 1950 and 1951

In the meantime, the Labour government had embarked on the enactment of its last major piece of domestic legislation. In October 1948 it introduced its bill to nationalize the iron and steel industry. Labour had pledged itself to nationalize steel in its 1945 election program. Its leaders contended that the steel oligopoly ought to be the servant and not the master of the people and that only nationalization could provide security against the operation of otherwise uncontrollable economic forces. The Conservative opposition had criticized earlier nationalization measures in a halfhearted manner, because in the case of coal and electricity Labour had so obviously built on Tory foundations. The opposition launched an all-out attack against this latest proposal, however, because steel was not an unprofitable public utility; it was a prosperous and efficient manufacturing industry in whose modernization and expansion large sums had recently been invested. Unlike the mines, its labor-relations record was good, and Conservative speakers could point to specific steel-union leaders who were antagonistic or apathetic toward nationalization. With the Labour majority in the House of Commons still huge, the steel nationalization bill passed easily; but the government did agree to a House of

Lords request that its operation be held up pending another general election.

Fearing a House of Lords veto, the Labour government had in 1947 introduced an act that limited the suspensive veto power of the upper house from two years to one. The bill became law in 1949. It followed the tradition of the Parliament Act of 1911, just as Labour's Representation of the People Act of 1948 followed the steps of the Reform Acts of 1832, 1867, 1884, 1918, and 1928. The act of 1948 eliminated the right of plural voting (for persons who had a home in one parliamentary district and a business in another) and the right, instituted under James I, of separate parliamentary representation for graduates of the universities of Oxford and Cambridge (and subsequently a few other British universities). There was also a complete redistribution of seats, and the number of M.P.'s was reduced from 640 to 625, each representing approximately 56,000 persons.

The Conservatives had long been looking forward to the general election that was held in February 1950. After initial discouragement, the party had, under the chairmanship of Lord Woolton, refurbished its national and constituency organization and revitalized its research bureau. From the time of the fuel crisis of early 1947, the Conservative opposition had, with increasing effectiveness, protested against government restrictions and the necessity of having to "Starve with Strachey and Shiver with Shinwell," the ministers of food and fuel respectively. The government was castigated for mismanaging the economy and Britain's position in the world and for placing, in the case of steel nationalization, ideology above the national welfare.

The Labour government defended its record by observing that the perils of postwar reconversion had been successfully weathered and that production totals had reached a point almost 50 percent above those of 1938. The country had remained free from large-scale unemployment and large-scale industrial unrest; and the government's social-insurance measures and National Health Service had guaranteed all British citizens against domestic perils not of their own making. Although 84 percent of the electorate voted, an all-time record, the election results were far from satisfactory to either side: Labour, 315; Conservatives, 298; Liberals, 9. Almost all the independents elected in 1945, including two Communists, were defeated.

The election had produced a virtual stalemate, but party discipline was sufficiently strong to enable the Labour government to limp along for another sixteen months and to pass its controversial steel-nationalization bill. A public corporation, the Iron and Steel Federation, took over the stock of the private companies, but for the moment their day-to-day management was little disturbed. The return of at least partial prosperity enabled the government to end many of the restrictions of the austerity period. Bread rationing had ended in 1948 and the rationing of clothing in 1949. In 1950 all limitations on restaurant meals were removed, and rationing ceased for milk, flour, eggs, and soap. London's fountains and bright lights were turned on again. The Festival of Britain in 1951 commemorated the hundredth anniversary of the Great Exhibition of 1851 with displays illustrating "British Contributions to World Civilization in the Arts of Peace." Although the exhibition was well attended and provided London permanently with the beautiful Royal Festival Hall, the spirit of overriding self-confidence of 1851 was absent.

The Labour cabinet of 1950–1951 was gravely weakened by the resignations of Sir Stafford Cripps and Ernest Bevin for reasons of health and by the resignations of Aneurin Bevan and Harold Wilson (1916–1995), the youthful president of the Board of Trade, for reasons of policy. Bevan and Wilson objected to the charges for spectacles and dentures that Hugh Gaitskell (1900–1963), who had replaced Cripps as Chancellor of the Exchequer, had proposed in his 1951 budget. That budget had also raised income taxes and sales taxes in order to pay for the rearmament made necessary by the creation of NATO and the onset of the Korean War. Labour's left wing was unhappy about both rearmament and the Attlee government's firmly pro-American foreign policy. Faced with a serious rift within his party which made it difficult to control Parliament with so slim a majority, Attlee decided in September 1951 to call for a new general election.

The campaign rehashed the issues of the year before. The government saw the choice as one between "Forward with Labour" and "Backward with the Tories." Churchill, accused by Labour's left wing of being a warmonger, was still seeking redress for the defeat of 1945 and spoke more moderately and more effectively than he had in 1945 or 1950. The Conservatives, he indicated, would accept the social services and almost all nationalization proposals already enacted except steel. The true choice, Churchill contended, was that Conservatives offered a ladder (on which everyone could rise), whereas Labour offered merely a queue (in which everyone took his turn). The results of the election were again very close: Conservatives, 321; Labour, 295; Liberals, 6. Labour still had a slim popular-vote plurality, and only one voter in eighty had switched from Labour to Conservative since the previous general election; but this was sufficient to make Winston Churchill prime minister again at the age of seventy-six.

In the course of six years, Labour had set the pattern of Britain's post–World War II world — at least through the 1970s: it had nationalized most of the service industries of the state; it had successfully presided over the dissolution of much of Britain's Asian empire; and, although it may not have transformed Britain into a "Socialist Commonwealth," it had made the welfare state a reality. Labour's policies had helped to make Britain a significantly more egalitarian society. Whereas back in 1910 some 5 percent of the people managed to acquire 43 percent of after-tax personal income, by 1949 the top 20 percent received 45 percent of that income. (The latter ratio was to remain virtually unchanged during the next three decades.) At the same time, Labour had transformed Britain into one of the world's most regulation-ridden and bureaucratic of lands: by 1951 more than 26 percent of its people were working for the government at a time that 17 percent of Americans and 14 percent of West Germans did so.

The End of Austerity

The narrow Conservative victory in the general election of October 1951 was to lead to thirteen years of Conservative rule, the longest continuous period of predominance by one party since before 1832. Few political leaders of either major party would have considered such a prospect likely in 1951.[12]

The very slenderness of the Tory triumph made it unlikely that a major policy turnabout was in store; and the early budgets of Richard Austen Butler, Churchill's new Chancellor of the Exchequer, so resembled those of Hugh Gaitskell, the last Labour chancellor, that the word "Butskellism" was coined. Yet, after the immediate international-payments crisis of 1951 had been resolved, there was a notable change in mood; in the course of the next few years, much of the remaining framework of postwar austerity was dismantled. In 1952 income taxes were cut. Ration controls were removed from one food item after another until in the summer of 1954 the British housewife, after almost a decade and a half, was given the right to throw away her family's ration books, while she and her husband were encouraged to invest in a new home. One of the ministry's proudest boasts was its success in promoting the construction of houses: 50 percent more each year than its Labour predecessor. As minister of local government and planning, Harold Macmillan (1894–1986) promoted private builders as well as local housing authorities. Small steps were also taken to ease the rent-control system that dated back to the First World War. The more fundamental transformations wrought by the postwar Labour government were, however, largely kept intact. The only significant change in the National Health Service was the addition of a minimal charge per drug prescription.

Except for the iron and steel industry and, in part, the trucking industry, the new Conservative government did not attempt to reverse the Labour program of nationalization. (An act of 1953 restored the steel industry to private hands under "an adequate measure of public supervision"; the actual process of denationalizing took a decade.) Nationalization was for the time being proving neither a cure-all nor a major drawback for either the coal industry or the railways. Mine productivity even rose slightly during the 1950s, although the market for coal was continuing slowly to decline. The railways, converting gradually from steam power to diesel or electric power, were hampered by a lack of capi-

---

[12]Relevant works include Anthony Seldon's *Churchill's Indian Summer: The Conservative Government 1951–55* (1981), Henry Pelling, *Churchill's Peacetime Ministry 1951–55* (1997), and providing a broader context, Kevin Jefferys, *Retreat from New Jerusalem: British Politics, 1951–64* (1997).

tal, by renewed motor vehicle competition, and by a public insistence that branch lines continue to operate even when, in strict economic terms, they no longer paid their way.

The oldest of Britain's nationalized concerns, the Post Office, retained its reputation for efficiency. The Post Office Savings Bank, which celebrated its centenary in 1961, utilized a central accounting system to enable any of its twenty-two million depositors to make deposits or withdrawals at any of the United Kingdom's twenty thousand post offices and became in this sense for a time the largest banking institution in the world. The most productive of the nationalized industries was the Central Electricity Authority which, among other things, pioneered in the utilization of nuclear energy for nonmilitary purposes with its power plant at Calder Hall, Cumberland, in 1956.

Diplomatic Achievements

The second Churchill ministry provided the opportunity not only for the relaxation of austerity measures but also for the evocation of a prewar note of pomp and circumstance in the solemn state funeral accorded to King George VI early in 1952 and in the triumphant coronation provided for his daughter Queen Elizabeth II in the summer of 1953. "I suppose that you and I have witnessed the coronation of the last British sovereign," wrote the historian Macaulay to a friend in 1838; but a century and a quarter later the monarchy, however altered as an institution, appeared as popular as ever in British life. Churchill, who had served in the army of Queen Victoria and had first been elected to Parliament in her lifetime, now had the satisfaction of leading his fellow Commonwealth prime ministers, including India's Nehru, in the royal procession that marked the crowning of Victoria's great-great-granddaughter. The Westminster Abbey ritual followed a tradition dating back in part to the Anglo-Saxon kings.

Like Elizabeth I, Elizabeth II became monarch in her twenty-sixth year, and people began to talk of a new Elizabethan Age. Although one of the new Elizabethans, Sir Edmund Hillary, conquered Mount Everest in 1953 and another, Roger Bannister, became in 1954 the first man to run the mile in less than four minutes, the new age provided relatively fewer opportunities for individual daring. In the diplomatic arena, it seemed to promise little but prolonged and often futile negotiations at the foreign-minister level. Churchill, who had been one of the statesmen most alert to the threat posed by the Soviet Union during the later 1940s, proved equally eager after Stalin's death early in 1953 to use diplomacy to ease Cold War tensions. He hoped to set up another Big Three meeting, but President Eisenhower of the United States was reluctant, Georgi Malenkov (Stalin's immediate successor) was insecurely established in Moscow, and Churchill himself was physically handicapped by the stroke that he had suffered in July.

Yet Stalin's death did lead to a Cold War thaw. It helped bring the Korean War to an end in the summer of 1953. A year later, the efforts of Sir Anthony Eden, Churchill's foreign secretary, brought at least a temporary close to the prolonged war that French forces had been fighting in what had been French Indo-China. Part of the area, North Vietnam, was acknowledged as under Communist control, but the others — Laos, Cambodia, and South Vietnam — retained varying degrees of autonomy.

From time to time, Britain also acted the role of diplomatic broker closer to home. Churchill had himself been a prime mover in the post–World War II forces working for a Western European Union; Britain had joined with France, Italy, Belgium, the Netherlands, and Luxembourg in an organization by that name in 1948. Britain did not, however, seize the postwar opportunity to create a western European customs union; its transoceanic ties, both economic and sentimental, still predominated over its links to the continent. Nor did Britain join the projected European Defense Community of 1952–1954, the purpose of which was to integrate the military forces of a rearming West Germany within a multinational European force. When the French parliament rejected the EDC project that its own government had helped to formulate, the American Secretary of State Dulles threatened "an agonizing reappraisal" of American commitment to Europe. Anthony Eden broke the resulting impasse by promising to keep British troops on the continent indefinitely as a pledge of support, provided the French would accept West Germany as part of the North Atlantic Treaty Organization. West Germany was admitted into NATO in 1955.

In order to give force to its own foreign-policy initiatives and in order to advertise to the world that Britain was still a great power, the Churchill government tested Britain's own atomic bomb in 1952 — the Labour government having earlier decided to undertake its production — and in 1955 Churchill announced that Britain would follow the American and Soviet example and also build its own hydrogen bomb — a weapon a thousand times as powerful as the nuclear bomb that had been dropped on Hiroshima. Such a weapon was successfully tested in 1957.

In April 1955 Churchill retired from the prime ministership in his eighty-first year. Only Palmerston and Gladstone had held the office at a more advanced age. Eden, Churchill's second in command for a decade and a half, was the obvious successor. The Conservative party could claim a number of economic and diplomatic successes; and Eden, suave and debonair in appearance and a respected if never genuinely popular figure, easily led his party to its second straight general-election victory in 1955. The Labour party had developed no dramatic new program, and its slogans of "Nationalization" and "Full Employment" had lost much of their appeal and novelty. The party was, moreover, internally divided by the left-wing Bevanite faction. The electorate proved relatively apathetic; only 76.8 percent voted. Both parties lost votes, but the Conservatives lost fewer and therefore led their rivals 49.6

percent to 46.4 percent in the popular vote and 347 to 277 in parliamentary seats.

The new prime minister was immediately involved in the type of activity for which he had won the greatest renown, diplomacy. In May 1955 the Big Powers agreed to an Austrian peace treaty, and after seventeen years of occupation — first German and then Russian and Western — Austria once again became an independent (and neutral) state. The Austrian peace treaty led to a Big Four meeting at Geneva in July 1955, with President Eisenhower, Prime Minister Bulganin (accompanied by Soviet party Chairman Nikita Khrushchev), Prime Minister Eden, and Premier Fauré of France in attendance. In the afterglow of "the spirit of Geneva," the two Russian leaders made a state visit to Britain. There, after a clash with a group of Labour party leaders, they informed incredulous journalists that, if they were British citizens, they would vote Conservative. The Geneva summit did not bring closer the possibility of German reunification on terms that both the Soviet Union and the Western powers would accept. Yet it did represent the implicit acknowledgment that a notable degree of diplomatic equilibrium had returned to the European scene and that co-existence was preferable to co-destruction.

A decade had passed since the end of the war. The scars of bomb damage were disappearing from the hearts of Britain's cities, and the spirit of austerity was gone. A generation of Britons had grown accustomed to a world in which large-scale unemployment was but a memory and in which a national network of social services was taken for granted. Abroad, the Cold War had subsided for the moment, and Britain played a respected diplomatic role. But even in as tradition-bound a society as Britain's, no generation was likely to remain permanently satisfied with the accomplishments of its predecessors. Nor could a world of three billion people or more be trusted to remain long in equilibrium. The decades that followed were destined to bring new challenges and new responses.

PART SIX

POST-IMPERIAL BRITAIN
1956 to 1979

MULTIRACIAL BRITAIN
London's Petticoat Lane *(Terry E. Eiler/Stock Boston)*

CHAPTER 20

The Decline of Empire and the Mood of the 1960s

The apparent complacency of the early 1950s was broken in 1956 by the Suez crisis, which seemed to illustrate — perhaps even to exaggerate — Britain's diminished role as a world power, and by the premiere of John Osborne's play *Look Back in Anger*. Its hero (or antihero), Jimmy Porter, takes for granted the social security provided by the welfare state but remains dissatisfied with his lot. "I suppose," he laments, "people of our generation aren't able to die for good causes any longer. We had all that done for us, in the thirties and the forties, when we were still kids. There aren't any good, brave causes left." These two unrelated events set the scene for the confusing decade and a half that followed: the increase of private affluence combined with economic uncertainty at the national level; the continued evolution (or devolution) of the British Empire into a Commonwealth of independent nations; and the search by British diplomats for a meaningful role in a nuclear age dominated largely by the United States and the Soviet Union. The period also brought a mood of self-questioning by a generation that either had forgotten or had never known the spirit of national self-discipline evoked by the Second World War. The result was a rebellion against traditional social values, a temporary worship of the vitality of youth, and a search for "good, brave causes" to work for within the framework of a materially successful twentieth-century society.[1]

---

[1]The events of the late 1950s and the 1960s are taken up in the books by Morgan, Sked and Cook, and Marwick cited earlier. The story may also be followed in prime ministerial biographies such as Vol. II of *Macmillan* (1988) by Alistair Horne. Among post-1945 prime ministers, the reputation of Harold Wilson has fared worst. Austen Morgan's *Harold Wilson* (1992) is highly critical; Ben Pimlott's *Harold Wilson* (1992) is distinctly more sympathetic. Christopher Booker provides a vivid if unduly schematic account of the cultural and social transformation that Britain underwent between the mid-1950s and the mid-1960s in *The Neophiliacs* (1969). See also Christie Davies, *Permissive Britain* (1975).

Suez and After

In the course of 1956, East-West relations, Britain's role in the Middle East, and Anglo-American friendship all received rude shocks. Although Britain had helped to inspire twentieth-century Arab nationalism, the Palestine dilemma of the 1940s had damaged British prestige in the area. Only long negotiations and an internal coup in Iran (encouraged by British and American secret agents) had enabled Britain to save the Anglo-Iranian Oil Company from the nationalization sought by premier Mohammad Mossadegh in the early 1950s. A military revolt in Egypt in 1952 replaced the complaisant King Farouk with the militant Colonel Abdul Gamal Nasser. In 1954 the latter obtained an agreement from Britain to withdraw the last of its military forces from Egypt in return for his promise to uphold the international convention of 1888 guaranteeing freedom of navigation through the Suez Canal.

By June 1956, when the last British troops withdrew from the Canal Zone, both Russian and American missions were already competing against each other in the Nile Valley. Doubtful about the manner in which Nasser was managing the Egyptian economy, Secretary of State John Foster Dulles announced in July that the United States would not, after all, contribute to the building of a high dam at Aswan. The British government followed suit. In violation of the spirit, if not the letter, of the 1954 treaty, Nasser retaliated by nationalizing the Suez Canal Company. Eden and many of his fellow Britons came to look upon the Egyptian dictator as a new Hitler prepared to bend the Middle East to his will, but British and French efforts to arouse world opinion against the seizure of the canal received only indifferent backing from the United States. Egypt had barred Israeli ships from the canal and was provoking border incidents; and it was partly in concert with Israel that the two European countries drew up secret plans for a military operation. On October 29, Israeli forces launched an attack across the Sinai desert. The next day Eden announced that France and Britain were intervening between Israel and Egypt and would temporarily occupy the Suez Canal. After destroying the Egyptian air force, Britain and France sent paratroopers to capture the city of Port Said. By the time a slow-moving Anglo-French amphibious armada had reached Egypt on November 6, the Egyptians and Israelis had stopped fighting, and the public justification of the intervention had become even less plausible.

The Suez intervention was to be criticized alternatively for its immorality and for its mismanagement. Clearly, Britain expected American acquiescence, if not support; instead the United States teamed up with the Soviet Union at the United Nations to condemn the Anglo-French intervention and to save Nasser at the very same time that Russian tanks were crushing a Hungarian revolution in the streets of Budapest. (At the cost of 30,000 — mostly Hungarian — lives, the Soviet Union preserved its empire in eastern Europe.) In London there was a run on the pound, and the International Monetary Fund promised a loan only if the fighting stopped. When the British and French governments agreed to a cease-fire on November 6, their forces had occupied only part of the Canal Zone, and the Egyptians themselves had blocked the waterway. In accordance with a face-saving formula, worked out primarily by Canadian Foreign Minister Lester Pearson, U.N. forces replaced the Anglo-French invaders.[2]

In the Middle East, the intervention marred a widespread British reputation for fair dealing, and its failure lowered British prestige. Back home, the affair sparked comparable criticism. Labour party leaders denounced the intervention; Aneurin Bevan, for one, condemned the use of "epic weapons for squalid and trivial ends." Labour found it difficult to capitalize on Eden's embarrassment, however, because many party followers proved clearly sympathetic to the assertion of British power. Conversely, the intervention pleased the diehard imperialists in the Conservative ranks, but at least forty Conservative M.P.'s threatened to desert the government unless the troops were withdrawn. Prime Minister Eden, whose vacillation had been at least partly responsible for the fiasco, now became physically ill, resigned his office in January 1957, and retired from active politics by moving to the House of Lords as earl of Avon.

For the first time since 1923, a monarch was given the duty of choosing a prime minister without an obvious candidate in sight. Richard Austen Butler seemed the most likely selection but, presumably acting on the advice of Lord Salisbury (the Conservative leader in the House of Lords) and Sir Winston Churchill, Queen Elizabeth nominated Harold Macmillan. A third-generation book publisher by profession, he was the grandson of a poor Victorian Scot who had risen from rags to riches. Macmillan's mother was the daughter of a small-town American doctor, his wife the daughter of a duke. He had first been elected to Parliament in 1924, and his book *The Middle Way* (1938) had promoted welfare-state inclinations within his party. He had won postwar renown as Churchill's housing minister, and he soon succeeded in restoring confidence both in his party and his country. As Macmillan insisted in 1958, "A national party like ours . . . must by its very character and tradition avoid sectional or extremist policies. It must, therefore, by definition occupy the middle ground."[3]

In the early months of 1957, public opinion polls had revealed a sizable shift toward the Labour party; but as the Suez crisis receded in the public memory and times remained prosperous, Macmillan's stock rose. Back during World War II, a knowledgeable American observer had privately contrasted the new prime minister with the old in these words: "Eden is the sheep striving to look like a man, Macmillan the man affecting to look like a sheep." An amiable, unflappable, Edwardian facade did

---

[2]Keith Kyle, *Suez* (1991), provides the fullest account. See also William Roger Louis and Roger Owens, eds., *Suez 1956: The Crisis and the Consequences* (1989).

[3]Cited in Brian Harrison, *Peaceable Kingdom: Stability and Change in Modern Britain* (1982), p. 334.

"Supermac"   *(1958 Cartoon by Vicky by permission of the Evening Standard)*

indeed hide a shrewd and at times ruthless politician who increasingly impressed his party followers as a veritable "Supermac." His Labour party counterpart in the 1959 general election was Hugh Gaitskell, the one-time economics instructor who back in 1955 had won a three-cornered parliamentary Labour party election to succeed Attlee as party leader. Gaitskell's intelligence proved to be no match for Macmillan's skills as a political campaigner, however. Nor did the Labourite find it easy to combat Conservative posters showing a smiling suburban couple next to a new car in front of a new house: "You've had it good. Have it better. Vote Conservative." In 1959, for the third consecutive time, the Conservative party won a general election; for the fourth time in a row, it gained seats. It attracted 49.4 percent of the popular vote to Labour's 43.7 percent. In the House of Commons it now possessed a majority of 365 to 258.

Twilight of Empire: Africa

Although the Suez crisis had no long-range political effects within Britain, it clearly did have long-range effects in the British Empire."I did not become the King's First Minister in order to preside over the liquidation of the British Empire," Winston Churchill had declared in 1942. And, indeed, he lived up to his word. In neither of his two ministries did any British dependency gain independence; the devolution of the greater part of the Asian empire had taken place during the Labour ministry. And, during Churchill's government of 1951–1955, Britain withstood assaults on its remaining empire by successfully suppressing a Communist revolution in Malaya and the Mau Mau revolt in Kenya.

During the second half of the decade, the situation changed. In 1956 the one-time Anglo-Egyptian Sudan was set up as an independent republic, and a long-drawn-out rebellion against French rule began in Algeria.

Nasser's survival of the Suez invasion strengthened his own prestige; and once Africa north of the Sahara had gained its independence, could Africa south of the Sahara be far behind? The Macmillan government, despite the reservations of some of its supporters, decided to embark on what proved to be a remarkably speedy program of independence within the Commonwealth for almost all of the African dependencies, rather than await the otherwise inevitable rebellions. As recently as the 1930s the British government had felt committed to the preservation of African tribal institutions. It was with initial reluctance, therefore, that the British acquiesced in the wishes of the newly urbanized and politically conscious African elites. Their leaders spoke of a future based not on tribal chiefs but on popular representation, political parties, and responsible government molded on the British example.

In few of these areas had British influence ever been as pervasive or as longstanding as in India; but in all of the new African countries — whose boundaries were often the accidental by-products of nineteenth-century European diplomacy — British economic, governmental, educational, and medical institutions had made some impact during the 1920s, 1930s, 1940s, and 1950s. Yet some of the older inhabitants of the new African states could still remember the era before European colonization. The West African state of Ghana (formerly the Gold Coast) was granted its independence in 1957. Nigeria, Britain's most populous West African dependency, gained self-government in 1960, as did British Somaliland, which became part of the republic of Somalia. Tanganyika, one of Britain's League of Nations mandates, gained its independence in 1961; three years later it formed a union with the erstwhile British protectorate of Zanzibar to become Tanzania. Sierra Leone, which had been founded as a colony for freed black slaves in 1787, became independent in 1961. Uganda, Kenya, and tiny Gambia followed in 1962, 1963, and 1965, respectively. In the euphoria of the early 1960s, voices such as those of historian D. K. Fieldhouse were little heeded. He predicted in 1964 that the end of empire in Africa was "more likely to lead to political dictatorship, economic decay, and even endemic minor wars than to brilliant new civilizations."[4] Back in London in 1966 the Colonial Office ceased to be a separate government ministry.

For a time, British members of both political parties harbored the hope that in a divided world the Commonwealth could act as a bridge between nations of different races and stages of economic development. In a tour of the Union of South Africa in 1960, Prime Minister Macmillan sought to convince the government of that country that it, too, should heed "the wind of change" that was sweeping the continent; but South Africa, controlled since 1948 by the (Boer) Nationalist party, adamantly adhered to its policy of *apartheid*, a system of legally enforced racial separation in which only whites were granted the right to participate in the

---

[4]D. K. Fieldhouse, *The Colonial Empires* (1966), p. 410. See also John Darwin, *Britain and Decolonization: The Retreat from Empire in the Post-War World* (1988).

nation's government. In 1961 South Africa declared itself a republic and severed all ties with the Commonwealth. South Africa remained part of the sterling area, however, and for the time being Britain maintained as dependencies the enclaves of Basutoland and Swaziland and, as a protectorate, the neighboring state of Bechuanaland. Even when all three states became independent late in the decade under black African auspices, they remained for geographical reasons dependent on South African goodwill.

Farther to the north, the British Colonial Office encouraged the development of a multiracial Central African Federation of the Rhodesias and Nyasaland. The racial strains proved too great, however, and in 1964 the federation split up. Northern Rhodesia became the independent state of Zambia and Nyasaland the independent state of Malawi. Southern Rhodesia (hereafter called Rhodesia), domestically autonomous since the 1920s, was the African state (other than the Union of South Africa) in which the largest number of Britons had settled. For the moment it remained under white settler control, and it was to cause successive British governments numerous headaches during the next decade and a half.

The process of imperial devolution was going on in other parts of the world, also. On the Mediterranean island of Cyprus, a prolonged struggle for reunion with Greece on the part of the leaders of its Greek-speaking majority was confused by the desire of the British to maintain the island as a naval base and by the fact that the Turkish minority on the island strongly opposed annexation by Greece. In 1960 Cyprus became an independent member of the Commonwealth and Britain retained its naval base, but sporadic outbursts of fighting between Greek and Turkish inhabitants continued to take place during the 1960s, and in 1974 an invasion by the Turkish army led to a *de facto* partition of the island into Turkish Cypriot and Greek Cypriot zones.

In the meantime, a contemplated Federation of the (British) West Indies broke down, but Jamaica and Trinidad-Tobago received independence as separate states in 1962. The process of independence for British Guiana (in South America) was complicated by the struggle for political predominance between the inhabitants of African and of East Indian descent. After a lengthy period of civil disorder and negotiation, British Guiana — under the name of Guyana — became independent in 1966. In East Asia, the territory of Malaya received its independence in 1957 and, after uniting with several former British dependencies on the island of Borneo, was transformed in 1963 into the Federation of Malaysia. The attempt to incorporate Singapore into the federation did not work out, and in 1965 that geographically tiny state was recognized as a separate member of the Commonwealth.

In some respects the Commonwealth of the 1960s was a face-saving device that cushioned the psychological impact on Britain of the renunciation of empire. Most of the political bonds that remained were so amorphous as to seem unreal, and the member states rarely formed a voting bloc at the United Nations. Yet those member states that did not declare themselves republics kept Queen Elizabeth II as their head of state and retained the office of governor-general. The citizens of some (such as the Australian states, New Zealand, Jamaica, Malaysia, and Singapore) also retained the right of final legal appeal to the Judicial Committee of the Privy Council in London.

Other ties remained. The use of the English language, facsimiles of British parliamentary institutions, and elements of the English legal and civil-service systems could be found in a majority of Commonwealth states. There were athletic ties in the form of international cricket matches and educational ties that stemmed from many African universities having begun as branch colleges of the University of London. Even in the 1990s, elementary education in countries such as Nigeria continued to be carried on in English, and many African high schools still sent their students' comprehensive written examinations to Cambridge for grading. In the meantime, tens of thousands of students from Commonwealth countries came to Britain to seek higher education; Malaysia, Nigeria, New Zealand, Sri Lanka (Ceylon), and Cyprus were represented in particularly large numbers in the 1960s and 1970s.

There also remained strong commercial bonds in that all Commonwealth countries except Canada (but including Eire, South Africa, Iceland, and several nations of the Middle East) were part of the sterling area and until the 1970s continued to settle all international payments in English pounds. The system of Commonwealth trade preference inaugurated at Ottawa in 1932 also continued, and during the 1950s more than 40 percent of Britain's exports and imports went to and came from Commonwealth countries. The proportion declined during the 1960s, but in 1967 27.4 percent of British imports and 30.4 percent of British exports still involved sterling-area countries.

During the postwar years the United Kingdom became for a time increasingly generous with loans and grants to foster the economic development of onetime colonies. The net annual expenditure on such loans and grants rose from £52 million in 1952–1953 to £150 million in 1960–1961 and remained at relatively high levels during the 1960s and 1970s. Only during the 1980s did the amount of such overseas aid grow more slowly than did the rate of inflation. Such aid involved teachers, technicians, and the British equivalent of the American Peace Corps. Military aid was provided as well in 1962, when India's frontiers were invaded by Chinese troops, and in 1964, when the newly independent governments of Tanganyika and Kenya asked for assistance in putting down internal army revolts. In similar fashion, military help was offered the Federation of Malaysia in the face of Indonesian aggression in the mid-1960s. The British government was less successful in resolving the perennial dispute between India and Pakistan over the status of Kashmir or in preventing the bloody civil war that wracked the Federation of Nigeria until the final collapse of secessionist Biafra early in 1970. Finally, the Commonwealth was held together by the custom of regular conferences among Commonwealth prime ministers, a tradition begun in 1887 and supplemented in 1965 by the setting up of a permanent Commonwealth secretariat.

The Macmillan Era

For a majority of the inhabitants of Macmillan's Britain, the Commonwealth remained a subject of only sporadic interest. They were more immediately affected by the pleasures and paradoxes of a new age of prosperity. Although some of the old industries, such as coal, shipbuilding, and cotton textiles, continued to languish, the oil refineries and the manufacturers of airplanes, electrical equipment, automobiles, and plastics flourished. The annual production of steel more than doubled between 1946 and 1964; and Britain maintained the largest nonferrous-metal industry in Europe and the largest woolen-textile industry in the world. As a result of higher productivity, the gross national product rose 32 percent between 1950 and 1961.

The lot of the average British family correspondingly improved. The 1950s witnessed a housing boom, and by 1961 one family in four lived in a post–World War II dwelling. The scars of war disappeared from central London and central Birmingham; a new cathedral replaced the one destroyed at Coventry; and if the new glass-and-concrete office buildings sometimes jarred with adjoining Edwardian, Victorian, and Georgian structures, the housing boom also meant a gradual decline in the number of slums that had for so long seemed a necessary consequence of city life. As recently as 1951 only two houses or apartments in five could boast indoor toilets, bathtubs, and hot and cold running water; by 1976 such amenities were to be found in nine dwellings out of ten. Although Britain could no more prevent the problem of suburban sprawl than could the United States, an insistence on "green belts" around the major cities and the development of distinct "new towns" under a parliamentary act of 1946 limited the disfigurement of the countryside.

The affluent society meant increasing Americanization: growing numbers of supermarkets and self-service stores; a sharp rise in the use of "hire purchase" (installment-plan buying) to acquire refrigerators, washing machines, and other appliances; the custom of annual paid vacation of at least two weeks (often on the continent) for most families; and by 1962 the ownership of a television set by four families in five. It also meant eleven million automobiles by 1964 and more cars per mile of road surface than could be found in any other country. It meant a gradual change of diet — a smaller consumption of potatoes and bread, a larger consumption of meat and eggs and fruit, and the largest consumption of chocolates and candy per person to be found anywhere in the world. It meant larger sums placed in savings accounts and invested in stocks, and still greater sums "invested" in football pools, horse-race betting shops, and bingo parlors (the last two having been legalized by the Betting and Gaming Act of 1960).

Affluence also implied a greater interest in education, especially at the university level. The growth of Britain's educational institutions did not parallel precisely the post–World War II college boom in the United States, but during these years all over the Western world the proportion of young men and women who attended institutions of higher education rose dramatically. In Britain in the early 1960s, a committee headed by economist Lord (Lionel) Robbins noted the continued existence of "large reservoirs of untapped ability in the population" and recommended that the number of full-time students in higher education (216,000) be increased two and a half times by 1980. This meant, in part, the rapid expansion of Britain's traditional, elite form of university education. By 1970 the 17 universities that had existed in Britain in 1945 had grown to 44. More than 170 teacher-training colleges and over 700 technical colleges of various types also provided educational opportunities beyond the secondary-school level. Although the universities remained self-governing, most of their expenses were underwritten by the National Exchequer, and for four out of five students both tuition and living expenses were provided by the state. The National Union of Students — a million strong by the late 1970s — became a formidable political pressure group.

In the meantime the population was still slowly growing by some two million persons per decade. Although there had been no large-scale emigration during the 1930s and World War II, the nineteenth-century pattern temporarily recurred between 1945 and 1960 as some two million Britons moved to Canada, Australia, New Zealand, and South Africa. During those same years, 200,000 eastern Europeans (a majority of them Poles) and an even larger number of Irish migrants moved permanently to Britain. For the first time also, significant numbers — 400,000 by 1962 — of black and brown migrants moved permanently to Britain from the West Indies and from Pakistan and India.

A partial explanation for the prosperity of the Macmillan era lies in the fact that postwar Britain produced at least half of its food on its own farms (as opposed to one-third three decades earlier). In contrast to the 1940s, the terms of trade also once again favored Britain. The cost of imports fell, and the value of exports rose. British investments abroad grew more quickly than foreign investments in Britain, and by the mid-1960s Britain was once again a net creditor country. (British investments in American companies, for example, rose from a little over one billion dollars in 1950 to almost three billion dollars in 1968; the citizens of no other country had so sizable an investment in the United States, a state of affairs that continues to hold true in the twenty-first century.)

A significant by-product of the new age of prosperity was an apparent mellowing of the class-consciousness that had once seemed to divide England into "two nations" and that even in the 1930s had appeared a permanent aspect of the British scene. Blue-collar wages were catching up with white-collar salaries; more significantly, the relative number of factory workers was steadily declining, and the number of salaried office workers, professionals, and people active in the service trades was significantly rising. If the mass of the British population had not yet become as outwardly middle class as that of the United States, many signs were pointing in that direction.

Troubles of the Early 1960s

Although the general election of 1959 had entrenched a Conservative government more strongly than at any time since the 1930s, the Macmillan era was not bereft of critics. Increasingly the fear was voiced, an echo of the century-old warnings of Thomas Carlyle and Matthew Arnold, that — in an age of commercial television (introduced in 1956) and ever more lurid advertising — British society was becoming purely materialistic. In a society in which only wealth gave satisfaction, could people ever feel secure in their status or content with their lot? Affluence seemed only to encourage juveniles like the "Edwardian" Mods and the leather-jacketed Rockers who vandalized several English seaside resorts; and the number of indictable crimes rose from 500,000 a year in 1947 to 800,000 in 1961.

What Britain seemed to require was a fundamental religious revival; but despite the temporary attraction of visiting American evangelists such as Billy Graham, postwar Britain underwent no such revival or even growth of regular churchgoing as took place in the United States. The Church of England still baptized and buried a majority of English men and women, but marriages were increasingly performed in registrars' offices, and only one adult in seven attended church on a regular basis. Yet six out of ten defined themselves as "religious," and the activities of the archbishop of Canterbury continued to receive much publicity —as when in 1960 he held the first meeting with a Roman Catholic pope since Henry VIII's break with Rome — but the effect of the Church on the day-to-day lives of its supposed members had largely been subordinated to a variety of secular influences. The Nonconformist denominations — now generally known as the Free Churches — remained part of the religious scene but (even if the Presbyterian Church of Scotland is included) could count less than three million active members. The Roman Catholic Church was still growing slowly, and by the end of the decade one Briton in nine (and one active churchgoer in three) was likely to be a Roman Catholic. However, as a result both of the changes in religious practice authorized by the Vatican Council of the early 1960s and of widespread intermarriage, Roman Catholics gradually ceased to constitute a distinctive subculture in British society. More than a third of the 1,200,000 western European Jews who had survived the Nazi holocaust made their home in Britain.

Finally, immigration from Pakistan and other countries was to make Islam the religion of several hundred thousand citizens of the United Kingdom by the end of the decade.

If some critics found Macmillan's Britain too materialistic, other critics found it too amateurish, too stuffy, and too elitist. As recently as 1955, one foreign commentator observed of Britain's writers: "Never has an intellectual class found its society and its culture more to its satisfaction." A year later *Look Back in Anger* took London by storm, and what one literary critic was to call "the Angry Decade" was well under way. One of the play's characters, Alison Porter, tells her Edwardian father, an army officer retired from the Indian service: "You're hurt because everything is changed. Jimmy is hurt because everything is the same. And neither of you can face it." The line exemplified the sense of outrage by numerous playwrights and novelists of the years after Suez that, in spite of the changes wrought by the postwar Labour government, Britain was still, in fact if not in law, ruled by an elite few. It became fashionable in books, in weeklies such as *Private Eye,* and in television programs like *That Was the Week That Was* to satirize that elite as "the Establishment," an amalgam of top people in government, in industry, in the BBC, in the Church of England, and in the offices of the *Times* of London. Nine-tenths of the recruits of Britain's Foreign Office posts still came from a few exclusive fee-paying public schools; so did 80 percent of all Conservative M.P.'s elected in 1955. A majority of Prime Minister Anthony Eden's cabinet were products of a single such school: Eton.

To playwrights such as Arnold Wesker and novelists such as Alan Sillitoe, who "rediscovered" the working class and took pride in their own proletarian origins, education symbolized this continued inequality. The Education Act of 1944 had seemed at last to make a reality of the theory of universal free secondary education for Britain's boys and girls. Yet the future careers of all schoolchildren were largely determined by the test they had to take in their twelfth year — the "eleven plus" examination — which destined three in four for the terminal "secondary modern" school while permitting but one in four to go on to the academically far more respectable grammar school and in due course perhaps to a university. Educational stratification seemed to confirm rather than to modify traditional class distinctions.

The old aristocracy had not disappeared, although the domestic servant class was now virtually extinct and although many a peer was now making ends meet by charging tourists a fee to tramp through his ancestral halls. "It was impossible to foresee in the spring of 1944," marveled Evelyn Waugh in 1960, "the present cult of the English country house. . . . The English aristocracy has maintained its identity to a degree that then seemed impossible." Yet any impression that there was no social mobility in Britain was misleading. More than half of Britain's thousand hereditary peerages had been created after 1906; and, measured in terms of the percentage of children of working-class parents who ended up in white-collar jobs (30 percent), there was as much social mobility in post–World War II Britain as in the United States. Moreover, the ease with which "New Left" critics found acclaim for their books and plays and acquired influential positions on the major newspapers and the increasingly less staid BBC belied the notion that the Establishment was as monolithic or powerful as they proclaimed it to be.

Public questioning of the Establishment was at least indirectly connected with Britain's increasing difficulty in asserting an independent position in world affairs. Prime Minister Macmillan's personal friendship with President Eisenhower, which dated back to World War II, did much to ease Anglo-American tensions in the late 1950s, and Macmillan worked hard to bring about another Big Four summit conference. He was unable to save the Paris Conference of 1960 from failure, however, after Chairman Nikita Khrushchev walked out because of the U-2 incident, the shooting down of an American spy plane over Russia. Eisenhower's successor, John F. Kennedy, although partly educated in and sympathetic to Britain, was more interested in the possibility of Big Two than of Big Four conferences. The British government thus found itself a concerned spectator of, but not a participant in, the Cuban missile crisis of 1962. After a worrisome week, that crisis was peacefully resolved when the Soviet government decided to withdraw the long-range missiles it had been secretly installing on Cuban soil in return for an American promise not to invade the island nation that had become a Soviet client-state.

The credibility of an independent British nuclear deterrent was undermined from the late 1950s on, as the long-range bomber was increasingly supplanted in military strategic thinking by the intercontinental ballistic missile. When the British government decided in 1960 to cancel, for reasons of expense, the further development of its own Blue Streak rocket, it became dependent on the American-manufactured Skybolt. The American decision in December 1962 to scrap the Skybolt project as unfeasible revived a latent spirit of anti-Americanism in Britain. At a hastily convened conference in Nassau, in the Bahamas, President Kennedy agreed to sell to Britain Polaris missiles, which could be equipped with British nuclear warheads and installed in British-built nuclear submarines. In Macmillan's eyes, Britain's independence as a nuclear power had been preserved; in the eyes of his critics, the island's military dependence on the United States had been reconfirmed. Yet in a world in which peace among the Great Powers apparently depended on the technical perfection of a succession of weapons that might not be used without risking global destruction, old-fashioned judgments as to military dependence or independence might well prove beside the point. An increased British reliance on nuclear weapons did have one quite practical consequence, however — the decision of the government to reduce expenditures for conventional weapons and in 1960 to end conscription. Britain's volunteer army, navy, and air force of the early 1960s, some 400,000 men and women, was only half as large as it had been a decade earlier. In the course of the next two decades it was to shrink to

300,000, and British spending on defense, which had constituted 10 percent of the gross national product in the early 1950s, dropped to 5 percent by 1970.

Even less concerned with British military power was the Campaign for Nuclear Disarmament organized in 1958. Led by an Anglican clergyman, Canon John Collins, and the octogenarian rationalist philosopher, Earl (Bertrand) Russell (1872–1970), the group gained the emotional commitment of a new generation of middle-class young people, just as the causes of the depression-era hunger marchers and the Spanish republicans had won the support of their parents. The aim of the CND was to "ban the bomb" on a worldwide basis and, if that were impossible, to win for Britain "the moral leadership of the world" by disarming unilaterally, ending its alliance with the United States, and taking refuge in strict neutrality between East and West. The annual protest marches to London from Aldermaston, the British Atomic Energy Authority's chief research laboratory, swelled year by year. In 1960 the unilateral disarmament forces even succeeded, by a narrow margin, in persuading the Labour party's annual conference to adopt their position. Hugh Gaitskell, the party's leader, who looked on unilateral nuclear disarmament as folly, succeeded a year later in having his party reverse course. The nuclear disarmament movement split in the early 1960s between civil-disobedience extremists and more moderate forces, and — except for a fleeting revival in the 1980s — it largely faded away after 1963, when Britain helped negotiate an international treaty banning nuclear-weapons testing in the atmosphere.

The nuclear disarmament movement had been fed by a sometimes overt and sometimes latent spirit of anti-Americanism, which during the 1950s had been given added force by the strength of "McCarthyism" in the United States and by the apparent ideological inflexibility of Secretary of State Dulles. The British also tended to deplore examples of American influence ranging from chewing gum to television serials and, initially, to rock music. The British Foreign Office, however, maintained close relations with the United States. Its diplomats did tend to view the United States as too much given to ideological rigidity — Britain, for example, had formally recognized as early as 1949 that the Communist movement had conquered mainland China — but they believed that they could more readily influence American policy as loyal allies than as a neutral third force. Successive governments during the 1950s and 1960s were also compelled to concede that during World War II and after, British spies such as Kim Philby recruited by the Soviet Union had sent thousands of secret documents to Moscow — thereby providing the Soviet Union with a detailed knowledge of British and American military power and diplomatic strategy and thereby enabling it to build its own nuclear weapons far more quickly than the West had expected.

Some of the critics of British society during the early 1960s were much less concerned with the decline — or immorality — of Britain's military power or with the supposedly baleful consequences of material prosperity than with the relatively slow pace of Britain's economic growth. The annual increase in the gross domestic product had averaged 3.5 percent between 1948 and 1955 but only 2.2 percent between 1955 and 1961. These figures, although impressive in comparison with certain earlier periods, were not nearly so high as those of several other European countries or Japan. They compared most unfavorably, for example, with the economic miracle of West Germany, which had overtaken Britain in 1955 as an exporter of motor vehicles. A year later Japan had become the world's leading shipbuilder. Britain's business managers seemed unduly bound by custom and too attached to the British tradition of exalting the amateur to attend (or to encourage the creation of) schools of business administration. The trade unions, in turn, were at least as conservative in outlook. They saw labor-saving machines and techniques far more as a short-run threat to their jobs than as a long-run means of enabling British industry to keep up with international competition and thereby maintain full employment.

The First Move to Join Europe

Although Britain was obviously participating in the pattern of unprecedented growth that marked the economies of the United States, western Europe, and Japan between the late 1940s and the early 1970s, the nation had not succeeded in combining such growth with both full employment and price stability. Thus, while personal income rose 106 percent between 1950 and 1961, retail prices went up 54 percent and successive Chancellors of the Exchequer seemed destined time and again to chart a "stop-go" policy. Low interest rates would encourage new investment in domestic business, but before long the volume of imports would rise more quickly than the volume of exports and thereby endanger Britain's international balance of payments. Foreign speculators would then withdraw their holdings of pounds sterling from British banks in order to profit from — and by their actions encourage — a devaluation of the currency. Because such a devaluation would upset world trade and endanger Britain's continuing role in furnishing one of the world's reserve currencies, the government of the day would take countermeasures. A new budget would impose steeper taxes, encourage higher interest rates, and reduce government expenditures. Such measures would restrain imports and improve the international balance of payments, but at the same time they would discourage domestic employment and the investments on which long-run economic growth depended.

The government had been forced to impose such an economic "stop" in 1955, and a rapidly growing international deficit forced it to do the same in 1961. Restrictive measures resolved the immediate crisis but, inasmuch as they retarded general economic growth, they did little to halt inflation. In Britain and the prospering countries of western Europe, as in the poorer nations of Asia and Africa, there was "a revolution of rising expectations" that caused first one group and then another to push for wage increases. Necessarily there was pressure on the government not to let its employees and old-age pensioners fall behind. As each element of the population successfully agitated for higher wages, the national income rose faster than national productivity; inflation was the result.

In the face of this inflationary spiral, pressure increased for a "national incomes policy," which would make the division of the national economic pie dependent more on national planning by government, union leaders, and employers than on the market pressure that a specific organized group could exert. In 1961, Chancellor Selwyn Lloyd recommended a temporary "pay pause," and soon thereafter the government established the National Economic Development Council — popularly known as "Neddy" — to formulate such a policy. It was the first of several similar attempts by both Conservative and Labour governments. Yet could any society hostile to authoritarian regulation develop by social consensus a workable national incomes policy? The answer remained, and remains, highly doubtful.

A reaction to the economic crisis of 1961 with far wider implications was Prime Minister Macmillan's announcement that summer that Britain was applying for membership in the European Economic Community (EEC), the Common Market consisting of France, West Germany, Italy, Belgium, the Netherlands, and Luxembourg. Since 1957 the Common Market had been embarking on a program of lowering economic barriers in such a fashion as to make a single economic (and potentially political) unit of western Europe. Britain had refused to join in 1957 but had instead set about creating a European Free Trade Association of Britain, Sweden, Norway, Denmark, Austria, Switzerland, and Portugal — the "Outer Seven" as opposed to the "Inner Six."

The Common Market proved to be politically the more meaningful and economically the more stimulating organization, and by 1961 the Macmillan government became convinced that it would be preferable for Britain to remain a strong power within this new European community rather than a weak power outside it. The decision to begin negotiations set off a political furor inside Britain. The government was criticized for forsaking the Commonwealth, for ignoring the interests of Britain's farmers, and for being willing to subordinate Britain's national sovereignty to the EEC's governing council without even first holding a general election. The government's decision did indeed raise one of the oldest questions in British history: whether Britain's destiny, as in Roman times and in the days of Henry II and Henry V, resided on the European continent, or whether in the tradition of the Elizabethan seafarers of the sixteenth century it lay, and continued to lie, beyond the seas.

Right-wing Conservatives (such as Lord Beaverbrook) joined hands with staunch Labourites (such as Lord Attlee) in opposing Britain's entry into the Common Market, and in October 1962 Hugh Gaitskell, appealing to "a thousand years of history," virtually committed the Labour party to opposing the plan. Yet it still seemed likely that the long-drawn-out negotiations that Edward Heath (1916–   ) was carrying on in Brussels would culminate in Britain's entry. A bracing effect on Britain's economy was expected to follow, as were such logical by-products of unity with Europe as the adoption of a common time zone, the metric system, a decimal coinage system, and the building of a tunnel under the English Channel. Then in January 1963 President de Gaulle of France vetoed Britain's entry. De Gaulle's own ideal, it was clear, was not a supranational community at all — the Common Market Treaty had been signed before he became president in 1958 — but a strong continental coalition dominated by France. He was suspicious of the non-European interests of "the Anglo-Saxons" (the British and the Americans) and of the "special relationship" that British leaders had sometimes claimed with the United States and that President Kennedy and Prime Minister Macmillan had apparently reaffirmed at their Nassau meeting.

By vetoing Britain's entry into the Common Market, de Gaulle had in his own fashion temporarily resolved a major political controversy within Britain — a controversy that was to re-emerge within five years — but only at the cost of damaging the reputation of the Macmillan government. De Gaulle's rebuff was widely interpreted as a major international defeat for Britain. The government's position was further undermined in the summer of 1963 by the Profumo affair. It turned out that Minister of War John Profumo and the Russian naval attaché in London had shared the same call-girl. Several earlier cases of successful Russian espionage in Britain had roused public suspicions, but in this instance no breach of military security was uncovered. There was a widespread outcry, however, when Profumo admitted that, in initially denying the affair, he had knowingly lied to his cabinet colleagues in private and to Parliament in public. This sense of shock was attributed alternately to British hypocrisy and to the high degree of confidence that British citizens retained in the rectitude of government officials.

John Profumo immediately resigned his post, and in September 1963 so did Prime Minister Macmillan, increasingly plagued as he was by physical and political ailments. The proliferation of crises — nuclear, economic, diplomatic, and moral — in the early 1960s had induced a national mood of introspection and, at times, of almost pathological self-criticism. Books proliferated with titles such as *The Stagnant Society, What's Wrong with the Unions?, What's Wrong with British Industry?,* and *Suicide of a Nation?* An affirmative answer to this last question seemed premature, to say the least, as the nation was introduced to a new prime minister and looked ahead to a new general election.

The Elections of 1964 and 1966

Macmillan's successor was a surprise: the slightly built and self-effacing foreign secretary, the fourteenth earl of Home (pronounced *Hume;*

1903–1995), who resigned his peerage to return to the House of Commons as Sir Alec Douglas-Home. A year earlier he could not have done this; but a battle fought by Anthony Wedgwood Benn (1925–), a Labour M.P., against being forced to enter the House of Lords (and resign his seat in the House of Commons) upon his father's death in 1960, had led to a new Peerage Act that relieved the members of the upper house of the political disadvantage of their titles. The House of Lords itself had been democratized a few years earlier, when in 1958 the first of numerous life peers, two of them women, were admitted to that venerable assembly. (The titles of life peers, as opposed to hereditary peers, lapsed with their death.)

In a divided Conservative parliamentary party, Douglas-Home had been the favorite second choice of many M.P.'s but the first choice of few, and some important party leaders, such as Iain Macleod, refused to join his cabinet. Sir Alec strove with considerable skill, however, to mend party fences and to reverse the underdog status to which opinion polls and by-election defeats had condemned his party. The president of the Board of Trade, Edward Heath, promoted business competition and aided the consumer by pushing through the House of Commons a bill to end retail price maintenance. At the same time, Reginald Maudling (1917–1979), Chancellor of the Exchequer, gave fiscal encouragement to a new economic boom. Douglas-Home put off the general election until the last legal month, October 1964, in the hope of staving off what appeared to be inevitable defeat.

The election was warmly contested. It involved not only Douglas-Home but also Harold Wilson, the man who had been voted Labour party leader after Hugh Gaitskell's untimely death in January 1963, and Jo Grimond (1913–1993), the leader of the small but temporarily revitalized Liberal party. Wilson muted socialist doctrine and sought to convey the image of a Kennedy-like "New Frontiersman" who intended to harness "the white heat of the technological revolution" on behalf of the people of Britain and to modernize the planning of their economy. While Wilson emphasized domestic issues, Douglas-Home placed greater stress on his party's experience in foreign policy matters and its commitment to an independent nuclear deterrent for Britain. The election results were very close: Labour, 317 seats; Conservative, 304; Liberal, 9. The total popular vote showed no swing to Labour, but disenchanted Conservative voters had switched to the Liberal party in sufficient numbers to provide the Labour party with a plurality of the popular vote and a slight parliamentary edge.

Harold Wilson, the new prime minister, was a man of acknowledged brilliance as parliamentary debater and tactician. He decided to treat the narrow margin of his party's victory as a popular mandate for positive economic action. The deputy party leader, George Brown (1914–1985), was appointed head of a new Ministry of Economic Affairs, whose task it was to work out a National Plan, according to which business and union leaders would agree on a "prices and incomes policy" within the framework of an economy growing steadily at 4 percent a year. A National

The New Prime Minister   Labour party leader Harold Wilson (on the right of the picture) hails his party's return to power in 1964. To his right are the deputy leader, George Brown, and Wilson's wife, Mary. *(Topham)*

Board for Prices and Incomes was set up to issue early warnings against unwarranted price and wage increases; these warnings were seldom heeded. In the meantime, the ministry demonstrated its working-class sympathies more immediately by raising old-age pensions, by eliminating all charges on National Health Service prescriptions, and by dismissing the cook at No. 10 Downing Street. Mrs. Wilson preferred to prepare the prime minister's dinners herself. The ministry encouraged social equality by promoting the substitution of "comprehensive" secondary schools for the earlier system that segregated academically oriented children from others at the age of eleven. By the end of the 1960s, one student in three attended such a comprehensive high school; by the end of the 1970s, four in five did so. (Comprehensive high schools were hailed at the time as a triumph of social equality; in retrospect, they came to be criticized for lowering academic standards and fostering student disorder.) Planning was also begun for the Open University, which was officially chartered in 1969 to enable adults to earn university degrees by a combination of radio and television courses, correspondence study, one-week residential summer schools, and nationally standardized examinations. It soon became the largest single teaching institution in the United Kingdom. In 1992 it opened its programs of study to students throughout Europe, and by 2000 it had conferred more than 200,000 degrees and could boast tens of thousands of active students.

Long-range changes in educational policy did not solve immediate economic problems, however, and Wilson's inexperienced government was forced almost at once to subordinate ambitious social goals to the necessity of coping with a giant gap in Britain's international balance of payments. The government decided to meet the new economic crisis not by devaluation but by the revival of a deliberate policy of deflation: a temporary surcharge on all imports, a rise in interest rates, and reliance on the aid of the International Monetary Fund to stabilize the pound. The budget of April 1965 sharply curtailed tax-free business expense accounts and imposed the first tax in British history on long-term capital gains. The continuing failure of the nation's international accounts to balance led in July to still further deflationary steps: the imposition of curbs on new capital investments and the tightening of consumer credit controls.

In the autumn the sense of economic crisis eased, but the ministry faced a major crisis in Rhodesia, whose government declared its unilateral independence from British rule. The Labour government would have been well satisfied to permit Rhodesia to advance along the road to independence as other African colonies had, but in a land of 225,000 whites and more than four million blacks it did not seem just to exclude the latter permanently from gaining the chance to attain a majority voice in the government of their country. Yet this was the condition that Prime Minister Ian Smith of Rhodesia insisted on, and Wilson failed to change Smith's mind. Although several Commonwealth countries urged the prime minister to suppress the Rhodesian rebellion by means of airborne invasion, he preferred to rely on a United Nations resolution that imposed economic sanctions on Rhodesia. Such sanctions damaged but did not cripple the Rhodesian economy, and with the aid of its neighbor, the Union of South Africa, a white-ruled Rhodesia proclaimed itself a republic and succeeded, for the time being, in securing its independence from Britain.

Early in 1966 Prime Minister Wilson decided to risk a new general election in order to strengthen his government's parliamentary majority. His party's program stressed planning for growth in industry, transportation, housing, and education, but — except for the steel industry — downplayed further nationalization. By then the Conservative opposition no longer was headed by Sir Alec Douglas-Home, who had resigned during the previous summer, but by Edward Heath. For the first time the Conservative party had chosen its leader by the formal balloting of its House of Commons members rather than by secret informal consultations within the party's inner circle; Heath had narrowly emerged as the victor over Reginald Maudling. In his social background — the son of a carpenter and a lady's maid — and in his reputation as a hardheaded professional, Heath resembled Wilson more than he resembled his somewhat casual aristocratic predecessor, Douglas-Home. Yet as the election campaign made clear, Wilson and Heath were far from identical. In his television appearances, Wilson looked and sounded like a national leader who truly understood and could cope with the grave problems of the day. Heath emerged as earnest and honest but somewhat dull; he found it difficult to arouse fervent enthusiasm in an audience. The election proved to be a solid Labour triumph. There was a significant swing to Labour in the total popular vote — 48 percent Labour, 42 percent Conservative —

and a still more obvious swing in the number of parliamentary seats: Labour, 363; Conservative, 253; Liberal, 12.

The Perils of the Pound

In his more sanguine moments in the spring of 1966, Prime Minister Wilson may well have believed that his government had survived its economic time of troubles and that in a calmer atmosphere it could go about encouraging the process of constructive social change. Instead, the years 1966–1969 continued to be shadowed by the problem of Britain's international balance of payments. Economically speaking, Britain appeared to be "the sick man of Europe," and the British public became accustomed to newspaper warnings that the pound was once more in peril. The intricacies of international finance are little understood by the average citizen, and so a prime-ministerial call to "save the pound" failed to evoke the same spirit of national unity that Winston Churchill had aroused with his defiant "We shall fight them on the beaches. . . . We shall never surrender."

The average citizen did become more immediately aware of the impact of world finance on his or her own daily activities when a six-week seamen's strike in May and June of 1966 precipitated a sharp reduction in exports and a new run on the pound. The government, which had entered office in 1964 on a pledge to end the "stop-go" syndrome, now instituted the stiffest and most deflationary "stop" of the post–World War II period. Again the bank interest rate was raised and installment-buying regulations were tightened in order to curb the supply of credit. Taxes on alcoholic beverages and gasoline as well as income were raised to soak up consumer purchasing power. A limit of £50 ($140) a year per person was placed on English tourist spending abroad. The Prices and Incomes Act of August 1966 imposed a six-month standstill on all wage, salary, and dividend increases, to be followed by a system of "severe restraint" for another six months.

These severe deflationary measures did have some success in curbing inflation and the growth of imports, but only at the expense of drastically curtailing the rate of economic growth envisaged in the National Plan. Early in 1967, Wilson's government made a new bid to have Britain join the Common Market; the decision won the approval of the House of Commons by a vote of 488 to 62 but was once again blocked by the opposition of President de Gaulle of France. Britain's economic recovery was further impeded by the Six-Day War between Israel and its Arab neighbors in June 1967. The consequent closing of the Suez Canal — for the next eight years — added £20 million a month to Britain's import bill; and a three-month embargo on oil shipments by Arab lands, whose leaders falsely accused the British government of having served as Israel's accomplice, complicated matters still further. Continuing economic difficulties led to the decision to curb overseas military expenditures, a major drain on the balance of payments, by closing Britain's last major military bases east of Suez by the mid-1970s. This decision involved Singapore and a number of small Arab states on the Persian Gulf. The protectorate over Kuwait had been ended in 1961, and the base on the tip of the Arabian peninsula at Aden was relinquished in 1968. Little thought was given to the prospect that such a decision would place Britain's oil imports during the 1970s in even greater peril. Yet the departure of British military forces "left behind a dangerous power vacuum in a region that supplied 32 percent of the free world's petroleum and that, at the time, held 58 percent of the proven oil reserves."[5]

Britain remained firm in regard to its bases west of Suez, however, and it resisted Spanish harassment designed to force the return of Gibraltar to Spain after 260 years. In September 1967, a referendum of Gibraltar citizens demonstrated that they preferred British to Spanish rule by a margin of 12,138 to 44 and confirmed the government's resolve. Wilson had indifferent success in his efforts to help extricate the United States from the Vietnam quagmire, but Britain helped negotiate the 1967 treaty banning nuclear weapons from outer space and the 1969 agreement curbing further nuclear proliferation.

The economic difficulties occasioned by the closing of the Suez Canal were compounded by a six-week-long dock strike in Liverpool and London in September and October 1967. A new "flight from the pound" led to the November decision that it would be necessary after all to devalue the pound in terms of the dollar (from $2.80 to $2.40) and other currencies. James Callaghan (1912–), the Chancellor of the Exchequer who had opposed devaluation, resigned and exchanged positions with Roy Jenkins (1920–), the home secretary. Jenkins soon made it clear that the government would not permit the chief advantage of devaluation — making British exports cheaper abroad — to be dissipated by the rapid growth of prices and wages at home. The Prices and Incomes Board retained the power to delay and restrain inflationary wage increases, and the April 1968 budget again raised income and sales taxes. Drug prescription charges were reimposed, and the implementation of a school-leaving age of sixteen (rather than fifteen) was postponed.

Later in the year Jenkins employed additional governmental tools to help bring bank credit expansion into line, and by the late spring of 1969 some light could at last be glimpsed at the end of the tunnel. The overall balance of payments was moving from deficit into surplus, and the rate of exports was growing more rapidly than that of imports. But the experience of Britain between 1964 and 1970 illustrates that economics remains a highly inexact science and that even a government that — unlike that of the United States — possesses the power to make rapid shifts in lowering or raising taxes and interest rates may yet find the task of

---

[5]Daniel Yergin, *The Prize: The Epic Quest for Oil, Money, and Power* (1990).

steering the national economy difficult and the immediate social and political consequences far from harmonious.

One of these consequences, from the summer of 1966 on, was a growing sense of disaffection in the trade-union movement, the backbone of the Labour party. Trade unionists might pay lip service to the concept of "socialist planning" but they wanted no government interference with "free collective bargaining." They disliked intensely Prime Minister Wilson's reminders that "one man's wage increase is another man's price increase" and that the only meaningful wage increases were those that resulted from increased economic efficiency. Union leaders became disenchanted with government restrictions that curbed the monetary expectations of their followers. In 1967 and 1968 the number of working hours lost as a result of strikes increased rapidly. A government White Paper on industrial relations, *In Place of Strife*, published early in 1969, noted that 95 percent of British labor disputes were wildcat strikes begun in defiance of the elected union leadership. The government proposed a compulsory twenty-eight day cooling-off period, a secret ballot of all union members before major strikes could begin, and ultimate penal sanctions. There was a storm of protest within his own party, and in June, in order to save his prime ministership, Wilson gave up on a proposed Industrial Relations Bill in return for a promise (which it lacked the power to fulfill) by the TUC General Council that it would prevent unofficial work stoppages.

A second consequence of the government's economic policies was an avalanche of political reverses. In twenty-nine parliamentary by-elections between 1966 and the end of 1969, the Labour party lost thirteen seats, retained six, and failed to win any of the remaining ten seats from the opposition. The party fared equally badly in local elections, and by 1969 it retained control of only a handful of elected borough and county councils throughout the nation. Within the House of Commons, Labour members became less hesitant than in previous decades to rebel against their party leadership on particular issues, although never in sufficient numbers to endanger the tenure of the Wilson ministry.

Not all of the electoral benefits of this political shift flowed to the Conservative opposition. In 1966 a Welsh Nationalist candidate won a parliamentary by-election seat, and in 1967 a Scottish Nationalist won another. Far more serious stirrings of discontent broke out in 1968 in Northern Ireland (see Chapter 21). Although neither the Welsh nor the Scottish Nationalist by-election victories were soon to be repeated, they provided the first signs in half a century or more of a widespread questioning of the underlying constitutional framework of the United Kingdom.

In the meantime, a form of nativism had emerged within England itself — a fear of and hostility toward a growing number of "black" immigrants from the West Indies, India, and Pakistan.[6] In the 1950s, at the very

---

[6]Catherine Jones, *Immigration and Social Policy in Britain* (1977).

time that British ties with the Commonwealth were loosening, an increasing number of Commonwealth citizens took advantage of their right to migrate freely to Britain, to find jobs there, and to exercise the full rights of citizenship (including the franchise). As their numbers increased beyond the half-million mark, their new English neighbors became less impressed with the manner in which they were alleviating an English labor shortage as doctors, nurses, hospital orderlies, bus drivers, and factory workers than with the manner in which they competed for available housing and changed the atmosphere of numerous urban neighborhoods. Although the British Isles had become the home of many groups of European exiles over the centuries, the English felt no historical reverence for the ideal of a pluralistic society; and the skin color as well as some of the customs of these newest immigrants testified to the fact that they were "simply not English." Popular pressure caused the Macmillan government to impose curbs in 1962. The Commonwealth Immigration Act of 1962 compelled potential immigrants to obtain work permits before being allowed to enter the country. Some 30,000 permits were issued in 1963, but by 1966 the number had been reduced to 8,500 a year. Because the dependents of earlier immigrants were permitted to enter freely, however, an average of 70,000 immigrants a year entered Britain during the 1960s and 1970s and 50,000 a year during the 1980s and 1990s. The continued immigration of relatives of Asians and West Indians already living in Britain and the relatively high birthrate in these communities was to increase their number to well over 3.5 million (at least 6.5 percent of the population) by the end of the century. By then more than half of the members of these communities had been born in Britain.

The Labour government that assumed office in 1964 heeded the fears of its supporters by taking stringent measures to curb further immigration. At the same time, with the Race Relations Acts of 1965 and 1968, it sought to prevent discrimination in housing, education, and employment against those immigrants and their children who were already in the country. A new problem developed in 1968 when the African Republic of Kenya began the process of expelling its residents of Indian origin. Because most of these still held British passports, many of them sought entry into the United Kingdom. The Commonwealth Immigration Act of 1968 permitted them to enter at the rate of no more than 1,500 per year. These measures were insufficiently restrictive for Enoch Powell (1912–1998), the former Conservative minister of health, who in the late 1960s broke with his own party leadership on the issue. Warning of "a dark and ever more menacing shadow," he pressed a program not merely of limiting immigration to Britain but of government-subsidized repatriation for those immigrants who had already come. His efforts won him considerable notoriety and some public support but little hope of success; he never held cabinet office again. Britons of the 1960s were learning, however, that problems of race relations could no more readily be conjured away with a magic wand than could political disaffection or the much publicized "perils of the pound."

The Permissive Society

When foreigners thought of London during the later 1960s, they were increasingly less likely to think of it as the capital of an empire or as the center of international finance than as the home of the fictional James Bond, the real-life Beatles, and the miniskirt. Black-suited, bowler-hatted, umbrella-carrying bankers on their way to Lombard Street or a Pall Mall club had apparently given way to long-haired youth dressed in the multicolored "mod" fashions supplied by Carnaby Street and Kings Road boutiques, on their way to join their "birds" at the local discotheque. Popular stereotypes are at best a partial key to a society or an age, but the prevalence in the 1960s of phrases like "the cult of youth" and "the permissive society" did denote a measurable shift in public attitudes and a new spirit of rebellion against earlier values.

Mary Quant (1934–) and other London fashion designers had at least temporary success in challenging the traditional predominance of Paris as the stylesetter for women's fashions; at the same time, four young men from Liverpool, the Beatles, were placing their imprint on the world of popular music. As one of the earliest of the major rock groups, they won the adulation of teenagers all over the world and proved that

The Beatles   Photograph taken in 1965 after Queen Elizabeth at Buckingham Palace officially granted them membership in the Order of the British Empire. *(UPI/Bettmann/Corbis)*

even in the age of television, pop music makers could fill a baseball stadium with enthusiastic — at times frenzied — admirers. Although not professionally trained, they demonstrated a high degree of musical originality in the songs they composed and performed and the films they made; of the twenty-five most widely sold record albums in the United States during the decade, the Beatles provided eleven. In their avant-garde hairdos and clothes, in their experiments with Indian mysticism and drugs, and in their perpetual search for novelty, they both influenced and reflected the mood of a whole generation of young people.[7] Although the four Beatles went their separate ways after 1969, similar groups such as the Rolling Stones continued successfully to elude moss all the way into the twenty-first century.

A 1960 court decision holding that D. H. Lawrence's novel *Lady Chatterley's Lover* could be published in its unexpurgated version inaugurated an age more tolerant toward what earlier generations had defined as obscene or pornographic. In the novel, the theater, the cinema, and to some degree on the television screen, sexual explicitness was increasingly in fashion. As the American weekly *Variety* phrased it, "British Prudery Out, Nudery In." At a time when Britannia no longer ruled the waves, she seemed increasingly willing to waive the rules.

Not only was London a home for strip clubs and gambling parlors but, with its National Theatre headed by Sir Laurence Olivier, its Royal Shakespeare Company, and its forty legitimate theaters, it was also the theatrical capital of the English-speaking world. London's musical scene was made up not only of rock groups and recording studios, but of five symphony orchestras, two opera companies, and several ballet companies, including the prestigious Royal Ballet, made famous throughout the world by Dame Margot Fonteyn and the Russian exile Rudolf Nureyev. Londoners were slower to appreciate the talents of the home-grown Henry Moore (1898–1986). Born near Leeds, Moore, the son of a miner, became known in his later years for his giant outdoor sculptures; they won him plaudits and commissions from all over the world. Fewer plaudits greeted many of the unornamented glass-and-concrete buildings that joined the London skyline during the 1960s and 1970s; numerous critics saw them as fundamentally inhuman. London was, however, becoming a cleaner and more smog-free city than it had been for centuries. An act of 1956 outlawed the burning of soft coal, and the grime of decades was blasted from the outer walls of public buildings. In due course, salmon were even induced to return to the waters of a purified Thames. Its variety of scene and activity and of musical and sartorial originality, combined with a lingering air of tradition and a still-dominant attitude of civility, caused *Time* in 1966 to dub London "the city of the decade." It was *the* place to live for actors, artists, musicians, writers,

---

[7]Philip Norman, *Shout! The Beatles in Their Generation* (1981).

and members of the "jet set," and a more temporary mecca for four million tourists a year.

The Labour government that took office in 1964 looked with an indulgent eye on many aspects of what one of its leading members, Roy Jenkins, preferred to call the "civilized" rather than the "permissive" society. In 1965 Parliament ended hanging as a punishment for murder for an experimental five-year period. Late in 1969 the ban on capital punishment was made permanent. In the words of the Labour lord chancellor, Lord Gardiner: "I think that human beings who are not infallible ought not to choose a form of punishment which is irreparable." A 1966 measure ended criminal penalties for homosexual activities among consenting adults. An act of 1968 legalized abortions for women whose physical or mental health was endangered by the prospect of additional children. A 1969 measure virtually eliminated the notion of plaintiff and defendant from divorce cases and made "the breakdown of a marriage" the key legal criterion. In the aftermath, the number of divorces per year rose from 27,000 in 1961 to 80,000 in 1971 and 158,000 in 1980. Powers of censorship that the Lord Chamberlain had exercised over the London stage since the 1730s were ended by the Theatre Act of 1968. The cult of youth was served by laws that, as of January 1, 1970, reduced both the voting age and the age of legal majority from twenty-one to eighteen. The feminist revival of the 1960s led to the Equal Pay Act of 1970, which was designed to ensure within five years equal pay and conditions for men and women doing similar work. It became increasingly common for married women to work outside the home; whereas only one in five had done so as recently as 1957, one in three did so by 1970, and three in five were to do so — at least part-time — by 1981. The constituent colleges of universities increasingly became coeducational and so did their residence halls. In "the era of the Pill," the ideal of premarital chastity (and, less often, that of marital fidelity) came to be dismissed as "Victorian." Children born out of wedlock became increasingly common — only 1 in 20 in the 1950s, but 3 in 10 as of 1991. Such social and legal changes all influenced (or were influenced by) similar movements for social change in the United States and continental Europe.

Not all of the legislative changes of the decade moved in the direction of greater permissiveness. Restrictions, however temporary, on wages, prices, and currency transfers clearly did not. Nor did the actions of Barbara Castle (1911–   ), the Labour minister of transportation, who in 1965 imposed an automobile speed limit of seventy miles per hour on British roads (where none had hitherto existed) and in 1967 imposed a "breathalizer" test on drivers suspected of alcoholic overindulgence. New restrictions were imposed on operators of gambling clubs, dealers in dangerous drugs, and businessmen found guilty of misleading advertising; and the private off-shore radio transmitters that had challenged the BBC monopoly on broadcasting with popular music and commercials were put out of business. At the same time, a 1967 act set up the Office of

Parliamentary Commissioner (or *ombudsman*, a Scandinavian term) to give aid to the ordinary citizen entangled in government red tape.

The "permissive society" was not lacking in critics who wondered whether its freedom ought not more justly to be termed "vulgarity" and its permissiveness "decadence." Rather than serving, like Athens in the Roman world, as a cultural beacon after its political power had declined, London was becoming "the Corinth of Europe ... where the serious Athenians would go for a good debauch." A decline of social discipline was manifested in a growth of drug addiction and of illegitimate births and in an ever-rising crime rate — from 800,000 offenses in 1961 to over 1,300,000 in 1969. The fact that even the latter figure compared favorably with figures for the United States, or for that matter the Britain of the early nineteenth century or the Middle Ages, provided cold comfort to those who remembered the law-abiding, nonviolent Britain of the 1930s. A combination of material well-being, social laxity, and plain boredom seemed to be involved in the growth of crime, in the increase of spectator melees at football games, and in a growing public acceptance of violence among youth gangs, political demonstrators, and university students. The welfare state had been achieved in its essentials, but the prevalent spirit of permissiveness did not seem to be accompanied by the requisite corollary of social responsibility. "Is it necessary," wondered one disenchanted commentator in 1969, "to abandon finally the cherished hopes of reformers who for centuries have believed that an improvement in man's material condition would bring with it enlightenment, humanity, generosity, decency, and even nobility?"[8]

Although for some Britons the 1960s constituted a decade of liberation, for others it was a decade of disappointment. On the one hand, the state was spending (even discounting inflation) an ever-greater percentage of the earnings of its citizens. By 1970 it was expending 50 percent more on the health of its citizens and 100 percent more on their education than it had twenty years before. In the course of a single decade, the amount spent in real terms for social services increased by two-thirds. On the other hand, the Wilson government lurched from one financial crisis to another and failed to inspire the economic boom that it had promised. A rate of economic growth that had averaged 2.9 percent per year during 1959–1964 fell to 2.2 percent during 1964–1970, and the material expectations of the nation's citizens seemed destined to continue to outpace economic realities.

---

[8]Arnold A. Rogow, *American Historical Review*, December 1969, p. 506.

CHAPTER 21

The Stormy 1970s: The Age of Stagflation

As the 1960s drew to a close, Britain seemed to be adjusting to its diminished role in world affairs and to an age in which government loomed larger in economic life but smaller in matters of personal morality. Britain's position in the world economy had apparently been stabilized, but no sooner was the new decade under way than it became clear that the twenty-five-year economic boom that had been experienced by much of the Western world since 1947 was at an end. It was followed for more than a decade by that combination of economic stagnation and of price and wage inflation (as well as levels of unemployment greater than any since the 1930s) that came to be known as "stagflation." The economy of the entire world was jarred by the explosion in oil prices dictated by OPEC (the Organization of Petroleum Exporting Countries) in 1973–1974 and again in 1979–1980. By the time the situation stabilized for a time in the early 1980s, the price of a barrel of oil had jumped from two dollars to over thirty, Third World nations had contracted gigantic debts, and the entire structure of international trade and banking had received a shock from which it did not recover for a decade or more.

Britain, which had shared in a significant, if unspectacular, fashion in the prosperity of the 1950s and 1960s, was to be very much affected by the economic roller coaster of the 1970s, when a rate of inflation that during the 1960s had seemed disturbingly high came to be looked back upon as an elusive ideal. During the 1970s, questions such as British membership in the European Economic Community and the proper role of powerful trade unions in a welfare-state society were to raise political and ideological passions in a manner reminiscent of the years before World War I. Both in the mid-1970s and again in the early 1980s, the tradition of two-party politics seemed about to give way to a political pattern less simple but more representative of the spectrum of public attitudes. Finally, the "Irish question," seemingly resolved fifty years earlier, cast its shadow upon the land once more; so did the analogous problem of how to assimilate peacefully into a fundamentally conservative British society the second generation of racially

418

mixed immigrants. For Great Britain, the decade turned out to be "the Stormy Seventies."[1]

The General Election of 1970

The Labour government had been battered by economic storms for more than four years, but in 1969 the essentially conservative fiscal and monetary tools employed by Roy Jenkins, Chancellor of the Exchequer, began to work. The international balance of payments showed a sizable surplus, foreign loans were being repaid, and the pound seemed no longer in peril. Jenkins found it possible to ease some of the restraints on wages, prices, and spending abroad; and although these steps set into motion a new inflationary tide, the atmosphere of prosperity brightened the government's political prospects.

For three years by-elections, local elections, and public opinion polls had all indicated a popular preference for the Conservative opposition; but early in 1970 the opinion polls reflected a shift in the public mood. They predicted a continuation of Labour rule and a distinct public preference for Harold Wilson over Edward Heath as prime minister. So Wilson, a faithful student of the polls, called for a new general election in June. The Labour party stood on its record — advancements in health care, pensions, social reform, and success in bringing overseas commitments into line with Britain's diminished resources. The published diaries of cabinet colleagues were to reveal a government given more to day-to-day improvisation than to long-range planning, but in public Wilson invariably appeared as the unruffled, slightly bemused Oxford don calmly puffing on his pipe. In a manner reminiscent of Conservative Prime Minister Harold Macmillan eleven years earlier, Wilson waged a quiet and almost complacent campaign; he did not think that the British people wanted "a lot of change and disturbance."

His Conservative alter ego reminded the electorate of "Labour's broken promises," of the government's failure either to halt inflation or to promote steady economic growth, and of its inability to curb wildcat strikes and to cope adequately with the growth of crime and public violence. Heath, the stiff and somewhat aloof election underdog, campaigned doggedly on, and when the votes had all been tallied, the pollsters stood red-faced as Edward Heath became the new occupant of No. 10 Downing Street. Personalities had proved less significant than issues,

---

[1]The books by Morgan, Marwick, and Sked and Cook cited earlier deal with various aspects of the decade. So do the biographies of Harold Wilson by Pimlott and Austen Morgan, as does Max Beloff and Gillian Peele, *The Government of the United Kingdom: Political Authority in a Changing Society* (2nd ed., 1985). Martin Holmes interviewed numerous participants for his book, *The Labour Government, 1974–79: Political Aims and Economic Reality* (1985), and Prime Minister James Callaghan provided his own account of his political career in *Time and Chance* (1987).

Leaders of the 1960s and 1970s The imposing figure of Sir Winston Churchill looms over Prime Minister Edward Heath and former (as well as future) Prime Minister Harold Wilson at the opening of Parliament after the general election of 1970. *(Bettmann/ Corbis)*

and Conservative party workers had proved far more efficient than their Labour counterparts in getting out the vote. The Conservatives won 330 parliamentary seats; Labour, 287; Liberals, 6; others, 7. Conservatives captured 46.4 percent of the total popular vote, Labour 43 percent.

Conservative Reform

What Prime Minister Wilson had called "the exciting new world of the '70s" was thus ushered in with a new prime minister and a party pledged not to maintain the status quo but to bring about specific changes. There was to be a reduction in taxes (which had risen by 80 percent during six years of Labour rule). "There has been too much government," declared Heath; "there will be less." Although the essentials of the welfare state were not to be undermined, the emphasis was to be on aid for the least well-off rather than for everyone. A proposed industrial relations bill would make trade-union contracts legally binding. Finally, the Conservative government would launch a new effort to make Britain part of the European Economic Community.

Heath was the same age as Wilson and of a similarly unaristocratic background, but the two men differed markedly in personality. Heath was a talented organist who had attended Oxford on a music scholarship, and he was an expert yachtsman whose victory in Australian waters in the 1970 Sydney-Hobart race confirmed his skill. He was also the first bachelor at No. 10 since A. J. Balfour in 1902–1905. His ministry was to resemble Balfour's in yet another way: its positive actions rather than its errors of omission were soon to reap the most bitter political opposition.

The Conservative government hoped that, by encouraging industrial competition and by reducing taxes, it would fuel a new economic boom. Thus, it lowered tax rates on income from investments as well as on wages and salaries, and it exempted from income tax altogether some four million of the lowest-paid wage-earners. During 1971 the ceilings on bank interest payments and restrictions on installment loans were lifted, and building societies (the British equivalent of American savings-and-loan associations) were encouraged to expand their mortgage loans. The anticipated boom did take place in 1972 when the national budget deficit rose sharply, industrial production grew by 10 percent, and the stock market index reached an all-time high. Many factories instituted overtime, and unemployment dwindled. Easily available loan funds tended to flow less into industrial investment, however, than into installment buying and into a real estate boom that in the course of two years doubled the market price of houses. By 1973 a shortage of skilled labor, a rapid rise in world raw materials prices, and increasing industrial turmoil at home caused economic expansion to reach a plateau.

By then the Heath ministry had enacted into law two other significant legislative reforms. The Local Government Act of 1972 for England and Wales and a comparable act in 1973 for Scotland established a fundamentally two-tier system of local government. The upper tier in England was made up of forty-five county authorities, in addition to the Greater London Council, each headed by a chief executive. The authorities would be elected at four-year intervals and were primarily concerned with education, police, and the administration of social services. Although many historic county boundaries (dating back to Anglo-Saxon times) were kept, some old counties were divided, others like Rutland disappeared altogether, and a number of new "metropolitan counties" were established in the industrial Midlands and in Yorkshire. The lower tier (with responsibility for local planning, housing, urban streets, and refuse collection) was to be made up of elective district or borough councils. A third tier of rural parish or city neighborhood councils was allowed for as well — less to serve as governing bodies than as forums for canvassing local opinion. Although far more dependent on the national government than are American states, British local authorities remained significant after 1972 if only because they spent three-tenths of all public funds. Of every pound they disbursed during the 1970s and early 1980s, however, forty-eight pence were provided by the national Exchequer; thirty-six pence came from local rates (property taxes on homes and businesses); and sixteen pence from fees and assessments for local services. Greater efficiency was the long-range purpose of local government reform, but the change did not come cheaply: thousands of electoral boundaries had to be

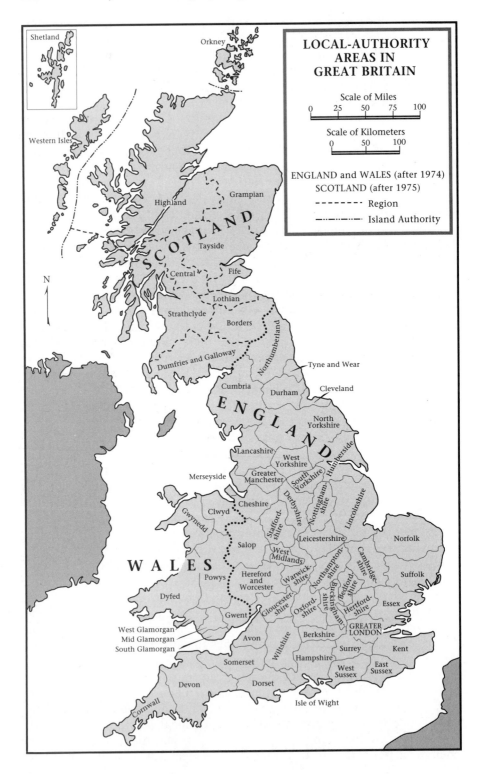

Shetland

Orkney

Western Isles

**LOCAL-AUTHORITY
AREAS IN
GREAT BRITAIN**

Scale of Miles

0   25   50   75   100

Scale of Kilometers

0   50   100

ENGLAND and WALES (after 1974)
SCOTLAND (after 1975)

- - - - - - -   Region
-·-··-··-··-   Island Authority

Highland

Grampian

S C O T L A N D

Tayside

Central   Fife

Lothian

Strathclyde

Borders

N

Dumfries and Galloway

Northumberland

Tyne and Wear

Cumbria   Durham   Cleveland

E N G L A N D

North
Yorkshire

Lancashire

West
Yorkshire

Humberside

Merseyside

Greater
Manchester

South
Yorkshire

Nottingham-
shire

Lincolnshire

Cheshire

Derbyshire

Clwyd

Gwynedd

Stafford-
shire

Leicestershire

Norfolk

Salop

West
Midlands

Northampton-
shire

Cambridge-
shire

W A L E S

Powys

Hereford
and
Worcester

Warwick-
shire

Bedford-
shire

Suffolk

Essex

Dyfed

Gloucester-
shire

Oxford-
shire

Buckingham-
shire

Hertford-
shire

Gwent

GREATER
LONDON

West Glamorgan
Mid Glamorgan
South Glamorgan

Avon

Wiltshire

Berkshire

Surrey

Kent

Somerset

Hampshire

West
Sussex

East
Sussex

Devon

Dorset

Isle of Wight

Cornwall

redrawn, and numerous historic place names and offices, such as that of alderman, permanently disappeared. The new boundary lines did not only undermine old community loyalties, but in the course of the next two decades they also unintentionally diminished the prestige accorded to local government officeholders.

Far more controversial than the Local Government Act was the Industrial Relations Act of 1971, a measure that sought to fit the process of collective bargaining between unions and employers into a framework of statute law comparable to that of other European countries and the United States. On the one hand, the act protected trade unionists from unjust dismissal or other unfair industrial practices. On the other hand, it gave authority to an Industrial Court and to lesser local tribunals to rule on labor disputes and, in emulation of American law, to order a sixty-day cooling-off period in the case of strikes that threatened to create a national emergency. In order to avail themselves of the benefits of the act, unions were asked to sign up with an official registrar. Many union leaders believed that they already possessed in practice the benefits the act avowedly gave them in law, and they objected to all government curbs on their activities. They persuaded the Trades Union Congress therefore to instruct member unions to refuse to register under the new act and to place pressure on employers to ignore the law as well. Relations between the Heath government and the unions soon became enveloped in a spirit of mutual distrust.

Britain Joins the EEC

The step that Heath expected would do most to stimulate the British economy and to give Britain a vital political role to play in the wider world was entry in the Common Market — the European Economic Community. Negotiations began at once, and a conference in Paris in May 1971 between Heath and Georges Pompidou, de Gaulle's successor as president of France, broke the logjam that had blocked Britain's admission during the previous decade. A common external tariff, a common farm policy, and a five-year period of transition were agreed upon once Britain's membership became official on January 1, 1973. What remained was for the House of Commons to approve the terms and the supplementary legislation. Throughout the summer and early fall of 1971 the question was debated and the limitations on national sovereignty that membership would impose were weighed against the opportunities that membership might provide and against the risks of permanent exclusion from an economic entity that, in productive capacity, might soon outrank the United States. As the debate progressed, most Conservatives chose to follow their leader, but Labourites grew increasingly antagonistic. When prime minister, Wilson had himself sought entry, but he now bowed to the influence of the Trades Union Congress and of the party's left wing, which viewed most EEC countries as "reactionary." Heath

European Wedding   The question of whether Great Britain would become a true partner of the European Economic Community remained uncertain until the national referendum of June 1975. The question was indeed still being debated twenty-five years after the "wedding." (The Guardian *[London], January 27, 1975*)

gave Conservative M.P.'s a "free vote" whereas the Labour opposition imposed a party whip. Thirty-nine Conservatives voted no, but sixty-nine Labourites, including Roy Jenkins, who was then the party's deputy leader, defied instructions and voted yes. The result was a decisive majority in favor of the Common Market, 356 to 244.

In the course of 1972, Parliament debated and ultimately approved the European Communities Bill, which gave the force of British law to existing and future EEC regulations. On January 1, 1973, the addition of Britain as well as Ireland and Denmark transformed the six-nation EEC (France, West Germany, Italy, Belgium, Netherlands, Luxembourg) into a nine-nation organization. Other steps had already been taken to "move into Europe." As early as 1950 Britain had agreed to the establishment of a European Court of Justice (sitting at Strasbourg, France), authorized to judge appeals from the citizens of all nations that (like Britain) gave the court authority to enforce the UN Convention on Human Rights. In the course of the 1970s the court became increasingly active in deciding cases ranging in subject from the caning of schoolboys to the dismissal of employees for refusing to join a closed shop. In 1971 the British coinage had been converted to a decimal system. No longer was the pound divided into twenty shillings and each shilling into twelve pence; the pound was now made up simply of one hundred new pence. During the 1970s the Fahrenheit system of measuring temperature gave way to the continental centigrade system, and inches, feet, yards, and miles were gradually supplanted by centimeters, meters, and kilometers. In accordance with EEC policy, Britain substituted a so-called Value-Added tax (an impost on a firm's business turnover) for the older form of purchase (or sales) tax. That Napoleonic pipe dream, a Channel tunnel, received a joint blessing from Britain and France in 1973 but, during the decade that followed, the project was derailed once more. The technology was available; the money was not. Only in 1985 did Britain and France sign a new treaty authorizing a private corporation to build a rail tunnel (with flatcars to transport automobiles), and only in 1994 did it become possible to board a train in London and to get off in Paris three hours later.

In some ways the timing of Britain's adhesion to the EEC was unfortunate; it coincided with the onset of an era of economic stagnation rather than of growth. Also, unlike some of the German and French founders of the Common Market — who saw it as the symbol of the triumph of a common feeling of Europeanness over the clashing nationalisms of its member states that had so often led to murderous war — most British advocates saw adhesion, more prosaically, as simply economic good sense. And, even in the short run, membership in the EEC did indeed alter the pattern of British trade. Back in 1960, 22 percent of British exports and 20 percent of British imports had involved the EEC nations; by 1979 the figures were up to 42 and 43 percent, respectively, and West Germany had become Britain's single most important trading partner. The number of trucks crossing the English Channel by car ferry more than doubled between the mid-1970s and the mid-1980s, and the number of Britons taking their vacations in EEC lands grew from fewer than 3 million to more than 7 million per year. In the meantime, exports to Commonwealth lands had fallen from 34 to 12 percent of the total, imports from 31 to 11 percent. A variety of Commonwealth ties remained, however. Thus, British investors were still the largest suppliers of capital to Australia, and Britain provided a quarter of all annual foreign aid to India. When Pakistan broke with the Commonwealth (for several years) after the successful revolt of Bangladesh (East Pakistan) in 1972, that poverty-stricken state was independently admitted to the Commonwealth of Nations. When Idi Amin, the dictator-president of Uganda, arbitrarily expelled all residents of Indian origin that year, Britain acknowledged responsibility for those who held British passports; 28,000 Ugandan Asian refugees were in due course admitted to England. Although the Immigration Act of 1971 ended all preferences extended earlier to Commonwealth immigrants, it restored the right of automatic entry to any person with at least one parent British by birth.

The Northern Ireland Question

Although Conservatives and Labourites differed on the regulation of trade unions and on Britain's entry into the Common Market, they were

EUROPEAN UNION [known earlier as Common Market, European Economic Community (EEC), and European Community (EC)] 2000

European Union Members (with dates of admission)

during the 1970s largely in accord as to how best to deal with the nagging problem of Northern Ireland, which had come to the fore during the Wilson ministry in the late 1960s. Since 1921, when the "Irish question" had been "solved" by partition, Northern Ireland had constituted the only portion of the United Kingdom with a federal form of government. In addition to sending twelve M.P.'s to Westminster, Northern Ireland had its own Home Rule parliament and prime minister. For almost half a century, that parliament had been dominated by the Unionist party, predominantly Protestant and pledged to preserve the area's ties with Britain and to prevent a union with the predominantly Catholic Irish Republic to the south. The fact that at least one-third of the people of Northern Ireland were Roman Catholics whose loyalty to the regional government was suspect provided cause for intermittent tension through the years. From 1963 on, a moderate Northern Ireland prime minister, Terrence O'Neill, sought reforms to ease the social intolerance as well as the political discrimination (at the local government level) that the Roman Catholic minority suffered; at the same time he promoted more cordial relations with the Irish Republic.

These reforms were adopted at too slow a pace to please a militant civil-rights movement that emerged in Northern Ireland in the late 1960s and far too quickly to suit an ultra-Protestant faction headed by Ian Paisley, a Presbyterian minister. Demonstrations and counterdemonstrations forced O'Neill to resign as prime minister in April 1969. They

Violence in Northern Ireland   Vehicles set on fire in Londonderry to mark a funeral for two I.R.A. members shot by undercover troops (1984). *(Topham/The Imageworks)*

reached a climax in August when barricades were set up in the streets of Belfast and Londonderry; 8 persons were killed and 740 were wounded. The Wilson government, which would have preferred that the Irish settle their own problems, felt compelled to send regular army troops to the province to help keep order. It also provided special economic aid to relieve housing and unemployment problems and pushed reforms intended to satisfy the Roman Catholic minority.

Catholics initially welcomed the British troops as protectors, and the situation might have been resolved had not the so-called provisional wing of the professedly Marxist Irish Republican Army supplanted the civil-rights movement. Its purpose was less to ease the lot of the Roman Catholic minority in Northern Ireland than to unite the entire island, if necessary by violence. The constitution of the Irish Republic envisaged the eventual incorporation of Northern Ireland, and a united Ireland remained the republic's long-range goal. At the same time successive Irish governments during the 1970s had no desire to force a million Northern Irish Protestants to become its unwilling citizens, and they had long since outlawed the I.R.A. as a dangerous nuisance. The I.R.A. was therefore publicly pledged to overthrow the legally elected governments of both Northern Ireland and the Irish Republic. Its campaign of terrorism did succeed in compelling the acquiescence of most Northern Roman Catholics and of turning many against what they called "the British occupation." A succession of I.R.A. attacks on British army units in the summer of 1971 led to a policy of internment without trial of I.R.A. leaders by the Northern Ireland government. This step led to even more violent attacks on troops and police and the beginning of a policy of random bombings of pubs, shops, and hotels. In March 1972 the Heath government concluded that, even with the aid of fourteen thousand British soldiers, the Northern Ireland government was no longer capable of preserving order in the area. The fifty-year-old constitution was therefore suspended, and William Whitelaw (1918–1999) became the first of a number of secretaries of state for Northern Ireland appointed by successive British ministries to govern the province directly.

That decision satisfied neither the I.R.A. nor the militant Protestant Vanguard Movement, which was becoming increasingly fearful that the British government was preparing to "sell out" the interests of Ulster and some of whose supporters were retaliating against the I.R.A. with bombings and murders of their own. In the course of 1972 more than ten thousand incidents of shooting and almost fourteen hundred explosions took place, and at the end of the year the four-year death toll stood at 676. Whitelaw attempted to steer a middle course. On the one hand, he sought to reassure the Northern Ireland majority that it could remain part of Britain as long as it wished; in a March 1973 plebiscite, three-quarters of the electorate so voted. On the other hand, Whitelaw sought to establish a formal tie with the Irish Republic, an appropriate step at a time when both Britain and Ireland were joining the Common Market. He also sought to set up a new Northern Ireland government that would, by means of proportional representation, give a voice to all factions. An assembly of seventy-eight members was elected in June 1973, two-thirds of them pledged to accept the principle of Protestant-Catholic power sharing. The assembly was to be headed by an eleven-person committee, the Northern Ireland Executive, made up of both Protestants and Catholics.

Scarcely had the new regional government taken office when a general election (called for reasons unconnected with Ireland) enabled the militant ultra-Unionists to capture eleven of twelve Northern Ireland seats at Westminster. Their determined opposition to power sharing and a fifteen-day general strike by Protestant workers in the province led in May 1974 to the collapse of Whitelaw's experiment. By the end of 1974, pubs and shops in Dublin, London, and Birmingham — where 21 people were killed and 160 injured — had been added to the list of I.R.A. targets. There were to be several additional attempts to set up a new elected assembly for Northern Ireland, but public attitudes had become too polarized to make possible a compromise settlement — at least during the 1970s and 1980s. A majority of Britons would have much preferred the Irish to bridge their sectarian differences, but for the time being successive British governments found no alternative but to diminish, if they could not eliminate, the level of violence by continuing to use the army to assist the local police and by continuing the direct rule of the province.

Economic Dilemmas

Although sharp ideological differences between the Conservative and Labour parties had been muted during the greater part of the 1950s and 1960s, they reappeared during the early 1970s. For Heath "it was in freedom, not in reliance upon the State, that Britain achieved greatness. It was the acceptance of personal responsibility, not dependence upon the central government, that made this small island so dominant in the world." It was the private and not the public sector of the economy that had triggered the "economic miracle" in Germany and Japan and that the Conservatives hoped to imitate. The state might and should help the poor, the old, and the unemployed, but for Conservatives the collective success of a society was ultimately based on the achievements of individuals. Labourites had much greater faith in the ability of the state to plan and direct society and distrusted most business executives as profiteers. Labour's fundamental concern was with the distribution of goods rather than with their creation, and in 1973 the party pledged itself to bring about "a fundamental and irreversible shift in the balance of power and wealth in favor of working people and their families." Under the influence of Michael Foot (1914–   ) and Tony (Anthony Wedgwood) Benn, the party unfurled anew the wrinkled banner of "nationalization."

The sense of ideological tension was accentuated by a heightened spirit of trade-union militancy. Strikes occurred with ever-greater

Modern Trade Unions: Heroes or Villains? (*above*) The wives of Derbyshire miners hand a letter to an official at the coal board at Hobart Place, January 18, 1972. (*Hulton Deutsch Collection*) (*left*) A cartoonist's version of the aims of the engine drivers' union that brought the British rail system to a temporary halt in 1982. (*Daily Express [London], January 15, 1982*)

frequency. In 1971 a strike of Post Office workers led to forty-seven days without mail, and a strike of British Ford Motor Company employees lasted nine weeks. Early in 1972 the first national coal strike since 1926 led to extensive electricity cuts and caused the layoff of more than 1.5 million workers; a national dock strike took place in July. As the graph on page 433 shows, the number of working days lost because of strikes in

1971 was four times as great as the average for the 1960s, and the total for 1972 was the highest since the general strike year of 1926. Increasingly unions relied on "mass picketing," "secondary picketing," "flying pickets," and other forms of direct action that the police were either unable or unwilling to restrain. Such militancy can be explained in part by the influence of Communist shop stewards, in part by a sense of alienation from the Conservative government, in part by a prickly insistence on preserving all existing wage differentials, and in part by an awareness that even a lengthy strike involved little immediate economic risk: a striker's family could readily obtain welfare aid. Many strikes were triggered by changes in work rules or by the firing of a single individual; fear of unemployment and loyalty to a "mate" outranked any awareness of the need to increase efficiency in a particular industry.

Such strikes did not merely injure the reputation for reliability of British exporters; they also led to ever-more-inflationary wage settlements, which led in turn to comparable price rises and to demands from other unions to catch up. As inflation made British exports more expensive, the international balance of payments (after three years of surplus) plunged into deficit again in 1972. Although it had long been felt that world trade depended on a fixed long-term relationship among different currencies, the World War II (Bretton Woods) agreement among the industrialized nations that had kept currency relations stable for a generation was breaking up in the early 1970s, and in the summer of 1972 the Heath ministry decided to permit the pound to "float" on the international money market. By 1974, this meant a 20 percent devaluation vis-à-vis the major western European currencies.

Although the floating of the pound temporarily aided British exporters and discouraged currency speculators, it did not solve the problem of inflation. Nor did a series of attempts by Heath to obtain a policy of voluntary price and wage restraints acceptable to both the Confederation of British Industries and the Trades Union Congress. The TUC insisted on price control but was unwilling to accept wage control, and early in November the talks broke down. As a consequence, in November 1972 Heath decided on a sharp U-turn in economic policy — from an attempt to rely largely on market forces to a strengthening of state regulation. He called for a ninety-day freeze on wages, prices, rents, and dividends. The Counter-Inflation Act that followed early in 1973 set up a Price Commission and a Pay Board and was designed to impose a rigorous limit on all increases. The turnabout in policy was a hard pill for the Conservative party to swallow; stock market prices began to plummet, and trade unions remained publicly uncooperative. Yet during 1973 the amount of industrial unrest did subside, and the rate of inflation did decline.

Inflation was not solely the result of domestic causes. It was also the consequence of a worldwide rise in the price of raw materials. The most dramatic example of such an increase came in November 1973 when the Organization of Petroleum Exporting Countries quadrupled the price of oil. As recently as World War II, 75 percent of the world's oil had been supplied by the United States, but by the 1960s a world using burgeoning quantities had become dangerously dependent on the cheaper oil from the Middle East. In 1973, using another Arab-Israeli war as a pretext, OPEC demonstrated its new power. Although Britain still utilized relatively more coal than did the United States or western Europe, more than half of its economy relied on oil, and virtually all of that oil was imported from the Middle East. The result was the onset of a worldwide economic recession and an overwhelming new threat to Britain's uneasy balance-of-payments position. British mineworkers decided to take advantage of the renewed importance of the coal that generated most British electricity by seeking wages far in excess of Heath's anti-inflation guidelines. In November the miners banned all overtime in the mines; this meant a 40 percent cutback in production. When electric-power and locomotive engineers also banned overtime work, the government declared a state of emergency, and on January 1, 1974, in order to save the diminishing coal supply, Heath put most of British industry on a three-day week. The resulting decline in production proved to be far smaller than anticipated, demonstrating the potential capacity of British industry when both labor and management worked at peak efficiency. Numerous last-minute negotiations failed to head off a total miners' strike in early February. Heath, who had seen the coal strike of 1972 foil his voluntary anti-inflation program, did not feel that he could permit a comparable strike in 1974. For him the question was "Who Governs Britain?" — was it a single powerful trade union or was it a constitutionally elected parliament? A new general election was called for on February 28 so that the electorate might provide the answer.[2]

The General Elections of 1974

A considerable portion of the electorate, which was asked to render a decision between the Conservative and Labour parties, had become disenchanted with both. Voters were unhappy with Heath's policy toward the unions, which vacillated between compromise and confrontation, and with Wilson's acquiescence in their militancy. As public opinion polls had suggested and as a number of dramatic by-elections in 1972 and 1973 had confirmed, the Liberal party, which had almost disappeared in the 1950s, had gained a new lease on life. Under the leadership of the urbane Jeremy Thorpe (1929–   ), it won the support of voters discontented with both major parties. Although it had been Heath's initial hope to focus the election on a single grave constitutional issue, a great variety of more

---

[2]John Campbell's *Edward Heath: A Biography* (1993) illuminates both the man and the era. See also Stuart Ball and Anthony Seldon, eds., *The Heath Government 1970–1974: A Reappraisal* (1997).

prosaic subjects, such as mortgage interest rates and real estate taxes, soon entered the debate. That articulate maverick, Enoch Powell, broke with the Conservative party because of its pro-Europe and compulsory price-control policies and ultimately urged his followers to support Labour.

The returns proved to be curiously indecisive. No party held an overall parliamentary majority (at least 318), but Labour, with marginally fewer popular votes, had won 301 seats, the Conservatives, 296. The resurgent Liberals, with more than 19 percent of the total popular vote, had obtained only 14 seats. Of Northern Ireland's 12 seats, which in earlier elections would probably have gone Conservative, 11 had been won instead by the United Ulster Unionists. Seven seats had gone to Scottish Nationalists and 2 to Welsh Nationalists. Once the results were in, Heath sought to form a Conservative-Liberal coalition and offered Thorpe a major seat in the cabinet. The latter refused to participate in anything except a "grand coalition" of all major parties, but this notion was rejected by Wilson. Heath thereupon handed in his resignation to the queen, and she called on Wilson to form a new government. Thus a Labour party, with only 37.2 percent of the popular vote, was able to form a government, the first minority ministry since MacDonald's in 1929–1931. Wilson felt sure that he could keep his ministerial ship afloat long enough to find a favorable opportunity to call a new election.

"Back to Work with Labour" had been Wilson's slogan, and early in March, after an eleven-week slowdown and a four-week strike, the coal miners went back to work on essentially the terms they had sought.

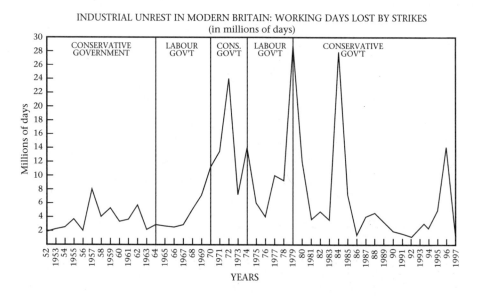

INDUSTRIAL UNREST IN MODERN BRITAIN: WORKING DAYS LOST BY STRIKES (in millions of days)

Derived from *Annual Abstract of Statistics* (1963, 1973, 1982, 1987, 1990, 1994, and 1999 editions).

Wilson's ministry retained some statutory controls over prices and strengthened controls on rent, but it repealed the Conservative Industrial Relations Act, and it abandoned all attempts to restrict wage increases except for a voluntary "social contract." According to that agreement, the Trades Union Congress promised to urge restraint on its members and have them limit their wage claims to a level that did no more than preserve their living standards. In practice, the policy led to a dramatic rise in the rate of inflation and an increasingly demoralized business community. Profit margins were squeezed yet further, investments declined, and bankruptcies were frequent. The London stock market suffered its most precipitous fall since the South Sea Bubble of 1720, and in December 1974 stock market averages, discounting inflation, plummeted temporarily to the level of the early 1920s. The annual budget deficit was higher than ever, and the international trade deficit for the year turned out to be £5.1 billion ($12.2 billion), by far the largest in British history. It was only a combination of foreign loans and large-scale Arab deposits in London banks that provided a short-term solution. For many Britons, moreover, the national economic crisis was disguised for several months; at a time when retail prices had risen by 19 percent, weekly wage rates for manual workers had gone up by an unprecedented 28 percent.

By autumn the national mood seemed sufficiently favorable for the politically pragmatic Wilson to justify a second general election within the same year, one that would, he hoped, provide the Labour party with an overall majority in the House of Commons. Although all parties promised to deal with inflation, only the Liberals were pledged to reimpose mandatory price and wage restraints. The October campaign echoed the February contest, but the election revealed a more apathetic electorate: 79 percent had participated in February, but only 72 percent did so in October. By the narrowest of margins, the electorate provided Wilson with an overall parliamentary majority.

SEATS AND PERCENTAGE OF POPULAR VOTE

Party	1970		Feb. 1974		Oct. 1974	
Labour	287	(43.0%)	301	(37.1%)	319	(39.2%)
Conservative	330	(46.4%)	296	(37.9%)	277	(35.9%)
Liberal	6	(7.4%)	14	(19.3%)	13	(18.3%)
Other	7	(3.2%)	24	(5.7%)	26	(6.6%)
TOTAL HOUSE OF COMMONS	630		635		635	

Although Wilson acknowledged that "Britain faces, and has for a considerable time been facing, the gravest economic crisis since the war," the program his party had presented to the electorate and that it now presented to the new Parliament seemed largely unrelated to that crisis. The 1964–1970 Labour government had sought to make the existing "mixed economy" work, but the Labour government elected in 1974 emphasized its acquiescence in union power and in socialist doctrine. A government that had won the allegiance of fewer than four voters in ten still felt it had a mandate to nationalize Britain's shipbuilding and aircraft industries and, in part, its oil industry. Tony Benn, secretary of state for industry, hoped to extend nationalization further by using a projected National Enterprise Board to offer funds to cash-starved private businesses in exchange for a share in their ownership and management. Denis Healey (1918–   ), the Chancellor of the Exchequer, promised a tax program that would elicit "howls of anguish" from the rich and a revised capital transfer and inheritance tax likely to warrant a similar reaction.

By the spring of 1975 it had become clear, however, that the apparently militant Labour majority was in fact sorely divided. In an effort to paper over earlier cracks in the party's program, Wilson had promised a constitutional innovation, a national referendum on the subject of whether Britain should remain in the Common Market. This apparent solution became a problem in turn, as the referendum campaign publicly pitted the prime minister and a majority of his cabinet — satisfied with "renegotiated" terms — against an unappeasable cabinet minority that won the support of a razor-thin majority of Labour M.P.'s and a substantial majority of trade-union leaders. Almost all Conservative and Liberal M.P.'s were united in favor of a yes vote, and in June 1975, after a lively newspaper and television debate, the British electorate gave the European Economic Community its seal of approval by a margin of more than two to one.

Although Wilson's cabinet had successfully weathered the Common Market referendum storm, it had clearly failed thus far to master the economy. The rate of inflation, the rate of unemployment, and the annual national budget deficit were all still growing. The social contract (or "social con-trick," as its critics called it) had proved so flexible as to lend justification to whatever wage increases union leaders were inclined to ask for. Although the TUC agreed to a program of limited wage increases for the year ahead, the government promised to impose no legal sanctions on member unions that exceeded those guidelines. Its price commission was to disallow, however, all price rises justified by pay settlements that did exceed the guidelines. In effect, the government sought to use private employers as police officers: either they would compel trade unionists to limit their demands or they would go bankrupt.

The policy did something to reduce a rate of inflation that had reached an all-time high in the summer of 1975, but it did little to restore business confidence. Nor did it aid Britain's international balance of payments; the pound was floating steadily downward in value vis-à-vis the American dollar and the major European currencies. It was in this environment that Harold Wilson surprised his country in March 1976 by resigning as prime minister. He justified the step on the grounds that, although he was only sixty, he had had a lengthy career as M.P. and prime minister and that his successor would need time to shape his ministry before the next election. His critics suggested that Wilson was fleeing a

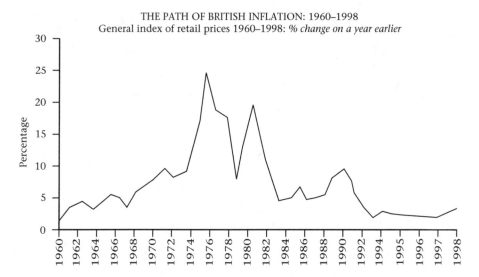

THE PATH OF BRITISH INFLATION: 1960–1998
General index of retail prices 1960–1998: *% change on a year earlier*

Source: H. M. Treasury, *Economic Progress Report* #184 (May/June 1986). More recent statistics are derived from the -
Annual Abstract of Statistics (1999).

sinking ship, leaving a heritage of economic mismanagement and deep political division within his own party. Their number increased after he received the Order of the Garter (and became Sir Harold) and his "resignation Honours List" was announced. He had recommended life peerages and other awards to a number of financiers and show-business tycoons whose contributions to the national welfare were apparent to few; he thereby evoked memories of the Lloyd George "Honours scandal" of the 1920s. Wilson thus left office under a cloud. In the words of David Marquand, "No modern Prime Minister has received more adulation on entering office or more execration on leaving it. No leader of the Labour Party has won more elections or disillusioned more followers."[3]

The Callaghan Years (1976–1979)

Wilson's resignation gave the Labour M.P.'s the novel opportunity of electing the next prime minister. Six nominees were in the running, and none won a majority on the first ballot; on the third ballot, however, James Callaghan, the candidate of the party's moderate center, defeated Michael Foot, the candidate of the party's left wing, by a vote of 176 to 137. The sixty-four-year-old party veteran had worked his way up the ranks, the first British prime minister successively (if not always successfully) to have headed all three major government departments: the

---

[3]*Times Literary Supplement,* Nov. 6, 1992, p. 11.

Exchequer, the Home Office, and the Foreign Office. He was untypical of his fellow Britons in being a chapelgoer, a teetotaler, and a nonsmoker, yet he soon won their affection. Even those who distrusted his policies found him more amiable, more magnanimous, and more in touch with the lives of ordinary people than his predecessor. He came to be known as "Sunny Jim."

The economic scene looked far from sunny, however, during the summer and fall of 1976 as the value of the pound continued to plummet and national budget deficits remained high. The international financial community privately came to fear that if Britain did not begin to live within its means, the nation would default on its outstanding loans, introduce rigid import controls, and unwittingly transform the world recession into a depression comparable to that of the early 1930s. Chancellor Denis Healey had already curtailed the funds his colleagues wanted to devote to welfare-state measures, but in November he was compelled to apply to the International Monetary Fund for the largest loan it had ever granted, in order to "save the pound." The IMF ultimately agreed, but only on the condition that Britain do much more to curb deficit spending. With great skill, Prime Minister Callaghan persuaded a reluctant cabinet to do so by reducing planned spending increases on education, food subsidies, housing, roads, overseas aid, and defense. A separate agreement with the United States (strongly supported by President Gerald Ford and Secretary of State Henry Kissinger) enabled the government to minimize speculation in pounds sterling, whose role as a major world currency was ebbing but had not entirely disappeared. Callaghan's economic problems were far from over, but the value of the pound stabilized for several years.[4]

In order to lower the rate of inflation, the government had to retain the goodwill of the major trade unions, and most of them did attempt to abide by voluntary wage-increase guidelines — at least until the fall of 1978. The Labour government dealt with the leaders of the major unions in as gingerly a fashion as did a medieval king with his chief barons: true, they had pledged their fealty, but at any moment they might turn unruly and order their private armies into battles that threatened the king's peace. Such union leaders continued to talk about the virtues of "free collective bargaining" and to see themselves as tiny islands in a sea of capitalist exploitation, but in fact three of every ten union members now worked for the government or for nationalized industries; in negotiations with private employers the cards were increasingly stacked in their favor. Unions had already gained so much influence over day-to-day operations on the factory floor that when the Bullock Commission recommended in 1977 that the boards of directors of private corporations include as many union representatives as shareholder representatives, the proposal fell on

---

[4]In *"Goodbye, Great Britain": The 1976 IMF Crisis* (1992), Kathleen Burk and Alec Cairncross contend that the episode served as catalyst to a profound change in British government economic policy and a prelude to the Thatcher approach of the 1980s.

deaf ears. Most union leaders preferred short-run victories over management to long-run responsibility for the viability and profitability of their companies.

In contrast to the American experience, the 1960s and 1970s had been an era of growth in British trade-union membership. Between 1966 and 1979 the numbers increased from 10.2 to 13.5 million, and the unionized proportion of the total work force went from 43 to 55 percent. Dependent on the support of the unions, the Wilson and Callaghan ministries did much to strengthen their privileges with new laws such as the Employment Protection Act of 1976. They decreed that only a union could initiate a legal process compelling an employer to pay the prevailing wage in his industry. Employers were given new encouragement to negotiate "closed shops" with their unions; if a worker fell out with his union and forfeited his membership card, his employer was compelled to fire him. Employers were to be fined heavily if found guilty of unfairly dismissing a worker; no employer was to be fined, however, for dismissing a worker who refused to join a union. Analogously, an employer had to give a ninety-day warning if he expected to lay off a hundred workers or more — provided they were union members.

The government sought to aid their union supporters in yet other ways, often with unforeseen consequences. Thus, the employer ordered to pay large compensation payments to any workers he had to let go was discouraged from hiring them in the first place. Analogously, the policy of permitting rent increases in council houses to lag 40 percent behind increases in worker earnings made it more difficult for local authorities either to maintain the public housing in which almost four in ten Britons lived, or to build more. The policy also discouraged the unemployed from seeking jobs elsewhere; so did a related rent-control statute that gave the tenants of private landlords so many legal privileges as to induce half the landlords to go out of business. The measures of nationalization taken by the Callaghan ministry, which involved airplane manufacturers, shipbuilders, and a new British National Oil Corporation, also satisfied union leaders, who had come to look upon nationalized industries as more likely to be bailed out by public funds in an emergency and therefore less likely to go bankrupt.

Other domestic measures were related less to union influence than to the Labour commitment to achieve yet greater degrees of social equality. The ministry took cognizance of an increasingly militant feminist movement by enacting the Sex Discrimination Act (1975) which provided for a permanent Equal Opportunities Commission to implement equal pay for equal work. The Employment Protection Act required employers to give all women workers a six-month maternity leave on request. In the meantime, the Education Act of 1976 hastened the transformation of tax-supported high schools into "comprehensives," and efforts were made to exclude all "pay beds," remnants of privately financed medicine, from National Health Service hospitals. The aim of equalizing wealth was central to the income tax rates as well. By 1977 the highest marginal tax rate had been raised to 83 percent for salaried income and to 98 percent for investment income — an invitation to the well-off either to evade taxes or to emigrate.

Such social legislation did not win the Labour government the electoral success it sought. By 1977 a series of by-election defeats had deprived Labour of its overall parliamentary majority, and during the next two years the Callaghan ministry became increasingly dependent on the two largest of the minor parties that had emerged from the general elections of 1974, the Liberals and the Scottish Nationalists. In January 1977, Callaghan and David Steel (1938–   ), the new Liberal leader, agreed on a "Lib-Lab" pact: Liberals did not enter the Labour government, but they were given the right to veto bills proposed by the cabinet prior to their introduction into Parliament. The plan lapsed in the summer of 1978. One of the sensations of the 1974 elections had been the sudden growth of a Scottish Nationalist party; in October it had captured eleven seats, one-sixth of Scotland's representatives. Proclaiming that the oil being discovered beneath the North Sea belonged by right to a Scotland that should become independent once more, the party seemed about to emulate the history of the Irish Nationalists in the 1880s. Eager to steal the Scottish Nationalist thunder, the Labour government prepared a Scottish "devolution" bill that — as amended — called for an elected assembly to meet in Edinburgh to make laws relating to local government, health, social services, housing, education, and the like; the head of the majority party would serve as prime minister. A proposed Welsh assembly was to have more restricted powers and no separate executive. Both peoples were to continue to send M.P.'s to Westminster as well. Most Conservatives were hostile to devolution, and many Labourites refused to support the plans until a clause had been added declaring that the assemblies would come into existence only if at least 40 percent of the registered Scottish and Welsh voters approved by referendum. In Scotland a sharp debate ensued between those who saw the plan as a just recognition of a revived Scottish nationalism and those who denounced it as a needless extravagance and potential bureaucratic nightmare. A small majority of Scottish voters favored the plan, but since they constituted only 33 percent of the total electorate, the plan failed. With only 12 percent support, the proposal for a Welsh assembly failed even more decisively. Once the results were announced, the Scottish Nationalists, like the Liberals, were prepared to turn out the Callaghan government at the earliest opportunity — "like turkeys voting for an early Christmas," commented the prime minister.

By the winter of 1979, the Callaghan government had also been undermined from within. It had slowed inflation and stabilized the exchange value of the pound, but it had not found the means of making British industry more efficient — at a time when it required twice as many British as German workers to manufacture the same automobile. Britain was therefore "deindustrializing," as year by year a larger proportion of motor vehicles and other manufactured goods was being imported from abroad. The number of unemployed had increased from 615,000 in 1974 to 1.3 million in 1979, and then, in the 1978–1979 "winter of discontent," the Callaghan government lost its chief claim to public confidence: the ability to limit union demands for inflationary wage settlements. Truck drivers, ambulance drivers, water workers, and others all struck in defiance of an attempt by the government to limit wage increases to 5 percent. Garbage lay uncollected in the streets; hospital workers switched off the boilers they tended; and in Liverpool gravediggers went on strike and left the dead unburied. Although Callaghan denounced the activities of his supposed supporters as "free collective vandalism," his government buckled. The Liberals and Scottish Nationalists supported a Conservative "no confidence" motion, and on March 28, by a vote of 311 to 310, the Labour government fell. For the third time in nine years, trade-union power had brought down a British ministry, and for the first time since 1924 the immediate agent of defeat had been not the electorate but the House of Commons itself. The vote reflected a long-smoldering popular revulsion against trade-union arrogance, and — as things turned out — brought to an abrupt end the era of Labour party government that had dominated British political life (with only a brief interruption) since 1964.

PART SEVEN

CONTEMPORARY BRITAIN

Since 1979

THE "LONDON EYE:" A TWENTY-FIRST CENTURY ADDITION TO THE CITY SKYLINE
(Bob Ecker)

CHAPTER 22

The Thatcher Era and After (1979–1997)

The election of 1979 may justly be compared with those of 1832, 1906, and 1945 in that it set the British ship of state on a distinctly new course. For the first time since the 1940s, a government came into power pledged to reverse the long drift toward a society in which government spent an ever-greater proportion of its people's earnings and regulated in ever-greater detail the economic aspects of their lives. Government planning was to give way to market forces, and nationalized industries were to give way to enterprises owned by private investors. During these same years, the essentials of the British welfare state were to change far less than advocates hoped or critics feared, but it remains appropriate to define this change of attitudes and policies as Thatcherism and to dub the 1980s "the Thatcher era." Margaret Thatcher (b. 1925) was to hold the post of prime minister for a longer continuous time, eleven and a half years (1979–1990), than any prime minister since the 1820s. She also was to become the first prime minister since British politics had become even partly democratized to lead a political party to victory in three successive general elections. Even after her fall from power, the waves that Margaret Thatcher had set into motion would jostle the ship that her successor, John Major, sought to steer with increasing difficulty during his own six-and-a-half-year prime ministership (1990–1997).[1]

The First Years (1979–1982)

In the general election campaign of 1979, Labour was led by Prime Minister James Callaghan. The Conservative party, however, was led not by Edward Heath but by Margaret Thatcher. In the aftermath of the two

---

[1]The historical surveys by Sked and Cook and by Morgan, cited earlier, both deal with the 1980s. Helpful contemporary accounts have been provided by Peter Riddell, *The Thatcher Era and Its Legacy* (1991), and by Hugo Young, *The Iron Lady: A Biography of Margaret Thatcher* (1989), as well as by Margaret Thatcher herself in *The Downing Street Years* (1993). Earl Reitan has furnished a dispassionate summing up in *Tory Radicalism: Margaret Thatcher, John Major, and the Transformation of Modern Britain, 1979–1997* (1997).

Margaret Thatcher   The prime minister listens to opening-day speeches at the Conservative party conference in 1984. *(Bettmann/Corbis)*

election defeats the party had suffered under Heath's leadership back in 1974, there was widespread grumbling in the party, but the only person who had held cabinet office who was willing to challenge him in 1975 in a contest for the party leadership was Margaret Thatcher. It was she who led her party to victory in 1979 with a campaign that articulated popular grievances against a government that had increased the role of the state in the economy but that had failed to curb either trade-union power or the growth of unemployment. Her hope was to transform Britain from a "wealth-consuming" to a "wealth-producing" nation, and she borrowed from Abraham Lincoln the dictum: "You don't make the poor richer by making the rich poorer." The daughter of a small-town grocer and mayor, Margaret Thatcher had been trained at Oxford as a research chemist; for four years she was also employed as a tax lawyer. First elected to Parliament in 1959, she had served from 1970 to 1974 as Heath's secretary of state for education and science. The first woman in Europe or North America to head a major political party, she became in May 1979 the first woman prime minister, and Britain became the first nation in history in which both the head of state, Queen Elizabeth II, and the head of government were women.

The election results showed that the Conservatives had gained 339 seats and 43.9 percent of the vote. Labour was reduced to 268 seats and 36.9 percent of the vote, the Liberals to 11 seats and 13.8 percent. Since 1974, three Liberals in ten and numerous abstainers had returned to the Conservative fold; almost four trade-union members in ten had voted

Conservative. For the time being, the Scottish and Welsh Nationalist parties were reduced to two M.P.s each.

The priorities of the new Thatcher government were clear-cut. The first was to provide incentives for private industry by reducing all income tax rates on individual wages (the highest marginal rate was reduced from 83 to 60 percent and later to 40 percent) and on corporations (for which the highest rate dropped from 52 to 35 percent). At the same time, inheritance taxes were reduced, and the movement of funds in and out of the country was freed from state regulation for the first time since before World War II. Inflation was to be kept under control by "monetarism," the use of government powers to curb the amount of money pumped into the economy. The growth of expenses on social services, education, and housing subsidies was to be restricted, and families who rented council houses (public housing administered by local housing authorities) were to be encouraged to buy them. In the course of five years, the number of people working for government, national and local, was scheduled to decline by 15 percent.

The new prime minister had little faith in the workability of mandatory price and wage controls and none in the willingness or ability of union leaders to agree on an "incomes policy." She sought instead to set fixed monetary limits on expenditures for civil servants and nationalized industries, and she hoped that union leaders would prefer smaller wage claims to job losses for their members. Her government launched no all-out assault on the legal immunities that trade unions had come to take for granted, but in 1980 and 1982 it began to chip away at those immunities: the number of picketers permitted at the site of a strike was restricted; secondary boycotts were banned; unions were encouraged to use secret ballots to elect officers and authorize strikes. Strikes that were clearly political were banned, and workers dismissed for refusing to join closed shops were allowed compensation.

The first three years of "Thatcherism" brought mixed results at best. There were successes. After an initial leap, spurred by the 1979–1980 OPEC oil price hike, the rate of inflation declined by 1982 to less than 8 percent, and living standards largely kept pace with inflation. A number of industries, such as aircraft construction, were denationalized once more, and the government strongly encouraged workers to become shareholders in the companies for which they worked. British industry was becoming significantly more efficient, and the international balance of payments showed a healthy surplus. That surplus was attributable in large part to oil from wells drilled 12,000 feet or more beneath the waters of the stormy North Sea. By 1981 Great Britain had become a net exporter of oil.

There were failures as well. Holding down inflation by monetarist means turned out to be far more difficult than expected. Despite the government's intentions, civil servants and employees in nationalized industries proved more successful in achieving their wage demands than did workers in private industry. A hefty pay raise for civil servants that was "in the pipeline" when Margaret Thatcher took office contributed significantly to the inflationary upsurge of 1980–1981. In the meantime, high interest rates had driven some businesses into bankruptcy and forced others to lay off workers. North Sea oil had indeed proved a mixed blessing: at the same time that it made Britain once more self-sufficient in energy it also caused the pound to be overvalued, thereby creating difficulties for other British exporters.

Even as the government spent less on subsidies to industry, it was compelled to spend far more on unemployment benefits. The generous level of such benefits in Britain constituted at least one explanation for why many of the long-term unemployed found no substitute jobs. Other reasons included the difficulty in finding accommodations to rent if one moved to another part of the country and the unwillingness of British union leaders (unlike American ones) to consider "give-backs" — that is, concessions in wage rates and working conditions in order to save jobs. During a period of world recession, businesses had not expanded sufficiently to absorb the available work force, and over the course of three years the rate of unemployment rose to over 11 percent (from 1.3 to over 3 million people by 1982); it leveled off at this percentage for several years before declining sharply for a time later in the decade. In the meantime Margaret Thatcher continued to battle what her secretary of state for employment, Norman Tebbit, called the "seven deadly delusions" (among them, "Pay rises, however high, do not affect unemployment"; "Strikes do not damage job prospects in the long run"; and "Restrictive practices preserve jobs"). For her numerous critics, however, she had become less "the Iron Lady" than "Attila the Hen" who was sacrificing a generation of young high school graduates and many older workers to a flawed economic doctrine.

Some critics blamed those economic policies for the riots that broke out during the spring and early summer of 1981 in the Brixton area of London, the Toxteth area of Liverpool, and in several other cities, where there were large settlements of immigrants from the West Indies and South Asia and their British-born children. Although many Britons remained uncomfortable about the way old neighborhoods had changed, the efforts of the National Front party to make political hay at the election of 1979 by fostering racial antagonism met with little success. It garnered less than 200,000 votes throughout the land, and it did not come close to electing any of its parliamentary candidates. Still, some members of the second generation of immigrants were not fitting easily into British society. At a time when crime in general was continuing to increase, street crime had risen precipitously in areas such as Brixton. Police officers seeking to contain such crime were themselves charged with "harassment" by bands of young blacks who smashed shop windows, burned cars and houses, and attacked the police with stones, broken bottles, and homemade gasoline bombs. Before the violence died down, they were joined by other young men, some of them white, from different neighborhoods. In the Liverpool and Manchester disorders, there was evidence of left-wing revolutionaries egging the rioters on. A series of race-relations statutes had yet to transform Britain into a harmonious multiracial society. The 1976 act, passed by a Labour government, had established a permanent Commission for Racial Equality to support local, voluntary race equality councils, investigate complaints, and issue nondiscrimination orders. In an independent report on the Brixton disturbances, Lord Scarman urged the promotion of closer police-community relations in multiracial areas and additional efforts by the police to attract black recruits. The riots shocked British opinion, but only one person had been killed, and a subsequent newspaper poll showed that 83 percent of the public remained convinced that their largely unarmed police were "still the best in the world."

The Split in the Labour Party

Margaret Thatcher's economic policies prompted some criticism from the "wets" within her own party — M.P.s such as her predecessor, Edward Heath, who remained aloof from the Thatcher cabinet and who was willing to risk greater inflation if it lowered a rate of unemployment he deemed "morally unjustified." Far more severe criticism came from the Labour opposition, but that opposition became sorely divided in the aftermath of the 1979 election. James Callaghan as leader gave way in 1980 to his deputy, the sixty-seven-year-old representative of the party's left wing, Michael Foot, who defeated the more moderate Denis Healey by a vote of 139 to 129. Under the influence of Tony Benn, the party abandoned its tradition of having Labour M.P.s choose future party leaders (and potential prime ministers). Instead, a party electoral college was set up in which Labour M.P.s were granted only three votes in ten; representatives of constituency party organizations had three votes as well, and major union leaders, four. Constituency organizations were also given the right to replace sitting Labour M.P.s with alternate candidates. Benn defended such changes as moves toward greater democracy, but in practice they meant that small groups of party militants could take over local party organizations and replace moderate M.P.s with those more closely attuned to their own ideas. By 1981 those ideas included unilateral nuclear disarmament, withdrawal from the EEC, steep protective tariffs, a new program of nationalization without compensation of private industries, a single-chamber parliament, and an enforced end to all private schooling and private medicine. At a time when the mass of the electorate seemed to find doctrinal socialism and "the class struggle between capital and labor" increasingly irrelevant, Labour militants adhered firmly to both. In many ways the party was turning its back on the actual policies of the Wilson and Callaghan governments.

In response to this move by the Labour party toward foreign policy neutralism and still greater state power, four former Labour party cabinet members — including Roy Jenkins and David Owen — resigned from their party in 1981 in order to form a new Social Democratic party. Its purpose was to serve as a new center force in British politics and to take the place of what Jenkins called "the ideological roller coaster" that the British public had ridden during the previous two decades. The leaders of the new party won dramatic by-election victories and then allied themselves with David Steel's Liberal party. The Alliance hoped to contest all British parliamentary seats at the next general election on a program of promoting "greater equality without stifling enterprise" and of substituting a system of proportional representation for Britain's traditional "first past the post" system in each parliamentary constituency. (As in the United States, the candidate who attracts the largest number of votes wins the seat even if those votes constitute fewer than a majority of all the votes cast.) For several months the Social Democratic/Liberal Alliance surpassed both Conservatives and Labourites in the public opinion polls, but in the long run the new Alliance found it impossible to break the mold of British politics, and ultimately it failed to replace Labour as the chief opposition party. Margaret Thatcher's Conservative government was to benefit greatly, however, from the deep rifts among her political opponents.

The Britain of the 1980s laid no claim to superpower status, but it remained very much involved with the EC (European Community), with NATO, and at times with obligations assumed when it had been the center of a worldwide empire. Although the Conservatives, unlike the Labourites of that era, were committed to remaining part of the EC, Prime Minister Thatcher made it a point to stand up for her country's interests. When the workings of the European agricultural subsidy plan mandated that Britain pay a larger sum into the community exchequer than did any other EC member, she took strong exception and eventually negotiated a better deal. Britain cooperated more willingly to create a directly elected European Parliament. Britain and Northern Ireland were divided into seventy-eight districts, and in June 1979 voters in each district elected their first M.E.P. (Member of European Parliament).

During these same years the Thatcher government adamantly opposed Soviet warmongering. It protested strongly in 1979 against the Soviet invasion of Afghanistan, and it increased the British defense budget (in real terms) for the first time in a decade. The government also resisted firmly a temporarily revived Campaign for Nuclear Disarmament whose advocates asserted that Britain would be safer with a policy of unilateral disarmament and removal of all American military bases rather than with the policy of close alliance with the United States and of mutual East-West nuclear deterrence that for more than three decades had averted war among the great powers. It agreed to "maintain a credible British strategic deterrent" by substituting, once they became available, Trident missiles for the outmoded Polaris missiles on British nuclear submarines. When the Soviet Union deployed medium-range nuclear missiles in eastern Europe in order to intimidate and neutralize western Europe, the Thatcher government cooperated with the Reagan administration to install American Cruise missiles on British soil.

Echoes of empire were heard in 1979–1980 when the British foreign secretary, Lord Carrington (1919–   ), found a solution for Rhodesia, whose white government had been involved in skirmishes with black guerrillas ever since it had unilaterally declared its independence from Britain back in 1965. Carrington secured first a cease-fire and then a constitutional conference that agreed on a new charter in which white voters were guaranteed a role for ten years. Churchill's son-in-law Lord Soames returned briefly to Salisbury as British governor while an election took place that determined that Robert Mugabe would take over as the first black prime minister of a nation that in 1980 became the independent state of Zimbabwe. Like most of Britain's erstwhile Asian and African possessions, Zimbabwe remained a member of the Commonwealth. Mugabe, like other leaders of former African colonies, sought in time to turn Zimbabwe into a one-party state, but in the famine-afflicted Africa of the 1980s and 1990s Zimbabwe remained relatively peaceful. In 1981 the Commonwealth was further expanded as the colony of British Honduras became the independent state of Belize. British troops remained on hand to protect it from possible invasion by neighboring Guatemala or Honduras.

The Falkland Islands War (1982)

Echoes of empire were heard loudly once more on April 2, 1982, when forces from Argentina invaded Britain's South Atlantic dependency, the Falkland Islands. Outnumbered by a ratio of twenty to one, British marines stationed there and on the yet more distant island of South Georgia were compelled to surrender. British involvement with the area dated back to 1690, when an English sea captain had landed on the Falklands, an area of peat bog, rock, and heather the size of Connecticut that he named for King William III's treasurer of the navy. Although claimed by Spain and France as well as Britain during the eighteenth century, the islands were inhabited only intermittently until 1833, when a permanent British settlement and British administration began. After World War II, Argentina reasserted pre-1833 claims to islands that lay 400 miles off its coast, and successive British negotiators — aware of how difficult it might be to defend the islands — had discussed possible ways of giving Argentina a role to play. There was no question, however, as to the firm desire of the eighteen hundred islanders, many of them sheep herders, to remain British. The invasion evoked a storm of protest in Britain against what even Michael Foot, the leader of the Labour opposition, called "an act of naked aggression carried out in the most shameful and disreputable circumstances." Members of Thatcher's own party criticized the government for having failed to foresee the invasion; Lord Carrington, the foreign secretary, took personal responsibility for that failure and resigned.

He was replaced by Francis Pym (1922–   ), who pledged: "Britain does not appease dictators."

For a few days Margaret Thatcher's future as prime minister hung in the balance, but she met the challenge with a shrewd combination of diplomacy and force. At British urging, the UN Security Council, by a vote of ten to one, demanded the immediate withdrawal of the invaders, and Britain's EC partners imposed trade restrictions on Argentina. Within three days Britain had improvised and begun to send to the South Atlantic a large naval task force to set up a blockade around the islands. Commercial vessels such as the *QE II*, the world's largest passenger liner, were commandeered to carry troops. After the mediation efforts of American Secretary of State Alexander Haig and the UN Secretary-General failed, British troops went into action. In late April they recaptured South Georgia. On May 21, 8,000 miles from their home base, they established a beachhead on East Falkland. Although outnumbered and exposed to air attack from the mainland, British troops advanced steadily on the Falkland capital, Port Stanley. An operation described by Prime Minister Thatcher as "boldly planned, bravely executed, and brilliantly accomplished" culminated on June 14 with the surrender of the Argentinian garrison of 11,000 troops.[2]

For Britain the costs included six ships sunk and 255 servicemen killed, but, except for the Tony Benn wing of the Labour party, most Britons rejoiced in the outcome. They saw their cause as an example not of colonialism or jingoism but as one of upholding international law, defeating aggression, and liberating the Falkland Islanders from alien rule. Within six months they also had the satisfaction of witnessing the overthrow of the military junta that had launched the invasion. Political democracy returned to Argentina, and the junta leaders who had initiated the war were ultimately sentenced to jail for "the military crime of negligence." Although in time the Falkland Islands faded once more into relative obscurity, the British victory had served as a reminder of British military skill and as a tonic to British pride. It enhanced the reputation of the Conservative government and established Margaret Thatcher as the most resolute prime minister since Winston Churchill.

The "Falkland factor" was to play a significant role in the general election that Margaret Thatcher requested in 1983. Two years earlier, at the depth of the economic recession, her party had ranked below both Labour and the new Social Democratic/Liberal Alliance in public opinion polls. Thatcher's spirit of determination, however, had won her a degree of respect, if not necessarily affection, that was to persist for the rest of the decade. At the same time, the Labour party appeared to be headed by a weak prospective prime minister and to be wedded to an unpopular pro-

---

[2]Max Hastings and Simon Jenkins, *The Battle for the Falklands* (1983). See also Lawrence Freedman and Virginia Gamba-Stonehouse, *Signals of War: The Falklands Conflict of 1982* (1990).

Thatcher Triumphs at the Polls   One view of the general election of 1983. *(Dick Wright/*The Providence Journal-Bulletin*)*

gram. The aging Michael Foot and his little dog Disraeli conducted an ineffectual campaign. Although Foot's promise to vanquish unemployment may have cheered the party faithful, pledges to disarm unilaterally, to leave the EC, to abolish the House of Lords, and to restore trade-union privileges tended to repel rather than to attract undecided voters and to cause one disenchanted Labourite to describe the party's manifesto as "the longest suicide note in history." The election results were clear-cut: Conservatives, 397 (42.4 percent); Labour, 209 (27.6 percent); Alliance, 23 (25.4 percent); Scottish and Welsh Nationalists, 4 (1.5 percent); Northern Ireland parties, 17 (3.1 percent).

Labour had managed to hang on to most of its seats in the industrial towns of northern England and Scotland, but in southern England (outside London) it managed to retain only two parliamentary seats out of 117 and in most races came in third. Not since 1918 had the Labour party secured so small a percentage of the popular vote. For the Alliance the election results were equally frustrating: not since the 1920s had a third party won so many votes while securing so few parliamentary seats. Although the Falkland factor may have been instrumental in making the Conservatives the single most popular party by far, it was the divisions among her opponents that enabled Margaret Thatcher's party to garner the largest majority in parliamentary seats that any party had achieved since 1945.

The Victors Come Home A cheering multitude at the port of Southampton in July 1982 welcomes the liner *Canberra* and British troops returning from the Falkland Islands War. *(Bill Warhurst/Times Newspapers Limited)*

Privatization

In the aftermath of the election of 1983, Prime Minister Thatcher reshuffled the cabinet to bring to the fore colleagues most in accord with her political approach. She also set into full gear the policy of privatization, denationalizing many industries that had been turned into public corporations by successive Labour governments since 1945. Hers was the first deliberate effort since World War II to return to the private sector of the economy businesses that, in the words of one advocate of the process, "perform relatively poorly in terms of their competitive position, use labour and capital inefficiently and are less profitable."[3] By 1987, ten major enterprises had been sold to private investors; they included seaport facilities, cross-channel ferries, the British Oil Corporation, Jaguar automobiles, British Airways, British Gas (the national gas-distributing utility), and — in the largest share offering ever — British Telecom (the entire telephone portion of the British Post Office). There were additional examples of privatization during the years that followed, including the companies that supplied British cities with water. In almost every case, greater efficiency resulted. Thus the once dilapidated British telephone system was transformed into one of the best-equipped in the world, and

---

[3]John Moore in John Kay et al., eds., *Privatisation and Regulation: The UK Experience* (1987).

electric power stations found it possible to operate successfully with half as many workers as before. Privatized industries paid taxes, rather than being subsidized by the taxpayer, as nationalized industries had been. Although critics insisted that the spur of competition was more important than the mere fact of ownership by private investors instead of government, it was indeed one of the government's purposes to increase the number of such investors. Many of the shares in privatized enterprises were sold to the men and women who worked in them; between 1979 and 1987, the number of British shareholders tripled from fewer than 3 million to about 9 million.

The government's efforts to encourage greater efficiency among those private sector manufacturers who had survived the "deindustrialization" of the 1970s and early 1980s also began to bear fruit: productivity, which had stagnated during the 1970s, rose dramatically (by 30 percent) between 1980 and 1986, placing Britain first among Europe's growth leaders rather than last. Admittedly the fact that the British steel industry needed only one-half as many workers in the mid-1980s to manufacture the same amount of steel as it had in the mid-1970s meant only that Britain was beginning to keep even (or partly catch up) with its major competitors; such improvement did not ease the problem of unemployment. The Thatcher government also had some success in encouraging new enterprises: twice as many new businesses were founded in 1985 as in 1975. Yet even in the later 1980s business management remained less prestigious in Britain than in the United States or Japan. That career still attracted fewer university graduates than it did in other large industrial countries.

While the proportion of the British work force employed in factories had declined steadily since the early 1950s, the number employed in banking and finance had steadily grown. Even during the era of stagflation, London maintained its role as one of the world's great centers of banking, insurance, and commodity trading. Its stock exchange ranked behind those of New York and Tokyo, but it remained the world's most important center for currency exchange, for insurance, and for trade in gold and silver. Income from financial services ranked more highly than ever during the 1980s in providing the British economy with "invisible" exports. Another form of invisible exports grew once more during the 1980s — dividends from overseas investments. By the end of World War II, Britain had become a net debtor country, but — after the Thatcher government lifted all controls on foreign exchange — there was a net outflow of investment capital. During the very decade that the United States became a net debtor country, Britain became the world's second largest creditor country — second only to Japan. Much of this money was being poured into the American economy. Thus in 1985, 24 percent of new foreign investment in the United States came from Britain compared to only 10 percent from Japan. The Japanese proportion increased later in the decade, but even during the 1990s, the total sum of investments by Britons remained larger than that of any other group of foreign nationals.

Analogously, Americans found it advantageous to channel more of their investments into the European Community economy via Britain than through any other EC member country.

Not all nationalized industries could readily be privatized, and not all aspects of the British economy glowed with the luster of high finance. The coal industry, nationalized since 1947, had been losing ground to oil and natural gas as a source of energy ever since the 1950s, and between 1947 and 1982 the number of coal miners declined from 700,000 to 200,000. At the same time, the National Union of Mineworkers had fought successfully to raise the wages of a diminishing work force and to resist every attempt to close mines — even if no market could be found for the coal produced. The coal strike of 1974 had, in effect, brought down the Heath ministry. In 1983, Margaret Thatcher appointed as head of the Coal Board Sir Ian McGregor, a Scottish-born American industrialist who, having turned around the money-losing British Steel Corporation, was asked to manage the coal industry in such a way that it would no longer require hefty subsidies from the British taxpayer year after year. His opponent was Arthur Scargill, the charismatic but militant Marxist president-for-life of the mineworkers' union. In 1984 Scargill launched a strike in the coal fields to stop all further pit closures and at the same time, if need be, to bring down the Thatcher government and initiate a "socialist revolution." Fearful that he could not persuade enough miners to strike, he did not call for the ballot required by the union constitution but encouraged miners all over the country to stop work. More than two-thirds of them did so, but others remained at work, whereupon Scargill sent groups of "flying pickets" about the country trying to intimidate nonstriking miners and to prevent the movement of coal to utilities. A number of bloody clashes resulted, and the strike lingered on from April 1984 until March 1985, when the remaining strikers straggled back to work. There was considerable public sympathy for the plight of individual miners but very little for the revolutionary Arthur Scargill, who had hoped to triumph by shutting down Britain's power stations and who remained adamant to the last. He found Margaret Thatcher as resolute, however, as had the Argentine junta in 1982, and, in the aftermath of the strike, many aging coal miners were persuaded with generous retirement benefits to leave the pits early. In the course of just seven years (1979–1986), the number of coal miners and collieries was reduced by 40 percent. Because of increasing productivity, however, those that remained still produced 85 percent as much coal as had been produced in 1979. Supply continued to outstrip demand, however, and by 1994 only twenty-two mines remained open and fewer than 15,000 coal miners were left in all of Great Britain. During an age increasingly concerned with global warming and environmental pollution, coal was steadily being replaced by oil and natural gas, and a once central chapter in Britain's economic history was drawing to a close.

A comparable defeat was suffered by London printers, who had long campaigned to block newspaper proprietors from using new technology.

In 1986 the Australian-born publisher Rupert Murdoch abruptly moved his four papers out of London's traditional Fleet Street to the eastern suburb of Wapping, where new computer word processors required only a third as many employees. After a year-long strike, the printers gave up. The failure of the strikes by the miners and printers and the legal requirement that unions poll their members by secret ballot (rather than by a raising of hands at open-air meetings) reduced the number of working days lost to strikes in 1986 to less than two million, the lowest number since the 1950s; 1991 proved to be Britain's most strike-free year since record-keeping began a hundred years before. In the course of fifteen years, the number of active union members also declined from over 12 million in 1979 to about eight million. Although more than 35 percent of Britain's work force remained unionized in the mid-1990s (as contrasted with 16 percent in the United States), the enormous political power wielded by trade-union barons during the 1960s and 1970s had faded, and individual union members were guaranteed by the Trade Union Act of 1984 a voice, by secret ballot at five-year intervals, in choosing their leaders. The mood of the day emphasized no-strike agreements, job flexibility, and consultation rather than confrontation.

Education, Health, and Housing

A number of public enterprises had been privatized by 1987, but there was minimal popular demand for removing from public hands two of Britain's most significant social services — education (from kindergarten through university) and the National Health Service. The Conservative government did insist, however, that market principles be introduced into both the health service and the process of education in order to make both schools and universities more efficient. A majority of schoolteachers and university lecturers disagreed, however, and they proved to be the most articulate of Mrs. Thatcher's critics. They condemned her for philistinism and for a failure to appreciate the significance of university-based research, and they applauded when Oxford University (her *alma mater*) voted to deny her the honorary degree it had awarded to most previous prime ministers. Reluctantly, university administrators agreed to alterations in staff/student ratios, to the restructuring of pay scales, and to the notion that not every university could specialize in every area of knowledge. Even as university administrators were asked to become more businesslike, the number of students in all forms of higher education was growing rapidly. In 1992 erstwhile polytechnic institutes were permitted to transform themselves into universities; by the mid-1990s there were 90 universities in the United Kingdom. Students whose living grants did not keep up in value with inflation were encouraged to take out loans.

In the meantime, the Education Act of 1988 sought to impose a national curriculum on primary and secondary schools designed to raise the level of student accomplishment in many subjects, especially science, mathematics, and English. Despite teacher-union protests, standardized tests were to be administered to pupils at ages seven, eleven, and fourteen, and "league tables" were to be issued to enable parents to compare the test results secured by specific schools. At the same time, the act allowed individual schools to opt out of the regulatory supervision of local educational authorities; their income from the national exchequer would depend on their ability to attract pupils and teach them successfully.

The Thatcher government also sought to introduce market mechanisms into the National Health Service, not by privatizing the service but by separating purchasers (primarily local health districts) from providers (hospitals and doctors) and allowing general practitioners to manage their own budgets; by 1994, one-third of all physicians had agreed to do so. In effect, physicians used their fixed annual budget to purchase drugs, laboratory tests, and nonemergency hospital care for their patients. With people over 65 now making up 15 percent of the population and medical technology becoming ever more complex, the costs of health care continued to increase without let up year after year, but in Britain at the end of the century such costs consumed only 7 percent of each year's gross domestic product (in contrast to the United States, where they consumed 14 percent).

The most popular of the Thatcher government efforts to introduce market mechanisms into the social services involved housing and old age pensions. Council house (public housing) tenants were given the right to purchase their own homes. In the course of fourteen years, some 1.5 million houses were sold to the tenants who lived in them, and by the mid-1990s some 67 percent of all families had become homeowners, while 23 percent still lived in rented council housing, and 10 percent rented apartments or houses from private landlords. The government also altered the law in order to encourage three-quarters of all working people to supplement their basic state-sponsored old age pensions with additional retirement benefits based on their investments in stocks and bonds.

The government was also responsible for a reform very much at odds with traditional conservatism, the Local Government Act of 1985. Repeatedly annoyed by the manner in which local government authorities exceeded government spending guidelines and infuriated by what it considered the spendthrift ways of the Greater London Council (controlled by a militant Labour party majority), the Thatcher government abolished the Council (first established in 1888 and enlarged in 1964). Elsewhere in the country, it abolished six of the metropolitan counties that had been set up by the Local Government Act of 1972. Most of the powers of these bodies were taken over by the next-lower tier of local government; in the case of Greater London, this meant thirty-two borough councils and the corporation of the original (medieval) city of London. The Conservative government seemed quite willing to weaken elective local government authorities, in part supplanting them with the ever-more numerous "quangos" (quasi-autonomous nongovernmental organizations whose members are appointed by central government ministers) that came to play an increasingly significant role in British administrative life.

The Northern Ireland Question Once More

Even before she took office in May 1979, Margaret Thatcher was reminded of one aspect of her governmental inheritance, the troublesome Northern Ireland Question.[4] In March of that year, one of her closest parliamentary aides was assassinated within the precincts of the House of Commons by Irish extremists. Four months later, members of the I.R.A. (Irish Republican Army) murdered the seventy-nine-year-old Earl Mountbatten of Burma while he was vacationing in the Irish Republic. The military funeral of this last viceroy of British India and one of Britain's greatest twentieth-century war heroes matched those given to Nelson and Wellington. Prime Minister Lynch of the Irish Republic condemned such I.R.A. actions as "brutal and horrific gangsterism" and urged Americans not to contribute to funds used to buy weapons for a terrorist group that remained illegal on both sides of the Irish border. In the course of the 1980s the I.R.A. made use to an increasing degree of weapons supplied by Libya's ruler, Colonel Muammar Qadaffi.

From May to October 1981 the I.R.A. recalled the flagging attention of the world to its cause by having members who were serving terms in a Belfast prison stage hunger strikes. Thatcher stood firm against the I.R.A. demand that their members be granted "political prisoner" status, and only after ten young men had taken their own lives by starvation did the I.R.A. give up the campaign. The I.R.A. did not give up bank raids in the Irish Republic, however, nor terrorism and intimidation in the North where in November 1981 it assassinated one of the elected Members of Parliament who represented Northern Ireland in the British Parliament. Although the level of violence remained much lower than it had been during the early 1970s, the I.R.A. clearly continued to hope that one day Britain would tire of the expense — well over two billion dollars per year — of governing a province afflicted by a stagnant economy as well as by intermittent terrorism. By 1982 Britons were indeed eager to rid themselves of responsibility for Northern Ireland, but, as the Ulsterites demonstrated at election after election by a margin of more than two to one, they preferred affiliation with Britain rather than with the Irish Republic.

On October 12, 1984, Margaret Thatcher herself became a near-victim of I.R.A. terrorism when a 100-pound time bomb went off in the middle

---

[4]See John Darby, ed., *Northern Ireland: The Background to the Conflict* (1987).

The Hunger Strikers   Relatives of the I.R.A. prisoners hold replica coffin lids at a vigil in London in 1980. The strike was given up a few days later. *(Topham)*

of the night in Brighton's Grand Hotel, where the Conservative party was holding its annual conference. Its intended victims were "the British cabinet and the Tory warmongers." Four people were killed in the blast, and the wife of Norman Tebbit, a member of the Thatcher cabinet, was permanently crippled; she died a few years later. Mrs. Thatcher escaped, and the next day she received a rapturous eight-minute-long standing ovation from conference members when she assured them that "all attempts to destroy democracy by terrorism will fail."

A year later she tried to tackle the Irish Question in a somewhat different manner. She reached an agreement with a cooperative prime minister of the Irish Republic, Garret FitzGerald, to set up a consultative Anglo-Irish intergovernmental conference in which the Irish Republic might put forward proposals on the place of the Roman Catholic minority in Northern Ireland affairs. At the same time, the Irish Republic formally recognized British sovereignty over Northern Ireland, pledged "that any change in the status of Northern Ireland would only come about with the consent of a majority of the people of Northern Ireland," and acknowledged "that the present wish of a majority there is for no change in that status." Although some Ulster Protestants might have been expected to feel reassured by such a pledge, they denounced the agreement instead as a betrayal, as the entering wedge for a sell-out to

Dublin, and Mrs. Thatcher herself as "an unprincipled and shameless hussy." As the prime minister had acknowledged two days after her near-assassination: "I can't think of a political initiative which would be acceptable to one side which would not be repugnant to the other. But we will have to keep on trying."

In 1984, in another part of the world, Britain laid the groundwork for severing most ties with the last populous portion of the British Empire, Hong Kong. That crown colony of almost six million people had become one of the great success stories of the post-1945 world: it boasted the highest per capita income of any of the "developing countries" and constituted an oasis of personal liberty and prosperity adjoining Communist China, the land from which many of its citizens had fled. Those of China's leaders who had survived the miseries inflicted by the Cultural Revolution of the 1960s and 1970s were beginning to liberalize the nation's command economy. They were aware that in 1997 the ninety-nine year lease that imperial China had granted to Britain for the mainland portion of Hong Kong would end. Although in 1842 the actual island of Hong Kong had been ceded to Britain in perpetuity, the treaty negotiated between the two countries in 1984 stipulated that the entire area would return to Chinese sovereignty in 1997. In return, China formally agreed to maintain Hong Kong for at least fifty years as a separate "special Administrative Region of China" with its own "social and economic systems and life style." A crackdown on dissidents within China in 1989 prompted new fears about Hong Kong's future, and Parliament in due course agreed to give refuge in Britain to at least 50,000 Hong Kong families should they ask for it.

The General Election of 1987

Since 1983, the Thatcher ministry had experienced both triumphs and difficulties, but its standing in the public opinion polls had never sunk as low as it had back in 1981. By the mid-1980s Margaret Thatcher had established herself as the Western world's most formidable and longest-serving head of government. Her five-day visit to Moscow in April 1987 was a diplomatic triumph in which "the Iron Lady from Downing Street" eased the path to a nuclear arms reduction agreement between the United States and Soviet Union. She had been the first Western leader to sense that Mikhael Gorbachev, who became the leader of the USSR in March 1985, marked a break with the Soviet past. "I like him," she declared. "We can do business together." At the same time, in a news conference telecast live, she reminded the Soviet people of the scope of Soviet military might and of the reasons for Western concern. Back in London early in May, Thatcher asked the queen to call for a new general election a month later.

She had two new opponents. Shortly after the 1983 election, Michael Foot, after three years as leader of the Labour party, had given way to Neil

Kinnock (b. 1942), a youthful Welsh M.P. who had not previously held cabinet or ministerial office. He was a congenial family man, however, with an engaging television personality; according to one biographer, he had won the leadership of his party by "telling good jokes." Although identified with his party's left wing, he devoted his first four years as leader to trying to mute party militants such as Arthur Scargill, and most observers concluded that he waged a far more effective "presidential-style" campaign in 1987 than his predecessor had in 1983. His manifesto no longer insisted on having Britain leave the EC, but it did promise many more social benefits, tax increases that would soak the rich, and the repeal of all laws that curbed trade-union privileges. It was Labour's "unilateral nuclear disarmament" plank that may have hurt his party most. When Kinnock suggested that, if the Russians subsequently took over a defenseless Britain, the British might resist as the Afghan guerrillas had done, many voters found the prospect unappealing.

In the meantime, the S.D.P./Liberal Alliance was facing difficulties of its own, policy divisions between its two leaders, David Steel of the Liberals and David Owen of the Social Democratic party. Margaret Thatcher necessarily campaigned on her record, which included a rate of unemployment still above 10 percent. As it had during the later 1930s, however, such unemployment coexisted with a sense of prosperity for the great majority of British families. Foreigners no longer depicted the country as an invalid afflicted by "the British disease." Between 1984 and 1990, the number of Britons who described themselves as self-employed was to increase by a third, and a spirit of free enterprise appeared to be reviving. Once the ballots were counted, it turned out that a larger portion of the electorate had voted than four years earlier but that there had been no pendulum swing against the Conservative government: the Conservatives had elected 375 M.P.s (with 42.3 percent of the popular vote); Labour, 229 (30.8 percent); Alliance, 17 (22.6 percent); Scottish and Welsh Nationalists, 6 (1.7 percent); Northern Ireland parties, 17 (2.6 percent). Labour had somewhat improved its status as the nation's second party, but its gains were made at the expense of the Alliance, and in much of England and Wales the party fared only marginally better than in the disastrous year of 1983. Its greatest success took place in Scotland, where Labour won 42.4 percent of the total vote and 50 of 72 parliamentary seats (thereby reviving talk of a separate Scottish assembly).

Thatcher's Last Years (1987–1990)

Her government's record of accomplishment and the continued division among her political opponents had enabled Margaret Thatcher to become the first person in post-1832 Britain to lead a political party to triumph in three successive general elections. During the next three and a half years, however, a combination of circumstances caused the prime minister's political luck to run out: the economic boom of the mid-1980s petered out; a daring reform of local government taxation, the "poll tax," aroused a storm of opposition; the chief opposition force, the Labour party, transformed itself once more into a plausible alternate government; and several of Thatcher's long-time cabinet colleagues turned against her.

For British as for American foreign policymakers — long intent on containing Soviet expansion and countering Soviet military power weapon for weapon — the later 1980s and early 1990s brought a series of triumphs in such rapid succession that the winners found it difficult at first to believe their good fortune. In the very process of reforming the economically moribund USSR, President Gorbachev found himself unwittingly undermining the very pillars — coercion and centralization — on which depended the Soviet state and its army, the world's largest. As soon as the powers of the Soviet secret police were held in check, then one after another the lands of the post-1945 Soviet empire (such as Poland, Czechoslovakia, and Hungary) overthrew the Communist overlords whom fear of Soviet military force had kept in place for decades. They abandoned the Warsaw Pact; they invited remaining Soviet troops to go home; and they sought to reintroduce free elections and a market system as well as to strengthen their economic and political ties with western Europe and the United States. The tearing down of the Berlin Wall in November 1989 symbolized the rending of what Churchill had dubbed "the Iron Curtain" and led within a year to the collapse of Communist East Germany and to its political (and, more gradually, its economic) reabsorption by Helmut Kohl's Federal Republic of (West) Germany. In Africa, Angola and Ethiopia ceased to be Soviet client states. In 1991 President Gorbachev was displaced as the Soviet Union broke up into its constituent republics. Russia, the largest and most powerful of these republics, turned its back on more than sixty years of Communist rule, but it seemed destined for a long period of political confusion and economic readjustment. Like other Western leaders, Margaret Thatcher was as much spectator as participant in a process that necessitated careful rethinking about the proper role of armaments and of alliances such as NATO in a post–Cold War world.

By the late 1980s Margaret Thatcher was convinced that the twelve-nation EC, of which Britain had been a member since 1973, was becoming not only a single free trade area but a single political entity as well. Although she reluctantly acceded to parliamentary approval of the Single European Act of 1986, the prelude to true economic integration, she long resisted British adhesion to ERM (the European exchange rate mechanism), and she opposed outright a system of majority (rather than unanimous) voting in the European Community council of ministers and the prospect of a single European currency. At a time when her people had become reconciled to EC membership for Britain as, on balance, far more a "good thing" than a "bad thing," she became an insistent opponent of tendencies that she denounced in 1991 as "the greatest abdication of national and parliamentary sovereignty in our history."

Although the prime minister's increasingly anti-Europe stance disturbed both her continental counterparts and several of her cabinet colleagues, it was the deterioration of the British economy that did more to damage her political popularity. A temporary stock market crash in October 1987 led to financial policies that caused the rate of inflation to rise sharply again. Mortgage interest rates (which in Britain, unlike the United States, tend to be variable rather than fixed) were then raised to heights that alienated some of the Conservative party's most loyal supporters. The annual national budget, after several years of surplus, lapsed into deficit once more, and in the autumn of 1990 the economy sank into recession. In the meantime, critics denounced every government effort to increase the efficiency of the health service and education as an attempt to undermine the welfare state. They appeared unaware that government spending on health and old-age pensions had gone up in real terms (that is, discounting inflation) by more than a third between 1979 and 1990. Because many voters took at face value the prime minister's oft-voiced opposition to state mollycoddling and her promotion of self-help, Lady Bountiful was repeatedly depicted as Mrs. Scrooge.

No projected government reform was condemned more harshly than was the "community charge," the form of local government taxation introduced into Scotland in 1989 and into England and Wales in 1990. Ever since the 1970s, the Conservative party had been pledged to find a substitute for the "rates," the traditional property taxes paid by householders that provided about a third of the income of the county and district councils that made up local government. Such taxes were levied in too erratic a fashion, and in many councils under Labour control, voters who (as renters) paid no rates were in irresponsible fashion electing high-spending councillors. A group of junior ministers and civil servants — none having direct experience with local government — persuaded the prime minister that they had found the ideal substitute tax in the new community charge. Subject to rebates only for welfare recipients, the old, and the disabled, the legislation required all adults living in a given district, whatever their income or the value of their homes, to pay an identical annual tax.

The result was what the *Economist* was to call "the most misguided piece of domestic policy produced by any British government in this century."[5] Critics, harking back to the events that led to the Peasants' Revolt of 1381, immediately dubbed the community charge a "poll tax," a regressive and fundamentally unjust imposition. It was instituted (and defied) first in Scotland and a year later in England and Wales where even many Conservative voters came to view it as a cure more painful than the disease it was intended to ameliorate. It also proved far more expensive and difficult to collect than its authors had anticipated, and in the spring of 1990 reaction to the tax led to the worst riot of the century in central London. The controversy caused Margaret Thatcher's popularity

---

[5]See David Butler et al., *Failure in British Government: The Politics of the Poll Tax* (1995).

as prime minister to plummet to the lowest percentage (20 percent) recorded in the five-and-a-half-decade history of the Gallup poll.

The poll tax issue did much to revive the fortunes of the Labour party headed by Neil Kinnock. His verbal clashes in the House of Commons with the prime minister could now not only be heard but seen by a wide public, as the historic chamber, which had permitted radio broadcasts of debates for a decade, as of 1988 permitted telecasts as well. Kinnock could not oust Thatcher from power, however. Pending a new general election, only her fellow Conservative M.P.s could do that, and by November 1990, her policy toward Europe and toward finance had alienated both her longtime Chancellor of the Exchequer, Nigel Lawson, and her longtime foreign secretary, Geoffrey Howe. It was neither of them, however, but Michael Heseltine, the man who had quarreled with her and resigned as secretary of defense four years earlier, who formally challenged her leadership in a secret ballot of Conservative M.P.s in the same fashion that fifteen years earlier she had challenged Edward Heath. Thatcher won the first ballot, but not by a sufficient margin, under the party's rules, to escape a second and perhaps more damaging ballot. Before that ballot took place, she chose to resign as party leader and therefore as prime minister. Half a year later she announced her decision not to stand for reelection in the House of Commons but to retain a political voice in the House of Lords as Baroness Thatcher. Thus late in 1990 Margaret Thatcher's eleven-and-a-half-year prime ministership ended with an abrupt but peaceful transfer of power.

Her ministry may not have constituted a revolution, but it had sharply altered the direction of British politics. "To exorcise the ghost of Attlee, she adopted a mixture of moral populism, businesslike efficiency and imperial nostalgia. Like Gladstone she was an incorrigible moralizer; like Churchill she loved grand strategy and political theatre; and like Chamberlain, she had used her unrivalled grasp of detail to control her Cabinet."[6] Ultimately most members of that cabinet — and a majority of Conservative M.P.s — privately concluded, however, that her conduct toward her colleagues had become too arbitrary and dictatorial. The party required a new leader.

The Election of 1992

As soon as Margaret Thatcher announced her resignation, the struggle for the succession became one between her initial challenger, Michael Heseltine, and two of her cabinet colleagues, Foreign Secretary Douglas Hurd and Chancellor of the Exchequer John Major. She gave behind-the-scenes support to Major, and a few days later he was chosen to be the new party leader and was therefore invited by Queen Elizabeth II to become

---

[6]Adrian Wooldridge, review of Peter Clarke, *A Question of Leadership: Gladstone to Thatcher* (1991), in the (London) *Times Literary Supplement*, April 26, 1991.

Britain's new prime minister. In several respects Major was an unexpected choice. Born in 1943, he was at 47 the youngest prime minister of the twentieth century and the first to have no personal memories of World War II. The son of a onetime circus trapeze artist and sculptor of garden gnomes, he had grown up in a small apartment in one of London's poorer boroughs. At age sixteen he had left school in order to take a job as a cement mixer to assist his parents with the family budget. By means of correspondence courses he qualified as an entrant into the world of banking. His evident understanding of finance, his equable temperament, and his ability to get things done all help explain his stunningly rapid rise to the top of the political ladder via election to the House of Commons (1979) and then appointment to a ministerial post (1982) and later to the cabinet (1989).

Major's political honeymoon coincided during the winter of 1990–1991 with the prosecution of Operation Desert Shield and Desert Storm, the successful war authorized by the United Nations to free Kuwait from invasion and occupation by Iraq. No European nation cooperated more promptly, more fully, or more loyally with the American-led military effort than did Britain, and John Major became the first Western leader to visit liberated Kuwait. In February 1991 the Irish Republican Army reminded the new prime minister that it disliked being eclipsed in the newspaper headlines when it launched, by remote control, a mortar bomb attack on No. 10 Downing Street; one bomb exploded in the garden behind the dwelling and shattered numerous windows. In March 1991, with the war in the Persian Gulf over, the new energy secretary, Michael Heseltine, announced on behalf of the government a plan to replace the detested poll tax with a new "council tax," a property tax based on both the value of a home and the number of people who lived in it.

Although Prime Minister John Major proved far less confrontational in manner than his predecessor, much of the autumn and winter of 1991–1992 was taken up by a sharp debate among the major political parties, a prelude to the looming general election. The Social Democratic/Liberal Alliance had fused into a single party, the Liberal Democrats, headed by the amiable Paddy Ashdown (1941–   ). This third party had scored significant successes in local government elections, but its appeal in national politics appeared to be fading even as that of the Labour party led by Neil Kinnock revived. Labour had expelled many of its militants, and it now approved of the sale of council houses to the tenants who lived in them. The party also now accepted many legal regulations of trade unions that it had once spurned and even acknowledged the freedom not to join trade unions. The party turned its back on its earlier policy of unilateral nuclear disarmament and now embraced membership in the European Community that it had once scorned. Labour remained committed to sharp tax rises for the rich, to significant rises in spending on health and education, and to setting up the country's first across-the-board national minimum wage. It had moved sufficiently toward the political center, however, to make it the likely winner in the election scheduled by John Major for April 1992.

Most public opinion polls agreed that Neil Kinnock would be the nation's next prime minister, and a week and a half before the election the Labour party leaders held a "victory party." That party proved premature, however, because for the fourth time in a row the Conservatives emerged with the largest number of M.P.s and popular votes: the Conservatives elected 336 M.P.s (with 41.9 of the popular vote); Labour, 271 (34.2 percent); Liberal Democrats, 20 (17.9 percent); Scottish Nationalists, 3 (1.8 percent); others (mostly Northern Ireland parties), 21 (4.2 percent). Postelection analysis suggested that the red-faced pollsters had failed to take into account both a last-minute swing toward the Conservatives and the impact of the insistent Conservative attack on Labour as a tax-and-spend party.

The Government of John Major (1990–1997)

If John Major had hoped for a time of political tranquillity after his unexpected electoral triumph, he was to be sorely disappointed, because during the next five years public opinion polls and by-election results recorded a steady decline in the popularity of his government.[7] For a time it was hurt also by the lingering effects of the longest economic recession since World War II. The severity of that downturn was enhanced for many of its supporters by the severe losses suffered by the society of insurance underwriters known as Lloyd's of London, an institution long famed for its willingness to insure risks that others would not. A series of weather disasters and gigantic pollution lawsuit settlements in the United States led to losses of more than £7 billion ($11.2 billion) for claims involving 1988–1991 alone.

In September 1992 the government's prestige was hurt badly by the need, after pledging firmly not to do so, to decouple the value of the British pound from the ERM (European Rate Mechanism), which the more ardent supporters of the European Community had hoped would eventually lead to a single currency for all member nations. The decision had a silver lining in that, once the value of the pound had fallen relative to the German mark, the Bank of England found it possible to lower interest rates, thereby helping to speed the country out of economic recession during 1993 and the years that followed. This traumatic event renewed the debate within Major's own party, however, as to whether the EC (European Community) should truly become the EU (European Union) called for by the treaty signed in December 1991 at Maastricht (in the Netherlands) by the EC nations. That treaty looked ahead to a yet

---

[7]See Peter Dorey, ed., *The Major Premiership: Politics and Policies under John Major, 1990–97* (1999), and John Major, *Autobiography* (1999).

John Major   The embattled
Conservative party leader served as
prime minister from 1990 to 1997.
(Sean Aidan/Eye Ubiquitous/Corbis)

stronger economic entity, a more meaningful European political federation in which the citizen of each state obtained the right to live and work
anywhere in the union, and a more influential European Parliament.
Some forty Euro-skeptics within his own party (including Baroness
Thatcher) compelled Major to devote much time during parliamentary
sessions in 1992 and 1993 to the delicate task of securing approval of the
Maastricht Treaty. He finally succeeded, but only at the cost of giving the
impression of a government and a party in disarray. By 1993 more than
half of Britain's trade was conducted with other EU members (compared
to less than a third in 1970), and a majority of Britons had come to accept
the continued link with Europe as an economic necessity. During the
1990s the European Union enlarged itself from twelve to fifteen nations
and began a long-term process of incorporating some of the lands of eastern Europe as well. For many continentals, the EU represented a triumph
of peaceful cooperation over ancient wars and hatreds, and yet the EU remained for many Britons more a cause for suspicion than a source of
pride.

The impression of governmental disarray was enhanced by contro-
versies evoked by spending plans on the social services and by the proposed privatization of both the British Post Office and parts of the railway system. The former process was halted, but the complex process of
privatizing the railways was badly managed and led to far more complaints than congratulations. The impression of confusion in government was deepened by the manner in which it handled mad-cow disease
(bovine spongiform encephalopathy), the most expensive catastrophe

ever to befall British agriculture. The mysterious affliction was first detected in the 1980s, and it was in due course attributed to the diseased chopped-up sheep that some cows had been fed as a protein supplement. In 1996 scientists concluded that a number of human beings — seventy-seven as of 2000 — had also died as a result of eating infected beef. By then the suspect protein supplement had been banned from cattle feed, well over four million head of cattle had been destroyed, and the European Union had banned the import of all British beef for a three-year period. Yet another cause of governmental unpopularity was a series of minor sex and financial scandals in which members of John Major's administration were involved; one after another they would capture the headlines of London's newspapers. According to one public opinion poll, the scandals persuaded three voters in five that the governing party was "very sleazy and disreputable."

Almost overlooked in the process were the successes of John Major's prime ministership. In August 1994, he secured a cease-fire on the part of the I.R.A. (see page 472). He presided over a five-year period during which the economy prospered and during which the rate of unemployment declined from more than 10 percent to less than 5 percent. His government-sponsored National Lottery provided a valuable new financial resource to organizations supporting British music, dance, theater, art, and architecture. His Citizen's Charter set forth targets of performance by which ordinary people might hold to account those who administered Britain's health and education and other public services.

Yet the carping within the ranks of the Conservative party remained so loud that in June 1995 Prime Minister Major flung down the gauntlet before his critics in Parliament and the press by deliberately resigning his party's leadership. One of his cabinet colleagues, John Redwood (b. 1951), thereupon formally challenged Major's reelection. After a spirited two-week campaign, however, Conservative M.P.s reelected Major by a vote of 218 to 89. He then reshaped his cabinet and named his most popular colleague, Michael Heseltine, to serve as deputy prime minister.

Although John Major was now safe as prime minister until the next general election, the results of parliamentary by-elections, local government elections, and public opinion polls continued to be unfavorable. The prime minister may have been accepted as a personally decent and amiable human being at home and as a skillful diplomat abroad, but his party remained sorely divided, and long before the general election of May 1997, it had become clear that eighteen years of Conservative rule at the national level were drawing to an all-but-inevitable close.

CHAPTER 23

Entering the 21st Century: The Tony Blair Era

T he dramatic results of the general election of 1997 opened a distinct new chapter in British history. It brought to the fore a new generation of political leaders headed by a new prime minister, the youthful, optimistic, and (for several years) immensely popular Tony Blair (b. 1953). Blair was not to alter to a significant degree the relationships of government to the economy or of Britain to the European Union as they had been fashioned by Margaret Thatcher and John Major. His government did, however, encourage the wonders of the new technology — such as personal computers and access to the Internet (the World Wide Web) as a source of information, as a method of personal and professional communication, and as a means of transforming the manner in which the entire world of business operated — and the prolongation of an era of economic prosperity. He also superintended the most dramatic changes in the constitutional structure of the United Kingdom (including Scotland, Ireland, and Wales) since the early years of the twentieth century or even longer. A majority of Britons therefore entered the new century (and the new millennium) in a mood of relative self-satisfaction. Even as some old institutions, such as the House of Lords, were subjected to dramatic alteration, others, such as the monarchy, were recovering their latent popularity.[1]

The General Election of 1997

By the spring of 1997, the government of John Major had the right to boast that Britain's economy had been growing steadily for five years, that the rate of inflation was far lower than it had been during most of the 1970s and 1980s, that income tax rates had been cut, and that the rate of unem-

---

[1]The information in this chapter is drawn largely from newspaper and periodical articles, from yearly chronicles such as the *Annual Register,* and from three annual publications of Her Majesty's Stationery Office: the *Annual Abstract of Statistics,* the more digestible *Social Trends* (published since 1971), and *Britain: An Official Handbook.* See also David Butler and Dennis Kavanaugh, *The British General Election of 1997* (1997).

A New Family at Number 10
Prime Minister Tony Blair, his
wife Cherie, and their three children move in after the election of
1997. A fourth child was born in
2000. *(AFP/Corbis)*

ployment was lower than in any other major European country. Yet, as
public opinion polls confirmed at regular intervals, the electorate had
grown tired of Conservative rule. At the same time, Tony Blair, the leader
of the chief opposition party, was eager to reassure the electorate that if it
turned to Labour, it would be choosing not a radical socialist but a centrist
social democratic alternative.

The son of a university lecturer and himself both a graduate of Oxford University — where for a time he played in a rock band — and a
trained lawyer, the youthful Blair had been elected as Labour party leader
in 1994. After a skillful campaign, he succeeded a year later in persuading
his party to repeal Clause Four of its constitution, its commitment to
doctrinal socialism and to the nationalization of banks and major industries that the party had first adopted back in 1918. He thereby did his best
to marginalize the party militants and to expunge the fear that a "New
Labour" government would confiscate wealth or raise taxes or undermine the revitalized market economy that served to undergird an only
slightly modified welfare state. With Blair frankly conceding that many
Thatcherite reforms had been "necessary acts of modernisation," the
spirit of ideological conflict that had reentered British political life during the 1970s and 1980s was once again giving way to a high degree of
consensus.

During the political campaign that immediately preceded the general election of May 1, 1997, Tony Blair emulated in several respects — in his populism; in his reliance on pollsters, focus groups, and sound bites; and in his electoral "War Room" — the successful campaigns that "New Democrat" William Jefferson Clinton had waged for the American presidency in 1992 and 1996. The campaign itself apparently changed the minds of only a few voters; yet the result, in turnover of parliamentary seats (if not of popular votes), constituted the most dramatic turnabout in British electoral history: Labourites, 419 (43.2%); Conservatives, 165 (30.7%); Liberal Democrats, 46 (16.8%); Welsh and Scottish Nationalists, 4 and 6 respectively (2.5%); others (mostly Northern Ireland parties), 20 (6.8%). The Conservative party had lost half of its parliamentary seats since 1992 and had suffered its worst electoral defeat since 1906; it retained not a single seat in either Scotland or Wales. In terms of parliamentary seats, the Labour party had scored the greatest victory in its history. The Liberal Democrats had won the largest number of seats since the 1920s, but their role as potential political power brokers had altogether disappeared. "New Labour" had been particularly successful in attracting first-time voters. Not only were the members of the newly-elected Parliament themselves youthful, but two-fifths of them had no previous experience in Westminster, and 120 of them were women, twice as many as in the previous Parliament and the largest number ever.

The Blair Honeymoon

An enthusiastic Tony Blair, at forty-four the youngest prime minister since 1812, his wife Cherie, and their three children happily moved into Number 10 Downing Street (and the house adjoining). His wife was a successful London trial lawyer (a Queen's Counsel) in her own right and the first prime ministerial spouse to maintain a distinct professional life. In 2000, they also became the first residents of Number 10 Downing Street in 152 years to become the parents of a new baby. Blair's informality — "Call me Tony!" — and his gift for ingratiating himself with a wide public helped ensure that, for the next three years, the new prime minister and his party would rank higher in the public opinion polls than had any prime minister or political party in modern British history.

Although Tony Blair promised to lead "one of the great radical reforming governments in our history," the Blair government made few dramatic changes in British domestic policy. It cheered the business community by adhering to the balanced budget and income tax rates set by its Conservative predecessor and by giving an independent Bank of England the right to set interest rates (a power similar to that wielded in the United States by the independent Federal Reserve Bank system). It surprised some of its supporters by ending the tradition of free tuition for all British university students. It cheered its more ardent Labour supporters by introducing, at £3.60 (about $5.75) an hour, the first comprehensive "minimum wage" law in British history. Its decision to incorporate the European Convention on Human Rights into English law seemed likely to enhance the power of the judiciary. In 1998 it outlawed "racially aggravated harassment," and, in the aftermath of an incident of mass murder at a Scottish school, it banned the ownership of all handguns by private citizens.

Blair insisted that continued membership in the European Union was central to his nation's future, but his government was unprepared, for the time being, to go along with eleven of the other fourteen constituent nations that, as of 1999, began the process of replacing national currencies such as the German mark and the French franc with the euro. Pending at least another general election and a popular referendum, coins and bills displaying Queen Elizabeth II would remain the only legal currency in the United Kingdom. In 1999, Prime Minister Blair became an even more enthusiastic champion than the United States of the NATO policy of using military threats and air attacks to induce Slobodan Milosevic, the president of Serbia, to halt a policy of "ethnic cleansing" in the largely Albanian province of Kosovo. British troops contributed to a significant degree to the subsequent military occupation of Kosovo and the continuing NATO presence in nearby Bosnia.

When it came to reforming welfare-state services — health, education, pensions, disability benefits, and the criminal justice system — the Blair government promised dramatic changes but found it politically easier merely to tinker with the details. According to one critic, Blair's was "a gravity-defying victory of style over substance," but for the first three years of his ministry, the Conservative opposition found it impossible to chip away at either his parliamentary majority or his broad popularity. Those Conservatives were no longer headed by John Major, who resigned his party's leadership right after the election of 1997. His fellow M.P.'s replaced him not with one of the leading members of the outgoing cabinet but with someone who had played only a minor role in the Major government, the thirty-six-year-old William Hague. He proved both energetic and articulate, but he often found thankless the task of leading a dispirited opposition still sorely divided over Britain's future role in Europe.

The Federalization of the United Kingdom

It was in constitutional rather than in social or economic policy that Prime Minister Blair followed a distinctly radical course, and within little more than two years he oversaw the restoration and the election of parliaments, each headed by a "first minister," in Northern Ireland and in Scotland, and the choosing of an assembly and a "first secretary" in Wales.

Ever since the suspension back in 1972 of the operation of the autonomous Northern Ireland Parliament, it had been the hope of successive British ministries to restore to Belfast such a Parliament on a power-sharing basis, one that would represent both ardent Unionists and the Sinn Fein, the political wing of the Irish Republican Army. The first step in that direction came in August 1994 when Prime Minister John Major achieved a cease-fire on the part of both the I.R.A. and the ultra-Protestant militants. It was only after Blair became prime minister, however, that prolonged negotiations began that involved representatives of all of Northern Ireland's political groups, including Gerry Adams, the leader of the Republican Sinn Fein. An American selected by President Clinton, former U.S. Senator George Mitchell, served as chief mediator, and in 1998 he secured the "Good Friday Agreement." It provided for a new Northern Ireland legislature selected by proportional representation and a cabinet nominated by the constituent parties in accordance with their political strength. The Unionists were once again promised that Northern Ireland would not be forcibly annexed to the Irish Republic unless a majority of its people so voted. At the same time, the Irish Republic formally removed from its constitution its claims to Northern Ireland. In return, the I.R.A. gained the release of those of its members who had been imprisoned for maiming and murder, the promise of a North-South ministerial link with the Irish Republic, and a reform of the Ulster police.

In May 1998, the agreement was approved by popular referendum in both Northern Ireland and the Irish Republic. Elections to the new Northern Ireland Parliament followed, and after yet further delays, David Trimble of the (Protestant) Ulster Unionists agreed to become "first minister"; his second-in-command was a (Roman Catholic) nationalist, and his cabinet included two members of the Sinn Fein. Many Northern Ireland Unionists remained deeply suspicious of the inclusion in the new government of men whom they saw as terrorists, and early in 2000 the entire settlement was suspended once more because of the failure of the I.R.A. to carry out the promised "decommissioning" of the weapons in its secret arsenal.[2]

The reconstitution of the first Scottish Parliament since the Act of Union of 1707 moved far more quickly than did the Northern Ireland peace process. The unpopularity of Margaret Thatcher and the Conservatives in the Scotland of the 1980s had led to a widespread sense of political alienation there and the formation of an unofficial "Scottish Constitutional Convention." The setting up of a parliament in Edinburgh became a major theme in the 1997 Labour election manifesto, and later that year — by popular referendum — 74 percent of Scottish voters approved such a devolution plan. The United Kingdom Parliament thereupon authorized the election of a Scottish Parliament of 129 members —

---

[2]According to David McKittrick et al., *Lost Lives* (2000), of the 3,633 victims of violent death in Northern Ireland from 1969 on, 59 percent were murdered by the I.R.A. and its allies, 29 percent by militant Unionists. The police (the Royal Ulster Constabulary) and British army patrols attempting to keep the peace were responsible for the remaining deaths.

to be chosen in part by proportional representation — to deal with such subjects as health, education, housing, transportation, and agriculture. Its budget would be furnished by the United Kingdom government, but it would have a limited authority to raise additional income taxes on its own. The first election for a Scottish Parliament in May 1999 resulted in a coalition government of Labourites and Liberal Democrats, with Donald Dewar, a Labour cabinet member, emerging as Scotland's "first minister." The Scottish Nationalists (who sought complete Scottish independence within the European Union and who received 28 percent of the vote) and the Conservatives (with 16 percent) became the chief opposition parties. One month later, Queen Elizabeth formally opened the new legislature.

For its supporters, the new Parliament represented a pragmatic response to popular pressure and an opportunity for Scots to play a more visible participatory role in governing their own land. It also served as a political validation of Scottish cultural identity in a world in which the great Victorian manufacturing industries and the British Empire (in whose settling and governing Scots had played so central a role) had both passed from the scene. For its critics, the new Parliament represented, at best, an additional and wholly unnecessary level of bureaucracy and, at worst, a giant step toward complete Scottish independence. The Labour party, for many years the strongest political party in Scotland, remained adamantly opposed to such independence — if only because its influence in the United Kingdom parliament at Westminster had so often been dependent on Scottish M.P.'s; the Blair cabinet itself included a large number of Scots.[3] For the same reason, Labour was reluctant to end Scottish overrepresentation in the United Kingdom Parliament (in terms of population) or to curb the continuing right of Scottish M.P.'s to vote on bills concerned solely with England.

In a comparable referendum in 1997, fewer than 51 percent of Welsh voters approved the creation of a consultative Welsh assembly. It was granted no legislative powers, but it was given the right to help determine how to spend the annual budget administered by the secretary of state for Wales. It too came into being in the spring of 1999. Yet another referendum (among Londoners in 1998) resulted in a decision by Labour to reverse the policy of the Thatcher ministry and to reconstitute an elected government for metropolitan London, the GLA (Greater London Authority). In the year 2000, Londoners were therefore granted their first opportunity directly to elect their own mayor (with special authority for police, transport, and development) and an assembly of twenty-five members. The victory of an independent Labourite, "Red Ken" Livingston (b. 1945) — with the Conservative candidate a strong second, and

---

[3]Blair was himself born and educated in Edinburgh, and his two leading cabinet associates, Gordon Brown (Chancellor of the Exchequer) and Robin Cook (foreign secretary), were both Scots.

the official Labour nominee a distant third — provided strong evidence that Prime Minister Blair's political honeymoon had ended.

The most dramatic constitutional change took place in 1999 when Parliament voted to expel from the House of Lords (except for a token ninety-two), the hereditary peers who had been summoned to that historic chamber since medieval times. (They retained both their titles and their estates.) There remained a widespread consensus in Britain that it was desirable to retain a second legislative chamber to serve as an unsalaried debating, reviewing, revising, and delaying body for House of Commons bills. Earlier attempts to reform the Lords had been held up, however, by an inability to agree as to what kind of body should be put in its place. Prime Minister Blair decided to remove the hereditary peers first, thereby leaving a House of Lords made up predominantly of the five hundred life peers appointed since 1958 and of the two archbishops and twenty-four senior bishops of the Church of England. The question of whether future members of the House of Lords should be elected rather than nominated by the incumbent prime minister was left unsettled. So was the prime minister's promise that the House of Commons would in the future be chosen on the basis of proportional representation rather than by the traditional "first past the post" system.

Prospect and Retrospect

The Britain that entered the twenty-first century remained in several respects a paradoxical society. Its people still spoke of the importance of social class, and they continued to display social-class distinctions in the manner in which they spoke. The richest person in the kingdom was, indeed, a hereditary aristocrat, the sixth duke of Westminster, the recipient by the time he turned twenty-one of five hundred proposals of marriage by admiring young women. At the same time Britain could provide more examples of upward social mobility than did most other societies; Prime Minister John Major served as a remarkable example. As the tribulations that the Labour party underwent during the 1980s suggested, social class had become an increasingly poor predictor of voting behavior, and it had never been a truly reliable one. At the turn of the twenty-first century, the professed purpose of Blair's "New Labour" was to transcend social class.

In the aftermath of the changes in social attitudes that characterized "the permissive society," British families at the turn of the century were six times as likely to be broken by divorce as had been the case during the 1950s, and — especially for the women involved — the immediate consequence was often severe economic hardship. At a time when only one Briton in four any longer disapproved of birth out of wedlock, the rate of illegitimacy had risen in the course of a generation from one in twenty to one in four; one direct consequence was a larger number of adolescent boys deprived of two-parent care and a concomitant heightened crime rate in city slums. Over sixty-five percent of women now did paid work outside the home, three-fifths of them on a full-time basis.

At the same time, by the end of the century an increasing number of families could take pride in owning their own home, in providing such homes with central heating rather than with the individual coal fires or electric heaters that had long been common, in filling them with all the latest household appliances (including microwave ovens, videocassette recorders, and personal computers), and in having a car parked at the door. Seven out of ten households now owned at least one automobile. Although not all groups benefited equally, the average income of such households had risen by sixty percent in the course of three decades, and nine families in ten (as contrasted to only four in ten as recently as 1970) owned telephones. Government spending (in real terms) on old-age pensions and other social benefits had tripled, and the number of students enrolled in post-secondary school education had more than doubled. Whereas in the mid-Victorian years, members of the upper classes tended to live a decade-and-a-half longer and to be five inches taller than the population as a whole, such differences had virtually disappeared by the year 2000. If old industries such as coal mining and textiles had declined, then others had prospered; and, under largely foreign ownership, even the manufacture of automobiles had recovered. Britain could claim the world's largest pharmaceutical drug company, and its largest wireless telephone company, and Europe's largest biotechnology industry, even as London remained Europe's prime financial center.

Although a relatively high rate of unemployment had added a note of insecurity to the Britain of the 1980s and early 1990s, unemployment figures had fallen to about five percent as the new century began. Examples of mob rowdyism at football matches and of racial discord had also become less frequent. Although the theft of property (including cars) was at least as common in Britain as in the United States, the homicide rate remained only a third as high, the rate of forcible rape one-fourth as high, and the rate of armed robbery one-fifth as high. Only one Briton in 167 was likely to be attacked violently in a given year, the lowest rate among the fourteen western European and North American countries surveyed. If the Britain of the early twenty-first century had not yet become a harmonious multiracial society, it had taken significant steps in that direction as numerous first- and second-generation immigrants prospered in business, sport, and politics. Thus Britain had elected its first Asian-born Lord Mayor (1985) and its first four nonwhite Members of Parliament (1987); four years later, Britain's largest trade union, the Transport and General Workers, chose its first black general secretary. Some of the implications of the partial transformation of Britain into a multicultural society became evident in the years after 1988, when Iran's Ayatollah Khomeini condemned to death (and British Moslems rioted in protest against) Salman Rushdie, the Indian-born British author of a novel, *The Satanic Verses*, that in their eyes blasphemed the prophet Mohammed. Rushdie felt compelled to go into hiding for several years under British government protection, even as his case stirred a new debate in Britain as to whether the goal of racial and religious harmony should ever curb cherished freedoms of speech and press.[4]

The Britain of the early twenty-first century was not only far more than twice as prosperous materially as it had been when Queen Elizabeth II ascended the throne in 1952; it was also a healthier and better-educated society, a society that, notwithstanding the vicissitudes of the Cold War, had emerged from the process of voluntary decolonization with remarkably few scars and that had avoided a major war for more than five and a half decades. World War II had come to be looked back on "as something rather glamorous they do amazingly well on television."

In 2000 London remained in many respects the theatrical, musical, and publishing capital of the English-speaking world, a distinction enhanced in 1982 by the opening of the Barbican Arts and Conference Center, "the greatest arts complex in Western Europe," and in the completion during the 1990s of the new British Library building, the single largest construction project in Europe. A replica of Shakespeare's Globe theater was completed in 1997. More controversial additions to the London metropolitan scene included the Tate Modern (the world's largest museum of modern art located in a giant former power station), the "London Eye" (a giant Ferris wheel), and the Millennial Dome at Greenwich, finished just in time to celebrate the coming of the year 2000. Resembling a giant squashed mushroom sprouting along the banks of the Thames, the Dome was the largest such structure in the world. The purpose of the exhibits inside was to entertain, to educate, and to serve (in the words of Prime Minister Blair) as "a triumph of confidence over cynicism."

In the meantime, British rock bands continued to prosper and London's dramatic and musical productions continued to play an influential role on Broadway. Composer Andrew Lloyd Webber had established a worldwide reputation with works such as *Jesus Christ Superstar*, *Evita*, *The Phantom of the Opera*, and *Sunset Boulevard*. His *Cats* (based on poems by T. S. Eliot) had indeed become the most commercially successful musical of all time. In the meantime, playwrights such as Tom Stoppard, David Hare, and Alan Ayckbourn remained active. Even as competition from transatlantic cable channels increased, both the BBC and Britain's commercial television companies remained among the world's most creative, especially in dramatizing aspects of life during Britain's earlier centuries — whether it be the court of Henry VIII, the early-nineteenth-century England of Jane Austen's *Pride and Prejudice*, the early-twentieth-century London of *Upstairs, Downstairs*, or the British raj in India of *Jewel in the Crown*. Britain was second only to the United States as an exporter of television programs to other countries, and the worldwide audience of one hundred twenty million who listened

---

[4]See Malise Ruthven, *A Satanic Affair: Salman Rushdie and the Rage of Islam* (1990).

The Millennium Dome   The gigantic exhibition center at Greenwich became a controversial (and probably temporary) addition to the world of metropolitan London. *(Reuters/Archive Photos)*

regularly to the BBC shortwave radio service of pop music and news remained greater than the combined audience for all comparable American, Soviet, and German broadcasts.

Nor were Britons of recent decades deficient in individual derring-do. Francis Chichester, who at the age of sixty-five circled the globe alone in a small sailing vessel in 1966, inspired a host of emulators, including Naomi James, who in 1978 became the first woman to accomplish such a feat, and David Scott-Cowper, who in 1982 became the first person to sail around the world successively in both directions. In the meantime, John Fairfax had rowed across both the Atlantic and Pacific oceans and Wally Herbert had led an expedition across the top of the world — from Alaska to Spitsbergen via the North Pole — by dog sled. In 1987 Richard Branson and a Swedish companion were the first to cross the Atlantic in a hot-air balloon, and in 1998 Brian Jones (with a Swiss partner) became the first successfully to circle the entire world in such a craft. In 1995 Alison Hargreaves became the first woman to reach the top of Mount Everest alone and without the aid of oxygen. In 2000, Barbara Cartland died at the age of ninety-eight after having written 723 romantic novels of which more than a billion copies had been sold worldwide in thirty-six languages.

While inspiring and celebrating new record holders, Britain remained also a land of ancient institutions. The most remarkable of the institutions to survive into the twenty-first century is the British monarchy, which dates back without significant break to early Anglo-Saxon and Celtic times. By 2000 the queen's reign had become the third longest monarchical reign of the past six centuries and had already surpassed in duration that of her collateral ancestor Elizabeth I. It symbolized continuity, stability, and devotion to duty. "Prime ministers have their season and then depart. The Queen remains on stage and the apparently effortless loyalty she commands is the envy of politicians." Thus wrote James Callaghan in 1982. He was the seventh prime minister of her reign even as Tony Blair is the tenth and as Winston Churchill was the first. Churchill's life spanned more than half the decades chronicled in this volume, and his death, observed with solemn pageantry in 1965, truly marked the end of an era. His country appeared a smaller place without him.

The Victorian Britain into which Churchill was born seems far removed from a world that even in the twenty-first century cannot altogether escape the shadow of potential nuclear destruction and in which economically successful nations live side by side with less fortunate and increasingly populous lands demanding as their birthright the benefits of modern technology and the miracles of modern science. Churchill the boy, born within the ancestral halls of Blenheim Palace, Churchill the soldier, who fought to win and hold the outposts of empire in Asia and Africa, and Churchill the statesman, who refused as prime minister "to preside over the dissolution of his Majesty's empire" — such a Churchill now belongs to history. But the Churchill who helped lay the foundations of Britain's welfare state before World War I and who steadfastly upheld the democratic cause against Hitler and Stalin in triumph and adversity remains immediately relevant to our times and inspired many commentators in 1999 to name him as "the person of the twentieth century."

The queen still confers privately with the prime minister once a week, and she continues to serve as head of a Commonwealth that, in her eyes, retains a valuable world role. Except for a scattering of islands, the British Empire old-style may have drawn to an end with the formal handover of Hong Kong to China in 1997, but the Commonwealth persists. As its secretary-general observed in 1986, the queen "believes that the Commonwealth helps reduce tension in the world . . . and that the Commonwealth helps bring different regions and races closer together." The queen also remains personal head of state of seventeen of the states that make up the Commonwealth and Britain's primary public link with many other nations. Thus in 1991, in the aftermath of Anglo-American cooperation in the Persian Gulf, she became the first British monarch in history to address a joint session of the United States Congress. In 1994 she formally inaugurated the opening of the tunnel under the English Channel, and in 1995 she led the festivities with which Britons marked the fiftieth anniversary of the end of World War II. When Australians were asked in a popular referendum in 1999 whether they preferred Elizabeth II as their head of state to a locally appointed Australian politician, they voted in favor of the queen.

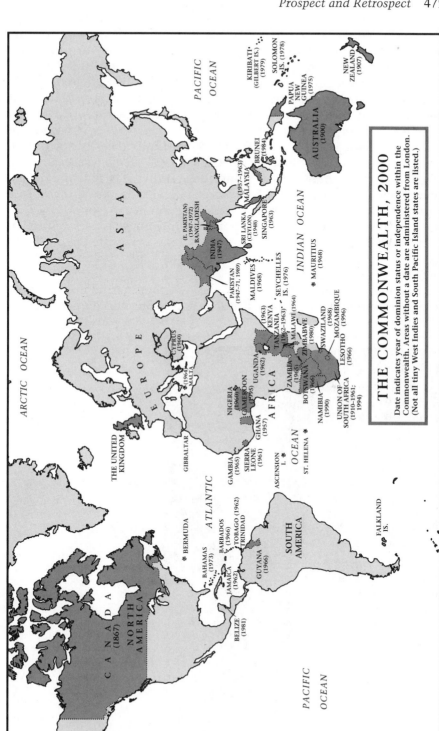

THE COMMONWEALTH, 2000

Date indicates year of dominion status or independence within the Commonwealth. Areas without a date are administered from London. (Not all tiny West Indies and South Pacific Island states are listed.)

The queen and her family continue also to provide a subject of obvious — at times obsessive — fascination and speculation to millions of Britons and others. Thus in July 1981 Prince Charles married a dazzling young Englishwoman, Lady Diana Spencer, in what was celebrated as the wedding of the century. Whereas only 2,000 people had been able to witness the last marriage of a Prince of Wales, that of the future Edward VII at Windsor in 1863, some 750 million television viewers in both hemispheres witnessed the solemn ceremony and joyful procession of 1981. In 1986 a wedding of almost equal splendor united the queen's second son, Prince Andrew (a helicopter pilot during the Falkland Islands war), with a commoner, Sarah Ferguson. In accordance with tradition, they were named the duke and duchess of York. Neither of the two couples was destined to live together happily ever after. Tabloid newspapers and tell-all books, tapped phone conversations, and cameras with telephoto lenses had made that clear by 1992. Both couples formally separated that year and were divorced four years later.

The media speculated excitedly as to whether marital discord in the royal family would soon lead to the abolition of Britain's monarchy, but a

The "Wedding of the Century"   Charles and Diana, the Prince and Princess of Wales, leave St. Paul's Cathedral in July 1981. *(Sygma)*

parliamentary system requires a head of state as well as a head of government (the prime minister). Who would take the place of the monarch? Britain's people appeared as eager as ever to have members of the royal family make public appearances and serve as patrons of charitable causes. In the 1980s, Diana, the princess of Wales, had become a model of poise and beauty on such occasions. Her face was seen on more magazine covers than any other, and by the 1990s she had become the best-known woman in the entire world. Prince Charles served as patron of scores of charities in his own right, and for a time he sparked a vigorous public debate with his pointed criticisms of post–World War II trends in British architecture. The public took a sympathetic interest in the life and education of the couple's elder son, the heir to the throne, Prince William, and their younger son, Prince Henry. In the meantime, Charles's sister, Princess Anne, traveled the globe as president (since 1970) of the Worldwide Save the Children Fund; his father, Prince Philip, remained the equally active president of the World Wildlife Fund. For many Britons the single best-liked member of the extended royal family was the "Queen Mum" (Elizabeth, the Queen Mother, the widow of George VI), who was born a subject of Queen Victoria in the year 1900, and who survived to celebrate her one hundredth birthday.

The British monarchy was thrust into headlines all over the world once again in September 1997 when Princess Diana and her male companion were killed in a car crash in a Paris tunnel. The result was an

The "Funeral of the Century" Princess Diana's cortege passes in front of Buckingham Palace in September 1997. *(Peter Turnley/Corbis)*

unprecedented week-long outpouring of popular emotion in Britain and elsewhere as tens of thousands of bouquets of memorial flowers dotted central London. The week ended with a moving funeral service in Westminster Abbey — televised live on every continent — that involved the entire royal family and a funeral cortege that wound its way through a crowded city. Thus the young woman who had been cheered at "the wedding of the century" back in 1981 and who in her inner torments as in her outer beauty and charm had captured the imagination of hundreds of millions was deeply mourned at "the funeral of the century" sixteen years later.[5] During the years that followed this event, memories of "the People's Princess" gradually faded, and the remaining members of the royal family once again rose in popular esteem. Prime Minster Blair, who had traumatically altered the makeup of the House of Lords, remained a staunch champion of the monarchy.

As the twenty-first century began, the age of Churchill had necessarily taken its place with earlier ages of English and British history — medieval, Elizabethan, Augustan, and Victorian — but Churchill's nation survives. This small island — seventy-fifth in size among the nations of the world — has spread English law and British institutions to every continent. The English language, spoken by fewer than 4 million people in Shakespeare's day, is now spoken by an estimated 350 million people as a first language and by an estimated 350 million more as a second language. Hundreds of millions more can speak some English, if only because it has become the international language of airline pilots and of navigators at sea. It has also become the prime international language of scientists and business people and of users of the World Wide Web. It is used more often than any other at the United Nations (where the United Kingdom remains one of the five permanent members of the Security Council) — and even in the European Union, because as of the year 2000 at least 83 percent of all EU secondary school pupils are expected to become proficient in English. When we consider the impact that Britain has had upon the world and when we ponder its unrivaled three-centuries-old national record of peaceful social and political change — often with heated rhetoric but without revolutionary violence — then we would be premature to conclude that the final chapter in its annals has yet been written.

---

[5]See Sally Bedell Smith, *Diana in Search of Herself: Portrait of a Troubled Princess* (1999), and Ben Pimlott, *The Queen: A Biography of Elizabeth II* (1996).

Appendix

POPULATION IN THOUSANDS

Year	England & Wales	Scotland	Ireland	United Kingdom
1831	13,897	2,364	7,767	24,029
1841	15,914	2,620	8,197	26,731
1851	17,928	2,889	6,574	27,391
1861	20,066	3,062	5,799	28,927
1871	22,712	3,360	5,412	31,485
1881	25,974	3,736	5,175	34,885
1891	29,003	4,026	4,705	37,733
1901	32,528	4,472	4,459	41,459
1911	36,070	4,761	4,390	45,222
			Northern Ireland	
1921	37,887	4,882	1,257[a]	44,026
1931	39,952	4,843	1,280[b]	46,075
1941	*no census*	—	—	—
1951	43,758	5,096	1,371	50,225
1961	46,072	5,178	1,425	52,676
1971	48,749	5,229	1,528	55,506
1981	49,011	5,117	1,510	55,639
1991	49,890	4,999	1,578	56,467

[a]1926 Census
[b]1937 Census

Victoria as "Grandmother of Europe"
A Simplified Genealogy

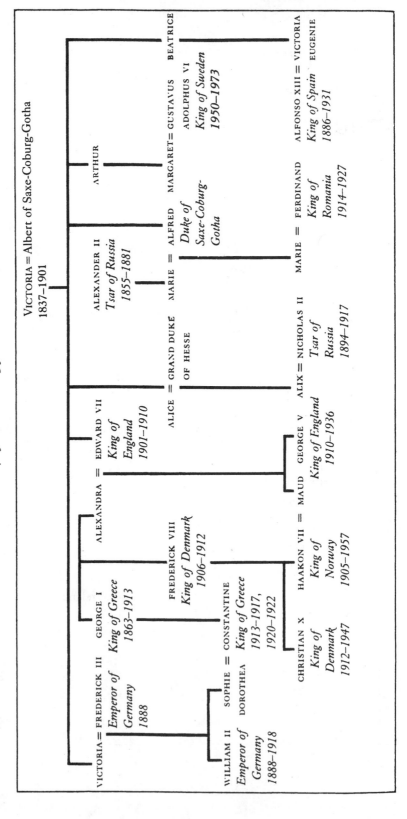

MINISTRIES SINCE 1830

Formed	Party	Prime Minister	Chancellor of the Exchequer	Home Secretary	Foreign Secretary	Other Ministers
Jan. 1828	Tory	Duke of Wellington	H. Goulburn	Robert Peel	Earl of Dudley / Earl of Aberdeen (1828)	
Nov. 1830	Whig	Earl Grey	Viscount Althorp	Viscount Melbourne	Viscount Palmerston	Lord Durham (Lord Privy Seal)
July 1834	Whig	Viscount Melbourne	Viscount Althorp	Viscount Duncannon	Viscount Palmerston	
Dec. 1834	Tory	Sir Robert Peel	Sir Robert Peel	H. Goulburn	Duke of Wellington	
Apr. 1835	Whig	Viscount Melbourne	T. Spring-Rice / Sir F. T. Baring (1839)	Lord John Russell / Marquis of Normanby (1839)	Viscount Palmerston	T. B. Macaulay (Secretary at War, 1839)
Sept. 1841	Tory	Sir Robert Peel	H. Goulburn	Sir James Graham	Earl of Aberdeen	W. E. Gladstone (Board of Trade, 1843)
July 1846	Whig	Lord John Russell	Sir C. Wood	Sir G. Grey	Viscount Palmerston / Earl Granville (1851)	
Feb. 1852	Tory	Earl of Derby	Benjamin Disraeli	S. H. Walpole	Earl of Malmesbury	
Dec. 1852	Whig-Peelite	Earl of Aberdeen	W. E. Gladstone	Viscount Palmerston	Lord John Russell / Earl of Clarendon (1853)	Sidney Herbert (War)
Feb. 1855	Whig	Viscount Palmerston	Sir G. C. Lewis	Sir G. Grey	Earl of Clarendon	

MINISTRIES SINCE 1830 *(continued)*

Formed	Party	Prime Minister	Chancellor of the Exchequer	Home Secretary	Foreign Secretary	Other Ministers
Feb. 1858	Tory (Conservative)	Earl of Derby	Benjamin Disraeli	S. H. Walpole / T. H. Sotheron-Estcourt (1859)	Earl of Malmesbury	
June 1859	Whig (Liberal)	Viscount Palmerston	W. E. Gladstone	Sir G. C. Lewis / Sir G. Grey (1861)	Lord John Russell	Sidney Herbert (War)
Oct. 1865	Whig (Liberal)	Earl Russell (formerly Lord John Russell)	W. E. Gladstone	Sir G. Grey	Earl of Clarendon	
June 1866	Tory (Conservative)	Earl of Derby	Benjamin Disraeli	S. H. Walpole / Gathorne Hardy (1867)	Lord Stanley	
Feb. 1868	Conservative	Benjamin Disraeli	G. Ward Hunt	Gathorne Hardy	Lord Stanley	
Dec. 1868	Liberal	W. E. Gladstone	Robert Lowe / W. E. Gladstone (1873)	H. A. Bruce / Robert Lowe (1873)	Earl of Clarendon / Earl Granville (1870)	Edward Cardwell (War) / John Bright (Board of Trade)
Feb. 1874	Conservative	Benjamin Disraeli	Sir Stafford Northcote	R. A. Cross	Earl of Derby (Son) (formerly Lord Stanley) / Marquis of Salisbury (1878)	Earl of Carnarvon (Colonial Secy.)

	Party	Prime Minister		Home Secretary	Foreign Secretary	
Apr. 1880	Liberal	W. E. Gladstone	W. E. Gladstone H. C. E. Childers (1882)	Sir William Harcourt	Earl Granville	Joseph Chamberlain (Board of Trade)
June 1885	Conservative	Marquis of Salisbury	Sir Michael Hicks-Beach	Sir R. A. Cross	Marquis of Salisbury	Lord Randolph Churchill (India)
Feb. 1886	Liberal	W. E. Gladstone	Sir William Harcourt	H. C. E. Childers	Earl of Rosebery	John Morley (Chief Secy. for Ireland)
Aug. 1886	Conservative	Marquis of Salisbury	Lord Randolph Churchill G. J. Goschen (1887)	Henry Matthews	Earl of Iddlesleigh (formerly Sir Stafford Northcote) Marquis of Salisbury (1887)	A. J. Balfour (Chief Secretary for Ireland 1887)
Aug. 1892	Liberal	W. E. Gladstone	Sir William Harcourt	H. H. Asquith	Earl of Rosebery	
Mar. 1894	Liberal	Earl of Rosebery	Sir William Harcourt	H. H. Asquith	Earl of Kimberley	
June 1895	Unionist (Conservative)	Marquis of Salisbury	Sir Michael Hicks-Beach	Sir Matthew Ridley C. T. Ritchie (1900)	Marquis of Salisbury Marquis of Lansdowne (1900)	Joseph Chamberlain (Colonial Secretary) A. J. Balfour (First Lord of the Treasury)
July 1902	Unionist (Conservative)	A. J. Balfour	C. T. Ritchie Austen Chamberlain (1903)	A. Akers-Douglas	Marquis of Lansdowne	Joseph Chamberlain (Colonial Secretary)
Dec. 1905	Liberal	Sir Henry Campbell-Bannerman	H. H. Asquith	Herbert Gladstone	Sir Edward Grey	David Lloyd George (Board of Trade) John Morley (India) R. B. Haldane (War)

MINISTRIES SINCE 1830 (*continued*)

Formed	Party	Prime Minister	Chancellor of the Exchequer	Home Secretary	Foreign Secretary	Other Ministers
Apr. 1908	Liberal	H. H. Asquith	David Lloyd George	Herbert Gladstone Winston S. Churchill (1910) Reginald McKenna (1911)	Sir Edward Grey	Morley & Haldane (as above) Winston S. Churchill (Board of Trade, 1908; Admiralty, 1911) Earl Kitchener (War, 1914)
May 1915	Coalition	H. H. Asquith	Reginald McKenna	Sir John Simon	Sir Edward Grey (now Lord Grey)	David Lloyd George (Munitions)
Dec. 1916	Coalition	David Lloyd George	Andrew Bonar Law Austen Chamberlain (1918) Sir R. Horne (1921)	Sir G. Cave Edward Shortt (1919)	A. J. Balfour Lord Curzon (1919)	Arthur Henderson (Educ.) Winston S. Churchill (Munitions, 1917; War & Air, 1919; Colonies, 1921) Stanley Baldwin (Board of Trade, 1921)

War Cabinet, 1916–1919

David Lloyd George	Neville Chamberlain (to 1917)	Jan Christian Smuts (1917–1919)
Lord Curzon	Arthur Henderson (to 1917)	George Barnes (1917–1919)
Andrew Bonar Law	Lord Milner (to 1918)	Austen Chamberlain (1918–1919)
		Sir Eric Geddes (1919)

Formed	Party	Prime Minister	Chancellor of the Exchequer	Home Secretary	Foreign Secretary	Other Ministers
Oct. 1922	Conservative	Andrew Bonar Law	Stanley Baldwin	W. C. Bridgeman	Lord Curzon	
May 1923	Conservative	Stanley Baldwin	Neville Chamberlain	W. C. Bridgeman	Lord Curzon	

Date	Party					
Jan. 1924	Labour	Ramsay MacDonald	Philip Snowden	Arthur Henderson	Ramsay MacDonald	Lord (R. B.) Haldane (Lord Chancellor) Sidney Webb (Board of Trade)
Nov. 1924	Conservative	Stanley Baldwin	Winston S. Churchill	Sir William Joynson-Hicks	Austen Chamberlain	Neville Chamberlain (Health)
June 1929	Labour	Ramsay MacDonald	Philip Snowden	J. R. Clynes	Arthur Henderson	
Aug. 1931	National (mostly Conservative)	Ramsay MacDonald	Philip Snowden Neville Chamberlain (1931)	Sir Herbert Samuel Sir John Gilmour (1932)	Lord Reading Sir John Simon (1931)	Stanley Baldwin (Lord President of the Council)
June 1935	National (mostly Conservative)	Stanley Baldwin	Neville Chamberlain	Sir John Simon	Sir Samuel Hoare Anthony Eden (1935)	Ramsay MacDonald (Lord President of the Council, to 1937)
May 1937	National (mostly Conservative)	Neville Chamberlain	Sir John Simon	Sir Samuel Hoare Sir John Anderson (1939)	Anthony Eden Lord Halifax (1938)	Winston S. Churchill (Admiralty, 1939)
May 1940	Coalition	Winston S. Churchill	Sir Kingsley Wood Sir John Anderson (1943)	Sir John Anderson Herbert Morrison (1940)	Lord Halifax Anthony Eden (1940)	Clement Attlee (Deputy P.M., 1942) Ernest Bevin (Labour)

War Cabinet, 1940–1945

Winston S. Churchill	Lord Beaverbrook (to 1942)	Oliver Lyttleton (1941–1945)
Neville Chamberlain (to 1940)	Sir John Anderson	Sir Stafford Cripps (1942)
Clement Attlee	Sir Kingsley Wood (to 1942)	Robert Casey (1942–1945)
Lord Halifax	Ernest Bevin	Herbert Morrison (1942–1945)
Arthur Greenwood (to 1942)	Anthony Eden	Lord Woolton (1943–1945)

MINISTRIES SINCE 1830 (continued)

Formed	Party	Prime Minister	Chancellor of the Exchequer	Home Secretary	Foreign Secretary	Other Ministers
May 1945	Conservative	Winston S. Churchill	Sir John Anderson	Sir Donald Somervell	Anthony Eden	
July 1945	Labour	Clement R. Attlee	Hugh Dalton / Sir Stafford Cripps (1947) / Hugh Gaitskell (1950)	Chuter Ede	Ernest Bevin / Herbert Morrison (1951)	Sir Stafford Cripps (Bd. of Trade, to 1947) / Aneurin Bevan (Health) / Herbert Morrison (Leader of Commons)
Oct. 1951	Conservative	Winston S. Churchill	Richard A. Butler	Sir David Maxwell Fyfe	Anthony Eden (also Deputy P.M.)	Harold Macmillan (Housing)
Apr. 1955	Conservative	Sir Anthony Eden	Richard A. Butler / Harold Macmillan (1955)	Gwilym Lloyd George	Harold Macmillan / Selwyn Lloyd (1955)	Richard A. Butler (Leader of Commons) / Marquis of Salisbury (Lord Pres. of Council)
Jan. 1957	Conservative	Harold Macmillan	Peter Thorneycroft / D. Heathcote-Amory (1958) / Selwyn Lloyd (1960) / Reginald Maudling (1962)	Richard A. Butler / Henry Brooke (1962)	Selwyn Lloyd / Lord Home (1960)	Duncan Sandys (Defense) / Richard A. Butler (Deputy P.M., 1962)
Oct. 1963	Conservative	Sir Alec Douglas-Home (formerly Lord Home)	Reginald Maudling	Henry Brooke	Richard A. Butler	Edward Heath (Board of Trade)

Date	Party	Prime Minister				
Oct. 1964	Labour	Harold Wilson	James Callaghan Roy Jenkins (1967)	Sir Frank Soskice Roy Jenkins (1965) James Callaghan (1967)	Sir Patrick Gordon-Walker Michael Stewart (1965) George Brown (1966) Michael Stewart (1968)	George Brown (Economic Affairs, to 1966) Barbara Castle (Transportation; Employment & Productivity, 1968)
June 1970	Conservative	Edward Heath	Iain Macleod Anthony Barber (1970)	Reginald Maudling Robert Carr (1972)	Sir Alec Douglas-Home	Margaret Thatcher (Education & Science)
Mar. 1974	Labour	Harold Wilson	Denis Healey	Roy Jenkins	James Callaghan	Anthony Wedgwood Benn (Industry)
Apr. 1976	Labour	James Callaghan	Denis Healey	Roy Jenkins Merlyn Rees (1976)	Anthony Crosland David Owen (1977)	Anthony Wedgwood Benn (Energy) Michael Foot (Leader of Commons)
May 1979	Conservative	Margaret Thatcher	Sir Geoffrey Howe Nigel Lawson (1983) John Major (1989)	William Whitelaw Leon Brittan (1983) Douglas Hurd (1985) David Waddington (1989)	Lord Carrington Francis Pym (1982) Sir Geoffrey Howe (1983) John Major (1989) Douglas Hurd (1989)	Lord Hailsham (Lord Chancellor, to 1987) Lord (William) Whitelaw (Leader of House of Lords, 1983–1987)
Nov. 1990	Conservative	John Major	Norman Lamont Kenneth Clarke (1993)	Kenneth Baker Kenneth Clarke (1992) Michael Howard (1993)	Douglas Hurd Malcolm Rifkind (1995)	Michael Heseltine (Environment; Bd. of Trade, 1992; Deputy P.M., 1995)
May 1997	Labour	Tony Blair	Gordon Brown	Jack Straw	Robin Cook	John Prescott (Deputy P.M.)

Bibliography

Selected Web Sites

http://www.libraries.rutgers.edu/rulib/socsci/hist/amhist.html
AMERICAN AND BRITISH HISTORY ON THE WEB. A site maintained by the Rutgers University Library with hundreds of links for students of Modern British History.

http://www2.h-net.msu.edu/~albion/
H-ALBION HOME PAGE. A site operated by the Michigan State University that includes an H-Net Discussion Network for British and Irish History.

http://www.Britain-Info.org
BRITISH INFORMATION OFFICE. A site that provides data about all aspects of British life today as well as links to current issues of major British newspapers.

http://www.bl.uk
THE BRITISH LIBRARY HOME PAGE. The British Library is the single largest library in the United Kingdom.

http://www.sixtiespop.com/
BRITISH POP CULTURE IN THE 1960s.

http://www.spartacus.schoolnet.co.uk/resource.htm
THE EMANCIPATION OF WOMEN. The site includes biographical information about scores of British women.

http://www.ihrinfo.ac.uk/search/
THE INSTITUTE OF HISTORICAL RESEARCH. The University of London's center for graduate study in History provides information on books, journal articles, historians, and doctoral dissertations (completed and in progress).

http://www.iath.virginia.edu/mhc/
MONUMENTS AND DUST: THE CULTURE OF VICTORIAN LONDON.

http://ota.ahds.ac.uk/
THE OXFORD TEXT ARCHIVE. This site contains thousands of digitized primary source materials.

http://landow.stg.brown.edu/victorian/victov.html
THE VICTORIAN WEB. A metasite developed by Professor George Landow of Brown University that contains primary sources as well as biographies of famous Victorians.

http://www.indiana.edu/~victoria/vwcont.html
> THE VICTORIA RESEARCH WEB. A collection of resources affiliated with a discussion network involving all aspects of Victorian culture.

http://www.winstonchurchill.org/
> THE WINSTON CHURCHILL HOME PAGE. A site maintained by the Winston Churchill Center in Washington, D.C.

> For further information, consult Todd E. Larson, "British History Web Sites," in Dennis Trinkle and Scott Merriman, eds., *THE HISTORY HIGHWAY 2000: A GUIDE TO INTERNET RESOURCES.* 2000.

Bibliographical and Reference Works

Arnstein, Walter L., ed. *Recent Historians of Great Britain: Essays on the Post-1945 Generation.* 1990.

Bellamy, Joyce M., and John Saville, eds. *Dictionary of Labour Biography.* 9 vols. 1972–1992.

Central Office of Information. *Britain: An Official Handbook.* Annual.

Chaloner, W. H., and R. C. Richardson, eds. *British Social and Economic History: A Bibliographical Guide.* 2nd ed. 1984.

Cook, Christopher, and John Stevenson, eds. *Longman Atlas of Modern British History.* 1978.

Dictionary of National Biography. 1882–

Freeman-Grenville, G. S. P., ed. *Atlas of British History.* 1979.

Griffiths, Dennis, ed. *The Encyclopedia of the British Press, 1422–1992.* 1992.

Her Majesty's Stationery Office. *Social Trends.* Annual since 1971.

Higham, Robin, ed. *A Nation at War: A Bibliography of British Military History.* 1970.

Kanner, Barbara, ed. *The Women of England from Anglo-Saxon Times to the Present: Interpretive Bibliographical Essays.* 1979.

Mitchell, Brian R. *British Historical Statistics.* 1988.

Rasor, Eugene L., ed. *British Naval History Since 1815: A Guide to the Literature.* 1990.

The Royal Historical Society. *Annual Bibliography of British and Irish History.* Since 1975.

The Royal Historical Society Bibliography: The History of Britain, Ireland, and the British Overseas [1901–1992]. CD-ROM. 1998.

Stenton, Michael, and Stephen Lees, eds. *Who's Who of British Members of Parliament, 1832–1975.* 4 vols. 1976–1981.

Weinreb, Ben, and Christopher Hibbert, eds. *The London Encyclopedia.* 2nd ed. 1992.

Winks, Robin, ed. *The Oxford History of the British Empire: Historiography.* 1999.

Nineteenth Century (to 1914)

Altholz, Josef. *The Religious Press in Britain, 1760–1900.* 1989.

Arnstein, Walter L., et al. "Recent Studies in Victorian Religion." *Victorian Studies* (Autumn 1989).

Brown, Lucy, and Ian Christie, eds. *Bibliography of British History, 1783–1851.* 1977.

Bruce, Anthony. *A Bibliography of the British Army, 1660–1914.* 1985.

Cevasko, George A., ed. *The 1890s: An Encyclopedia of British Literature, Art, and Culture.* 1993.

Cook, Chris. *The Longman's Companion to Nineteenth-Century Britain.* 1999.

Cook, Chris, and B. Keith, eds. *British Historical Facts, 1830–1900.* 1975.

Hanham, H. J., ed. *Bibliography of British History, 1851–1914.* 1976.

Kanner, Barbara, ed. *Women in English Social History, 1800–1914: A Guide to Research.* 3 vols. 1987–1990.

Mitchell, Sally, ed. *Victorian Britain: An Encyclopedia.* 1988.

Tucker, Herbert F., ed. *A Companion to Victorian Literature and Culture.* 1999.

Twentieth Century (since 1914)

Butler, David, and Gareth Butler, eds. *Twentieth-Century British Political Facts, 1900–2000.* 2000.

Gallup, George H., ed. *The Gallup International Public Opinion Polls: Great Britain, 1937–1975.* 2 vols. 1975.

Havighurst, Alfred, ed. *Modern England, 1901–1984.* Conference on British Studies Bibliographical Handbook. 2nd ed. 1988.

Robbins, Keith, ed. *Bibliography of British History, 1914–1989.* 1996.

General Works

Devine, T. M. *The Scottish Nation, 1700–2000.* 2000.

Ensor, R. C. K. *England 1870–1914.* Vol. XIV. Oxford History of England. 1936.

Harrison, Brian. *Peaceable Kingdom: Stability and Change in Modern Britain.* 1982.

Inwood, Stephen. *A History of London.* 1998.

Schuyler, Robert L., and Herman Ausubel, eds. *The Making of English History.* 1950.

Nineteenth Century (to 1914)

Ausubel, Herman. *The Late Victorians.* 1957.

Beales, Derek. *From Castlereagh to Gladstone, 1815–1885.* 1969.

Briggs, Asa. *The Age of Improvement, 1783–1867.* 2nd ed. 2000.

Burn, W. L. *The Age of Equipoise.* 1964.

Clark, G. Kitson. *An Expanding Society: Britain 1830–1900.* 1967.

———. *The Making of Victorian England.* 1962.

Douglas, David C., gen. ed. *English Historical Documents.* Vol. XII. Pt. I (1833–1874). 1956. Pt. II (1874–1914). 1977.

Evans, Eric J. *The Forging of the Modern State, 1783–1870.* 1983.

Gash, Norman. *Aristocracy and People: Britain 1815–1865.* New Oxford History of England. 1979.

Gourvish, T. R., and Alan O'Day, eds. *Later Victorian Britain, 1867–1900.* 1988.

Halévy, Elie. *History of the English People in the Nineteenth Century.* 2nd rev. ed. 6 vols. 1949–1952.

Hoppen, K. Theodore. *The Mid-Victorian Generation, 1846–1886.* New Oxford History of England. 1998.

Powell, David. *The Edwardian Crisis, 1901–1914.* 1996.

Read, Donald. *The Age of Urban Democracy: England 1868–1914.* Revised ed. 1994.

Robbins, Keith. *Nineteenth-Century Britain: Integration and Diversity.* 1988.

Roberts, David. *Paternalism in Early Victorian England.* 1979.

Schneer, Jonathan. *London 1900: The Imperial Metropolis.* 1999.

Tocqueville, Alexis de. *Journeys to England and Ireland.* Translated by George Lawrence and K. P. Mayer. Edited by K. P. Mayer. 1958.

Woodward, E. L. *The Age of Reform, 1815–1870.* Vol. XIII. Oxford History of England. 1938.

Young, G. M., ed. *Early Victorian England, 1830–1865.* 2 vols. 1934.

———. *Victorian England: Portrait of an Age.* 1936.

Twentieth Century (since 1914)

Bogdanor, Vernon, and Robert Skidelsky, eds. *The Age of Affluence, 1951–1964.* 1970.

Briggs, Asa, ed. *They Saw It Happen, 1899–1940.* 1960.

Churchill, Winston S. *History of the Second World War.* 6 vols. 1948–1954.

———. *The World Crisis.* 4 vols. 1923–1929.

Clarke, Peter. *Hope and Glory: Britain 1900–1990.* Penguin History of Britain. 1996.

Dangerfield, George. *The Strange Death of Liberal England.* 1935.

Gilbert, Bentley B. *Britain Since 1918.* 2nd ed. 1980.

Havighurst, Alfred F. *Britain in Transition: The Twentieth Century.* 4th ed. 1985.

Hennesy, Peter. *Never Again: Britain, 1945–51.* 1992.

Lloyd, T. O. *Empire, Welfare State, Europe: English History, 1906–1992.* 4th ed. 1993.

Morgan, Kenneth O. *The People's Peace: British History, 1945–1989.* 1990.

Mowat, Charles Loch. *Britain Between the Wars, 1918–1940.* 1955.

Nowell-Smith, Simon, ed. *Edwardian England 1901–1914.* 1964.

O'Day, Alan, ed. *The Edwardian Age: Conflict and Stability 1900–1914.* 1979.

Raymond, John, ed. *The Baldwin Age.* 1960.

Read, Donald, ed. *Edwardian England.* 1982.

Riddell, Peter. *The Thatcher Decade.* 1990.

Sissons, Michael, and Philip French, eds. *The Age of Austerity, 1945–1951.* 1963.

Taylor, A. J. P. *English History, 1914–1945.* Vol. XV. Oxford History of England. 1965.

Thorpe, Anthony. *Britain in the 1930s: The Deceptive Decade.* 1992.

Williamson, Philip. *National Crisis and National Government: British Politics, the Economy, and the Empire, 1926–1932.* 1992.

Wilson, Trevor. *The Myriad Faces of War: Britain and the Great War, 1914–1918.* 1986.

Winter, J. M. *The Experience of World War I.* 1989.

———. *The Great War and the British People.* 1986.

Legal, Constitutional, and Political History

Blake, Robert. *The Conservative Party from Peel to Thatcher.* 1985.

Butler, (Lord) Richard A., gen. ed. *The Conservatives: A History from Their Origins to 1965.* 1977.

Checkland, Sidney. *British Public Policy 1776–1939.* 1983.

Clarke, Peter. *A Question of Leadership: Gladstone to Thatcher.* 1991.

Cook, Chris. *A Short History of the Liberal Party.* 1978.

Emy, H. V. *Liberals, Radicals, and Social Politics, 1892–1914.* 1973.

Fair, John D. *British Interparty Conferences: A Study of the Procedure of Conciliation in British Politics, 1867–1921.* 1980.

Hardie, Frank. *The Political Influence of the British Monarchy, 1868–1952.* 1970.

Harrison, Brian. *Separate Spheres: Opposition to Women's Suffrage in Britain.* 1978.

———. *The Transformation of British Politics, 1860–1995.* 1996.

Harvie, Christopher. *Scotland and Nationalism: Scottish Society and Politics, 1707–1994.* 1994.

Hutchison, I. G. C. *A Political History of Scotland, 1832–1924.* 1986.

James, Robert Rhodes. *The British Revolution 1880–1939.* 2 vols. 1977.

McLeod, Roy, ed. *Government and Expertise: Specialists, Administrators, and Professionals, 1860–1919.* 1988.

Marquand, David. *The Progressive Dilemma: From Lloyd George to Kinnock.* 1991.

Moore, Roger. *The Emergence of the Labour Party, 1880–1924.* 1978.

Parris, Henry. *Constitutional Bureaucracy: The Development of British Central Administration Since the Eighteenth Century.* 1969.

Pelling, Henry. *A Short History of the Labour Party.* 10th ed. 1993.

Prochaska, Frank. *Royal Bounty: The Making of a Welfare Monarchy.* 1995.

Pugh, Martin. *The Making of Modern British Politics, 1867–1939.* 1982.

———. *The Tories and the People, 1880–1935.* 1985.

Radzinovicz, Leon. *A History of English Criminal Law and Its Administration from 1750.* 5 vols. 1948–1986.

Searle, G. R. *The Liberal Party: Triumph and Disintegration, 1886–1929.* 1992.

Smellie, K. *A History of Local Government.* 4th ed. 1968.

Stevens, Robert. *Law and Politics: The House of Lords as a Judicial Body, 1800–1976.* 1978.

Waller, P. J. *Democracy and Sectarianism: A Political and Social History of Liverpool, 1868–1939.* 1981.

Nineteenth Century (to 1914)

Adonis, Andrew. *Making Aristocracy Work: The Peerage and the Political System in Britain, 1884–1914.* 1993.

Anderson, Olive. *A Liberal State at War: English Politics and Economics During the Crimean War.* 1967.

Arnstein, Walter L. *The Bradlaugh Case: A Study in Late Victorian Opinion and Politics.* New ed. 1984.

Bagehot, Walter. *The English Constitution.* [1867] 1967.

Barker, Michael. *Gladstone and Radicalism: The Reconstruction of Liberal Policy, 1885–1894.* 1975.

Biagini, Eugenio F. *Liberty, Retrenchment and Reform: Popular Liberalism in the Age of Gladstone, 1860–1880.* 1992.

Brent, Richard. *Liberal Anglican Politics: Whiggery, Religion, and Reform, 1830–1841.* 1987.

Brock, Michael George. *The Great Reform Act.* 1973.

Conacher, J. B. *The Aberdeen Coalition, 1852–1855.* 1968.

_____ . *Britain and the Crimea, 1855–56: Problems of War and Peace.* 1987.

_____ . *The Peelites and the Party System, 1846–1852.* 1972.

Cooke, A. B., and John Vincent. *The Governing Passion: Cabinet Government and Party Politics in Britain, 1885–86.* 1974.

Cornford, James. "The Transformation of Conservatism." *Victorian Studies* VII (September 1963).

Cowling, Maurice. *1867: Disraeli, Gladstone, and Revolution: The Passing of the Second Reform Bill.* 1967.

Cox, Gary W. *The Efficient Secret: The Cabinet and the Development of Political Parties in Victorian England.* 1987.

Emsley, Clive. *The English Police: A Political and Social History.* 1991.

Finn, Margot C. *After Chartism: Class and Nation in English Radical Politics, 1848–1874.* 1993.

Fulford, Roger. *Votes for Women.* 1957.

Gash, Norman. *Politics in the Age of Peel.* 1953.

_____ . *Reaction and Reconstruction in English Politics, 1832–1852.* 1965.

Green, E. H. H. *The Crisis of Conservatism: The Politics, Economics and Ideology of the British Conservative Party, 1880–1914.* 1995.

Hamer, D. A. *Liberal Politics in the Age of Gladstone and Rosebery.* 1972.

_____ . *The Politics of Electoral Pressure: A Study in the History of Victorian Reform Agitation.* 1977.

Hanham, H. J. *Elections and Party Management: Politics in the Time of Disraeli and Gladstone.* 1959. With new introduction, 1978.

_____ , ed. *The Nineteenth Century Constitution, 1815–1914.* 1969.

Hardie, Frank. *The Political Influence of Queen Victoria, 1861–1901.* 1935.

Hawkins, Angus. *British Party Politics, 1852–1886.* 1998.

_____ . *Parliament, Party, and the Art of Politics in Britain, 1855–1859.* 1987.

Hollis, Patricia. *Ladies Elect: Women in English Local Government, 1865–1914.* 1987.

Jenkins, T. A. *Gladstone, Whiggery and the Liberal Party, 1874–1886.* 1988.

Kelley, Robert. *The Transatlantic Persuasion.* 1969.

Kent, Susan Kingsley. *Sex and Suffrage in Britain, 1860–1914.* 1986.

Kinzer, Bruce L. *The Ballot Question in Nineteenth-Century English Politics.* 1982.

Koss, Stephen. *The Rise and Fall of the Political Press in Britain: The Nineteenth Century.* 1981.

Krein, David F. *The Last Palmerston Government.* 1978.

Kuhn, William. *Democratic Royalism: The Transformation of the British Monarchy, 1861–1914.* 1996.

Le May, G. H. L. *The Victorian Constitution.* 1979.

Lubenow, W. C. *Parliamentary Politics and the Home Rule Crisis.* 1988.

———. *The Politics of Government Growth: Early Victorian Attitudes towards State Intervention, 1833–1848.* 1971.

MacDonagh, Oliver. *Early Victorian Government, 1830–1870.* 1977.

Machin, G. I. T. *Politics and the Churches in Great Britain, 1832–1868.* 1977.

Mandler, Peter. *Aristocratic Government in the Age of Reform: Whigs and Liberals, 1830–1852.* 1990.

Marsh, Peter. *The Discipline of Popular Government: Lord Salisbury's Domestic Statecraft, 1881–1902.* 1978.

Midgley, Clare. *Women Against Slavery: The British Campaign 1780–1870.* 1992.

Moore, David Cresap. *The Politics of Deference.* 1976.

Newbould, Ian. *Whiggery and Reform, 1830–41: The Politics of Government.* 1990.

Parry, Jonathan. *The Rise and Fall of Liberal Government in Victorian Britain.* 1993.

Pelling, Henry. *The Origins of the Labour Party, 1880–1900.* 2nd ed. 1966.

———. *Popular Politics and Society in Late Victorian Britain.* 2nd ed. 1979.

Poirier, Philip. *The Advent of the British Labour Party.* 1958.

Rover, Constance. *Women's Suffrage and Party Politics in Britain, 1866–1914.* 1967.

Saab, Ann Pottinger. *Reluctant Icon: Gladstone, Bulgaria, and the Working Classes, 1856–1878.* 1991.

Searle, G. R. *Entrepreneurial Politics in Mid-Victorian Britain.* 1993.

Shannon, Richard. *The Age of Disraeli, 1868–1881: The Rise of Tory Democracy.* 1992.

———. *The Age of Salisbury, 1881–1902.* 1996.

———. *Gladstone and the Bulgarian Agitation of 1876.* 2nd ed. 1975.

Smith, E. A. *The House of Lords in British Politics and Society, 1815–1911.* 1992.

Smith, Francis Barrymore. *The Making of the Second Reform Bill.* 1966.

Smith, Paul. *Disraelian Conservatism and Social Reform.* 1967.

Steele, E. D. *Palmerston and Liberalism, 1855–1865.* 1991.

Vernon, James. *Politics and the People: A Study in English Political Culture, c. 1815–1867.* 1993.

Vincent, John. *The Formation of the British Liberal Party, 1857–1868.* 2nd ed. 1976.

Wiener, Martin J. *Reconstructing the Criminal: Culture, Law, and Policy in England, 1830–1914.* 1991.

Williams, Richard. *The Contentious Crown: Public Discussion of the British Monarchy in the Reign of Queen Victoria.* 1997.

Twentieth Century (since 1914)

Adams, R. J. Q. *Arms and the Wizard: Lloyd George and the Ministry of Munitions.* 1978.

Ball, Stuart. *Baldwin and the Conservative Party.* 1988.

Ball, Stuart, and Anthony Seldon, eds. *The Heath Government 1970–1974: A Reappraisal.* 1997.

Beloff, Max, and Gillian Peele. *The Government of the United Kingdom: Political Authority in a Changing Society.* 2nd ed. 1985.

Bernstein, George L. *Liberalism and Liberal Politics in Edwardian England.* 1986.

Bogdanor, Vernon. *The Monarchy and the Constitution.* 1995.

Butler, David, et al. *Failure in British Government: The Politics of the Poll Tax.* 1995.

Butler, David, and Dennis Kavanaugh. *The British General Election of 1997.* 1997.

Coetzee, Frans. *For Party or Country: Nationalism and the Dilemmas of Popular Conservatism in Edwardian England.* 1990.

Cook, Chris. *The Age of Alignment: Electoral Politics in Britain, 1922–1929.* 1975.

Cook, Chris, and John Stevenson, eds. *Trends in British Politics Since 1945.* 1978.

Cowling, Maurice. *The Impact of Labour, 1920–1924.* 1971.

Crewe, Ivor, et al. *The British Electorate, 1963–1987.* 1991.

Dorey, Peter, ed. *The Major Premiership: Politics and Policies under John Major, 1990–97.* 1999.

Graubard, Stephen. *British Labour and the Russian Revolution, 1917–1924.* 1956.

Hazlehurst, Cameron. *Politicians at War, 1914–1915.* 1971.

Holton, Sandra S. *Feminism and Democracy: Women's Suffrage and Reform Politics in Britain, 1900–1918.* 1986.

Hume, Leslie Parker. *The National Union of Women's Suffrage Societies, 1897–1914.* 1982.

Jackson, R. M. *The Machinery of Justice in England.* 7th ed. 1978.

Jefferys, Kevin. *Retreat from New Jerusalem: British Politics, 1951–64.* 1997.

Jenkins, Roy. *Mr. Balfour's Poodle.* 1954.

Johnson, Paul Barton. *Land Fit for Heroes: The Planning of British Reconstruction, 1916–1919.* 1968.

Keith-Lucas, Bryan, and Peter G. Richards. *A History of Local Government in the Twentieth Century.* 1978.

Koss, Stephen. *The Rise and Fall of the Political Press in Britain: The Twentieth Century.* 1984.

Lawlor, Sheila. *Churchill and the Politics of War, 1940–1941.* 1994.

Laybourn, Keith, and Dylan Lee Murphy. *The History of Communism in Britain.* 1999.

Lee, J. M. *The Churchill Coalition, 1900–1945.* 1980.

Lowe, Rodney. *The Welfare State in Britain Since 1945.* 1993.

Lyman, Richard. *The First Labour Government.* 1958.

McKibbin, Ross. *The Evolution of the Labour Party, 1910–1924.* 1974.

McKie, David, and Chris Cook, eds. *The Decade of Disillusionment: British Politics in the Sixties.* 1972.

Morgan, David. *Suffragists and Liberals: The Politics of Woman Suffrage in England.* 1975.

Morgan, Kenneth O. *Consensus and Disunity: The Lloyd George Coalition Government, 1918–1922.* 1979.

———. *Labour in Power, 1945–1951.* 1984.

———. *Wales in British Politics.* Rev. ed. 1970.

Pederson, Susan. *Family, Dependence, and the Origins of the Welfare State: Britain and France, 1914–1945.* 1993.

Pelling, Henry. *The Labour Governments, 1945–51.* 1984.

Phillips, Gregory D. *The Diehards: Aristocratic Society and Politics in Edwardian England.* 1979.

Pugh, Martin. *Electoral Reform in War and Peace, 1906–1918.* 1978.

Ramsden, John. *The Age of Balfour and Baldwin, 1902–1940.* 1978.

———. *The Age of Churchill and Eden, 1940–1957.* 1995.

———. *The Winds of Change: Macmillan to Heath, 1957–1975.* 1996.

Reitan, Earl A. *Tory Radicalism: Margaret Thatcher, John Major, and the Transformation of Modern Britain, 1979–1997.* 1997.

Rosen, Andrew. *Rise Up, Women! The Militant Campaign of the Women's Social and Political Union, 1903–1914.* 1974.

Rowland, Peter. *The Last Liberal Governments, 1905–1915.* 2 vols. 1968, 1971.

Savage, Gail. *The Social Construction of Expertise: The English Civil Service and Its Influence.* 1996.

Searle, G. R. *Corruption in British Politics, 1895–1930.* 1987.

Sked, Alan, and Chris Cook. *Post-War Britain: A Political History.* 3rd ed. 1990.

Skidelsky, Robert. *Politicians and the Slump: The Labour Government of 1929–1931.* 1967.

Stevenson, John, and Chris Cook. *The Slump: Society and Politics During the Depression.* 1978.

Stewart, Graham. *Burying Caesar: Churchill, Chamberlain and the Battle for the Tory Party.* 1999.

Tanner, Duncan. *Political Change and the Labour Party, 1900–1918.* 1990.

Thompson, J. A., ed. *The Collapse of the British Liberal Party: Fate or Self-Destruction?* 1969.

Tiratsoo, Nick, ed. *The Wilson Governments, 1964–1970.* 1993.

Tomlinson, Jim. *Democratic Socialism and Economic Policy: The Attlee Years, 1945–51.* 1997.

———. *Public Policy and the Economy Since 1900.* 1990.

Turner, John. *British Politics and the Great War: Coalition and Conflict, 1915–1918.* 1992.
Wilson, Trevor. *The Downfall of the Liberal Party: 1914–1935.* 1966.

Economic and Social History

Ashworth, William. *The Economic History of England, 1870–1939.* 1960.
Barker, Theodore, and Michael Drake. *Population and Society in Britain, 1850–1980.* 1982.
Beckett, J. V. *The Aristocracy in England, 1660–1914.* 1986.
Bédarida, François. *A Social History of England, 1851–1975.* 1979.
Briggs, Asa. *A Social History of England.* 1983.
Brown, Henry Phelps. *The Origins of Trade Union Power.* 1984.
Bruce, Maurice. *The Coming of the Welfare State.* 4th ed. 1968.
Burnett, John. *Plenty and Want: A Social History of Diet in England from 1815 to the Present.* 1966.
_____ . *A Social History of Housing, 1815–1970.* 1978.
Cannadine, David. *The Decline and Fall of the British Aristocracy.* 1990.
_____ . *Lords and Landlords: The Aristocracy and the Towns, 1774–1967.* 1980.
Chinn, Carl. *Better Betting with a Decent Feller: Bookmakers, Betting, and the British Working Class, 1750–1990.* 1991.
_____ . *They Worked All Their Lives: Women of the Urban Poor in England, 1880–1939.* 1988.
Clapham, J. H. *An Economic History of Modern Britain.* 2nd ed. 3 vols. 1930–1938.
Coleman, David, and John Salt. *The British Population.* 1992.
Cronin, James E. *Industrial Conflict in Modern Britain.* 1979.
Daunton, M. J. *Royal Mail: The Post Office Since 1840.* 1985.
Dyos, H. J., and D. H. Aldcroft. *British Transport: An Economic Survey from the Seventeenth Century to the Twentieth.* 1969.
Floud, Roderick, and Donald N. McCloskey, eds. *The Economic History of Great Britain since 1700.* 2nd ed. 3 vols. 1994.
Gillis, John R. *For Better, for Worse: British Marriages 1600 to the Present.* 1985.
Gourvish, T. R., and R. G. Wilson. *The British Brewing Industry, 1830–1980.* 1994.
Hobsbawm, E. J. *Industry and Empire: An Economic History of Britain since 1750.* 1968.
_____ . *Labouring Men: Studies in the History of Labour.* 1964.
Holmes, Colin. *John Bull's Island: Immigration and British Society, 1871–1971.* 1988.
Holt, Richard. *Sport and the British: A Modern History.* 1989.
Howe, Anthony. *Free Trade and Liberal England, 1846–1946.* 1997.
Johnson, Paul. *The Working-Class Economy in Britain, 1870–1939.* 1985.
Jones, Helen. *Health and Society in Twentieth-Century Britain.* 1994.

Lees, Lynn Hollen. *The Solidarities of Strangers: The English Poor Laws and the People, 1700–1948.* 1998.

Lewis, Jane. *Women in England, 1870–1950: Sexual Divisions and Social Change.* 1984.

Owen, David. *English Philanthropy, 1660–1960.* 1964.

Pelling, Henry. *A History of British Trade Unionism.* 5th ed. 1992.

Perkin, Harold. *The Rise of Professional Society: England Since 1880.* 1989.

Pollard, Sidney. *Britain's Prime and Britain's Decline: The British Economy, 1870–1914.* 1989.

Pollard, Sidney, and Paul Robertson. *The British Shipbuilding Industry, 1870–1914.* 1979.

Porter, Roy. *London: A Social History.* 1995.

Price, Richard. *Masters, Unions and Men: Work Control in Building and the Rise of Labour, 1830–1914.* 1980.

Rose, Michael E., ed. *The English Poor Law, 1780–1930.* 1971.

Rostow, W. W. *The Stages of Economic Growth: A Non-Communist Manifesto.* 3rd ed. 1990.

Rubenstein, W. D. *Capitalism, Culture and Decline in Britain, 1750–1990.* 1992.

———. *Elites and the Wealthy in Modern British History.* 1987.

Schmiechen, James, and Kenneth Carls. *The British Market Hall: A Social and Architectural History.* 1999.

Seccombe, Wally. "Working-Class Fertility Decline in Britain." *Past & Present* 126 (February 1990).

Shkolnik, Esther Simon. *Leading Ladies: A Study of Eight Late Victorian and Edwardian Political Wives.* 1987.

Simmons, Jack, and Gordon Biddle, eds. *The Oxford Companion to British Railway History.* 1997.

Smout, T. C. *A Century of the Scottish People, 1830–1950.* 1986.

Soloway, Richard Allen. *Birth Control and the Population Question in England, 1877–1930.* 1982.

Stone, Lawrence. *Road to Divorce: England, 1530–1987.* 1990.

Szreter, Simon. *Fertility, Class and Gender in Britain 1860–1940.* 1996.

Thompson, F. M. L., ed. *The Cambridge Social History of Britain, 1750–1950.* Vol. I: *Regions and Communities;* Vol. II: *People and Their Environment;* Vol. III: *Social Agencies and Institutions.* 1990.

Vamplew, Wray. *Pay Up and Play the Game: Professional Sport in Britain, 1875–1914.* 1988.

Vicinus, Martha. *Independent Women: Work and Community for Single Women, 1850–1920.* 1985.

Watson, James L., ed. *Between Two Cultures: Migrants and Minorities in Britain.* 1977.

Nineteenth Century (to 1914)

Anderson, M. *Family Structure in Nineteenth-Century Lancashire.* 1977.

Arnstein, Walter L. "The Survival of the Victorian Aristocracy." In *The Rich, the Well-Born, and the Powerful,* ed. F. C. Jaher. 1973.

Ashton, Owen, et al., eds. *The Chartist Legacy.* 1999.

Auerbach, Jeffrey A. *The Great Exhibition of 1851: A Nation on Display.* 1999.

Bailey, Peter. *Leisure and Class in Victorian England.* 1978.

Banks, J. A. *Prosperity and Parenthood.* 1954.

Banks, J. A., and Olive Banks. *Feminism and Family Planning in Victorian England.* 1964.

Banks, Olive. *Becoming a Feminist.* 1990.

———. *Faces of Feminism: A Study of Feminism as a Social Movement.* 1981.

Barrett-Ducrocq, Francoise. *Love in the Time of Victoria: Sexuality, Class, and Gender in Nineteenth-Century London.* 1991.

Benson, John. *The Penny Capitalists: A Study of Nineteenth-Century Working-Class Entrepreneurs.* 1983.

Best, Geoffrey. *Mid-Victorian Britain, 1851–1875.* 1971.

Branca, Patricia. *Silent Sisterhood: Middle-Class Women in the Victorian Home.* 1978.

Briggs, Asa, ed. *Chartist Studies.* 1959.

———. *Victorian Cities.* 1963.

———. *Victorian Things.* 1989.

Brundage, Anthony. *The Making of the New Poor Law.* 1978.

Bythell, Duncan. *The Sweated Trades: Outwork in Nineteenth-Century Britain.* 1978.

Caine, Barbara. *Victorian Feminists.* 1992.

Chapman, Stanley. *Merchant Enterprise in Britain: From the Industrial Revolution to World War I.* 1992.

Checkland, S. G. *The Rise of Industrial Society in England, 1815–1885.* 1964.

Clark, Anna. *The Struggle for the Breeches: Gender and the Making of the British Working Class.* 1995.

Conway, Hazel. *People's Parks: The Design and Development of Victorian Parks in Britain.* 1993.

Copelman, Dina M. *London's Women Teachers: Gender, Class, and Feminism, 1870–1930.* 1996.

Cowherd, Raymond G. *Political Economists and the English Poor Law.* 1977.

Crow, Duncan. *The Victorian Woman.* 1972.

Cunningham, Hugh. *Leisure in the Industrial Revolution, 1750–1880.* 1980.

Daunton, M. J. *House and Home in the Victorian City: Working-Class Housing, 1850–1914.* 1983.

Davidoff, Leonore. *The Best Circles: Society, Etiquette, and the Season.* 1973.

Davidoff, Leonore, and Catherine Hall. *Family Fortunes: Men and Women of the English Middle Class, 1780–1850.* 1987.

Deane, Phyllis. *The First Industrial Revolution.* 2nd ed. 1981.

Digby, Anne. *Pauper Palaces.* 1978.

Driver, Felix. *Power and Pauperism: The Workhouse System, 1834–1884.* 1993.

Dyos, H. J., and Michael Wolff, eds. *The Victorian City: Images and Realities.* 2 vols. 1973.

Eshtain, Jean Bethke. *Public Man, Private Woman: Women in Social and Political Thought.* 1981.

Farnie, D. A. *The English Cotton Industry and the World Market, 1815–1896.* 1979.

Fox, Alan. *History and Heritage: The Social Origins of the British Industrial Relations System.* 1986.

Fraser, Derek, ed. *The New Poor Law in the Nineteenth Century.* 1976.

Freeman, Michael. *Railways and the Victorian Imagination.* 1999.

Gartner, Lloyd P. *The Jewish Immigrant in England, 1870–1914.* 1960.

Gerard, Jessica. *Country House Life: Family and Servants, 1815–1914.* 1994.

Haas, J. M. *A Management Odyssey: The Royal Dockyards, 1714–1914.* 1994.

Haley, Bruce. *The Healthy Body and Victorian Culture.* 1978.

Hammond, J. L., and Barbara Hammond. *The Age of the Chartists, 1832–1854.* 1930.

Harris, Jose. *Private Lives, Public Spirit: Britain, 1870–1914.* 1994.

Harrison, Brian. *Drink and the Victorians: The Temperance Question in England, 1815–72.* 1971.

Harrison, J. F. C. *The Early Victorians, 1832–1851.* 1971.

———. *Late Victorian Britain, 1875–1901.* 1990.

Hartwell, R. M. *The Industrial Revolution and Economic Growth.* 1971.

Henriques, Ursula. *Before the Welfare State: Social Administration in Early Industrial Britain.* 1979.

Holcombe, Lee. *Victorian Ladies at Work.* 1973.

———. *Wives and Property: Reform of the Married Women's Property Law in Nineteenth-Century England.* 1983.

Hollis, Patricia, ed. *Class and Conflict in Nineteenth-Century England, 1815–1859.* 1973.

Horn, Pamela. *Pleasures and Pastimes in Victorian Britain.* 1999.

Howe, Anthony. *The Cotton Masters, 1830–1860.* 1984.

Howell, David W. *Land and People in Nineteenth-Century Wales.* 1978.

Hughes, Kathryn. *The Victorian Governess.* 1993.

Hunt, E. H. *British Labour History, 1815–1914.* 1981.

Jalland, Pat. *Death in the Victorian Family.* 1996.

———. *Women, Marriage, and Politics, 1860–1914.* 1987.

Jones, G. Stedman. *Outcast London.* 1971.

Joyce, Patrick. *Visions of the People: Industrial England and the Question of Class, c. 1848–1914.* 1993.

———. *Work, Society, and Politics: The Culture of the Factory in Later Victorian England.* 1980.

Kynaston, David. *The City of London.* Vol. I: *A World of Its Own, 1815–1890.* 1994; *Golden Years, 1890–1914.* 1995.

———. *King Labour: The British Working Class, 1850–1914.* 1976.

Lewis, Jane. *Women and Social Action in Victorian and Edwardian England.* 1991.

Lewis, Judith S. *In the Family Way: Childbearing in the British Aristocracy, 1760–1860.* 1986.

Lynd, Helen Merrell. *England in the Eighteen-Eighties.* 1945.

McCord, Norman. *The Anti-Corn Law League, 1838–1846.* 1958.

McCrone, Kathleen E. *Playing the Game: Sport and the Physical Emancipation of English Women, 1870–1914.* 1988.

McLaren, Angus. *Birth Control in Nineteenth-Century England: A Social and Intellectual History.* 1978.

Malchow, H. L. *Gentlemen Capitalists: The Social and Political World of the Victorian Businessman.* 1992.

Malone, Carolyn. "Gendered Discourses and the Making of Protective Labor Legislation in England, 1830–1914." *Journal of British Studies.* April, 1998.

Marcus, Steven. *The Other Victorians: A Study of Sexuality and Pornography in Mid-Nineteenth-Century England.* 1966.

Margetson, Stella. *Victorian High Society.* 1980.

Mason, Michael. *The Making of Victorian Sexuality.* 1994.

Mather, F. C. *Public Order in the Age of the Chartists.* 1959.

Meacham, Standish. *A Life Apart: The English Working Class, 1890–1914.* 1977.

_____ . *Toynbee Hall and Social Reform, 1880–1914: The Search for Community.* 1987.

Messinger, Gary S. *Manchester in the Victorian Age.* 1985.

Mingay, G. E. *Rural Life in Victorian England.* 1978.

_____ , ed. *The Victorian Countryside.* 2 vols. 1981.

Mitchell, Sally. *Daily Life in Victorian England.* 1996.

Mokyr, Joel, ed. *The British Industrial Revolution: An Economic Perspective.* 1993.

Morgan, Marjorie. *Manners, Morals and Class in England, 1774–1858.* 1994.

Morris, R. J. *Class and Class Consciousness in the Industrial Revolution, 1780–1850.* 1979.

Mowat, Charles Loch. *The Charity Organisation Society, 1869–1913: Its Ideas and Work.* 1961.

O'Brien, Patrick, and Roland Quinault, eds. *Industrial Revolution and British Society.* 1993.

Offer, Avner. *Property and Politics, 1870–1914: Landownership, Law, Ideology and Urban Development in England.* 1981.

Olsen, Donald J. *The City as a Work of Art: London, Paris, Vienna.* 1986.

_____ . *The Growth of Victorian London.* 1976.

Perkin, Harold. *The Age of the Railway.* 1971.

_____ . *The Origins of Modern English Society, 1780–1880.* 1969.

_____ . *The Structured Crowd: Essays in English Social History.* 1981.

Perkin, Joan. *Victorian Women.* 1993.

_____ . *Women and Marriage in Nineteenth-Century England.* 1989.

Peterson, M. Jeanne. *Family, Love, and Work in the Lives of Victorian Gentlewomen.* 1989.

_____ . *The Medical Profession in Mid-Victorian London.* 1978.

Plumb, J. H., ed. *Studies in Social History.* 1955.

Prothero, Iorwerth. *Radical Artisans in England and France, 1830–1870.* 1997.

Raverat, Gwen. *Period Piece.* 1960.

Reader, W. J. *Professional Men: The Rise of the Professional Classes in Nineteenth-Century England.* 1966.

Richter, Donald C. *Riotous Victorians.* 1981.

Robbins, Michael. *The Railway Age.* 1962.

Roberts, David. *Victorian Origins of the British Welfare State.* 1960.

Rostow, W. W. *British Economy of the Nineteenth Century.* 1948.

Rubinstein, David. *Before the Suffragettes: Women's Emancipation in the 1890s.* 1986.

St. George, Andrew. *The Descent of Manners.* 1993.

Saul, S. B. *The Myth of the Great Depression in England.* 1969.

Schmiechen, James A. *Sweated Industries and Sweated Labor: The London Clothing Trades, 1860–1914.* 1984.

Searle, G. R. *Morality and the Market in Victorian Britain.* 1998.

Semmel, Bernard. *Imperialism and Social Reform.* 1960.

Sharpe, Pamela, ed. *Women's Work: The English Experience 1650–1914.* 1998.

Sheppard, Francis. *London, 1808–1870: The Infernal Wen.* 1971.

Shiman, Lilian L. *Crusade Against Drink in Victorian England.* 1988.

Smith, Francis Barrymore. *The People's Health, 1830–1910.* 1979.

Spring, David. *The English Landed Estate in the Nineteenth Century: Its Administration.* 1963.

Taylor, A. J. *Laissez Faire and State Intervention in Nineteenth-Century Britain.* 1972.

——— . *The Standard of Living in Britain During the Industrial Revolution.* 1975.

Taylor, P. A. M., ed. *The Industrial Revolution in Britain: Triumph or Disaster?* 2nd ed. 1970.

Tholfsen, Trygve R. *Working Class Radicalism in Mid-Victorian England.* 1977.

Thompson, F. M. L. *English Landed Society in the Nineteenth Century.* 1963.

——— . *The Rise of Respectable Society: A Social History of Victorian Britain, 1830–1900.* 1988.

Vicinus, Martha, ed. *Suffer and Be Still: Women in the Victorian Age.* 1972.

——— , ed. *A Widening Sphere: Changing Roles of Victorian Women.* 1977.

Walkowitz, Judith. *Prostitution and Victorian Society: Women, Class and the State.* 1980.

Ward, J. T. *Chartism.* 1973.

——— . *The Factory Movement.* 1962.

——— , ed. *Popular Movements, 1830–1850.* 1970.

Wilson, Charles. "Economy and Society in Late Victorian Britain." *Economic History Review* XVIII (August 1965).

Wohl, Anthony S. *Endangered Lives: Public Health in Victorian Britain.* 1983.

——— . *The Eternal Slum: Housing and Social Policy in Victorian London.* 1977.

——— , ed. *The Victorian Family.* 1977.

Twentieth Century (since 1914)

Aldcroft, Derek Howard. *The Inter-War Economy: Britain, 1919–1939.* 1970.

Alford, B. W. E. *British Economic Performance, 1945–1975.* 1988.

Beddoe, Deirdre. *Back to Home and Duty: Women Between the Wars, 1918–1939.* 1990.

Blythe, Ronald. *The Age of Illusion.* 1963.

Booker, Christopher. *The Neophiliacs.* 1969.

Bragg, Melvyn. *Speak for England: An Oral History of England, 1900–1975.* 1977.

Branson, Noreen. *Britain in the Nineteen Twenties.* 1975.

Branson, Noreen, and Margot Heinemann. *Britain in the Nineteen Thirties.* 1971.

Braybon, Gail, and Penny Summerfield. *Out of the Cage: Women's Experiences in Two World Wars.* 1987.

Brookes, Barbara. *Abortion in England, 1900–1967.* 1988.

Burk, Kathleen, and Alec Cairncross. *"Goodbye, Great Britain": The 1976 IMF Crisis.* 1992.

Calder, Angus. *People's War: Britain 1939 to 1945.* 1969.

Chester, Norman. *The Nationalisation of British Industry, 1945–1951.* 1975.

Christmas, Linda. *Chopping Down the Cherry Trees: A Portrait of Britain in the 80s.* 1990.

Church, Roy. *The Rise and Decline of the British Motor Industry.* 1994.

Clarke, Peter. *The Keynesian Revolution in the Making, 1924–1936.* 1988.

Cronin, James E. *Labour and Society in Britain, 1918–1979.* 1984.

Davies, Christie. *Permissive Britain.* 1975.

Dewey, Peter. *War and Progress: Britain, 1914–1945.* Longman Economic and Social History of Britain. 1997.

Fraser, Derek. *The Evolution of the British Welfare State.* 1973.

Gilbert, Bentley. *British Social Policy, 1914–1939.* 1970.

_____ . *The Evolution of National Insurance in Great Britain.* 1966.

Glynn, Sean, and John Oxborrow. *Interwar Britain: A Social and Economic History.* 1976.

Graves, Robert, and Alan Hodges. *The Long Week-End: A Social History of Great Britain, 1918–1939.* 1940.

Gray, Nigel. *The Worst of Times: An Oral History of the Great Depression in Britain.* 1985.

Halsey, A. H. *British Social Trends Since 1900.* New ed. 1988.

Hancock, W. K., and M. M. Gowing. *British War Economy.* 1949.

Hopkins, Harry. *The New Look: A Social History of Britain in the 1940's and 1950's.* 1964.

Johnson, Paul, ed. *Twentieth-Century Britain: Economic, Social, and Cultural Change.* 1994.

Jones, Catherine. *Immigration and Social Policy in Britain.* 1977.

Kynaston, David. *The City of London.* Vol. 3: *Illusions of Gold, 1914–1945.* 1999.

Marwick, Arthur. *Britain in the Century of Total War, 1900–1967.* 1968.

_____ . *British Society Since 1945.* Rev. ed. 1991.

_____ . *The Deluge: British Society and the First World War.* 1965.

_____ . *The Home Front: The British and the Second World War.* 1976.

_____ . *Women at War, 1914–1918.* 1977.

Milward, Alan S. *The Economic Effects of the Two World Wars on Britain.* 1984.

Norman, Philip. *Shout! The Beatles in Their Generation.* 1981.

Owen, Geoffrey. *From Empire to Europe: The Decline and Revival of British Industry Since the Second World War.* 1999.

Pedersen, Susan. "Gender, Welfare, and Citizenship in Britain During the Great War." *American Historical Review* (October 1990).

Pollard, Sidney. *The Development of the British Economy, 1914–1990.* 4th ed. 1992.

Richardson, Harry W. *Economic Recovery in Britain, 1932–1939.* 1967.

Robson, William A. *Nationalised Industries and Public Ownership.* 1960.

Ruthven, Malise. *A Satanic Affair: Salman Rushdie and the Rage of Islam.* 1990.

Seccombe, Wally. *Weathering the Storm.* 1993.

Smith, Harold L. *Blighty: British Society in the Era of the Great War.* 1996.

———. *Britain in the Second World War: A Social History.* 1996.

———, ed. *War and Social Change: British Society in the Second World War.* 1987.

Stevenson, John. *British Society, 1914–45.* 1984.

Thane, Pat. *The Foundations of the Welfare State.* 2nd ed. 1996.

Thompson, Paul. *The Edwardians: The Remaking of British Society.* 1975.

Thorpe, Andrew. *A History of the British Labour Party.* 1997.

Intellectual, Religious, Educational, and Cultural History

Alderman, Geoffrey. *Modern British Jewry.* 1992.

Altick, Richard D. *The Shows of London.* 1978.

Armytage, W. A. G. *Four Hundred Years of English Education.* 1965.

Bindman, David, ed. *The Thames and Hudson Encyclopaedia of British Art.* 1986.

Caldwell, John. *The Oxford History of English Music.* Vol. 2: *c. 1715 to the Present Day.* 1999.

Cannadine, David. *The Rise and Fall of Class in Britain.* 1999.

Currie, Robert, and others. *Churches and Churchgoers: Patterns of Church Growth in the British Isles Since 1700.* 1978.

Ehrlich, Cyril. *The Music Profession in Britain since the Eighteenth Century.* 1985.

Gilbert, Alan D. *The Making of Post-Christian Britain.* 1980.

Harrison, J. F. C. *Learning and Living, 1790–1960: A Study in the History of the English Adult Education Movement.* 1961.

Himmelfarb, Gertrude. *The Demoralization of Society: From Victorian Virtues to Modern Values.* 1994.

Mandler, Peter. *The Fall and Rise of the Stately Home.* 1997.

Minihan, Janet. *The Nationalization of Culture: The Development of State Subsidies to the Arts in Great Britain.* 1977.

Norman, E. R. *Church and Society in England, 1770–1970: A Historical Survey.* 1976.

Pittock, Murray G. H. *The Invention of Scotland: The Stuart Myth and Scottish Identity, 1638 to the Present.* 1991.

Wiener, Martin J. *English Culture and the Decline of the Industrial Spirit, 1850–1980.* 1981.

Williams, Raymond. *Culture and Society, 1780–1950.* 1958.

Nineteenth Century (to 1914)

Altholz, Josef. *The Liberal Catholic Movement in England: The Rambler and Its Contributors, 1848–1864.* 1962.

———, ed. *The Mind and Art of Victorian England.* 1976.

Altick, Richard D. *The English Common Reader.* 1957.

———— . *Victorian People and Ideas.* 1973.

Anderson, R. D. *Education and Opportunity in Victorian Scotland.* 1983.

Arnstein, Walter L. *Protestant Versus Catholic in Mid-Victorian England.* 1982.

Bebbington, D. W. *The Nonconformist Conscience: Chapel and Politics, 1870–1914.* 1982.

Behrman, Cynthia Fansler. *Victorian Myths of the Sea.* 1977.

Binfield, Clyde. *So Down to Prayers: Studies in English Nonconformity, 1780–1920.* 1997.

Bossy, John. *The English Catholic Community, 1570–1850.* 1975.

Brightfield, Myron C. *Victorian England in Its Novels* [1840–1870]. 4 vols. 1968.

Brinton, Crane. *English Political Thought in the Nineteenth Century.* 2nd ed. 1949.

British Broadcasting Association. *Ideas and Beliefs of Victorians.* 1949.

Brose, Olive J. *Church and Parliament: The Reshaping of the Church of England, 1828–1860.* 1959.

Brown, Lucy. *Victorian News and Newspapers.* 1986.

Chadwick, Owen. *The Victorian Church.* 2 vols. 1966, 1970.

Clark, G. Kitson. *Churchmen and the Condition of England, 1832–1885.* 1973.

———— . "The Romantic Element, 1830 to 1850" in *Studies in Social History,* edited by J. H. Plumb. 1955.

Clarke, Peter. *Liberals and Social Democrats.* 1978.

Collini, Stefan. *Public Moralists: Political Thought and Intellectual Life in Britain, 1850–1930.* 1991.

Connell, Joan. *The Roman Catholic Church in England, 1780–1850: A Study in Internal Politics.* 1984.

Crook, J. Mordaunt. *The Rise of the Nouveaux Riches: Style and Status in Victorian and Edwardian Architecture.* 1999.

Culler, A. Dwight. *The Victorian Mirror of History.* 1985.

Feldman, David. *Englishmen and Jews: Social Relations and Political Culture, 1840–1914.* 1994.

Foldy, Michael S. *The Trials of Oscar Wilde: Deviance, Morality, and Late-Victorian Society.* 1997.

Ford, Boris, ed. *The Cambridge Guide to the Arts in Britain.* Vol. 7: *The Later Victorian Age.* 1989.

Freeden, Michael. *The New Liberalism: An Ideology of Social Reform.* 1978.

Girouard, Mark. *Life in the English Country House: A Social and Architectural History.* 1978.

———— . *The Return to Camelot: Chivalry and the English Gentleman.* 1981.

———— . *The Victorian Country House.* Rev. ed. 1979.

Greene, John. *Darwin and the Modern World View.* 1961.

———— . *Science, Ideology, and World View: Essays in the History of Evolutionary Ideas.* 1981.

Halévy, Elie. *The Rise of Philosophical Radicalism.* 1928.

Harrison, J. F. C. *Robert Owen and the Owenites in England and America.* 1969.

_____ . *The Second Coming: Popular Millenarianism, 1780–1850.* 1979.

Helmstadter, Richard J., and Paul T. Phillips, eds. *Religion in Victorian Society.* 1985.

Hempton, David. *The Religion of the People: Methodism and Popular Religion, c. 1750–1900.* 1996.

Heyck, T. W. *The Transformation of Intellectual Life in Victorian England.* 1982.

Hilton, Boyd. *The Age of Atonement: The Influence of Evangelicalism on Social and Economic Thought, 1795–1865.* 1988.

Himmelfarb, Gertrude. *Marriage and Morals Among the Victorians.* 1986.

_____ . *Poverty and Compassion: The Moral Imagination of the Late Victorians.* 1991.

_____ . *Victorian Minds.* 1972.

Holmes, J. Derek. *More Roman Than Rome: English Catholicism in the Nineteenth Century.* 1978.

Honey, J. R. de S. *Tom Brown's Universe: The Development of the English Public School in the Nineteenth Century.* 1977.

Houghton, Walter. *The Victorian Frame of Mind.* 1957.

Hurt, John. *Education in Evolution: Church, State, Society and Popular Education, 1800–70.* 1971.

Hynes, Samuel. *The Edwardian Turn of Mind.* 1968.

Inglis, K. S. *Churches and the Working Classes in Victorian England.* 1963.

Irvine, William. *Apes, Angels, and Victorians.* 1955.

Jann, Rosemary. *The Art and Science of Victorian History.* 1985.

Jordan, Robert Furneaux. *Victorian Architecture.* 1966.

Knight, Frances. *The Nineteenth-Century Church and English Society.* 1995.

Koss, Stephen. *Nonconformity in Modern British Politics.* 1975.

Laqueur, Thomas Walter. *Religion and Respectability: Sunday Schools and Working Class Culture, 1780–1850.* 1976.

Levine, Philippa. *Victorian Feminism, 1850–1900.* 1987.

Lubenow, W. C. *The Cambridge Apostles, 1820–1914: Liberalism, Imagination, and Friendship in British Intellectual and Professional Life.* 1998.

Mackenzie, Norman, and Jeanne Mackenzie. *The First Fabians.* 1977.

Macleod, Dianne Sachko. *Art and the Victorian Middle Class: Money and the Making of Cultural Identity.* 1996.

McLeod, Hugh. *Class and Religion in the Late Victorian City.* 1974.

_____ . *Religion and Society in England, 1850–1914.* 1996.

Marsh, Peter, ed. *The Conscience of the Victorian State.* 1979.

Newsome, David. *The Victorian World Picture.* 1997.

Norman, Edward R. *Anti-Catholicism in Victorian England.* 1968.

_____ . *The English Catholic Church in the Nineteenth Century.* 1984.

_____ . *The Victorian Christian Socialists.* 1987.

Parsons, Gerald, et al., eds. *Religion in Victorian Britain.* 4 vols. 1988.

Paz, D. G. *Popular Anti-Catholicism in Mid-Victorian England.* 1992.

Poovey, Mary. *Uneven Developments: The Ideological Work of Gender in Mid-Victorian England.* 1988.

Reardon, Bernard M. G. *Religious Thought in the Victorian Age.* 1980.

Richter, Melvin. *The Politics of Conscience: T. H. Green and His Age.* 1965.

Rose, Jonathan. "Willingly to School: The Working-Class Response to Elementary Education in Britain, 1875–1914." *Journal of British Studies* (April 1993).

Rothblatt, Sheldon. *The Revolution of the Dons: Cambridge and Society in Victorian England.* 1968.

_____ . *Tradition and Change in English Liberal Education.* 1976.

Royle, Edward. *Radicals, Secularists and Republicans: Popular Freethought in Britain, 1866–1915.* 1980.

_____ . *Victorian Infidels.* 1974.

Ruse, Michael. *The Darwinian Revolution.* 1979.

Sanderson, Michael. *The Universities in the Nineteenth Century.* 1975.

Schmiechen, James A. "The Victorians, the Historians, and the Idea of Modernism." *American Historical Review* (April 1988).

Smout, T. C., ed. *Victorian Values.* 1992.

Soffer, Reba N. *Discipline and Power: The University, History and the Making of an English Elite, 1870–1930.* 1994.

_____ . *Ethics and Society in England: The Revolution in the Social Sciences, 1870–1914.* 1978.

Somervell, D. C. *English Thought in the Nineteenth Century.* 1929.

Stansky, Peter. *On or About December 1910: Early Bloomsbury and Its Intimate World.* 1996.

_____ . *Redesigning the World: William Morris, the 1880s and the Arts and Crafts.* 1985.

Taylor, M. W. *Man Versus the State: Herbert Spencer and Late Victorian Individualism.* 1992.

Temperley, Nicholas, ed. *The Romantic Age, 1800–1914.* Vol. V of the Athlone History of Music in Britain. 1981.

Tickner, Lisa. *The Spectacle of Women: Imagery of the Suffrage Campaign, 1907–1914.* 1988.

Trudgill, Eric. *Madonnas and Magdalenes: The Origins and Development of Victorian Sexual Attitudes.* 1976.

Turner, Frank. *Between Science and Religion: The Reaction to Scientific Naturalism in Late Victorian England.* 1974.

_____ . *Essays in Victorian Intellectual Life.* 1993.

Vincent, David. *Literacy and Popular Culture in England, 1750–1914.* 1989.

Wallis, Frank H. *Popular Anti-Catholicism in Mid-Victorian Britain.* 1993.

Waters, Chris. *British Socialists and the Politics of Popular Culture, 1884–1914.* 1990.

Watts, Michael R. *The Dissenters.* Vol. 2: *The Expansion of Evangelical Nonconformity, 1791–1859.* 1995.

Webb, R. K. *The Working Class Reader, 1790–1848.* 1955.

West, E. G. *Education and the Industrial Revolution.* 1975.

Wiener, Joel H., ed. *Papers for the Millions: The New Journalism in Britain, 1850's to 1914.* 1988.

Twentieth Century (since 1914)

Badham, Paul, ed. *Religion, State, and Society in Modern Britain.* 1989.

Briggs, Asa. *The BBC: The First Fifty Years.* 1985.

Ford, Boris, ed. *The Cambridge Guide to the Arts in Britain.* Vol. 8: *The Edwardian Age and the Inter-War Years.* 1989.

_____ . Vol. 9: *Since the Second World War.* 1988.

Freeden, Michael. *Liberalism Divided: A Study in British Political Thought, 1914–1939.* 1986.

Fussell, Paul. *The Great War and Modern Memory.* 1975.

Halsey, A. H. *Decline of Donnish Dominion: The British Academic Profession in the Twentieth Century.* 1992.

Harrison, Brian. "Mrs. Thatcher and the Intellectuals." *Twentieth Century British History,* 5:2 (1994).

Hewison, Robert. *In Anger: British Culture in the Cold War, 1945–60.* 1981.

Hollander, Paul. *Political Pilgrims: Travels of Western Intellectuals in the Soviet Union, China, and Cuba, 1928–1978.* 1982.

Hornsby-Smith, Michael P. *Roman Catholics in England: Studies in Social Structure Since the Second World War.* 1987.

Hynes, Samuel. *The Auden Generation: Literature and Politics in the 1930s.* 1976.

_____ . *A War Imagined: The First World War and English Culture.* 1990.

Kennedy, Thomas C. *The Hound of Conscience: A History of the No-Conscription Fellowship, 1914–1919.* 1981.

LeMahieu, D. L. *A Culture for Democracy: Mass Communication and the Cultivated Mind in Britain Between the Wars.* 1988.

Messinger, Gary S. *British Propaganda and the State in the First World War.* 1992.

Murphy, Robert. *Realism and Tinsel: Cinema and Society in Britain, 1939–1948.* 1989.

New Oxford History of Music. Ch. 4: "Music in Britain: 1918–1960." 1974.

Nicoll, Allardyce. *English Drama 1900–1930: The Beginnings of the Modern Period.* 1973.

Robertson, James C. *The Hidden Cinema: British Film Censorship in Action, 1913–1972.* 1989.

Taylor, Richard. *Against the Bomb: The British Peace Movement, 1958–1965.* 1988.

Veldman, Meredith. *Fantasy, the Bomb and the Greening of Britain: Romantic Protest, 1945–1980.* 1994.

Winter, Jay. *Sites of Memory, Sites of Mourning: The Great War in European Cultural History.* 1997.

Imperial, Diplomatic, and Irish History

Albertini, Luigi. *The Origins of the War of 1914.* Eng. trans. 3 vols. 1952–1957.

Allen, H. C. *Great Britain and the United States: A History of Anglo-American Relations, 1783–1952.* 1954.

Andrew, Christopher. *Her Majesty's Secret Service: The Making of the British Intelligence Community.* 1985.

Beckett, J. C. *The Making of Modern Ireland, 1603–1923.* 3rd ed. 1966.

Beloff, Max. *Imperial Sunset.* Vol. I: *Britain's Liberal Empire, 1897–1921.* 2nd ed. 1987.

Bew, Paul. *Conflict and Conciliation in Ireland, 1890–1910: Parnellites and Radical Agrarians.* 1987.

Boyce, D. George. *Nationalism in Ireland.* 3rd ed. 1995.

Brantlinger, Patrick. *Rule of Darkness: British Literature and Imperialism, 1830–1914.* 1988.

Cambridge History of British Foreign Policy. 3 vols. 1922–1923.

Cambridge History of the British Empire. 8 vols. 1929–1963.

Coleman, Terry. *Passage to America.* 1973.

Dewey, Clive. *Anglo-Indian Attitudes: The Mind of the Indian Civil Service.* 1994.

Fieldhouse, D. K. *The Colonial Empires.* 1966.

Foster, R. F. *Modern Ireland, 1600–1972.* 1988.

Halstead, John P. *The Second British Empire: Trade, Philanthropy, and Good Government, 1820–1890.* 1983.

Hayes, Paul. *The Twentieth Century, 1880–1939.* Modern British Foreign Policy Series. 1978.

Headrick, Daniel R. *The Invisible Weapon: Telecommunications and International Politics, 1851–1945.* 1991.

Hoppen, K. Theodore. *Ireland Since 1800: Conflict and Conformity.* 1989.

Hutchins, Francis. *The Illusion of Permanence: British Imperialism in India.* 1967.

Kee, Robert. *The Green Flag: A History of Irish Nationalism.* 1972.

Kennedy, Paul M. *The Realities Behind Diplomacy: Background Influences on British External Policy, 1865–1980.* 1981.

_____ . *The Rise and Fall of British Naval Mastery.* 1982.

Lee, Joseph. *The Modernisation of Irish Society, 1848–1918.* 1973.

Lloyd, T. O. *The British Empire, 1558–1983.* 1984.

Lowe, Peter. *Britain in the Far East: A Survey from 1819 to the Present.* 1981.

Lyons, F. S. L. *Culture and Anarchy in Ireland, 1890–1939.* 1979.

_____ . *Ireland Since the Famine.* 2nd ed. 1973.

McCaffrey, Lawrence J. *The Irish Question: Two Centuries of Conflict.* 1996.

Mansergh, Nicholas. *The Commonwealth Experience.* 1969.

_____ . *The Irish Question, 1840–1921.* 3rd ed. 1975.

Metcalf, Thomas. *Ideologies of the Raj.* 1994.

Moon, Penderel. *The British Conquest and Dominion of India.* 1989.

Moorhouse, Geoffrey. *India Britannica.* 1983.

O'Neill, Timothy P. *Life and Tradition in Rural Ireland.* 1977.

O'Sullivan, Patrick, ed. *The Irish World Wide.* 5 vols. 1992.

Perham, Margery. *The Colonial Reckoning.* 1963.

Porter, Bernard. *The Lion's Share: A Short History of British Imperialism 1850–1995.* 3rd ed. 1996.

Spear, Percival. *India: A Modern History.* 3rd ed. 1972.

Swift, Roger, and Sheridan Gilley, eds. *The Irish in Britain, 1815–1939.* 1989.

Taylor, A. J. P. *The Struggle for Mastery in Europe, 1848–1918.* 1954.

Thornton, A. P. *The Imperial Idea and Its Enemies: A Study in British Power.* 1959.

Townshend, Charles. *Political Violence in Ireland: Government and Resistance Since 1848.* 1983.

Wilson, Monica, and Leonard Thompson. *The Oxford History of South Africa.* Vol. II (1870–1966). 1971.

Woodcock, George. *The British in the Far East.* 1969.

_____ . *A Social History of Canada.* 1989.

Woodruff, Philip. *The Men Who Ruled India.* 2 vols. 1954.

Nineteenth Century (to 1914)

Adams, E. D. *Great Britain and the American Civil War.* 2 vols. 1925.

Bartlett, C. J. *Britain Pre-Eminent: Studies of British World Influence in the Nineteenth Century.* 1969.

Belich, James. *Making Peoples: A History of the New Zealanders from Polynesian Settlement to the End of the Nineteenth Century.* 1997.

Bourke, Austin. *"The Visitation of God?" The Potato and the Great Irish Famine.* 1993.

Bourne, Kenneth. *The Foreign Policy of Victorian England, 1830–1902.* 1970.

Bowen, Desmond. *The Protestant Crusade in Ireland, 1800–1870.* 1978.

Burton, Antoinette. *At the Heart of the Empire: Indians and the Colonial Encounter in Late Victorian Britain.* 1998.

_____ . *Burdens of History: British Feminists, Indian Women and Imperial Culture, 1865–1915.* 1994.

Cain, P. J., and A. J. Hopkins. *British Imperialism: Innovation and Experience, 1688–1914.* 1993.

Chamberlain, Muriel E. *"Pax Britannica"?: British Foreign Policy, 1789–1914.* 1988.

Connell, Brian, ed. *Regina vs. Palmerston.* 1961.

Crook, Paul. "Historical Monkey Business: The Myth of a Darwinized British Imperial Discourse." *History* (Oct. 1999).

Curtis, L. P. *Coercion and Conciliation in Ireland, 1880–1892.* 1963.

David, Lance E., and Robert Huttenback. *Mammon and the Pursuit of Empire: The Political Economy of British Imperialism, 1860–1912.* 1986.

Eldridge, C. C. *England's Mission: The Imperial Idea in the Age of Gladstone and Disraeli, 1868–1880.* 1973.

_____ . *Victorian Imperialism.* 1978.

Fieldhouse, D. K. *Economics and Empire, 1880–1914.* 1972.

Gooch, Brison D., ed. *The Origins of the Crimean War.* 1969.

Hachey, Thomas E. *Britain and Irish Separatism: From the Fenians to the Free State, 1867–1922.* 1984.

Hammond, J. L. *Gladstone and the Irish Question.* 1938.

Hayes, Paul. *The Nineteenth Century, 1814–1880.* Modern British Foreign Policy Series. 1975.

Headrick, Daniel R. *The Tools of Empire: Technology and European Imperialism in the Nineteenth Century.* 1981.

Heyck, Thomas William. *The Dimensions of British Radicalism: The Case of Ireland, 1874–95.* 1974.

Hibbert, Christopher. *The Great Mutiny of India, 1857.* 1978.

Hoppen, K. Theodore. *Elections, Politics, and Society in Ireland, 1832–1885.* 1984.

Howard, Christopher. *Britain and the Casus Belli, 1822–1902: A Study of Britain's International Position from Canning to Salisbury.* 1974.

Hyam, Ronald. *Britain's Imperial Century, 1815–1914: A Study of Empire and Expansion.* 2nd ed. 1993.

Imlah, Albert H. *Economic Elements in the Pax Britannica.* 1958.

Jenkins, Brian. *Britain and the War for the Union.* 2 vols. 1974–1980.

Kennedy, Paul H. *The Rise of Anglo-German Antagonism, 1860–1914.* 1980.

Larkin, Emmet. "Church, State, and Nation in Modern Ireland." *American Historical Review* (December 1975).

———. "The Devotional Revolution in Ireland, 1850–1875." *American Historical Review* (January 1972).

———. *The Making of the Roman Catholic Church in Ireland, 1850–1860.* 1980.

———. *The Roman Catholic Church and the Creation of the Modern Irish State, 1878–1886.* 1975.

Lees, Lynn Hollen. *Exiles of Erin: Irish Migrants in Victorian London.* 1979.

Lowe, C. J. *The Reluctant Imperialists, 1870–1902.* 1968.

McCaffrey, Lawrence J. *Irish Federalism in the 1870s.* 1962.

Martin, Kingsley. *The Triumph of Lord Palmerston.* 1924.

Medlicott, W. N. *The Congress of Berlin and After.* 1938.

Metcalf, Thomas. *The Aftermath of Revolt, India, 1857–1870.* 1965.

Miers, Suzanne. *Britain and the Ending of the Slave Trade.* 1975.

Millman, Richard. *Britain and the Eastern Question, 1875–1878.* 1979.

Mokyr, Joel. *Why Ireland Starved: A Quantitative and Analytical History of the Irish Economy, 1800–1850.* 2nd ed. 1985.

Morris, James. *Pax Britannica: The Climax of Empire.* 1968.

Norman, E. R. *The Catholic Church and Ireland in the Age of Rebellion, 1859–1873.* 1965.

O'Brien, C. C. *Parnell and His Party, 1880–1890.* 1957.

O'Day, Alan. *The English Face of Irish Nationalism.* 1977.

———. *Irish Home Rule 1867–1921.* 1998.

———. *Parnell and the First Home Rule Episode.* 1986.

———, ed. *Reactions to Irish Nationalism, 1865–1914.* 1987.

Ó Gráda, Cormac. *The Great Irish Famine.* 1989.

———. *Ireland: A New Economic History, 1780–1939.* 1994.

———. *Ireland Before and After the Famine.* Rev. ed. 1993.

Pakenham, Thomas. *The Scramble for Africa: White Man's Conquest of the Dark Continent from 1876–1912.* 1991.

Perkins, Bradford. *The Great Rapprochement: England and the United States, 1895–1914.* 1968.

Platt, D. C. M. *Finance, Trade, and Politics in British Foreign Policy, 1815–1914.* 1968.

Porter, Andrew, ed. *The Oxford History of the British Empire: The Nineteenth Century.* 1999.

Robinson, Ronald, John Gallager, and Alice Denny. *Africa and the Victorians.* 1961.

Schreuder, D. M. *The Scramble for Southern Africa, 1877–1895.* 1980.

Schroeder, Paul W. *Austria, Great Britain, and the Crimean War.* 1972.

_____ . *The Transformation of European Politics, 1763–1848.* 1994.

Semmel, Bernard. *The Rise of Free Trade Imperialism: Classical Political Economy and the Empire of Free Trade, 1750–1850.* 1970.

Seton-Watson, R. W. *Britain in Europe, 1789–1914.* 1937.

_____ . *Disraeli, Gladstone, and the Eastern Question.* 1935.

Solow, Barbara. *The Land Question and the Irish Economy, 1870–1903.* 1971.

Stokes, Eric. *The English Utilitarians and India.* 1959.

Strobel, Margaret. *European Women and the Second British Empire.* 1991.

Swartz, Marvin. *The Politics of British Foreign Policy in the Era of Disraeli and Gladstone.* 1985.

Temperley, Howard. *British Anti-Slavery, 1833–1870.* 1972.

Vaughan, W. E. *Landlords and Tenants in Mid-Victorian Ireland.* 1994.

_____ , ed. *A New History of Ireland* Vol. VI: *Ireland Under the Union II, 1870–1921.* 1996.

Webster, C. K. *The Foreign Policy of Palmerston, 1830–1841.* 2 vols. 1951.

Wheatcroft, Geoffrey. *The Randlords: The Men Who Made South Africa.* 1985.

Winks, Robin, ed. *British Imperialism: Gold, God, Glory.* 1963.

Woodham-Smith, Cecil. *The Great Hunger.* 1963.

Twentieth Century

Adams, R. J. Q. *British Politics and Foreign Policy in the Age of Appeasement, 1935–1939.* 1993.

_____ , ed. *British Appeasement and the Origins of World War II.* 1994.

Adamthwaite, Anthony P. *The Making of the Second World War.* 2nd ed. 1979.

Anderson, Terry H. *The United States, Great Britain, and the Cold War, 1944–1947.* 1981.

Barker, Elizabeth. *The British Between the Superpowers, 1945–50.* 1984.

Barnett, Corelli. *The Collapse of British Power.* 1973.

Bell, P. M. H. *France and Britain, 1900–40.* 1996.

_____ . *France and Britain, 1940–1994: The Long Separation.* 1997.

_____ . *The Origins of the Second World War.* 1986.

Beloff, Max. *Dream of Commonwealth, 1921–42.* 1990.

Bew, Paul, et al. *Northern Ireland, 1921–1996: Political Forces and Social Classes.* 1997.

_____ . *The State in Northern Ireland, 1921–1972.* 1979.

Boyce, D. G. *Englishmen and Irish Troubles: British Public Opinion and the Making of Irish Policy, 1918–22.* 1972.

Brown, Judith M. *Modern India: The Origins of an Asian Democracy.* 1985.

Brown, Judith, and Wm. Roger Louis, eds. *The Oxford History of the British Empire: The Twentieth Century.* 1999.

Cain, P. J., and A. G. Hopkins. *British Imperialism: Crisis and Deconstruction, 1914–1990*. 1993.

Cowling, Maurice. *The Impact of Hitler: British Politics and British Policy, 1933–1940*. 1975.

Cross, Colin. *The Fall of the British Empire, 1918–1968*. 1968.

Darby, John, ed. *Northern Ireland: The Background to the Conflict*. 1987.

Darwin, John. *Britain and Decolonisation: The Retreat from Empire in the Post-War World*. 1988.

Deighton, Anne. *The Impossible Peace: Britain, the Division of Germany, and the Origins of the Cold War*. 1990.

Dockrill, Michael, and J. Douglas Gould. *Peace Without Promise: Britain and the Peace Conferences, 1919–1923*. 1981.

Dockrill, Michael, and John W. Young, eds. *British Foreign Policy, 1945–56*. 1989.

Drummond, Ian M. *British Economic Policy and the Empire, 1919–1939*. 1972.

Edwardes, Michael. *The Last Years of British India*. 1963.

Edwards, Jill. *The British Government and the Spanish Civil War, 1936–1939*. 1979.

Eubank, Keith. *The Origins of World War II*. 2nd ed. 1990.

_____ , ed. *World War II: Roots and Causes*. 2nd ed. 1992.

Gilbert, Martin. *The Roots of Appeasement*. 1967.

Gilbert, Martin, and Richard Gott. *The Appeasers*. 1963.

Gordon, R. *Conflict and Consensus in Labour's Foreign Policy, 1914–1965*. 1969.

Gowland, David. *Reluctant Europeans: Britain and European Integration 1945–1998*. 2000.

Hathaway, Robert M. *Ambiguous Partnership: Britain and America, 1944–1947*. 1981.

Hinsley, F. H., ed. *British Foreign Policy Under Sir Edward Grey*. 1977.

Hogan, Michael J. *The Marshall Plan: America, Britain, and the Reconstruction of Western Europe, 1947–1952*. 1987.

Hyam, Ronald, ed. *The Labour Government and the End of Empire, 1945–51*. 1992.

Jeffrey, Keith. *The British Army and the Crisis of Empire, 1918–22*. 1984.

Joll, James. *The Origins of the First World War*. 1986.

Jones, Bill. *The Russia Complex: The British Labour Party and the Soviet Union*. 1977.

Kedourie, Elie. *England and the Middle East: The Destruction of the Ottoman Empire, 1914–1921*. 1956.

Kimball, Warren F. *Churchill and Roosevelt: The Complete Correspondence*. 3 vols. 1984.

_____ . *Forged in War: Churchill, Roosevelt and the Second World War*. 1996.

Kyle, Keith. *Suez*. 1991.

Lafore, Laurence. *The End of Glory*. 1970.

_____ . *The Long Fuse*. 1965.

Lash, Joseph P. *Roosevelt and Churchill, 1939–1941: The Partnership That Saved the West*. 1976.

Longford, Lord (Frank). *Peace by Ordeal* (The Anglo-Irish Treaty of 1921). 1972.

Louis, William Roger. *The British Empire in the Middle East, 1945–1951.* 1985.

———. *Imperialism at Bay: The United States and the Decolonization of the British Empire, 1941–1945.* 1978.

Louis, William Roger, and Hedley Bull, eds. *The Special Relationship: Anglo-American Relations Since 1945.* 1987.

Louis, William Roger, and Roger Owen, eds. *Suez 1956: The Crisis and the Consequences.* 1988.

Lowe, J. C., and M. L. Dockrill. *The Mirage of Power: British Foreign Policy, 1902–1922.* 3 vols. 1972.

Lowenheim, Francis L., ed. *Peace or Appeasement? Hitler, Chamberlain and the Munich Crisis.* 1965.

McKittrick, David, et al. *Lost Lives: The Stories of the Men, Women and Children Who Died as a Result of the Northern Ireland Troubles.* 2000.

Medlicott, W. N. *British Foreign Policy Since Versailles, 1919–1963.* 2nd ed. 1968.

Monger, George W. *The End of Isolation: British Foreign Policy, 1900–1907.* 1963.

Monroe, Elizabeth. *Britain's Moment in the Middle East, 1914–1971.* 1981.

Moran, Sean Farrell. *Patrick Pearse and the Politics of Redemption: The Mind of the Easter Rising, 1916.* 1994.

Moser, John E. *Twisting the Lion's Tail: Anglophobia in the United States, 1921–48.* 1999.

Murray, Williamson. *The Change in the European Balance of Power, 1938–1939: The Path to Ruin.* 1984.

Nicolson, Harold. *Peacemaking 1919.* 1933.

Northedge, F. S. *Descent from Power: British Foreign Policy, 1945–1973.* 1974.

———. *The Troubled Giant: Britain Among the Great Powers, 1916–1939.* 1967.

Orde, Anne. *British Policy and European Reconstruction after the First World War.* 1990.

Padfield, Peter. *The Great Naval Race.* 1974.

Pandey, B. N. *The Break-Up of British India.* 1969.

Rothwell, Victor. *Britain and the Cold War, 1941–1947.* 1982.

Steiner, Zara S. *Britain and the Origins of the First World War.* 1978.

Stevenson, David. *The First World War and International Politics.* 1988.

Taylor, A. J. P. *The Origins of the Second World War.* 1961.

Taylor, Telford. *Munich: The Price of Peace.* 1980.

Thomas, Hugh. *Armed Truce: The Beginnings of the Cold War, 1945–1946.* 1987.

———. *The Suez Affair.* 1967.

Thorne, Christopher. *The Approach of War, 1938–1939.* 1967.

Tolstoy, Nikolai. *The Secret Betrayal, 1944–1947.* 1978.

Ullman, Richard W. *Anglo-Soviet Relations, 1917–1921.* 3 vols. 1966–1973.

Wasserstein, Bernard. *Britain and the Jews of Europe, 1939–1945.* 2nd ed. 1999.

———. *The British in Palestine: The Mandatory Government and the Arab-Jewish Conflict, 1917–1929.* 2nd ed. 1991.

Watt, D. Cameron. *Succeeding John Bull: America in Britain's Place.* 1984.

Wheeler-Bennett, J. W. *Munich: Prologue to Tragedy.* 1948.

Wheeler-Bennett, J. W., and Anthony Nicholls. *The Semblance of Peace.* 1972.

Williamson, S. R., Jr. *The Politics of Grand Strategy: Britain and France Prepare for War, 1904–1914*. 1969.

Woodward, E. L. *British Foreign Policy in the Second World War*. 1962.

_____ . *Great Britain and the German Navy*. 1935.

Yergin, Daniel. *The Prize: The Epic Quest for Oil, Money and Power*. 1990.

Military and Naval History

Beckett, F. W. *The Amateur Military Tradition, 1558–1945*. 1992.

Howard, Michael. *The Continental Commitment*. 1972.

Marder, Arthur J. *The Anatomy of British Sea Power: A History of British Naval Policy in the Pre-Dreadnought Era, 1880–1905*. 1940.

Nineteenth Century (to 1914)

Barker, A. J. *The Vainglorious War, 1854–1856*. 1970.

Beeler, John F. *British Naval Policy in the Gladstone-Disraeli Era, 1866–1880*. 1997.

Farwell, Byron. *The Great Anglo-Boer War*. 1976.

_____ . *Mr. Kipling's Army: All the Queen's Men*. 1981.

_____ . *Queen Victoria's Little Wars*. 1973.

Fay, P. W. *The Opium War, 1840–1842*. 1975.

Gollin, Alfred. *The Impact of Air Power on the British People and Their Government, 1909–1914*. 1989.

_____ . *No Longer an Island: Britain and the Wright Brothers, 1902–1909*. 1984.

Hamilton, C. I. *Anglo-French Naval Rivalry, 1840–1870*. 1994.

Harries-Jenkins, Gwyn. *The Army in Victorian Society*. 1977.

Myerly, Hughes Scott. *British Military Spectacle: From the Napoleonic Wars through the Crimea*. 1996.

Pakenham, Thomas. *The Anglo-Boer War*. 1979.

Rich, Norman. *Why the Crimean War? A Cautionary Tale*. 1985.

Semmel, Bernard. *Liberalism and Naval Strategy: Ideology, Interest, and Sea Power During the Pax Britannica*. 1986.

Spiers, Edward M. *The Late Victorian Army, 1868–1902*. 1992.

Strachan, Hew. *From Waterloo to Balaclava*. 1985.

Sumida, Jon Tetsuro. *In Defense of Naval Supremacy: Finance, Technology, and British Naval Policy, 1889–1914*. 1989.

Woodham-Smith, Cecil. *The Reason Why*. 1954.

Twentieth Century (since 1914)

Adams, R. J. Q., and Philip P. Poirier. *The Conscription Controversy in Great Britain, 1900–1918*. 1987.

Barker, A. J. *Dunkirk: The Great Escape*. 1977.

Bennett, Geoffrey. *The Battle of Jutland*. 1964.

Bond, Brian. *British Military Policy Between the Two World Wars.* 1980.

Brown, Anthony Cave. *The Bodyguard of Lies.* 2 vols. 1965.

Bryant, Arthur. *Triumph in the West, 1943–1946.* 1959.

———. *The Turn of the Tide, 1939–1943.* 1957.

Burk, Kathleen. *Britain, America, and the Sinews of War, 1914–1918.* 1984.

Falls, Cyril. *The Great War: 1914–1918.* 1959.

Freedman, Lawrence. *Britain and the Falklands War.* 1988.

Freedman, Lawrence, and Virginia Gamba-Stonehouse. *Signals of War: The Falklands Conflict of 1982.* 1990.

Fuller, John Frederick C. *The Second World War, 1939–1945.* 1959.

Fuller, J. G. *Troop Morale and Popular Culture in the British and Dominion Armies, 1914–1918.* 1991.

Gilbert, Martin. *Second World War.* 1989.

Guinn, Paul. *British Strategy and Politics, 1914–1918.* 1965.

Hastings, Max, and Simon Jenkins. *The Battle for the Falklands.* 1983.

———. *The Korean War.* 1987.

Hinsley, F. H. *British Intelligence in the Second World War.* Abridged ed. 1993.

Hough, Richard. *The Great War at Sea, 1914–1918.* 1975.

James, Robert Rhodes. *Gallipoli.* 1965.

Lawlor, Sheila. *Churchill and the Politics of War, 1940–1941.* 1994.

Marder, Arthur J. *From the Dreadnought to Scapa Flow: The Royal Navy in the Fisher Era, 1904–1919.* 5 vols. 1961–1970.

Massie, Robert K. *Dreadnought: Britain, Germany and the Coming of the Great War.* 1991.

Middleton, Drew. *The Sky Suspended.* 1962.

Overy, Richard. *Why the Allies Won.* 1995.

Pelling, Henry. *Britain and the Second World War.* 1970.

Reynolds, David. *Rich Relations: The American Occupation of Britain 1942–45.* 1995.

Roskill, Stephen. *British Naval Policy Between the Wars.* 2 vols. 1968, 1976.

Shay, Robert Paul. *British Rearmament in the Thirties.* 1979.

Simkins, Peter. *Kitchener's Army: The Raising of the New Armies, 1914–1916.* 1988.

Thorne, Christopher. *Allies of a Kind: The United States, Britain and the War Against Japan, 1941–1945.* 1978.

Townshend, Charles. *The British Campaign in Ireland, 1919–1921.* 1975.

Travers, Tim. *The Killing Ground: The British Army, the Western Front, and the Emergence of Modern Warfare, 1900–1918.* 1987.

Tuchman, Barbara. *The Guns of August.* 1962.

Van der Vat, Dan. *The Atlantic Campaign: World War II's Great Struggle at Sea.* 1988.

Weinberg, Gerhard L. *A World At Arms: A Global History of World War II.* 1994.

Wheatley, Ronald. *Operation Sea-Lion.* 1958.

Wilmot, Chester. *The Struggle for Europe.* 1948.

Woodward, E. L. *Great Britain and the War of 1914–1918.* 1967.

Biography

Nineteenth Century (to 1914)

Anderson, Nancy Fix. *Woman Against Women in Victorian England: A Life of Eliza Lynn Linton*. 1986.

Annan, Noel. *Leslie Stephen: The Godless Victorian*. 1984.

Bell, H. C. F. *Palmerston*. 2 vols. 1936.

Bennett, Daphne. *King Without a Crown: Albert, Prince Consort of England, 1819–1861*. 1977.

Bew, Paul. *C. S. Parnell*. 1980.

Blake, Robert. *Disraeli*. 1966.

Bowler, Peter J. *Charles Darwin: The Man and His Influence*. 1992.

Boyce, D. George, and Alan O'Day, eds. *Parnell in Perspective*. 1991.

Bradford, Sarah. *Disraeli*. 1982.

Brent, Peter. *Charles Darwin: A Man of Enlarged Curiosity*. 1981.

Briggs, Asa. *Victorian People*. 1955.

Cecil, David. *Melbourne*. 1954.

Checkland, Sydney G. *The Gladstones: A Family Biography, 1764–1851*. 1971.

Clive, John. *Macaulay: The Shaping of the Historian*. 1973.

Cole, G. D. H. *Life of Robert Owen*. 1925.

Davis, Richard W. *Disraeli*. 1976.

———. *The English Rothschilds*. 1983.

Desmond, Adrian. *Huxley: The Devil's Disciple*. 1994

———. *Huxley: Evolution's High Priest*. 1997.

Edsall, Nicholas C. *Richard Cobden: Independent Radical*. 1986.

Ellmann, Richard. *Oscar Wilde*. 1987.

Feuchtwanger, E. J. *Gladstone*, 1975.

Finer, Samuel. *Life and Times of Edwin Chadwick*. 1952.

Finlayson, Geoffrey B. A. M. *The Seventh Earl of Shaftesbury*. 1981.

Fulford, Roger. *George the Fourth*. Rev. ed. 1949.

Garvin, J. L., and L. Amery. *Joseph Chamberlain*. 6 vols. 1932–1970.

Gash, Norman. *Peel*. 1976.

———. *Sir Robert Peel*. 2 vols. 1961–1972.

———, ed. *Wellington: Studies in the Military and Political Career of the First Duke of Wellington*. 1990.

Gilley, Sheridan. *Newman and His Age*. 1990.

Gilmour, David. *Curzon*. 1994.

Hawkins, Angus. "Lord Derby and Victorian Conservatism: A Reappraisal." *Parliamentary History* [1987].

Hinde, Wendy. *Richard Cobden*. 1987.

Jackson, Patrick. *The Last of the Whigs: A Political Biography of Lord Hartington, Later 8th Duke of Devonshire*. 1994.

James, Robert Rhodes. *Lord Randolph Churchill*. 1959.

———. *Rosebery*. 1963.

Jenkins, Roy. *Asquith: Portrait of a Man and an Era*. 1964.

_____ . *Gladstone.* 1995.

Jenkins, T. A. *Disraeli and Victorian Conservatism.* 1996.

Judd, Denis. *Radical Joe* [Joseph Chamberlain]. 1977.

Kaplan, Fred. *Thomas Carlyle: A Biography.* 1983.

Ker, Ian. *John Henry Newman: A Biography.* 1989.

Koss, Stephen E. *Asquith.* 1976.

_____ . *Fleet Street Radical: A. G. Gardiner and the Daily News.* 1973.

_____ . *Lord Haldane: Scapegoat for Liberalism.* 1969.

Lockhart, J. G., and C. M. Woodhouse. *Cecil Rhodes: The Colossus of South Africa.* 1963.

Longford, Elizabeth. *Queen Victoria: Born to Succeed.* 1965.

_____ . *Wellington: Pillar of State.* 1973.

Lyons, F. S. L. *Charles Stewart Parnell.* 1977.

McCarthy, Fiona. *William Morris: A Life for Our Time.* 1995.

McCrum, Michael. *Thomas Arnold, Headmaster: A Reassessment.* 1990.

MacDonagh, Oliver. *The Emancipist: Daniel O'Connell, 1830–1847.* 1989.

Mackay, Ruddock F. *Fisher of Kilverstone.* 1974.

Mackenzie, Norman, and Jeanne Mackenzie. *Dickens: A Life.* 1979.

Magnus, Sir Philip. *Gladstone.* 1954.

_____ . *Kitchener: Portrait of an Imperialist.* 1958.

Marsh, Peter T. *Joseph Chamberlain: Entrepreneur in Politics.* 1994.

Matthew, H. C. G. *Gladstone, 1809–1898.* 1997.

Meacham, Standish. *Lord Bishop: The Life of Samuel Wilberforce.* 1970.

Miles, Dudley. *Francis Place, 1771–1854: The Life of a Remarkable Radical.* 1988.

Mill, John Stuart. *Autobiography.* 1873.

Mitchell, L. G. *Lord Melbourne, 1779–1848.* 1997.

Monypenny, W. F., and G. E. Buckle. *Life of Disraeli.* 6 vols. 1910–1920.

Morgan, Kenneth O. *Keir Hardie: Radical and Socialist.* 1975.

Morley, John. *Life of Gladstone.* 3 vols. 1903.

Orton, Diana. *Made of Gold: A Biography of Angela Burdett Coutts.* 1980.

Packe, Michael St. John. *John Stuart Mill.* 1954.

Prest, John. *Lord John Russell.* 1972.

Read, Donald. *Cobden and Bright: A Victorian Political Partnership.* 1967.

Ridley, Jasper. *Lord Palmerston.* 1970.

Robbins, Keith. *John Bright.* 1979.

Roberts, Andrew. *Salisbury: Victorian Titan.* 1999.

Roberts, Brian. *Cecil Rhodes: Flawed Colossus.* 1987.

Rolt, L. T. C. *Isambard Kingdom Brunel: A Biography.* 1968.

_____ . *The Railway Revolution: George and Robert Stephenson.* 1962.

Rotberg, Robert I. *The Founder: Cecil Rhodes and the Pursuit of Power.* 1988.

Rubinstein, David. *A Different World for Women: The Life of Millicent Garrett Fawcett.* 1991.

Semmel, Bernard. *John Stuart Mill and the Pursuit of Virtue.* 1984.

Shannon, Richard. *Gladstone.* 2 vols. 1982, 1999.

Smith, E. A. *Lord Grey, 1764–1845.* 1990.

Smith, F. B. *Florence Nightingale: Reputation and Power.* 1982.

Smith, Paul. *Disraeli: A Brief Life.* 1996.

Stansky, Peter. *Gladstone: A Progress in Politics.* 1979.

Steele, David. *Salisbury: A Political Biography.* 1999.

Strachey, Lytton. *Eminent Victorians.* 1918.

_____ . *Queen Victoria.* 1921.

Thompson, E. P. *William Morris.* Rev. ed. 1977.

Trevelyan, George Macaulay. *Life of John Bright.* 1913.

_____ . *Lord Grey of Fallodon.* 1937.

_____ . *Lord Grey of the Reform Bill.* 1920.

Wallas, Graham. *Francis Place.* 1908.

Webb, Beatrice. *My Apprenticeship.* 1926.

_____ . *Our Partnership.* 1948.

Webb, Robert K. *Harriet Martineau: A Radical Victorian.* 1960.

Weintraub, Stanley. *Disraeli.* 1994.

_____ . *Prince Albert.* 1998.

_____ . *Victoria: An Intimate Biography.* 1987.

Wilson, John. *CB: A Life of Sir Henry Campbell-Bannerman.* 1973.

Woodham-Smith, Cecil. *Florence Nightingale.* 1951.

_____ . *Queen Victoria, 1819–1861.* 1972.

Ziegler, Philip. *King William IV.* 1973.

_____ . *Melbourne.* 1976.

Twentieth Century (since 1914)

Adams, R. J. Q. *Bonar Law.* 1999.

Addison, Paul. *Churchill on the Home Front, 1900–1955.* 1992.

Bentley-Cranch, Diana. *Edward VII: Image of an Era.* 1992.

Blake, Robert. *The Unknown Prime Minister: The Life and Times of Andrew Bonar Law.* 1954.

Blake, Robert, and Louis William Roger, eds. *Churchill: A Major New Assessment of His Life in Peace and War.* 1993.

Bonham-Carter, Violet. *Winston Churchill: An Intimate Portrait.* 1965.

Bradford, Sarah. *George VI.* 1989.

Brown, Judith M. *Gandhi: Prisoner of Hope.* 1990.

Bullock, Alan. *Ernest Bevin.* 3 vols. 1960–1983.

Callaghan, James. *Time and Chance.* 1987.

Campbell, John. *Aneurin Bevan and the Mirage of British Socialism.* 1987.

_____ . *Edward Heath: A Biography.* 1993.

Chalfont, Alun. *Montgomery of Alamein.* 1977.

Charlton, David. *Anthony Eden: A Biography.* 1982.

Chisholm, Anne, and Michael Davie. *Beaverbrook: A Life.* 1992.

Churchill, Randolph, and Martin Gilbert. *Life of Winston Churchill.* 8 vols. 1966–1989.

Dilks, David. *Neville Chamberlain.* Vol. 1: *Pioneering and Reform, 1869–1929.* 1984.

Donaldson, Frances. *Edward VIII.* 1974.

Douglas-Home, Alec. *The Way the Wind Blows: An Autobiography.* 1976.

Dugdale, Blanche E. C. *Arthur James Balfour.* 2 vols. 1936.

Dunleavy, J. E., and G. W. Dunleavy. *Douglas Hyde: A Maker of Modern Ireland.* 1991.

Dutton, David. *Austen Chamberlain: Gentleman in Politics.* 1987.

Eden, Sir Anthony. *Memoirs.* 3 vols. 1960–1965.

Feiling, Keith. *Neville Chamberlain.* 1946.

Foot, Michael. *Aneurin Bevin.* 2 vols. 1962–1973.

Gilbert, Bentley Brinkerhoff. *David Lloyd George: A Political Life.* 2 vols. [to 1916]. 1987, 1992.

Gilbert, Martin. *Winston Churchill: A Life.* 1991.

Gollin, A. M. *Proconsul in Politics: A Study of Lord Milner.* 1964.

Grigg, John. *Lloyd George* [to 1916]. 3 vols. 1973–1985.

Harris, José. *William Beveridge: A Biography.* 1977.

Harris, Kenneth. *Attlee.* 1982.

Horne, Alistair. *Harold Macmillan.* 2 vols. 1988.

Howard, Anthony. *RAB: The Life of R. A. Butler.* 1987.

James, Robert Rhodes. *Anthony Eden.* 1987.

––––––. *Churchill: A Study in Failure, 1900–1939.* 1970.

Jones, Thomas. *Lloyd George.* 1951.

Lacey, Robert. *Majesty: Queen Elizabeth II and the House of Windsor.* 1977.

Leventhal, Fred M. *Arthur Henderson.* 1989.

Macleod, Ian. *Neville Chamberlain.* 1960.

Magnus, Sir Philip. *King Edward VII.* 1964.

Major, John. *Autobiography.* 1999.

Marquand, David. *Ramsay MacDonald.* 1977.

Middlemass, Keith, and John Barnes. *Baldwin.* 1969.

Morgan, Austen. *Harold Wilson.* 1992.

Nicolson, Harold. *Diaries.* 3 vols. 1966–1968.

––––––. *King George V.* 1951.

Pelling, Henry. *Winston Churchill.* 2nd ed. 1989.

Pimlott, Ben. *Harold Wilson.* 1992.

––––––. *The Queen: A Biography of Elizabeth II.* 1996.

Robbins, Keith. *Sir Edward Grey.* 1971.

Rose, Kenneth. *King George V.* 1984.

Rowland, Peter. *David Lloyd George.* 1975.

Russell, Bertrand. *Autobiography.* 3 vols. 1967–1969.

St. Aubyn, Giles. *Edward VII: Prince and King.* 1979.

Schneer, Jonathan. *George Lansbury.* 1990.

Skidelsky, Robert. *John Maynard Keynes.* 2 vols. [to 1937]. 1983–1994.

Smith, Sally Bedell. *Diana in Search of Herself: Portrait of a Troubled Princess.* 1999.

Taylor, A. J. P., ed. *Lloyd George: Twelve Essays.* 1971.

Weiler, Peter. *Ernest Bevin.* 1993.

Wheeler-Bennett, J. W. *King George VI: His Life and Work.* 1958.

Williamson, Philip. *Stanley Baldwin.* 1999.
Woolf, Leonard. *Autobiography.* 5 vols. 1960–1969.
Wrigley, Chris. *Lloyd George.* 1992.
Young, Hugo. *The Iron Lady: A Biography of Margaret Thatcher.* 1990.
Young, Kenneth. *Arthur James Balfour.* 1963.
Ziegler, Philip. *King Edward VIII: A Biography.* 1990.
———. *Mountbatten.* 1985.

Index